THE TRUMPS

THREE GENERATIONS OF BUILDERS
AND A PRESIDENT

—◦◦◦—

GWENDA BLAIR

SIMON & SCHUSTER PAPERBACKS
NEW YORK • LONDON • TORONTO • SYDNEY • NEW DELHI

SIMON & SCHUSTER PAPERBACKS
An Imprint of Simon & Schuster, Inc.
1230 Avenue of the Americas
New York, New York 10020

First Simon & Schuster Paperback Edition November 2015

SIMON & SCHUSTER PAPERBACKS and colophon are
registered trademarks of Simon & Schuster, Inc.

Photo credits appear on page 593.

For information about special discounts for bulk purchases,
please contact Simon & Schuster Special Sales:
1-800-456-6798 or business@simonandschuster.com.

DESIGNED BY KEVIN HANEK

Manufactured in the United States of America

10

The Library of Congress has cataloged the Simon & Schuster edition as follows:
Blair, Gwenda.
The Trumps : three generations that built an empire / Gwenda Blair.
p. cm.
Includes bibliographical references and index.
1. Trump, Donald, 1946– 2. Trump, Friedrich, 1869–1918 3. Trump, Fred, 1905–1999
4. Businesspeople—United States—Biography. 5. Real estate developers—United
States—Biography. I. Title.
HC102.5.T78 B53 2000

333.33'092'273—dc21
[B]   00-041931

ISBN 978-0-684-80849-9
ISBN 978-0-7432-1079-9 (pbk)
ISBN 978-1-5011-3936-9 (ebook)

To my children, Sasha and Newell, and to my parents,

Newell and Greta Blair

―⁓―

CONTENTS

Contents

—⁓—

On Tuesday, June 16, 2015, two days after Donald Trump's 69th birthday, his daughter Ivanka, wearing a tailored sleeveless white dress, stepped onto a temporary stage in the lobby of Trump Tower. Eight American flags stood at attention along the back of the stage, which had a speaker's podium faced with bright blue and edged with red. Across the front of the podium, in large white letters, was the name *Trump*, a website address, and a presidential campaign slogan, Make America Great Again!, recycled from the 1980 campaign of the nation's last celebrity candidate, Ronald Reagan.

It was the culminating moment in an only-in-America story, the three-generational rise of a family dynasty based on doing whatever it took to win, never hesitating to push the envelope, and never giving up.

Donald Trump's grandfather Friedrich, who came to New York from Germany as a 16-year-old in 1885, amassed a nest egg—the first Trump fortune—by mining the miners during the gold rush era. Starting in Seattle and ending up in the Yukon, he established the Trump MO: scope out the best location (it tended to be in the red-light district); open a business (in his case, restaurants, at times on land to which he had no legal right); and offer customers (mostly rootless newcomers who had yet to see their first nugget) some right-now comfort in the form of booze and easy access to women. When he later attempted to move back to Germany, he massaged this history, insisting that he was a quiet sort who avoided bars and that he had been in the United States during the years he would have been subject to compulsory German military service solely because he wanted to support his widowed mother. But German authorities saw him as a draft dodger and sent him back where he came from—the same fate his grandson would propose for undocumented immigrants more than a century later.

Donald's father, Fred, became a multimillionaire by exploiting every loophole when constructing government-backed housing in Queens and Brooklyn. When payment for federal projects was by the unit instead of the room, he upped the number of efficiencies and one bedrooms, even though the architects had intended larger apartments and the buyers, many of them GIs returning from World War II, needed more space for their growing families. Later, when building apartments subsidized by New York State, Fred set up shell equipment companies and billed the state for trucks and cement mixers he rented from himself at inflated prices.

A generation later, Donald refined the family formula by adding new techniques, including celebrity branding and extreme self-praise. While he heeded classic business basics like "location, location, location," his personal mantra would be "exaggerate, exaggerate, exaggerate"—and he used it to become a billionaire through high-end building; casino gambling; and his reality TV show, The Apprentice. As fresh-faced young contestants competed for a job with the Trump Organization, he played the archetypal boss, pouncing on mistakes and dismissing excuses, ever aware of the bottom line.

But what few contestants or viewers knew was that behind this role lay a life story with more twists and turns than any television producer could possibly imagine. Nor did they know that Donald himself had been a lifelong apprentice to a powerful man whom he admired, rebelled against, studied, competed with, and eventually surpassed—his father, Fred, who had made his money building ordinary homes for ordinary people, not by constructing super-luxury apartments, running casinos, or becoming a television star. One of the most celebrated figures of his time, Donald, the erstwhile apprentice lived in the center of photographers' cameras, but his master existed outside the media's glare. The two men's lives were vastly different—as different as business in the middle of the twentieth century from that of the early decades of the twenty-first, as different as America during and after World War II from what the country became in the post–cold war era.

This apprentice did not always follow his master's advice. When Donald ignored his father's old-fashioned all-brick aesthetic in favor of modern glass-walled skyscrapers, he achieved great success; when he disobeyed his father's financial precepts and signed personal financial guarantees for nearly $1 billion, he brought about a near disaster. But unlike other magnates of the time, Donald emerged from financial turmoil to create a second, virtual empire. He no longer owned everything with his name on it; instead he marketed himself as the embodiment of the American dream of wealth and fame.

Perhaps the biggest difference was that Fred put his name on only one development: Trump Village, a cluster of 23-story middle-income apartment buildings in Coney Island. It was his tallest project as well as his last.

Everything Donald built was far taller; and every pitch for every venture hyped not just the project at hand but the Trump name itself, which a prescient ancestor had changed from Drumpf. Starting with Trump Tower, his signature building in Manhattan, everything—from the 12-inch-tall Apprentice Talking Donald Trump Doll, a pint-sized personal mentor, bearing the pursed mouth and bushy eyebrows, to the 98-story Trump Tower Chicago, the 16th-tallest structure in the world—would bear the Trump name front and center in large, shiny letters, seemingly a guarantee of success when attached to any business undertaking. Now, as TV cameras and reporters clustered in front of the podium, Donald and the rest of the country were about to find out whether that magic, presumed to attach to his name in business, would carry over to the political realm.

And who better to hand him off to the public than his daughter Ivanka, a former model with her own line of jewelry, perfume, and clothing? Now 33 and the mother of two, she was also an executive at the Trump Organization, as were her two brothers from Donald Trump's first marriage, Donald Jr., 37, and Eric, 31.

With her brown eyes and her long blond hair tucked up in a neat chignon, Ivanka bore a marked resemblance to her mother, Ivana, also a former model. But when Ivanka began speaking, she was her father's daughter. Radiating self-confidence, she said she was introducing a man who needed no introduction; nonetheless, she spent five minutes lauding his success, vision, brilliance, passion, strength, boldness, and independence. When she finally finished, a recording of Canadian singer Neil Young's rendition of "Rockin' in the Free World" reverberated from the cavernous lobby's peach-colored marble walls.

Then, as is customary at the announcement of a candidacy, the contender appeared. But rather than enter from the wings, as is traditional, Donald Trump stood at the top of a gilded escalator with his third wife, Melania, yet another former model, also wearing a white dress. Gazing out, they seemed for a moment like a royal couple viewing subjects from the balcony of the castle.

Donald waved, flashed two thumbs up, and slowly descended to take his place on the podium. He was heavier and more jowly than when he first stepped into the national spotlight some four decades earlier, and his hair—blond in childhood, then light brown, and later, infamously, an improbable orange—was now a subdued blond comb-over. As usual, he was wearing a white shirt and a bright red tie, but he had traded his habitual black Brioni suit for a navy number; on the video clips that played around the world in the days that followed, the combination of podium, attire, and flags produced a television-savvy cornucopia of red, white, and blue.

On most such occasions, the next step would be for Trump to declare his candidacy for the Republican nomination. But the first thing on his agenda was to establish that his announcement was better than those of his rivals and that they were nincompoops.

"Whoa," he began, looking out into the lobby. "That is some group of people. Thousands." In fact, there were only a few hundred people, but no matter. "This is beyond anybody's expectations. There's been no crowd like this." By contrast, he said, at their own announcements, the other candidates didn't know to check out the air conditioner or the room size and "they sweated like dogs"—proof positive, evidently, that they were hapless idiots with no idea how to get even the simplest thing done. Seemingly, these shortcomings gave him permission to leap to a spectacular conclusion: "How are they going to beat ISIS?" he said. "I don't think it's going to happen."

It was vintage Trump. What mattered wasn't whether his opponents were liberal or conservative, prochoice or prolife, or ultimately whether they were Democrats or Republicans. What mattered was that he was a winner and everyone else was a loser—in his mind, the only categories that counted. Indeed, the entire Trump family history—grandfather Friedrich; father, Fred; and now Donald himself—has been one of focusing relentlessly on winning and doing everything possible to come out on top.

It wasn't the first time Donald Trump had shown an interest in the Oval Office. In 1987, as part of a publicity campaign for his first book, *Trump: The Art of the Deal*, he took out full-page newspaper ads declaring that the United States needed more backbone in its foreign policy, gave a speech in New Hampshire during primary season, and distributed bumper stickers that said I ♥ Donald Trump. In 2000, he made another presidential feint with the sketchy set of policies enumerated in a quickie new book, *The America We Deserve*; and in 2004,

2008, and 2012 he hinted that a run for the White House might be in the offing. But now, after a lifetime of devoting himself to being a winner in the business world, he was ready to run—to use his real-world expertise and no-holds-barred approach on the nation's behalf.

"Our country is in serious trouble," he said at Trump Tower. "We don't have victories anymore." It was time for America to return to the winner's circle, and he was the one person with the strength and the skills to make that happen.

He began immediately by declaring that Mexico was sending drugs, criminals, and rapists across the border. Predictably, the ensuing hubbub forced NBC, Univision, and ESPN to cancel their contracts with him—which in turn allowed him to seem a man of heroic proportions, willing to take risks and make sacrifices to get America back on track. (In addition, the canceled contracts gave him an out from shows with declining viewerships and opened the door for him to file potentially lucrative lawsuits, a tactic he often employs.)

And that was just his first day on the campaign trail. The next month, when Senator John McCain said that Trump was firing up all the crazies, Trump shot back that McCain wasn't a war hero because real heroes don't get captured. During the first Republican debates, after CNN news anchor Megyn Kelly asked Trump about his record of calling women derogatory names, he said she was overrated and unprofessional and retweeted a post calling her a bimbo.

Political experts said that he had written off the Hispanic vote; the military vote; and, even though he had a history of hiring women executives at the Trump Organization, the female vote. But he was targeting a different audience—the millions of disaffected, alienated, and above all angry Americans who felt their lives were going nowhere and longed for someone to help them get the respect and prosperity they deserved.

And they heard him. With each poll, his ratings increased. The nomination that was supposed to be Jeb Bush's for the asking began to seem like it might be within the grasp of the brash billionaire who told the disenfranchised what they wanted to hear—that they had a legitimate beef and that he could and would take care of it.

Throughout his career, Trump has been a master builder, a master negotiator, and a master salesman. But perhaps what he is most masterful at is finding the leverage point in any situation.

In his first big project, the transformation of a decrepit midtown Manhattan hotel into the Grand Hyatt in the 1970s, he wangled an unprecedented tax abatement by leveraging the desperation of New York City, then in financial meltdown, to get rid of a highly visible eyesore and to launch a major construction project. In the early 1990s, when his own ever-expanding empire was on the ropes, he leveraged the Trump brand to persuade creditors not to foreclose, which would have meant removing his name and the perceived value that went with it, and instead to lower interest rates and work out a repayment schedule. In effect, he had made himself too big to fail, a status that allowed him to emerge similarly unscathed from subsequent corporate bankruptcies in 1999, 2004, and 2009.

Now he was leveraging the global celebrity he had gained from *The Apprentice* to roll over the rest of the Republican candidates. Whenever any of them criticized him, he tossed out a stinging remark that in ordinary circumstances would have seemed petty but now appeared as further evidence that he would not let anything, including what he sneeringly referred to as "political correctness," get in the way of his efforts on behalf of his supporters. He wasn't being rude or thoughtless or insensitive; rather, he had elevated himself to a special truth-teller status that permitted him—even required him—to talk that way.

It was a realm where policy details—exactly how he planned to deal with Iran, Iraq, Afghanistan, ISIS, Syria, Israel, Egypt, terrorism, Mexico, China, Japan, border security, illegal immigrants, health care, education, unemployment, climate change, tax policy, and all the other things he said the Obama administration was totally mishandling—were unnecessary and distracting. His plan, it seemed, boiled down to little more than *Trust me, I can handle it and I'll take care of it.*

Because he was so wealthy, he insisted, he would not be beholden to donors—which raised the question of whether someone who had made his fortune by using other people's money would actually pour that fortune into his own campaign. For the moment, the calculus seemed to be that he would leverage his fame so that large ad buys would be unnecessary, and after he won the nomination the Republican Party would be obliged to pay.

The rollout followed the Donald Trump playbook—the manual that had allowed him to become, as it were, the people's billionaire. He was born rich, had become even richer, and lived in a 53-room penthouse crammed with marble and mirrors and gilded furniture and crystal chandeliers, yet he would hold fast to the blunt, uncensored demeanor that allowed him to come across not as some refined upper-class snob—the kiss of death in politics—but as an ordinary guy who tells it like it is and happens to be the biggest winner in the world.

But after writing a book about Donald Trump, his father, and his grandfather, I think other factors played a pivotal role in his election to the presidency.

There's a Trump family culture of ruthlessly pressing any advantage. His German immigrant grandfather, who operated restaurants in gold rush–era Seattle and the Yukon, amassed a nest egg by offering miners alcohol, food, and proximity to women; his father greatly increased the family fortune by exploiting loopholes in New Deal government subsidies; and Donald used a billion-dollar loss of borrowed money and four corporate bankruptcies to build a global brand and avoid paying personal income taxes for nearly two decades.

That family culture includes an adherence to the success-oriented theology of Dr. Norman Vincent Peale, author of the 1952 bestseller *The Power of Positive Thinking*. In his book, Peale emphasizes the supreme importance of self-confidence, a notion that Donald has weaponized with a winning-at-all-costs, scorched-earth approach that has more than fulfilled his own father's fierce injunction to be a "killer" in every pursuit. But Donald has also contributed his own special flourishes.

For example, his much-ridiculed hair. For years it has been a highly effective trademark, a humanizing bit of vanity that made him the people's billionaire rather than a remote tycoon, and on the campaign trail, his coiffure made him the perpetual center of attention.

Ultimately Trump's success may have hinged on his voice. "I am your voice," he said in his acceptance speech at the Republican National Convention in July 2016—and there's more to that claim than might have been apparent at that moment.

Despite his obsession with showing that he is the most powerful person on earth, his speech doesn't have the archetypal tough-guy edge. Although he's shown he's more than capable of shouting in classic rabble-rousing style, more often than not what comes out when he opens his mouth is not traditional alpha-male talk. Instead of insistently bellowing or pounding his chest, he's tapping into the image of a counter-intuitive strongman who tosses off some of his most devastating comments with a malevolent sneer. His vocabulary is extremely simple, almost to the point of being childish, and his use of incomplete thoughts and sentence fragments has an unmediated, stream-of-consciousness feel.

It is this combination—the hint of menace beneath the surface added to what appears to be an unpolished immediacy—that millions of listeners take as evidence of Trump's authenticity and spontaneity. The way he talks reminds them of the voice inside their own heads—a rich and sometimes dark stew of conversational snippets and memory scraps, random phrases and half-thoughts—and by extension, it somehow seems as if they're hearing the voice inside his head.

To many, the way Trump talks has been evidence of his lack of seriousness, of focus, of discipline. But to his supporters, it is proof that he is the real deal—not focus-grouped, not mediated, not hiding behind a mask of calculation and manipulation. They admire and, in some cases, envy Trump for openly expressing a deepest self that seems to mirror what they think and feel but don't dare reveal to the world.

Donald Trump launched his presidential candidacy at a moment when technology provided him with the perfect megaphone, in the form of Twitter. Even more than the substance of his words, it is the apparent immediacy, even intimacy, of this inner voice that makes his denunciations of "political correctness" strike such a powerful chord.

In fact, there is nothing authentic or spontaneous about what Donald Trump says; everything is considered, strategic, and, as even a casual look at his rallies on YouTube reveals, repeated continually. The impression of having a direct line to what he's thinking is proof to his supporters of his underlying honesty—a vital clue to understanding how it is that this man, the most artificial of creatures, has come to represent "telling it like it is" to voters.

Gwenda Blair
November 2016

PAST AND PRESENT

LONG BEFORE THE STORE OPENED, people were waiting outside, clustered beneath a thicket of umbrellas. Midtown Manhattan, with its mob of skyscrapers and canyonlike streets, can be surprisingly nasty during a downpour. The sheets of water slant in, driving from the side, hitting the pavement hard enough to kick up a knee-high spray. The crowd huddled against the steady downpour, turning this way and that in a doomed effort to keep their backs to the storm, trying to edge closer to the building in the vague hope that it would provide some sort of protection. But nobody complained. They were there to see the most famous man in America, if not the world.

The people who had come by cab or limousine had arrived only lightly doused during the mad dash from the curb across the white marble plaza of the General Motors Building to the entrance of FAO Schwarz. Those who came to the nation's most exclusive toy store by subway or bus had to hike at least a block through the spring deluge, and they were already drenched. But class distinctions had long since disappeared; everyone had merged into one uncomfortable, sodden-shoed, soggy-socked mass.

Once the store opened, the line disappeared inside and up the escalator onto the main floor. There it grew longer. And longer. And then longer still. By late morning it wound back past the enormous

Lego castle and Lego dragon, around the radio-controlled race cars and the miniature Mercedes with the two-horsepower engine, all the way down to Patio Party Barbie and Oscar the Grouch and Babar and the seven-track toy train set with illuminated tunnel and working coal hopper and flag-waving signalman. In New York City, which recognizes all manner of religious occasions, Tuesday, May 16, 1989, was not a holiday, but the crowd included truant schoolchildren with gleeful smiles.

Downstairs the store was empty. A colossal Paddington Bear, majestic yet still cuddly in his six-foot-tall splendor, and the life-size stuffed animals, some of which cost more than coats made from actual pelts, were alone. An in-store juggler, flesh and blood in a bowler hat, gazed yearningly up at the crowd on the second floor.

At the head of the line was a media inferno of flashing lights, waving microphones, whirring cameras, shouted questions. At the center of the commotion was a calm, apparently oblivious man in an immaculate navy blue suit of a conservative cut. His tie, made of rich silk, was red and wide. A blue felt-tip pen with a wide nib protruded from his neatly tended hands. His face—an indoor face, handsome and clean-shaven but heavy jowled—was intent. He was performing a favorite task. Large black wingtips firmly planted on his personal square of immaculate white carpet, he was signing his name: Donald Trump.

His face was everywhere, smiling and confident, his longish blond hair carefully arranged to cover a thinning spot in back, something about his pursed mouth reminiscent of another preternaturally famous American, Elvis Presley. Indeed, he was autographing his face, which adorned thousands of black game boxes the size of an unabridged dictionary. Each box held a game, the object of which was to be like Donald Trump. Like a movie, the game was having its premiere, and the star was taking a turn. The games were stacked everywhere, and on each and every one was a word in two-inch letters: TRUMP.

"Love, Donald," he wrote in one place. In another he inscribed, "Win! Donald Trump."

He was proud of his name and had put it in every conceivable venue, building it into a national symbol of luxury and sybaritic excess. He had gone to court to protect it from being used by anyone else in connection with real estate, including those who had it as a legal surname from birth.[1] He had, in effect, trademarked it. Every time his name appeared in the papers—and Donald Trump took care to see that it appeared on a daily basis—it invoked an aura of opulence, of privilege, of success heaped upon success.

Yet Trump the trademark was not a symbol of aristocracy. He had built the name into an emblem of the American dream itself, of an ordinary fellow with ordinary tastes but extraordinary savvy, of a boy from Queens who had become a real estate developer and risen swiftly to the penthouses of Manhattan, of a billionaire who was married to a beautiful former model, flew in private helicopters, hobnobbed with the glitterati, but somehow had kept his common touch. And bearing this weight, the name was truly potent.

In a sense, Donald Trump had merely polished to the highest of glosses what was already there. "Trump" is a wonderful word, a marvelous name. A name Dickens would surely have given to a prominent character if only he had thought of it, "Trump" evokes trump card, trump hand, trump suit—all terms associated with winning. Whether Donald Trump could have had the same success with any other name is an intriguing question. How fortunate that "Drumpf," the unresonant original version, evolved over the centuries to the current orthography.

Now, at FAO Schwarz, each time Donald Trump signed his name on a shiny black game box, the customer who had purchased it would pick it up and stare at the signature. Mouths commonly fell open; not a few tongues darted out to lick lips. Owners held out their autographed boxes in front of themselves, as if the name were combustible. And it was: the fat vertical strokes were Fame itself, reduced to its essence.

The nation's most famous developer was sitting at a table in front of an enormous eight-foot mock-up of Trump: The Game. Hovering next to him were several private security guards, beefy, anonymous men in large dark suits. To his left, a special kiosk set up that morning was doing a land-office business selling the new game. To his right was a white grand piano being played by pianist Christopher Mason. A regular at parties given by café society in New York, Mason made his living by turning out topical lyrics by the yard. After a few ivory-tickling flourishes, he began with the anthem for the day:

Donald Trump's brought out a game
And you'll never guess its name
It's called Trump: The Game and it's in the stores
And to buy it folks are breaking down the doors. . . .

Big bucks will never seem the same
After you've played Trump: The Game. . . .
If you should forget that Trump's his name
You'll see it 553 times in the game . . .

Trump: The Person, Trump: The Game, and Trump: The Song sat in the middle of a large circle formed by reporters and television crews. As boom mikes bobbed up and down like fishing poles and camera crews filmed, reporters for ABC radio, Associated Press, United Press International, the *New York Post*, the *New York Daily News*, WABC-TV, German and French television, a documentary filmmaker, and a dozen other outlets interviewed people in line, scribbled in notebooks, and shouted out questions to Donald Trump.

"Yo, Donald, can't you stop this rain?"

"Donald, what about a match between you and Milken?"

"Donald, how much money do you make a minute, anyway?"

A number of the autograph seekers brought their own cameras to record the event. Three women, unsuccessful at striking a pose next to the developer, instead stood next to a poster advertising the promotion as a fourth snapped their photograph. "Mr. Trump, your picture is on my desk!" a grandfather gushed as he held out his game for a signature and aimed his Polaroid. Next was a proud papa who whipped out an Instamatic, handed his small son across the table, then snapped half a dozen shots as the blond tycoon gamely held the tyke and flashed a smile.

"Donald Trump for president!" shouted a man in a business suit. Scattered applause came from the line.

An assistant stood by, keeping an even flow of games across the developer's table. Busy bestowing his trademark broad-stroke signature on the games, he ignored most of the reporters' queries. One of the few he answered directly concerned the sale of the Eastern Airlines Washington–New York–Boston shuttle. Would Northwest Airlines beat him out in the heated negotiations to scoop up the jewel of Eastern's tottering empire?

"No, they won't get it because they don't plan to keep on union members," he said. "They'd just let all those guys go, and I just don't think you can treat people that way. Besides, I don't think they've got the financing." Waving away the questioner with a "Sorry, fellas, I've got work to do" nod, he bent again over the seemingly endless stream of black boxes.

——〰——

It is a truism that people become famous today not because of what they accomplish, but because of their skill in selling themselves on television. Donald Trump, in the view of George Ditomassi, was a genius at this kind of salesmanship. The president of Milton Bradley Toys, Ditomassi, a trim, middle-aged figure wearing a dark suit and a club tie, was there to witness the launch of what he hoped would be his newest blockbuster. Each year his company introduced about thirty new toys, and about twenty-eight or twenty-nine flopped. But if just one made it, then you had a Scrabble, a Candyland, a Chutes & Ladders, a Parcheesi—cash cows that had made Milton Bradley the nation's largest toy maker, with 40 percent of the game market.[2] Trump: The Game had a fair shot to join this pantheon.

To be sure, this would require beating the odds. Games based on celebrities have a poor track record. Most end up like Flip Your Wig, a Beatles spin-off put out by Milton Bradley in 1964 and now a forgotten oddity traded by old Beatles fans. Milton Bradley's game based on Gorbachev was another dud.

But it seemed to Ditomassi that Trump: The Game was in another category altogether. For one thing, it had the name. And it had a few other things going for it as well. Its creator was Jeff Breslow, a toy pro from Chicago who had created merchandise associated with Lucille Ball, Doug Henning, and Evel Knievel, as well as the noncelebrity board games Operation, Mousetrap, Simon, and Hands Down. As soon as he read the developer's book, *The Art of the Deal*, Breslow saw a board game that would give players the fantasy of sharing Donald Trump's opulent lifestyle and charisma. Breslow's previous celebrity games had all fizzled, but it seemed to George Ditomassi that this one was different. He rushed it into production for Toy Fair, the industry's major sales event, held each February in New York, and arranged a $4 million ad budget, the largest in toy history.

Unlike Monopoly, another real estate game, Trump: The Game has only a small number of properties, bought at the beginning of the game, and the play focuses on postpurchase wheeling and dealing, coups, bankruptcies, and, inevitably, double crosses. The currency is different, too. The lowest denomination is $10 million, and Donald Trump's face and name appear on every bill. The cover on Monopoly reads, "Real Estate Trading Game Equipment"; the Trump box declares, "It's not whether you win or lose, it's whether you win!"

During the long months of preparation, all plans remained secret. The day before Toy Fair began, word broke that Milton Bradley and the developer were talking about a game. Then came the not-so-secret weapon: Donald Trump. When he walked into the Toy Fair showroom, Breslow was amazed. The media were slavering at his feet. He was signing autographs and giving interviews to reporters from all over the country. It was pandemonium, a crowded but essentially humdrum trade show suddenly invaded by Fame.

There was more to come. Donald Trump unveiled the game on February 7 during a press conference in the six-story pink marble atrium of his flagship Fifth Avenue building, Trump Tower. Again it was a mob scene, but he presided over the event with cheerful magnanimity. After pulling a gold cloth off the giant Trump: The Game mock-up later used for the FAO Schwarz promotion, the developer tossed a pair of fourteen-carat-gold dice for the cameras. His game, he declared, was not only more sophisticated than Monopoly, it was better than an MBA program. "I think that if you can do well at this game," he told one interviewer, "you can sort of determine in your own mind whether or not you're going to be a good businessman."

Despite the crowd, things were still not hot enough in Donald Trump's estimation. To Ditomassi's amazement, the developer suddenly announced that his share of any profits would go to charity. In almost the same breath, he proclaimed that Trump: The Game would be *"the* game for the nineties."

Three long, dangerous months stretched between the game's debut at Toy Fair and the national rollout in May. A segment on *48 Hours*, reported by Dan Rather, was a boost. Through a continuous stream of press releases, Milton Bradley managed to place mentions of the game here and there. Then, in the early spring, Donald Trump visited the company's factory in East Longmeadow, Massachusetts, a suburb of Springfield. Alighting from his helicopter on the lawn, he waved to the large crowd that had gathered, then strode across the grass to the entrance. Behind him trotted reporters, camera crews, and security guards.

Inside the gleaming glass-and-brick building, he announced that he wanted to head for the assembly line. "I came up here because I wanted to see the people who do the work," he declared as he shook hands with employees who every day cut and trimmed millions of bills bearing his likeness. "The hell with the executives!" That evening TV viewers saw the tycoon at the plant, and the next day newspaper readers read about his field trip.

Now, three months, one week, and two days after its debut, Trump: The Game was finally sitting on the first store shelf. Even at FAO Schwarz's premium price of $35 per unit, $10 more than Toys "R" Us and Kmart would be charging, sales were brisk on this rainy Tuesday morning. Each party in line purchased a game, and many bought extras and had them personalized as gifts.

On the far side of the room, away from the press and the line, an old man stood quietly in a wet, slightly bedraggled raincoat. His hair and elegantly waxed mustache were bright red, with a touch of magenta. His eyes were a brilliant blue, almost turquoise. He held three games under his arm.

"Where can I pay for these?" he asked one of the tycoon's security guards.

"Oh, that's all right," the guard answered. "You don't have to pay, Mr. Trump."

"That's not right," the old man said stubbornly. "I want to pay."

"Mr. Trump, I said it's *all right*," said the guard. "He's your own son, and you don't have to pay."

The man in the raincoat was Fred Trump, Donald's father. Like his son, he was in real estate. Also like his son, he was immensely wealthy. Indeed, his son had relied on his father's wealth in several tight situations that he didn't often discuss with reporters. But Fred Trump had not made his money by turning himself into an image of celebrity and cavorting in multimillion-dollar penthouses. Instead he had built ordinary homes for ordinary people in Brooklyn and Queens. Whereas the son made vast sums by running casinos in Atlantic City and through financial manipulations, the father had made his producing houses and apartments with government subsidies. Whereas the son lived in the center of photographers' lenses, the father had kept his personal life out of the media's glare. The two men's lives were vastly different—as different as business in 1940 and business in 1989, as different as America itself had become in that time.

In turn, Fred Trump's life was far different from that of his own father, Friedrich Trump, who became a real estate entrepreneur in New York City near the end of his life. Friedrich Trump had no tax shelters to take advantage of and none of the government housing schemes that would create homes for millions of Americans. He had only his bare hands, but he went at the business of becoming rich with the single-mindedness that has run through all three generations of the family. Born a vintner and trained as a barber, he had through a combination of circumstance and sheer grit become a Gold Rush–era saloonkeeper whose customers depended on him for food, liquor, and women. Hard living and hard drinking, Friedrich laid the foundation for the fortune that now, almost a century later, was personified in red-haired Fred, standing at the edge of the spotlight and staring; and full-cheeked Donald, signing box after box as the morning wore on. Three men; three empires; three different times: the whole constituting a singular history of American capitalism itself.

That day at FAO Schwarz, Fred Trump, the middle man who built the middle empire, still wanted to go by the old rules, the rules that said a customer waited his place in line and paid for the merchandise. In cash. He started to walk toward the special kiosk.

"Come on, Mr. Trump, let's go back here," said the guard, taking the old man by the elbow. "There's a nice, quiet little room, away from all these people." As they walked around the corner, away from the crowd, Fred Trump looked back over his shoulder. His son, still autographing games, did not look up.

—⁓—

As he had predicted at FAO Schwarz, Donald Trump took final possession of what had been the Eastern Shuttle three weeks later. In exchange for a loan of $365 million from a consortium of banks led by Citibank, he was free to paint his name on the tails of twenty-one aircraft. For the first and only time, he chose to do so in red rather than gold. It was the sole touch of modesty; as soon as he took possession, the operation underwent a makeover that included faux marble bathrooms, all-leather seats, strings of pearls on all female flight attendants, concierge service at terminals, and its own in-flight magazine, called *Trump's*.

In less than a year, Trump: The Game would disappear from American toy stores and memories, and an economic recession would begin to cast a long shadow over the nation and, especially, its most high-flying entrepreneurs. Eventually, because Donald Trump would be unable to make the interest payments on the massive debt he undertook when purchasing the shuttle, his creditors would require it to be sold. Much of the rest of the empire he had assembled would share the same fate. But unlike other magnates of the time, he would emerge from financial turmoil to create another empire. He would manage, construct, enhance, oversee, renovate, glamorize, publicize, market, and, by his general presence—his Trump-ness, as it were— add value to property after property, although he would not exactly own many of them. Yet displayed across the front of each and every part of that empire would be the name *Trump*, larger, shinier, and, literally, more brassy than ever.

THE TRUMPS

Part I

THE FOUNDER:
FRIEDRICH TRUMP

CHAPTER ONE

THE NEW WORLD

ON OCTOBER 17, 1885, a thin, gangly sixteen-year-old boy watched from the rail of the SS *Eider* as it approached the island of Manhattan. He had traveled alone to America, leaving behind his family, his homeland, and his obligation to enter into his country's military service. He did not intend to return. He had jammed a few clothes into a small suitcase; otherwise he had left every scrap of his past life behind. If he had second thoughts, they did not show. He wanted to become rich, he was in a hurry about it, and he knew that America was the place to be. His name was Friedrich Trump.

America at last! New York! It was like no place he'd ever seen— no place any European had ever seen. Dozens of ships shoved each other aside for space in the vast, rotting port, and mates and long-shoremen screamed themselves hoarse on wharves that were among the world's busiest and most poorly maintained. Noisy, chaotic, bustling, a place of violent activity and indescribable filth, New York Harbor was everything Friedrich Trump had hoped for. It was a monument to commerce and to the possibility of getting ahead.

The *Eider* anchored, and her 505 steerage passengers lined up for a lengthy interrogation and medical inspection. Bellowing instructions, customs agents pawed through the hundreds of shapeless bags that were the worldly goods of these new immigrants. This was Friedrich Trump's first exposure to democracy, American style; the cabin-class passengers went through inspection and customs while

the ship was still entering the harbor, thus bypassing the humiliating
public perusal.

After a seemingly endless interval, officials herded the tired, hungry newcomers onto a pair of 150-ton barges. The blue sky of Indian
summer stretched above the vessels as they heaved their way toward
an immense circular structure at the southern tip of the island. Thick
walled and bristling with cannons, Castle Garden had been built to
defend New York Harbor during the Napoleonic Wars.[1] Fortunately
its utility had never been called into question, for it resembled less a
mighty fortress than the stage set for an opera buffa. After Waterloo,
the city fathers rented out Castle Garden for public events, but in
1855 the government made it the official entry point for immigrants,
stirring protests from neighbors. Commodore Cornelius Vanderbilt,
the shipping and railroad tycoon whose ancestors had arrived a respectable two centuries earlier, complained bitterly that he would
suffer when the newcomers' pestilential odors wafted across the
street into his palatial home.

Vanderbilt wasn't merely being snobbish. Friedrich Trump and
his fellow travelers *did* stink. "Ship," the perfume created when unwashed bodies mix for several weeks in an unventilated space with
seasickness and a lack of sanitary facilities, pervaded the *Eider* and
everything and everyone on it; long after they disembarked, the odor
still clung to those who had crossed the Atlantic in steerage. When
the *Eider*'s passengers stepped onshore, authorities immediately ushered them into Castle Garden's gigantic lavatory and urged them to
wash themselves in the rows of basins and huge twenty-foot tubs full
of constantly running water.

Beyond the baths were lines of desks. Immigrants crowded
around them, begging in half a dozen languages for instructions about
changing money, buying railroad tickets, and making their way
around the city. Above them, an old iron staircase led from a former
stage to the superintendent's office, and uniformed men ran upstairs
and down, waving documents and clanging their boots. Friedrich
Trump presented his papers, had them stamped, and found himself
shoved into the grimy central rotunda. In the eerie half-light of
gas lamps, officials shouted the names of those who had mail or, if
they were fortunate, friends and relatives there in person. When
"Friedrich Trump" rang out, the slim, light-haired youth jumped up

and dashed over to the waiting room. His older sister, who had Americanized her name to Katherine, and her husband, Fred Schuster, stood there, smiling and teary eyed. They had not seen Friedrich for two years.

Katherine had been in the United States long enough to know the drill. New immigrants were hot commodities. Almost by definition, they could be relied upon to work hard and to lack street smarts in the matter of pay scales, qualities that endeared them to many businesses and administrative organizations, including the federal government.[2] Next to the waiting room was the Labor Exchange, where employers waited to get first crack at the newcomers.[3]

Advancing into the throng of bawling voices, Friedrich Trump quickly made the happy discovery that many were shouting in German and that some of the German speakers were looking for a barber. Friedrich Trump had apprenticed as a barber. He made contact, learned an address, found out when to show up for work. It was dizzying; just hours after his arrival he had a new home and a new job. It was true—anything could happen in this raw new land.

In fact, the Trump family's adventures in America had hardly begun.

—◈—

Friedrich Trump was not leaving home so much as fleeing three centuries of barbaric European history. He was born and raised in the village of Kallstadt, in the region of southwestern Germany called the Pfalz, or the Palatinate in English. Today the Pfalz, a lush, pleasant, affluent place, shows little sign of its nightmarish past. But in Friedrich Trump's time, memories were fresh, and young people with poor prospects tried to escape as soon as they could.

The Pfalz sits athwart a stretch of sandy soil and clay in the foothills of the Haardt Mountains. Protected from excessive rain and cold by mountain and forest, the slopes are cool and moist by night and sunny by day—perfect conditions for growing grapes. Kallstadt has been known for its viniculture since Roman times. Located some forty miles west of the Rhine River, the "highway of Europe," the village was easily able to transport its wine to the rest of Europe.

Unfortunately, its proximity to the Rhine meant that the rest of Europe also had easy access to Kallstadt—with dreadful results. Over the centuries the Pfalz was invaded, sometimes more than once, by Spain, Austria, Prussia, Russia, and France. Murderous squabbles among the dozens of competing German principalities filled interludes between foreign occupations. For centuries the good people of Kallstadt unwillingly supplied occupying armies with provisions, housing, and, at times, troops. In return, the invaders periodically burned the village to the ground.

In 1608 Hanns Drumpf, an itinerant lawyer, showed up in Kallstadt, then a muddy settlement of fewer than six hundred people. Most were involved in winegrowing and did not welcome newcomers into the vineyards. But soon after Drumpf's arrival, the Thirty Years' War engulfed Germany and ushered in one of the worst periods in Kallstadt's bloody history. The village burned to the ground at least five times—the period was so chaotic that nobody is sure of the exact number—and at one point only ten families remained in residence. By war's end in 1648, about 40 percent of its inhabitants had died, and economic activity came to a standstill.[4] It was a scene of near total devastation; it was also an opportunity, however unbidden, for Drumpf's family to gain entry into Kallstadt life. By the end of the century a winegrower named John Philip Trump—the family changed the spelling of its name in the course of the war—was a taxpayer in good standing. Although their holdings were never more than modest, the Trumps had become part of the village's social elite.

While European powers withdrew from the old Holy Roman Empire and embarked on the long road to becoming modern nation-states and colonial empires, Germany marched in the opposite direction, fragmenting into ever-smaller mini-nations. By 1789, as a famous phrase has it, Germany had 1789 different governments. Most of these statelets were tiny, just a castle and a village or two; the majority were politically unstable; all had more or less autocratic nobles in charge.[5] These petty lords tended to aggrandize themselves by bickering with their neighbors and imposing upon their subjects constant levies, conscriptions, and outright seizures. Kallstadt endured its share of these hardships. Unlike most such villages, however, it was never subordinate to any one ruling house, which perhaps contributed to the sense of independence and sturdy self-reliance for which its inhabitants were known.[6]

Napoleon unified some of the German states in 1790, when he conquered everything west of the Rhine. But the French occupation was far from gentle. Soldiers raped and looted. Innocent bystanders, including a Trump relative named Richard Bechtloff, were shot in the street, and the town had to devote its resources to providing food and shelter for the occupying forces. Wine makers were hardly immune, for they produced the village's most valuable product. The Trumps saw their casks emptied by soldiers again and again.

By this time many Pfalzers had already fled. Indeed, so many had immigrated to America that until after the Revolutionary War, German speakers in the United States were routinely referred to as "Palatines," the Anglicized version of "Pfalzers."[7] Fearful of the population drain, local officials in the Pfalz virtually banned emigration. But Pfalzers circumvented the restrictions by pretending that they were only going on short trips and then, at a train station en route, picking up the suitcases they had stored there. By the close of the eighteenth century the Pfalz was the only region in Germany with a diminishing population. The end of French occupation in 1814 did not mean liberation for Kallstadt and the other villages, which still had to provide food and shelter to foreign troops. Victorious soldiers from the alliance of Russia, Prussia, Bavaria, and Austria camped there while their leaders tried to figure out where to redraw the frontiers that Napoleon had obliterated. In 1815 the Congress of Vienna awarded the Pfalz to the state of Bavaria. Fourteen years later, when Friedrich Trump's father, Johannes, was born, the Bavarians were still in charge.

Johannes Trump grew up in a community that was vibrantly proud of its long wine-making tradition. Pfalzers regarded themselves as the aristocrats of German agriculture, a people who did not have to bow down to anyone. In return, Bavarian nobles made known their disapproval of people they saw as loud, crude, wine-loving hotheads. Viewed from the royal court in Munich, where splendid dress was the norm, the Pflaz fell particularly short in the matter of appearance. Other German-speaking groups might pride themselves on elaborate festival costumes, but Pfalzers were stubbornly plain. Men refused to wear anything more formal than simple white linen shirts and wide blue pants, and by the time Johannes Trump reached manhood, they resisted hats as well.[8]

Bavarian rule was more than a matter of clashing styles of dress, of course. The court at Munich issued one dictatorial edict after another. Sporadic rebellions erupted; officials quickly reacted; bursts of emigration followed. The emigrants were not always poor; many well-to-do, even wealthy, folk left. They may not have wanted a revolution, but they could not accept the lack of any reforms whatsoever. Bavarian rule finally ended when Otto von Bismarck, prime minister of Prussia, forcibly merged the various states into one. On January 18, 1871, Wilhelm I of Prussia was crowned emperor in the Hall of Mirrors at Versailles, and modern German history began.[9] New, Bismarck-inspired decrees made three years of military service compulsory, and the penalty for draft dodging was jail.[10]

Johannes Trump was forty-two years old when the modern German state was born, and he had been sick, probably with emphysema, for more than ten years. Coughing and gasping, he insisted on working in the family fields as long as he could, despite the dense clouds of noxious fertilizer fumes that blanketed the valley. The family was all too familiar with tragedy. Two boys had died in infancy, and recently Johannes's brother had been killed when a tree he was cutting down fell on him. Now the desperate family borrowed and borrowed again in a frantic attempt to find the right doctors and medicines. All manner of magic potions and elixirs were available in pharmacies and shops, but the new cures promised far more than they could deliver. One doctor after another came to the sick man's door. Nonetheless, Johannes Trump died on July 6, 1877, at the age of forty-eight, leaving a family ruined by debt.

Friedrich Trump was just eight years old at the time. The fourth of six children, he was born on March 14, 1869. By modern standards his childhood was hard, but he did not think of himself as deprived. He was a frail but spirited child, the younger of the two boys and babied a little for that reason. The family lived comfortably in a two-story house, half-timbered in Hansel and Gretel fashion, on Freinsheimstrasse, a cobbled street not far from the village center. From the room that the thin, light-haired boy shared with several of his siblings, he could hear the bell in the tall, onion-shaped dome of the central Lutheran church. It regulated the day for everyone in Kallstadt from before sunrise until long after dark. The family holdings, located in the hills, were still small, but their plots of wine grapes provided enough income for the Trumps to give generously to the church. In 1868, the year before Friedrich Trump was born, his father's church taxes were three florins and thirty-four kreuzer, the equivalent of a month's income for a laborer at the time.

Despite the family's relative prosperity, Friedrich Trump had no money for elaborate games or toys. Nor did he have the time. His day-time hours were filled to the brim with the demands of church, school, and the family arbors. A Kallstadt child's closest brush with indulgence occurred a few weeks before Christmas, when Pelznickel, a local resident tricked out in tatters, patrolled the cobbled streets. Stopping at every household, Pelznickel would ask about each child's behavior for the previous year. Those who had been nice received apples, nuts, and gingerbread; those who hadn't received a thrashing from Pelznickel's sidekick, another local resident dressed in rags.[11]

All the Trumps, young and old, worked in the fields. Wine producers might regard themselves as the aristocrats of agriculture, but it was still a hard life. Farming methods, tools, vessels, and machines had changed little since the Roman occupation. Although the new German chemical industry had recently introduced the artificial fertilizers that cost Johannes Trump his health, Kallstadt farmers had no pesticides or fungicides. When pests invaded their crops, the Trumps, like farmers since medieval times, raced into the fields to paint each individual leaf with copper sulfate. The job was time-consuming, laborious in the extreme, but of utmost urgency, and sometimes even delicate Friedrich had to work late at night, lamplight glowing on the bucket of stinking copper sulfate at his side. Even with the day's most advanced fertilizers, the vines grew only thigh high; as a result, picking grapes was backbreaking work.[12]

After the harvest, the whole village celebrated All Souls' Day on November 2 with a parade and an enormous feast. But with Johannes Trump's death, everything changed for his family. At forty-one, Friedrich's mother, Katherina Kober Trump, had six hungry children and ruinous debts.[13] Although she was the daughter of a winegrowing family and no stranger to hard labor, she could not work a vineyard on her own. Katherina, fifteen; Jakob, thirteen; and Luise, twelve, did what they could; Friedrich, eight, was too frail to work, and Elizabetha, four, and Barbara, only one, were too young. Katherina scratched together a tiny income by baking bread for the neighbors, but the Trumps were on the edge of disaster.

As soon as it was possible, Katherina shipped Friedrich off to learn a trade. In 1883, at the age of fourteen, he went to the nearby town of Frankenthal, where a barber named Friedrich Lang needed an apprentice. In its way, this was a modern step. Before unification, Germany's byzantine political structure had placed formidable difficulties before those trying to improve their lot by moving from one place to another. Now tens of thousands of people whose families had lived in the same place and had the same occupation for generations were suddenly able to look for new cities and new jobs. Friedrich Trump was one of them.

A small center of porcelain manufacture in the eighteenth century, Frankenthal had become an industrial town of perhaps twenty thousand people. Friedrich Trump saw little of it. Seven mornings a week he opened up the barbershop before dawn; seven evenings a week he swept up the day's cuttings. In between he ran errands, unpacked supplies, maintained and sharpened tools, brought meals and snacks, and slowly mastered the art of using a straightedge razor to shave a beefy burgher without a nick. After two and a half years he satisfied the terms of his contract. Now a man with a profession, he returned to Kallstadt in the fall of 1885.

The homecoming was brief. Katherina's fortunes had not improved, and she still could not afford to feed another mouth. Neither could Friedrich support himself barbering in Kallstadt, for there was not enough work. Eventually he would have to serve in the army, but three years of grinding routine in a remote outpost was not an attractive prospect. If he refused to serve, he would be clapped in jail. The stifling lack of opportunity in the village seemed to close in on him. Without any apparent opportunity for a better life, he saw what lay ahead as dreary, difficult, and poor. He seemed to have no choice but to leave. "I agreed with my mother that I should go to America," he later wrote.

"Agreed" might be the wrong word. According to family lore, he simply wrote a note to his mother explaining that he was off to the New World, enclosed his last day's earnings of one mark, thirty-two pfennig to be returned to his boss, and slipped out in the middle of the night. Katherina woke up to find Kallstadt's population reduced by 1. It was now 985 souls.

Friedrich Trump's act was risky, but hardly foolish. For more than fifty years Germans had been the single largest immigrant group in the United States, and by now they were a well-established presence, courted assiduously by aspiring politicians. In the 1850s Abraham Lincoln went so far as to buy a German newspaper and even tried to learn the language.[14] Eager to entice good German workers, American states and industries launched recruitment campaigns, especially in the Pfalz.[15] The Northern Pacific Railroad, which needed people to live along its sparsely populated lines and to produce freight to be shipped, insisted that North Dakota's capital be named Bismarck after the German chancellor. In addition, the railroad hired agents across Europe to distribute more than half a million copies of company publications and place ads in newspapers extolling the virtues of the American Great Plains.[16] Germans responded; more than a million immigrated between 1880 and 1890.

One reason Friedrich joined the exodus was Germany's inheritance laws, introduced by Napoleon, which required that property be parceled out among children in strictly equitable fashion.[17] For families with little land, like the Trumps, this practice meant that children inherited uselessly small pieces of land. In the United States, on the other hand, the Homestead Act, passed in 1862, ensured that anyone—anyone!—could get title to 160 acres in exchange for working the land for five years. It sounded like an amazing deal to people whose holdings were ever dwindling.

Equally important, Friedrich Trump was not going to be alone. His oldest sister had immigrated to New York a year earlier, at twenty-three. There she joined her fiancé, a shipping clerk from Kallstadt who had changed his own name, Friedrich, to the more American Fred. He had come to America after two older cousins set up a wine business in New York City. Now married and working as a maid, Katherine had an infant daughter and seemed to be prospering. Friedrich Trump planned to stay with her while he set himself up in one of New York's many German neighborhoods.

He left from Bremen, nearly 350 miles north of Kallstadt. The first port to require posted schedules and to take steps to ensure passenger safety and well-being, Bremen now lived off the north German immigrant trade. Like all German cities, it was a bustling but orderly place.[18] All visitors spending more than twenty-four hours in the city were required to register with the police, and the streets were so clean that one could almost literally have eaten off them. Friedrich Trump spent his last days on German soil in one of Bremen's scores of boardinghouses, all filled to capacity with would-be Americans,[19] as well as an abundant supply of *Bauernfanger* ("trappers of greenhorns"), ready to take advantage whenever possible.[20]

For about $20,[21] Friedrich Trump bought not a berth but a space in steerage class on the SS *Eider*, the next boat out from the North German Lloyd Lines. On October 7, 1885, he boarded what was a modern steamship and soon was in the gray, frigid North Sea. Conditions were better than they had been before the steam age, but the voyage was still crowded and unpleasant for Friedrich.[22] In calm weather the ship provided one scanty meal a day. Everything else was up to the passenger, who could cook on the deck if the ocean spray did not swamp the fire. Drinking water was in short supply; water for baths was nonexistent.[23] The stink of "ship" quickly pervaded the air, and the sight of steerage passengers huddled over the weak fires on deck was depressing.

Ten days after his departure, Friedrich Trump stood on the deck, a hawk-faced boy beneath a sheaf of light hair, waiting for his first glimpse of New York Harbor.

—⁂—

Not far from Castle Garden stood the station for the elevated train. During rush hour it cost the same as the streetcar, five cents, and the rest of the time it was ten cents. It was noisier and dirtier than streetcars, but it was also modern, fast, and convenient. The pea green steam locomotives chuffed up and down Manhattan from dawn to midnight, rattling on overhead tracks at up to thirty miles an hour and spewing sparks and ashes on passersby.[24] Friedrich Trump couldn't help but be bowled over by the elevated—an actual train passing directly over a city! It was everything he had come to New York to find, and he must have climbed aboard with a soaring anticipation.[25]

As the steel-rimmed wheels squeaked shrilly up Second Avenue, Trump brushed the grit from his clothes and peered through the smoky windows while the city flowed beneath him. Endless rows of five- to seven-story cast-iron buildings passed beneath his gaze, their brick facades gritty from the wood and coal smoke that was playing silent havoc with the lungs of New Yorkers. Behind them, barely visible in the smog, rose the steeple of Trinity Church, the monstrous eleven-story headquarters of the *New York Tribune,* and the city's greatest architectural wonder, the soaring span of the Brooklyn Bridge.

By European standards the whole enormous city of more than a million people had been thrown up in a single violent instant. Shaped in the endlessly boiling cauldron of capitalism, it was a monument to the chaotic growth, change, and destruction unleashed when the pursuit of wealth proceeds virtually untrammeled. Buildings went up and were torn down in an instant; roads were paved, smashed, and finished again. Thick cables crisscrossed in a dense, unsightly spiderweb of electrical, telephone, and telegraph lines.[26] And everywhere Friedrich Trump looked, he saw the crackling raw energy of people making money. Opportunity shone from the streets like the new incandescent lights now bathing Broadway, and the thrilled young man in the elevated train was determined to seize it.

Things were different at ground level. The Trump-Schuster party exited at Grand Street, in the middle of what would later be called the Lower East Side. Fighting through the by-now-familiar shower of ashes, they walked into a scene out of Bedlam. Sidewalks and pavement alike were buried beneath foul heaps of garbage, mud, tobacco juice, and animal excrement, for in addition to its many cows and horses, New York City had ten thousand feral swine. Stagecoach and pushcart drivers bellowed at each other, and the streets, paved with huge, uneven cobblestones, were so bumpy that at least one doctor refused to let convalescent patients travel on them. The result was constant confusion, countless accidents, frequent runaway horses, and general pandemonium.

The Schuster apartment, at 76 Forsyth Street, was just a block away, but it was in an oasis of comparative calm. Dozens of Kallstadt folk lived in the neighborhood, where they had carved out a little piece of the Pfalz in the Lower East Side. Whenever Friedrich walked down the street, he heard a familiar German dialect, and on Sundays the air was thick with the smell of the same breads and cakes, made from rosewater-flavored *Hefeteig* dough, which his mother had produced back home.

Nonetheless, even these familiar touches did not offset the discomfort of the Forsyth Street building, whose owner, one John Wetterau, had replaced the two smaller buildings previously on the lot with a single larger and more profitable structure. Five stories tall, it was plastered against its neighbors and extended two-thirds of the way back from the street, an arrangement that maximized the rental space within its four walls. Because the new building was sandwiched in between two others like it, it had no side windows. Each floor was sliced into two long, narrow apartments, with four and five rooms strung one after another like the cars on a train; unsurprisingly, New Yorkers dubbed them "railroad" apartments. The arrangement provided each flat with two small windows, one at either end, but the inside rooms, lacking light and air, were stifling in the warm Indian summer weather.[27] The layout made privacy impossible, for traversing the apartment required tramping through every room.

Friedrich Trump reported for work the day after his arrival. Because it was a Sunday, most jobs would not have required him to come in, but barbershops stayed open seven days a week. Germans dominated the profession, which, given that the barber's role was one part lathering and shaving and one part dispensing gossip and advice, gave German culture a major toehold in everyday life. Next to the saloon, the barbershop was the primary hangout for working-class men, the place where coworkers who labored hard the rest of the week relaxed, smoked cigars, and schmoozed. The fixtures were black walnut, old carpet covered the chairs, and often a few canaries chirped in the background as the tonsorial masters turned out a succession of Galways, Van Dykes, County Downs, and other popular hair and beard styles. To supplement his income, the owner often installed a tobacco counter, signaling its existence by placing a wooden Indian on the sidewalk next to the traditional striped barber pole.[28]

Friedrich Trump did not work twenty-four hours a day. Young, unattached, and modestly solvent, he could devote his few spare hours to exploring the giant, throbbing metropolis in which he intended to reestablish his family. New York was a social world unto itself, inconceivably more complex than anything Trump had previously encountered, At the bottom of the ladder were the city's thousands of homeless, jammed into the Bowery. Often they holed up in "stale beer dives," rough saloons that bought the last suds from empty kegs and sold this flat brew for a few cents per mug. Homeless customers slaked their thirst for next to nothing and then passed out in large numbers on the sawdust-covered floor, which functioned as a de facto dormitory and shelter. For those without even the little money required for stale beer, the only hope was Mr. Fleischmann's lower Broadway bakery, which handed out day-old bread at midnight to scores of the destitute.

Just above the homeless were the Gypsies who camped out on Broadway in the Fifties, the streetwalkers who lined up by the hundreds along Sixth Avenue, and the gangs of young men who preyed on them and their customers. Prostitution was especially rampant; block after block, house after house, displayed red blinds. Street gangs, too, proliferated. To walk through Hell's Kitchen on the West Side of Manhattan or the Gas House district on the Lower East Side was a risky matter, for there was no telling when a dozen thugs would suddenly swoop down, brandishing pistols and knives, bricks and stones.[29]

At another level altogether were immigrant workers like Friedrich and Katherine Schuster and Friedrich Trump. Many worked in the fast-growing garment industry; others toiled as domestic help in middle- and upper-class households, day laborers in the busy construction industry, even cowboys, like the shouting riders who drove herds of Texas longhorns down 14th Street to the slaughterhouse. However they made their way through the world, these arrivals became solid members of the labor force and, once they had fulfilled the residency requirements, citizens and voters. Anxious to do well but fearful of failing, they worked long hours for low pay and had little time or money for paid amusements.

Then, as now, at the other end of the social scale were those with wealth or, more exactly, the appearance of wealth, an effect New York's upper crust was highly skilled at producing. "Extravagance," contemporary journalist James McCabe bemoaned, "is the besetting sin of New York society. Money is absolutely thrown away."[30] Thrown away, yes, but strategically, with maximum fanfare. Often this meant a lavish party; the most famous was the $250,000 costume ball given in March 1884 by Mrs. William Vanderbilt, daughter-in-law of the sharp-nosed transportation magnate Commodore Vanderbilt. The costumes alone, ranging from Mary Stuart to Electric Light (diamonds on white satin), came to another $30,000 and kept 140 dressmakers sewing for five weeks, and the opening "hobby horse quadrille" featured life-size stuffed horses made of real hides.

Such activities received acres of coverage in New York's scores of newspapers. Back in 1860, as Abraham Lincoln himself was the first to admit, Matthew Brady's noble photos had helped elect an unknown congressman from Illinois to the presidency—a lesson not lost on future seekers of fame, fortune, or political office. Framed photographs of notables sold briskly, as did newspapers carrying exhaustive accounts of their lives, loves, and luxurious wardrobes. The same American ethic of individualism—expressed first in terms of religious preference, then in capitalist initiative and westward expansion—that had attracted millions of Europeans, including Friedrich Trump, was now fueling the growing celebrity business.

The man who was the archetypal celebrity, who gave the notion of fame for fame's sake a whole new dimension, was a New Yorker named Jim Fisk. The son of a Vermont wagon peddler, he was a big, fat man renowned for doing everything publicly and to excess. Every day the papers carried accounts of the vast quantities of food and drink he consumed, the diamonds he wore on his fingers, the jewel-studded costumes he designed for himself, and the marble and gilt decorations that ornamented his yachts and residences. "His monogram was placed on everything he owned or was connected with," wrote McCabe. "He had little regard for morality or public sentiment, and hesitated at nothing necessary to the success of his schemes. His great passion was for notoriety, and he cared not what he did so it made people talk about him."[31] His place in the superstar pantheon was ensured when he committed the deliciously horrifying sin of abandoning his wife and children to set up house with a bosomy actress. To the delight of the tabloids, Fisk was shot to death in a hotel lobby by a jealous rival for the actress's affections and buried in the uniform of his own private navy.

Then as now, behavior that would have been insufferable in

someone of modest means became instead audacious, perhaps even admirable, when writ so very large and unapologetic. Fisk violated every ethical principle Americans supposedly held dear. Yet many saw in him the epitome of American individualism, of a determination, grit, and unshakable self-assurance that seemed critical for the success of the free enterprise system. He did what they wanted to do, and they applauded.

Jim Fisk and Friedrich Trump never met, of course. But the two men did have a peculiarly American connection. Friedrich Trump was infected by the dream of instant wealth that Fisk embodied. Being a barber wasn't enough for the young immigrant. He wanted money on a grander, faster scale, the scale of Jim Fisk. He wouldn't make it. But a century later his grandson Donald would, in a sense, *become* Jim Fisk.

<hr />

In Kallstadt, the first of May meant the beginning of spring, but in New York it was moving day. It was the day that annual residential leases expired and thus the day when addresses changed. On May 1, 1886, Trump and his relatives joined the local rite of spring by boxing up their belongings and moving about a mile and a half up Manhattan to 606 East 17th Street.

With the addition of Friedrich Trump to the household, the flat on Forsyth Street had been full to bursting. Pooling their joint incomes, the siblings and the brother-in-law had sent money to the widow Trump and asked another sibling, Luise, to join them. A move was now imperative, but having another wage earner under the same roof meant they would have more resources and could send more funds back to Kallstadt. Moreover, because their new home, in a commercial structure with storage on the lower floors and living quarters above, was owned by Fred Schuster's cousins George and William Schuster, the combined Schuster/Trump household could get a break on the rent.

Only a few decades earlier, 17th Street had been empty landfill off the East River; now it was covered with new dwellings, and the

city's northern edge had moved past 42nd Street. No one had ever anticipated having development this far up the island. At the beginning
of the century, when City Hall went up near Manhattan's southern
tip, its builders left the white Massachusetts marble that sheathed
the eastern, southern, and western faces off the northern side because everyone assumed that not many people would be looking at
the building from that direction.[32] But real estate speculators kept
pushing their way up the island, erecting new buildings along the
path of the elevated trains that snaked along Ninth, Sixth, Third, and
Second Avenues. When the elevated had first been proposed, critics
had sneered that no one would climb the steps up to the platform.
Now the only reason not to climb the steps was that they were too
crowded.[33]

Not all the expansion was to the north; in a manner even more
unanticipated, the city also grew to the east and west. As European
settlers produced a city, they also, in the natural course of events, produced garbage. At first people simply filled ditches with it. Soon the
city was paying carters to haul it away to the nearest dumps, which
were the Hudson and East Rivers. The amount to be hauled grew at a
prodigious rate, increasing eightfold in a single four-year period from
1856 to 1860 and even more thereafter.[34] In 1858, after great public
outcry, the city finally barred any further dumping in the rivers.
Meanwhile, however, so much had already been dumped that cur-
rents were permanently altered and the Manhattan shoreline on both
the East and Hudson Rivers vastly extended. By October 1885, when
Friedrich Trump stepped ashore, Manhattan was nearly 25 percent
bigger than it had been when Peter Minuit purchased the island from
the Indians.[35]

The new land initially served for smelly but necessary functions,
such as slaughterhouses and tanneries, as well as factories and dock
facilities. Most important for the city's fortunes, railroad yards and
storage depots also appeared there. As more new land was created, the
overcrowded city continued to push out at the edges, shoving these
heavy-duty industries ever farther out and allowing their space to
be taken over by new residential, commercial, and light industrial
structures, including the Trumps' new home. Along the way, small
entrepreneurs, like the Schuster cousins, became slightly larger

entrepreneurs, and large entrepreneurs—the Van Cortlandts, the Rutgers, the Livingstons—became the old money of the city.

At midcentury there was still a vast empty space between lower Manhattan and Harlem, the charming rural settlement a few miles to the north. Between 42nd Street and 125th Street was a territory populated by old mansions along the shorefront and occasional isolated homes. Here and there, squatters' wooden lean-tos perched atop tall rock outcroppings that were accessible only by homemade ladders. Winding through the landscape were inland waterways, consisting of creeks and ponds, which could be used to cross the island by rowboat. Out in the East River, fishermen still caught lobsters, squid, blackfish, and striped bass, as well as hard and soft clams.[36]

By the mid-1880s, when Friedrich Trump arrived, the rush uptown was under way. With the elevated train from the tip of Manhattan to 129th Street taking just forty-five minutes,[37] and downtown lots ever less available and more costly, vacant northern expanses underwent what afterward seemed like overnight development. Residences shot up from nowhere in former fields; tenants from nowhere followed. The farther north a building was, the lower the rent, which served as a powerful inducement for families to keep heading up the island every May 1.

On May 1, 1887, Friedrich, his next oldest sister—who now spelled her name Louise—and the Schusters again made a long move uptown, this time to an apartment on the third floor at 2012 Second Avenue, near the corner of East 104th Street. A four-story brick tenement, it had stores on the ground-floor front and held eight families. Two months after the move, Emma Katherine, then two years old and Katherine and Fred Schuster's only child, suddenly became sick. The little girl developed a fever and an irregular pulse; she lay down and did not want to move. By the time the flush spread over her body, the diagnosis was certain: acute meningitis.

Katherine Schuster, six months pregnant, tried everything she could think of or afford. Nothing helped, because she was fighting againsty her own living conditions. The Schusters' new building was called a "dumb-bell" because it was so shaped, wide at the ends and pinched in at the middle to create desperately needed airshafts. But the shafts were too small to provide much light or air, and in any case most people still believed that open windows were unhealthy. Someone nearby had been attacked by meningitis, and in the crowded, unsanitary tenement it was passed on. Kathie Schuster, the first of the Trump family to be born in the New World, was also the first to die.

The grief-stricken parents found distraction in October, when Louisa Schuster came into the world. Once again the coos and squalls of a baby filled the apartment. Things seemed to return to normal. The men commuted downtown to work, and Katherine took care of the child.

All the time, though, dissatisfaction was growing in Friedrich Trump's breast. He was impatient with the slow progress he was making. He earned a living wage, but that was all. He was tired of the seven-day-a-week routine at the barbershop. The unhappiness went with him when the Schusters moved again in May 1890, this time to an apartment at the corner of West 145th and Main Street (now Amsterdam Avenue). After the turn of the century, blacks pushed out of Manhattan's West Side began renting apartments in Harlem, but at this time the area was full of European immigrants, especially Germans.[38] As on 104th Street, the landlord was German, in this case a former milk dealer, Jacob Raichle. His was a brand-new building, much more elegant than anything the family had lived in before. For the first time they had a dumbwaiter and an Otis elevator.

Friedrich Trump did not enjoy the family's newfound luxury for long. Within a year he set off again on his own to make his fortune. This time, though, he wasn't going to do it little by little. He was determined to find a place where somebody with grit and determination could become a rich man fast.

CHAPTER TWO

SEATTLE DAYS AND NIGHTS

FRIEDRICH TRUMP BECAME TRULY AMERICAN in the fall of 1891. On November 9 of that year he bought his own little piece of the American dream: one cash register, one range, one iron safe, one counter, twenty-four stools, twenty-four chairs, and a cupboard full of silverware and dishes. The price was $600 "lawful money of the United States."

These homely items constituted the fixtures of the Dairy Restaurant, located at 208 Washington Street in Seattle, Washington. The first commercial Trump enterprise in the New World, it was a modest affair, smaller than any of the other eating establishments nearby. But it was more than enough to show that this twenty-two-year-old immigrant, speaking a second language and only recently arrived in a new city a continent away from any family, knew the importance of location. Running one block south of Yesler Way—the city's main drag—Washington Street, a hotbed of sex, booze, and money, was the indisputable center of the action in Seattle. Known as the Line, its three blocks of saloons, casinos, and whorehouses were infamous all over the Northwest. The nickname came from the tacit understanding that along the Line anything went, but north of it vice would not be tolerated.[1]

After five years in New York with his sisters, the slight German lad had become a young man. His hair was darker now, and he had reached his full adult height of five feet nine inches. He fleshed out his appearance with an imposing handlebar mustache. The metamorphosis extended to his name: he now called himself by the plain American "Fred."* Supplied with funds from relatives and savings from barbering, he set off in time-honored fashion to seek his fortune on the frontier. In the 1890s this meant the Pacific Northwest.

Seattle's history as an American city dates back to November 13, 1851, when a small party of midwesterners disembarked on a lonely stretch of windswept beach at Puget Sound, the great natural harbor in the northwest corner of what is now Washington State.[2] Led by Arthur Denny, a dour, ascetic twenty-nine-year-old from Illinois who had already tried farming, teaching, and surveying, the ten adults and twelve children landed in pouring rain. The only sign of human habitation was a small, unroofed cabin. Many in the party immediately burst into tears. The situation seemed to go from bad to worse when the neighbors showed up. They were Salish Indians, and their near nakedness shocked the pious white visitors. Worse, to ward off the chill, the Indians swathed their bodies with vile-smelling dogfish oil. The new arrivals were repulsed, blissfully ignorant that in their own seasick and unwashed state they surely smelled just as bad to the Indians.[3]

The newcomers quickly recovered their aplomb. Within a month the Denny party was exporting lumber to San Francisco. They had big plans, as suggested by the name picked for their first landing spot, New York.[4] Soon afterward they moved across the bay to a spot they christened Seattle, after an Indian chief, and demanded that Congress recognize a separate territory north of the Columbia River and carved out of Oregon Territory. Despite the small population of four thousand whites and seventeen thousand Indians, Congress granted the requested status. Ten years later Seattle had tree stumps, muddy streets, pugnacious pioneers, and a white-columned university. Founded on land donated by the civic-minded Denny, the University of Washington sat high on a hill overlooking Puget Sound and provided distinction to a town sorely in need of it. Due to the absence of any college-age students, however, the university did not produce its first graduate for fifteen years.

Of more immediate impact was the construction of one of the re-

---

*From this point, he will be referred to by the Americanized "Frederick" in order not to confuse him with his son, also known as "Fred."

gion's few steam-powered sawmills, which provided a base for future economic growth. A steady stream of workers, drawn by new employment opportunities, began to appear and, in short order, provide customers for another Seattle institution making its debut that year. An unpainted frame building down by the waterfront, it was called the Illahee, after a Chinook word for "earth" or "homeland," and it was a whorehouse. The owner was a San Franciscan named John Pennell, a dapper, smooth-talking entrepreneur with a penchant for flowered vests. He had been in the same line of business along the Barbary Coast and had worked out a surefire formula for profits. Customers danced for free with the women, many of whom were Indians traded by local chiefs in return for Hudson's Bay blankets. For drinks, though, and for the other services performed in the small rooms along one side of the floor, customers had to pay hard cash.

Although prostitution was part and parcel of frontier life, the Illahee's size, organized arrangements, and relative cleanliness distinguished it, and Seattle, from the other new settlements in the area. After Tacoma, thirty-five miles to the south, won the intense competition to be the Northern Pacific's westernmost stop, Seattle citizens had rallied and developed local industries that included meatpacking and furniture manufacture. Determined to avoid second-class status, they even built their own short-haul line to nearby coal mines, and Seattle became the West Coast's major coaling port. But a key factor in Seattle's survival was Pennell's ability to attract free-spending types. Town officials, including the sheriff and the God-fearing but practical-minded Denny, kept their distance, and the Illahee flourished. Lumberjacks and miners poured into Seattle, cashed their paychecks with Pennell, and launched spending sprees that didn't end until they'd parted with their last cent. Such commerce gave rise to a bawdy section known, after London's red-light district, as Whitechapel and centered on the Line. Two decades later Frederick Trump would set up shop there.

———

For the eastern half of the nation, the last four decades of the nineteenth century were dominated by fundamental economic and political shifts caused by the Civil War. In the West, however, the great watershed event was the coming of the railroad. For its first century the nation had been a loose collection of localities so autonomous that many of them proudly kept their own time; by the mid–nineteenth century Illinois had twenty-seven different time zones, Indiana twenty-three, and Wisconsin thirty-eight. By linking place to place, and reducing and standardizing how long it took to travel between them, the iron horse brought order to the American experience of time and place. Further, because railroads required orderly timekeeping, their appearance eventually caused the adoption of four time zones for the entire U.S.[5]

Although railroads had an enormous positive impact on the nation, their creation was chaotic. The problem was that in building them, the country faced a chicken-and-egg problem of epic proportions. In order to transport people and materials to build up the West, the nation needed rail networks; yet until such development had occurred, there would be few towns and markets to support the new lines. Well after the railroads were finished, many would run trains from nowhere to nowhere.[6]

Building this great transcontinental network clearly required government assistance, but in what form was a matter of debate. In 1862 the Pacific Railroad and Telegraph Act authorized construction of a route that lay roughly across the middle of the country, with the Union Pacific building west from Nebraska and the Central Pacific going east from California. This monumental effort was underwritten by large land grants, government bonds, and federal loans with easy repayment terms. Two years later, with the line far from complete, Congress decided the nation needed a second line at a safe distance from Confederate forces and chartered the Northern Pacific Railroad. But because the financing of the first line was under attack as a giveaway, Congress provided no direct financial assistance. Instead it granted the new railroad millions of acres of land to build on.

The provisions reverberated for decades. Lacking direct government financing, the Northern Pacific was badly crippled. It would never have put down a single mile of track had it not caught the eye of Jay Cooke, the renowned financier whose sales of U.S. bonds abroad had funded the North's troops in the Civil War. So powerful that he could demand the president come to dinner at his fifty-two-room mansion in Philadelphia, Cooke forced Congress to enlarge the Northern Pacific's land grant to an astounding sixty million acres, an area six times the size of New England. As a reward, he took a hefty portion for himself. Then, because the railroad was not allowed to raise capital by mortgaging its land, Cooke set to work selling it. He was an imaginative pitchman, famously describing Minnesota's harsh climate to prospective buyers in such rapturous terms that people later referred to the state as "Jay Cooke's Banana Belt." Eventually his efforts would end up creating hundreds of thousands of new property owners, including Frederick Trump, in what was arguably the biggest real estate deal of all time.

The completion of the second trancontinental system, the Northern Pacific, on September 8, 1883, at Gold Creek, Montana Territory, was a world historical event. Attending the final ceremonies were some 362 honored guests, including a dozen governors and former governors, scores of legislators and journalists, and representatives of half a dozen European governments. Hosted by Henry Villard, an immigrant from the Pfalz who had become the president of the Northern Pacific, they traveled to the festivities on five first-class trains.[7]

But behind the splendid trappings, the railroad was on the verge of chaos. The final spike was not gold but rusty iron, all that the railroad could afford. A few months later Villard resigned in disgrace as the line slipped into bankruptcy. Nor was it alone. By that time Congress had granted dozens of railroads more than one hundred million acres to build on.[8] But because there were nowhere near enough goods to ship on all these lines, what had become America's biggest business was in big trouble. Overexpanded, underutilized, inefficient, thoroughly corrupt, and financed by watered stock—according to one estimate, by 1885 up to a third of the nation's rail capitalization was obtained by fraudulent means—the roads were strangling each other and their bondholders.[9]

The era of consolidation was at hand. J. P. Morgan, whose many credentials by this time included a seat on the Northern Pacific board, proceeded to reorganize that line and, along the way, the entire industry. Scaling down fixed liabilities, consolidating operations, persuading bondholders to take bonds of lesser yield or exchange them for stock, he was inventing what would become known as the tools of finance capitalism, putting the sick railroads of the country through workouts long before that term had been invented. These tools would save the railroads; they would also lay the foundation for the unprecedented twentieth-century economic expansion that would sweep up Trump's son and grandson and carry them to the top of the financial heap in the course of the next century.[10]

Eight years after that grand moment at Gold Creek, the Northern Pacific carried nearly half the westbound passengers across the United States, far more than any other railroad. Its total for fiscal 1891 alone was nearly three million people.[11] In all likelihood, one of them was Frederick Trump.

Like his trip from Kallstadt to New York, his journey across North America would have occurred in several stages. Because there were no tracks heading due west from New York, he would first have gone south, to Philadelphia, on the Pennsylvania Railroad's distinctive burgundy red train. In the City of Brotherly Love he would have transferred to a Chicago-bound train, likely the Chicago, Burlington, & Quincy.

At last he would have been heading west; more than that, he would finally be leaving Germany. In New York he had been in a sort of mini-Kallstadt, amid relatives and friends who were speaking Pfalzer dialect, wearing Pfalzer-style clothes, cooking and eating Pfalzer food, drinking Pfalzer wine. But now he would truly be in another country, one where other Germans were but one of many ethnic groups. He would speak English, wear stiff denim pants and red longjohns, and eat steak and eggs. Instead of a "Kraut," he would be a "Yank."

Once in Chicago, he would have boarded yet another train, likely the Wisconsin Central, to the Union Depot in St. Paul, Minnesota. Here he would at last climb onto the dark green Northern Pacific and begin the major and final portion of the journey. Those who could afford to pay $60 could travel in first-class luxury. This provided fully appointed sleeping accommodations, outfitted, according to advertisements, with everything from combs and brushes to "a uniformed colored porter." For Frederick Trump and most other passengers, though, the likely option was a second-class ticket, which cost $35 and provided space in one of the "emigrant" cars.[12] These carriages offered steam heat, electric lights,[13] and pull-down beds; passengers had to bring or rent their own bedding and to supply their own food.[14]

Looking out the window after St. Paul, passengers saw little but an enormous empty prairie, dry and windblown. Every hundred or so miles the train stopped to let riders stretch their legs and buy a snack or, occasionally, a souvenir from local craftspeople or Indians.[15] Some passengers were alarmed at high trestle bridges, particularly that at O'Keefe Canyon, 112 feet above ground, and another, at Murattes Canyon, that sat 263 feet up in the air. They had good reason, for washouts delayed many a train. Snowdrifts, too, could be a problem; often crews issued shovels to passengers and invited them to go out and start digging. Then, as the train approached the Cascades, the country changed again, to a mountainous world filled with monstrous conifers. Passengers saw Douglas fir up to eight feet in diameter and cedars as much as fifteen feet around. Older trees rose for a hundred feet before the first branch.[16]

Seattle, too, was novel terrain. For one thing, snow-capped Mt. Rainier loomed nearby, a backdrop so spectacular that it looked to newcomers like a gigantic stage set. For another, although the city was forty years old, its downtown area was brand new. A disastrous fire in June 1889 had leveled most of the central city, creating both a financial disaster and a grand urban planning opportunity. With one fell swoop the dilapidated wooden structures of the first settlers were gone, taking with them, according to one estimate, perhaps one million rats. In their place rose a fire-resistant city, its streets lined with brick and stone buildings designed in a Victorian-Romanesque pastiche that was the latest style.[17]

Seattle's makeover was total. During the city's first decades its streets had been a muddy, pockmarked nightmare, with gaping holes that turned into small lakes during rainy weather. Worse, builders of the sewage system, which drained directly into Puget Sound, had little regard for tides; the inevitable and appalling result twice a day at high tide was sewage backed up in pipes and toilets throughout much of the city. The "solution" had been to mount toilets on pedestals up to a dozen feet high, which meant users had to climb a ladder. After the fire, planners pushed through an ordinance raising the street level in affected areas above the high-water line, doing so by filling in the streets so that the second floor became the ground floor. After a confusing few years of a split-level downtown, with shops and sidewalks in use below- and aboveground, the city settled into aboveground life and the old quarters were sealed off.

From 1880 to 1890 Seattle's population increased from 3,500 to 43,000, a jump of 1,200 percent. The army of single, rootless men who had been enticed west by glib railroad and Chamber of Commerce promises of quick gain found that they faced the same job shortages, low wages, frequent layoffs, and lack of prospects they had been fleeing. Timber and minerals, the main industries of the West, depended on distant markets that contracted as often as they expanded, stranding anyone without a safe cushion of capital.

After the Northern Pacific went bankrupt for a second time, in 1881, a financial panic engulfed the region and then the country. Those who did not find the new opportunities they had been seeking felt furious and betrayed and began scapegoating Chinese laborers who had come slightly earlier to work on the railroads. Whites had considered the Chinese, perhaps four to five hundred in number, unscrupulous and unreliable even in prosperous times but had tolerated them because they were willing to do the dirtiest and hardest jobs for low wages. But when the job market shrank, the Chinese became the competition, regularly described in the press as "scurvy opium fiends," "rat eaters," and "treacherous lepers."[18]

The market for prostitution, gambling, and drinking continued unabated, regardless of the city's economic vicissitudes. Reform movements waxed and waned; a typical mid-1880s campaign slogan denounced "rum vendors and pink-cuff hoodlums," a reference to gamblers' customary garb. But the Line and what civic-minded types called the Lava Beds survived handily. After the 1889 fire, prostitutes whose places of business had gone up in smoke fanned out over the city, but residents in other sections complained, and the hookers soon found new quarters back where they had started. City officials, eager to return the prostitutes to Washington Street, allowed wooden construction there although it was now illegal in the rest of the city because of the fire hazard. Soon the Line and the area in its immediate vicinity sported a new supply of "cribs," long rows of wooden rooms just large enough for a narrow cot and a trapdoor in the back to eject unlucky johns.

Before the fire, city officials labeled these accommodations "Female Boarding" on official town maps; afterward the quarters bore somewhat more honest identification as saloons. The women, however, were called "dressmakers" and had to pay a special "dressmaking" tax that was said to be a major source of city revenue for some years. According to one urban legend, flower pots on windowsills above the first floor were illegal because idle "dressmakers" sometimes dropped them on passersby and then scurried down to relieve the stunned victims of their possessions.

By November 1891 the Line had roared back from the fire. Up one side of Washington Street and down the other were saloons, gambling parlors, pawnshops, bawdy houses, bookie dens, vaudeville theaters, loan offices, opium parlors, cheap hotels and dives, secondhand clothing stores, and the ubiquitous prostitutes' cribs. On the north side of Washington Street, wedged between Rippley and Ehle's Standard Oyster House and Henry Baumann's Second-Hand Goods, was a two-story brick building with a skylight. On the plate-glass front window, shiny new letters spelled out "Dairy Restaurant, prop. Fred Trump."

A small, crowded box with unpainted wooden walls, the Dairy was a place where hungry men could get away from the constant winter drizzle. On one side a perpetual fire blazed and guttered. Steam rose from the garments of the customers seated nearby, and the room was thick with the smells of wet cloth, hot meat, sour beer, and unwashed human flesh. Frederick Trump had a hard way with a nickel and spent little on ambiance. The sawdust he sprinkled on the floor every morning lay in muddy, manure-dotted clumps by noon; a few notices hung tacked on the wall, greasy with wood smoke and the soot from lanterns. The wiry, energetic proprietor darted among the long tables, his head filled with orders taken and filled and calculations of profit and loss. Ten to twelve hours a day he carried pitchers of beer and plates of food, attended the shouted commands of customers and friends, stuffed slips of paper and heavy silver dollars into the pocket of his denim trousers. At sunset the lamps went on, and sometimes candles were lit on the table. The din continued without break. People kept lining up well into the night, and Frederick Trump provided food and liquor nonstop.

Finally, when the Dairy closed, he staggered one fetid block through the rain to his flophouse, up the rude wooden staircase and down a narrow, unlit hallway to his cold, shabby room. Early the next day he woke up to the tumult of people yelling, horses and wagons clattering, and vendors peddling their wares. In the same drizzle he hurried back to the Dairy and once again swept the floor, laid sawdust, started the fire, prepared food, and refilled wooden kegs of beer.

Frederick Trump had bought the equipment in this culinary parlor from Benjamin A. Foster, a barkeeper, who had purchased it a year earlier from one Spiro Bisazza. Under Bisazza's hand, the establishment was called the Poodle Dog. It was a restaurant in those days, too, and specialized in oysters. "Everything new, neat, and first-class," boasted one advertisement. "All Meals prepared by First-class Cooks only." But the Poodle Dog's ads also mentioned its other specialty: "Private Rooms for Ladies." As everyone who read the ads knew, the "ladies" in question were prostitutes. Perhaps Frederick Trump eliminated this service. In all likelihood, though, he did not. This was not an area where anyone with prudish inclinations would gravitate, much less open a business. All around the Dairy Restaurant were buildings chockablock with saloons and brothels, for the simple reason that those were what the clientele wanted. For Frederick Trump to offer anything else at the Dairy Restaurant would put him at a punishing competitive disadvantage. If the young man had any sense, in other words, at the first outpost in the Trump family empire, private rooms and the services offered therein remained in place.

On the Line and everywhere else in Seattle, business was thriving. Beneath the magnificent dome of Mt. Rainier, streetcar lines laced the streets, electric lights illuminated homes and offices, and gasworks rose in the central city.[19] Washington State, too, was about to take its place on the national stage.[20] Democrats had blocked Washington's admission to statehood for more than thirty years because they did not want to make this Republican-leaning territory a full-fledged member of the Union. But in 1888 Republicans finally took Congress and the White House, and the stalemate ended. In one sweep, six new states joined the Union. The next year Washington voters approved a new state constitution that took away from women the vote they had exercised in territorial days. The issue was less an ideological than a practical one, with the antiwomen side led by saloon and liquor interests who feared that prohibitionist forces would persuade women to outlaw alcoholic beverages.

Thus, in 1892, when residents of Washington received the right to vote in a presidential election for the first time, only male citizens were allowed to register. The chance to step up to the ballot box in November 1892 proved irresistible to male immigrants. During the last days of October, applicants for citizenship and witnesses jammed the corridors, courtrooms, and clerk's office in Seattle's superior court. To keep up with the unprecedented demand, there was talk of judges giving up their lunch hours to swear in new citizens, but instead the court opened its offices from seven to nine in the evening.

On Thursday, October 27, the day before registration closed, Frederick Trump joined the line that wound all the way down the marble front steps of the courthouse. Accompanying him were Hannibal Henry Blewett and Joseph G. Smith, two acquaintances who had agreed to be his witnesses. Blewett, a twenty-two-year-old laborer, had come to Seattle about the same time as the young German; Smith was a fellow barber, cutting hair and trimming beards at the Green Tree, a combination saloon/boardinghouse. Located across the street from the Dairy Restaurant, the Green Tree concerned itself with "female boarding" before the great fire; most likely it was now involved in the profitable "dressmaking" trade.

After hours of waiting, the three men reached the head of the line in the county clerk's office, where they filled out a naturalization affidavit. Perhaps because of the crowd and tumult, Frederick Trump wrote the wrong date for his entry in the United States. After he swore that he was under eighteen when he arrived and renounced any vestige of loyalty to Germany or the kaiser, Blewett and Smith declared that they were well acquainted with him, that he had lived in Washington State for at least a year, and that "during all of said time he has behaved as a man of good moral character."

Clutching his citizenship papers, he headed for the even longer line at City Hall. Every eligible voter in Seattle had to register there, and most, like the newly naturalized restaurateur, had left this task until the last possible moment. The line stretched for hundreds of yards down the street and around the corner, and it must have looked to Frederick Trump as if everyone in Seattle were in line in front of him. People shoved and pushed; soon-to-be voters squabbled over politics; and, as usual, industrious Seattle entrepreneurs sold peanuts and pretzels.

The heavy turnout was hardly a surprise, for reminders appeared throughout the newspapers. "Do not disenfranchise yourself by neglecting to register before 12 tonight," the Seattle Press-Times had warned its readers. "Register before midnight, or lose your vote." Evidently such admonitions worked. When registration books closed, on October 28 at the stroke of midnight, some 3,800 new names had been added, bringing the grand total of registered voters in Seattle to 13,383. The city's bitter rival, Tacoma, had only 10,790 voters, and the next morning's edition of the Tacoma Star charged that 3,000 of Seattle's names were fraudulent. In response, Seattle's chief clerk hotly insisted that his office had kept the official seal under constant vigilance during daylight hours and had locked it in the vault each night.

On Tuesday, November 8, there was an impressive turnout. City-wide, the vote was fairly evenly divided between electors pledged to the Republican incumbent, Benjamin Harrison, and those pledged to the Democratic candidate, former president Grover Cleveland. But this election was about more than numeric returns. Thousands of men stayed up all night, dashing from publicly posted bulletins to the nearest saloon, running home briefly, then racing back to check out the latest notice. Yelling, groaning, and drinking constantly, they were marking Seattle's entry onto the national political stage. Equally important, if not equally obvious, they were also marking Seattle's emergence into the national economy. From now on Seattle would be an integral part of the American free enterprise system. It would be a place where great fortunes would be won and lost, but it would also be a place where it would take money to make money and where those who started small were almost certain to end up small.

Frederick Trump did not really understand this yet. After a year in Seattle, he itched to make it big and go to the biggest mining boomtown in the nation. A gold and silver town north of Seattle, it was named Monte Cristo. He knew nothing about mining, but he had a distinct advantage over most people going there: He had absolutely no intention of looking for either metal.

CHAPTER THREE

TALES OF MONTE CRISTO

Some three years earlier, in 1889, at the beginning of June, a tall, thin man in his mid-thirties with brown hair and a sandy mustache had climbed to the crest of a steep ridge in the Cascade Mountains.[1] His name was Joe Pearsall. He had been a schoolteacher, but he wasn't in that line of work anymore. Ninety miles to the southwest, the smoke was just clearing from the great Seattle fire. The great bay of Puget Sound glittered to the west. To the northeast, he had a clear view of the huge volcanic cone of Glacier Peak. None of this interested Pearsall. He was looking for something else. His battered binoculars went this way and that. Then, suddenly, he dropped his field glasses in amazement.

Pearsall had left the classroom a decade earlier when he got word of a gold strike in Leadville, Colorado. He didn't find anything, but he was hooked. Even though, as he later told a reporter, he "went broke, you know, oh, hundreds of times," he kept looking for a big strike.[2] By now he was looking for silver as well as gold. Deciding to check out the Northwest, he had climbed in the uncharted territory between Troublesome and Silver Creeks, east of what is now the town of Index, Washington. Threading his way through heavy brush and past towering firs and cedars, sliding on occasional muddy spots, patches of remaining snow, and glacial ice, he had stopped at about five thousand feet for a rest and a look around.

Bright red streaks splashed on the side of a faraway summit had caught his attention. He wiped off the binoculars and looked again. The reflection of the sun on the glittering surface of that distant peak was causing an immense glare. Slowly he realized that he was looking at what seemed an entire mountain made from an ore called galena. There was little commercial value in the sulfurous content that caused the red streaks, but as markers for galena they immediately captured Pearsall's attention. He knew that galena is often found with gold and silver. If that was the case here, Pearsall could be looking at the biggest find in his prospecting career.[3]

Pearsall did the first thing any wise prospector would do. He immediately went to Seattle to get money and support. Within a month he was back on the crest with Frank Peabody, another prospector, and Mac Wilmans, a backer. Wilmans took one look and reportedly burst out, "Brother, the world is ours!" On July 4 the three men staked their first claims. They left when grim winter weather drove them out. The next year Pearsall and Peabody returned with Mac's brother, Fred Wilmans, and half a dozen workers, staked more claims, and built a cabin. Inspired by the adventure-filled book Fred Wilmans had in his pocket, *The Count of Monte Cristo* by Alexandre Dumas, they named the spot Monte Cristo.[4]

With every day of reconnoitering and digging, Monte Cristo's mineral resources looked more promising and the terrain more daunting. As the men struggled with pack animals to haul food and gear through some of the roughest country in the Northwest, the problems of transporting mining equipment and getting ore to the market loomed large. To Wilmans, Pearsall, and Peabody, there was only one possible solution: a railroad. Only a railroad could carry up the heavy equipment needed for lode mining; only a railroad could carry down the vast mineral wealth they were convinced they would find. Accordingly, in the summer of 1891 they went calling on the one man they knew of who might be able to get a railroad built.

His name was Henry Hewitt Jr., and he was already involved in one of the most ambitious development schemes in the Northwest. Born in England in 1840, Hewitt had grown up in Wisconsin and followed the then-legal custom of paying someone to take his place in the Civil War. The son of a successful timber dealer, Hewitt made a considerable fortune in the logging business, then headed west to the land of virgin timber. By 1890 he had settled in Tacoma and amassed a larger fortune as a partner in the St. Paul and Tacoma Lumber Company, which owned almost one hundred thousand acres of prime northwest timber and had just built the world's largest and most modern sawmill. Determined to find more ways to turn a profit, that summer he hired local Indians to paddle him around Puget Sound in a canoe. When he found abundant timber and a good natural harbor sixty miles north of Tacoma, he started buying land there.[5]

Back in Tacoma, he ran into an even richer acquaintance, a New Yorker named Charles Colby. Hewitt had first met him when Colby was in Wisconsin supervising his family's extensive railroad interests. Now Colby had come out to the coast in his private railroad car to set up the western division of one of his many business ventures. Soon the two men were talking about founding a major industrial center. Hewitt would provide the location and local contacts, and Colby would supply his connection to the one person in the country who could bankroll such a project: John Davison Rockefeller Sr., owner of Standard Oil and the wealthiest man in America.

Colby and his business partner, Colgate Hoyt, had special access to Rockefeller. Both were members of the executive committee of the Northern Pacific Railroad at a time when Rockefeller was the majority stockholder. Better yet, both were also fellow parishioners with the oil tycoon at the Fifth Avenue Baptist Church in New York. Hoyt, a banker and broker from an old Cleveland family who sat on numerous corporate boards, was a shrewd and stylish operator. Before work he frequently stopped in at Rockefeller's home, at 54th Street and 5th Avenue, and would accompany him to his office, at 26 Broadway, at the southern tip of Manhattan. Sitting next to the magnate, a slender, dignified figure with close-cropped sandy hair and mustache and gray eyes, Hoyt rhapsodized about the boundless possibilities awaiting in the Northwest.[6]

Having overworked for twenty straight years, Rockefeller was on the verge of a nervous breakdown. Worse, he was deluged by requests for donations to worthy causes. "Neither in the privacy of his home, nor at table, nor in the aisles of his church, nor on his trips to and from his office, nor during his business hours, nor anywhere else, was Mr. Rockefeller secure from insistent appeals," his chief assistant, a lapsed Baptist minister named Frederick Gates, wrote later. "[The magnate was] constantly hunted, stalked, and hounded almost like a

wild animal." Alarmed at Rockefeller's appearance, his doctors demanded that he stay away from his office and delegate all possible
tasks.[7]

Because Hoyt and Colby were fellow investors, their attentions
and suggestions seemed like a breath of fresh air. At last, someone
was suggesting a scheme that would *make* money, rather than cost
it. Figuring that these two energetic young men would not commit
their own resources without proper investigation, Rockefeller un-
questioningly added his capital to their projects in Wisconsin, Michigan, Minnesota, Cuba, and now Washington. For Rockefeller, whose
own financial shrewdness was legendary, it was an extraordinary
show of trust.

Coded messages went back and forth between 26 Broadway and
Colby and Hoyt's office, then out to Henry Hewitt on the coast. Rockefeller's name never appeared in any public documents, but it dominated the secret communications. The ambitions of Hewitt and his
eastern partners kept growing. Then, in mid-1891, the prospectors
from Monte Cristo showed up at Hewitt's office. After he sent two
engineers up into the mountains to take a look and received a positive
account, he sent the news on to New York. Colby and Hoyt dispatched a team of mining experts to Monte Cristo for yet another
opinion. Their reports were also highly favorable, although they
noted that no deep mining had yet taken place and so any analysis
could be based only on surface findings. The galena ore had a relatively low mineral content but seemed accessible in such quantities
that processing could retrieve profitable levels of both gold and silver.[8]

"There is here in Monte Cristo the ear marks [sic] of one of the
greatest mining camps in the United States," prominent mining expert Alton L. Dickerman told the *Everett Times*.[9] The mines, he told
another reporter, would "rival the Comstock in production and send
down silver enough to pave the streets [of the proposed new town]."[10]
Coming from the man who had plumbed the rich Gogebic iron mines
in Michigan, this exuberant assessment confirmed Colby and Hoyt's
enthusiasm. Like overeager investors throughout history, they listened to the abundant positive and filtered out any cautionary negatives.

It's not hard to see why. Only one year earlier the federal government had approved silver coinage, which meant that this metal was now a hot commodity. The Monte Cristo mines would be literally digging *money* out of the hills. Hewitt, Colby, and Hoyt would have the biggest gold and silver mine in the nation, and they would create a coastal metropolis, named Everett after Colby's oldest son. There they would expand old industries and create new ones, manufacture equipment of all sorts, feed supplies and miners going into Monte Cristo, and process the gold and silver coming out. Inevitably, they believed, Everett would become the western terminus of the third transcontinental railroad, James Jerome Hill's Great Northern, then nearing completion. The new city would soon dwarf Seattle and Tacoma.

Such a vision, as well as the name of its illustrious financial angel, could not remain a secret. As word spread that Rockefeller was investing in Everett, so many people flocked in that the local undertaker joked that his coffins were being used as bunks.[11] People bought and sold lots in a dizzying spiral of ever-higher prices, enriching all participants in a Ponzi-like process that they believed would continue indefinitely. One piece of property, bought by Hewitt from an old-timer for $4,000 and then sold to his brother-in-law, changed hands again a few months later for $128,000 and then for $500,000.[12] The trees came down, the buildings went up, and wharves covered the shoreline. With awesome speed, the Everett Land Company, led by its spirited president, Henry Hewitt Jr., was hacking an entire new city out of the wilderness.[13]

In November 1891, as Frederick Trump was acquiring the fixtures for the Dairy Restaurant, a syndicate of New York investors dominated by Rockefeller, who owned an 80 percent interest, formally launched the Monte Cristo Mining Company and the Everett & Monte Cristo Railway. Using the methods of vertical integration honed in setting up Standard Oil, the Everett Land Company created some two dozen overlapping corporations that would mask future profits. What had begun as an all-but-impossible dream for a few western miners and their backers had now been absorbed into the empire of the man who embodied the awesome power of the free enterprise system.

By this point, Everett, headquarters for the railroad and the mining company, was a rip-roaring boomtown. It was crowded with saloons and prostitutes, and its muddy streets stank from manure, garbage, and seepage from a grossly inadequate sewer system. A dire housing shortage meant that hundreds of residents had to sleep in leaky tents night after rainy night. But the endless rumors of the unimaginable riches that would soon pour down on the city and the region kept the newcomers flooding in. According to one report, Rockefeller was planning to sell off all other interests in order to concentrate solely on the Northwest. Another touted a mining expert's prediction that there would be enough ore to keep the world's largest smelter busy for one hundred years.[14]

Almost no ore had actually been mined, but the nail factory in Everett had already produced a spike from Monte Cristo silver. It was a tantalizing indication of the riches to come.[15] Miles from the town site, crews working on the railroad stumbled on a rich vein of copper, further proof that the entire area was bursting with valuable minerals.[16] If ever there was a sure thing, Monte Cristo seemed to be it.

Sure things were a popular topic everywhere, and nowhere more so than Seattle in the 1890s. By the end of 1892 buzz about Monte Cristo and its astonishing potential had reached the Line, and Frederick Trump became entranced by the fabulous tales of what this remote mining town had to offer. By a stroke of luck, the owner of the Dairy Restaurant happened to have an inside source from whom he could glean further details: Henry Blewett, a witness at his naturalization and a relative of Ed Blewett, a mining investor who put money into Monte Cristo early on. With Rockefeller himself investing millions, Trump concluded, Monte Cristo seemed a risk well worth taking. Because he wanted to get in on the ground floor, he would put in some capital of his own.

On August 30, 1892, his older brother, Jakob, then twenty-nine, married Elizabetha Boeringer, twenty-four, in Kallstadt. Jakob's marriage was the occasion chosen by Katherina Kober Trump to divide up her holdings among her children. She would continue to live in the same house, but it was now Jakob's property. Barbara and Elizabetha, the two sisters remaining in Germany, received equivalent shares, and Katherine, Louise, and Frederick, the three children in the United

States, received cash amounts. Since coming to America, Frederick Trump had operated on a relatively small margin, ever watchful for a chance to make his fortune. With his share of his mother's worldly goods, he had found his golden opportunity.

On February 10, 1893, he sold the fixtures in the Dairy Restaurant. Two weeks later, on February 24, he bought forty acres of land from the Northern Pacific Railroad. The parcel, which was about a dozen miles east of Seattle, was part of the huge federal land grant that the railroad had received in lieu of direct cash subsidies some three decades earlier and had been continually selling off ever since. In early 1893 the perennially strapped line was in particularly dire straits, and Trump was able to pick up the property at the bargain price of $200, or $5 an acre.[17]

The property had one small shack on it and was otherwise unimproved or even cleared. But it was the first piece of real estate in what would become the family empire. It was located on the Pine Lake Plateau, an area that had already attracted many land speculators, each armed with insider information that because of logging, or minerals, or a new town, or another rail line, this land was going to take off in value, just like that farther north, around Everett and Monte Cristo.[18] This was only the beginning of a new chapter in Frederick Trump's life. One week after buying the lot, he left Seattle for Monte Cristo itself.

———————

Winter meant the suspension of operations there, but as soon as the weather warmed up, blasting and tunneling would be going full tilt. Prospectors and suppliers, shopkeepers and carpenters, even a self-styled public-relations agent,[19] had poured in along the wagon roads built from "puncheon," felled trees split lengthwise and laid side by side across the roadway to form a continuous wooden surface.[20] A sawmill was finally in place and would resume transforming the boundless timber resources of the area into usable lumber. Tramways, then under construction, would carry the ore from the mines, which were being sunk above the town site, down to the gigantic ore processor now under way. This mechanism, known as a "concentrator," would refine ore before shipping it by the railroad, yet unfinished, to the smelter, which was nearing completion 55 miles away in Everett.

Although the winter population had been well under one hundred, Monte Cristo expected a year-round settlement of at least two to five thousand.[21] Three hundred miners were sleeping in the streets of the closest town, Silverton, eager for enough snow to melt so they could start work at Monte Cristo. Four restaurants were also poised to get under way, and thirty-two applications for liquor licenses were pending.[22] It would be a long wait, for during the first week of May a blizzard dropped twelve feet of snow on Monte Cristo.[23]

Frederick Trump did not intend to wait. Backpacking in supplies through the deep snow, he staggered into a small, scarred mountain valley with a motley collection of smoky shacks and tents. Land was going for as much as $1,000 an acre, much more than he could afford. So he found a piece of property he wanted and promptly discovered gold on it or, at any rate, said he did. The land was a parcel of scrub right next to the future train depot, the nearest thing Monte Cristo had to a town center, and was also flat enough to build on, a rarity in that mountain terrain. Claiming he was going to use it to mine gold gave Trump control of this prime real estate without having to endure the unpleasant process of paying for it. After staking out the corners of the spot, he recorded his claim on April 29, 1893, at the county auditor's office in Everett. He swore that he was making a "placer" claim, that he had found "color," the legal term for ore, and that nobody else had mineral rights to the property.

Not one of these statements, it seems, was true.

By definition, a placer claim is an assertion that minerals have been found on the surface, which, since they originally formed underneath the surface, means that they must have been removed from their original site, usually by a stream. It was hardly an obscure category, for, as everyone in Monte Cristo knew, a placer claim had set off the 1848 gold rush at Sutter's Mill. The Triangle Placer Claim, as Trump called his filing, gave him exclusive mineral rights to the land; because he was not actually purchasing the site, however, he did not have surface rights, which meant that he could not build on it or log it. The claim also provided an option on an annual renewal contingent on his having done at least $100 worth of work since the last renewal.[24]

But Frederick Trump had no intention of mining. For one thing, Monte Cristo had no minerals on the surface. All legitimate claims were "lode" claims, in which the minerals were embedded in rock and had to be drilled and blasted free, a far more expensive process.[25] For another, the Triangle Placer Claim lay within a larger parcel already claimed by someone else, Nicholas Rudebeck of Everett. A German immigrant, the thirty-eight-year-old Rudebeck had built the first office building in Everett, a large, gingerbread-covered affair on the main street, and had also invested in mining properties.[26]

The usurper had nothing to fear, for such falsehoods were commonplace in Monte Cristo. Despite its utter lack of color, placer claims covered the main town site. Like Fred Trump, almost everyone else there saw no reason actually to put down cash money for a piece of land when they could control it through staking a claim; if and when valuable minerals were discovered nearby, they could then sell off the claim for a profit. Similarly, if and when any problems arose, they could almost certainly be resolved through informal financial settlements, readily facilitated through or even by the notoriously corrupt U.S. Land Office.

Frederick Trump lost no sleep over the issue. Two weeks before filing his claim, he had bought five thousand board feet of lumber from the Monte Cristo Mining Company in Everett for $125 in cash. Ignoring the inconvenient fact that his placer claim gave him no actual right to build on the property, he soon put a boardinghouse on the Triangle Placer Claim.

It was a shrewd move. Rather than go into the risky business of prospecting for minerals himself, he built a hotel for those more willing to take such a chance. He was mining the miners, as it were. The actual prospectors might or might not find gold or silver, but they would pay him for their bed and board, no matter what the outcome. Frederick Trump, at twenty-four, was an apt pupil in the ways of the free enterprise system. Unfortunately, however, he was still only a pupil. The system had more lessons to teach him, and some of them would be harsh.

—ɷ—

In 1890 the American economy began to contract. The immediate cause was the failure of Baring Brothers and Company, a British financial house that bit the dust because of Argentinian financial upheavals. Alarmed, British brokers sold off their American stocks and bonds. As U.S. stock and bond prices fell, Americans rushed to buy these securities, causing an outflow of gold to the sellers back in Europe. As gold supplies decreased and securities lost value, Americans found it increasingly difficult to borrow money. Rising interest rates were a problem for the entire nation, but especially so in the West, where an expanding economy desperately needed a flow of cheap cash. By the fall of 1890 money was in such short supply that interest rates had risen to extraordinary levels. At times credit was virtually suspended. Both Everett and Seattle were in the bizarre position of being boomtowns with no money.

Fortunately, a poor wheat and cotton harvest forced Europe to make large purchases in American markets and therefore to rescue the U.S. economy.[27] But because wheat and cotton do not come from the Northwest, recovery came to that area more slowly. Some places, including Seattle and Everett, were still slumping three years later, when the next panic hit.

On May 4 of that year two of the nation's largest brokerages, Henry Allen & Co. and B. L. Smythe & Co., failed, shaking public confidence.[28] Wall Street went into convulsions as stocks went into free fall. "[Crowds] yelled themselves hoarse in attempts to sell," the *Seattle Press-Times* reported. "The going and coming brokers' messengers ran as if Satan were after them."[29] A week later the decline had spread to the Midwest, and banks in Illinois and Indiana closed their doors.[30] By June the panic had hit the Northwest.

Henry Hewitt had spent the spring planning an elaborate reception to celebrate the arrival of the first Great Northern train in Everett. His dream of Everett as the terminus for the Great Northern Railway had been for naught, as this plum was going to Seattle, but he stubbornly insisted on a party anyway. The culminating moment was to be the presentation to Great Northern president James J. Hill of a commemorative plate made of solid Monte Cristo silver and set in velvet.[31] But Hill sent last-minute regrets, and the highlight of the month was not a party, but the bankruptcy of three of the town's five banks.

Within two months the Northern Pacific was bankrupt and the Great Northern had suspended all building operations. In Everett the spanking new smelter sat idle, and half the town's population had vanished, leaving behind debts and unpaid mortgages.[32] The centerpiece of Hewitt's efforts, the Everett Land Company, was broke. To pay off creditors, the New York partners issued $1.5 million in bonds, payable at a tough 8 percent interest. Nobody bought them. Luckily Rockefeller stepped in. He purchased the entire issue, providing the desperate Hewitt with the hope that the downturn was only temporary. After all, if Rockefeller stood behind a venture, there must be some merit to the idea.[33]

High up in the mountains, the railway crews, the miners, and the shopkeepers paid no attention to the panic. That summer the settlement had grown to 1,200 residents living in sixty houses, scores of tents,[34] and a handful of hotels and boardinghouses, including Frederick Trump's. Workers were planking the streets, new buildings were springing up everywhere,[35] and this once quiet spot reverberated with the noise of men and machines. Near the depot the construction of the concentrator, designed to be 185 by 60 feet and a mind-boggling five stories high, continued.[36] Up in the mountains, tunneling, blasting, and sinking of new mine shafts went full tilt ahead.

One of the houses belonged to Joe Pearsall, whose discovery of this location only four years earlier had led to all that was now taking place. An inspiring example of hard work bountifully rewarded, he sat on modern furniture, read the latest periodicals and novels, ate fresh fruit from California, and slept in an embroidered nightshirt. "Mr. Pearsall," said the *Everett News*, "knows how to spend his money like a sensible thoroughbred."[37]

Pearsall was exceptionally fortunate. Most of the miners made just $3 a day. They spent it energetically, though, pouring their wages into a muddy, mountain version of the Line. Fred Trump's boardinghouse sat right in the center of what the *Everett News* called "a regular White Chapel [sic] . . . where dance hall and crib sirens are supposed to lure men to moral and financial destruction." Because the salaries were so low, the paper said, "the girls are not buying seal skins and diamonds this fall" and would "be in luck if they don't have to do their own washing and cooking."[38] Still, saloons like the Rattler and the Blazing Stump proliferated, many run from tents because proprietors didn't want to wait for actual buildings.[39] Periodically scandals broke and charges flew over selling liquor without a license, selling fake licenses, favoritism in the granting of licenses, and law enforcement officers having their hands around, behind, or in the bar till.[40]

In such a frontier environment, it was hard to say precisely what went on in any particular establishment. Few records remain. As with his Dairy Restaurant in Seattle, it's possible that Frederick Trump never served anything stronger than chamomile tea and refused to admit any unmarried woman. But the young German immigrant was no fool, and not one to be scared of vice. Sleeves rolled up, he stood at the cash register, taking in a constant, if not overwhelming, stream of profits.

The railroad finally reached Monte Cristo in August 1893 amid a steady flow of upbeat pronouncements. In late September the *Everett News* announced that the amount of ore to be processed would be so immense that already, before the first concentrator had handled even a single carload, machinery for a second concentrator was on order.[41] Regular U.S. mail service had begun, telephones were on the way, school had opened, the Presbyterian Church was on hand, and a weekly newspaper called the *Monte Cristo Mountaineer* had started publishing. Untouched by the economic upheaval devastating the nation, the juggernaut that was Monte Cristo rolled on—or seemed to.

In November 1893 Congress repealed the Sherman Silver Purchase Act and cut back the amount of silver coinage. This sudden change in the nation's currency suggested instability and created vast alarm. Europeans began demanding that big loans be repaid in gold. Americans cashed in so many bills for gold that the nation's reserves in the U.S. Treasury shrank by three-quarters. There was a run on the banks. All across the nation, but particularly in the Northwest, they began to topple.

Meanwhile Monte Cristo encountered a second, more direct disaster: the weather. That fall, as always, it rained buckets. The simplest operation became torturously slow. Worse yet, the downpour flooded the rail yards and damaged the roadbed. The railroad's route, some sixty miles long, lay along the south fork of the Stillaguamish River. To avoid floods, residents and engineers had recommended placing the line on the cliffs above the river, rather than along its edge, even though the latter course was much cheaper. But Colby and Hoyt, facing railroad cost estimates close to $2 million, had made a fateful decision and put the track on the river's banks.[42] The lower route was so breathtaking that a round-trip train ride to Monte Cristo became a popular day trip for people throughout the area in good weather. In bad weather, however, the same ride was a disaster. River floods regularly closed down the line, and in winter, when the rain turned to snow, huge drifts piled up on the tracks and falling rocks plugged the many tunnels. Engineers and crews worked heroically to keep the trains moving, but they were fighting gravity, nature, and an annual snowfall of several hundred inches.

Like so many operations at Monte Cristo—the mines, the concentrator, the tramways, the various pulley systems, the tunnels— the railroad was an irresistible force confronting an immovable object. That it ran at all was an extraordinary feat. But large-scale mining operations were impossible. So was shipping in adequate supplies to maintain the town. Faced with the imminent prospect of serious shortages, most residents hightailed it out of town until spring.[43]

Among the hardy souls who remained in Monte Cristo was Frederick Trump. An immediate reason to stay was to protect his building against the elements. The snow accumulation was so great that it often literally flattened unattended buildings. More important, his initial scam had come back to haunt him. At the end of December, Nicholas Rudebeck, who held the first claim to the property on which Frederick Trump's boardinghouse stood, incorporated the Rudebeck Land Company with several wealthy and influential investors in Everett. To Frederick Trump this meant one thing and one thing only: He was going to get hit up for back rent. On New Year's Day 1894 he made a countermove. He filed a second placer claim, adjacent to the first. Clearly the idea was to argue that his boardinghouse was somehow on *that* land and not on Rudebeck's property.

Because the ground was under more than ten feet of snow, the required survey did not occur until April.[44] Produced by a complaisant surveyor, it mentioned that Frederick Trump's new property contained a two-story boardinghouse, twenty-two by fifty feet, worth $800. In a proper placer claim this information would be incidental, because it had nothing to do with mining. To Frederick Trump, though, the assertion was vital, for the boardinghouse was the sole reason for the claim. Expanding his authority to make this bald assertion, he informed R. L. Polk & Co., the nation's leading compiler of local directories, that their first Monte Cristo edition should include the following listing: Trump Frederick, real estate. In this way—to beat out a landlord—the Trump family formally entered the real estate business.

In June and July Frederick Trump made two further placer claims, this time above town on Sylvan Creek. Because they were on a creek, they could plausibly be called placer claims. But the shoreline there had no gold. The claims were useful only as attempts to nail down turf near other claims.[45]

In July Rudebeck obtained what is called a "patent" on his claims, which made them into his private property. He now had free and clear control of 3.74 acres, including the land underneath Frederick Trump's boardinghouse. It was an ideal spot to locate a business, which is precisely why Frederick Trump had chosen it. Rudebeck promptly sent an agent to collect $10 per month in rent from the many people who occupied dwellings on his land. The move was unpopular. *Very* unpopular. "A great roar is now being made and what the result will be no one can tell," the *Everett Herald* reported.[46] The type of people who would be attracted to Monte Cristo were not the type to pay attention to fiddling details like legal titles. A week after Rudebeck tried to dun those whom he now considered his tenants, a local vigilante group tore down the jail, which was still under construction, and tossed it into the river. "We want no jail here," the group announced. Nor did the citizenry want absentee landlords in Everett.[47]

But back in New York there was now a far bigger problem for Frederick Trump and everyone else in Monte Cristo. John D. Rockefeller had recovered from his partial breakdown and taken back the wheel of his business empire. For the first time, the tycoon took a sharp look at the Colby-Hoyt operation. Uncle Sam's current posture on silver made mining it far less attractive than previously. The question was whether Monte Cristo in particular had something else to recommend it. Determined to have a reliable answer, he dispatched his top aide to examine the score of investments into which Colby and Hoyt had led Rockefeller.

Frederick Taylor Gates, a tall, lean figure with shaggy hair, a handlebar mustache, and a sharp eye for figures that didn't add up, returned with a portrait of a disaster. A succession of wily promoters had wined and dined Colby and Hoyt in elegant fashion, dazzling them with the prospect of enormous profits raining down on all sides. At every turn Gates discovered financial losses, misrepresentation, and deceit. Claims turned out to be worthless, mortgages did not include what they were supposed to cover, and inflated cost estimates had provided extra funds to be skimmed off. Like Rockefeller, Colby and Hoyt had been remarkably naive; now, however, they had quietly sold out their interests, leaving their backer to deal with the messes they had initiated.

Amid charges of incompetence and fraud, the Everett Land Company had already replaced Henry Hewitt as president and ejected him from its board of directors.[48] By summer he faced bankruptcy proceedings.[49] Summoned to New York to meet with Rockefeller, the man known as the father of Everett was forced to hand over all of his stock in the Everett Land Company.[50]

While Hewitt was traveling east, Gates went west, arriving in Everett on August 1, 1894. Although it meant writing off a considerable loss, he immediately sold Rockefeller's interest in the land company, the hotel, and the street railway. Soon Rockefeller was also out of the pulp and paper company. With most of the town's assets dumped onto the market, the Everett bubble burst. When townsfolk complained that they sank their own life's savings into Everett because of the Rockefeller connection, Colby, who had replaced Hewitt but was himself to be thrown out within months, replied firmly that Mr. Rockefeller had not forced anyone else to get involved.[51]

The Everett & Monte Cristo Railway and the mining operations were also a sinkhole for Rockefeller, but his leavetaking of these enterprises would be staged more carefully. Gates quickly ascertained that the fabled mineral wealth had been far from a sure thing. The expertise of the chief mining authority, Alton Dickerman, whose opinion and authority had convinced Rockefeller to invest millions of dollars, was about iron mines in northern Michigan; he knew little about gold and silver and had never worked in the Pacific Northwest. During his brief foray at Monte Cristo, he had, in fact, seen veins of minerals, all of it a few feet from the surface. After that, though, the vein disappeared, fractured by the sort of volcanic activity rarely seen in Michigan. In other words, the traces of valuable minerals seen in the first loads of ore from near the surface were not the sign of more to come; deeper drilling revealed nothing more than additional traces. Indeed, Dickerman himself had concluded that too little was known to be sure just how valuable the site was and for that reason had declined the offer of a job as chief mining engineer.[52]

Gates told Monte Cristo nothing of what he had learned. Instead he spoke of hopes for an upturn in the situation and actually increased Rockefeller's investment by a small amount. He authorized repairs of equipment, new railroad cars, improvements to the track, and a new snow shed. The concentrator opened and finally sent its first carload of ore and timber to the Everett smelter.[53] Although not enough profitable minerals were being extracted to make a profit, Monte Cristo ore was finally becoming bullion and being shipped to the U.S. mints.[54] Saloons and dance halls opened round the clock, the raucous cries within blending with the blasting of dynamite, the grinding of the concentrator, and the clang and screech of the tramways and pulleys.[55]

Electrification was on its way. A school building was going up for the town's children.[56] The Monte Cristo Telephone Exchange had twenty-one subscribers paying $4 a month.[57] High-quality asbestos had just been discovered nearby, opening up a whole new field for exploitation.[58] Everything was growing. The notion that Monte Cristo might one day be a paying proposition began to seem like a distinct possibility.

On the heels of this optimism, on December 1, 1894, Frederick Trump stepped up and bought the same property from Rudebeck that he had tried to acquire through placer claims.[59] What Frederick Trump did not know was that the confidence expressed by Rockefeller's most high-level executives was an elaborate charade. Gates had already decided to pull the plug and to remove Rockefeller's backing from both railroad and mines. Now he was biding his time, waiting for the moment to cut the losses in the least unprofitable fashion.

Two American beliefs were in play at Monte Cristo. The first was that the sort of initiative and self-sufficiency Frederick Trump and others brought to Monte Cristo should have been sufficient to secure their future. It was not. The United States encouraged the Frederick

Trumps of the world to pursue their own paths to fortune, but this was not the reason it had become a major economic power. The nation owed its astounding financial growth to its ability to tap into capital, most of it in Europe. Americans had borrowed enough capital to build a national transportation and communication network, attract and absorb a large number of skilled immigrants, promote new technologies, and develop huge natural resources. They had profited enough to create their own centers of capital, which could then invest in enormous extractive projects such as Monte Cristo. Although people like Frederick Trump were necessary to carry out these projects, their outcome ultimately rested not with these facilitators, but with whoever controlled the capital, in this case John D. Rockefeller.

The second belief was the meritocratic one that those who possess abundant capital must owe it to their superhuman wisdom and power. Because Rockefeller was involved in Monte Cristo, people there assumed that the enterprise must be foolproof and discounted any suggestion that such might not be the case.

In February 1895 Everett papers reported that earlier in the month the *New York Sun* had received a telegram signed by one William E. Everette, who identified himself as a Tacoma metallurgist hired by "eastern millionaires" to investigate the Monte Cristo mines. In the telegram, Everette said that he had spoken to Rockefeller in New York, that the tycoon had already lost $1.5 million in the enterprise, and that the mines were not a feasible proposition. By mid-February news of the telegram had appeared in newspapers all over the country. If anything, this communiqué understated the true state of affairs, but nobody in the greater Everett vicinity wanted to believe that the richest man in America could have made a misstep. Accordingly, follow-up stories in local newspapers did not explore whether Everette existed or had done any such investigation or whether, as seems likely, the telegram was a fiction but its content was fact, inspired by knowledge of what Gates had found during his probing. In any case, the local press instead provided a glowing assessment of Monte Cristo's potential from a local mining expert "of unquestioned integrity" and denials by Rockefeller representatives that any interview with Everette had taken place.[60]

Evidently appeased, Everett and Monte Cristo went back to business as usual. And, in fact, to all outward appearances, prosperity continued to be just around the corner. In the spring of 1895, the Monte Cristo school opened, electric lights appeared, and new equipment for the concentrator arrived and was installed. There were rumblings of discontent among underpaid mine workers, but mine operators quickly quelled outbreaks of unrest. That fall, local prognosticators, citing observations that squirrels, mountain rats, and rabbits hadn't stored winter provisions with their usual care, forecast a mild winter.[61] Some three hundred hardy souls, more than double the previous winter's total, elected to stay, and among their number was Frederick Trump. Their reward was a two-week storm in December that knocked down scores of trees and dumped eleven feet of snow on the ground. Four more feet of snow fell on Christmas Day alone, turning the usual five-hour train trip from Everett into a seventy-hour ordeal. The snow was so heavy that it smashed in a shed, killing six horses. It also crushed the roof of Frederick Trump's boardinghouse.[62]

He could do nothing about it for days. The storm kept raging, and the snow got deeper and deeper. It didn't stop until the first days of 1896. When the snow let up, the remaining miners resumed burrowing ever-deeper, ever-longer tunnels, hunting the minerals that they were still convinced must be there. Frederick Trump turned to the daunting task of digging out his ruined business, replacing the smashed timbers, and reshingling the roof. It was enough to make anyone long for a vacation. In April he sublet the business and returned to Kallstadt for the wedding of a younger sister.

Elizabetha had been a pigtailed twelve-year-old when he'd left Kallstadt. Now she was twenty-three, a young woman. She married Karl Freund, a local butcher, on June 20, in a lovely church ceremony that was everything her older brother had run away from. She was doing what she was supposed to, marrying into a good local family, filling her assigned slot. Her brother was an American now, impatient with the orderly predictability of village life. There were few surprises in Kallstadt, bad or good. In this familiar little village he would never have his roof crushed by snow, but he would also never strike it rich. There were few risks, and Frederick Trump had developed a taste for risk.

After the wedding festivities were over, Trump returned to Monte Cristo in time for the fall elections. Across the nation, that year's presidential contest was unusually bitter, but nowhere more so than in the Northwest, which still remained locked in recession. The reason was that although the region's natural resources were enormous, they required investments on a scale unavailable either nationally, now that European bankers had pulled money out of banks back east, or locally, once eastern banks had in turn pulled money out of their western counterparts.[63] When the populist Democrat William Jennings Bryan ran for president as a champion of a financial scheme called bimetallism, which seemed to many in the Northwest like the last hope for economic recovery, Washington became Bryan country.[64]

Bryan's eloquent articulation of the feelings of depression and discontent sweeping the nation had already won him a seat in Congress from usually Republican Nebraska. Champion of the agrarian West and South, Bryan inspired adulation and awe in his followers. Within the eastern financial establishment, however, he aroused great alarm. As the election neared, old-line monetary interests flexed their muscles, driving up gold prices and interest rates. The message to the capital-starved West was clear: Vote for Bryan, and things will get even worse.[65]

Bryan was hugely popular in Monte Cristo, where gold and silver were not simply shiny coins but actual minerals, embedded in pieces of ore, that could be hewn out of the earth, concentrated, smelted, and made into bullion for shipment to the U.S. mint to be made into money. Bryan's bimetallism plan would, in effect, more than double the price of silver, a godsend to this increasingly desperate location in the mountains. Like almost every town in the county, Monte Cristo formed a Silver Club, and its members fervently boosted Bryan's candidacy.[66]

Apparently galvanized by the election fever surrounding him, Frederick Trump, too, plunged into politics, running for justice of the peace. On November 3, 1896, Bryan carried the state, although not the country. In Monte Cristo he won 2 to 1. But Frederick Trump did even better, winning by a decisive margin of 32 votes to 5.[67] At twenty-seven he had become not just an American, but a city father.

CHAPTER FOUR

MINING THE MINERS

BACK IN KALLSTADT FREDERICK TRUMP had listened to stories of those who had left for America and figured out how to do likewise. Once in New York he listened to sagas of the West and picked up what he would need to head that way. In Seattle he listened to descriptions of Monte Cristo and set himself up there. And now, in Monte Cristo, he listened to the tales miners were telling one another about gold strikes in Alaska and, especially, in the Yukon.

No one knew much about these remote and mysterious places. Most people in Washington referred to them interchangeably and assumed that the Yukon Territory, Canada's northwesternmost extension, was part of the United States. But this state of geographical ignorance mattered not one whit. By the spring of 1896, so many men had left Monte Cristo for the frozen North that the town experienced its first labor shortage.

Frederick Trump was tempted to follow. When two Monte Cristo mining veterans, Paul Hebb and Ed Monohan, declared that they were heading north, Trump joined in their plans. Although he was too deeply involved in Monte Cristo to fling himself headlong into anything so speculative, he cut a deal. He would help pay for Hebb and Monohan to reach the rumored gold fields. In return they promised to stake claims in his name. Frederick Trump was taking a flier, but not an enormous one. In the meantime, he would continue to pursue his business in Monte Cristo, which still seemed to him a more likely source of future revenues.

The next summer everything changed. On July 15, 1897, a steamer called the *Excelsior* landed in San Francisco. It was full of Yukon gold. Rumors spread that another steamer, then bound for Seattle, was bringing more. The *Portland* arrived in Puget Sound before dawn on Saturday, July 17, and was met by a boatload of reporters. One year earlier the first tales of Yukon gold had arrived; here was actual evidence that those wild stories were true. Aboard was more than $700,000 worth of gold nuggets from the Klondike River, a salmon stream that joined the Yukon River 1,200 miles north of Seattle.

Within hours the *Post-Intelligencer* came out with the first of what would be three extra editions.[1] Five thousand people jammed the Seattle waterfront to welcome the *Portland* and its booty. When its passengers stumbled down the gangplank, bent under the weight of their Klondike gold, Seattle exploded with excitement.

These sixty-eight grizzled, sunburned prospectors,[2] their suitcases and gunnysacks and coffee cans spilling over with precious metal, were not distant, Olympian figures of unimaginable wealth. They were ordinary working people: laundrymen, bookkeepers, farmers, ministers, stablemen, housewives. They looked tired and grubby, distinctly frayed around the edges. Very quickly, each of the five thousand people standing on the dock grasped the exciting fact that he or she could be one of these sixty-eight people. He or she could become rich. Turning into a Rockefeller or a Morgan was no longer a ridiculous fantasy that would draw a few hundred dreamers to Monte Cristo. It could happen. Here was the proof.

As newspaper stories over the following weeks explained, gold mining in the Yukon was different. It was not a lode strike, as in Monte Cristo, which required dynamite to blast out valuable minerals from surrounding rock. Instead the Yukon had placer strikes. *Lots* of placer strikes. Real ones. Soil and water erosion and glacial movement had already pried the gold loose. Now it lay on the surface, there for the taking. Often it had washed into streambeds, where it could be scooped up with a plain metal pan. You didn't need miles of mine shafts or hundreds of workers. You didn't need a concentrator or a smelter or a $2 million railroad. In short, you didn't need to be rich already. All you needed was grit, and poor people had plenty of that.

By the end of that Saturday word of the *Portland*'s cargo filled dinner tables throughout the Northwest. That morning Frederick Trump's contribution to Hebb and Monohan's grubstake had been a flier. That night it was the most prescient thing he'd ever done. By the time he was eating supper, his priorities had turned upside down. Now the Yukon was on the top of the list. Monte Cristo, it seemed, was merely a dress rehearsal, preparing him for the real thing in the North. But after four years in Monte Cristo, pulling up stakes was not a simple matter. It would be some weeks before he could leave, and in that time he pondered how to exploit the new discovery.

At Monte Cristo he had never expected to find precious metal himself, whereas in the Yukon he might have a shot at it. But he had seen scores of Monte Cristo claims come to nothing, and he had learned that there is always one sure thing in any mineral rush: The prospectors need rooms, refreshments, and female companionship. In Monte Cristo he had made a profitable business for himself out of providing hundreds of miners with all three. If the gold-mining prospects in the Klondike were anywhere near as good as people said, these things would be even more valuable there.

Frederick Trump, like everyone else who was thinking about the Yukon, wanted to get rich. He wanted to make a million dollars. But unlike the others, he realized that the best way to get what he wanted was to lay down his pick and shovel and pick up his accounting ledger.

In the time it took him to close up shop in Monte Cristo, Seattle was transformed. By midmorning on the day of the *Portland*'s arrival, downtown was in an uproar that would last for months. Mailmen, teachers, streetcar operators, and the mayor himself quit their jobs and started packing. On July 21 the city council held a special session to consider raising police salaries so that the entire department would not desert.[3] On the outskirts of town, crops withered on the vine because there was no one to pick them. Shipping companies were frantic because their vessels, abandoned by gold-crazed crews, sat stranded in distant ports.[4] Eight thousand people left Seattle in the first six weeks after the *Portland* landed. They paid no attention to warnings from transport companies and the U.S. secretary of the interior that traveling so close to winter was hazardous.

Few knew the precise location of the Klondike. Even fewer knew how to spell it. Nonetheless, when advertisements appeared offering opportunities to back mining expeditions to the Yukon, thousands jumped in. Within two weeks eight mining companies had been formed in New York with combined resources of over $25 million.

Happy days are here again, the *Seattle Post-Intelligencer* declared three days after the *Portland* landed. "So far as Seattle is concerned, the period of depression, which has lasted fully four years, is at an end," the paper rhapsodized. Seattle threw itself into the fierce competition with every other major West Coast city to be the gateway to the goldfields. Two days after the *Portland's* arrival, the Seattle Chamber of Commerce held a packed meeting to hammer out plans to nail down a U.S. Assay Office for Seattle.

The Chamber of Commerce established task forces to help Seattle grab the lion's share of Klondike-related trade. Already this was shaping up to be a different kind of gold strike from any that had come before. There was more gold, there were more people, and there was more frenzy. But what was to set this event apart more than any other single factor was the Chamber of Commerce's appointment of an unemployed journalist from Connecticut named Erastus P. Brainerd to head the special committee for advertising.[5]

Reasoning that word of the gold rush would spread without his help, Brainerd instead concentrated his formidable energy on making sure that anyone thinking about the Yukon would think about Seattle as well. "All advertising, anything that tends to give publicity, is good, but newspaper advertising is best," he declared. Then he set about proving it on an unprecedented scale. Brainerd filled the country's print media, some 6,000-plus papers and magazines, with ads. In Illinois alone, blurbs for Seattle ran in 488 papers.[6] The most spectacular advertisement was a six-column spread, enormous for that time, in the *New York Journal*, which had the nation's largest circulation. Within six months he had arranged a staggering total of nearly fifty million ads pointing out that any Yukon expedition had to buy equipment in Seattle, use the unique services of Seattle, and launch itself from Seattle.[7]

At the same time, he sent almost one hundred thousand reprints of a special *Seattle Post-Intelligencer* Klondike edition to every postmaster, public library, and mayor in the country. Brochures and letters poured out of Brainerd's committee. How to get there? Via Seattle, of course. Whom to ask for advice? Why, any merchant in Seattle. Where to buy equipment? Seattle!

And then there were the letters home. Every newcomer to Seattle was urged to write a note about Seattle to the old hometown newspaper. To make this easier, the committee conveniently provided form letters and postage; all the "letter writers" had to add was the address and their signature.[8]

Brainerd produced the first modern gold rush, guiding it with his public-relations savvy and marketing genius. It was a smash success, and thousands of gold seekers poured in every week. Every hotel was jammed, and new businesses opened all over town. Competing for attention, shopkeepers hung up so many ads and banners and flags that few were actually readable.

Everything that could float headed north, but demand far outstripped capacity. Although the price of boat tickets shot up, they all disappeared—just as well, perhaps, because transport companies no longer had enough clerks to handle sales. Like so many others in Seattle, they, too, had joined the rush northward.

Anything with the name *Klondike* on it sold out immediately. Footwear suddenly became "Klondike boots," coats became "Klondike jackets," and tents became "Klondike cabins." The prospectors-to-be paid ridiculously inflated prices for horses barely capable of standing, as well as burros, ponies, goats, even reindeer and elk, desperately hoping that these creatures could carry the ton of supplies considered necessary for survival in the northern wasteland. Dogs disappeared from Seattle, for those that weren't sold were stolen. "Seattle has become a cat's paradise," reported the *Seattle Argus*.[9]

No one in the city complained. "May [this situation] continue," the *Seattle Times* asked in an editorial plea to the Almighty. "[May] the difficulties of obtaining the yellow metal [be] of such magnitude, as to require an [sic] hundred thousand men twenty-five years to exhaust these newly discovered mines."[10] Seattle merchants were ecstatic. In September the flow of new assets into the city's banks was up 65 percent over the previous year.

Frederick Trump did his part. Thousands of visitors, all in a hot-brained hurry, were passing directly in front of him, and he again opened a restaurant to feed them. Located at 207 Cherry Street, it was a one-story wooden building with a skylight and a twelve-foot ceiling.¹¹ For $400 he purchased from another restaurateur the fittings: 47 chairs, 11 oak tables, 6 stools, 53 yards of linoleum, 8 hat racks, 3 ice-boxes, a lunch counter, and a full complement of kitchen equipment, dishware, and serving utensils. ¹²

His new eatery was three blocks away from his first, but in the four-year interim Seattle had so expanded that Cherry Street was in the center of the action.¹³ Just up the block from his restaurant, at Cherry and Third, was one of the most popular spots in town, the Seattle Theatre. Headliners there included such attractions as Professor Bristol's Educated Horses and the Georgia Minstrels. In between acts there was an early version of moving pictures, including, in August 1897, a "veriscope" of the Corbett-Fitzsimmons championship fight. Night after night crowds filled the downtown streets, providing a steady flow of customers for Frederick Trump.¹⁴ Business was so good that he paid off the entire mortgage within four weeks.

He shared in his customers' excitement more directly than most Seattle merchants because he was already personally involved in the gold rush. On July 7, ten days before the *Portland* reached Seattle, Edward Monohan and P. H. Hebb—his Monte Cristo mates—staked a claim in his name on Hunker Creek, a tributary of the Klondike. Named after Andrew Hunker, a German immigrant from Wittenberg, Hunker turned out to be one of the world's richest placer gold creeks.¹⁵ But Frederick Trump did not get a share of this bounty, because his partners sold his claim one day later for $400. Having paid $15 to register it, they made a 2,500 percent profit in twenty-four hours while still keeping half the land. How much of this sum reached Frederick Trump is unclear. Presumably his partners were following his instructions, although the signature on the claim and sales documents is not his. In any event, staking and then selling off immediately was usually the smart move. As it happened, though, several weeks later, Mark Pierce, who bought half of Trump's claim, sold a quarter of the original claim for $1,000.

Monohan and Hebb were busy taking care of their own interests. On July 6 they staked claims for themselves on what they called

Monte Cristo Gulch, a feeder off Boulder Creek. Two months later, on September 20, they staked another claim in Frederick Trump's name, this one on Deadwood Creek, a tributary of the Yukon River three miles below Dawson, the capital of Yukon Territory.[16] Three weeks later, on October 11, they sold half of Frederick Trump's second claim for $150. Three days before Christmas they unloaded the other half for $2,000.

On paper, Frederick Trump came out even better in this exchange, for Deadwood had no gold. As with the Hunker claim, it is unclear how much of this amount reached him, or when, but perhaps it did not really matter. His cash register was ringing night and day.

Frederick Trump did not go to the Yukon until he was good and ready. Over the fall and winter of 1897–98, he assembled the formidable list of supplies necessary for the trip.

Alarmed by the appearance of so many unprepared newcomers in the frigid North, the Canadian government had enacted new rules that required every newcomer to bring a year's supply of food, which amounted to about 1,150 pounds. In the storage area of his restaurant, Trump gradually stockpiled the requisite provisions and equipment, including 400 pounds of flour, 200 pounds of bacon, 100 pounds each of beans and sugar, 35 pounds of rice, and 50 pounds each of corn-meal, onions, and oatmeal. For vitamins there were another 50 pounds of potatoes and 25 pounds each of dried apples, peaches, and apricots. Stacked next to them were whopping amounts of candles, baking powder, yeast, salt and pepper, matches, soap, coffee, tea, and so forth. Recommended equipment included a stove, buckets, frying pans, coffeepot, hatchet, shovels, files, ax, chisels, nails, compass, and canvas tent, as well as enough sturdy, warm clothing to make it through months of aching, bitter cold and what would seem like near total darkness.

Then he sold off his restaurant and, just before departure, took care of one final detail. He transferred his three lots in Monte Cristo and the forty acres he had purchased from the Northern Pacific Railroad six years earlier to his sister Louise. Prudent Frederick Trump was not about to leave any loose threads behind. If something happened to him in the Yukon, he wanted to be sure that a family member could handle his affairs. Ten days later he filed the papers in the county clerk's office. The boy who was too frail to work in the vineyards was ready to take off for the most physically demanding experience of his life.

He had planned well. It was the end of March, the small annual window of opportunity between the end of impassable winter and the horrendous mud that accompanied warmer weather. Even in this favorable interval, though, he had to traverse more than a thousand miles of icy wilderness. And when he reached his goal, he would be in one of the strangest and most lawless communities on earth.

Leaving Monte Cristo during the first season it actually produced gold or silver had been a gamble for Trump. As it turned out, though, staying there would have been a disaster. In November 1897, record high temperatures melted the snow, causing the worst floods and avalanches in the area's history. They flattened railroad trestles and tunnels and destroyed more than five miles of roadbed. Facing the complete loss of all rail connection to the outside world, Monte Cristo rapidly became a near ghost town.

A month later, Frederick Gates, Rockefeller's principal henchman, declared that there would be no reconstruction of the railroad. During the spring of 1897 he began a systematic effort to consolidate Rockefeller's Monte Cristo holdings, foreclosing on mortgages held on the various independent mining operations that had developed there.

The following June Rockefeller himself finally visited the Northwest but got only as far as the outskirts of Everett. There he met in a private railroad car with James J. Hill, head of the Great Northern. In one afternoon Rockefeller sold all his Everett properties except the smelter to Hill, who went on to foster the development of the area's rich potential as a timber town.[17] Over the next few years Gates adroitly managed to sell off parts of the railroad to the Northern Pacific and rebuild enough of what was left to allow the resumption of

what appeared to be modestly profitable mining operations in Monte
Cristo. This seeming prosperity benefited the Trumps, for in 1900
Frederick Trump's sister Louise was able to sell his Monte Cristo
property for $250. It also benefited Rockefeller; in 1903 Gates man-
aged to unload the Everett smelter and what was now the Monte
Cristo Mining Company on a trust controlled by another major entrepreneurial clan, the Guggenheim steel family. They had no interest in the smelter. Simply wanting to eliminate competition, they
dismantled what had once seemed proof positive of Everett's sunny
prospects.[18] Gates used the proceeds to buy huge stands of timber in
Washington and British Columbia and eventually sold what would be
Rockefeller's last northwest investment for nine times what it had
cost.[19]

Through an extraordinarily elaborate and carefully staged with-
drawal, Frederick Gates was able to turn around what had been a major financial disaster. More than a decade after Rockefeller first
invested in the Northwest, he finally exited, having cleared a handsome profit of several million dollars. Although the oil tycoon and
the restaurateur never met, they were among the small and select
company of those who actually profited from Monte Cristo, although
on vastly different scales. Indeed, Rockefeller was the only original
large-scale investor to make money; too late to be of any help to anyone else, he had finally vindicated the naive trust Frederick Trump
and so many others had in his golden touch.[20]

CHAPTER FIVE

KLONDIKE FEVER

LIKE THE OTHER THOUSANDS OF GOLD RUSHERS in Seattle, Frederick Trump faced an awesome logistical task to get to the Klondike. After a long trip in a crowded boat from Seattle to the panhandle of southern Alaska, he would have to haul his crushing burden of supplies on an overland voyage that would take many weeks. Once having landed on the Alaskan coast, he would have to go over mountains, through the Canadian border patrol and customs, and then across a strip of British Columbia into Yukon Territory and the shore of Lake Bennett. There, at the headwaters of the Yukon River, he would have to build a boat from scratch, then float his supplies north—that is, downstream—on the Yukon and through rapids to the town of White Horse. At last he would be at the southernmost stop on the steamboat line to Dawson, the biggest city in the Yukon and 465 miles further. Going by steamer, he could reach Dawson in relative comfort, but if he were a prospector, he would then face the arduous task of actually digging a mine.

Frederick Trump had no plans to mine himself, but he still had to plan the trip just right. He had to get over the ten-thousand-foot-high mountains between the Alaska coast and Lake Bennett while the ground was still frozen hard. Warmer weather would turn the path into an impassable sea of mud, and it would be far harder to trek around Lake Bennett's long, uncleared shoreline than to cross it on ice. On the other hand, if he started the trip too early, he could end up

having to cool his heels at Lake Bennett, eating up his valuable supplies while waiting for the Yukon River to thaw. The trick was to
time the journey so as to arrive at Lake Bennett just before the thaw.

Trump's first sight of Alaska would have been of greenish gray
slopes, striped with old avalanche scars, silently disappearing into
low clouds. Every gold rusher passed countless tree-covered islands,
their rocky shores lined with oysters and the purple starfish that feed
on them. Coming into "civilization," in the form of Skagway and
Dyea, the Alaskan ports used by most gold rushers, was a shock. A
chaos of screeching gulls, bellowing stevedores, and roaring fires
abruptly replaced the low chuckle of waves. Dense smoke covered
the towns and reached out into the water, stinging the eyes of new arrivals. Through the smog, Trump could see an ugly jumble of tents
and shacks staggering uphill from the water, with horses and human
beings mired in the narrow, muddy streets. The passengers, startled
into wakefulness by the tumult, crowded the gangplank, pushing and
shoving in their eagerness to get ashore and get about the business of
becoming rich.

The first problem for Frederick Trump and every other newcomer
was keeping track of the supplies that had been so painstakingly
assembled and were now dumped on wharves and beaches helter-
skelter. Then there was the teeth-gnashing realization that much of
the "genuine" Klondike gear purchased back in Seattle was useless.
Greenhorns, one wrote in a letter home, "look as if they were gotten
up to represent a character on stage—[and] very much overdrawn at
that."[1] Klondike boots, complete with spurs and other paraphernalia,
were ridiculously cumbersome; another traveler, noting how envi-
ous everyone was of his lightweight tennis shoes, joked that he could
have sold a thousand at $5 a pair.[2]

Worse, both towns were almost completely lawless, and the sole
occupation of all inhabitants seemed to be extracting money from
travelers. Thus instead of resting up and regrouping for the next phase
of the journey, the new arrivals had to make every effort to press on
immediately. The next hurdle for these "cheechakos," as newcomers
were called in Inuit, was the mountain passes, which, as per Canadian government order, had to be crossed with a year's supply of food.
At the summit, which was also the U.S.-Canada border, North West
Mounted Police vigorously enforced this regulation, forcing those

without twelve months of grub to turn back.[3] The preferred method of transport was to break the supplies into fifty-pound lots, then move them along, load by painstaking load. The stashes of prospectors lined both sides of the trail and were understood to be absolutely inviolate; anyone who touched someone else's cache could be shot. En route, exhausted travelers camped out in tents but had to be sure to have enough wood for an all-night fire to scare away timber wolves.[4]

Frederick Trump could cross the mountains by one of two routes. At thirty-two miles in length, the Chilkoot Pass was the shorter, more direct way, but it was a hellish climb.[5] Even with sleds, it took weeks to scramble up to the final one-thousand-foot stretch of the trail, which angled up at a steep thirty-five-degree slope. With 1,500 steps cut into the ice and a cable attached to the mountainside so that climbers would have something to hold, the ascent still remained appallingly difficult. The weather was bitter cold, the winds cut like blades, and avalanches could happen at any moment. Each step toward the top was agony. Because the pass was far above the timberline and any greenery was buried under many feet of snow, all that could be seen was a vast, terrifying whiteness.

All winter long the single file of people stretched along the trail. Travelers had to step aside to pause for even a moment. To get back in line, they then had to wait for a break, which might not occur for hours. Because no one had yet invented lightweight, cold-weather clothing, people wore as many layers as they could manage, which added to their discomfort. And because no one had yet invented garments that wicked away perspiration, the layers got soaking wet. When perspiration reached the outer surfaces it froze, covering climbers in a frosty chain mail. To prevent condensation from their breath freezing onto mustaches and beards and forming a mask of ice, men shaved religiously, despite the discomfort of using a frozen razor.[6]

In all likelihood Frederick Trump took the alternative route, the White Pass. Essentially a narrow canyon with a stream at the bottom, it, too, was a nightmare. At forty-three miles this route was longer than the Chilkoot. But the White Pass did allow the use of pack animals, and when the stream was frozen and could be walked on, the climb itself was arduous rather than horrendous. Unfortunately the steep 1,500-foot rock walls of the canyon made it a natural echo chamber, which caused a constant reverberating din. Far worse, the beasts of burden were so expensive to buy and feed that everyone worked them literally to death. Owners whipped horses, donkeys, mules, oxen, and dogs until they dropped. The bodies were not buried or even moved; owners simply stripped the animals of their load and moved on. Travelers coming up the trail behind them had no choice but to walk over the remains.

As the months went by, the walls of the pass were stained dark red from the blood. Underfoot, entrails, bones, and skin, mashed together with the manure of surviving animals into an indistinguishable, vile slush, covered the ground. The revolting experience of Samuel Graves, a banker from Chicago who later became Frederick Trump's landlord in the Yukon, was typical. One morning, as he headed up the trail on a reconnoitering trip, he saw a horse drop to the ground. A few hours later, on his return trip, he saw the head of the horse on one side of the trail and the tail on the other, with the rest of the body having been ground into pulp by the constant traffic.[7]

By the time Frederick Trump crossed the pass, more than two thousand packhorses had died on what was known as the Dead Horse Trail, and at least one thousand more would perish there.[8] Most people saw the horse carcasses as the sickening evidence of human brutality. To Frederick Trump, this frozen horseflesh could have other possibilities. Stampeders were tired and hungry, and certain provisions were there for the asking. Opportunity was knocking, and Trump was listening. In the spring of 1898 he joined another cheechako named Ernest Levin in running one of the dozens of tent restaurants that dotted the trails. Six or eight men would crowd into a small canvas tent, wolf down a meal, then be replaced by another six or eight, all day long, day after day. A frequent dish was fresh-slaughtered, quick-frozen horse.

It is, of course, possible—barely—that Frederick Trump somehow shipped in hamburger from Seattle and owned the sole tent restaurant *not* to serve horsemeat. But if he was like everyone else, he did what the locals did—went out and cut up a piece of old Nelly. After a day of hauling heavy packs up the trail, no cheechakos were going to argue about prices. In fact, they willingly paid up to a dollar just to stand in the doorway of a restaurant, out of the cold and snow.[9] In addition to horsemeat, Frederick Trump's larder undoubtedly included sourdough biscuits and pancakes made from the little can of fermented starter dough that prospectors kept at their side. At trail eateries, one seasoned traveler wrote, "The menu is not elaborate, containing chiefly an assortment of beans, sometimes a suggestion of the poor dead horses on the trail, known locally as 'beef,' and generally a very greasy species of salt pork, with some very dried fruits by way of concession to the fastidious requirements of tenderfeet."[10]

Frederick Trump's career in the tent restaurant business was brief. By May 1898 he and Levin had crossed over to the Canadian side of the pass and were heading down to the raw new town of Bennett. It had sprung up almost instantly on the shore of Lake Bennett when thousands of stampeders appeared, threw up tents, and began putting together the boats they needed for the series of waterways that led to Dawson. Soon, of course, all the nearby timber was gone, so boatbuilders had to go some distance to find wood. Then, because the small sawmill in Bennett could not possibly meet the demand for milled wood, most Klondikers had to cut it into boards with two-person whipsaws, a frustrating, infuriating, painfully slow process. The vessels these inexperienced shipwrights produced, ungainly and often unseaworthy, did not inspire confidence; one observer called them "more like coffins than anything else."[11] But none of this seemed to deter the cheechakos. From May 1897 to July 1898 more than 18,000, including 631 women, came through Bennett and left by boat.[12]

The town's Main Street, a muddy, potholed thoroughfare that ran parallel to the shore, sported a Presbyterian church, a bakery, and the New Arctic Restaurant and Hotel, which Frederick Trump and Ernest Levin opened at the end of May. The two men had paid top dollar for the milled lumber used to construct the two-story frame building with its peaked roof. In the larder was salmon and an extraordinary variety of meats, including duck, ptarmigan, grouse, goose, and swan, as well as caribou, moose, goat, sheep, rabbit, and squirrel. Incredibly, the New Arctic served fresh fruit: red currants, raspberries, strawberries, blueberries, blackberries, even cranberries. A small oasis of luxury, the Arctic's menu was a vast improvement over what the two restaurateurs had been able to offer on the trail. Soon the restaurant gained a reputation as the best in town.[13]

Nonetheless, the bulk of the cash flow came from the sale of liquor and sex. This was hardly surprising in a town where the population, overwhelmingly male, existed in a perpetual state of boredom and anxiety. "There are two basic activities in Bennett," the *Victorian Colonist* commented in the spring of 1898. "Frantically building boats, and then once that is completed, sitting on thumbs waiting for the ice to clear." As in Seattle, Frederick Trump's establishment included accommodations for prostitutes. Newspaper advertisements in the *Bennett Sun* touted the Arctic's kitchen as the "Best Equipped in Bennett," with "All Modern Improvements," "Every Delicacy in the Market," and "Fresh Oysters in Every Style." But the ads also noted that the Arctic was open twenty-four hours a day and had private boxes for ladies—facilities that here included not only a bed, but a scale for weighing the gold dust used to pay for services.[14] Indeed, the Arctic owed its renown to its raunchiness as much as to its food. "For single men the Arctic has excellent accommodations as well as the best restaurant in Bennett," remarked one writer in the *Yukon Sun*, "but I would not advise respectable women to go there to sleep as they are liable to hear that which would be repugnant to their feelings and uttered, too, by the depraved of their own sex."[15]

Still, in comparison with Skagway or Dyea, life in Bennett was restrained. Public drunkenness was unusual, and the sole gambling allowed was blackjack.[16] The difference was due to the North West Mounted Police (NWMP), whose own discipline was legendary. A perfectly pressed uniform, for example, was so important that commanders were known to have been carried to inspections in order to preserve the knife-sharp crease in their trousers.[17] There were occasional tales of NWMP misbehavior; one stampeder from San Francisco complained that a Canadian customs officer added an extra "sinkerage" fee to the duties being charged. "Handing over five dollars, I asked him what 'sinkerage' was," the stampeder reported later. "For this," the customs agent answered as he dropped the money in his pocket.[18]

Unlike the situation in the Alaskan ports, however, reports of official corruption or public disorder were rare. An ultimately practical bunch, the Mounties seem to have been willing to put up with vices conducted in a nondisruptive manner. As long as there was no drinking, gambling, or chopping of kindling on the Sabbath, women did not consume liquor in saloons, and prostitutes remained in their own quarter, the Mounties stayed mum.[19] They kept the peace in a peaceful way, and entrepreneurs who did likewise, including Frederick Trump, were free to begin making their fortune long before they got to the Yukon itself.

———————

At 4:15 P.M. on Wednesday, June 8, 1900, Mrs. Zachary Taylor Wood, wife of the NWMP superintendent, stood at the foot of Main and Front streets in the town of White Horse,[20] Yukon Territory, nearly one hundred miles north of Bennett. Fifteen minutes earlier, locomotives from the White Pass & Yukon Railroad (WP&YR) had steamed up on newly completed tracks. Mrs. Wood hit the final spike,[21] and then the small crowd of onlookers and WP&YR officials dispersed. In another two months, an intermediate section of the line would be finished.[22] Then the railroad would carry passengers from Skagway to White Horse, which was located on the Yukon River just downstream—that is, north—of a treacherous series of rapids. Because the river was navigable from this point on, traffic could continue by steamboat all the way to Dawson, hundreds of miles farther north.

For the moment, that traffic would still have to go part of the way from Skagway by water, but passengers would no longer have to provide any transport of their own. They would not have to hike over icy passes, they would not have to carry anything on their backs, and they would not have to build boats. A train would take them through the mountains and across the tundra, and steamers would carry them the rest of the way. With the tapping of that last iron peg, the cost of transport from Skagway to White Horse dropped from $1 per pound to $.04 per pound, and a new era had begun.[23]

Watching the proceedings, Frederick Trump had every reason to be happy. Across the street from the train depot, the Arctic Restaurant was opening for business. Along with most of the other business folk in Bennett, he and Levin had followed the railroad and relocated in White Horse. Indeed, Trump had been scoping out the next location within six weeks of opening his restaurant in Bennett. On July 14, 1899, he had crossed Lake Bennett on the *Australian*, one of the fleet of medium-size freighters that carried passengers and goods on their way north, to take a look at White Horse.

The next spring he and Levin literally moved their business to the railroad terminus. Taking advantage of their lakeside location in Bennett, they dragged the hotel to the river and loaded it onto a scow. Slowly and majestically, the wooden building floated across the water. Unfortunately, because there was no highway or railroad yet and the river turned into rapids before reaching White Horse, there was no way this two-story edifice could arrive there intact. Once it had gone as far by scow as possible, the two owners salvaged the lumber, a rare commodity so far north, for use in the Arctic Restaurant's next incarnation, on Front Street in White Horse.

The town sat in a relatively pleasant spot. In addition to being directly en route to the goldfields of the Klondike, it had promising copper deposits quite nearby. And, with most of its rainfall blocked by the Gray Mountains to the east, the area received less than two feet of snow in winter,[24] and in summer the climate was dry enough for dust storms. Nearby there was actually a small desert, complete with sand dunes and tiny northern succulents.

White Horse thought of itself as a boomtown. The town site had been little but empty bush in the winter of 1899, but by the next spring a street grid cut neatly through stands of trees. Although the streets were muddy, they were wide and free of debris, and wooden sidewalks kept pedestrians clean and dry.[25] Two- and three-story frame buildings and tents were going up all around as merchants, railroad and steamboat officials, and hotel and restaurant owners scrambled to cash in on the railroad trade. With the opening of a brickyard that used local clay,[26] construction increased even more. Plans were already afoot for an electric light plant and a telephone service. A local board of trade had been formed, an athletic club materialized, and the post office was in operation.[27] A weekly paper, the *White Horse Tribune*, made its debut; soon afterward the *Bennett Sun* turned into the *White Horse Star*. By the end of June town lots that had sold in early spring for $300 to $500 went for $2,000 to $2,500.[28]

But the boom was a hollow one. Unlike Dawson, where gold was produced and circulated on the spot,[29] the White Horse copper mines had no significant output. "The boom was being conducted principally on credit, assisted with effusive proclamations about the glori-

ous future, while ready money in the town was exceedingly scarce,"
a prospector named Stratford Tollemache wrote later. Whenever a
train arrived, Tollemache recalled, townsfolk eagerly inspected the
passengers in search of "capitalists," meaning anyone with at least
$100 in cash, upon whom they could palm off town lots and mining
claims at inflated prices.[30] Indeed, as soon as a car full of passengers
pulled into the station, steamer captains and crews descended on the
hapless arrivals and competed furiously for their business.[31]

Unfortunately, by the time the owners of the Arctic arrived at
White Horse, Klondike gold—that endless, glimmering mountain of
wealth—was running out, or at least the relatively easily accessible
placer deposits were. What was left was deep in the hills and would
require the same expensive, capital-intensive methods needed for
White Horse copper or Monte Cristo silver. Not only that, prospectors had discovered gold on the beach in Nome, Alaska, over two
thousand miles away. Twenty thousand people who would have come
to Dawson were instead camped out in Nome, and thousands already
in Dawson were headed there as well.[32] Although more gold was
taken out of the Klondike creeks in 1900 than ever before,[33] it came
from claims that had long been staked out. There was little left for
newcomers.[34]

But most people in White Horse did not know this in June 1900.
With sunlight practically around the clock, land that had seemed
stark and forbidding to Frederick Trump only a short time earlier was
covered with greenery and wild flowers. The only unwelcome note
was the Klondike mosquito. Because the permafrost keeps groundwa-
ter trapped at the surface level, the entire countryside becomes an in-
cubator for these pests. Hardier, noisier, and more needle-nosed than
their brethren in warmer climes, the mosquitoes of the Yukon do not
retreat from wood smoke; on the contrary, campfires seem to draw
them. Nor do they seem to mind if, say, the hand they are biting is
immersed in water; they simply bite all the harder.[35]

But even the mosquitoes couldn't slow the newest Trump-Levin
enterprise. Almost as soon as Mrs. Wood hit that last spike, the Arctic Restaurant was up and running. Its tiny lot, just twenty-four feet
wide and sixty-six feet deep, was part of a forty-acre parcel that en-
compassed the entire waterfront of White Horse. In March 1910 the
Canadian government had transferred it to Duncan Cameron Fraser,

a barrister from Nova Scotia and Liberal member of Parliament, and after two weeks Fraser sold it to WP&YR president Samuel Graves. The new owner didn't bother to register title to it until nearly a year later, at the end of May 1901. In the meantime, an old Yukon hand named Patty Martin set up the Arctic Trading Company on the northern half of block 6, lot 3, located at First Avenue near Main Street. Although Martin, who sold groceries, paints, oils, and other supplies, did not actually own the property for another quarter century, he then proceeded to turn over the southern half of the lot to Frederick Trump.[36]

The Arctic Restaurant began its third incarnation just like its first, as a tent. But unlike the eatery on the trail, the restaurant in White Horse had a wooden facade and a wooden frame inside the tent reinforcement. Described in the *White Horse Star* as the principal restaurant in town as well as the biggest, it was open round-the-clock and boasted that it could serve some three thousand meals in the course of a day. To produce this prodigious amount of food, it had one of the largest steel ranges in the Yukon. The menu featured local game and fish and, in the warm months, local produce. Winter meant canned and dried food. Several bakeries in town provided bread, and water arrived in big barrels filled from the Yukon.[37] For certain supplies, Frederick Trump still had to go to Skagway, a trip that became easier when the WP&YR was finished.[38]

Wearing a clean white apron over his boiled white shirt and tie, the proprietor was also waiter, sometime cook, and, when necessary, bouncer. Overhead were kerosene lanterns, and there was a brand-new set of oak furniture. Along one side of the main room was a long wooden lunch counter with stools. A newsstand carried fresh fruits, cigars, tobaccos, late papers, and magazines.[39] The main floor area had tables and carved straight-back chairs, and along the opposite side of the room and in the back were accommodations for gamblers and for what were called "sporting ladies," curtained areas where prostitutes could entertain miners in privacy.[40] Finally, in the backyard was an outhouse, undoubtedly a two-seater to accommodate the lunch and dinner crowds.[41]

Unfortunately, trouble was brewing inside the Arctic Restaurant. Ernest Levin, a fractious type, was not getting along with his partner. In the first week of February 1901 Levin went for what the *Star* called "a short visit to outside points." Three weeks later, on February 25, Frederick Trump publicly dissociated himself from Levin, announcing in a notice printed in the *Star* that Levin was out of the restaurant operation and that he would not be responsible for any debts contracted by Levin.

By April the two men had reconciled, but there were other strains on the business. Major Zachary Taylor Wood was preparing to suppress gambling and liquor sales. Worse, he declared his intention to banish "the scarlet women" from the center of town. Frederick Trump and the other merchants petitioned the central government in Ottawa, pleading that they would be stuck with a huge inventory of unsold liquor and the town would be saddled with unemployed gamblers and prostitutes. In response, Wood postponed the date of this new regulation from March 16 to June 1.

Upon hearing of the postponement, the *Star* reported, "the town was painted a mild vermilion." That night, the faro tables were busy, "the girls were on the strees in squads dressed in their best bibs and tuckers," and many good citizens of White Horse displayed "that happy smile which good news and wine can bring about." A contest was promptly mounted offering a gold nugget bracelet and brooch to the ladies making the closest guess as to the precise moment the ice would break up on the stretch of the Yukon adjacent to White Horse.[42]

Regardless of the upbeat mood, Frederick Trump saw that it was time to leave. If Major Wood actually enforced the laws regarding prostitution, gambling, and liquor, hotels and restaurants would be far less profitable. Not only that, the economic boom was bound to be short-lived. There was not nearly enough solid economic development to absorb these newcomers in any long-term way; when the placer deposits were emptied, they would go back home. Without the umbrella of gold, other local industries would not be strong enough to keep going on their own and compete with cheaper sources farther south.[43] The boom was over, Frederick Trump realized.[44]

But probably the most pressing and immediate reason to leave was the continued deterioration of his relationship with Ernest Levin. Their reconciliation was short; by the end of April Frederick Trump was packing to leave and Levin was filing court papers to compel the landlord, Patrick Martin, to turn over the land under the restaurant to him. He was also continuing to tangle with the law. At the beginning of May Levin and nine other men were arrested for being "nuisances," a charge that generally meant "drunk and disorderly." Levin's companions, who included the president of the board of trade and a barrister, were prominent types, which may explain why the entire group was found not guilty.

Perhaps because Frederick Trump did not actually have a lease on the property, or perhaps because of Levin's brushes with the law, the court eventually awarded the restaurant to George S. Fleming and Harry Chambers. Fleming, a telegraph operator, worked at the railroad depot, and Chambers had a livery stable as well as a business buying and selling all kinds of property, including dogs, horses, feed, and wood. Originally from New York, "Shorty" Chambers was a bank robber and cattle rustler who had raced across the border one step ahead of the U.S. marshals only a year earlier. Now there were bad feelings between Levin and Chambers, and in June 1901 those feelings spilled over. Levin was arrested for theft and unlawful entry, and the complainant was Chambers. At the trial, held the same day, Levin's counsel was Willard Phelps, one of Levin's fellow miscreants back in March. Fortunately for Levin, Phelps was an able lawyer and got him off with a suspended sentence.

For the next nine months Levin continued to run the Arctic, although Fleming and Chambers held title to the land under it. An uneasy situation, it came to an abrupt halt on Saturday, March 1, 1902. That evening Levin and a newsdealer from Dawson went to the hotel room of three French prostitutes, and the entire party got gloriously drunk. In the course of a long, inebriated night, suitcases went flying out of windows, jewelry disappeared and then reappeared in the two men's pockets, and both of them ended up in jail despite their insistence that the whole episode had been intended as a prank.

Bad as he'd been, Levin was still one of White Horse's founding fathers. Before court opened the next morning, nearly every businessman in town signed a petition for clemency. Obviously impressed, the judge meted out the lightest possible sentence, a month's imprisonment in the guardroom. It was not Levin's only punishment; within ten days Sergeant John A. Macdonald of the Royal Canadian Mounted Police was appointed receiver for the Arctic Restaurant, and Levin was out of a job. The story spread throughout the entire region;

in March an account ran in the *Ketchikan Mining Journal*. "Looks like a very clumsy attempt at blackmail," the paper sermonized, "but then there are those who will say, 'serves 'em right for being found in bad company.'"[45]

Frederick Trump left just in time. He avoided the uproar when his erstwhile partner hit the skids, and he avoided the economic decline that would soon sweep over White Horse. Once again, in a situation that created many losers, he managed to emerge a winner. He had made money; perhaps even more unusual in the Yukon, he had also kept it and departed from White Horse with a substantial nest egg. He had accomplished this goal of making and saving enough money to marry. But he had no intention of doing so in America. For this important moment, he would have to return to Germany.

CHAPTER SIX

HERE TO STAY

FREDERICK TRUMP RETURNED TO KALLSTADT in 1901 a wealthy man. The business of seeing to his customers' needs for food, drink, and female companionship had been good to him. The slight lad with one shabby suitcase had become a mature man of thirty-two surrounded by a mountain of luggage and packages. When he left Kallstadt, he had been a work in progress; now the features that had swum about when he was a teenager had resolved themselves to produce a long, thin, straight-nosed face with a prominent chin and, of course, the handlebar mustache that was such a signature of that era. Sixteen years earlier he had slipped out of his home in the dead of night, running away to a new life in the New World. Now he was returning to the Old, planning to fashion a life for himself that would be both old and new.

Although he had become an American citizen in 1892, like other emigrants he had always felt part of his birthplace. From New York City he had helped support his mother with his earnings as a barber. In 1896, when his older sister Elizabetha married Karl Freund, he returned for the wedding. Now, five years later, he came back for a wife of his own.

Elizabeth Christ had lived across Frankenheim Strasse from the Trumps since her birth on October 10, 1880. Because she was only five when Frederick Trump left Kallstadt for America, they hardly knew of each other's existence. To her, he had been, at best, a distant name; to him, she had been one more small child on a street full of small children. Despite their proximity, the families were not close. The Christs, who owned less land than the Trumps and were thus unable to support themselves from their vineyards, occupied a rung several steps below the Trumps on the ladder of Kallstadt society. Philip Christ, Elizabeth's father, sold pots and pans and other household items from his home, a trade that earned him the nickname of "Gscherr Christ"—Tinker Christ[1]—and the scorn of Katherina Kober Trump. Poor and humiliated, the Christs were not a happy family. To many in Kallstadt, Elizabeth's mother, Ana Maria Anton, seemed a cold, domineering woman, and Philip so despondent and depressed that they suspected suicide when he died in 1908.

Katherina Trump was appalled when Frederick, the boy who made good, picked Elizabeth out of all the eligible females in Kallstadt. The widow tried to steer him toward other candidates, but her efforts were to no avail. He was completely smitten by the young woman walking out of the house across the street. Blonde and blue eyed, she had a heart-shaped face, round pink cheeks, clear smooth skin, and the hourglass figure that was the hallmark of turn-of-the-century beauty. By the end of his visit, Frederick Trump and Elizabeth Christ were engaged.

A year later he returned to Kallstadt, and their wedding was on August 26, 1902. As a legacy of the Napoleonic era, a legal marriage had to include a civil ceremony. Ordinarily the mayor of Kallstadt would have performed the honors. But because the groom had become an American citizen, higher authority was required, and the ceremony took place before the registrar in the nearby town of Ludwigshaben. Laurence Stauch, a barber there who may have been a haircutting colleague of Trump's when he was a teenager, acted as witness, confirming the identity and Protestant religion of both bride and groom. After returning to Kallstadt for a family celebration and party, Frederick Trump and his bride were on their way to a new world and a new life.

Although Frederick Trump promised Philip Christ that he would bring Elizabeth back to Kallstadt if she did not like the United States, it seemed impossible to him that anyone would not embrace the land of opportunity. He had made careful arrangements for her arrival. In part to help make her feel at home, they would be doing what he did when he first came to New York: living with his sister Katherine, who now resided at the busy intersection of Westchester Avenue and Southern Boulevard in the Bronx. During this period, Katherine's husband, Fred, worked a variety of jobs, including shipping clerk, driver, and shopkeeper. Evidently Frederick Trump stuck to what he knew, barbering, and restaurant and hotel management. Compared with the Klondike, the Bronx was an easygoing, tranquil place, and he seems not to have minded the opportunity to take a rest.

Not long beforehand, this part of the Bronx had been empty farmland, on which large estates had only recently been divided into more modest holdings. By the end of the nineteenth century, though, the South Bronx had become urbanized, with paved streets, noisy factories, and big-city vices. Those favoring consolidation with New York City in 1898 painted a picture of a place riddled with corruption and pockmarked with so many gambling halls and saloons that it was a veritable Skagway on the Hudson. According to the *New York Tribune*, there was one gin mill for every eight people.[2] Consolidation, it was argued, would bring effective law enforcement, in addition to connecting the Bronx to New York sewers and subways, thereby raising property values.

Within four years of consolidation, developers were building across the South Bronx. It was in one of these newer structures that Frederick and Elizabeth Trump made their own home, in the German neighborhood of Morrisania.[3] There were new city-style amenities, such as public phones and trolleys; in addition, there was a zoo with a herd of bison and an amusement park that offered a roller coaster, a Wild West show, and an opportunity to try exotic new edibles like peanut butter. There were also new urban problems: rats, vandals, and shortfalls in overburdened school budgets. The newlyweds were moving into a place that was a far cry from either Elizabeth's home in Kallstadt or the Lower East Side tenement that had been her husband's first home in the city. With hot water, steam heat, electricity, and a private bathroom, the Trumps' Westchester Avenue residence was a new sort of dwelling, with a new name to underscore its novelty. It was called an "apartment house."[4]

Running a household in the days before telephones or supermarkets was an elaborate, seven-day-a-week job. On Mondays Elizabeth did the wash in a large copper-bottomed tub. Into the boiling water went a little kerosene to cut the dirt, as well as soap made at home from rendered fat and lye, excellent for removing spots and also a layer or two of the skin of whoever was doing the washing. Tuesdays were for ironing, and the rest of the week was taken up with endless rounds of cleaning, scraping, mopping, rubbing, polishing, and rug beating. To order groceries, she sent a postcard to the grocer in the morning, and, thanks to having three mail deliveries each day, she would receive what she had requested by midafternoon. In between these ongoing tasks, she would deal with the milkman, the fishman, tinkers, umbrella repairmen, fruit and vegetable vendors, the pack peddler with dress goods, and the tea and coffee salesman.[5]

For Elizabeth, life at 1006 Westchester Avenue was busy, noisy, bustling—but not entirely strange. The language and many of the customs, including local breweries for those who did not care for American-style beer, were German. Friends and relatives from Kallstadt lived nearby. Frederick Trump's sister Louise worked in Gramercy Park as a cook in the well-to-do household of Samuel Cooper, brother of the inventor and politician Peter Cooper. Fred Schuster's cousins George and William lived in Mt. Vernon, not far north of the Bronx, and his brother Carl lived in Manhattan.[6] Still, it was not Kallstadt; it was New York City. Although Frederick Trump was a U.S. citizen, Elizabeth remained a German. After a year in her new home, she was desperately homesick for Kallstadt. She was also pregnant. On April 30, 1904, she gave birth to a daughter, named Elizabeth. As soon as they could travel, Frederick Trump honored his commitment to Philip Christ. By the end of June, mother, father, and infant were on board a ship, headed for Bremen and home.

Frederick Trump brought to Kallstadt his savings of eighty thousand marks. A stupendous sum in Kallstadt at the time, it would still be a handsome amount today, worth just over $350,000 in purchasing power.[7] He promptly deposited the money in the village treasury, an act that surely contributed to the warm welcome he received from village officials. His wife was ecstatic to be back home, and it seemed possible that in newly industrialized Germany there might be a place for go-getters such as Frederick Trump. Soon after his arrival, he asked permission to remain permanently in Kallstadt and regain his original citizenship.

But although Kallstadt had not changed much while Frederick Trump had been away, Germany had. In addition to becoming more industrialized, it had become more militarized. After years of Prussian domination, the traditional Junker emphasis on hierarchy, order, obedience, and social discipline had permeated the entire nation. Into the twentieth century Germany marched, its factory chimneys belching and its military banners waving.

The army, no longer an ad hoc organization that materialized when the nation was at war, had become a permanent fixture of national life. Every able-bodied man had to serve; indeed, having been in the army was virtually a condition for male citizenship. "All the young men receive a discipline which transforms louts and boobies into trim and intelligent men," one contemporary account noted approvingly. "For the German military course is not one of drill of the body only, but of mental drill as well. Consequently, all of the manhood of the country is brought to discipline, subordination, and the sense of interdependence."[8]

Under Kaiser Wilhelm II, who reigned from 1888 to 1918, the size and disposition of the military machine was a national obsession. Wilhelm was passionately attracted to the military life; one of his favorite pastimes was war games, which, of course, he always won. Obsessed by uniforms, he dressed almost exclusively in full regalia, favoring coats covered with gold braid and multiple insignias. By 1904, the year of Frederick Trump's return to Kallstadt, Wilhelm had reportedly redesigned the uniforms of his army thirty-seven times.[9]

Into this environment stepped Frederick Trump, draft dodger. In 1885, when he had left Kallstadt, the defining characteristic of German citizens was industriousness. This he had to spare. By the time of his return, however, military zeal had become the sine qua non. Unfortunately, in this second category Frederick Trump had nothing to offer.

Initially, the process of repatriation seemed no problem. The local village government heartily endorsed the move. "He and his wife have led a solid life, have their own residence in Kallstadt, and he is able to care for himself and his family," the local council enthused in its endorsement of his repatriation. The hometown boy had done well, the hometown was glad to see him, and both expected that would be the end of it. Trump forwarded his request, and the district authorities at Durkheim joined the Kallstadt town council in approving it. "Trump has not given any reason for complaints," reported the district police station. "He has obliging manners, avoids bars, leads a quiet life, and is against alcoholic beverages."[10] Good notices for a former supplier of liquor and women, Trump must have thought.

Then, on Christmas Eve, a shadow fell across his hopes. It came in the form of a communication from the Department of the Interior, which operated at a national level and was in Speyer. "It seems noteworthy that Trump wants to return permanently to his native land, now that he is at an age at which he can consider himself released from his military obligation," Speyer wrote to Durkheim. "Since the assumption is not unfounded that said Trump had at the time of his emigration the intent of avoiding military service, his request for naturalization cannot be granted. On the contrary, there are reasons to examine whether said Trump should not be expelled from the kingdom."[11]

Frederick Trump was stunned. "The news that the High Royal Ministry of the Interior had decided that we were to leave our current home [has] suddenly hit us like lightning from a clear sky," he wrote to Speyer. In the ensuing flurry of letters and reports back and forth at local, district, and national levels, he explained, apologized, begged, and pleaded. "[Because of the decision] we were as if paralyzed by fear," he wrote, "and our happy family life was cast over by dark clouds."[12]

The basis for rejecting him was a regulation adopted on August 3, 1886, nearly a year after he had left Germany. Resolution of the Royal Ministry of the Interior No. 9916, "Emigration to North America of persons liable for military service," decreed that those who left to avoid the army would be stripped of their citizenship and expelled.[13] Such a rule seemed to be sorely needed. "Many men, rather than serve these three years, run away to America, or England, and the drain in this way of able-bodied men is so serious as to perplex the authorities greatly," lamented the contemporary account.[14] From the perspective of Speyer, the Frederick Trump situation was open and shut: young man leaves, waits until he's overage, then wants to return to hearth and home, scot-free, with the nest egg he amassed while on the lam.

Frederick Trump also saw it as open and shut: innocent virtue (his) battered by bureaucratic bungling (everyone else). Backed by affidavits from Friedrich Ludwig Schroeder and Philip Christ, whom Trump described as two "leading Kallstadt citizens," he claimed that he had instructed his mother before February 1886—that is, before his seventeenth birthday and before Resolution 9916 had been adopted—to obtain his release from Bavarian citizenship. In other words, he and his supporters maintained, he had tried to relieve himself of the obligation to serve *before* that obligation became due.

"I did not immigrate to America in order to avoid military service, but to establish for myself a profitable livelihood and to enable myself to support my mother," he declared to Speyer. "It was my intention to remain in America forever."[15] He had, he added, "never even thought about returning to Germany as a permanent resident, since I thought I was making more money in America than I could ever make back home."[16] Accordingly, his mother had submitted a request to the local government clerk, a certain Duttenhoeffer.

As the months went by, Katherina Kober Trump repeatedly asked Duttenhoeffer, who was also the village schoolmaster, about the status of her request. "She even made the attempt to pay the costs incurred," recalled Schroeder, "since she was of the opinion that the matter had been concluded."[17] Two years later she finally discovered that Duttenhoeffer had never lifted a finger and that her application had never been looked at. In 1889, after she submitted another application, her son was released from Bavarian citizenship. To Frederick Trump, this was three years after he had completed his part of the process by applying for the release; to Speyer, this was three years after the cutoff date imposed by Resolution 9916. For Duttenhoeffer, the clerk, the delay was an oversight. For Frederick Trump, it was a disaster.

At another time, it would perhaps have been possible to negotiate a compromise. But again, his timing was unfortunate. For some time, Wilhelm II and Bernard von Bulow, his chancellor, had been complaining that Germany, which had no European allies and few colonial possessions, was encircled by a ring of hostile states. France, the German king and chancellor declared, was particularly antagonistic. In 1905, just as Frederick Trump was making his final, frantic appeal for a stay of the order of expulsion, von Bulow persuaded the reluctant Wilhelm to interrupt his spring cruise on the Mediterranean and pay a three-hour visit to the sultan of Morocco in Tangier, then within the French sphere of influence. Wilhelm proceeded to demand free access to the area for Germany. He was rebuffed, but the incident, in which the king of Germany had bypassed French officials on their turf, electrified Europe and led to an international conference to discuss the independence of Morocco. The conference endorsed French influence over Morocco, and Germany again found itself isolated.[18] Feeling embattled, the kaiser announced that military preparedness was more essential than ever before.

Frederick Trump's request for reconsideration went nowhere. So did the plea from Kallstadt's mayor, who pointed to "Trump's tax and investment capacity."[19] Neither man could change the fact that Frederick Trump had not served in the German army, had become a U.S. citizen, and had stayed away until he was no longer eligible for conscription. Nor could they change the even more damning fact, from Speyer's point of view, that he was a Pfalzer, native of a hotbed of subversive republican ideas.

Letter after letter went to Speyer. "The continued residence of the family Trump is not a small matter with regard to the local treasury and community taxes respectively, considering their substantial wealth," the mayor of Kallstadt wrote.[20] "There does not seem to be any cause to expel Friedrich Trump from the Kingdom based on Resolution No. 9916," declared the district authority in Durkheim.[21] "We are loyal Germans and stand behind the high kaiser and the mighty German Reich," Frederick Trump insisted, noting that he and his wife were happy to invest their money in Kallstadt and pay taxes. "What should our fellow citizens think if upright and solid subjects are hit with such a resolution, not to mention the great material loss."

Flinging himself on the kaiser with all the obsequiousness he could muster, he made a final appeal: "All that is left for the most obedient and loyal signatory to do is to turn to the Much Beloved, Noble, Wise, and just Father of the Country, Our Solemn Ruler . . . who reigns so nobly, just, and wise, and so full of clemency, and who is sincerely and intensely loved because of it. . . ."[22]

It was all to no avail. Speyer's ear was deaf, and deaf it remained. The Trumps were granted a few extra months in Kallstadt because of illness. Then, on June 30, 1905, they left, for the last time. Elizabeth was five months pregnant with her next child, Frederick Christ Trump. The Trumps were to be Americans, after all.

PART II

THE BUILDER:
FRED TRUMP

CHAPTER SEVEN

————

BORN TO WORK

Q UIETLY, POLITELY, AND FIRMLY, Frederick Christ Trump
pushed his way into the back of a hot, packed courtroom on the
afternoon of Monday, January 15, 1934. Surrounding him were dozens
of anxious, frightened people who had recently discovered that they
had lost their life savings. Small investors for the most part, they had
found themselves left holding the bag in the biggest bankruptcy anybody could remember. Today, summoned by tiny-print newspaper
ads, certified letters, and word of mouth, they had gathered at the
Main Post Office Building in Brooklyn, which also served as the federal courthouse.¹ Court officials had expected a quiet judicial proceeding. To their dismay, more than three thousand people showed
up, overflowing the three-hundred-seat courtroom and clogging the
marble-lined corridors and the stairwells. A front-page story in the
next day's *Brooklyn Eagle* called it the largest courthouse crowd in
borough history.²

To accommodate the mob of unhappy creditors, officials had
propped open the heavy courtroom doors, which were covered in dark
leather and studded with brass nails. It was cold outside and chilly on
the floors below, but here the severe crowding made the area un-
pleasantly warm and stale with the smell of overdressed, sweating
bodies. Only someone determined could have shoved a way inside.
But twenty-eight-year-old Fred Trump, tall and slim, with a mustache
and straight blond hair, was very determined.

Courtroom 727, a recent addition to the post office, was an elegant room with a twenty-foot ceiling, patterned marble floors, and large windows that looked west toward the Brooklyn Bridge and the East River. Rich mahogany paneling covered the walls, and terracotta wreaths and decorative molding festooned the ceiling. But on this mid-January day no one was paying attention to the decor. Some of the people seemed too dazed to speak and simply stared into space. Others talked incessantly in loud, angry voices. Often the conversations were in German or German-accented English.

Waiting for the proceedings to begin, these spectators were outraged and vulnerable, equally ready to lash out in fury or burst into tears. The Depression had already lasted more than four years. It had long since taught them the cruel lesson that no job was safe, that a factory with production lines working double shifts one week could close the next, and that if you couldn't pay the rent, you were on the street even if you had no place to go. But through the stock market crash, the unemployment lines, and the bank holidays, this group had clung to the apparent stability provided by a handful of corporate enterprises based in downtown Brooklyn and run by a German-American family called Lehrenkrauss.

Known as the House of Lehrenkrauss, this family conglomerate had begun back in 1878, twenty years before the city of Brooklyn merged with Manhattan. In a tiny closet in what was then Brooklyn City Hall, Julius Lehrenkrauss, a recent German immigrant, opened a travel bureau that sold steamship tickets to other Germans who wanted to bring their families to America. Because transferring funds abroad was a complex affair, he became his clients' de facto private banker, holding their money, sending funds overseas, making investments on their behalf.[3] As Germans continued to pour into the United States, the Lehrenkrauss operation expanded to fill a five-story building across the street from Borough Hall, as the old City Hall was renamed after Brooklyn was incorporated into New York City in 1898. In addition to the travel agency and private merchant bank, the business now included a safety deposit box department, an insurance company, and mortgage brokering.

After World War I Lehrenkrauss developed a brisk trade in what was known as "guaranteed" or "certificated" mortgages. To pay for the residential properties going up all over New York City, mortgage banks and title companies began to "certificate" mortgages—that is, to divide them into shares that were then sold to the general public like so many bonds. Available in denominations of $1,000 and up, these certificates appealed to people who wanted to cash in on the economic bonanza of the 1920s but had little money to invest. Although mortgage certificates would never create the overnight windfalls of the stock market, they returned a guaranteed 6 percent interest at a time when banks paid only 3 percent and were not insured by the federal government.[4]

In the early 1930s, as the nation plunged into economic turmoil, certificated mortgages from Lehrenkrauss appeared to retain their value. The firm, now headed by Julius's son, also named Julius, held $30 million in Brooklyn and Queens mortgages, had forty thousand regular customers,[5] and maintained five branch offices around the city as well as correspondents in more than a dozen European cities.[6] Modest wage earners who had turned over their little nest eggs to Lehrenkrauss remained secure in the knowledge that on the first of every month an interest check would arrive in their mailboxes.

But on December 1, 1933, Lehrenkrauss investors reached into their mailboxes and found them empty.[7] The fifty-five-year-old House of Lehrenkrauss had crashed to the ground, apparently without any warning whatsoever. Soon screaming headlines in the *Brooklyn Eagle* revealed that Julius Lehrenkrauss had been running a deficit operation for years, covering expenses and salaries with a haphazard assortment of schemes that included issuing watered stock, writing up mortgages based on either inflated or nonexistent evaluations, selling mortgage certificates worth more than the mortgages they represented, and taking out bank loans against mortgages that had already been certificated.[8] When the Depression caused the mortgage market to contract, the Lehrenkrauss operation lost its cash flow—the constant inflow of new dollars that kept it afloat—and ended up drowning in a sea of financial obligations.

By law, bankruptcy falls under federal jurisdiction and regulations. Accordingly, Lehrenkrauss's creditors had gathered at the U.S. District Court for the Eastern District of New York—in other words, the federal court in Brooklyn—to exercise their legal responsibility. As most of them were learning for the first time, they were not only entitled, but actually obliged to meet and elect trustees who would parcel out the company's remaining assets. Shortly after two, a man in his mid-thirties who had a mustache and wore his thick brown hair plastered down and parted in the middle called the meeting to order. His name was Theodore Stitt, and he was the court-appointed referee in charge of the Lehrenkrauss bankruptcy case.[9]

After the crowd settled down, Charles J. McDermott, a prominent retired judge in his late sixties, began speaking. For the past six weeks he had been working on this case as a receiver, an interim official whose job was to inventory assets as bankruptcy proceedings unfolded. Standing in front of the room, he wasted no time getting down to business. The affairs of the House of Lehrenkrauss were so tangled, he said, that it was impossible to give even a general status report.[10]

To disguise the firm's dire straits, Julius Lehrenkrauss had ordered the accountant to cook the books. Thus, for example, one division's $19,000 deficit had magically turned into a net worth of $1.8 million.[11] Julius regularly made out corporate checks to cash, with no accounting for where the money went. Whenever he could get away with it, he paid dividends by issuing more worthless Lehrenkrauss stocks. He left dozens of deeds unfiled, misfiled, and, in some cases, missing altogether. As a result, almost all McDermott could say was that the Lehrenkrauss bankruptcy was "the most interwoven, intricate and hopelessly muddled-up mess that I have ever had anything to do with."[12]

"Appoint a trustee!" shouted one creditor in the mob.

"Who stole the money?" yelled another. "Put them in jail!"[13]

At this point, a short fat man with thick gray hair and a cigar stub in his hand stood up in front of the room. Archibald Palmer, a lawyer, had devoted his career to bankruptcy cases, a field that made up for its low prestige with handsome fees. Now in his forties, he had trained as a bantamweight fighter and was well-known for his combativeness in the courtroom. "I have to be punching all the time, even if I get licked," he once said.[14] Speaking on behalf of the creditors, he charged that family greed had caused the Lehrenkrauss downfall. The final collapse had turned into disaster and disgrace, he thundered, because of Julius Lehrenkrauss's unwillingness "to face the music" when financial ruin was inevitable. "He was looking for a miracle," Palmer said in a ringing voice. "God doesn't send miracles to bad people."[15]

The crowd applauded wildly when Palmer reported that police had recovered mining stocks that Julius had pocketed, but the lawyer quickly discouraged their jubilation. "Applause won't do you any good because they owe you so much money," he said, adding that the restored stock "would be of as much consequence as one wrinkle more or less on an old lady's face."[16] Indeed, he said, "in this muddle we are doing a public service if we can salvage anything at all and more than anything at all from this mess."[17] The press, he declared, had covered only a small fraction of the "dirt and filth" involved, for it would take four newspapers to cover all the crimes committed.[18]

Unlike everyone else in Courtroom 727, Fred Trump could not have been happier. The eldest son of Frederick Trump, he was well acquainted with the intricacies of New York real estate. As he stood and listened, he became increasingly interested in one particular Lehrenkrauss operation, the mortgage-servicing department. For a small fee, J. Lehrenkrauss & Sons, the core company of the Lehrenkrauss conglomerate, had managed the buildings on which it held mortgages, providing maintenance, collecting interest, paying taxes, and handling routine administrative matters. Because this operation was still making money, court-appointed officials would sell it off to satisfy claims. Presumably it would continue to make money for the buyer. Better yet, it could lead to far greater profits in the future. To the knowledgeable observer, the list of mortgages maintained by the company could be a gold mine, for it identified hundreds of properties that in these Depression times were liable to foreclosure and subsequent auction at tax sales.

After the Lehrenkrauss hearing, the young observer boarded the elevated train out to Woodhaven, Queens, where he lived with his widowed mother. Riding past the old Lehrenkrauss building at the corner of Fulton and Myrtle, now dark and shuttered, he pondered how to proceed. It could be risky; he had learned firsthand that building had its down periods. And with such high stakes, there would be serious political, legal, and financial infighting. But he had already made his decision.

———

If Elizabeth Christ Trump had gotten her way, her son Fred would never have been in that Brooklyn courtroom, because he would never

have been in America. But in July 1905, after her husband was unable
to regain German citizenship, he, Elizabeth, and their one-year-old
daughter returned to New York aboard the SS *Pennsylvania*. Three
months later, on October 11, one day after her twenty-fifth birthday,
Elizabeth gave birth to her second child and first son. His name on his
birth certificate was Frederick Christ Trump, but he was known as
Fred from the start.

The newborn's parents had set up housekeeping at 539 East 177th
Street. It was next to the recently electrified Third Avenue elevated
train and not far from the Westchester Avenue apartment where they
had lived with the Schusters.[19] The new neighborhood was quiet, but
because the building had been built under old zoning laws, the
Trumps had only cold water and shared a bathroom with their neighbors. Two years later they had a third child, John George, and moved
about fifteen blocks south to a spanking new five-story brick building
on a corner lot in a newly developed section named Woodstock.
There were six families on each floor and porcelain washbasins, bathrooms, and iceboxes in each apartment. Because they were on top of
a hill, there was also a view out over the South Bronx. A dumbwaiter
conveyed coal and wood to each apartment from a storage bin in the
basement.[20] A large farm at 152nd Street and Prospect Avenue provided fresh vegetables to the whole neighborhood, and a nearby Chinese hand laundry did the wash.[21]

After his return from Germany, Frederick Trump dusted off his
barber tools and supported his growing family by giving shaves and
haircuts. At first he lathered and snipped at home in the Bronx, but
within a few years he had rented a room at 60 Wall Street, a large office building in lower Manhattan, and hired a tonsorial staff.[22] The
chairs in his shop were seldom empty, for the modern safety razor
was not yet in general use, and being shaved by a barber was part of
any successful businessman's daily routine.

But Frederick Trump was no more content to remain a barber
now than he had been back in Germany two decades earlier. He
worked, he saved, and he searched for a spot where a quick, energetic
fellow who'd already knocked around the globe a bit could use what
he'd learned, where things were still open and there was a chance to
get in on the ground floor. His sister Katherine would move back to

Manhattan, where her husband, Fred Schuster, would continue a succession of low-paying clerk jobs. His other sister, Louise, would marry an older, well-to-do Schuster cousin, George, and move north of the city to Mt. Vernon. But Frederick Trump was still looking for the right opportunity for himself and his nest egg. By the end of 1906 he had found it. He was ready to stake his future on the growth of a section of western Queens called Woodhaven.

Before doing so, Trump made one last stab at returning to Germany. On December 20, 1906, he wrote again to the Royal Ministry of the Interior. Unlike previous unctuous missives, this letter was brief and to the point. He said that his life in America had been good and he had never intended to return to Germany, but his wife was unable to adjust to the New World. He did not emigrate to avoid military service, he said, but because he wanted to have "a profitable life" and to support his mother. He was "a quiet, peaceful man," and his family was of a high moral character. The flowery closing of the previous pleas was reduced to a perfunctory "Obediently."

In short order, the answer came back. The Royal Ministry was sticking to its guns. In a resolution dated January 10, 1907, the crown proclaimed him unwelcome as a resident in Bavaria. On March 13 the mayor of Kallstadt informed the Royal Ministry that he had given the required notice to this effect to Katherina Kober Trump and to Elizabeth's father, Philip Christ. Two days later, on March 15, Frederick Trump opened an account at the Hillside Bank, a new institution on Jamaica Avenue in Queens. He had stopped looking back. His future, and that of his family, would not be across the Atlantic Ocean in Germany, but across the East River in Queens.

It was hardly a wild gamble. As the rest of the city had urbanized, Queens had remained "the cornfield borough,"[23] a source of fresh produce and unspoiled countryside. As a result, although it was the largest borough in terms of land area, it had by far the smallest population, just 152,999 inhabitants, or 4 percent of the city's total, in 1900.[24] In large part this was because Manhattanites could reach the borough only by ferry or via Brooklyn. But now the city was building the Queensboro Bridge over the East River, and the Pennsylvania Railroad was digging a tunnel under it. When they were finished, Queens would be as accessible as the South Bronx. Surely, Frederick

Trump reasoned, the real estate development that had occurred in the rest of the city would then touch Queens, creating opportunity for - people like himself.

In September 1908, nine months before the completion of the Queensboro Bridge, he made his move, beginning the family's New York holdings by purchasing a modest two-story frame structure in Woodhaven. It was on the north side of Jamaica Avenue, the Indian track that had served as the main east-west road across Long Island for more than two centuries. The first acquisition in a real estate portfolio that would expand manyfold over the next century, the building was in an area called Union Terrace in honor of a nearby racetrack, now gone, named Union Course.[25] In choosing this site, Trump had, as in his northwest ventures, followed the primary rule of real estate: Location, location, location. With an electric trolley that ran down the center of Jamaica Avenue, this site was perfect for business. But his purchase violated real estate's second rule: Never use your own money. He paid cash.

The next year the fledgling real estate magnate got a job as a manager at the Medallion Hotel, on the east side of Sixth Avenue at 23rd Street. The Medallion was one of many prosperous, thoroughly German business establishments in New York, and its majordomo was a champion sharpshooter named Gustav Zimmerman who was from Baden and lived near the Trumps in Morrisania. He saw in Frederick Trump the experienced hand he needed at the newly renovated hotel, which had just obtained a liquor license and was expanding its restaurant and bar operations. As always, the restaurant and hotel business meant long hours, made longer by the task of getting the new operation up and running. Frederick Trump spent most of his time at the hotel, and in the fall of 1909 he cast his vote in the city's mayoral elections from that address.[26]

By 1910, however, he and his family were in Queens. After a few alterations, the Trumps moved into the building on Jamaica Avenue and rented out one floor to another barber and his family. Unfortunately the building was not well suited for housing. All day long Jamaica Avenue rang with the noisy clamor of commerce, including busy workers rushing to and fro and knickered boys hawking newspapers. The trolley roared deafeningly outside the windows, and Elizabeth worried about letting her young children outside to play. After months of fretting, Frederick Trump moved his business a few blocks farther east on Jamaica Avenue and bought a nearby house and vacant lot next to it. Located just south of Jamaica Avenue on First Street, the new Trump residence, a two-story frame dwelling, was in the middle of what had been Union Course, and the neighborhood was often referred to by that name.

Unlike the family's previous address, this section was a quiet enclave, dotted with Queen Anne–style homes. The streets were unpaved and ungraded, the potholes so huge that a twelve-year-old girl supposedly fell into one and almost drowned just a few blocks from the Trumps' house.[27] Aside from such perils, though, First Street in 1908 was a wonderful playground for Elizabeth, now eight, as well as five-year-old Fred and three-year-old John. Every evening until twilight, they played tag on streets that still had few cars. It was time to go home when the lamplighter came and reached his long pole up to the wick of the gas lamps.[28] Up First Street and across Jamaica Avenue was P.S. 97, the red brick elementary school all three children attended.

In winter they ice-skated and rode sleds on the golf course at nearby Forest Park; in summer they played games like ring-a-levio and cat, in which one team hit a stick up in the air and then tried to get to bases before the opposing team retrieved the stick. On Halloween boys turned their jackets inside out, scrawled on them with chalk, and then whacked each other with socks filled with flour.[29] A few days later, on election night, families went to Forest Park and huddled around huge bonfires as the local newspapers projected results on special screens. Four weeks later, on Thanksgiving morning, children would dress as ragamuffins and go from door to door collecting fruit and candy before returning home and tucking into turkey.[30]

Such pleasant conditions ensured the borough's rapid growth.[31] Between 1910, when the bridge was finished, and 1915, Queens's population increased 40 percent.[32] Land prices soared, nearly all of the borough's remaining farms quickly disappeared, and builders, most of whom worked on a small scale, began constructing one- and two-family homes and small apartment buildings.[33]

Frederick Trump had high hopes for the future, for he had his own savings to invest as well as possible funds from his sister Louise, who had backed his real estate ventures in the West. Weekday mornings he would walk the few blocks to his office, dressed, as was customary for businessmen at the time, in a spotless boiled white shirt, formal tie, and three-piece tailor-made gray suit. Often he stopped at a little two-room building across the street to visit Carl Louis Voeller, a first-generation German American who was fluent in German and English and specialized in second mortgages. Although Frederick Trump had now spent more than a quarter of a century speaking English, he preferred German and did considerable business, including his own will, with Voeller.[34]

Doing business in German was hardly unusual in Queens. As of 1900, one in four New Yorkers was German or of German ancestry, which added up to the world's second largest population of Germans after Berlin.[35] Queens was especially Teutonic, and along Jamaica Avenue German was at least as common as English. A few blocks from the offices of Trump and Voeller was the Triangle Hofbrau, a center of local gemütlichkeit. The restaurant's wooden barrel heads came from Neustadt, a village only a few kilometers from Kallstadt, and carvings across the front boasted of wine from the Pfalz.[36] Like many of their neighbors, the Trumps used German at home, and their children did not use much English until they went to school.[37]

Frederick Trump was working on Jamaica Avenue at a time of almost inconceivably rapid change.[38] When he arrived, Long Island farmers still traveled the old road, taking produce to Manhattan at night in horse-drawn wagons. By 1915, though, the weeping willows and chestnuts that had lined Jamaica Avenue were gone, replaced by mounds of dirt from the construction of the elevated train. The farmers' highway had become an urban landmark, a gloomy tunnel-like passageway on which the sun never shone and over which the elevated now roared with an unabated clatter.

With this enclosure of the old plank road, yet another wave of suburbanization ensued, bringing development and subdivision to the farther reaches of Queens.[39] In keeping with the borough's new, modern profile, Queens adopted a street-labeling system known as the "Philadelphia grid." Gone were Suydam, Shaw, and other references to the Dutch and English inhabitants whose farms once covered Queens. Gone also were other plain but familiar street names, replaced by sequential numbers. The Trump home, originally 154

First Street (also known, in an era more familiar with Latin, as Unum Street), became 154 87th Road, amended later, as lots subdivided, to 1540 87th Road.

But the greatest changes occurred in August 1914, when World War I erupted. Americans were neutral at first. As time went on, though, they lined up with the British and against the Germans—and, inevitably, against German-Americans. On May 5, 1915, a German submarine sank the *Lusitania*, a British liner sailing under a U.S. flag. All 1,200 passengers died, including 124 Americans. So did any remaining American neutrality.

Well before the United States officially entered the war in April 1917, the country yanked up the *wilkommen* mat for what was now perceived as the domestic Hun. The German music that had filled concert halls and opera houses vanished. Cities with German names changed them. Ground meat, formerly called "hamburger," became "Salisbury steak," patties made from it turned into "Wilsonburgers" and "liberty sandwiches," and "sauerkraut" became "liberty cabbage." More than a dozen states summarily dropped German instruction in school, and others severely limited it. German-language newspaper editors and advertisers received threats, postal workers misdelivered their publications, and Boy Scouts burned German papers in huge public bonfires. Teddy Roosevelt, the former president who had originated the notion of the hyphenated American, now denounced anyone who qualified. President Woodrow Wilson banned German males over fourteen from all boats other than ferries as well as airplanes, balloons, and all areas of military import, including Washington, D.C. The government also ordered six hundred thousand German aliens to register with local police and not to change residences.[40]

Unlike their neighbors, the Trumps did not change their name. Theirs had always been a German-speaking household, and so it remained. Hunkering down to avoid suspicion, Frederick Trump and his sister Katherine stayed in contact with their Kallstadt relatives, and after the war was over, Katherine Trump Schuster and her daughter Elizabeth went back to Kallstadt for a visit.[41] But the bitter experience of having been tarred by their German ancestry had left scars on the Trump children. Years later, the older son, Fred, would quietly promote the notion that the family was actually Swedish.

The American Trumps survived the war, but they did not escape tragedy from another source: *Blitzkatarrh,* or influenza. At first the number of influenza deaths in the spring of 1918 set off no alarms, for people died of influenza and pneumonia every spring. Without a public health network continually coordinating national statistics, it was impossible for the medical community to know that fatalities were higher than usual, much less that one of the most fearsome epidemics in history was about to cut down millions around the world.[42] The cases seemed to divide into two types, both fatal. Those who were sick for up to ten days or so before dying developed classic pneumonia, in which the normally whisper-thin membranes of the lungs become thickened, inelastic, unable to do their vital work of cleaning the blood of poisonous gases and providing it with oxygen. But those who died within only a day or two after the first sneeze had lungs full of a terrifying watery red liquid that poured out of the body and turned whole mattresses red.[43]

One Wednesday at the end of May 1918, Frederick Trump and his older son strolled down Jamaica Avenue. It was the eve of Memorial Day, and Fred, who was eleven, was delighted to honor the U.S. Civil War dead if doing so meant staying home from school. The next day there would be a big parade along this same street, and Fred could hardly wait. He and his father were doing what they often did in the afternoon, stopping in to chat with half a dozen realtors in the small storefront offices that now dotted Jamaica Avenue.

As Fred Trump recounted it many years afterward, his father turned to him and said he felt sick. They walked home, and the older man went to bed. "Then he died," Fred Trump said later. "Just like that. It seemed so sudden to me." At first, he said, he couldn't believe that as the parade was marching down Jamaica Avenue, his father was lying dead upstairs. "It just didn't seem real," he said. "I wasn't that upset. You know how kids are. But I got upset watching my mother crying and being so sad. It was seeing her that made me feel bad, not my own feelings about what had happened."[44]

The cause of death was listed on the death certificate as "pleno pneumonia, dextra et sinistra": full pneumonia, right and left lungs. Five days later, infected lungs caused the death of Frederick Trump's brother-in-law Fred Schuster. To the Trumps, it seemed a sad coincidence. By the end of the summer, though, it was clear that both men had almost certainly been early victims of what came to be known as

"Spanish influenza." Ultimately, the influenza epidemic of 1918 claimed twenty-one million lives—six million more than all of World War I.[45]

———

Five and a half years later, on Tuesday evening, January 30, 1923, Frederick Christ Trump stood in the auditorium of Richmond Hill High School. Looking self-conscious in his formal attire, the thin blond youth marched into the hall to the strains of Mendelssohn, listened to the valedictorian expound on "Investment of Our Heritage," received his diploma, and marched out to Sousa's Washington Post March. He was through with his formal education.

Richmond Hill High, the largest in Queens, was about two miles from Woodhaven. Founded in 1898, it was one of the first tangible rewards Queens received for its incorporation into New York City. In a grand gesture, city officials had laid a cornerstone containing a set of U.S. coins, an engraving of the battleship *Maine,* and a portrait of Admiral Dewey and his fleet. Unlike a modern high school, this one had no cafeteria; students went home for lunch, brought their own, or ate in a diner attached to the school. But the school did boast a domed observatory, the only one in a city high school, and a brand-new $6,000 telescope. In the early years school life centered around the German club—Der Deutsche Kreis—and social events often featured German games, dances, songs, and readings.[46] However, by 1918, the year Fred Trump entered Richmond Hill, the school had become Anglicized and German was rarely spoken.

Because there was little truancy and no vandalism, students did not have individual lockers. They simply left their coats and supplies in a coatroom, and apparently nothing was ever stolen.[47] Rules were strict. There were no makeup tests, which meant that no matter how sick they might be, students either showed up for final exams or repeated the course. Teachers still scrupulously followed the classical curriculum, and the school papers bristled with literary allusions and Shakespearean wordplay.[48] There were a few black students and a handful of Jews, but for practical purposes the school was white and Christian, with a Protestant majority.

Everything seemed to suggest that Queens would continue to grow and to improve, but not to change. Indeed, in many ways the area was still a nineteenth-century enclave. Some residents made forays into Manhattan, to see jazz at Gray's Drugstore or the Pennsylvania Grill or take in plays on Broadway. But most saw that borough, known throughout Queens as "the City," as a foreign land, distant and intimidating, and preferred to stay put amid traditional suburban familiarity.[49]

In early June, on Anniversary Day, the community celebrated its own existence.[50] Local schools and businesses closed. Parents dressed children in white and decorated baby carriages. Here and there, groups got up a small float for the occasion. People congregated at their churches, joined an informal parade through the streets to Forest Park, and then circled back to the churches for ice cream.[51] It was a glorious occasion, a moment to look around and savor a way of life so innocent and pleasant, it seemed that it would never end.

But it did. Economic development, population movement, and growth would inexorably change the face of all of New York City. As new businesses opened, new people would arrive. When Frederick Trump had come to America, he had naturally headed for the tenements of the Lower East Side and then out west, where opportunity was beckoning. But now new arrivals to New York, often from other parts of the United States, wanted to stay in the city and to have their own homes. As Fred Trump came of age, he saw an opportunity for himself in providing them.

When Frederick Trump died, his estate included the family's two-story, seven-room home in Queens, five vacant lots, $4,000 in savings and life insurance, $3,600 worth of stock, and fourteen mortgages. The net value was estimated at $31,359, the equivalent of about $345,000 in 1999 dollars.[52] He had come from nothing, and he had left something for his wife and children. Had he lived, he would probably have left much more. But he had accomplished a great deal in the time that he had. Above all, he had redirected the course of his life and that of his family and the descendants who would follow. Instead of being German, part of the Old World and the old order, they were American, in place to assume leading roles in the century now unfolding. By establishing his family in Queens and becoming involved in real estate, he had set the stage for what was to come.

Unfortunately his financial legacy quickly diminished, consumed by the drastic postwar inflation of 1919–20, during which consumer prices spiked up more than 50 percent. His small but thriving real estate business shrank to its outlines, forcing the family to scramble. As it turned out, his widow had a remarkable talent for doing just that.[53] Beginning with the lot next door to her home, she arranged for a local contractor to build houses on the empty property remaining in her husband's business, sell the houses, and provide home mortgages to buyers. For the time being, she would support her family with the income from the mortgages and whatever she could make by taking in sewing. Then, when her children finished school, they would continue the family business. Her older son, Fred, then fifteen, would be the builder; her younger son, John, thirteen, would be the architect; and her daughter, Elizabeth, sixteen, would run the office and keep the books.

Everything seemed to go according to her plan. Young Elizabeth left high school early, not an unusual step at that time, and enrolled in secretarial school. John busied himself with his schoolwork. Fred, who would have been happy to drop out of school, complied with his mother's request that he obtain a diploma, but he did not let being a full-time student interfere with getting the head start he craved.[54] While classmates belonged to school clubs and played on sports teams, he earned money caddying at the local golf course, whitewashing curbstones, and delivering groceries and papers to his Woodhaven neighbors.

For as long as he could remember, he had been drawn to building, partly out of respect for his father, but also because it seemed like the most interesting thing in the world. "I always wanted to be a builder," he said years later. "It was my dream as a boy, just as some kids want to be firemen." Now he took night courses at the local YMCA in carpentering and reading blueprints, and he studied plumbing, masonry, and electrical wiring in correspondence courses. He also built a garage for a neighbor. "Probably not the greatest garage ever put up," he later acknowledged, "but the experience reinforced my hope of doing something creative with wood and bricks and cement."[55]

He did not study any more than he had to. Unlike his younger brother, John, an excellent student and a member of his high school honor society, Fred Trump settled for average marks. He had no time to study, much less to practice the violin that sat gathering dust in his room. The yearbook entry under his name says simply "X"; he had no extracurricular activities. Next to his name appeared the phrase "Even the good Homer sometimes nods his head in sleep," presumably referring to Fred's exhaustion after working and attending night classes.

As soon as he graduated, he obtained full-time employment in construction. His first job was as a "horse's helper" for a local builder. At the time, horse- and mule-drawn delivery wagons hauled construction materials to building sites along streets paved with flat wooden blocks fitted tightly together. The smooth surface meant easy travel in warm months but disaster in winter, when ice sheeted the roadway. On level ground the animals slipped and slid, and on hills they could not move at all.[56] To keep Queens from closing down altogether, strapping young men like Fred Trump had to pull the loads themselves. "I replaced a mule," he said later.[57] Every day he towed lumber up steep hills too icy for horses to ascend safely and thought about the fact that those high school classmates who had pursued business courses were making $35 a week compared with his $11 paycheck.[58]

He got work as a carpenter and took courses at Pratt Institute in Brooklyn in engineering, estimating, and other construction-related subjects. "I learned how to frame walls more efficiently than other people, how to read a blueprint more accurately and faster," he said years later. "They weren't huge skills, but they gave me an edge. It meant I could offer something different, something the others couldn't offer."[59] He learned his craft well. Within two years of his graduation he had built his first house, a simple one-family home in Woodhaven, and then two more in Queens Village.

The financial end of the operation was more problematic. Because he was still under twenty-one, his mother incorporated the business, known as E. Trump & Son, and signed checks.[60] A more difficult hurdle was inadequate sources of credit. Even before the Depression, small-scale builders like Fred Trump had little access to what are known as "construction loans"—essentially the temporary bank loans used to cover architect fees, materials, and other construction costs.* The only place they could borrow money was from money-lenders who crowded the sidewalks across from Brooklyn's Borough Hall year-round, rain or shine. Known as "the Court Street boys," they had deep pockets and offered financing on a handshake. Their customers included the major developers of the day, whose office buildings lined Court Street and were beginning to fill lower Manhattan. But the interest rates charged by the Court Street boys went well into the double digits, far more than Fred Trump could pay.

Instead he contrived his own financing. He began one house, sold it before he had finished it, then used the money to get a second one going while finishing the first, constantly stretching funds to cover the costs that just as constantly threatened to overtake his fledgling operation. He worked from dawn to dusk. He raced the payment clock. By 1926, three years out of high school, he had managed to put up nineteen more homes in Hollis, another Queens neighborhood.

Ceil Raufer was a new bride when she and her husband bought one of these houses from Fred Trump in July 1926 for $7,500. Their house was one in a row of seven detached frame dwellings he built on 199th Street. Obviously designed by the same hand, all had two stories plus an attic and a basement, a driveway to the side, and a garage in the back. Yet each had distinct details: three windows across the second-floor front, three little steps leading up to the front door, a dormer, an asymmetric bit of cornice, a decorative touch on a front porch.

"Fred Trump was too young to be at the closing, so his mother came," Raufer recalled years later. She knew that her house was in the builder's first development, but she had no qualms. Raufer knew the family, as her younger sister had been a classmate of John Trump's in elementary and high school. More important, she was impressed

---

*Upon completion of a project, such loans, usually from commercial banks that lend on a short-term basis and at a relatively high interest rate, are replaced by "permanent loans" from insurance companies, pension funds, or other institutions able to place money at a lower rate and for longer periods. At that time, banks loaned at most about two-thirds of construction costs, forcing even well-established builders to seek preliminary financing outside formal channels.

by Fred Trump's attentiveness to his customers. "He used to come around all the time and ask if I needed anything," she said. "Once he connected something in the kitchen so I could turn on the hot water all the time. He always said, 'Don't tell the neighbors, but I'll do it.'"[61]

All over Queens, groups of Fred Trump's homes began to appear. With each cluster, the houses were a little larger and a little better designed. In part, this was because the Trumps learned firsthand of any shortcomings. After the mid-1920s the family became real estate gypsies, living in a succession of Fred's own newly finished houses all over Queens. As Elizabeth Trump had planned, her daughter worked as a secretary, for an import-export firm. John worked at General Electric and, with some help from his brother, began studying architecture at Brooklyn Polytechnic Institute. But he soon found that working with his older brother was not easy. To Fred Trump, building was a business proposition that required selling each house as soon as possible, regardless of its state of completion, in order to get enough capital to start the next one. To John, building was an aesthetic act that meant finishing each house down to the final touches before putting it on the market. Over and over the older brother prevailed, and John became increasingly disenchanted. By the end of his freshman year he departed from his mother's script and switched his major to engineering.

In June 1929 the younger Elizabeth Trump, then twenty-five years old, married William Walter, thirty-five, a tall, dark-haired bank trainee. His parents came from Germany, and his father, like Elizabeth's, had been a barber. The newlyweds moved to another of Fred Trump's Hollis homes, an expanded version of Ceil Raufer's house with everything nicer, bigger, and better made. Fred Trump, just twenty-three, had already built scores of residences and had hundreds of satisfied customers. Now he was carving large building lots out of the undeveloped sections of Jamaica Estates, a rolling, wooded area near the Long Island border.[62] Seeing an increase in demand for high-priced homes, he planned to build what he called "authentic architectural reproductions" of English manor and Georgian Colonial dwellings in stone, stucco, and brick. They would have up to five bedrooms and four bathrooms and sell for as much as $30,000.[63]

Frederick Trump's sisters, Louise Trump Schuster and Katherine

Trump Schuster, remained oriented to Manhattan. Both were widows, and their lives revolved around the Glad Tidings Tabernacle, a modest Pentecostal church in the Hell's Kitchen neighborhood of "the City." Geographically the parish was only a borough away from the Queens Trumps. But sociologically and economically, Glad Tidings, with its butchers and bakers, its mail carriers and store clerks, was light-years removed from the bankers and lawyers who came to live in Jamaica Estates.

But the Trumps did stay in touch. Louise and Katherine and their families came to dinner now and then, occasions Katherine's grandchildren remembered fondly years later because of Tante Elizabeth's excellent cooking and, especially, her apple torte. In the summer there were family outings to North Beach, to the fairgrounds and dance pavilions, later replaced by LaGuardia Airport, where German oompah music still rang out. Frederick Trump's children never met his mother, Katherina Kober, who died in Kallstadt in November 1922 at the age of eighty-six, shortly before Fred's graduation from high school. But they accompanied their own mother on a trip to Germany in 1929, just before the Depression made such journeys an impossible luxury.

That October, the stock market crashed, signaling the end of good times. Fred Trump kept putting up mock Tudor mansions, but the real estate market was drying up. The inflationary 1920s had been forgiving times, particularly in real estate; eager to clinch deals, banks had been willing to embrace chancy ventures because any cost overruns could be recouped in a seemingly ever-expanding economy. In the deflationary 1930s, though, banks became allergic to even modest risk taking. Almost no one could obtain capital. Abandoning residential real estate, Trump opened a food market in Queens. He modeled it on King Kullen, a new store a mile away. Unlike the old German-style markets, where customers handed a shopping list to a clerk and waited for it to be assembled, here they could walk around and select cans from the shelves and precut meat from a refrigerator case.[64] It was one of the first modern supermarkets in the city.

To attract customers, the erstwhile builder placed ads for Trump Market in local papers and published his own broadsheet advertising special bargains. But when his staff told him they could arrange his store better than that of his competitor, he told them not to bother. "I don't want to do it better than King Kullen," he said. "I just want to do it just as well."

What could have been a new career was only a stopgap for Fred Trump. He wanted to build, not manage.[65] It was the only time in his life that he did not put his utmost into what he was doing. His heart was in real estate, not refrigerator cases. The whole time he was running the supermarket, he kept looking for a way to return to his first love. With some energetic maneuvering amid the ruins of the House of Lehrenkrauss, perhaps he would be able to leave the grocery store behind.

Chapter Eight

SAVVY IN A BROOKLYN COURTROOM

THE BEGINNING OF 1934 was not, at first glance, a propitious time for a relative outsider to try to get anywhere in a court proceeding so tied into the backroom politics of Brooklyn. Indeed, even insiders were having trouble. With the election of Republican Fiorello LaGuardia as mayor the previous November, the Democratic establishment that had long run New York City politics was undergoing a seismic shift. For the first time in many years, exactly how to get a favor done—where to go and whom to see—took some figuring out.

Since the turn of the century politics in Brooklyn had proceeded in a clear, top-down fashion. Although Thomas Nast's brilliant caricatures of Tammany boss William Marcy Tweed had made Tammany Hall in Manhattan the nation's most infamous political machine, its counterpart in Brooklyn, led by boss John Henry McCooey, was almost as powerful in its own sphere. One measure of this power was McCooey's ability to keep Tammany leaders out of Brooklyn. Another was his success at teaming up with the same leaders when it came to wresting federal patronage for New York City.[1]

Controlling who won in local politics meant controlling who ran, i.e., controlling political clubs where nominations occurred. In 1905, McCooey, a shipyard worker called "Little Buttercup" for a character in the popular Gilbert and Sullivan operetta *H.M.S. Pinafore* whose cherubic looks mask deceit, took charge by founding his own Democratic political organization. Like the other neighborhood political clubs that dotted Brooklyn's two dozen or so state assembly districts,* the James Madison Club offered voters in its community, Flatbush, everything from a Thanksgiving turkey to a job in exchange for their electoral loyalty and the spoils of electoral victory.[2] For new immigrants facing unfamiliar customs and, for many, a new language, such assistance was vital, and they willingly threw their support behind the club's candidate in the next election.

As a result, long after the Irish in Brooklyn had lost the numerical edge to incoming Italians and Jews, McCooey managed to capture and retain the top party job for the whole borough—county leader. As such, he had a lock on contracts, insurance brokerage, and patronage jobs, which at the time meant posts from the lowliest clerk right up to city commissioner. In the meantime, he continued to be appointed to a series of lucrative government posts for which he was totally unqualified, despite occasional flurries of public outrage over the blatant conflicts of interest. Before him streamed a steady flow of politicians and favor seekers, as many as two hundred in a day, seeking his help and providing in return other considerations and favors that he could use to his advantage.[3]

Had the Lehrenkrauss debacle occurred even two years earlier, a non-Brooklynite like Fred Trump could never have muscled in on the action. McCooey already had one foot in the Lehrenkrauss door because he had placed a Madison Club surrogate, a plumber named Anthony Jordan, on the corporate board of directors. Moreover, one of the plummiest prerogatives of the surrogate's court, of which he was chief clerk, was the designation of officials to preside over bankruptcy proceedings. But McCooey was no longer the man in charge. Two years earlier he had backed the wrong presidential primary candidate, ex–New York governor and Tammany Hall veteran Alfred E. Smith. When the antimachine candidate, New York governor Franklin Delano Roosevelt, won, McCooey backed him to the hilt, but it was too late. Only prenomination help counted, and McCooey lost the federal patronage he needed to keep his hold on Brooklyn.

---

*The exact number of districts changed after every decennial census, when seats in state and national legislatures were reapportioned according to new population figures.

The political landscape was in upheaval. As governor, Roosevelt had an up-and-down relationship with Tammany and the Brooklyn machine, avoiding them when possible and using them when unavoidable. As president, he looked on them with even more disfavor.[4] Things were no better at home, where the new Republican mayor, Fiorello La Guardia, elected in November 1933 on an antimachine platform, was determined to control patronage himself.[5] In the short period before La Guardia took office, the machines maneuvered frantically to salvage as much as possible. Brooklyn Democratic leaders divvied up the remaining spoils in a secret hotel room meeting in December. When reporters burst in, the machine bosses straight-facedly insisted they were only celebrating one participant's eighteenth wedding anniversary.[6]

At the Madison Club, political skirmishing turned bitter. Meetings to pick a new district leader produced fistfights, black eyes, and threats of court action.[7] Then, on January 21, 1934, three weeks after La Guardia's inauguration and only five days after the first Lehrenkrauss creditors' meeting in Brooklyn, John McCooey died. An estimated thirty thousand people lined the streets at his funeral, where Al Smith, current Governor Herbert Lehman, and U.S. Postmaster General James A. Farley were honorary pallbearers.[8]

It was a moment of uncertainty, of openings and rare opportunities, for Fred Trump and everyone else. With the old power networks in disarray, doors that would have been closed to someone who had never built in Brooklyn might now be opened. Fred Trump had been trying to figure out how to get on the inside track for weeks. Now he would try even harder.

The court case had officially opened on Tuesday, December 5, 1933. Four days after the Lehrenkrauss Corporation failed to pay dividends to holders of mortgage certificates, lawyer Archibald Palmer acted on their behalf. He filed a petition of involuntary bankruptcy against Julius Lehrenkrauss and the other partners, charging them with insolvency, and asked for the appointment of a receiver to preserve the remaining assets. Palmer also requested that the court conduct a hearing under bankruptcy laws into the affairs of the corporation.[9]

This meant hearing directly from Julius Lehrenkrauss, a short, balding man in his mid-sixties who wore pince-nez and formal morning attire.[10] Called to the witness stand in Courtroom 727, the head of the House of Lehrenkrauss, who had been working there since he was thirteen, reluctantly began to reveal his way of doing business.

His tale was staggering. Day after day, front-page stories in the *Brooklyn Eagle* presented Julius's account of how he certificated mortgages, sold the shares—often above their face value—and then certificated the same mortgage again and resold it, over and over. When customers came in to buy certificates, one accountant testified, "We just handed them anything that was handy."[11] Using high-pressure sales techniques that included enthusiastic testimonials from nonexistent investors and facsimiles of their dividend checks, Lehrenkrauss salesmen convinced hundreds of naive customers to invest in worthless stock. The frauds were so varied and plentiful that unraveling them was nearly impossible, not least because deeds for mortgaged properties and other assets were missing. Julius had shuffled funds from one corporate bank account to another to give the appearance of healthy balances, and he and another senior executive had routinely extorted kickbacks from builders before advancing them construction loans. After two weeks of devastating testimony, the corporate partners wearily agreed to declare their business officially broke, and the proceedings advanced to the next stage.

Theodore Stitt, an experienced bankruptcy referee, then took charge of what amounted to mopping-up operations.[12] A Republican, Stitt was well connected and well seasoned, but the Lehrenkrauss affair would stretch his resources to the utmost. At one time a state assemblyman, he had later been a reporter for the *Brooklyn Standard-Union* and the *New York Sun*, covering the City Hall beat. On January 16, three weeks after his appointment, Stitt sat in Courtroom 727, facing the angry creditors and, in the back of the courtroom, Fred Trump. After Archie Palmer had finished speaking, Stitt named three trustees. They would not directly decide what happened to the mortgage servicing and other assets, but their opinion would be important. All three were connected to the Madison Club, demonstrating that even in its current tumultuous state, it could not be counted out.

By the second meeting of creditors, on January 29, John McCooey was dead and buried, and the machine was squabbling over his successor. The trustees, bleary-eyed after long days of sorting through a mountain of paper, reported to referee Stitt that foreclosure actions were already pending on some 450 Lehrenkrauss mortgages.[13] Not only had the mortgages been sold many times over, but the original mortgagees were going into default. It would take months, the trustees reported, to take a full inventory, and in that time hundreds more homeowners would default on their obligations.

Fred Trump took it all in. For two months he'd been learning all he could about who handed around the jobs and the favors and how, about patronage and appointments and contracts. He'd visited the Madison Club and its powerful cousin, the Seneca Club. Shortly before the great man's death, he'd met John McCooey, then attended the crowded funeral and wangled a lunch with McCooey's apparent successor, Frank Vincent Kelley, a former bank teller and athlete whose elegant style was in marked contrast with that of Little Buttercup. Fred Trump wanted to do business in Brooklyn, and he knew that meeting and greeting, seeing and being seen, were necessary steps along the way.[14]

On March 1, Julius Lehrenkrauss, who stood accused of having diverted more than $500,000 in corporate funds, pleaded guilty to first-degree grand larceny. Although he might have committed "a technical wrong," he said, the plea was not admission of "a public wrong," and he was making it only "to spare the county the extra expense of a trial." A week later he stood with bowed head in front of a packed and furious courtroom to hear his sentence. Penniless and nearly friendless, he had already spent five days in jail because he could not make bail. After the judge gave him five to ten years in prison, the pale, sobbing defendant was handcuffed to a common burglar, taken away for mug shots and fingerprinting, and hustled through a swarm of reporters and photographers into a black police car.[15]

Justice had been served, but Fred Trump was paying little attention. His eyes were on what was to come. The next day, March 9, he wrote to the three trustees, formally bidding for the Lehrenkrauss mortgage-servicing business. Writing on F. C. Trump Construction Corporation stationery and displaying the same boldness his father had shown back in Monte Carlo when registering claims already owned by someone else, Fred Trump, who was then running a supermarket, presented himself as the very model of a modern real estate executive. Indeed, his logo featured a cozy half-timbered bungalow. Claiming with more enthusiasm than accuracy that he had "been engaged for many years in the servicing of mortgages," he announced that he would immediately reorganize and move from Queens to a central location in Brooklyn if he was the successful bidder. Although he was not on the list of brokers the trustees had contacted, he had obviously seen the requirements for a bid and supplied the requested information.

The trustees had to act quickly. Only three months earlier, the mortgage-servicing department, which was the most valuable part of the business, had been worth $26 million. Now so many mortgage holders had taken their business elsewhere that the figure had fallen to only about $6 million. It was what bankers called a "shrinking asset," and it was getting smaller by the day. If it was not sold soon, it would vanish. Accordingly, the trustees put the mortgage-servicing department on the block the next Monday.

On the appointed day, March 12, a late winter storm dumped six inches of snow on the city, and the crowd that had overflowed Courtroom 727 in January stayed home. Nonetheless, there were still about a dozen bidders for the servicing prize. Fred Trump was the only one to represent himself. Doing so was evidently unusual, for the stenographer automatically listed him in the transcript as "Fred Trump, Esq."[16]

For the next several hours, bidders maneuvered for advantage. They argued about whether offers should remain sealed, whether they could be changed, whether all those making bids were competent, whether a title company could be in the running. But Fred Trump was silent. As he was now working in a supermarket, hadn't built anything in two years, and had only serviced mortgages on the homes he had built, it was probably a good idea to keep a low profile.

Comparing the proposals in strictly monetary terms was tricky. If, as seems likely, no more than $2 million worth of mortgages was involved, Fred Trump was the second-highest bidder. He offered $1,750 for the mortgage-servicing lists and the right to service contracts up to $1 million, an additional $500 for each additional unit of $250,000 worth of mortgages, and $750 on acceptance of his terms.[17]

The top offer came from William A. Demm, the only other bidder from Queens and also the only other bidder with similarly sketchy credentials. Demm's letter of intent cryptically claimed he had serviced mortgages "for the last several years," was in the real estate and insurance business, and ran "a large office." For the lists, he offered $2,100—$350 more than his Queens rival—plus the same sums for additional units.[18]

But no outsider was going to win this prize easily. A Brooklyn bidder complained pointedly of "two individuals who, there is no doubt in my mind, do not run a servicing company at all."[19] Although Trump had specifically offered to move operations to Brooklyn, referee Stitt noted that a Queens office would be inconvenient for many clients. Two of the trustees said firmly that the mortgage-servicing operation should go to the outfit best able to handle it rather than strictly to the high dollar bid.

Then again, one trustee added in an apparent afterthought, maybe Henry Davenport of the Home Title Guaranty Company had made the best bid. At $750 for the first million and $750 for each $250,000 thereafter, it would surpass Demm and Trump *if* more than $2 million in mortgages remained. And even if there wasn't that much left, Home Title, with twenty-seven years of experience in mortgage servicing, was the heavy hitter among the contenders. Its long-standing connection to the Madison Club had already won Home Title the servicing of $60 million worth of mortgages from the State Department of Insurance. These mortgages had come from a gilt-edged list of insurance and banking clients that included Aetna Life, Connecticut Mutual, Bowery Savings, Connecticut Fire, and the National Bank of Troy.[20]

Unlike Trump, Demm had a lawyer, a dark-haired athletic-looking young man named William Hyman.[21] At the first sign that the Brooklyn machine was preparing to shove his client aside, Hyman stepped in. He abruptly raised Demm's contingency offer from $500 to $750 for each additional unit of $250,000. It wasn't cricket, but it worked. Rival bidders squawked that Demm's lawyer had no right to increase his bid after hearing what the others were proposing, but that failed to move Stitt. Sales in federal court, Stitt said dryly, are likely to be "very unsatisfactory from the standpoint of bidders, because the attitude of the federal court has invariably been to have the widest kind of competition, and the man that puts in the highest figure last wins."

With that, Stitt seemed to have relegated Fred Trump's offer to third, less than Demm's and perhaps less than Home Title's. The next day, Fred Trump fired off a letter to the trustees that opened with the startling claim that he was a ten-year veteran of building, real estate, and mortgage servicing; in fact, ten years earlier he had been a high school senior. The methods by which he would handle the Lehrenkrauss mortgages, he explained glibly, "are now being worked out and will be completed within twenty-four hours after notification that I . . . [am] the successful bidder." He had "tentatively" selected a downtown location and "tentatively" engaged experienced staff. He had "spent thousands of dollars for advertising [and] the name Trump in connection with real estate is very well know [sic] throughout Queens County."²²

He didn't stop there. Knowing that he could not match Home Title's advantage in experience and that nobody from Queens could match its political clout, he met with Demm and his lawyer. Demm knew of Fred Trump, who had built houses near his office. Moreover, although Demm had greater financial resources, he was impressed by the other man's newly minted Brooklyn contacts. In short order, the two outsiders decided to join forces. Together they would be unbeatable.

That is, if the sale took place at all. Every Thursday night since mid-January, hundreds of anguished creditors, including mortgage investors, stockholders, bondholders, and the rest of the Lehrenkrauss victims, had plotted strategy at Bushwick High School, a huge red brick, neo-Gothic fortress deep in northeast Brooklyn. Because they believed that reorganizing the Lehrenkrauss Corporation and pulling it out of bankruptcy was their best shot at recouping their investments, they strenuously objected to selling off the corporation's few remaining assets. If the trustees kept the mortgages, they argued, Lehrenkrauss could once again be a going concern.²³

In fact, the creditors were suffering from a bad case of wishful thinking. But they could still put a crimp in the plans of Fred Trump and William Demm, as both men quickly grasped. The longer the mortgage-servicing situation remained unresolved, the more mortgage holders would take their business elsewhere, and eventually the Lehrenkrauss servicing business would become worthless. The Queens bidders had to neutralize the creditors, and quickly.

The very next Thursday, March 15, Fred Trump, William Demm, and Bill Hyman trooped out to Bushwick and sat in the cavernous school auditorium listening to the aggrieved investors. Halfway through the meeting, Fred Trump tugged on the lawyer's sleeve. He and Demm had the solution. Why not offer a buyback provision? If the creditors wanted to fantasize about a reorganization, let them. To the same monetary terms Hyman had proposed on March 12, the bidders would add an offer to sell back the servicing business for their costs in the event of successful reorganization. In return, the creditors would endorse their bid. Because the trustees would not want to be seen apparently squashing the hopes of the Lehrenkrauss victims, this maneuver would give Fred Trump and William Demm a powerful advantage over Home Title and the other contenders. Smiling broadly, Hyman rose, straightened his wide shoulders, and presented the proposal to the assembly.[24]

With the support of the creditors, the two bidders and their lawyer needed only nine days to hammer out the details with the creditors' lawyers. In the event of a buyback, Fred Trump and William Demm would be repaid whatever they had advanced plus an additional $1,000 in compensation. On Saturday, March 24, Fred Trump hand-delivered a letter to the trustees withdrawing his original bid and outlining the new proposal.

On the next Monday afternoon, March 26, at two o'clock, lawyers, trustees, bidders, and creditors gathered once again in the mahogany-paneled courtroom on the seventh floor of the post office. The trustees presented the bids, endorsing the one from the Queens bidders. This public approval indicated that the proposal also had the support of Frank Kelly, the likely successor to McCooey. Home Title backed off, not even bothering to send a representative to this meeting. Everything seemed to be coming together quite neatly for Fred Trump. But then the unexpected occurred: A new, unknown bidder showed up. Abraham J. Hammer, a real estate man in midtown Manhattan, offered more money—$400 more for every million dollars' worth of mortgages—and promised to abide by the buyback arrangements in case of a Lehrenkrauss reorganization.

An uneasy ripple went through the front of the courtroom as the tidy arrangements made over the weekend suddenly appeared on the verge of unraveling. Referee Stitt, who had two weeks earlier explained that courts favored "the man who puts in the highest figure" no matter when he does it, now blandly described this last-minute offer as "quite embarrassing." The head of the reorganization committee, previously keenly interested in getting the best possible monetary deal, now haughtily dismissed the thought of making a decision based on a few hundred dollars' difference.[25] A member of the stockholders' committee, who noted that he was a former neighbor of Fred Trump's, called Hammer's bid "outrageous" and "the most unfairest piece of work that ever was put before a Referee."[26] Although the trustees had earlier looked upon the two men from Queens as suspicious non-Brooklynites with somewhat vague credentials, Demm and Trump now heard themselves described as "estimable gentlemen with good financial reports."[27]

Finally, throwing caution to the winds, Archibald Palmer unsubtly reminded Stitt that as "a man of determination, firmness, and character," he should keep the bidding closed. Palmer then pushed for a binding vote on the spot.

This was one push too many. Although Stitt had been a courthouse fixture for years, he was close lipped, sometimes taciturn, and independent in his decisions. He had favored Fred Trump and William Demm, but he did not want to appear to give in to pressure. His decision, Stitt declared, would be not "on any basis of vox populi," but in the best interests of the creditors. Overriding the trustees' objections that "the longer we wait, the less we have to sell," he adjourned the meeting until the next morning.

Everyone reassembled promptly at 9 A.M. The trustees reiterated that Hammer's finances and prospects were inadequate. A lawyer for the creditors spoke warmly of the "personality" shown by Fred Trump and William Demm. None of the officials spoke for Hammer. Because, as Stitt put it, most of the creditors were "ten o'clock scholars"—that is, absent—they could not be polled. Finally Stitt gave up and awarded the servicing to the two men from Queens. Fred Trump was back in real estate for good.

CHAPTER NINE

WASHINGTON
TO THE RESCUE

LIKE HIS FATHER, FRED TRUMP WAS DETERMINED to better his station in life by the fastest route possible. By the time Fred Trump came of age, however, the physical frontier where his father met his biggest success was gone. So the son found another wealth-providing frontier: government. As he soon discovered, this frontier had many virtues, chief among them that, in the mid-1930s, it was not disappearing but growing. Greatly expanded by a host of New Deal programs, government offered rich opportunities to those, including Fred Trump, who proved particularly adept at figuring out how to use these programs to their own maximum advantage. This was not illegal or even particularly sneaky. Indeed, Fred Trump did exactly what the government hoped all the Fred Trumps in the land would do. And in so doing, he joined the ranks of entrepreneurs who constitute one of the oldest fraternities in the Republic: multimillionaires who owe their fortunes to subsidies from a grateful government.

Although he did not know it at the time, he set out on this new road shortly after nine o'clock on the morning of Tuesday, March 27, 1934, when the Brooklyn Federal Court approved his purchase of the Lehrenkrauss mortgage-servicing business. Although he would be managing a fraction of the mortgages once held by Lehrenkrauss, the

fee—one-half of 1 percent of all monies collected on what remained—
would allow him to leave the supermarket business.[1] Even better, he
would have an inside line on properties about to be foreclosed and
available on the cheap at court auctions. With this one favorable nod,
the court had provided him with what he needed to relaunch his real
estate career. It was an enormous plum, for he would be reentering
the field with access to a steady cash flow, permitting him to escape
the perpetual mad scramble of the small-scale builder. At last he
would not need to race the clock, frantically trying to sell each new
house in order to pay off construction debts left from the last one.

That was how Fred Trump got his second start. What allowed
him to keep going after the Lehrenkrauss purchase was that in short
order he would receive a second and even larger plum. While he had
been scheming to obtain control of the one salvageable piece of the
Lehrenkrauss wreckage, New Deal economists in the nation's capital
were setting about the task of resurrecting the Depression-racked
home construction industry. In the process they created a set of circumstances—in effect, a new frontier—in which builders could make
money. Almost as an aftereffect, housing would be built.

The one thing developers like Fred Trump couldn't do on their
own was to stimulate consumer demand. Even Fred Trump's formidable energy could not produce home buyers in the middle of the Depression. As an individual entrepreneur, he did not have the power.
But national policy makers did. The same home-building industry
collapse that had dealt a blow to Fred Trump had been a disaster to
the country. To government officials trying to revive a moribund
economy, helping the construction industry back on its feet was a
high priority. They wanted to put the blueprints and bricks back in
Fred Trump's hands as much as he did.

Accordingly, at the same time Fred Trump was maneuvering in
federal court in Brooklyn, President Roosevelt's inner circle was trying to figure out how to jump-start the home-building business. After
months of feverish discussion and sometimes bitter negotiation, they
created the Federal Housing Administration (FHA), and within the
next year the entire industry underwent a drastic change. What had
been a relatively low-key, local affair became a bustling, large-scale
enterprise. In the process, those who could adapt to the changed political and regulatory landscape had an enormous competitive advan-

tage. One of the most successful among them would be Fred Trump. Over the next two decades he would use the FHA to provide homes, to enrich himself, and to help create a new quasi-suburban way of life in the outer boroughs.

---⁓---

By early 1934 there was no argument about the enormity of the nation's financial crisis. From 1929 to 1933 income had fallen by 36 percent, which meant that, accounting for fluctuations in the value of the dollar, per-capita income was almost as low as it had been in the depression year of 1908. One out of every four workers in the nation was unemployed.²

The whole U.S. economy seemed in near free fall, but real estate was especially badly hit. Almost one-third of the jobless—the largest single category—were in the building trades.³ New housing starts, which had hit an all-time high of 937,000 units in 1925, plunged to 93,000 in 1933.⁴ One out of ten home mortgages in the United States was in default, and many more were in serious trouble.⁵

Meanwhile banks, the source of the capital needed for mortgages and new construction, were failing at an unprecedented rate. Those that stayed open were continuing to hemorrhage from withdrawals of cash by insecure American depositors and withdrawals of gold by jittery foreigners.⁶ By March 1933, on the eve of Roosevelt's inauguration, the banking system was in such chaos that about half the states had declared bank "holidays," the popular euphemism for official permission to keep the doors shut. Three days later the new president declared an unprecedented national bank holiday. In fact, it was more like a bank spring vacation, as it lasted more than a week. This hiatus provided breathing space and time for Congress to crank out emergency banking legislation, but it did not cure the country's financial ills. Of the 17,800 commercial banks in the United States, more than 5,000 delayed reopening, and of these over 2,000 closed permanently.⁷

Everywhere the nation's bankers were trying desperately to keep their institutions afloat. But out in Utah one of their number went further. Scrambling to keep his own establishment open, Marriner Eccles unexpectedly began formulating questions about the nation's financial underpinnings that would shock his colleagues, intrigue the president, and have a profound effect on Fred Trump's future. From the outside he seemed an unlikely innovator; the thirteenth of twenty-two children born to a practicing polygamist, he was a devout Mormon, a high school dropout, and a conservative Republican. A successful man who managed a number of family businesses, Eccles had never doubted the conventional economic wisdom that enough budget cutbacks would cure even the worst economic ills.

Then, one day in the early 1930s, he faced a run on his own Ogden bank. On the day it was expected, he opened every window and coached tellers to look up every signature card, use small bills, and count slowly. When three o'clock approached and people were still in line, Eccles stood on top of a black-and-gold marble counter and announced that the bank would not close that evening as long as anyone desired service. The next day he reversed orders. The bank opened two hours early, and clerks ignored signature cards and made fast dispersals with big bills. No lines formed, and a business-as-usual atmosphere prevailed. "That was the end of that run," Eccles wrote later. "I thanked God for the nerves I inherited from my father and mother."[8]

Although his tightly scripted series of moves had saved his own bank, he began to question the traditional notion that continuous belt-tightening would eventually bring the economy around. Rather than helping, he said later, this policy seemed to be "throwing a double loop around the throat of an economy already gasping for breath." Departing ever further from his past assumptions, Eccles declared that government should not be considered in the same light as a business or a family. The latter needed to balance their books or they would go bankrupt, but the government had the unique power to issue money, levy taxes, and in general change the rules of the game.

In fact, Eccles asserted, the government's job wasn't to balance the budget, but rather to put people and money to work. From there it was only a short leap to the distinctly heretical notion that getting the economy moving again meant accepting, and even embracing, an unbalanced budget, at least for the short term. At the same time, Eccles remained firmly on the side of private enterprise and a limited role for government. He wanted to get the country moving again by strengthening the private sector and using its resources, not by having the government sweep in and pick up the tab.

In February 1933, as Fred Trump was arranging supermarket shelves in Queens, Eccles attended an economic conference sponsored by the Senate Finance Committee. One after another, leaders of industry, finance, and labor reiterated that the best medicine for the economy was no medicine other than occasional relief for creditors and investors. When the man *Fortune* would later describe as a prophet spoke up and suggested a deliberately unbalanced budget, his audience was startled. Then he went on to speak of relief not for creditors, but for debtors—that is, the unemployed, laborers, and farmers. By the time he got to minimum wage laws and higher income and inheritance taxes, his listeners were thoroughly alarmed.[9]

Unrepentant, Eccles headed to New York to meet an economics professor at Columbia University named Rexford Guy Tugwell. The circumstances did not bode well. Tugwell was late because he had been sitting in a dentist's chair. Obviously feeling guilty, he asked Eccles to share a lunch of sandwiches at a drugstore booth. Tugwell, his jaw throbbing, popped pain pills, listened as the renegade western banker outlined his unorthodox proposals, and then sent him on his way without comment. Unbeknownst to Eccles, the prominent English economist John Maynard Keynes had already advanced similar ideas, and Tugwell was receptive to them. But Eccles knew nothing of this until nine months later, when Tugwell, then serving as assistant secretary of agriculture, abruptly summoned him to Washington.

For three exhausting days Tugwell trotted Eccles around to meet other top Roosevelt administration officials, including Secretary of Agriculture Henry Wallace and Secretary of the Interior Harold Ickes. Because of what Eccles later called "my bizarre status as a reputed millionaire banker and industrialist who preached the gospel [of planned government deficits]," they were willing to listen to him.[10] To Eccles's dismay, they were not willing to implement his ideas immediately. But they did want him on board. After he returned to Utah he received an invitation to become a special assistant to Treasury Secretary Henry Morgenthau Jr., and in early 1934 he reported for duty.

In the meantime, a working group known as the National Emer-

gency Council met in the Oval Office with the president to disman-
tle the Civil Works Administration, a public works effort whose price
tag was frightening the old-line budget balancers. When Roosevelt
was asked for more money, he threw up his hands in horror and asked
with dismay if there was any way to get the government out of the
whole lending and relief business. "Sure," one of the men gathered
around the president's desk piped up. "A housing program." And thus
began what was to become the Federal Housing Administration,
provider of homes for American families and fortunes for American
entrepreneurs.[11]

In March of 1934 a national housing task force got to work. Like
everything else in Washington, the guest list was heavily WASP. "It
was all Jimmy Stewart in those days," said one New Deal veteran afterward.[12] The group included Secretary of Agriculture Wallace, Secretary of Labor Frances Perkins, railroad magnate and Democratic
Party bigwig W. Averell Harriman, and Rexford Tugwell. Less well-
known was the group's economist, Winfield Riefler, a statistician
who had come to the Federal Reserve after working as a commercial
banker in Baltimore.[13] Colleagues had already singled out Riefler, a
tall, skinny blond, as the ablest economist in the entire Fed. He
proved it immediately by hiking over to the Treasury and asking Eccles about housing. For the rest of the day and well into the evening,
they dissected the nation's financial paralysis. In the process, each
found in the other someone willing to question economic shibboleths
and to consider unconventional solutions.

When the two men finished talking, Eccles had signed up for the
task force. But when he attended a meeting, he was dismayed to find
what he called "social service worker" thinking, in which "housing" meant public housing, financed and owned by the government.
When he pointed out that the group's members were long on enthusiasm but short on actual know-how for producing real homes for
real people, he became head of yet another subcommittee to get the
job done.

Together Eccles and Riefler planned what would become the Federal Housing Administration. Among other distinguishing features,
the FHA would bear no resemblance to the federal government's only
previous such effort, the thirty thousand housing units built for shipyard workers and their families during World War I and sold off at

war's end.[14] Convinced that government-built housing could not generate enough financial activity to make the economy hum again, Eccles wanted private banks to pony up funds for private construction. Riefler, who had experimented with the idea of mortgage insurance back in Baltimore, suggested the extraordinary notion of having the federal government insure private banks against losses when making loans to home buyers. As Roosevelt had requested, the government itself would thus be out of the lending business. It would not actually lend or give away a dime. Instead it would act as a guarantor of last resort, promising banks they would no longer have to assume all the risk. Bankers could then turn on the fiscal spigots, and construction could resume.

On June 27, 1934, the Seventy-third Congress of the United States passed the Eccles-Riefler plan in the form of the National Housing Act. Title I, the smallest and most quickly operational section, insured bank loans of up to $2,000 for home and office modernization. Within months these loans, which did not require collateral, put nearly $1 billion into the spending stream.[15]

Title II changed forever the way houses were built and financed in America. Fearing losses, banks had traditionally avoided giving mortgages for more than half of the appraised value of a home. Because most buyers did not have the cash for the other half of the purchase price or for the extortionate interest rates charged by those building and loan associations that provided bigger loans, they had to take out second and third mortgages. Worse, these loans were generally short-term, usually for no more than five years, and payments covered only the interest. When the loan was up, the borrower would hand over a whopping "balloon payment" on the principal and get the loan renewed. Even in the best of times many homeowners remained stuck in an endless cycle of overlapping mortgages, never able to finish paying off their homes.

Title II changed this practice completely. Banks could lend as much as 80 percent of the value of a home and lot, up to a maximum of $12,800, a generous sum at a time when half that amount would provide solid middle-class comfort. Moreover, there was a ban on balloon payments. The interest rate could not be higher than 5 percent, and the loan was both long-term and amortized—that is, payments applied to both interest and principal.[16]

If banks agreed to follow such radically different rules, the government would insure the loans. For this service, the buyer would pay an extra one-half of 1 percent of the unpaid balance of the loan. The premium or insurance fee would cover FHA administrative costs and also provide a pool to cover any defaults. The same terms would apply to rental housing, but until after World War II the FHA covered mainly single-family homes.

In less than three months Eccles and Riefler had come up with an entirely new approach to home building, figured out the administrative framework, made provisions for financing, and seen the final product through Congress. Now it was the official law of the land. But they were still short people who knew how to build houses.

In early May of 1934 a thirty-six-year-old architect named Miles Lanier Colean was hurtling toward the nation's capital in the backseat of an old jalopy. By virtue of the fact that he and several unemployed colleagues were willing to cover the cost of the gas, they were the official delegation from the Chicago chapter to the national convention of the American Institute of Architects. Colean, a lanky man with thick black hair and an architecture degree from Columbia University, was so broke that even his share of the expenses was a budget buster. The trip was a wild, desperate gamble that something would turn up.[17]

Upon arriving in D.C., the travelers crashed a party at a hot nightclub called the Troika. Because the host was Wisconsin's Robert La Follette, who had inherited his name, his liberalism, and his Senate seat from his late father, the guest list was full of young New Dealers. Colean managed to snag an invitation to the next housing task force meeting and soon was on staff. As a student Colean had looked at grand projects, not middle-class housing, and he had later worked on some of the most spectacular examples of overbuilding, including the Palmer House and the Stevens Hotel (later the Conrad Hilton) in Chicago. But unlike most of his colleagues, he had at least thought about large-scale housing development, which he had begun to explore as the building industry of the 1920s shuddered to a dead halt.[18]

By the fall of 1934 the FHA had perhaps a hundred employees, scattered in empty government offices around downtown Washington. Many were in an upper floor of the spanking new post office building, a neoclassical columned behemoth at Pennsylvania Avenue and 12th Street. Decorated with elaborate sculptural programs, dozens of murals, mahogany wall panels, and cut-glass chandeliers, it was part of a complex known as the Federal Triangle. Originally planned by the Hoover administration as a central location for government employees, it was now crammed with New Deal agencies.[19]

Surrounded by near imperial splendor, Colean and others on the FHA staff labored all day and half the night, six and sometimes seven days a week, to come up with design and financing guidelines for modest single-family homes all across America. A standard joke around the office was to ask whether there was a doctor in the house—a ridiculous remark because the core staff was composed largely of Ph.D.'s unable to find academic employment.

Once a week they trooped over to the University Club, a few blocks away, and over lunch they filled each other in on what they'd accomplished over the past seven days. To save time they ordered in advance, skipped dessert, and brought along a secretary who entered the men's club by a separate door and took notes on their discussions.[20] On Sunday nights the planners gathered again at the home of Fred Babcock, an insurance underwriter and Republican from Chicago. Exhausted from work and homesick, the men who were going to put the building industry back on its feet relaxed over a home-cooked meal and listened to Babcock, a portly fellow who was blind in one eye, play violin and piano trios with his children.[21]

Early Monday morning they started right back in again arguing and negotiating over how to go from half a dozen pages of legislation to concrete procedures that would attract loans and prevent cheating. The one thing they all agreed on was the need for rules that were, in the words of one participant, like a good farm fence—"pig tight and bull high."[22]

One major departure was to focus not only on the builder's ability to command a loan, but also on what was being built. For the first time, there was an emphasis on land planning rather than simply adopting a standard gridiron plan. There was also research on which designs had the best track record. They collected data showing that

small, well-planned, well-built houses that adhered to simple standards, like making the bathroom accessible without having to pass
through a bedroom, held value better than large, elaborate homes that
became white elephants in a slump.[23] Market studies on the number
and cost of houses in different parts of the country were another innovation. Ernest Fisher, a bespectacled older economist from the University of Michigan, sent researchers to Charleston, West Virginia, to
ring every doorbell—including those in the large red-light district—
and ask questions.[24]

Fred Babcock pioneered another important change. Every day he
came in, carefully removed his jacket, rolled up the sleeves of his
white shirt, and worked on the first nationwide standards for real estate appraisal. In part, this meant figuring out how to assess the cred-
itworthiness of the borrower. Determined to avoid the stranglehold
of loans made for unrealistically short time periods, Babcock devised
a system of level payments that stretched out over a number of years
and covered both interest and principal. To figure out if a mortgage
had an acceptable level of risk, a lender could check whether the
prospective buyer made enough money to cover the monthly payment—now a routine procedure, but novel at the time. Using this approach, borrowers could feel secure that by paying the same amount
each month for a set number of years, they would eventually own
their homes, and lenders could feel assured that monthly payments
would arrive and they would not have to resort to foreclosure.[25]

Babcock and Colean also worked on methods to assess the real estate itself. Colean made sure there was an architectural examiner in
each local FHA office, hardly a problem in the depths of the Depression. "I became known as the relief agency for the architectural profession," Colean said later.[26] Because many areas lacked building
codes, the FHA put together its own minimal standards for key elements like indoor plumbing, fire protection, sewage disposal, lot size,
and subdivision planning. In doing so, it was essentially providing the
first nationwide structural standards.[27]

Colean and Babcock's chief concern was for the economic soundness of FHA-insured mortgages, not for those who would actually be
buying the houses. Indeed, they and their colleagues regarded the
FHA not as a do-good government agency, but as an independent, professional insurance program, run on sound businesslike principles.

Real estate refugees who had fallen on hard times made up much of the staff, and they understood their clients to be other members of the same real estate fraternity—that is, builders, mortgage bankers, and insurance brokers. Hardly surprising, the culture that developed within this new agency was oriented toward business interests rather than toward consumers or social reform. Thus, for example, the FHA had firm guidelines on what was called "neighborhood homogeneity," based on the premium Babcock's risk appraisal system placed on communities whose families had similar economic, religious, ethnic, and racial backgrounds. In practice this meant that the FHA went along with the restrictive covenants against Jews, Armenians, and other minorities that were common in that era. Its underwriting manuals also strongly discouraged "inharmonious uses of housing," a code phrase for selling homes in white areas to blacks.[28]

Wary of the FHA's unconventional approach and unconvinced by the businesslike nature of the enterprise, the large insurance companies continued to hold back. It was an enormous problem, for they alone had the resources to lend on a nationwide basis. "The FHA was still a brand-new outfit, with people bumbling around trying to figure out what to do," recalled Philip Brownstein, an FHA staffer and later agency head. "Here you had this crazy Roosevelt determined to bankrupt the entire country—most people thought this program was just too risky."[29]

Then Stewart McDonald, a car manufacturer who had at one time been police commissioner of St. Louis, took charge. A big, fat man, he considered himself, probably correctly, to be tougher and richer than most of his critics. "This job wouldn't keep me in cigarettes, if I smoked cigarettes," he once told a hostile congressional committee.[30] Appointed FHA administrator on September 5, 1935, he quickly dispatched junior underwriters to beat the bushes for prospective FHA customers. At community centers and schools, churches and civic groups, the staffers touted what the FHA had to offer. When they couldn't find a meeting to address, they called one themselves.[31] Gradually smaller insurance companies jumped in and started making money. Soon major league outfits in New York City were wading in as well.[32] By 1939, five years after Win Riefler went over to the Treasury and talked to Marriner Eccles, the agency that came from their efforts was insuring about one-quarter of all new homes in the country. In 1935, the FHA's first full year of operation, it insured only about twenty-three thousand home mortgages; in 1941, it was covering over two hundred thousand loans.[33]

In turn, mortgage banking changed from a strictly local form of investment to a nationwide industry. Mortgage bankers could handle FHA-insured loans at the local level, then sell the mortgages on the so-called secondary market to large national institutions like insurance companies and big northeastern banks. Because of FHA standards as to the quality of construction and the terms of financing, FHA-insured mortgages were now marketable commodities all over the country. For the first time, capital in large financial centers could flow out to local banks and home buyers in distant locations.[34]

One of the busiest locations for FHA-insured mortgages would be New York City, and one of the most active builders there would be Fred Trump. Working in Brooklyn and using FHA-insured mortgages, he produced two thousand single-family homes between 1935 and 1942. Well designed and well built, these dwellings became known as Trump homes. As the public grew to know the name as a symbol of quality, within real estate and financial circles it was becoming known for shrewd business practices and entrepreneurial skill.

CHAPTER TEN

HOME BUILDING'S HENRY FORD

TUCKED DEEP INTO THE RECESSES OF PAGE THIRTY-SIX, *The New York Times* on August 12, 1936, carried a brief story, just three paragraphs long, that laconically described the most important event of Fred Trump's life.[1] At eleven o'clock the day before, Thomas G. Grace, New York State Federal Housing Administration director, had officially inaugurated the Trump Holding Company's new development in a section of central Brooklyn known as East Flatbush. Standing before more than one hundred invited guests, the FHA director waved his arm at an immaculate one-story model house and declared the first forty-eight homes open. Then he presented Fred Trump and his new partner, Charles A. O'Malley, with a plaque commemorating FHA approval of their 450-home project.

In the audience that hot, muggy day was Fred Trump's wife, Mary Anne, a twenty-four-year-old with brown hair and bright blue eyes.[2] Born Mary Anne Macleod and the youngest of ten children, she had emigrated six years earlier from Stornoway, an island in Scotland's Outer Hebrides known for herring, sheep, and Harris tweed. Scot Gaelic was her first language, and when she arrived in New York, on the day after her eighteenth birthday, she spoke English with a heavy burr. Unskilled and unemployed, she lived with her married sister in Astoria, Queens. One night she went with her sister to a party and met a blond man with a mustache who was half a dozen years her senior. His name was Fred Trump, and when he went home that night he told his mother he'd just met the woman he was going to marry.

Mary Anne was immediately attracted as well. On a visit to Scotland soon afterward, she told her parents she had met her future husband. They married in 1936 on the second Saturday in January, celebrated at the Carlyle Hotel, and went to Atlantic City for their honeymoon. Characteristically, Fred Trump was too busy to take more than the weekend off. On Monday he was back at work, and Mary Anne had become a housewife. Now it was eight months later, and she was four weeks pregnant with her first child. Smiling graciously despite the August heat, she greeted her husband's friends and colleagues.

Also present at the dedication was Elizabeth Christ Trump. Fifty-six years old, her blond hair turning gray, she was a well-dressed and imposing figure. Just before the bottom fell out of the building industry, she had returned to Germany to see her family and show off her children. Looking around at them today, she felt even more proud than before. By working hard, her older son had found his way back into real estate. Her daughter's husband, Bill Walter, had become a successful banker, and they had produced two grandchildren, both boys. Her younger son, John, had a doctorate in electrical engineering, an appointment as an assistant professor at MIT, and a wife named Elora Gordon Sauerbrun. A church organist in Queens, she, too, was from a German background.

Fred Trump was happy to have his entire family in attendance. But the real proof of his success was the men who were there because they did business with him. Charles O'Malley, who had replaced William Demm as Trump's partner, was sixty years old, exactly twice Trump's age, and the official real estate appraiser for New York City. O'Malley brought big-league credibility and status to the partnership, for he had appraised $2 billion worth of property, including the remains of the House of Lehrenkrauss.[3] Bill Hyman, the real estate lawyer Trump had met during the Lehrenkrauss hearings and subsequently retained, was also there. Other guests included the district director and main underwriter for the FHA's Brooklyn office.

The biggest coup was the personal appearance of Tommy Grace. A lawyer from Bay Ridge, near Coney Island, Grace, thirty-eight years old, had received an appointment as the first state FHA director the previous year. A decorated war veteran, law professor, and, despite his diminutive stature, former football coach, he had rung doorbells, tallied support, and pulled out the vote on election day. As recognition for his unstinting effort, the local Democratic machine had pushed for his ascension to the FHA.[4]

As with the awarding of the Lehrenkrauss mortgage-servicing business, politics and, especially, the Madison Club played a major role in the history of the new development in East Flatbush. "Freddy," as Trump was called by Madison pals, never missed a political event, willingly shelled out for every dinner and benefit, and occasionally paid a personal visit to the three-story brownstone that served as club headquarters. Downstairs was a big meeting room full of folding chairs and a lounge with old leather-covered seats; upstairs, in a warren of tiny offices, club officials worked the phones and the mimeograph machines. Out on the surrounding streets, ambitious young club members like Abraham Beame, a high school accounting teacher and later mayor of New York, spent their evenings dropping in on registered voters to see what could be done to keep them in the Democratic fold.[5]

Through these political contacts, Trump had explored the status of a large vacant tract on the southern edge of Madison Club territory. A stretch of old swampland, it was in East Flatbush and had been the dumping ground for dirt excavated during the construction of the Nostrand Avenue subway. Each year the Ringling Brothers circus camped there for a few weeks after its run at Madison Square Garden. The rest of the time local residents used the area for truck gardens and ball fields—soccer in the fall and baseball every spring.

Working out of one of the unsold houses he had built in Jamaica Estates, a sizable mock Tudor stucco affair on Devonshire Road, Fred Trump had learned all he could about two things: the new FHA mortgage insurance program and the Flatbush site. Over the months he tracked down individual properties that were either in foreclosure or about to be, including some from the Lehrenkrauss connection. In the past, he had built on a relatively small number of lots at any one time, sometimes only a single parcel. But with the FHA behind him, he was able to get loans based on the soundness of his plans rather than the size of his bank account. As a result, for the first time he could put together whole packages of adjacent lots.

Finding out exactly who owned what was a complicated business, and more than once Bill Hyman had to trace titles back to the original Dutch land grants. It was also a delicate business, for if owners found out that they had the last few parcels within a larger area, they - could hold out for higher prices. But creating such packages was a business Hyman was good at. Poring diligently over dusty records and then standing unobtrusively at the back of city auctions, he was able to buy up tax liens, many on old farmland on which owners had stopped paying taxes long ago. To avoid detection, he used pseudonyms, stand-ins at auctions, even dummy subsidiary corporations.[6] He would do whatever it took. "Whenever you went to a closing with your dad," Fred Trump later told Hyman's son David, "the deal always closed."[7]

Once Trump had secured the East Flatbush tract, he hired an architect and put him to work with a set of the FHA guidelines produced by Miles Colean. They spelled out official requirements, such as the inside bathroom reachable without going through a bedroom; elsewhere Trump learned about the unofficial requirements, like a brick exterior. Plans in hand, he then went to Tommy Grace. For the initial development of 450 houses, Grace approved $750,000 in mortgage insurance, making Fred Trump one of the first New York builders to get such an FHA commitment. He could then proceed to a commercial bank such as Dime Savings, with which he had established a close relationship, and get the money he needed to go into high gear.[8]

By mid-1936 Fred Trump had four hundred workers digging out the foundations for houses that would be priced from $3,000 up to $6,250. Unlike many other builders, he did not hire someone else to oversee his jobs. Instead he acted as his own general contractor, reporting to the job site every morning at seven-thirty and watching his crews frame the houses one by one. Within crews, which were all white and a hodgepodge of nationalities, specific craft was usually a matter of ethnic origin. Thus, for example, Swedes were woodworkers and Italians were plasterers. But Fred Trump, who had constructed whole houses by himself, knew how to do every job. Whenever he spotted something being done badly, he stepped in and showed how to do it better and faster.[9]

To get maximum value out of the land, he built attached row houses with common walls. He avoided corner lots because they were expensive; fortunately East Flatbush blocks were so long that there was room for dozens of row homes to stack up in the midblock sections. Every weekend eager buyers crowded his sales office. Within months he had expanded to similar projects in other Flatbush neighborhoods, again using FHA mortgage commitments to obtain construction loans from banks. To speed up the work, he installed floodlights and hired a second shift of workers to put up houses, lay sidewalks, and pave streets.[10]

By the time he opened his first section of houses, in August 1936, he was looking into doing more projects nearby. Soon long rows of what became known as "Trump homes" dotted central Brooklyn. Built of dark red brick, they had a distinctive, recognizable look: a beach-towel-size swatch of front lawn, three front steps, and a tiny porch. At the same time, each house was slightly different from those of its neighbors. Faux gables and peaks ornamented the roofline, but not in a uniform fashion. Rusticated stone surrounded a window here and a door there, and minichimneys sat on top of some houses but not others. Every so often one or two homes sat a few feet closer to the street, breaking up the solid line of house fronts. The brick balustrades in front of the porches had a variety of patterns, including stylized key slots or crosses that created long stretches of large capital *T*'s, prefiguring his son's constant use of both initial and name.

Inside the houses there was a similar attention to detail. The front door did not open directly into the living room, but into a minuscule foyer with a coat closet that had a mirror inside the door. Between the small living room and the smaller dining room was a rounded archway rather than the standard squared-off opening. Instead of using linoleum, Trump laid down hardwood parquet floors, and around the kitchen sink was ornamental tilework. The plumbing fixtures used high-quality copper pipes, and in some houses the stairs came carpeted.[11]

Sitting beneath each house was the emblem of the twentieth century, a garage. Entered by a steep ramp from the street, it had heat in the winter and its door was wonderfully visible year-round. The garage was a source of pride for Fred Trump's customers, even though most could not afford a car and did not know how to drive. Indeed, one of the big draws of Fred Trump's first development was its proximity to the Nostrand Avenue subway and the Utica Avenue bus. Nevertheless, said Marian Kelley, who in 1936 bought the second home Fred Trump built in East Flatbush, the garages meant that these houses "were the big thing—the modern home."[12]

The garage was hardly the only up-to-date touch. Instead of old-fashioned dormer windows, the houses had casements with small glass panes. In the bathroom the tub was framed with chrome, and there was a hand-painted landscape on the wall instead of the usual wallpaper. Some houses had stall showers, a novelty at the time; others had living rooms with shallow false fireplaces and electric logs that lit up when plugged into an outlet. The basements were not rough storage areas, but finished "recreation rooms" that could be rented out to help pay off the mortgage. Many had a bar with a mirror and a little foot rail in front. "Back then," said homeowner Kelley, "that was real class."

This classiness, which came from Fred Trump's sense of craft, was his new competitive edge. The FHA had launched several builders in Brooklyn, and the most direct competition came from two brothers named Match. "We'd have a front porch, and the Matches would put in a front porch," Fred Trump later told one interviewer. "We'd have a back porch, they'd have a back porch. Toilet upstairs, toilet downstairs. In the beginning, our houses sold for $2,990, $300 down, but they were always quality. . . . Do you know what I mean?"[13]

The people who lived in Trump homes were the middle of the middle class, or "middle-middle" as one former resident described her neighbors. Mostly young married couples with kids, they included teachers, lawyers, doctors, dentists, middle managers, small-business owners, accountants, a funeral director, and lots of housewives. The center of social life was the porches. All day long kids climbed over, under, and across them. At dusk their parents and, in some cases, grandparents sat there and talked as the kids threw and kicked balls against stoops and up and down the sidewalk and street. "Moving there was a nice step up," said novelist Lynne Sharon Schwartz. "My parents would say proudly, 'We live in a Trump home.'"[14]

As he had done earlier in Queens, Fred Trump periodically returned to the neighborhoods he had built, checking on how the houses were holding up. Dressed in a coat and tie, he would drive around the streets in a late-model car—at one time a red convertible, later a black Cadillac—and talk with his customers. When he visited Marian Kelley, he would chat with her husband, a store manager for A&P, about the supermarket business. Two years after they purchased the house, he helped them switch to gas heat, which was cleaner than the coal they had been using. "We were young, and we knew nothing about purchasing a house," she said. "He was so pleasant and reliable—it meant a lot to us."[15]

—◆◆◆—

Within a year after that August day when Fred Trump opened his first Flatbush home, the country was once again in a recession.[16] The rosy picture at the end of 1936—270,000 new homes that year, and predictions of another 400,000 to 450,000 in the year to come—turned dark only a few months into 1937. By April it looked as though the country would be lucky to stay at 1936 levels. A worried Marriner Eccles lobbied the president to do something, and they both began looking to the FHA to get the economy moving again. Coming back from a White House meeting, FHA administrator Stewart McDonald relayed to his staff their marching orders: "Tell the old girl to paint her face, pull up her skirts, and get out on the stage."

Early in 1938 Congress passed liberalized FHA regulations. Borrowers could have up to twenty-five years to pay back mortgage loans, which could cover up to 90 percent of the purchase price for homes costing $6,000 or less. Such changes had a salutary effect, but they worried agency staffers. The FHA had barely gotten started, and this was an enormous new burden. The FHA's original purpose was to stimulate construction by helping bank activity reach normal levels. Now the agency was supposed to rev up the entire economy.[17]

Fred Trump had no such qualms. Despite his optimistic comments to the press, he had taken a hit during the economic downturn. Now, though, with changed FHA regulations, he was back in business. In March 1938 he joined other builders to form the Brooklyn Home Builders Association, a trade group intended to promote FHA-

insured mortgages. Immediately the FHA committed $1 million in
mortgage loans for another cluster of Trump homes in Flatbush.[18]

That July Fred Trump made his five hundredth sale in Brooklyn,
and the *Eagle* hailed him as "the Henry Ford of the home-building industry."[19] It was an apt description. Although he was in an industry
long dominated by small operators working off the back of an envelope and still worked that way himself, he belonged to the new breed
of producers who were putting together their own version of mass
production. He built in multiple units, which allowed economies of
scale such as ordering bricks by the carload and equipment in large
enough shipments to earn discounts. Similarly, he bought lumber in
bulk quantities and cut it to size in his own lumberyard, paid in cash
to lower costs, and staggered construction to keep crews busy year-
round.

By 1938, Fred Trump reported proudly, these methods had lowered his costs from twenty-nine to twenty-five cents a cubic foot.[20] By
keeping costs down and taking advantage of the new FHA regulations, he was able to produce good homes at such low prices that people were literally jamming the streets to buy his projects—or so he
bragged to the *New York Evening Post*. Indeed, the builder claimed,
there was such a commotion one day at his sales office that he had to
call in the police to handle the mobs of eager buyers.[21]

In 1941 he was working on three hundred homes at once and took
in $1 million in sales.[22] Having run out of empty land in East Flat-
bush, he had moved his operation to Brighton Beach, on the other side
of Brooklyn and one block from the Atlantic Ocean. There he unleashed tractors, derricks, steam shovels, and cement mixers on land
that had once been a terminal on the Long Island Railroad.[23] Working
day and night, hundreds of bricklayers, carpenters, painters, and
plumbers raced to meet tight deadlines. To keep up morale and pro-
ductivity, he installed bathing lockers so workers could go swimming
on their breaks,[24] and to keep sales up, he promoted his homes constantly. Once he put on a public wedding ceremony for four couples
and offered prizes for babies born in Trump homes; other ploys included a push to get "Own a Home" on license plates, a beachfront
barge with Trump ads, and, at Coney Island, the release of balloons
with coupons for $50 off on one of his $4,990 bungalows.[25]

Stories on every one of these initiatives appeared in the media, for

Fred Trump had learned how convenient newspapers found short news releases for filling news holes. He generously provided item after item. Brief summaries of his sales reports, his market predictions, his "survey" of what had attracted buyers to his homes, and his opinions about everything from family values to national defense went to local media, which often reprinted the pronouncements verbatim. In this way New York newspaper readers learned, among other things, that Fred Trump considered it a patriotic act to build one-family homes—but not apartments—for Americans[26] and that in his opinion renters were mere drifters capable only of brief friendships. To be well-balanced, he declared, children needed to grow up in homes owned by their parents; luckily, his developments were especially child-friendly. Elsewhere he explained that in inflationary times, instead of postponing buying a home, people should snap one up right away as a hedge against further inflation.[27] He did not limit his remarks to industry concerns; when Roosevelt overturned historical precedent and ran for a third presidential term, Fred Trump sent a letter of endorsement to home-builder organizations across the country.[28]

Within Brooklyn and Queens, Fred Trump had become a public figure. In June 1937, when a stooped and shabby Julius Lehrenkrauss emerged from Sing-Sing prison with $20 to his name, Fred Trump was a highly prosperous businessman. Only in his mid-thirties, he had already built more than two thousand houses and expected to erect thousands more. By 1943, when Lehrenkrauss died alone and impoverished, Trump had become a millionaire.[29] Now a father, he would pass on this wealth and property to his children. He would also pass on to them something else equally valuable: what he had learned about the usefulness of the media.

—⁓—

Soon the gathering conflict in Europe would sweep up nearly everyone in the country, including Fred Trump. In January 1941, six months after the fall of France, the president established the Office of Production Management (OPM). Its mandate was to mobilize American industry for defense. Across the nation it impounded construction materials, and most private housing came to a dead halt. Fortunately for Fred Trump, the presence of the Brooklyn Navy Yard allowed the borough to qualify as a "defense housing area." In order to provide homes for defense workers, Brooklyn builders could still obtain supplies and FHA mortgage insurance.[30] In October 1941 the first OPM priority in New York for a major building operation went to Fred Trump for a new project in a section of Brooklyn called Bensonhurst. He had paid cash for a fifty-five-acre tract on which he proposed to build seven hundred houses, the biggest project so far for him and for the New York FHA office.[31]

Bensonhurst would also be his first project to fall behind schedule. After the bombing of Pearl Harbor in December 1941 and the American declaration of war, the OPM hurriedly withdrew Brooklyn's priority, and local construction sputtered out. But Fred Trump was hardly in trouble. The government had asked him and other developers from the New York area to build defense housing at Norfolk, Virginia, the center of naval operations for the entire East Coast. To sweeten the invitation, Congress added a new provision to the National Housing Act, used to create the FHA back in 1934. Known as Section 608, it provided generous mortgage insurance for multifamily rental housing—apartment houses—for war workers, particularly when located near war plants.[32] Fred Trump patriotically decided that the nation needed more apartment buildings.

His turnabout on the desirability of apartments rapidly followed his discovery that building them would let him be an owner, not just a builder. After he finished a development, he would not simply visit every now and then. He would collect rent every month, and he would have equity. Duty had called, and Fred Trump had answered with alacrity. Even before the enactment of Section 608, he was supervising five hundred construction workers at a new apartment complex. Called Oakdale Homes, it was located in what had been an old barroom and red-light district outside the Norfolk Naval Base and Naval Air Station in coastal Virginia.[33]

Norfolk, an ice-free, deepwater port at the south end of Chesapeake Bay, had long been an important center for shipping and shipbuilding. Over the years the city had expanded at a slow and stately pace, growing to about 140,000 inhabitants at the time of the 1940 U.S. census. But when Fred Trump arrived only two years later, the city had nearly doubled in size and was a boomtown bursting at the seams. During the frantic last-minute American defense buildup, the Pentagon had sent 30,000 men and women in uniform to Norfolk-area bases, and the city continued to swell with the arrival of more soldiers, sailors, shipyard workers, and their families. "There were so many servicepeople here, I hardly knew anybody who had a spare room who didn't take people in," recalled Carol Melton, a Norfolk grande dame who was a young housewife at the time. "You never drove anywhere without picking up sailors or servicepeople. I wore out the upholstery in my new car the first year."[34]

Fred Trump was stunned. "Norfolk is like a beehive," he told the *New York Herald Tribune.* There were long lines at stores, and it was standing room only at the movies every night. When it was his turn at a phone booth, getting a call through to New York could take hours. The housing shortage was so drastic that landlords resorted to "hot beds," rooms rented to one tenant during the day and another at night. Local builders had responded with a sprinkling of new homes, but they couldn't possibly meet the overwhelming need on their own. Nor did they want to. They had been stuck with empty housing after a big buildup during World War I, and they were wary of ending up in the same predicament once again.[35]

For Fred Trump and other outside builders coming to Norfolk, the overcrowding meant he was in the right place at the right time. "Rents are still soaring here," he reported elatedly to the *Herald Tribune.* Newcomers were so desperate for housing, they weren't waiting to see finished apartments. They lined up for the privilege of renting and signed leases based on blueprints. The previous weekend, Trump noted, forty naval officers showed up at his job site looking for places to live.[36] Nearly half a century earlier Frederick Trump had found Seattle and the Yukon to be where the action was; now his son Fred was discovering the same thing in Norfolk.

Fred Trump's partner in Norfolk was James Rosati, a former plastering contractor in Queens. After the Depression Rosati had switched to road construction and had supervised the relocation of dozens of homes that were in the path of the Van Wyck Expressway and Idlewild Airport (later renamed for John F. Kennedy). Watching as war fever mounted across the United States, Rosati headed for Norfolk just before Pearl Harbor and snapped up property near the naval base. When Fred Trump, who had met Rosati in New York, arrived soon afterward, the two builders from Queens teamed up to develop Rosati's land.

Although they were both New York born and bred and only three years apart in age, they were an unlikely pair. The older of the two, Rosati was short and chubby with dark hair, dark eyes, and a big nose. A gregarious man, he was so outgoing that almost as soon as he arrived anywhere he knew everybody's name. Trump, his blond hair turned light brown, was reserved, a ramrod-straight figure with little to say. When he did speak, though, people listened, for his voice was loud and commanding.[37] "He was already wealthy, but he wasn't flashy," said Rosati's son, James Jr., years later. "He never tried to impress anybody with his wealth. He didn't seem to care if anybody had ever heard of him."

Each man brought something important to the table. James Rosati had a talent for locating land in a new place, and Fred Trump had a track record of having successfully financed large developments through the FHA. Both were experienced at dealing with large projects and deadlines, something Norfolk builders had never before encountered. Both also knew the value of lining up local politicians, and they quickly made their way to the offices of key figures in Norfolk city government. "Nobody down there had ever seen the level of production and amount of work that went into the way things were done in New York," said James Jr. "It really took outside people coming in to get things moving the way they had to move."

Attorney Bill Hyman came south as well, and he and Fred Trump rented houses near the ocean at the resort community of Virginia Beach. Hyman brought his family, including two young sons who went to school at Virginia Beach, while Trump tried commuting back and forth to New York by train, plane, and, occasionally, his big black Cadillac.[38] But driving nearly five hundred miles on preinterstate, two-lane roads took much too long, and getting priority for train and plane travel was too difficult. Eventually Mary Anne and the three children joined him.[39] They were a handful: Maryanne, named after her mother, was five years old and ready for kindergarten, but Fred Jr. was only three, and Elizabeth, named after her paternal grandmother and born shortly after her father had begun building in Norfolk, was an infant.

Almost every day the children of the neighborhood played on the wide, white beach. But the most exciting activity was to watch as the navy practiced amphibious landings and sailors manned the machine-gun emplacements installed at the end of residential streets. "Thousands of sailors would be running up and down the beach," David Hyman recalled years later. "Norfolk was a sea of white hats, wherever you went. My father would come home from work and his little Chevy coupe would be like a circus car, filled with sailors on their way to Virginia Beach and the amusement park."[40]

As the children searched the skies for Messerschmitt planes, Fred Trump was silent about his own German background. Although he had spoken German when he had visited Kallstadt just before the Depression, in America only his parents' generation spoke the language in public. He began to deny that he knew German and did not teach it to his children. Eventually he started telling people that he was of Swedish ancestry.[41] Mindful of the growing prominence of Jews in the real estate industry and local politics, he became so active in Jewish philanthropies that people often assumed he belonged to that faith.[42]

While Fred Trump was building housing for American military families, his brother was also contributing to the war effort. John Trump, who led the MIT High Voltage Research Laboratory, had already made a name for himself through his work with Robert J. Van de Graaff on the first million-volt X-ray generator. Used for radiation therapy, this invention would prolong the lives of cancer patients around the world. During the war John Trump worked on microwave radiation and served as director of the British branch of the legendary MIT Radiation Lab. There he played a key role in the development of high-resolution radar, the same technology that would replace the citizen plane spotting so eagerly provided by the young Hymans and Trumps.[43]

Oakdale Homes, Fred Trump and James Rosati's first project, was half a mile from the Norfolk navy base and consisted of 216 garden apartments. Seemingly overnight, block after block of trim two-story brick buildings with two complete three-room apartments on each floor began to appear amid vast muddy expanses that would someday be tidy swaths of green. It was Fred Trump's biggest development yet, and one of the largest in eastern Virginia. It was also his baptism in multifamily rental housing.

Working with his partner, several secretaries, and a handful of superintendents in a small office on the outskirts of Norfolk, Fred Trump was in his element. "He knew more about construction even back then than most people," James Rosati Jr. recalled later. "My father was an expert. He knew so much himself that most people came to him for advice, but he looked up to Fred Trump. Fred was one of the only people my father would listen to." Years afterward Rosati Jr., still remembered his awe when he saw Fred Trump add up long columns of figures in his head.[44] Trump also knew more about how to get what he needed than most people. When sudden shortages occurred, as they did frequently in everything from toilets to steel girders, he used his clout back home to get items like steel stairwells, fabricated in steelworking facilities in New York, rerouted to Norfolk.

Rosati was hardly the only one who found Fred Trump's facility with numbers and details awesome. "He was like a computer," said W. Taylor Johnson Jr., whose father handled Trump's insurance in Norfolk. "He ran everyone else ragged. How he could keep all these facts and figures in his head was just unreal. Different locations, different trades, dealing with union people—he could just keep changing gears and still keep the conversation going. I almost never saw him refer to notes."[45] Co-owner as well as builder, Fred Trump monitored his buildings for waste day and night, turning out lights and getting up on a stepladder to remove any bulbs he deemed unnecessary.[46]

Norfolk would provide many New York builders with their first experience working on low-cost, high-volume housing. One Long Island builder, Bill Levitt, who had done only custom homes, found this new focus an intriguing novelty. As Fred Trump was building Oakdale Homes, Levitt was finishing off Oakdale Farms, a nearby development of 750 two- and three-bedroom houses. Little more than a roof and four walls, these bungalows were his first with carports, a money-saving garage substitute that would become a signature on future Levitt homes.[47] "Our marching orders were to come up with the cheapest livable housing that could be done," Levitt said many years later. "It gave us a whole new slant on life." After the war, this experience would produce Levittown, an enormous Long Island suburban development that would become an important symbol of the postwar era.[48]

Fred Trump had already built enough low-cost, high-volume housing to be dubbed "Brooklyn's outstanding builder" by the *Brooklyn Eagle*. But now he had a large, cheap labor force, little competition, and a drastically expanded market, and he was building even bigger, even faster, and even more inexpensively.[49] Talbot Park was his second Norfolk project. Although it had only 496 units, the cost was $4 million, a new high,[50] and the buildings, which housed from eight to twenty families, were the largest he had ever constructed.[51] In a newspaper interview he heaped praise on the FHA's liberal new provisions for mortgage insurance, which included advances during construction and no limit on rates of return for builders. "Red tape is cut to a minimum," he said excitedly, "and costly delays are eliminated."[52]

By 1944 Fred Trump had built 1,360 units, nearly 10 percent of all the wartime housing created in Norfolk.[53] As long as there was a housing shortage, he declared, he would put up at least 2,000 units a year.[54] Or maybe more. His goal, he told the *Eagle*, was "to achieve the same position in the field of building homes for war workers that Henry Kaiser now occupies in shipbuilding."[55] And Fred Trump was doing everything he could to accomplish it.

CHAPTER ELEVEN

PUTTING A ROOF OVER GI JOE'S HEAD

B Y THE SUMMER OF 1944 Washington had pulled the plug on the war housing program that had brought Fred Trump to Norfolk. He scrapped his third large-scale project, sold Talbot Park for $1 million, and moved his wife and three children back to one of the large houses he had built in Jamaica Estates. That fall the government lifted wartime restrictions on local building in order to provide homes for vets, and he assumed he would be putting up block after block of one- and two-family Brooklyn homes backed by FHA mortgage guarantees.

For nearly three years he had worked seven days a week, disrupted his home life, and postponed his own plans in order to help the national struggle against fascism. Now he was ready to return to normalcy and started making plans to resume building in Bensonhurst and to acquire another large site in Brighton Beach. But the nation wasn't ready. As armed conflict ended, first in Europe and then in the Pacific, an intense bidding war developed over scarce civilian goods. With the fervid demand driving up prices, Fred Trump found it almost impossible to buy bricks, cement, pipe, or any other building necessities. He raced around the city, begging, borrowing, wheedling, and paying extortionate prices for what few items he could find. Maddeningly, there was lots of construction going on, mostly by big business, which had far deeper pockets. All around the frustrated builder, he saw what Wilson Wyatt, the man President Roosevelt appointed to solve the housing crisis, called "a rash of racetracks, mansions, summer resorts, bowling alleys, stores, and cocktail bars"—everything, that is, but homes.[1]

Fred Trump was not alone in his dismay. The lack of homes for returning vets had caused an enormous public outcry. When the fighting stopped, more than six million GIs, most of them young men, had come home to begin civilian lives and found an unprecedented housing shortage.[2] Eager to start families, these returning heroes ended up living in storage rooms, food cellars, farm sheds, even boxcars. Twenty-five thousand homeless vets walked the streets of Washington, D.C., and Chicago had four times that number. In Atlanta an ad for a single vacancy drew two thousand people. An enterprising soul in Omaha offered to rent living quarters in a big icebox.[3]

It was an intolerable situation. President Harry Truman's solution was to tap Wilson Watkins Wyatt, the chain-smoking former mayor of Louisville, Kentucky, and a city-planning advocate, as the country's first national housing expediter. As such, his job was to head up a crash effort to solve the nation's housing crisis. Wyatt quickly devoured construction statistics, conferred with incensed groups and outraged committees, and came up with the basis for the Veterans Emergency Housing Program (VEHP). Approved on May 26, 1946, it reimposed price controls on building materials, raised the cost-per-room ceiling for Section 608 mortgage-insured property, and extended the program to veterans. It also changed the definition of building cost from "reasonable replacement cost" (itself a more generous substitute for an earlier "economic soundness" test) to the still more liberal "necessary current cost." Builders could now add possible inflation and shortages in materials and labor to their cost estimates, which resulted in larger mortgages on their projects.[4]

Assuming that he would now be able to buy supplies cheaply and sell his houses for higher profits, Fred Trump offered cautious approval for Wyatt's work. "The worst is over," he told the *Brooklyn Eagle*. "The sailing will be much smoother from now on."[5]

The exuberant Wyatt declared that the VEHP was in "high gear." As far as he was concerned, the target of 2.7 million homes within two years was practically in the bag.[6] But when price controls were enacted, the result was the exact opposite of what he and Fred Trump had hoped. Manufacturers and builders suddenly had a choice. They could produce for the housing market, which was subject to tough controls that would eliminate profits. Or they could produce for business, where a roaring demand was generating huge profits. In other words, Wyatt's price controls, enacted to encourage housing, had instead created a perverse incentive to discourage it.

His naiveté didn't help. "Wyatt was a phenomenon all his own," said Miles Colean, who had drawn up FHA design standards a decade earlier. "I don't think in my experience in Washington I had ever seen such a combination of vigor, enthusiasm, and complete ignorance."[7] Worse, disputes between labor and management in lumber, steel, coal, and railroads, suppressed in wartime, were bursting out into the open, and waves of strikes were disrupting the flow of materials.[8] Desperate to make his 2.7-million-home quota, Wyatt tried unsuccessfully to take over an enormous Chrysler-Dodge plant in Chicago and turn out steel prefab components.[9]

Fred Trump had a reputation for being able to find anything, anytime. But by the spring of 1946 even he couldn't put his hands on a reliable source for bathtubs and radiators. He had to wait three weeks just for bricks.[10] To get the necessary six-inch soil pipes, he had to dispatch trucks to Ohio.[11] And after two months without nails, he sent crews to outlying areas in New York, Connecticut, and New Jersey with instructions to buy nails any way they could, including, if necessary, by the handful.[12]

He was fed up. He had followed the VEHP mandates. He had observed the price ceilings, and he had given preference to GIs. And he had gotten nothing in return.[13] When his wife gave birth to their fourth child, a boy named Donald John, Fred Trump was looking at materials shortages he called "the most critical ever faced by the home-building industry." Not even a third of Wyatt's target number of homes could possibly appear, the builder fumed to reporters. Without a quick end to the crippling bottlenecks, he predicted grimly, "1946 will be gone before Mr. Wyatt's program is even started."[14]

In July the disheartened builder asked the FHA to raise the price ceiling on some new homes in Bensonhurst on which veterans had made deposits pending a final price decision. Unless he could increase the price from $14,200 to $16,000, he claimed, he would be forced to sell these two-family houses at less than the cost of construction. When the FHA turned him down, he refused to sell the homes, telling the vets he would return their deposits. The would-be buyers, furious at losing out on precious housing, charged that the builder had quoted to them the as-yet-unapproved higher price, a gross violation of official regulations. Equally furious, Trump insisted that he had not done so, but that such an action would have been justified. He insisted that his homes, which had an additional bedroom and a separate basement apartment that could cover monthly mortgage payments, were larger and better made than other two-family homes available at the official lower price for this category of dwelling.[15]

Similar feelings of chagrin and helpless frustration were starting to well up across the country. To a nation eager to leave the war behind, price controls—the very emblem of the war effort—had become anathema. On November 5, 1946, the Democratic Party lost control of Congress, in large part because of opposition to these restrictions. Rather than waiting for the new Republican Congress to end them, Truman chose to perform the deed himself. Four days after the election he lifted all controls other than those on sugar, rice, and rent, effectively ending the short, unhappy life of the VEHP.

Three weeks later Wilson Wyatt submitted his resignation and returned to Louisville to practice law.[16] "He left Washington so much more quietly than he had come in that there was hardly a stir," Miles Colean said. "There wasn't even a hole to look at."[17] The nation's housing crisis still loomed, but it would not be solved through centralized and government-controlled means.

The day Truman acted, Fred Trump issued his own press release. Although he would naturally like to see housing costs reduced, he said, he thought such a development was unlikely. Even without price controls he expected materials to remain in short supply because there would be so much competition for them. As a result, he foresaw high housing costs for at least the next five years. All of which meant, in his view, that the very two-family homes he was already building made even more sense because owners could finance their purchase through rental of the basement unit.[18]

Apparently home seekers agreed. A few months later, when Trump had new homes ready in a nearby Brooklyn neighborhood called Bath Beach, buyers thronged the model house. They were ready to take whatever Trump had to offer, and there were no more complaints about his prices.[19]

The price control battle was the latest round in a long political struggle over that most basic of human needs, shelter. The issue had come to the attention of Capitol Hill during the Depression because of the desire to save the banks and to lower unemployment by reviving the construction industry and related businesses like furniture manufacture. The FHA, designed to meet such goals, did so, raising housing standards in the process. Subsequently, the agency's impressive success managed to set into motion a further political struggle. On the one side, liberal politicians and organizations argued that the FHA's government-insured mortgages were not enough and that the only way the poor would ever be housed was if the government built the housing itself. Such public housing would not hurt private builders, the reformers said, because the beneficiaries could never afford privately built homes. On the other side, the real estate industry insisted that, except during rare circumstances like the Depression, public housing was a fundamentally flawed idea. By definition, the industry argued, it put government in competition with private business, a rivalry that would distort the market and lead to misguided, paternalistic decisions from Washington.

Throughout the 1930s and 1940s the real estate industry had prevailed. Despite the efforts of three of the Senate's most powerful members, Democrats Robert Wagner of New York and Allen Ellender of Louisiana and Republican Robert Taft of Ohio, public housing legislation languished. Indeed, the real estate lobby was so violently opposed to government involvement that even measures that might support it indirectly came under bitter attack. Thus, for example, as part of a major defense buildup, in 1940 Congress funded seven hundred thousand dwelling units for defense workers but at the insistence of real estate interests stipulated that after the war all such housing had to be sold or demolished. It could not be used for low-income public housing.

Perhaps the real estate industry's greatest success lay in setting the terms of the debate. Specifically, the industry managed to convince many Americans to see public housing, a program that helped the poor, as a government handout, but FHA mortgage guarantees, a program that helped builders, as routine assistance to private enterprise. In reality, though, FHA mortgage guarantees were more than a help. They had been the means by which the building industry recovered from the Depression.[20] Without the FHA Fred Trump would have been running a supermarket. With the FHA he was the biggest builder in Brooklyn, employing hundreds of construction workers and turning out four hundred homes a year.[21]

With Wyatt's departure, the real estate lobby had won a decisive victory. But the nation was still desperately short of houses.[22] Angered, Truman summoned FHA commissioner and National Housing Agency administrator Raymond Michael Foley. A former journalist from Michigan, Foley had long been a solid supporter of the construction industry.[23] When he arrived at the Oval Office, Truman literally pounded his desk and demanded to know why builders weren't producing more housing. They would, Foley pledged, and immediately set about making this promise a reality.[24]

At his direction, FHA staff members began fanning out across the country in early 1947 to encourage builders and bankers to jump on board. To spur on his staffers, he announced that their grade—which determined their salary—would be tied directly to the amount of new mortgage insurance they brought in.[25] In lengthy memos he promised that he would alter bothersome regulations and that the government's new goal was to have builders and bankers make money by creating houses.[26] Accordingly, the agency simplified applications and cost estimation procedures and lowered initial mortgage payment requirements.[27] Builders could circumvent the official $5 million mortgage ceiling by splitting rental housing developments into several projects. They could budget a 6 percent return on investment after expenses, and they could use a higher rate of depreciation for income tax purposes.[28] They could negotiate formerly non-negotiable regulations like "Minimum Property Requirement for Three or More Living Units." "A great opportunity and a great challenge is before us," Foley advised his field offices. "Don't make it tough; make it easy."[29]

As Foley realized, although the construction industry needed the

FHA to ensure financing of large projects, the FHA depended on the construction industry to justify its existence. Already a government reorganization in mid-1946 had dropped the formerly independent housing administration into a newly created Housing and Home Finace Agency (HHFA). The FHA could be further parceled out, perhaps even disappear, unless builders got cracking. But most builders were doing nothing of the sort. Even in New York they failed to see the potential of the new FHA largesse. By mid-1947 the New York regional office, the largest in the country, had only 2,822 apartments in the pipeline and a paltry $22 million in mortgage commitments.[30]

Fortunately, however, at least one builder grasped Foley's message. Before the press, the politicians, and many of his colleagues, Fred Trump saw that under the new FHA regime the home-building game had changed. In late spring he walked into Grace's office with plans for the largest private rental project in Brooklyn under his arm.[31] On June 17 he filed plans for the first section of the new development, which was to be called Shore Haven. Four days later, Grace, who had awarded the builder his first FHA project eleven years earlier, officially unveiled Trump's first project under the new regulations. Using his experience putting up garden apartments in Norfolk, the builder planned to construct 32 six-story elevator buildings that would sprawl over fourteen acres and overlook New York Bay and the Atlantic Ocean.[32] The complex would have 1,344 units, ranging from two rooms, which would rent for $60 a month, to five rooms, for $110 a month, and would also have 700 heated basement garage spaces for rent.[33]

As shown in hurried sketches by Seelig & Finkelstein, a Brooklyn architectural firm, the squat red brick structures were in the utilitarian style that Tom Grace's brother George would later call "just go ahead and do it fast."[34] They would occupy only about a quarter of the site, leaving the remainder for lawns, gardens, and walkways. In addition, Shore Haven would have its own shopping center with half a dozen stores, an innovation that required a zoning change and sparked a brief protest by neighboring property owners.

From his office at 90 Church Street in Manhattan, Tom Grace explained the financing to reporters. In order to provide $9 million in mortgage loans, the FHA was making three commitments of $3 million each, to be handled through the Bank of Manhattan. Fred Trump, interviewed at his desk in a temporary building on the construction site, declared that work would begin the next day. To be done like "a belt-line production," Shore Haven would require staggering amounts of material: 18 million bricks, 7 million board feet of lumber, 1 million feet of flooring, 3,000 tons of steel, 100,000 bundles of rock lath, and 10,000 cubic yards of concrete.[35]

The *New York Herald Tribune* described Shore Haven as "a village," but it was a kind of village no one in Brooklyn had ever seen before. Most villages did not spring up overnight, mushroom style. They did not start out with five thousand inhabitants, blocks of identical structures, and instant shopping areas. But this was not a traditional settlement, slowly growing and changing over successive generations. It was for vets and families who needed a place to live right now.[36] Including the 600 one- and two-family houses he had built next door, Fred Trump was providing homes for perhaps seven thousand people—in effect, a small modern city. Indeed, the *Brooklyn Eagle* called the area "Trump City."[37]

Down in Washington, Grace's boss, Clyde L. Powell, who had met the builder back in his Norfolk days, approved the application in record time.[38] Within two months the list of prospective tenants had grown to eight thousand names and was temporarily closed.[39] As construction on Shore Haven revved up, Fred Trump, the man who had once vilified apartment dwellers as unwholesome types, extolled multifamily living. The economics of the construction industry had changed, he explained. With the skyrocketing cost of materials, rental apartments had become the best way to give home seekers "a better break."[40]

Before the year was out, Fred Trump would be involved in a second large development. In December 1947 his lawyer, Bill Hyman, finished assembling a huge fifty-acre tract, the equivalent of eight hundred lots or twelve average city blocks, near Brighton Beach. The builder immediately announced preliminary plans for a second project. Located near Shore Haven,[41] it would be named Beach Haven and would have 1,860 apartments in twenty-three buildings. Like those at Shore Haven, they would be six-story elevator structures, officially fireproof and designed by Seelig & Finkelstein. Again there would be

underground parking garages and a shopping center. Evidently confident of FHA approval, the builder was already digging the miles of
sewer lines needed for the new complex.[42]

His efforts were anomalous. Nationwide, builders remained wary
of the FHA program, and tens of thousands of vets and their families
remained without a place to live. With the 1948 presidential elections
looming, the FHA pushed for still more generous terms in the coming
reauthorization of the 608 program. It got them, although only until
March 1950. Trump, whose application for Beach Haven had been
held up pending new FHA legislation, was jubilant.[43] With one
Trump City under way, another was about to begin. A forest of six-
story towers, Shore Haven and Beach Haven would bristle over the
entire waterfront of Gravesend and Sheepshead Bay. As with Shore
Haven, the construction loan would be from the Bank of the Manhattan Company, and the builder split the $16 million mortgage into six
pieces in order to stay under the FHA ceiling.[44]

To ensure that money flowed smoothly, Fred Trump was particularly attentive to the local FHA establishment. He took care to eat at
the Hamilton, the restaurant owned by Tom and George Grace, and
he cultivated their political mentor, Democratic district leader
Kenny Sutherland. For years the builder joined the Graces at the annual brunch for Sutherland's political club, where an apron-clad
Sutherland served a huge feast to loyal precinct workers. The builder
was also a fixture at the formal installation of club officials, where
one thousand people bought tickets and wore tails and floor-length
gowns, and he let Sutherland place tenants in Trump-built apartments.[45]

To keep the paperwork moving through the FHA bureaucracy, the
builder, often with an architect or auditor in tow, was a frequent visitor at the FHA office on Church Street in Manhattan. It was filled
with staff architects, underwriters, accountants, and field inspectors,
all working at a frenzed pace. "The FHA was an exciting place in
those days," said Alex Naclerio, who eventually succeeded Tom
Grace as regional director. "I loved my family and I loved weekends,
but I also loved Monday mornings because going to my job wasn't
like going to work. People, including the big names, like Fred Trump,
were lined up outside my office on their knees, waiting to get in for
two minutes."[46] Occasionally the builder also went to FHA head-

quarters in Washington, D.C. He was known there as "a real Cossack," according to Ben Holloway, then an FHA evaluator and later president of Equitable Life Insurance Company. "He had a reputation for knowing how to cut corners," Holloway said. "But he got things done, and he didn't waste time."[47]

When Fred Trump wasn't at the FHA, he was at the job site. By habit a hands-on boss, he was now running what amounted to a military operation. Moving squads of workers around the huge sites was a major task, and scheduling framers, bricklayers, electricians, and plumbers required a detailed timetable. From project headquarters, a three-room shack he had built at one corner of the site, the builder coordinated the complex sequence of events and the awarding of subcontracts. Because he was building on filled-in land that had once been marsh, preparation for each structure began with the sinking of deep piles, sixty-five-foot lengths of creosote-covered logs, on which the buildings would rest.[48] Aboveground, traditional labor-intensive methods prevailed, for building cranes did not yet exist; instead ropes and pulleys hoisted floor timbers up to framers and carpenters.[49]

Every day Trump inspected the entire site. "He was courteous, but he never spent time just chatting," recalled John Hyman. "He didn't yell or shout, but he made it clear what he wanted. Things had to be done, and they had to be neat. If there was a mess anywhere, it had to be cleaned up right away, and he wouldn't let us come into the office with our shirts off, even on really hot days."

A critical part of maintaining order was keeping the lid on problems with the local Mob. At Beach Haven the key to avoiding such conflicts was a small, slender mason named James Tomasello, who was the bricklayer contractor and a limited partner. One reason for the arrangement was that Tomasello was able to ensure good relations with one of the most powerful forces in the local contruction industry.[50] Another, as the builder later acknowledged, was that Jimmy Tomasello was a source of readily available capital while other financing was pending.[51] The source of that capital was something Trump didn't inquire about too closely. According to the Organized Crime Task Force in the 1950s, a complex web of relationships linked Tomasello to the Gambino and Genovese crime families as well as to Lucky Luciano.

Fred Trump also hired Tomasello's son-in-law, a new immigrant, as an assistant foreman. Although the builder usually demanded that his workmen earn their pay, this young man's role, a transparently made-up job, was to stand atop the scaffolding and yell, "More mortar! More mortar!" to tenders who already knew what was needed. Many Beach Haven bricklayers were, like Tomasello's son-in-law, nonunion, another suggestion of Tomasello's Mob connections, for ordinarily unions closed down jobs that hired nonmembers.[52]

The FHA had taken pains to ensure that an experienced builder like Trump was all but guaranteed to make money on a project like Beach Haven with Section 608 mortgage insurance. But the man who had spent his career gaining an edge wanted one here, too. As usual, he would provide special features, and because he had noticed that when couples looked at his homes and apartments, women seemed to cast the deciding vote, he would aim his marketing directly at the woman of the house.[53] He hired a Manhattan-based public relations firm to make sure she heard about all that Beach Haven had to offer and purchased radio time to get the message across. On-air personalities Tex McCrary and Jinx Falkenburg began pitching Beach Haven on their popular program. Press releases went out, and a steady stream of housewife-oriented newspaper stories began to appear.

Readers learned, for example, that each Beach Haven unit would have a "modern, scientific, fully equipped kitchen" with gas range and refrigerator,[54] and there would be "ultraviolet clothing dryers" in the basements.[55] Some apartments would come with furniture at a surcharge; at the end of the initial lease, tenants would own the furniture, even if they moved.[56] The sidewalks would be wide enough for two baby carriages to pass abreast, and buildings would occupy only 20 percent of the land, leaving the balance for landscaping—the equivalent of a twenty-four-acre city park, according to the builder.[57] Possibly best of all, reported the *Brooklyn Eagle*, with the opening of the new Brooklyn Battery Tunnel, "wifey can drive hubby" direct from this dream abode to a job in Manhattan and return home in under an hour.[58]

More stories followed as Trump announced plans for a baby-sitting service, added storage areas for baby carriages, and built playgrounds.[59] On Mother's Day in 1950 he presented every prospective mother in his buildings with a dozen roses.[60] He turned over space for public school classrooms[61] and a five-hundred-seat auditorium where adults listened to lectures on child care and atomic energy and a children's orchestra gave concerts.[62] He scheduled recreational programs for children and adults,[63] put on movies and dances for teenagers,[64] made arrangements for an all-night service station,[65] and provided arts and crafts classes.[66]

The strategy was successful. The wealth of services and bonuses provided a sense that Beach Haven would be not just a place to sleep, but a community and a way of life, and tenant waiting lists were always filled. Unlike the press coverage garnered by his son Donald a generation later, that given to Fred Trump contained little personal information. Occasionally he spoke out on matters of public concern, as when he publicly threw his support behind new federal credit curbs to slow inflation and dampen the black market in building materials.[67] In turn he received awards and citations for community contributions[68] as well as for design.[69] Gossip columnists referred to him as "Fred Trump, the builder" and floated his name as a possible political candidate.[70] In the fall of 1950 he garnered what amounted to a tribute to his PR savvy, a spot alongside Dwight D. Eisenhower, General George C. Marshall, and baseball star Phil Rizzuto on a fashion industry publicist's list of the nation's best-dressed men.

Trump's understanding of how to use mass media was unusual in real estate. He saw that media generated respect, which generated financial success, which in turn generated media, and acted accordingly. Without the media he might have been equally successful; with it he had become one of Brooklyn's better-known figures, and within the borough his name constituted something close to a brand denoting sturdy, reliable housing.

Meanwhile, though, Fred Trump never forgot his local political ties.[71] In February 1949 Bill Hyman died of a heart attack in a subway station. The builder still used Hyman's partner, Matthew Tosti, but also retained Court Street lawyer Richard Charles, who was close friends with Brooklyn borough president John Cashmore. Fred Trump and Charles often lunched at the Court Cafe, just below Brooklyn Democratic Party headquarters and across from Borough Hall. There they sat at a large round table with the loose-knit group of political leaders, local elected officials, and judges who had been dubbed "the knights of the Round Table." Tom and George Grace were regulars, and Cashmore, a florid-faced, glad-handing pol, stopped by occasionally.

Lunchtime was basically a Democratic affair, but Fred Trump was careful to keep up his contacts on all fronts. Periodically he and his wife hosted big parties at clubs and hotels. The whole family attended, Elizabeth Christ Trump riding herd on grandchildren as Fred and Mary were busy meeting and greeting le tout Brooklyn and Queens. A major donor to philanthropies, Trump pitched in as treasurer for an Israel benefit concert held at Ebbets Field featuring Robert Merrill, Roberta Peters, and Benny Goodman.[72] He was a trustee of Jamaica Hospital and a board member at Brooklyn Borough Gas Company, the Bank of the Manhattan, and Kew Forest School.[73]

By the end of 1953 Fred Trump was the picture of American success. Only a few months later he would appear to be on the verge of losing it all.

CHAPTER TWELVE

THE PERILS OF SUCCESS

O N MONDAY, JULY 12, 1954, AT TWO O'CLOCK in the afternoon, Fred Trump walked into the Banking and Currency Committee hearing room on the third floor of the Senate Office Building
in Washington, D.C. His face was damp with sweat, in part because
of the city's seasonal humidity and in part because his plane had been
hours late. But the main reason for his anxiety was that he was coming to testify before men who were accusing him in front of the entire
country of having done something terribly wrong.

Moving through the news cameras, he made his way to the long
witness table and sat down in the middle one of three dark wooden
chairs. The chamber's large size, white marble walls, and rich neoclassical decor underscored the solemnity of the proceedings. Fluted
columns lined the walls, and massive crystal chandeliers and an elaborately carved and gilded ceiling loomed overhead. At each end of the
room, marooned on top of a wide cornice that stretched from one side
of the room to the other, sat an antique model sailing ship. Now in
permanent dry dock, the tiny vessels looked out onto a room full of
reporters, photographers, congressional staff members and aides,
ranking bureaucrats, political power brokers, and those members of
the public who had been first in line for the few available seats.

They hadn't been disappointed. The morning session had already
provided its store of drama. For months President Dwight David
Eisenhower, members of the cabinet, high-ranking federal officials,

and congressional leaders had been denouncing "real estate profi-
teers" who had used the Section 608 program as a vehicle to reap vast
windfall profits. Top FHA brass had lost their jobs and found themselves pilloried in the press, along with the 608 developers. Trump
had been horrified to see himself fingered in a *New York Times* list of
thirty-five metropolitan area builders accused of milking the government.[1] A front-page article in the *Brooklyn Eagle* charged him with
pocketing a $4,047,000 windfall from his government loans.[2]

Decrying what he called the scandal of the century, Senator
Homer Earl Capehart, an Indiana Republican and chairman of the
Senate Banking and Currency Committee, had now launched a full-
scale hearing, complete with explosive press conferences and dire-
sounding charges that produced lurid front-page headlines.[3] That
morning he had again denounced FHA builders for making exorbitant
sums at public expense. "Talk about your Teapot Dome," he declared
in a loud, penetrating voice, referring to the illegal oil leases on government land in the 1920s that had become a symbol of graft and corruption in high places. "They were Sunday school affairs compared
with this situation."[4] Then he spoke darkly of efforts to protect the
evildoers. There was heavy pressure on Congress to drop efforts to
curtail future excess housing profits, he said. But Capehart was res-
olute. In a firm voice he assured the nation that he would never
knuckle under.

For six days developers and industry leaders, subpoenaed from
around the country, had answered hostile questions about apartments
built under the now disgraced Section 608. One witness, a real estate
insurance broker from Norfolk who counted Fred Trump among his
clients, had a heart attack after being hauled in front of the committee.[5] The New Jersey builder who appeared immediately prior to Fred
Trump refused to testify, and his lawyer hotly defended his right to do
so. "We did nothing wrong," he shouted at Senator Capehart. "We're
not charged with the crime." Pounding the witness table, his face
flushed and perspiring from the camera lights, the attorney denounced Capehart for relying on "inference and innuendo" and
"shooting off his mouth" about alleged windfall profits by developers.[6] Now it was Fred Trump's turn to step up and defend himself
from public accusation.

Turning the housing shortage around had required an enormous effort by Fred Trump and other builders. In record time they put up nearly half a million apartments and received nationwide applause. Then, seemingly overnight, these public benefactors found themselves branded as greedy crooks. Once esteemed for having rescued veterans and their families, developers were now excoriated for having betrayed them. The reason was that in the course of providing desperately needed housing, they had become millionaires. Even more infuriating, they had used legal means—the gaping loopholes in government mortgage guarantees—to do so.

Like many of those builders, Trump was chagrined and humiliated. The scandal seemed to have come from nowhere. As he was receiving plaques for his civic contributions, obscure government functionaries whom he had never met or heard of were chasing rumors of a possible technical violation of the tax code. Casting a net that would haul in dozens of FHA officials and hundreds of developers, the functionaries had set out to prove their case. Later there could be indictments and formal judicial proceedings. At the moment, though, the accused faced trial in the court of public opinion. Some yelled and pounded tables. Others hung their heads in shame. Sitting before the committee that hot July day, Fred Trump looked directly at his accusers and politely but firmly insisted that he had simply participated in the same free enterprise system the war had been fought to defend.

—⁓—

Exactly three months earlier, FHA commissioner Guy Tilghman Orme Hollyday had taken the afternoon train from Washington, D.C., to New York City. He was headed to the Commodore Hotel, site of that year's annual convention of the Mortgage Bankers Association of America (MBA). A silver-haired patrician from Maryland, Hollyday was a World War I cavalry veteran, a mortgage banker and former MBA president, and, at sixty-one, a vigorous sportsman who managed a working farm in his spare time. A Democrat, he had switched allegiances in 1952 and organized local Democrats-for-Ike activities in Baltimore. After the election he received the FHA post courtesy of ex–MBA president Aksel Nielsen, the Denver banker who had been a close friend of Mamie Eisenhower's father and whose Colorado hunting lodge was Ike's favorite hideaway.[7]

En route to New York City that April day, Hollyday stopped to deliver a speech in Trenton, New Jersey. It went well, as all of his speeches did. On the way out he was summoned to the telephone. Sherman Adams, presidential chief of staff, was on the line. The message was short and stunning: Hollyday was canned. The cause: rampant abuses under FHA programs.[8]

The real estate industry responded with a howl of protest over the cavalier treatment given one of their best and brightest. Despite some lapses, industry leaders declared, the $3.4 billion mortgage insurance effort, which had ended three years before Hollyday came to Washington, built nearly half a million apartments.[9] But the government's problem was not what Hollyday had done. It was what he had not done, which was to clean house when he took office.[10] From all accounts, Hollyday was "a good Christian gentleman," as his boss, Housing and Home Finance Agency (HHFA) administrator Albert Cole, said when making the announcement of Hollyday's "resignation." He was also too generous, too naive, or both. Rather than routinely replacing his predecessor's top staff, he kept them on and believed what they told him. When their reassurances proved worthless, he had to pay.

For years Washingtonians had whispered about possible illegalities at the FHA.[11] In January 1950 *Architectural Forum*, a leading magazine in the building industry, denounced the program's builders for squeezing exorbitant profits and sacrificing quality.[12] But with Section 608 scheduled to expire in two months and builders scrambling to climb aboard the departing gravy train, no one within the FHA had time to consider the architects' complaints, much less respond. On the last day, recalled former FHA evaluator Ben Holloway, fifty new applications appeared on his desk.

Both inside and outside the FHA, the program's beneficiaries far outnumbered its critics. By 1949, as Fred Trump was making a major push on Beach Haven, the FHA had become the nation's builder, backing 70 percent of the apartment buildings started that year.[13] In turn, FHA activity underlay the jobs of three million workers in construction and three million more in building materials.[14] Most important, Section 608 worked. Whatever the ethics of its operations, returning veterans finally had a roof over their heads. Builders were happy. Veterans were happy. The FHA was happy. But deep within the Internal Revenue Service, an agent named Arnold J. Levine was not, because he suspected that the builders were getting away with not paying all the taxes they owed.

The situation was complex, as was the logic Levine applied to it. In brief, the FHA provided mortgage insurance according to estimates and schedules furnished directly by the builders, and banks in turn provided actual funds based on the amount of insurance provided. The FHA also pegged future rents, intended to pay off the mortgage, to the same estimated costs. If builders finished their projects more cheaply and faster than they originally proposed, there was no legal requirement to return the extra mortgage monies or to have the allowable rents lowered. Instead builders could use these unexpended funds to pay off the loan. Through this practice, known as "mortgaging out," they could save on interest payments and begin issuing dividends to the official sponsors of their projects, namely themselves. In addition, if they finished early, they could keep any rent they collected before the commencement of the official lease. The extra profits per apartment might seem small, but multiplied over thousands of tenants, it could run into millions of dollars. Moreover, these extra profits could qualify as capital gains instead of income—a major consideration in an era when those in the upper brackets faced income tax rates as high as 85 percent but paid only 25 percent on anything that could be called capital gains.

The sticking point was whether or not the builders' profits were really capital gains. To qualify, these proceeds would have to be of an unforeseen, noncustomary, onetime nature, or what is known as a "windfall." With so many builders reporting precisely the same kind of revenue, though, the IRS suspected it was looking not at a windfall, but at a regular business practice. Such a determination would turn the profits from mortgaging out into straight income and thus subject to the higher tax rate.

Enter Arnold Levine. A longtime IRS inspector, he was a chubby fellow, about five feet ten, with dark hair, a sallow complexion, and sharp features. He was also a frustrated fellow. He had gotten nowhere when he had pursued the matter with Ray Foley, Cole's predecessor. Foley had asked FHA commissioner Franklin D.

Richards how often builders mortgaged out, and Richards said hardly ever. That was what his top people had told him, and Richards, a conservative title lawyer and devout Mormon, was not in the habit of suspecting anyone of wrongdoing. After Eisenhower's election, the new FHA commissioner, Guy Hollyday, asked the same top people the question again, and heard the same response. Richards and Hollyday had believed them, but Levine did not.

One day in August 1952 Levine poked his nose into the office of an FHA staffer named Hilbert Fefferman.[15] A young lawyer from New York who specialized in drafting legislative proposals for the FHA, Fefferman had learned that mortgaging out was a serious problem when speaking with Charles Abrams, a prominent New York developer. He told Fefferman that his friends were mortgaging out right and left. Without naming his sources, Fefferman had promptly passed the story along to Ray Foley. Later he had given the same information to Albert Cole. But nothing happened. "We were sitting there trying to figure out what the hell to do about all these facts we had," Fefferman recounted years later. "I can't snitch on my sources, and the FHA people are stonewalling, and we're completely stuck. Then one day in walks the solution—wearing a trench coat, the whole bit—and his name is Agent Levine."

Each had only half the information necessary to determine whether mortgaging out was widespread. The FHA knew builders' estimates, because the agency used them for mortgage insurance, but it did not know the actual costs; the IRS had the actual costs, as reported on tax returns, but not the estimates. Thus the FHA knew how much Fred Trump had predicted he would spend to build Shore Haven and Beach Haven, and the IRS knew what he paid out to get the jobs done. Unlike tax returns, which were confidential information, FHA cost estimates were a matter of public record, and the IRS could have obtained them without Fefferman's assistance. But what the IRS couldn't get on its own was an understanding of how Section 608 mortgage insurance actually worked. Accordingly Fefferman suggested a way that he and Levine could help each other but protect builder confidentiality. They could average builder estimates and costs for each of the six FHA regions in the country and compare the results for an overall picture.

As it happened, however, neither Levine nor anyone else at the IRS had time to do the averaging. Instead, in mid-March 1954 Fefferman provided a list of the names, and Levine pulled the associated tax returns and, incredibly, simply cut off the corners with identifying information. On March 19 he gave the returns to Fefferman, leaving them in the same order in which they had been pulled—in other words, in the same order as the names on Fefferman's list. When Fefferman matched up his list to Levine's returns and checked the actual and estimated costs, he could hardly believe his eyes. He had his smoking gun.

In the past, he would have been uncertain what to do next. But now his boss was Housing and Home Finance Agency administrator Albert Cole, a square-jawed, conservative former congressman who wound up at the housing agency after losing a bid for reelection. Back when he was on the Hill, he had argued against every piece of pro-government housing legislation Fefferman had drafted. During the previous year, however, the two had spent time together on the SS *America* en route to a housing conference in Europe. "We argued all day and spent evenings discussing Orwell and Balzac," Fefferman recalled. "Cole's wife mended my garters. Al and I got to be friends on the crossing, and by the time he had served a year or two as head of the agency he was so pro-government housing that Eisenhower thought he'd gone native."

Armed with the IRS data, Fefferman triumphantly burst into Cole's office. "The FHA is either ignorant or covering up," Fefferman said, "and we can prove it." Because he and Cole did not want to violate taxpayer confidentiality, they simply reported to the White House that a tremendous amount of mortgaging out was going on. In Fefferman's view the scandal would eventually have come out. "Cole's head would have rolled if Arnold Levine hadn't come in," Fefferman said later. "But now Cole was a man who acted, while everybody else at the FHA was standing still."[16]

By the morning of April 12, as the unknowing Hollyday was headed to New York, tales of FHA-related misconduct were spreading through the Washington rumor mill. On Capitol Hill, Virginia Democratic senator Harry Flood Byrd, suspecting that the Republican administration would try to paint any FHA scandal as a Truman legacy, determined to launch his own exposé of the situation. As chair of the obscure Joint Committee on the Reduction of Non-Essential Federal Expenditures, he said that he would hold hearings himself.[17]

At the Justice Department, Attorney General Herbert Brownell Jr., whose own law firm, Lord, Day & Lord, had counseled many 608 developers to take the very capital gains route now under investigation, held a series of urgent meetings. Over the weekend he summoned Bill McKenna, a Los Angeles lawyer and fellow Yale Law School graduate. Lean and self-confident, with receding red hair that encircled his head like a monk's tonsure, McKenna had shown himself an unflinching investigator when he had worked for the House Joint Committee on Racketeering and faced down Jimmy Hoffa.

As soon as he got to his Washington hotel room, McKenna started in on an enormous stack of 608-related documents and read until dawn. "The stuff was fascinating," he said later. A World War II vet himself, he was particularly incensed that his fellow GIs had ended up paying higher rents to cover developers' mortgaging out. "When I finished reading, I told Eisenhower's people that the 608s were being terribly abused by people who must have had confidence their heads - weren't going to be lopped off. They would have been scared to do this kind of thing without some kind of arrangement, because Eisenhower didn't tolerate shenanigans. Somebody was getting paid off, and it had to be somebody in Washington."[18]

Early on the morning of April 12, Cole went to the White House and met with Eisenhower's chief of staff, Sherman Adams, a former governor of New Hampshire known as the Great Stone Face because of his stern, rectitudinous attitude.[19] Adams already knew from Brownell that Senator Byrd was investigating FHA abuses and likely to go public at any moment. Now Cole was telling him about hard evidence of widespread profiteering. Appalled, Adams immediately took Cole into the Oval Office. The president was at his desk, an oversize antique made from Lord Nelson's warship. As Eisenhower stood to greet them, Adams related Cole's allegations.

At that point, Cole later told McKenna, Eisenhower blew his top. His face turned bright red and he screamed, "Why haven't you fired those sons of bitches?" Then he told Cole and Adams to get rid of Hollyday by sundown.[20] They did. Shortly afterward, McKenna met with the president to explain the details. After McKenna went over the story several times, Eisenhower gave McKenna carte blanche to carry out an investigation and then headed off for opening day at Griffith Stadium, where he was scheduled to throw out the first ball for the Washington Senators.[21]

McKenna took a cab to FHA headquarters and set up shop. Within days he had put together a staff of more than one hundred people.[22] He soon learned that the desire of FHA officials to encourage builders and the desire of builders to be encouraged had produced behavior that was highly questionable and perhaps illegal. To keep the apartment total rising, for instance, the FHA allowed builders to calculate costs in terms of housing units, rather than by rooms. This change passed unremarked when approved in August 1948, but it made a huge difference to people like Fred Trump. Instead of roomy three- and four-bedroom apartments, he produced more one-bedrooms and studios. Architects complained that they were too small for families or even young couples, but the practice continued because it allowed builders to receive maximum estimated costs for the housing that was least expensive to produce.[23]

Other variations on FHA regulations included allowing the minimum room size and ventilation standards established by Miles Colean to become maximums—in other words, targets that builders were allowed to miss. Eager to boost total units built on their watch, some FHA staffers condoned ruses like running exposed beams across the ceiling of a large room and calling it two rooms and shaving a few inches off supposed room measurements so as to cut costs and shoehorn in extra units.

In return, said FHA veterans, grateful builders bestowed upon staffers small considerations: candy, gift certificates, the odd ten-dollar bill, and, at the Christmas party at FHA headquarters, ties for men, nylons for women, and magazine subscriptions for everyone.[24] "People in the FHA were busting their butts trying to get buildings up and, all things considered, doing a pretty good job of it, " Ben Holloway later recalled. "Everybody knew some people took gifts they shouldn't have and passed buildings for inspection they shouldn't have. Guys got cases of whiskey or TVs. My supervisor got a television even though he never watched it. But I never saw any real wrongdoing." In his view, a lot of the so-called scandal was "just a big goddamn joke."

Other participants had a less sanguine view. "Builders paid off FHA underwriters," one New York developer recounted many years afterward. "It was part of the cost of doing business. You couldn't get a mortgage unless you paid a fee." He recalled another builder who would come into the New York office and call in the underwriters. "The office partitions were part glass," the developer said. "You could see everything that was going on. It was understood that the underwriters would get theirs. And what did it matter to them if a builder got a higher mortgage commitment in exchange?"[25]

As McKenna dug into the agency, he found a disturbing pattern of interlocking relationships among lawyers, builders, and FHA officials.[26] Overall, developers had built more than 7,000 rental housing projects and made profits greater than the amount mandated by FHA mortgage insurance guidelines on 1,410, or about 1 out of 5. The total surplus profit was over $110 million, and Fred Trump had made more than $4 million of it, one of the biggest individual shares.[27] To builders such profits were a necessary and well-deserved incentive. To McKenna they were excessive and outrageous. And to the Republican administration, energetically wielding its new broom, they were a perfect example of the legacy left by the Democrats, the party of communism, corruption, and Korea.

In McKenna's view, the only possible explanation was something wrong at the top. Accordingly, he focused on Tom Grace, who had approved more 608 projects than any other FHA state commissioner in the country. There were plenty of explanations, among them that Grace's seventeen-year tenure in the job was longer than that of any other commissioner. In addition, New York City was already an apartment town, and many local developers had learned how to build quickly and on a large scale doing wartime construction in Norfolk. But to McKenna, what mattered most was that a New York law firm named Grace & Grace handled more FHA projects and more mortgaging out than any other firm in the country.[28] Tom Grace and his brother George had started the firm, and now George was the principal attorney.

In George's view there was no ethical problem in one brother/ partner having power of approval over applications submitted by the other brother/partner or in Tom's continued place on the firm's front door and at the top of its masthead. Because his brother was "inactive," George explained to the Senate Committee on Banking and Commerce, there was no conflict.[29] "Everyone knows that to get something done, you have to pass a little green," George said years later. "It's been that way ever since God put green on this earth. And it was that way with FHA and 608." Like most government programs, he said, 608 was "designed to help someone get ahead, to make money. But the developers were the ones who made a lot of money. I just got a fee." With his brother serving as state FHA director, George acknowledged, "some people were ready to come and drop an envelope of money on my desk. But they didn't need to. My brother was honest, and I was like Caesar's wife. I probably lost rather than gained business for clients."[30] Still, Tom had resigned from the FHA in August 1952 to avoid conflict-of-interest charges.

To McKenna the resignation did not end the matter. He vigilantly scrutinized anyone who had crossed the brothers' path and noticed a man who was a political associate, a patron at their restaurant, and a recipient of much FHA largesse: Fred Trump. Indeed, the developer and the two brothers went way back. Soon after his FHA appointment, Tom Grace was the guest of honor at the opening of Fred Trump's first project, and Grace had continued sending FHA mortgage insurance the builder's way. More recently, the Redevelopment Builders of New York, a trade group organized and chaired by Fred Trump, had hired George Grace, and Fred Trump was also an investor in a federally funded slum clearance project in Brooklyn that paid Grace & Grace $20,000 as a retainer.[31]

All of which, George insisted, was meaningless. The whole idea of the Redevelopment Builders, he later said, was "a joke." As he described it, people who did redevelopment projects got together, put up $1 for each unit they had built, and hired Grace as their lawyer. "When government attorneys said they were going to subpoena the records of the group," he said, "I said, 'Fine,' and sent over the file. It was just old bank statements—that's all there was. That was the end of that one." He was untroubled by the apparent implication that either he was lying or the builders paid him well for little or no work, and he was equally dismissive of his relationship with Fred Trump. "Freddy was what I call 'a phoner,'" he said. "He was the kind of guy who calls a lot and always says I just have to check something out. Twenty minutes later you're still on the phone, but you can't bill them. That was Freddy all right."[32]

But George Grace could not dismiss McKenna's other findings: the fees that had not been recorded in Grace & Grace accounts, the Grace & Grace checks made out to "cash," the Grace & Grace checks that were missing from the books, the tens of thousands of dollars for which there was no accounting. Nor could George explain the large checks he had made out to another real estate lawyer named Abraham Traub.

The firm Dreyer & Traub was a Court Street fixture in Brooklyn. Senior partner Alfonso Dreyer had died before the FHA started, but junior partner Abe Traub had made the firm into Grace & Grace's only significant competition for FHA business. A big man with a big voice, big features, and a big head of wavy gray hair, Traub was known for his remarkable energy. Clients picked him up at home before dawn and conferred with him on the way to his morning stop at the Italian barbershop on Court Street. There more clients would be waiting, whispering in his ear as he walked, freshly shaven, to his office.[33]

Traub also had a reputation for being able to sit down in a conference room filled with bankers and lawyers and close a deal. "No matter how many roadblockers there were, he'd come up with a solution," said Murray Felton, a former partner at Dreyer & Traub. In part this was because to make a deal work, he occasionally guaranteed a loan himself, a practice that took him to the brink of ruin in 1948. He disappeared for a week, then reappeared in a frantic phone call to a client from a hotel room in Philadelphia. He was about to jump out of a window, he said. His friends and clients lent him enough to avoid bankruptcy.[34]

By the middle of 1954 Traub was again in trouble. After months of stalling, he grudgingly handed over some of his books to McKenna. They showed that he was probably closer to Clyde L. Powell, the former FHA assistant commissioner in charge of rental housing, than any other lawyer in the country. He and Powell had talked on the phone at least once a week for years, and they visted each other often. The books also showed over $1 million in unaccounted-for dispersals and a number of blank check stubs. Like George Grace, Traub was astonished to find such records missing and was at a loss to account for them. To William McKenna, though, there was no mystery. He was sure the two lawyers had used funds from 608 builders in New York to pay off Clyde Powell, and he set about to prove it.

Powell, a short, baby-faced midwesterner, was known as a natty dresser and a strong-willed administrator. "He was really a tyrant," said FHA staffer Alex Naclerio. "When he visited the New York office, everyone ducked and ran for cover."[35] Under Powell's management, though, builders produced housing on time and on budget. As McKenna discovered, Powell managed this impressive achievement despite a lengthy criminal past that included charges for check fraud and embezzlement and a conviction for jewel theft. He had also lost large sums at the track, where he was a habitual gambler. In recent years he had deposited in his bank account more than $100,000 for which he had no explanation. McKenna called him "the czar of the nation's postwar rental housing program" and charged that the money came from bribes.[36]

Few disagreed. "Powell was on the taking side," said Philip Birnbaum, an architect for many prominent New York builders, including Fred Trump and, later, his son Donald. "He was a terrific actor. He'd come to New York and he'd look at a project and say, 'Let me think about it, you need to make changes.' But it was all prearranged."[37] Likewise, Traub's former law partner Murray Felton recalled Powell as "one of Abe Traub's major sources in 608s. There's no doubt in my mind that plenty of money was exchanged there." Sometimes Powell asked builders to place bets for him and repaid them only if the horse won. Sometimes he offered to place a bet himself and pocketed it instead. Sometimes he pressured others to pay back his gambling debts. But the result was always the same: bigger mortgages, windfall profits, and higher rents for the public.[38]

———— ᨊ ————

As one of the biggest 608 builders in the city that was at the center of McKenna's inquiry, Fred Trump would inevitably have come under scrutiny. As a developer who had a long history with the Graces and Abe Traub, he came under further investigation. And as someone who had dealt directly with Clyde Powell, Trump ended up high on the list of targets in the report McKenna prepared for the Senate investigation chaired by Homer Capehart.

Powell, McKenna charged, had showered personal attention and approval on Trump's projects. In 1949 Powell had signed off on a decision to let Trump off the hook when he left out some numbers during a routine audit of the Shore Haven books.[39] Trump had also received special permission to start Beach Haven before the loans to finance it were closed. This meant he could finish the buildings six months before the first loan payments were due, and the $1.7 million in rent that he collected in the interim went directly to him.[40]

In his written report, McKenna cited Trump several times for serious unethical behavior.[41] During his lead-off testimony before the Senate Committee on Banking and Currency, he used Trump as an example of the abuses under investigation. It was an opinion Capehart seemed to share. As McKenna spoke, the committee chair told one reporter in an aside that Trump's actions at Beach Haven had been "nauseous."[42]

Now, facing the cameras and the assembled senators, it was Fred Trump's turn to confront his critics and, especially, Capehart. At his side as he sat before the committee were Matthew Tosti, his usual attorney, and Orrin Grimmell Judd, a prominent New York Republican who had been New York's solicitor general under Governor Thomas Edmund Dewey.[43] But Judd's Republican credentials seemed to make little difference to the Indiana legislator who would conduct the inquiry.

Despite differences in appearance and style, the fat, rumpled Homer Capehart and the slender, well-dressed Fred Trump actually had much in common. Both had ended their formal education with high school graduation, spent some time on the financial ropes during the Depression, and emerged as millionaires. Both had an aptitude for innovation, the builder for putting up housing better, cheaper, and faster than most of the competition, the senator for producing jukeboxes and radios. Both were also skillful salesmen; the builder sold everything he ever put up, and *Fortune* dubbed the senator "one of the highest-powered, highest-pressure salesmen this country has ever produced."[44]

In short, both were experienced and successful entrepreneurs who knew how the business world operates. Indeed, given that Capehart's son was a lawyer who specialized in 608 business and that the senator himself had been involved with home building and mortgage banking for decades, it seems unlikely that he was as naive about mortgaging out as he claimed. His dramatic look of shock as he heard how Fred Trump had pocketed the difference between the estimated and actual cost was surely as calculated as his decision to spread the hearings over several months and hold them in six different cities. In the process, he produced such an ongoing spectacle that the nascent television networks broadcast some of the hearings live, a rare event at the time.

The committee itself did no independent investigation and instead depended on McKenna's spadework. At hearings, committee lawyer William Simon's job was to grill witnesses while Capehart listened. "He was a plain old shoe," said Simon, a corporate attorney from Chicago. "No airs, no pretensions. When he asked questions, it was because he didn't like the answers I was getting." Unfortunately for Fred Trump, when he was on the stand, Capehart asked a lot of questions.

As with most of the witnesses, much of the dialogue between builder and committee chairman had to do with differences of definition. Repeatedly Simon asked about such seemingly clear-cut matters as land costs, construction costs, contractor's fees, architect's fees, materials, and taxes. And just as repeatedly Fred Trump and his lawyers said these matters were anything but clear and that the date, the time, the place, the people involved, and any number of other details had to be specified before the builder could answer.

Take the issue of land cost. Trump bought the land for Beach Haven in 1944 and 1945 from two real estate companies and the city of New York for a total of $34,500. But this sum, the purchase price, did not include broker's commissions, surveyor's bills, back taxes, back assessments, and penalties for those taxes and assessments. When all these charges were included, the cost of the land came to about $180,000. This was not the same as the value of the land when construction actually commenced, which the IRS pegged at $260,000. It was also not the same as the value of the land after construction, which the FHA estimated at $1.5 million, or about forty-three times more than the original purchase price.

Worse, Beach Haven's buildings and land were not owned in common. Six different corporations owned the buildings, but the area under them belonged to a trust administered for the benefit of Trump's five children by William Walter, Fred Trump's brother-in-law. The trust had leased the land for ninety-nine years to the corporations, which paid an annual rent of $60,000—almost twice the purchase price. Such an arrangement seemed outrageous to Simon and Capehart. It was even more infuriating that although federal guarantees had enabled projects that made the acreage worth forty-three times what Fred Trump had paid for it, he still owned the land.

It was bad enough, the counsel and the senator argued, that FHA mortgage insurance had been given on the basis of estimated costs, rather than actual costs, allowing builders to mortgage out and reap staggering profits. But in this case the builder had managed to make an end run around provisions that were already almost criminally generous. He had noticed that Section 608 assumed that building and land ownership went together and granted mortgage insurance on this basis but did not actually require it. What, Capehart asked, did Fred Trump have to say about such a bold-faced attempt to avoid the intent of this benevolent program?

Doing so, Fred Trump replied, allowed him to make larger rooms and better apartments. Infuriated, Capehart sputtered and then concluded weakly, "It is not a complaint against him [Trump], particularly, it is a complaint against FHA, it is a complaint against the whole business."

For the rest of the afternoon Simon and Capehart continued to point at disparities between estimates and actual costs, and Fred Trump continued to justify them. Asked whether he was entitled to the general contractor's fee, supposedly a separate subcontract, when he had done that job himself, Trump made an analogy to the job of a tailor. Whether the tailor himself does all the work of making a suit or has an assistant do it, he said, the suit is worth the same and the tailor is entitled to charge the same price. Likewise Trump pointed out that when he estimated the architect's fee at 5 percent of the total cost (the maximum allowable under FHA guidelines), but paid less than 1 percent (as did most builders), he had broken no rules.

As to the charge of pocketing $4 million in surplus profits, Trump angrily insisted that he had done nothing of the kind. The accusation, he said, was "very wrong, and it hurts me. The only thing I am happy about is that it is not true."[45] Because of this baseless accusation, he said truthfully, tenants were trying to withhold rent, and he was suffering "untold damage to my standing and reputation."[46] Yes, there was $4 million. Yes, it was sitting in the bank. Yes, Trump had loaned some of it to himself and paid it back. But, he insisted, he had not paid himself from this money or withdrawn it or pocketed it, so he was not a profiteer.

Technically, at least, his explanation was accurate. As long as the money remained deposited in the Beach Haven account, it served as a reserve, available to pay off the mortgage in case of a default. If Trump withdrew this $4 million, then it would be considered a windfall profit. But until then it was not.

Finally Simon threw up his hands in frustration and asked whether the original estimates—the numbers on which the FHA's entire commitment was based—meant anything at all. It was the moment Fred Trump had been waiting for. "The big problem is, when you file with FHA, it takes from six months to a year to get a commitment," he said. "Now, no one knows what is going to happen in that six months to a year. I would say six months is a very, very short time [for approval, so] we don't know what we are up against." Because there could be inflation, he said, a builder must build in a cushion to cover contingencies. He may be able to do the architectural supervision himself and pay the designers less, but, for example, tile for the bathroom could cost twice what he expected.

All true. Indeed, contingencies generally did lead to higher costs for developers. But this had not happened. To begin with, the projects were so big that they had created economies of scale that the FHA had not expected. The per-unit cost of appliances, for example, was far less if ordered in the hundreds or the thousands than one by one. More important, though, the program took place in an economy that was in mild deflation—an unexpected contingency, and one that turned everything upside down.

Prices had risen sharply after World War II, just as they had after World War I, but unlike the earlier era, they had not come back down. Worried about shortages and further inflation, manufacturers began increasing inventories of supplies for fear that they would cost much more on the morrow, and builders obtained FHA mortgage guarantees for maximum amounts. "It was just like shooting ahead of a moving target, such as a plane," Hilbert Fefferman later explained. "With maximum mortgages we were shooting ahead of the inflation we expected."

But no shortages materialized, manufacturers found themselves stuck with huge inventories, and prices went down. As time went by, goods and services cost less, not more, than budgeted. For most builders this meant that actual costs turned out to be at least somewhat lower than the estimated costs. For efficient, experienced builders like Fred Trump, they were a lot lower.[47] And what had been prudent contingency planning by the FHA now seemed shortsighted and irresponsible.

In a sense, good fortune had smiled on Fred Trump and the other 608 developers. What outraged McKenna was that they had pocketed the rewards of this serendipity rather than sharing them with the public and, especially, with veterans. "An honest person would have applied the unexpected extra profit against the mortgage," McKenna said later. "That would have lowered the rent. Instead, these builders raised the rent by getting the maximum mortgage and then mortgaging out. These vets, who had risked their lives for their country, had barely enough to feed their babies. The whole idea was to provide cheap housing to them while they went to school, which was why charging them higher rents seemed to me so wrong and what made Eisenhower so mad."

To Hilbert Fefferman, though, the real problem was not the developers, but the laws he had helped write. "We were at fault for not requiring actual cost certification at the end of construction," he said. "If Trump could build more cheaply than he estimated, more power to him, providing he built a good house. The drop in actual cost created a windfall we could have prevented with a better law. I'd give him a pat on the back, not a kick in the teeth." In Fefferman's view, any kicks should go instead to Capehart and his committee. "Putting Trump before a camera, asking him things they already knew, implying he broke the law when he was only the beneficiary of a change from inflation to deflation, is demagoguery at its worst," Fefferman said. "Trump created the value. That's all that matters. That's what free enterprise means."

Or, at least, that was how Fred Trump chose to interpret it. Curiously, it was also the way Homer Capehart had once interpreted it. In the past he had been a loyal supporter of Section 608. Each time it had come before the Senate for extension and expansion, he had voted aye.[48] Now, however, no one mentioned his voting record.

But perhaps the memory of how Section 608 had come about had not altogether faded from his mind. After the cameras were off and the reporters were gone, perhaps he was able to recall how he had championed the program at its inception, how he had dismissed critics who had testified that the program's loopholes were dangerously large. Perhaps that's why late on that same July afternoon in 1954, after the Senate Committee on Banking and Currency had recessed for the day and he had gone to National Airport to catch a plane and saw Fred Trump across the lobby, he called out to him.

"Fred!" Capehart yelled. "Hey, Fred! Keep up the good work. We need that housing, you know."[49]

CHAPTER THIRTEEN

CLASHING VISIONS

Nearly two decades after Friedrich Trump came to America and a year before his first son, Fred, was born, another boy landed at New York Harbor. Just over five feet tall, with thick dark hair and large brown eyes, he was fifteen, a year younger than Friedrich had been upon his arrival. Like Friedrich, he had traveled alone and left behind his family, his homeland, and his obligation to enter into his country's military service. And he, too, did not intend to return.[1]

His name was Abraham Eli Kazan, and the country he left was Russia. In the coming decades, he, like Fred Trump, would become a real estate developer in New York, building apartments in a city with a desperate need for housing. In the late 1950s the two men each sought to build on the same stretch of Coney Island. Located at the southern tip of Brooklyn, the site was the object of a long and bitter struggle between Kazan and Trump that eventually entangled the highest levels of city government. But it was more than a battle between two well-connected businessmen. Trump and Kazan were leaders in two separate movements battling for effective control of the way the city would grow—and because New York City was a bellwether for the rest of the nation, the way that cities all over the country would grow. Ultimately, on this patch of Coney Island, not far from the famous amusement rides, Fred Trump helped carve the template of the urban future.

Jewish by birth, Kazan grew up outside Kiev. His father managed a large estate owned by a general in the czar's army. In 1904 Russia and Japan went to war, and Russian commanders, who had been supremely confident of their military superiority, soon found themselves on the losing end. Reeling in shock, they rushed troops to the front, hoping to turn the tide in their favor by sending out waves of human cannon fodder. Kazan, who was liable to conscription, had no intention of dying on the front. Not waiting for the army's agents to appear, he traveled to the French port of Cherbourg and boarded a transatlantic vessel called the *Aurania*. His only contact in New York was a distant relative. Unlike Friedrich, who was greeted upon his arrival by his older sister, young Kazan had to cool his heels at immigration for three long days before the relative could take a day off from work and claim him. Kazan then moved in with him in a Lower East Side flat just blocks from Friedrich's first address. Like many new immigrants, he had no marketable skills, only a rudimentary education, and few words of English. This fitted him for work in the rag trade, and he became an errand boy at the International Ladies' Garment Workers' Union.[2]

As Friedrich, giving way to the pleas of his homesick young bride, was preparing his first futile effort to migrate back to Germany, Kazan was settling in to stay. Indeed, the rest of his family crossed the ocean within a few years. For a while the youth joined his widower father and his siblings on a farm in southern New Jersey. But rural life and his father's religious orthodoxy held little attraction for young Kazan, who had become a thoroughly secular city dweller. He returned to New York City and by 1918 had become a householder, a husband, and a father.

At that time he was financial secretary of the Joint Board of the Amalgamated Clothing Workers, which was the organization for workers who made men's garments. During and after World War I, when sugar and flour were scarce and expensive, Kazan organized union buying clubs to obtain these staples at wholesale prices. Eventually the clubs evolved into a credit union, a welcome innovation in an era when consumer credit was not readily available elsewhere.

Encouraged by this success, Kazan focused on another postwar shortage, the lack of affordable homes for poor working families. With a small group—a knee pants maker, a coat tailor, a cloth cutter,

a millinery worker, a shirt cutter, and several midlevel union officials—he met in a tiny space next to the freight elevator at union
headquarters. Just as the buying clubs had cut the price of staples by
eliminating the retail grocer, the group decided to cut the price of
housing by eliminating commercial builders and landlords. Instead of
paying private companies to construct and maintain their homes,
they would become a species of co-owners that they called "tenant-
cooperators." Pooling their money, they would form a union cooperative that would build and run the places where they lived. When
tenant-cooperators moved out, the co-op would refund the money
they had put in and recruit replacements, who would in turn add
their share of funds to the common pool.

Unfortunately Kazan's idealistic little band had no resources, no
experience in housing, and a plan so novel and untried that they were
sure the union would reject it if they asked for support. Instead they
simply incorporated themselves as the ACW Corporation, choosing
the union's initials, as Kazan later wrote in an unpublished autobiography, "to give the impression we had a Big Brother behind us in this
effort." Obtaining affordable property—they finally located a parcel
near the end of the subway line in the Bronx—took several years.
Meanwhile many within the union scoffed at Kazan's grandiose plans
as financially unrealistic. "Even close friends at the union used to
make fun of me," he wrote, "saying that a co-op house would last
from Monday to Thursday."

Only in 1926 did the situation begin to change. Governor Al
Smith, whose own impoverished childhood gave him a strong bond
with the ill housed and the needy, proposed giving state tax abatements on new housing when owners agreed to limit profits and forgo
raising rents. When Smith's measure passed, the union endorsed
Kazan's group.[3] The abatement was given, and the next fall the first
Amalgamated Houses opened.[4] On a cold, rainy November day, garment workers slogged through what seemed an endless expanse of
mud to move into 6 five-story buildings clustered around a large
courtyard. Soon Kazan added more buildings to the campus Gothic-
style complex and put up a second building, also called Amalgamated
Houses, on Manhattan's Lower East Side. When the Depression
forced him to suspend building, he had constructed a total of 856 low-
cost cooperative apartments.[5]

The Depression also forced Fred Trump, who had so far done only privately financed construction, to stop building. But when the first federal housing assistance appeared in the mid-1930s, in the form of FHA mortgage insurance, he was able to move back into development almost immediately. By contrast, Kazan spent the 1930s keeping what he had already built afloat.[6] Ultimately both Amalgamated Houses survived, in large part because those who were still employed chipped in to help those who were not. On Sunday mornings an elementary school student named Harold Ostroff had a job delivering staples to families who were destitute. "I would put the bag down in front of the apartment door, ring the bell, and run," Ostroff remembered afterward. "There was a committee that ferreted out who was desperate, but to protect people's dignity everything was done anonymously." After the war Kazan returned to construction and, like Fred Trump, used government programs for large apartment complexes. Because his projects, in the Bronx and on the Lower East Side, did not fit FHA categories, he did not receive mortgage insurance but instead continued to rely on state and city tax abatements.[7]

Although Kazan's goal was to keep charges for tenants low rather than profits high, he pressed as hard as Fred Trump to save money. A favorite target for economizing was the electric bill, which he held down by building his own generators and being ever vigilant about ways to curb kilowatt usage. "Once he asked my wife why she couldn't get along with just one kitchen ceiling fixture," Donald Martin, a longtime Kazan associate, recalled years later. "His eyes lit up at the thought of all he could save with one less bulb per apartment." Frugality also dictated the installation of only two elevators per building, regardless of the number of residents, and making them what was called "skip-stop," meaning that one elevator stopped on even floors and the other on odd floors. Such an arrangement was annoying to tenants but allowed the use of low-power elevator motors.

For his first postwar project, Hillman Houses, an eight-hundred-unit complex on the Lower East Side, Kazan asked for help from a new source: City Construction Commission head Robert Moses, who was a dominant figure in New York politics and well launched on a career of reshaping the city's landscape through massive slum clearance and highway projects.[8] A towering, Yale-educated Republican, Moses was not impressed by the short, slight union builder, who had a thick Russian accent, a minimal education, and socialist ideas. When the patrician commissioner learned that Kazan, who did not know how to drive, had asked his architect to take him to Moses's headquarters, he scoffed at the immigrant developer for not having a private car and chauffeur.[9] Hillman Houses, Moses declared, was "speculation," "without merit," and "preposterous," and he refused to provide any support.[10] But after Kazan finished the project at the low cost he had promised, Moses recognized him as a builder who could be relied on.

Having the backing of Robert Moses—acknowledged by even his most bitter critic, Lewis Mumford, as having more influence on American cities than anyone else in the twentieth century[11]—was a major coup for Kazan. Over the years that followed, Moses earmarked for Kazan a number of development sites that qualified for the federal urban slum clearance program known as Title I.[12] Among them was a sixty-one-acre plot of land, much of it vacant, on Coney Island. Kazan was thrilled. He immediately envisioned the world's largest cooperative, a huge complex that would contain 12 twenty-story buildings and more than five thousand apartments, and proposed naming it after a founder of the American cooperative movement, Dr. James Peter Warbasse.[13] The official sponsor of Warbasse Houses would be the United Housing Foundation (UHF), a nonprofit corporation established by Kazan when the Amalgamated Clothing Workers Union moved out of the housing field.[14] But just as UHF was about to apply for final approval and city real estate tax exemption, a rival claimant—the first in Kazan's entire building career—stepped forward.

Fred Trump was still the biggest builder in Brooklyn, but the past three years had taken a toll. During the summer of 1954 one newspaper article after another had broadcast to the world the Capehart committee's claims that he had profiteered on postwar housing. Although his oldest son, Fred Jr., passed off the stories by joking to friends that his father was going to hole up in the Caribbean to avoid testifying before Congress, the headlines were devastating to the Trumps.[15] According to a classmate of Maryanne Trump, then starting her first year in college, the accusations seemed to hang like a dark cloud over the family.[16] Worse yet, the scandal also cast a long shadow over Fred Trump's business interests. Beach Haven tenants were suing for rent rollbacks, the FHA was threatening to take over Shore Haven, and the agency put Fred Trump on its blacklist for future work. As a result, he could not obtain federal financing for his next major project, an apartment complex on the site of Luna Park, a celebrated Coney Island amusement center that had burned down ten years earlier.[17]

Fred Trump had kept busy. He produced a handful of smaller, privately financed apartment buildings in his home borough of Queens and gave them elegant English names like Saxony and Wexford. He put in the winning bid for a foreclosed 608 development that was one of the biggest apartment complexes on Staten Island.[18] He built University Towers, his first Title I project and part of the newly developed Brooklyn Civic Center. But none of these projects was close to the scale he'd had in mind. To reestablish himself and his good name, he needed to do something else. Something big. Then he learned about the sixty-one-acre parcel in Coney Island.

—⁓—

On August 12, 1957, with no prior notice of his intentions and only two days before UHF was scheduled to present its Warbasse plans at a City Planning Commission hearing, Fred Trump filed a formal objection. His verbal assault began at the hearing, which he attended with attorney Richard Charles. In a two-page statement read by Charles, he declared that the UHF proposal was an "outright giveaway" that would allow "a favorite few"—that is, 5,184 union families—to avoid paying their full share of taxes. Unlike his own projects, Trump claimed, Warbasse would take "money out of the pocket" of taxpayers and ask them "to subsidize more luxurious housing than they themselves enjoy."

Abraham Kazan was dumbfounded. What should have been a routine event was a fiasco. The approvals process for the UHF's most ambitious development skidded to a halt. In press releases and letters to officials, Trump and Kazan attacked each other's positions and boosted their own. Eventually Trump offered to match Kazan's proposal. He would build the same number of apartments in the same number of buildings on the same site, provide equivalent shopping facilities, and use the same form of partial tax abatement, which was

available under a state program called the Redevelopment Companies
Law. But he would take $2.2 million less in tax abatements than
Kazan, making up the difference by charging higher rents to tenants.

Charges and countercharges flew back and forth. Numerous ad-
justments to the proposals were announced, but the basic differences
remained unchanged. Trump's proposition included less tax abatement, higher rents, and no tenant investment, whereas that from
Kazan stipulated higher tax abatements, lower rents, and tenant
down payments of $500 a room.[19]

The stalemate continued for more than two years. On one side
were Brooklyn's biggest builder and his allies, a host of borough
politicians determined to protect one of Brooklyn's own against an in-
vader. Vigorously portraying himself as the embattled defender of free
enterprise, Fred Trump claimed repeatedly that low rents at Warbasse
would pull tenants from Shore Haven and Beach Haven, even though
these projects had long waiting lists and Warbasse's $500-per-room
deposit would discourage defection from Trump's buildings. On the
other side stood Abraham Kazan, nearly alone, doggedly repeating
that because he was offering homes to families who could not afford
Fred Trump's rents, he needn't stoop to partisan politics and alliance
building. "Housing should not be subject to politics," he wrote. "It's
too basic."

A noble stand, but unviable now that Kazan was alone. In earlier
UHF projects he had the support of the unions and Moses. Given this
powerful backing, politicians had gone along with the idea of projects
on which no one made money. But the labor unions were not initial
sponsors on Warbasse,[20] and Kazan had opted not to go for the Title I
financing that would have brought the project under Moses's oversight. The ostensible reason was that the land cost was so low, it was
unnecessary.[21] The real reason, however, was that it would be impossible to involve Moses without antagonizing Mayor Robert Wagner,
who was increasingly unhappy about the commissioner's extraordinary power over city affairs.

When Kazan had first begun planning Warbasse, city comptroller
Larry Gerosa and City Planning Commission head James Felt had
called the UHF head into Felt's office and read him the riot act. "They
wanted it clear that the dogged and fiery Moses was not to have War-

basse as another of his huge list of metropolitan credits," Kazan later recalled. "Not caring very much who got credit for what, so long as housing was getting built, and thinking that these men should fight out their own political battles, I went along."[22]

Kazan's single-mindedness, heretofore an asset, would now prove his undoing. Although he realized that Moses did not want to leave Warbasse out of the Title I program, he never asked why. Nor did he take heed when Moses noted that there might be political problems if Kazan operated without his protection, including "a stiff fight from a builder named Trump."[23] And Kazan seemed oblivious of the fact that he was constructing a huge project in Brooklyn, a place he had never worked before and one where Fred Trump had been consolidating his political ties for a quarter of a century. Still a regular at fundraising events, the Brooklyn builder stayed in constant touch with the borough's political movers and shakers and had recently introduced himself to the new Democratic county leader with a $1,000 check.

This local power base had not protected Fred Trump against the Capehart committee's accusations, but after the probe was over, Brooklyn's political heavies remained at his side. Among the most supportive was John Cashmore, the longtime Brooklyn borough president. He had gotten to know Fred Trump while lunching with the Knights of the Round Table at the Court Cafe, and the two had worked together on the centerpiece of Cashmore's twenty-year administration, the new Brooklyn Civic Center.[24]

But what may have been the strongest connection between Cashmore and Trump came from yet another quarter: Abraham Maurice Lindenbaum, a genial real estate lawyer who was one of the best fixers in the history of Brooklyn politics.[25] Lindenbaum, dubbed "Bunny" because of his rotund appearance and soft, warm manner, was famous for never raising his voice or openly disparaging anyone. "Whenever he saw you, he'd have his arm around your shoulder in a second," said one political insider. Another described him as looking as though he always wore bedroom slippers.[26] In 1949, after more than a decade at the commercial insurance company used by most Brooklyn landlords and years of dutiful doorbell ringing for the Madison Club, Lindenbaum had struck out on his own with another lawyer, Sidney Young.

Although their first office was in a single room so tiny that Young's desk was in the closet, their first client was Fred Trump. With Lindenbaum's talent for getting things done, the firm quickly grew to occupy an entire floor at 16 Court Street, the preeminent address for anyone involved in commercial real estate in Brooklyn.[27]

There Lindenbaum & Young serviced a growing number of Brooklyn real estate potentates. Young had cut his legal teeth working with Abe Traub, the other major fixer of the era, and he specialized in going before tax commissioners to appeal real estate taxes, a little-known maneuver that saved significant sums for Fred Trump.[28] Bunny's talent was putting people who could help each other in contact, occasionally by introducing them at his office.[29] More often Lindenbaum, the consummate rainmaker, the man who could always explain why what he wanted was good for you, was touching base at Borough Hall and City Hall, holding lunchtime meetings at the 21 Club, an elegant, high-profile restaurant in midtown Manhattan, and juggling his numerous professional and civic posts.[30] In January 1956 Mayor Wagner appointed him a member of the New York City Housing Authority. Four days later that same body approved the purchase from Fred Trump of the Luna Park site for a housing project.[31]

The idealistic Kazan detested fixers like Lindenbaum and Traub and insisted virtuously that good, low-cost housing for moderate-income families should make sense to every politician. But to the politicians who were doing the deciding, housing was a business, not a sacred trust. Kazan was just another operator building up a power base, and his pious words about not making trade-offs were simply a sign that he had gotten too big for his britches.[32] Pro-Warbasse petitions signed by more than three thousand prospective residents, the pro-Warbasse crowd that overflowed a Board of Estimate hearing on the dispute, and even labor leaders' phone calls to the Brooklyn borough president seemed to have no impact.[33] When Kazan finally obtained an appointment with Cashmore, he refused to commit himself about the site and instead talked for an hour about his support for the new state of Israel and how good a friend he was to the Jews.

Cashmore sat on the Board of Estimate with the other borough presidents, the city comptroller, and the mayor. Twelve times Cashmore exercised his prerogative as president of the affected borough to block consideration of the UHF tax abatement.[34] Each time Mayor Robert Wagner, a Kazan ally in the past, refused to confront Cashmore. Whether or not mayoral intervention would have helped was unclear; what was clear was that Wagner himself needed help on a far more pressing problem, the overwhelming presence and power of Robert Moses. Because Kazan's backing came from Manhattan and the Bronx, areas where the mayor was already strong, backing him would not advance Wagner's own anti-Moses agenda. Fred Trump, on the other hand, had the support of political forces in Brooklyn, the borough in which the mayor was weakest. If Wagner was ever to loosen Moses's hold on New York City, he needed to be able to trade a favor with Fred Trump's allies.

Put simply, to build up capital in the favor bank, he would have to obtain approval for Trump. This meant that he would have to produce another two ayes on the Board of Estimate, and the Manhattan and Bronx borough presidents would not provide them. The only possible source was the snowy-haired, Italian-born millionaire Larry Gerosa, who by virtue of his position as city comptroller had two votes. A combative figure who liked to boast that he never ran away from a fight, Gerosa was already on record as backing Kazan. On the other hand, he shared Wagner's antipathy to Moses.[35]

Possibly with the help of Bunny Lindenbaum, Wagner reflected on these complicated and pertinent facts. Then he sent a delegation to Los Caballeros Ranch, the resort in Arizona where Gerosa was vacationing, to explain to him why backing Trump was good. Apparently the delegation was persuasive, for Gerosa came home on the return flight. With Gerosa's support for Kazan eliminated and no possibility of Cashmore withdrawing his opposition, the UHF head agreed to a compromise. The new plan, reportedly worked out with the help of Robert Moses and Gerosa's successor as city comptroller, Abe Beame, divided the site, with the better and larger portion going to Fred Trump for a mix of rental and co-op units.[36]

Nine days after final Board of Estimate approvals on the Trump and UHF projects, Bunny Lindenbaum replaced Moses on the City Planning Commission. Pushed aside by Wagner, Robert Moses went off to become president of the World's Fair, scheduled for Queens in 1964. And the next fall, when Robert Wagner launched his third mayoral campaign as an independent and reformist effort, one reason he felt confident enough to do so was that he seemed to have found favor in Brooklyn at last.

———

Fred Trump had launched his attack with the complaint that tax abatements forced city taxpayers who did not live in Warbasse to foot the bill for it. A year later he reversed directions and went after the same tax abatements for the complex he would call Trump Village. For a while it seemed that outside taxpayers would be footing the bill for both projects. Then, not long after the final compromise between Trump and Kazan was hammered out, yet another program would render moot the debate over who should pay for middle-income housing. A whole new method of financing would come into being, pouring immense sums into construction and altering methods of public finance across the nation.

Until November 1958, such a program would have been unthinkable. But that fall, while Fred Trump and Abraham Kazan were duking it out over who would develop some five dozen acres in Brooklyn, a battle was under way elsewhere for who would control the 49,112 square miles that constitute New York State. The incumbent governor, William Averill Harriman, the scion of a wealthy railroad family, was facing a challenge from Nelson Aldrich Rockefeller, the scion of the even wealthier family that founded Standard Oil. Ultimately Harriman, a stiff, sixty-six-year-old patrician, was no match for the exuberant fifty-year-old Rockefeller. Week after week a grinning Rocky rolled up his shirtsleeves, plunged into the crowds, and greeted everyone he saw with, "Hiya, fella!" On November 4, 1958, voters went to the polls and elected him governor. In the years that followed, he would show himself to be the most energetic, ruthless, and determined politician the state had seen since the young Robert Moses.

Unwilling to observe either precedent or ordinary budgetary constraints, Rocky cheerfully rolled over whatever problems emerged in his path. Rather than be hampered by low government salaries when recruiting top staff members, he simply reached into his own pocket to pay distinguished figures like Henry Kissinger, who came over from Harvard to be one of the new governor's top advisers. Similarly, when Rocky saw that existing funding mechanisms were too limited for his ambitious construction agenda, he created a new means and folded older programs into it.[37] To be known as the New York State Housing Finance Agency (HFA), this new entity raised funds through the sale of bonds to the public and loaned the proceeds to private developers of certain types of middle-income housing. Because HFA bonds were exempt from federal taxation,[38] they would attract investors looking for ways to limit their taxable income; because of the tax exemption, buyers would be willing to accept a relatively low interest rate. Thus the HFA could afford to charge builders low rates on what they borrowed, which in theory would translate into lower home prices.

But the new agency still had to face the debt limitations set by the state constitution. For years housing officials had bypassed these limits by holding referendums to approve special bond issues. Recently, though, such referendums had gone down to defeat at the polls, suggesting that this venerable mechanism could no longer be relied upon.[39] As usual, Rockefeller refused to bow to seeming inevitability and instead quietly placed a bond lawyer named John Mitchell on retainer and told him to figure out a way around the debt ceiling.

Physically imposing, reserved, and utterly unflappable, John Newton Mitchell had played semiprofessional hockey, graduated from Fordham Law School, and, during World War II, commanded a squadron of naval torpedo boats that included the legendary *PT 109*, skippered by Lieutenant John Fitzgerald Kennedy. After the war Mitchell had gone on to become a well-regarded expert on the arcane regulations governing state and municipal bonds. Later he would become nationally famous as Richard Nixon's campaign manager and attorney general, but within the tight-knit world of public finance, he would earn renown for his ingenious solution to the dilemma posed by Rockefeller.

Traditionally the state backed its revenue bonds with its "full faith and credit," meaning that in case of default, the state was legally required to make good on the bonds. Mitchell's breakthrough was to create bonds backed instead by the state's "moral obligation," a seemingly subtle distinction that meant the state was not legally required to pay them off. As a practical matter, in order to protect its credit rating, the state would have to cover these bonds; nonetheless, because they technically were not a state obligation, they did not count against the constitutionally mandated debt ceiling and hence did not require voter approval. Government agencies could create as many such issues as they wanted; the only limitation would be whether or not Wall Street could move them.

"I drafted the boilerplate for HFA bonds, but John added the moral obligation twist that made it work," recalled Al Walsh, an attorney in the state housing department who was assigned to work with Mitchell. "Neither of us recognized it as genius right away—it just seemed like one more improvement to make bonds more marketable and get a lower interest rate." But when this novel form of bonds earned an AA rating from Standard & Poors and the first issue sold out instantly, Walsh's office received calls from around the country asking for copies of the legislation. Soon state after state had adopted a version of the New York model. Indeed, John Mitchell, later excoriated as a friend to wealthy elites, played an essential role in making decent housing available to millions of middle-income families all over America.[40]

Among the first to use these new financial instruments were Fred Trump and Abraham Kazan. In early 1962 both developers asked to transfer their projects from city administration under the Redevelopment Companies Law to the state-run HFA. As he had done a decade earlier at FHA offices in Manhattan, Fred Trump now spent months making the rounds of state agencies, his arms loaded with blueprints and his pockets full of cigars to hand out.[41] In May he broke ground on the new development. It was to be the largest project in Brooklyn, with 3,800 apartments, and it was also the tallest, comprising 7 twenty-three-story buildings.

He had been so eager to get moving that he had purchased some parcels within the site directly from owners instead of waiting for the official condemnation process. Still impatient, he was now barreling ahead before final HFA approval and covering construction costs with down payments from co-op buyers, even though by law these funds were supposed to remain in escrow. But his confidence was well placed, for in December the agency sold a bond issue earmarked for the first section of Trump Village.[42] By the next fall the HFA was in full swing and had committed itself to providing over $50 million for Trump Village and $36 million for Warbasse, now reduced to 2,484 units.[43]

By then, though, Fred Trump had encountered an unexpected difficulty. Although Shore Haven and Beach Haven were large-scale developments, they were only six stories tall and used wooden flooring everywhere but the ground floor. To erect them, Fred Trump had used a "skip"—a temporary freight elevator mounted on a building's exterior wall. Construction workers used the skips to lift building supplies and, later on, bathtubs, sinks, and other apartment fittings to upper floors. But the twenty-three-story buildings at Trump Village called for completely different procedures. At such heights, floors and ceilings were flat concrete plates reinforced with steel, and tall boom cranes with caterpillar treads and diesel motors hoisted materials to workers. Such construction also meant rigid, minute-by-minute scheduling for crane use or "hook time," for until the concrete hardened, the crane was the only way up.[44]

Fred Trump, who had started out as a carpenter, had balked at the idea of new materials and methods.[45] "I know what I can do and what it costs," he reportedly said when a structural engineer tried to convince him to use reinforced concrete. "I would be a damn fool to change my spots at this age." Later the engineer told an acquaintance that Fred Trump was the hardest sell he ever had. But finally, faced with the impossibility of proceeding otherwise, the builder went with the engineer's suggestions. Keeping up the habits of a lifetime, he still met regularly with the architect and contractors, spent hours each day on the site, kept a phone by his side at all times, ate lunch at his desk, and insisted that everyone on the job had to toe the mark. His working method, he told one reporter, remained unchanged: "You have to follow up and follow up and follow up and follow up."

But this time, following up was not enough. For the first time, the man who had been building before he graduated from high school, whose success in the construction field was based on knowing every step himself, often better than those he hired to do it for him, did not know how to do something. Through political connections cemented over many years, he had been able to wrest more than half the site from Abraham Kazan. But as construction on Trump Village and Warbasse went forward, it was Kazan, who had been creating high-rise buildings for years, who was the old hand. For the first time, Fred Trump had to ask for help. The job cost more than he had thought, and there were job overruns, which meant that he needed a bigger construction mortgage. He had already been conferring with HRH Construction Company, a major building outfit that had been one of the first in the New York area to use reinforced concrete for apartment buildings. When he got to the fifteenth floor of the first two buildings, he asked HRH to take over as general contractor and to put up the bond the state required for the job.

Trump Village, the one project to bear the developer's name, was the only one of his projects that he did not actually build himself. But he was still the boss. He collected $3.8 million, or about four-fifths of the total builder's fee of $4.8 million, and HRH received only one-fifth, or $1 million. In press accounts he did not mention HRH's role but instead spoke proudly of being four months ahead of his construction schedule. He boasted about being the first developer to follow the city's 1961 zoning ordinances, which required using only a small portion of the site for buildings and the rest for landscaping, play areas, and walkways. He pointed out that Trump Village, visible from twenty miles at sea, had displaced Coney Island's 250-foot-high parachute jump as the first thing sea travelers could identify. And he mentioned frequently that the high-profile architectural firm of Morris Lapidus, Kornbluth, Harle & Liebman was the project's designer.[46]

Back in the 1930s, Morris Lapidus, a Columbia University–trained architect, had rejected both the neoclassical look still prevailing in respectable design circles and the sleek white modernism of Le Corbusier and other Europeans. Instead he had gone into store design and begun creating compelling retail spaces through the use of dramatic lighting, curving walls, and eye-catching displays. In the early 1950s he used the same flair to produce the Sans Souci, the first of a series of sensational, flamboyant hotels that made Miami Beach into a national symbol of luxury and fun. "It made quite a stir," Lapidus said afterward of the rococo, over-the-top style that became known as Mediterranean Modern. "I was designing for the people, not the critics. My work was hated by every architectural writer in America." His later Miami confections—most notably the Fontainebleau Hotel with its Boom-Boom Room and Poodle Lounge—drew even more stinging reviews. But instead of ruining Lapidus's career, the storm of attention brought him business. "All hotel owners cared about with architecture was whether it was going to put heads in the beds," recollected Alan Lapidus, Morris's son, also an architect. "Everywhere people were talking about the Fontainebleau and lining up to make reservations."[47]

Fred Trump had always dismissed the thought of wasting money on fancy architects. But when he saw Lapidus's drawing power, he asked him to do a lobby like the Sans Souci's for a small apartment house in Queens. Lapidus was initially disdainful of such a pedestrian assignment. But the builder persisted, and the architect eventually produced an elegant, dramatically lit expanse with an all-glass entrance, sunken seating areas and mirrored walls, tropical plantings, and suspended birdcages with warbling songbirds. "Most lobbies you just walk through to the elevator," he said later, "but here you have to stop and look. I wanted something that would make people feel good about living there, that would actually merchandise the building."

A building that blew its own horn had great appeal to the man who had been promoting his work through billboards, newspaper advertisements, and endless press releases for decades. Fred Trump promptly signed Lapidus on for several other apartment buildings and, eventually, Trump Village. At nearby Warbasse, built of white brick because it was cheaper than red, Kazan had skimped on what he considered nonessentials in order to include central air-conditioning. As a result, facades were institutional, lobbies were spartan, and elevators were skip-stop. By contrast, Trump bragged that he was turning a sprawling, dilapidated area of Coney Island into a "miracle mile [of] luxury housing" featuring "a Taj Mahal of aesthetically appealing apartment houses [which would] combine resort living with city life."

The reality fell somewhat short of this description. "The aesthetics of that job were not great," Lapidus's partner, architect Harold Liebman, said afterward. "But with Fred Trump, everything always came down to money, money, money. We could never lose sight of the costs." Still, although Trump Village did not offer air-conditioning, in modest ways it was less bare-bones than its neighbor. Outside, occasional blue ceramic tiles and creative arrangements of red brick relieved the facades; inside, the hallways were carpeted. There were four elevators rather than two, they stopped on every floor, and they were painted in coordinated color schemes. In addition, there was recorded music in public areas, a security system that used closed-circuit television monitors, and lobby–apartment intercoms.[48]

By the fall of 1964 Fred Trump had completed Trump Village and rebounded completely from the difficulties of the past decade. The FHA scandals and the loss of Luna Park were behind him. So were the problems of adjusting to new construction methods. He had turned back potentially threatening competition—Kazan never built in Brooklyn again—and reestablished himself as the major builder in the borough. Once again Fred Trump seemed to be on a roll.

—∿∿∿—

The reason Abraham Kazan never built the Warbasse Houses he had originally envisioned was Brooklyn borough president John Cashmore; the reason Fred Trump did build Trump Village was New York City mayor Robert Wagner. A polite man as well as a practical one, Trump was more than ready to express his gratitude if and when such an occasion arose. So was his lawyer, Abraham Lindenbaum, whose seat on the City Planning Commission had been a mayoral appointment.

Such a moment arrived at a luncheon held on September 27, 1961, for the real estate community. Intended to honor the mayor, it took place in a private dining room at Sakele's, a restaurant in the Court Street area. After the meal, toastmaster Bunny Lindenbaum reminded the assembled guests why they needed to reelect Robert Wagner for a third term that November. Then he asked for campaign contributions. One by one, forty-three builders and realtors rose and made pledges totaling $25,000. Fred Trump committed himself to $2,500, the second-largest donation of the afternoon. Then Mayor Wagner stood up and gave his own thank-you remarks.

The next morning, newspaper headlines demanded Wagner's and Lindenbaum's heads for the unseemliness of the solicitation. Fred Trump and two other developer-donors also came under fierce attack because they had pending business before the City Planning Commission. Louis Lefkowitz, attorney general and Republican candidate for mayor, called the luncheon "political highway robbery" and "extortion." City Comptroller Larry Gerosa, who had broken ranks with Wagner and was now running for mayor on the independent Citizens Party line, referred to the luncheon as a "political shakedown." Prominent civic groups demanded that Wagner can Lindenbaum, who had set up the gatherings.

Lindenbaum was devastated. Protesting that he had done nothing wrong, he resigned from the City Planning Commission five days later. Wagner accepted his departure with alacrity. Three days later, in what was described as "an emotion-charged hearing," the commission met for the first time without the Brooklyn attorney. Apparently Wagner's damage control had worked. There was no objection to granting Lindenbaum's client, Fred Trump, the technical zoning change he needed for Trump Village, and Wagner won reelection by a comfortable margin.[49]

Everyone, including Lindenbaum himself, had assumed that his career was over. As it turned out, though, the Sakele's episode launched him as never before. For many in the real estate business, the take-home lesson was not about his ethics, but about how well connected he was. "Instead of being a disaster, the whole thing was a godsend," said Murray Feiden, Lindenbaum's brother-in-law and a Brooklyn Superior Court judge. "No one anticipated that this would be the best thing that ever happened to Bunny. As a member of the City Planning Commission, he was limited, but now he could do whatever he wanted, including practice in front of it."

By 1965, with Bunny Lindenbaum back in business at 16 Court Street and Trump Village completed, Fred Trump was once again in the market for a major project. He didn't have to look far. That spring, for the first time since 1897, Steeplechase Park did not reopen. Located only a few blocks away from Trump Village, it was the oldest of the fabled Coney Island amusement pavilions and the sole survivor.[50] Named after a popular carnival ride where customers on brightly painted mechanical horses zoomed around a circular racetrack, it was also home to arcade games, a gondola ride, and the towering parachute jump.[51]

Changing tastes in public entertainment, the escalating cost of maintenance, and a more mobile population had taken their toll on Coney Island. So had increasing racial tension as city agencies moved poor blacks and Latin Americans displaced by urban renewal elsewhere into Coney Island's residential areas, and they began to attend what had always been a white resort area. Sadly, the place known for decades as the nation's playground had become a gritty, dispirited slum. Huge new housing developments, including Trump Village and Warbasse Houses, loomed in the background. Once part of a flourishing seashore complex, Steeplechase was now the sole attraction, a dilapidated money loser whose longtime owners wanted out.

In July Fred Trump bought the 12.5-acre site for about $2.5 million. Using what had become valuable land for an outdated amusement park unable to pay its own way no longer made sense, he said. The parcel should go to housing. His plans were realistic and sensible, but they were also completely unacceptable to many at Coney Island and elsewhere. Fred Trump was offering the red bricks and mortar of the present; they wanted the fantasies and stardust of a long-vanished past. Bristling at the specter of yet more stark high-rise apartment buildings, members of Coney Island's Chamber of Commerce and Board of Trade, the City Planning Commission, the City Council, and community groups of all stripes dug in their heels and demanded that the site continue to be used for recreation.

Once again Fred Trump found himself in a tug-of-war in which his political ties appeared to give him the edge. His most important connection was to city comptroller and mayoral candidate Abraham Beame. A diminutive London-born accountant who had been part of the old Madison Club crew, Beame had replaced Larry Gerosa on the Wagner ticket in 1961 and was expected to win the mayoral race in the upcoming fall election. Fred Trump also had a strong connection with Abe Stark, who had become Brooklyn borough president after John Cashmore died of a heart attack in 1961. Stark, an elementary school dropout who went on to become the owner of a successful men's clothing store, was known throughout Brooklyn for the sign next to the Ebbets Field scoreboard offering any Dodger who hit it a free suit.[52] As soon as Trump's purchase of Steeplechase was announced, Stark enthusiastically backed his plans.

Come November, though, what had seemed a sure thing became

less sure. In a surprise election upset, Beame lost the race for mayor to John Vliet Lindsay, the liberal Republican congressman from the Upper East Side district better known by its "Silk Stocking" nickname. The patrician, Yale-educated mayor-elect, who owed nothing to Democratic powers in Brooklyn, saw no reason to change Coney's status from recreational, and Thomas Hoving, his parks commissioner-designate, dismissed the idea of tearing down Steeplechase well before Inauguration Day. Not wanting to offend the popular new mayor, Stark backpedaled on his support for Fred Trump's plans.[53]

Worse, the builder quickly became ensnarled in accusations set off by the final settling of accounts with New York State for Trump Village. Two years earlier, an auditor for the New York State Division of Housing named Leo Silverman had inspected a state-financed apartment building being constructed for the staff of a hospital in Buffalo.[54] At the site, Silverman noticed a new type of derrick that could be disassembled when a floor was finished and then reassembled on the next floor. Because he thought some of the builders he audited might want to know about this useful piece of equipment, the conscientious Silverman visited a dealer who quoted him the price to buy such a derrick. Some time later, Silverman, the auditor for Trump Village, was going over paperwork and noticed that Fred Trump had submitted a bill for renting the same derrick from something called the Boro Equipment Company. The amount listed as the monthly rental charge was the same amount Silverman had been given as the entire purchase price. He refused to authorize payment, which provoked a heated argument from Trump's office and from HRH.

Silverman also mentioned the matter to another state employee named Joseph Fisch when he saw him at a Knights of Pythias meeting. Only a few years out of Harvard Law School and the U.S. Army, Fisch was an attorney at a watchdog public agency called the State Investigation Commission (SIC). An offspring of the law-and-order administration of Governor Thomas Dewey, the SIC had been upgraded under Governor Harriman but still had no prosecutorial authority, which meant that it could expose malefactors through investigations and public hearings, but it could not try them.[55] Nonetheless, the tenacious, street-wise Fisch had used SIC probes of hospitals, police departments, and school construction authorities to force major cleanups, dismissals, and indictments.

Silverman's story intrigued Fisch. Poking around, he learned that Boro Equipment, which charged equally exorbitant rents for the bulldozers, tile scrapers, backhoes, and dump trucks used at Trump Village, was owned by Fred Trump. Now Fisch started digging in earnest. Working all day and half the night—during one memorable stretch he put in nineteen such days in a row—he found that Fred Trump had spent $8 million less than his estimated cost, itself inflated by the high equipment rental charges. Because the 7.5 percent builder's fee was based on this estimated figure rather than actual cost, he ended up with a windfall of $598,000.[56]

There was also the matter of Bunny Lindenbaum's bill for land condemnation and relocation of the 681 families living on the site. The final tab was $520,000, the largest such fee submitted in the entire state housing program. As Fisch learned, Bunny and his firm had done almost nothing to earn it. Lawyers from the office of the Corporation Counsel—the legal division of the mayor's office—had handled the condemnations and related court appearances, and a private relocation firm had taken care of moving the families elsewhere. In fact, when Lindenbaum submitted his bill to the New York State Division of Housing, he had to ask the relocation firm for the names and addresses of the tenants because he had never dealt with them.

On Tuesday, January 26, 1966, public hearings began at the SIC's Manhattan offices. Once more Fred Trump was in the headlines because he had made a windfall profit from overestimating his costs in a government program that paid on the basis of estimates. Once more he had to push his way through reporters and cameras into a large government chamber, sit down at a table where he was flanked by his lawyer, and face a bank of disapproving stares belonging, in this case, to the four commissioners who sat on the SIC.

On January 27 Fred Trump raised his right hand, swore to tell the truth, and began answering Joe Fisch's questions.

No, he had not used political connections to force another developer—that is, Kazan—to surrender part of his site because the site was not that developer's property to surrender.

No, the fees charged for rental equipment were not excessive because, compared to other costs for the massive project, they amounted to "peanuts."

"DUTCHTOWN" In 1885, when newly arrived German immigrant Friedrich Trump came to 76 Forsyth Street, New York's Lower East Side, now known as Chinatown, was a German area known as Dutchtown.

SETTING OUT Instead of bringing Friedrich into the family wine-making business, his mother, Katherina Kober Trump, sent him off to be a barber's apprentice. Friedrich's life course changed yet again when, at sixteen, he ran away from home and headed for America and a future as an entrepreneur.

1

2

3

THE LITTLE GIRL NEXT DOOR Elizabeth Christ, whose family lived next to the Trumps, was only a small child when Friedrich struck out for the New World.

THE BIG GIRL After Friedrich amassed a nest egg in the Klondike gold rush, he returned home, found that the girl next door had grown up, and married her.

4

5

GIVING CUSTOMERS WHAT THEY WANTED In 1893, Friedrich Trump opened the Monte Cristo Hotel in this bustling, Rockefeller-backed gold-and-silver town northeast of Seattle. There he provided miners with the necessities of life: food, shelter, liquor, and women.

6

FREE RIDE By 1898, Friedrich was in Bennett, British Columbia, offering food and female companionship to would-be miners en route to the Klondike. When a new boomtown called White Horse opened further along the trail, he floated his Arctic Hotel part way, then salvaged whatever could be used for his next venture.

THREE THOUSAND BLUE PLATE SPECIALS Trump's next gold rush establishment, the Arctic Restaurant, was the largest in town. In a possible precedent for his grandson's legendary habit of exaggeration, Friedrich boasted that he could prepare three thousand meals a day.

7

DRAWN CURTAINS
Inside the Arctic, co-owner Trump stands proudly at the bar. Across the room and in back were curtained areas where local ladies of the night entertained miners in privacy. *Courtesy of Paul Erlham*

8

BORN TO BUILD
By the time Friedrich's son Fred (second row, center) graduated from a Queens high school in January 1923, he was well on his way to a career as a builder.

9

TWO CHIEFS Fred Trump in his office at Trump
Village. On the walls are clippings and plaques from
his building career; at his side is one of his beloved
cigar-store Indians, the traditional symbol of barber
shops and a reminder of his father's original trade.

10

PUBLIC GOOD-BYES
To push along plans to raze
Steeplechase, the last of the fabled
Coney Island amusement parks, so
that he could build on the site,
Fred Trump hired local beauties to
appear at a "farewell ceremony" in
which guests threw bricks at the
old entertainment center.

11

TRYING TO FILL THE
OLD MAN'S SHOES
Fred Trump's older son,
Fred Jr., in the empty
shell of Steeplechase's
main pavilion. Fred Jr.
had the name to carry on
the family business, but
it was Donald who had
the drive.

12

DREAM HOUSE After Fred and Mary Trump had their fourth child, Donald, in 1946, Fred built what would eventually be a twenty-three-room mansion in the upscale Queens suburb of Jamaica Estates.

13

PORTRAIT OF THE TYCOON AS A TODDLER Long before he sent out this invitation to his fiftieth birthday party, Donald Trump was sizing up the world and trying to get it to do things his way.

14

SHAPING UP At New York Military Academy, Donald Trump found the structure he needed to transform himself from a discipline problem into a model cadet.

BLUEPRINTS IN THE BLOOD At twenty-seven, Donald was ready to take over the family business. Behind Donald and Fred is Trump Village, Fred's last and largest project.

15

BEFORE *Left* In the mid-1970s, as New York City reeled under a major fiscal crisis, the dilapidated Commodore Hotel, next door to Grand Central Station, was one of Manhattan's most distressing eyesores.

AFTER *Below* Helped by a huge tax abatement, Donald Trump gave the Commodore a shiny new glass skin and an eye-catching overhanging restaurant. Reopening as the Grand Hyatt, it became one of the city's most successful hotels.

17a

18
GRAND ENTRANCE The Grand Hyatt's sumptuous new lobby helped set a glitzy, glamorous tone.

17b

On His Way Donald Trump at home in his penthouse bachelor pad on the day the New York City Council approved the tax abatement for what would be the Grand Hyatt.

19

20

Donald's Debut The groundbreaking for the Grand Hyatt, June 28, 1978. Those in attendance included (from left) Bill Frentz (Equitable Life), Rusty Crawford (Bowery Bank), Donald Trump, New York Governor Hugh Carey, unidentified, Jay Pritzker (Hyatt Hotels), Jordan Gruzen, former mayor Abe Beame, Der Scutt, and Vito Pitta (hotel workers' union).

The Twenty-eight-Sided Logo
The city waged an unsuccessful struggle to deny Donald Trump a tax abatement for Trump Tower, the twenty-eight-sided skyscraper he erected next door to Tiffany & Co. on Fifth Avenue.

21

MR. & MRS. TRUMP
Donald and Ivana in their eight-room apartment at 60th Street and Fifth Avenue in 1980. In each other, they had each finally found someone else with the same energy and love of competition.

22

23

TOP ENTREPRENEUR In 1985, Fred Trump received the Horatio Alger award for his contribution to America's free-enterprise system. At the ceremony were (from left) family members Robert, Fred, Donald, Ivana, Maryanne, and Mary. They were joined by close family friend Roy Cohn, far right, whose influence helped put Maryanne on the federal bench in 1983.

THE CAN-DO KID
Donald Trump's renovation of problem-plagued Wollman Rink made him a hero to New Yorkers and an irritant to Mayor Ed Koch. At the November 1986 dedication were (from left) skating champions Dick Button and Aja Zanova, Koch, Trump, banker Robert Douglas, Manhattan Borough President David Dinkins, and Parks Commissioner Henry Stern.

24

PROUD FATHER, PROUD SON
Donald and Fred Trump outside the Plaza
Hotel, July 1988. After Donald had become
a national figure, he still relied on his
father for support and advice.

THE ROYAL COUPLE Donald and Ivana sit
amid the regal splendor of their Florida trophy estate, Mar-a-Lago, as the staff stands
in attendance behind them.

25

26

IN MOURNING
The Trump family at
Ivana's father's funeral in
October 1990. Sharing
their grief were (from left)
Donny Jr., twelve; Ivana;
Eric, six; Donald; and
Ivanka, nine.

27

GEORGIA PEACH
Marla Maples's Delta
Airlines ad displays
the charms that won
Donald Trump's
heart.

RELAX

Fly Delta to Florida · the Bahamas

28

WEDDING BELLS
On December 20, 1993, three months
after the birth of their daughter,
Tiffany, Donald and Marla finally wed
in a lavish ceremony at the Plaza
Hotel.

HAPPY BIRTHDAY
Donald, Marla, and his four children at
his fiftieth birthday party. Helping
their father celebrate are Donny Jr.,
eighteen; Eric, twelve; Tiffany, two;
and Ivanka, sixteen.

29

ENDURING POVERTY Intended to end urban decay in Atlantic City, legal gambling instead added huge casinos, including the Trump Taj Mahal and the Showboat, to the city's blighted landscape.

IN THE CENTER OF THE RING Because big-name boxing brought big gamblers to Atlantic City, Donald Trump backed such fights. In January 1988, promoter Don King (second from right) helped set up a match there between challenger Larry Holmes (second from left) and world heavyweight champion Mike Tyson (far right).

ABRACADABRA In April 1990, Donald Trump rubbed a lamp and opened the Taj. Atlantic City's largest and most expensive casino, it failed to break even and cannibalized Trump's other two casinos. Two months later, he was in secret meetings with bankers to fend off bankruptcy.

Doonesbury   BY GARRY TRUDEAU

COMIC FIGURE Trump's brief appearance on the presidential campaign trail in 1987 made his autobiography, *The Art of the Deal*, a best-seller and earned him a place in "Doonesbury."

COVER BOY By the end of the 1980s, Donald Trump had been on the front of so many magazines they covered a wall in his office.

FLYING HIGH In the fall of 1988, Donald extended the Trump franchise—and his debt level—with the purchase of the Eastern Shuttle. At the time, Frank Lorenzo, shown here with Trump, presided over this strike-plagued fleet of twenty-one aging Boeing 727s.

36

37

TRUMP: THE GAME By 1989, Trump's fame brought him endorsement deals for cars, ballpoint pens, sunglasses, business cards, and a board game with his photograph on the box. A year later, the games were on remainder shelves and the developer was facing bankruptcy.

LIFESAVER Facing a tidal wave of debt, Donald Trump hired financial wizard and onetime opponent Steve Bollenbach, shown here with Trump and daughter Ivanka at a 1991 U.S. Open tennis match, to save him.

38

TRUMP CITY In 1985, Donald Trump first unveiled plans for what came to be known as Trump City, a huge complex on Manhattan's West Side that included the world's tallest building and led to a long-running battle with local community members.

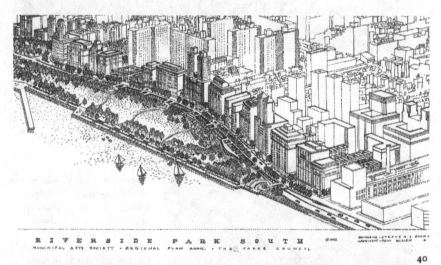

RIVERSIDE PARK SOUTH
MUNICIPAL ARTS SOCIETY • REGIONAL PLAN ASSOC. • THE PARKS COUNCIL

RIVERSIDE SOUTH In 1990, Trump's West Side opponents came up with a smaller, alternative scheme called Riverside South. Financially strapped, the developer was willing to compromise in exchange for alliance help in obtaining zoning changes.

41a

THE FINISH LINE In October 1993, Donald Trump stood in the New York City Council balcony next to Riverside South strategist Richard Kahan (seated to his right), and watched the next-to-last vote on the project.

41b

GOING THE DISTANCE In 1999, a quarter century after Donald Trump first pursued the West Side site, construction was finally under way.

TRUMP PLACE Although Donald Trump no longer controlled the site, it would bear his name.

PASSING THE TORCH In June 1999, Fred Trump died at the age of ninety-three. Coming down the church steps after his funeral were (from upper left) his former daughter-in-law, Ivana Trump; Lisa Desmond, wife of his grandson David Desmond, son of Maryanne Trump Barry by her first marriage; son Robert Trump and (to his right) daughter-in-law Blaine Trump; son Donald Trump; grandson David Desmond; and daughter Elizabeth Trump Grau (in profile).

43

44

THINKING GLOBAL In keeping with what he calls "the most important address in the world," Donald Trump placed a stainless-steel globe outside Trump International Hotel and Tower. City officials refused to allow signage on the globe because they considered it to be advertising, but the large shiny letters above the building's entrances ensure that no visitor will miss the name *Trump*.

No, it was not a conflict of interest that he owned the equipment rental company or that he had failed to note this on any documents where he had listed the name of the company.

No, there was nothing untoward about owning so many of the subcontracting outfits involved in the job because he was the sole stockholder in a lot of things—forty-three corporations, to be exact— and "these things escape my memory sometimes."

No, there was nothing wrong with having used co-op buyers' deposits for construction expenses rather than leaving them in escrow as was legally required because it was the state's fault for taking too long to process the financing.

No, there was no problem about equipment rented for Trump Village with public money having been used on other jobs because the several incidents that had been reported must have been single and isolated, and if there were more such incidents, they were the fault of the observers for not blowing the whistle at the time, and he was "very hurt" that they had not done so.

Above all, his huge profits were not unethical because he had been able to save money on the original cost estimates. That was what he was good at, and that was the way it should be. "Trump Village has the finest reputation," he said proudly. "We finished eight months ahead of schedule, millions of dollars under anticipated constructions costs, and I don't think there will ever be another job in the city that will be able to shine a candle up against Trump Village."[57]

The commissioners were not impressed. Just that morning they had heard testimony from Abraham Kazan about how under the same program and in the same place he had built a comparable project for a fraction of the cost.[58] Fred Trump's record, one commissioner exploded angrily, was "outrageous" and "unconscionable," "greedy" and "grasping." At another point he blurted out, "Is there any way of preventing a man who does business in that way from getting another contract from the state?" For five days the SIC continued to gather public testimony and newspaper ink. Then the commission recessed the hearing and began turning out a final report that enumerated Trump's infractions, characterized him as "a pretty shrewd character," and noted his "talent for getting every ounce of profit out of his housing project." It concluded by calling for tighter administration

and more accountability in the state housing program—but not for indictments.[59]

As with the FHA's 608 program, there was no statutory penalty
for such unanticipated profits. Nor was there any legal requirement
that funds appropriated on the basis of overestimates be paid back.[60]
In practical terms, the only penalty a developer might encounter was
for underestimating his expenses, for if a project ended up costing
more than expected, the government did not make up the difference.[61] As a result, the New York State program, like the federal program that preceded it, created an incentive for overestimation. But
now that it was becoming clear—and public—that this policy contained such a large, developer-friendly loophole, state officials had to
denounce it.

The results of the investigation were meager. Joe Fisch sent what
he had unearthed to the office of the Brooklyn district attorney,
where it proceeded to gather dust. Although Fred Trump had to lower
rental charges slightly, he kept his windfall profits and, ultimately, all
the other contested fees, plus interest. Bunny Lindenbaum had to
wait some years for the final payment on his fee and to face a number
of inquiries and obstacles, but eventually he also received the full
amount, plus interest. Abraham Kazan, who had surmounted the first
serious setback in his construction career, continued initial work on
his most ambitious undertaking, Co-op City, a fifteen-thousand-unit
complex in the Bronx.

One of the few directly affected was Leo Silverman, who retired
early a few years later. "I was completely fed up with how the office
was run and who got favors," he said. "After I lost every single battle,
I got out." The SIC itself was also affected, although more positively.
Later that year, for the first time in SIC history, the governor of New
York extended the commission's next two-year term well in advance.[62]

But the UHF was far less robust than it had appeared at the hearings. The reason was not the loss of part of the original Warbasse site,
but what the Warbasse experience revealed. It was the first time either Fred Trump or Abraham Kazan had confronted another developer
over a site, and the conflict highlighted the differences between the
two. Once the dust had settled, though, it was possible to see that
Fred Trump and Abraham Kazan were remarkably similar. Robert

Moses once described Kazan as "about as flexible as high-speed steel,"[63] and the same could easily have been said about Fred Trump. Both builders were tough-minded businessmen who were impatient with rules and regulations, always wanted to go faster, and had no tolerance for doing things any way but their own. Neither ever settled for anything but the lowest prices and best deals. No matter how impossible a job might seem, they got it done. Despite the fact that one sought profits and the other didn't, both were entrepreneurs. As such, they faced one ultimate test: whether their competitive advantage— that characteristic that let them succeed where others failed—was replicable.

Fred Trump's strength was his ability to figure out where the extra profits lay and how to get them—what regulations could be safely skirted, where the give was in financial arrangements, which politicians and officials to approach and what to say, how to minimize friction along the way. With this savvy he created a successful, profit-making organization. And it is in the nature of such organizations that if the head steps aside or dies and an adequate successor is not at hand, the business can be given a monetary value and sold and then someone else with the necessary entrepreneurial skills can take over.

By contrast, Abraham Kazan's edge was his cooperative leadership. It was what made co-workers and cooperative managers accept low salaries and what made tenants go along with UHF management and with the requirement that if they moved, they had to sell their apartments back for no more than they had paid for them. It was what allowed this stubborn Russian immigrant to buck the very ethos of American capitalism, to scorn the notion of profits, and yet to build more housing units than anyone else in American history, including Fred Trump.

But the one thing Kazan's cooperative leadership could not do was provide for an orderly succession. When the head of a cooperative institution leaves, the transfer of control is less clear, and finding someone of comparable skills to hold the enterprise together is a lot harder than finding someone who can make money. That is why, all over the country, cooperative movements have faltered, for it has been impossible to replace the small number of idealistic figures who got them started. And it is also why, ultimately, it is wise to encourage and, at times, to provide public subsidies to the Fred Trumps of the land—not because private development is morally good, but because it will keep going. There will never be a problem finding the next Fred Trump if this one dies or bankrupts himself—the market will keep pushing them along. They may or may not be as clever or shrewd or good or wise or inspiring as the Kazans, but they don't need to be in order to get the job done.

As it happened, though, the market didn't need to provide a successor to Fred Trump. He had a son, Donald, who wanted to be a developer and was more than capable, and thus the Trump Organization could go on building. At the UHF, though, there was no one in the next generation able to take hold of the reins, no one with Kazan's combination of cooperative vision and leadership skills. When construction at Co-op City proved more difficult and expensive than anticipated, Kazan was too old to impose his authority on the situation, and tenant-cooperators did not rally round. They did not accept the UHF request to raise rents and levy additional surcharges; they did not even heed regulations about noise and pets. They saw management not as an ally, but as an adversary, and ultimately they ejected UHF from its own project. After this crushing defeat, the UHF, an institution based on trust and mutual respect, never built again.

This did not mean, however, that all went smoothly for Fred Trump. Indeed, his next project, building on the old Steeplechase site, never happened, for he could not get the zoning variance necessary for high-rise buildings. He could not overcome New Yorkers' abiding nostalgia for the Coney Island that was, and his old political connections could not deliver as they once had. The result was that the man who had excelled at figuring his way around any impasse was stopped cold.

Still, he did not give up easily, despite advice from many quarters to do so. "You could never tell Fred Trump what to do," recalled lawyer Sidney Young. "You could tell him how to do it, but not what to do. He was very strong willed."[64]

First Trump tried honey. He pledged that he would not commit himself to building housing without listening to the Coney Island community. He said that he would make a careful study of all options. He promised to talk to amusement park operators about re-opening Steeplechase.

Nothing happened.

Then he switched to vinegar. He suggested that if he couldn't build, he would tear down the much-beloved parachute jump that had been installed at Steeplechase after a debut at the 1939 Chicago World's Fair. He hinted that if he couldn't build, he might let large discount stores open on the site.

Still nothing happened.

He switched gears altogether and hired Morris Lapidus to sketch out a large-scale overhaul of Coney Island. Extending over a vast area that totaled about 120 acres, this master plan placed a skating rink and a convention center on the 12 acres Trump actually owned. At one end of the huge redevelopment zone was an enormous entertainment center with carnival rides, shops, and the original Nathan's hot dog stand; at the other end, on city-owned land that carried the appropriate zoning, were six tall apartment buildings. Trump and Lapidus unveiled sketches of the proposal at a press conference at the Americana Hotel, another flashy Lapidus-designed building in mid-town Manhattan. The presentation focused on the entertainment complex, which was dominated by a modernistic, glass-and-plastic-covered pleasure dome and flared, ribbed tower. But even these fantasy structures, which looked like terminals at an international airport, could not disguise the fact that the whole grandiose scheme was Trump's way of exchanging a site on which he could not build for one where he could. Coney Island officials and dignitaries in the audience remained stone-faced.[65]

Once again nothing happened.

Two months later Trump sent the same officials and dignitaries an engraved invitation to a "V.I.P. Farewell Ceremony" for Steeplechase Park at noon on September 21, 1966.[66] When the guests arrived at the Pavilion of Fun, the enclosure around the old Steeplechase entertainments, they found champagne, half a dozen bikini-clad models, TV cameras, and a wrecker's bulldozer. With all the rides sold and carted off, one of the few remnants of the past was the huge grinning clown's face painted on the pavilion's enormous glass window.[67] Despite a steady drizzle, the bathing beauties posed with Fred Trump in the bulldozer's scoop and pulled down pieces of the pavilion that had been attached to ropes. At one point the new owner passed out bricks and encouraged guests to pitch them at the smiling face that had greeted generations of Steeplechase customers and served as the park's logo. Then the bulldozer got to work.

With the shattering of the panes, Fred Trump breathed a sigh of relief. At last he had exorcised the ghost of Coney Island past and could proceed with what he saw as the island's present and future. But such was not to be. Although he redid his plans several times, he remained unable to obtain the necessary zoning changes. "I'm fighting a lost cause," he said after another year-long standoff. "There isn't much hope in the atmosphere." Eventually the city voted to take over the property and awarded Fred Trump $3.7 million for the site.[68] He banked $1.4 million, but doing so was bittersweet. Fred Trump wanted to make his money building, not as compensation for not building. Now he had lost the struggle to do so, and he was exhausted. It was time for someone else to take over—someone with the energy and hope he once had.

His second son, Donald, would not solve the problems at Coney Island. Neither would he devote himself to finding a less problematic building site elsewhere in Brooklyn. Instead he would leave behind the place where his father had made the family fortune and where a well-marked career path now lay ready and waiting for him. He would take off for new territory, for a place where both the obstacles and the rewards were truly immense. He would go where only the sky was the limit. He would go to Manhattan.

PART III

THE STAR:
DONALD TRUMP

CHAPTER FOURTEEN

BORN TO COMPETE

ON JUNE 14, 1946, THE DAY DONALD JOHN TRUMP was born, school bands and Boy Scouts marched up Fifth Avenue, and there were plenty of American flags waving—a festive touch, although in honor not of his birth, but of Flag Day.

He came into the world with thousands of other babies, as part of the first onrush of what is now called the baby boom. Given that America's biggest war had just ended, and hundreds of thousands of GIs and sailors had only recently returned home after years away, demographers were hardly surprised by the upsurge in births. But they were astonished by its duration, as measured, in the precomputer Census Bureau, by endless streams of punch cards riffling noisily through the sorters and mechanical tabulators of unit calculators. The best counters in existence, these jerry-built contraptions, dishwasher size, with wires sticking out everywhere, showed that instead of dropping to normal levels after a few years, the number of births remained high. Outside the Census Bureau, the nation adjusted to crowded playgrounds, overstuffed classrooms, and bigger Scout troops; inside, office pools, pegged to when the birth level would drop, grew steadily larger.[1]

By the 1950s, the UNIVAC, an early computer the size of a two-bedroom apartment, had taken over tabulation duties and found that the birth rate still had not slackened. In 1964, when the level finally decreased, the statisticians got to work. During the baby boom, they learned, the nation's population rose by almost seventy-six million—

about eighteen million more than had been expected.[2] The country had experienced many population increases, but this was the first time immigration played only a minor role. Unlike the 1880s, when Friedrich Trump and millions of other newcomers arrived in New York Harbor, between 1946 and 1964 almost all new Americans were born in the United States. Perhaps in part for that reason, membership in the baby boom—that is, belonging to the largest demographic cohort in American history—would affect the lives of millions of children more deeply than anyone could have anticipated.

Although this generation's primary identity would be as members of their own families, they would also develop a secondary role as members of the baby boom family. Together with their boomer sisters and brothers, they would grow up on television, rock and roll, and the cold war. But for those born, as Donald Trump was, at the beginning of the boom, there may have been something more.[3] Because the war had interrupted normal patterns of marriage and childbearing, children born in the first few years of the baby boom included a higher than normal proportion of firstborns. In turn, instead of having the full range of personality attributes associated with children of a variety of birth orders, children in that first wave of the baby boom would tend to have a similar, firstborn character: assertive, ambitious, and, above all, successful. Further, because of this heavily firstborn environment, a kind of herd effect may have taken over, with playmates and classmates who were not firstborns acting as if they were.[4]

Donald Trump was one of these faux firstborns. Although the fourth-born in his family, by all accounts he was self-assured, determined, and positive from the start. Obviously his own genes and family contributed mightily to the person who emerged. But it just may be that growing up among more firstborns than had ever before gone through childhood together had a shaping influence on the man who would come to define success to so many.

—⁓—

It was a good time to be born. America was on a roll. Wartime price controls would soon be lifted, and cars were once again rolling off Detroit's assembly lines. A small bank in Brooklyn was readying

Charge-It, the nation's first third-party credit plan, which allowed customers to charge purchases within two blocks of the bank and led eventually to the modern consumer economy.[5] Ethel Merman was starring on Broadway in the new feel-good musical *Annie Get Your Gun*, Dr. Benjamin Spock published his first book on baby and child care, and NBC provided the few thousand Americans with television sets one of their first live broadcasts, a welterweight bout at Madison Square Garden.[6]

At the time of Donald's birth, Fred and Mary Trump and the older children—Maryanne, nine, Fred Jr., seven, and Elizabeth, four—lived on Wareham Street in Jamaica Estates. Fred Trump had built their home, a two-story mock Tudor shoehorned into a tiny lot, almost twenty years earlier; now, with four children, it was bursting at the seams. Fortunately the solution lay right outside the back door. On a double lot that backed onto the Wareham property and fronted on a wide, tree-lined boulevard called Midland Parkway, Fred Trump began to build his dream house.

A red brick colonial-style structure with white shutters at the windows and door, the Trumps' new home was far larger than the house on Wareham. But because it also covered almost the full width of the plot on which it stood, it had the same sandwiched-in look. In front, a winding brick walkway led up from the street past a pair of grinning lawn jockeys to a large portico-style entrance porch. Six thick, two-story columns flanked the front door and supported a large classical pediment decorated with an iridescent ornamental shield. To the right, a driveway led into a large garage on the basement level, an echo of the little garages Fred Trump had tucked under his first attached houses back in East Flatbush. Above the foyer rose a domed ceiling. In the library, which had more shelves than books, there was one of the neighborhood's first television sets, a huge console with a tiny screen. From the foyer, a formal curved staircase led up to the second-floor landing, bedrooms, and a back staircase for the children's use. There was also an intercom system, unusual in a residence at the time.

But mainly there were rooms: twenty-three of them, plus nine bathrooms, by the time Fred Trump finally finished building. They were not particularly sumptuous or even all that spacious. Because this was the house of a developer, not an architect, there were built-in cabinets in the dining room and neat detail work in the living room, but no cathedral ceiling or grand drawing rooms. Instead Fred Trump had enlarged and repeated a relatively ordinary floor plan, creating what was in essence an enormous bungalow/ranch house/tract home. It was the home of a man who made his money himself and had not tried to distance himself from that fact.[7]

Finally, there was plenty of space for the family, which added a fifth and last child, Robert, on August 26, 1948. There was also room for a maid, a middle-aged white woman named Emma, plus a black chauffeur named George and two Cadillac limousines with license plates that read FT1 and FT2.

Fred Trump did not take much time off to enjoy his new home. He often left for work before dawn, driving from one site to another and keeping on top of things with an early car phone. After he came home, twelve or thirteen or maybe even fourteen hours later, he sat in the library and returned phone calls. "The telephone was always ringing," recalled Jan von Heinigen, one of Fred Jr.'s classmates. "It was always for Fred's father, and it was always about business. My impression was that this was normal—you know, doesn't everyone do this, we're awake so we must be working."

"My father never had any hobbies," Maryanne Trump Barry said many years later. "He never thought about anything but work and family." Whenever possible, he would combine the two. Thus weekends meant taking the kids along to look at properties or meeting with his sister Elizabeth's husband, William Walter, an accountant at Manufacturers Hanover Bank, to go over company books. Presumably because they were both engaged in commerce, Fred Trump sometimes seemed closer to his brother-in-law than to his own brother John. Known as "the Boston Trumps," the MIT professor and his family were an intellectual crew, respected for their academic accomplishments but considered to have little practical sense. "He had the brains," Fred Trump once said gloatingly to a mutual acquaintance, "but I made the money."[8]

And he seemed to be doing so round the clock. "Dad was always checking on some building or construction site," said Maryanne. "What else would he do on a Saturday, hang around the house?" Robert Trump, too, remembered weekends as family workdays. "Even when [I was] through college," he said, "we would go check out his buildings. Dad would take the elevator to the top floor and then walk down. He would look at each landing and the incinerator and boiler room. Supers had to be there, because weekends were when you rented."

Worldly success notwithstanding, Fred Trump was often shy and uncomfortable in private. "He was awkward and hated to speak in front of any group of people," Maryanne said. "He took a Dale Carnegie course back in the fifties, and we kidded him about it, but it didn't help." When one elder from the Trumps' Presbyterian church in Queens came to the family home to ask for a pledge, he found Fred Trump generous but shy almost to the point of being tongue-tied.[9] But what he may have lacked in public speaking and conversational skills he made up for with his steadfast belief in the power of positive thinking. Long before Norman Vincent Peale's best-selling book, *The Power of Positive Thinking*, published in 1952, made this notion a national cliché, Fred Trump had been living by it and drilling it into his children. "'You can do it if you try,' that was his motto," Maryanne remembered. "If we wanted to stay home from school [because of illness], he'd always say, 'Go, you'll feel better in two hours.'"

Mary Trump was also busy—so busy that she worked herself almost to exhaustion. Even with a maid, five children and volunteer work at Jamaica Hospital so filled her days that she sometimes looked pale and felt unwell. After Robert was born she started to hemorrhage and had to be rushed to the hospital for what turned out to be an emergency hysterectomy. Using his car phone and his clout as a hospital board member, Fred Trump contacted a surgeon at Columbia University Medical School and fetched him in person for the procedure. Afterward Mary Trump developed peritonitis, a severe abdominal infection, and had several more operations. "There were four in something like two weeks," recalled Maryanne, who was an adolescent at the time. "My father came home and told me she wasn't expected to live, but I should go to school and he'd call me if anything changed. That's right—go to school as usual!"

Her mother recovered, although her health remained precarious, and she continued her role as chief homemaker. She had another role as well: family entertainer, the one around whom family occasions revolved. Donald later spoke of her as a source for his sense of showmanship. "She always had a flair for the dramatic and the grand," he wrote in his autobiography, *The Art of the Deal*. Maryanne, too, saw her mother as someone who loved the spotlight. Even when she was ill, Maryanne said, she would rally for family parties and events. "When the lights went up, she was the star," her daughter said.

The other major figure in the Trump children's lives was their paternal grandmother. From the start Elizabeth Christ Trump had helped her son in his business, and well into her seventies she still collected the coins from Laundromats in Trump buildings in Queens and Brooklyn. After her son's marriage she left the house they shared, but there was no rupture in their relationship; he would remain close to her for the rest of her life. She continued to live nearby in Queens and eventually moved to an apartment building that her son built across Midland Parkway from his own house.

Impeccably dressed and hardworking, the family matriarch seemed a stern figure to neighborhood children. "She wasn't a grandmother you'd leap on for kisses," recalled Heather MacIntosh Hayes, who was a year older than Donald and grew up in the house next door. Evidently her older son, too, had a rather formal demeanor. A meticulous dresser, he disdained wearing a bathrobe and slippers in the morning even on weekends and instead always got fully dressed. Every evening he came home from work, showered, and then dressed all over again for dinner in a jacket and tie. He discouraged nicknames, correcting anyone who called and asked for "Lizzie" instead of Elizabeth,[10] and he also looked down on the use of terms he considered indelicate for female conditions. "Years later, when I was pregnant," Maryanne recalled, "I said something about my state and my father said, 'Your mother had five children and never used that word.'"

Inside the big house on Midland Parkway, there were curfews and lots of rules, including, for Maryanne, no lipstick. "You didn't utter a curse word in that house, or you'd get your neck broken," recalled Louis Droesch, a friend of Fred Jr. Cookies or other snacks between meals were forbidden. When Fred Trump came home at night, Mary gave him a report on who had done what to whom during the day, and then he would mete out whatever disciplinary actions seemed called for. Depending on the seriousness of what had occurred, malefactors might be grounded for a few days; according to the children's friends, occasionally wrongdoers were also paddled with a wooden spoon.

Fred and Mary Trump made sure their children knew something about the value of a dollar. Sometimes it seemed that life's highest priorities were to remember to turn out all the lights, to eat every single mouthful on their plates, and to be ever mindful of all the poor, starving children all over the world. Whenever they visited one of their father's building sites, they collected empty bottles to turn in for the deposits. They all had summer jobs, and the boys had paper routes; when it rained or snowed, Fred Trump made a single concession—he let them make their appointed rounds in a limousine. "The first time I ever realized that my father was successful," Maryanne said, "was when I was fifteen and a friend said to me, 'Your father is rich.' I was stunned. We were privileged, but I didn't know it."

Within the family, what mattered was not financial success per se, but the family itself. With the exception of Robert, the children shared not only the family surname, but also first names; thus, in order of their birth, the Trump children were named after their mother (Maryanne), father (Fred Jr.), grandmother (Elizabeth), and maternal and paternal uncles (Donald John). When Maryanne was expecting a child of her own, she later recalled, she asked her father for suggestions for names. "He said, 'Oh, a proper name like Elizabeth or Maryanne,'" she said. "That was it, that was the entire list of proper names." Hardly surprising, family would remain the highest loyalty for this generation; indeed, for at least one member, Donald, it was a source of warmth and security that nothing else in life could ever quite match.

—◆—

In the late twenties, when Fred Trump began building in Jamaica Estates, it was a remote, genteel enclave, almost a square mile in size, without stoplights or streetlights.[11] Much of the area was undeveloped woodland dotted with springs and streams. There were old stone walls and even a stone bridge. Splendid old oaks, elms, chestnuts, and maples surrounded the few houses, and there was plenty of room for rose gardens and vegetable patches. Each spring pink and purple azalea and rhododendron bushes lit up the wide median strip that ran the length of Midland Parkway, and each fall the red and orange leaves of the hardwood trees set the gently rolling landscape ablaze. Visitors registered at a small copper-roofed gatehouse at the corner of

Midland Parkway and Hillside Avenue, and a guard called ahead to make sure they were expected. The Jamaica Estates Association sponsored a sleigh and carolers at Christmas, a community picnic and fireworks on July Fourth, and ladies' luncheons and dinner dances throughout the year.

By 1946, when Donald was born, the woodlands were gone, there was a parochial school on Midland Parkway, and there were red lights at intersections. The once bucolic refuge had become a magnet for successful professionals, with so many doctors that the local public school's PTA stamped its envelopes "Dr. or Mr." But it was still a relatively homogeneous white area, with one or two black families, no Asians, and little truly conspicuous consumption. It was still a place where people knew each other, where each winter the kids all sledded together down Midland Parkway.

Nobody bothered to lock doors, and nobody minded when children wandered over to a neighbor's house in search of adventure. Almost every day the three younger Trump children, Donald, Elizabeth, and Robert, all blond and fair skinned, visited the lady next door, Bernice Able MacIntosh, and her daughter, Heather. Some years earlier, Bernice's mother, who spoke German, had been friends with Fred Trump's mother. Her father, a retired jeweler and land developer who had been one of the earliest residents in the area and had sold Fred Trump the lots on Wareham and Midland Parkway, was surrogate grandfather to these towheaded neighbors. He made them toy boats and hung a swing from a high tree branch in the backyard. On summer mornings his daughter would wake up to its squeak as the Trumps went for an early ride.

"It seemed like every morning I would have two or three Trumps at the breakfast table with Heather," Bernice MacIntosh said many years later. "There were three cookie jars, and they were always open. So was the refrigerator. The Trumps didn't have that [freedom] at their house, so they came over to mine." The Trumps also had no pets, so they came over to play with the MacIntoshes' kittens and rabbits. Heather's specialty was dirt bombs, made from a mixture of dirt and water and molded in empty egg cartons. After the bombs had dried in the sun, the children pelted each other with them and then started all over. Donald's special passion, Bernice MacIntosh recalled, was toy vehicles. "Every Christmas and for each birthday I'd buy him the strongest truck I could find," she said. "He'd always take it apart immediately. By the time my daughter got home from his birthday party, he'd have dismantled it. 'Oh, Mom, he's got it all in pieces,' she'd say."

When Donald was three he went to the Carousel Pre-School, a new nursery program in Jamaica Estates. "Donald was a beautiful little boy, very blond and buttery," recalled the director, Shirley Greene. "He was a nice size for his age, very attractive, social, and outgoing. He wasn't fat, but he was sturdy, and really quite jolly." After being trained at two of the leading schools in the field of early childhood education, Columbia University's Teachers College and Bank Street College of Education, Greene had set up a model nursery school in an old house and put into practice her studies about child-centered curricula. Considered avant-garde at the time, Carousel emphasized individual development and hands-on learning experiences from gardening and outdoor play to collecting snowflakes and, especially, building with blocks.[12]

Among Donald's closest playmates at the time was his younger brother, Robert. When they weren't next door with Heather or her grandfather, they were down in the family playroom with their toys: cars, trucks, model trains, and toy construction equipment. Two years younger than Donald, his hair slightly darker, his build more slight, and his manner more quiet and easygoing, Robert usually ended up doing things Donald's way. When Donald was an adult, one of his favorite childhood stories was about using all his own blocks on a particularly ambitious structure and then borrowing all of Robert's to complete it. When Donald finished he was so pleased with the results that he glued everything together. "And that was the end of Robert's blocks," he later remembered.[13] It was also the model for how things would continue to go between the brothers, who would play and work together for years to come—always under Donald's direction.

At five Donald went to Kew Forest, the private school in nearby Forest Hills attended by his older siblings. Unlike Carousel, it was a traditional, structured environment where children sang hymns at morning assembly and wore uniforms. For boys this meant a navy blazer with the school crest on the pocket, charcoal pants, and the school tie, and girls wore navy blue jumpers with a white blouse. Although the Trump children did not seem to realize it, their father's success, reflected by the limousines, the chauffeur, and the many billboards around Queens and Brooklyn advertising Trump buildings, had already distanced them from other children in Jamaica Estates; similarly, his wealth set them apart at the First Presbyterian Church in Jamaica, where they attended Sunday school and were confirmed. "Their house was noted by people," recalled Ann Rudovsky Kornfeld, who grew up a few blocks away. "They'd say, 'Oh, the Trumps live there.' People knew who they were. They were really separated, cut off." The station wagon that appeared every morning to pluck the Trump children off to Kew Forest made that separation manifest.[14]

Kew Forest was where Donald met his best friend for many years, Peter Brant, the son of another wealthy man.[15] With his short, chunky build and dark coloring, Peter was the physical opposite of Donald, a tall youngster with a fair-haired, choirboy look. But in every other respect they seem to have been a perfect match. Like Donald, Peter grew up hearing accented English, for his parents were refugees from war-torn Spain. Although both boys could have been able students, they were in the bottom half of the class. It was outside the classroom, as athletes, that they excelled, playing on all the teams and bringing home medals and trophies.[16] "Sports was our whole life then," Peter Brant said afterward. "We were in our own world. After school we would look through sporting goods catalogs and see if we could buy equipment. We would go to stores together and look at the best possible mitt we could afford. Our life revolved around watching the Brooklyn Dodgers play."

Equally important, although both lived the life of rich children, with families who went to Florida on vacation and stayed at the Fontainebleau, they had been taught not to show off this fact. Like Donald, Peter had a paper route and rounded up used bottles for the deposits. One of their favorite games was Land, which consisted simply of drawing a line in the dirt, then throwing a pocketknife at it and seeing who could get closest. Once Donald and Peter both wanted a particular baseball glove that cost $28, a hefty sum in the 1950s, and each got an emphatic "no" from his father. Peter asked relatives and raised enough money to buy it on his own; Donald got a new glove that was a simpler model.

"The two of them were very similar," said another classmate, Fina Farhi Geiger. "They were extremely competitive and had to be on top whichever way they could. They really pushed the limits in terms of authority and what they could get away with." They got into mischief constantly, throwing spitballs, cracking jokes, doing whatever they could to get attention from classmates and a rise out of the teachers. As punishment they had to stay after school, and more than once they were summoned to the principal's office. "We grew up at a time when everyone basically went by the rules, which means being respectful," Geiger said. "Peter and Donald didn't do that. They weren't respectful. They did their own thing. Donald was very sharp and knew just what he could get away with."

In seventh grade the two boys had crew cuts and wore pegged pants and black shoes. "Donald was not the best dresser then," Peter said. "He had these Thom McAn black flapjack shoes with a piece of metal that ran up the tongue so you'd step in the shoe and it snapped shut. This was the doo-wah period, but these were awkward looking, like something Jerry Lewis would wear." That year kids started having coed parties, where they would stack up Elvis Presley, Chuck Berry, and Bill Haley 45s on little RCA record players and stand around wondering whether to dance. "You'd be looking at girls," Peter said, "but not really admitting you were interested. I don't ever remember having a conversation with Donald about girls."

One of the things they liked to do best was ride the subway into Manhattan on Saturdays and go to a magic store at West 49th Street and Broadway. There they bought stink bombs and smoke bombs and plastic vomit. Another favorite was hot peppered gum, which they gave to unsuspecting schoolmates. After seeing *West Side Story*, they became fascinated with switchblades. "A switchblade knife was an exciting thing for an eleven-year-old to have," Peter said. "We bought a little one, then a bigger one, and finally we were up to an eleven-inch knife. There was nothing bad in it, we just wanted to play Land and listen to the noise of flicking the blade."

One day their parents found the knives. Fred Trump, an active member of the school's board of trustees, was already disturbed by the reports he received about Donald's behavior in the classroom. At church, too, Donald had managed to annoy his elders, including Sunday school teachers and youth group leaders. Discovering the switchblades and learning that the boys had been going into New York was the last straw. "That was the incident," Peter said, "that turned Donald's father into thinking he should go away to school."

—⁄⁄⁄—

Occasionally the family piled into the limousine and drove to the Concord, a sprawling Catskills institution about ninety miles northwest of New York City.[17] One of the largest of hundreds of hotels in what was called the Borscht Belt, the Concord was a vast hodgepodge of tennis courts, swimming pools, golf courses, putting greens, and dozens of brick buildings connected by covered walkways. Catering to a mostly Jewish clientele, the Concord offered city families a chance to take a drive, breathe in the pine-scented air, then disappear inside familiar-looking buildings and re-create a scaled-down version of the urban scene they had just left. Fred Trump saw men he knew from business and politics, and his kids hung out with their kids. Then the family ate dinner together at tables piled with platters of kosher food and watched entertainers who included comedian Buddy Hackett and crooner Vic Damone.

But for the Trump children, summer really meant two adjacent Catskill camps.[18] Founded by Everett "Chief" Hillman, who had graduated from Richmond Hills High a few years ahead of Fred Trump, Camp Hilltop offered eight weeks of healthy outdoor activities to boys, and Camp Hill Manor did the same for girls. The camps were expensive, explicitly Christian,[19] and exceptionally carefully supervised, a matter of some concern to Mary Trump. "I hated to see the children go away," she said later, "but we knew they would be taken care of."[20]

Every morning boys and girls, who were strictly segregated despite the fact that they shared facilities and were within hailing distance of each other all day, put on the camp uniform: gray shorts and green shirts for boys, green shorts and white blouses for girls. Then they made their beds, stood for cabin inspection, and trotted off to a busy day of sports and crafts. In the evening counselors in each cabin filled out "poop reports," in which they noted what children did and ate, how they felt, whether they had brushed their teeth, and, most important, whether they had had a bowel movement that day. The chief's wife, known as Aunt Helyne, read the reports and responded to any hint of a problem with an immediate bunkside visit.

Even in such a well-regulated environment, though, certain kids found ways to assert themselves. Fred Trump Jr. toed the line himself but induced others to misbehave. "He would come up with some mischief he'd like to see, then plant the idea in another kid's mind and watch what happened," said Richard Hillman, a son of the owners and a camp counselor. Usually the mischief was fairly innocent, things like short-sheeting another kid's bed. Sometimes Freddy and his cabin mates sneaked out and met girls from Hill Manor. Once they hitchhiked into a nearby town in the middle of the night and then on the way back had the misfortune to be picked up by Aunt Helyne. As punishment they had to strip down to their underpants, lean over a sawhorse, and get spanked with a paddle.

Donald found camp life boring, but he learned from his brother's experience. Instead of creeping into town and risking a paddling, he concentrated on doing only what he wanted to do around camp. "He was an ornery kid, the kind that tried to get out of activities whenever he could," recalled Stanley Hillman, another of the owner's sons, "He figured out all the angles." One safe outlet was to paint "Don Trump 59" inside the door of his cabin. Whenever camp got to him, he could lie down on his bunk and look over at the sight of his own name—a reassuring sight, perhaps, for a boy about to be swept into the uniformed impersonality of military school.

—✳—

In 1959, when he was thirteen, Donald Trump went off to New York Military Academy (NYMA).²¹ Situated on the edge of Cornwall-on-Hudson, a tiny hamlet about fifty-five miles north of New York City and next door to West Point, it had first opened its doors in 1889. The founder, Colonel Charles Jefferson Wright, was a Civil War veteran. Believing that an orderly mind requires an orderly environment, he set out to curb unruly young spirits by taking over an old summer hotel and turning it into a miniencampment. Over the ensuing seventy years NYMA staff and students created an institution that in the fall of 1959 resembled a child's toy soldier set. At the center of the campus, a series of crenellated, fortress-style barracks enclosed a central quadrangle. Flags and pennants fluttered from rooftops, old cannons sat neatly on the edge of smooth lawns, and off in the distance stretched green playing fields. In the afternoons and on weekends, squads of uniformed cadets marched up and down, back and forth, as the school band steamed through one military march after another.

Inside the barracks, cadets rose before dawn to the sound of a bugle, put on a gray shirt and pants and maroon tie, and marched to meals, chapel, classes, and military drills. Taped to the inside of the door to every dorm room were typewritten instructions and a diagram that showed how to fold and where to stow sheets, towels, and clothing. A complete ban on civilian clothing made the task somewhat easier. Cadets wore NYMA-issue garments, from gym shorts to formal dress uniforms. For Saturday morning inspections they had to sweep, dust, wash, and wipe every square inch of their rooms. Then they put on their white dress gloves and scrubbed white hatbands and white cartridge belts in the sink until gloves, bands, and belts were snowy. They gave their black shoes the requisite glasslike sheen by adding spit to polish and rubbing until it seemed their hands would fall off. Afterward they got out metal polish and shined brass buttons, buckles, ornamental eagles, and breastplates.

As soon as they arrived, cadets found themselves immersed in the discipline of learning how to march, salute, and perform military maneuvers. Upperclassmen ordered them to stand at attention, recite NYMA rules and traditions, run errands, do push-ups, eat in the squared-off manner, and carry out the many onerous demands made of them when they had first showed up. "It's not an easy task for a boy away from home, having people barking at you, do this, do that, get in step, keep your mouth closed, take a shower, do your homework, go to bed, get up," said Colonel Ted Dobias. A weathered-looking World War II veteran known as "Doby," he had graduated from NYMA and then stayed on as a tactical training officer and athletic coach. "Kids would burst into tears and beg to go home."

But somehow, what might have been utterly Dickensian was not. After a few dazed weeks the cadets rallied and began to compete for cleanest room, shiniest shoes, most impeccable uniform. Parents of cadets visited and took their sons and friends whose parents weren't there out to Sunday dinner. By Thanksgiving most cadets had gotten more or less used to the routine. "After a while, you're on your way," Doby said. "It builds character in a boy, teaches them to be organized, to know exactly what they're doing all the time."

For the first time, Donald was in a place that encouraged and channeled competitiveness and aggression instead of tamping it down. In the barracks he could compete for neatest room and help boost his company's rating. In the classroom he could compete for grades and actually managed to get the highest grades in geometry. And on the athletic field he could compete in every sport and be a star. Unlike Kew Forest, NYMA considered sports the main event. At last Donald was in a place where winning really mattered, and he poured himself into doing better than everyone else at everything.

By any measure, Donald was a success at NYMA.[22] He did his best to fit in, once even refusing to let his parents visit unless they left the chauffeur at home,[23] and he participated in the usual adolescent group events. Like boys everywhere, the cadets had contests for who would be the first one to have a wet dream, spread rumors that the school put saltpeter in cadets' food to keep testosterone under control, and carried condoms that remained unused but left a small round mark of distinction on leather wallets.[24] During spring break senior year, Donald went on a chaperoned trip to Bermuda with other cadets, and they all rode around on rented motor scooters and met socially appropriate girls on chaperoned trips from their own prep schools. That year classmates voted Donald "Ladies' Man," although like the other cadets, he saw girls only at mixers and occasional school dances.

Nonetheless he never had truly close friends. "He wasn't that tight with anyone," said Ted Levine, Donald's roommate their first year at NYMA. "People liked him, but he didn't bond with anyone. I think it was because he was too competitive, and with a friend you don't always compete. It was like he had this defensive wall around him, and he wouldn't let anyone get close. He didn't distrust everybody, but he didn't trust them, either."

Donald seemed closest to Coach Dobias. "He caught my eye right away because he was so aggressive but so coachable," Doby said. "Lots of kids you can talk to until you're blue in the face and nothing happens, but Donald would react to instructions. If you told him he wasn't throwing the baseball correctly, he'd do it right the next time. If you said he wasn't blocking a tackle high enough, he'd correct it.

He was very sure of himself, but he also listened." Like many of the teachers at NYMA, Doby took an active interest in cadets he considered particularly promising, and he pushed Donald constantly, checking that he was keeping up his grades and, during his senior year, making him unofficial assistant baseball coach.

As Donald remembered it, he "finessed" Doby by showing that he was respectful of the coach but not scared of him. Perhaps Doby finessed him as well. By protecting and promoting him, he elicited a performance and level of self-discipline well beyond what the young man from Jamaica Estates had seemed capable of. When Fred and Mary Trump came up to see their son, as they did nearly every weekend, they found him transformed. "The academy did a wonderful job," she said afterward. "I would never have sent Robert there, he was too sensitive. But Donald was different. He was never homesick, or at least if he was, he never let on. He loved it."

What Donald seemed to love most was the military environment itself. Far from being daunted by the strict discipline at NYMA, a former roommate recalled, Donald seemed to welcome being in a place with clear-cut parameters, a place where he could focus on figuring out how to come out on top and get what he wanted. Indeed, he seemed drawn to Doby precisely because, as he later wrote in his autobiography, *The Art of the Deal*, the coach "didn't take any back talk from anyone" and "if you stepped out of line, Dobias smacked you, and he smacked you hard."[25]

When Donald and his senior-year roommate, David Smith, hung out in their room, Donald liked to "hit the beach" by putting an ultraviolet bulb in the ceiling fixture, lying down on his bunk, and pretending that he was basking in the Florida sunshine. Smith had only the vaguest notion of his own future, but Donald seemed to know exactly where he was headed. Dropping the usual Trump family reticence about their wealth, he pegged his father's worth at $30 million and bragged that the number doubled every year. "Donald had a sense of how he wanted to be viewed," Smith said. "He really wanted to be a success. He was already focused on the future, thinking long-term more than present. He used to talk about his dad's business, how he would use him as a role model but go one step further."

He had started doing so back on visits to construction sites when he was a kid and saw his father's attention to details as minor as picking up and recycling unused nails. As a teenager he worked on the maintenance crew at Gregory Apartments, a foreclosed FHA project his father had bought in Seat Pleasant, Maryland, and saw the emphasis on regular daily upkeep. "I wore a T-shirt and worked in the machine shop," he said years later. "I loved it, working with my hands, and I saw a different world, the world of the guys who clean and fix things."[26] He collected coins from laundry rooms.[27] He ran errands. He hosed down dust at the Trump Village construction site. He chauffered his father and saw that even when Fred Trump stopped for a coffee break at a neighborhood luncheonette, he was busy scribbling in a notebook and doing paperwork. Day in and day out, Donald Trump watched, worked, and learned. "You could already see the motor running in his head," said an early Trump Village tenant.[28]

"He was a real eager beaver, a go-getter," remembered Trump Village architect Morris Lapidus. "Whenever his father gave him something to do, he would be off and running. You could tell that he was going to get somewhere."

For his first two years of college Donald Trump attended classes in business administration at Fordham University, a Roman Catholic institution in the Bronx, and commuted to his parents' home on Midland Parkway.[29] Run by the Jesuit order, Fordham, like NYMA, did not seem an obvious choice for Donald Trump. But the reason for going there, he said later, was simple. "I'd been away at school for five years, and I wanted to see my parents," he said.[30] When Maryanne was asked why her brother went to Fordham, she offered another explanation: "That's where he got in."

By Donald Trump's own account, what may have been one of his most important lessons occurred just after he started college at Fordham. One rainy, cold day in November 1964 he accompanied his father to opening ceremonies for the Verrazano-Narrows Bridge, which joined Staten Island and Brooklyn and was the longest and highest suspension bridge in the world. It was also City Construction coordinator Robert Moses's last hurrah, and its opening day was an occasion for politicians to deliver remarks and, mainly, receive applause, regardless of whether they had actually backed the project. But what Donald Trump noticed was that Othmar Hermann Amman, the eighty-five-year-old Swiss-born immigrant who designed the Verrazano, George Washington, Whitestone, and Throgs Neck bridges, was alone and ignored. "I realized then and there," the young developer-to-be told a reporter many years later, "that if you let people treat you how they want, you'll be made a fool. I realized then and there something I would never forget: I don't want to be made anybody's sucker."[31]

At Fordham he would not be a sucker, although he would be out of place in many ways. For starters, his military bearing stuck out in a civilian setting. In addition, he was not Catholic, and with his little red sports car and well-tailored clothes, he was obviously wealthier than most of his classmates. In an era in which cigarette smoking was the symbol of sophistication and independence, Donald Trump did not smoke; more unusual, in a school culture where alcohol played a big role, he was a teetotaler. On the squash team, which he joined his fresh-man year, he never slammed his squash racket into the wall after los-ing, like some of the other players. "He had a certain aura," said Rich Marrin, a teammate. "He didn't have tantrums, and he was never late. If anything, he was more of a gentleman than we were, more refined, as if brought up in a stricter family, with more emphasis on manners. We weren't that rowdy, but we didn't always know the right forks."

At the same time, Donald Trump wanted to be part of the crowd, and he made an effort, for the most part successful, to fit in. Although squash was new for him, he worked hard at it, doggedly squeezing into a station wagon with his teammates to ride to practice day after day. Eventually he won a spot on the first-string team. When the squash team traveled to matches in Washington, D.C., he seemed like just one more hell-raising college kid. Along with his teammates, he stayed out late and went to parties to meet girls; the only difference was that he handled himself better. "Most of us had come from parochial schools and were socially not at ease," Marrin recalled. "We sometimes acted like jerks or were shy or just got drunk. He didn't seem to come with that baggage. He could talk easily and get girls' at-tention. He had a certain savoir faire."

Occasionally that savoir faire showed through in other ways. Whenever *The Wall Street Journal* or *The New York Times* was lying on a bench at practice, he'd grab it and start scanning the pages. When the squash team went to Washington, he tried out the new set of golf clubs that was in his car trunk and hit half a dozen new balls into the Potomac River without a second thought—a gesture that seemed so extravagant, his teammates remembered it decades later. By the end of sophomore year he was ready to move on. He was interested in business development, which he called "the what-if kind of stuff," and business connections, and he could learn more about both at the place he was going next: Wharton, the University of Pennsylvania's business school.[32]

To many of the young people in or around American colleges or universities in the fall of 1966, it might have seemed a curious choice. At the time, Wharton was perched on the edge of the campus both geographically and culturally.[33] Opposition to the Vietnam War was beginning to heat up at schools around the country and within Penn's own liberal arts division, but the business school remained resolutely unaffected by the signs of impending change. Wharton students still wore coats and ties to classes, and those enrolled in ROTC wore their military uniforms to class without incident. The only protest at Wharton occurred when authorities canceled Skimmer Weekend, two days of crew races and beer drinking, because of excessive rowdiness; instead of marching, students simply reversed the letters and renamed the event "Remmiks Weekend," and the administration let the event go ahead as planned.

But Donald wasn't there to participate in the counterculture. He didn't care that Wharton students were the most straight-arrow in all of Penn. Nor did he care that as a transfer student he was ineligible to play on varsity sports teams and that he seemed to have even fewer friends at Wharton than at previous schools. What he cared about was that Wharton had one of the few real estate departments in American academia. Indeed, his older brother, Fred Jr., had identified the school as the top choice for Fred Sr.'s successor, but the older boy had been unable to gain admission. Heeding Freddy's example, Donald had not applied to Wharton straight off but had instead spent his senior year at NYMA, leafing through the dozens of college catalogs he kept in a little duffel bag under his desk. Now, after two years of respectable grades at Fordham and an interview with a friendly Wharton admissions officer who was one of Freddy's old high school classmates, Donald was able to transfer there.

"My father wanted me to finish and get a degree," Donald said later. "[Real estate] was the only thing I could see studying." It was Wharton's smallest division, with only one professor and six students, most of them there because their families were in the industry. For the next two years Donald and his classmates studied finance, mortgages, accounting, and money and banking. Working together in teams, they learned how to analyze neighborhoods and make appraisals by walking around and going into bars to see what ethnic groups were there. For those Wharton students who had chosen to major in more popular fields like marketing and industrial management, real estate seemed obscure, even somewhat esoteric. But for Donald it was familiar and welcome territory. For the first time in his life, what he was studying seemed relevant. Finally there was a classroom competition he wanted to win.

Doing so was easy after a lifetime of visiting his father's building sites, listening to his father's evening and weekend telephone calls, and working on his father's construction projects during the summers. "It didn't take me long to realize that there was nothing particularly awesome or exceptional about my classmates," he later wrote in his autobiography, *The Art of the Deal*. "I could compete with them just fine."[34] Sometimes the department's lone professor and Donald would have asides as to what was really going on in the business. "I remember the professor talking to Donald like one insider to another," said Peter Gelb, another real estate major. "We were the students, and they were the pros."

Although he was barely old enough to vote, Donald Trump had already won what might have been the toughest competition of his career.[35] On his dresser at NYMA was a photograph of his older brother standing next to an airplane. As Donald and his roommate lay on their backs and discussed the future, Donald talked about how Fred Jr., who was nearly six years older than Donald, had decided to opt out of the family business and become a pilot. This choice—which Donald hastened to say he would never have made—left him next in line to take over. Before he had finished high school, in other words, what could have been the biggest and most difficult conflict of his entire career was over, and he had come out on top.

It wasn't supposed to turn out that way. Frederick Christ Trump Jr. was the obvious heir apparent in a family where an older sister was not considered a candidate.[36] The problem was that he did not act like an heir apparent. Skinny, blond, and nervous, he was a live wire, always active, always moving, always doing something. Even when sitting down, he would invariably be tapping his toe or jiggling his chair. Freddy was closer to Maryanne, who was a year and a half older, than he was to his other siblings. He played with her and, more often than not, lost to her—the usual outcome between older and younger siblings, but with Freddy it seemed to happen way too often. Like his father and his younger brother, he was fiercely competitive; unlike them, he did not have the skills or the strategic sense to get what he wanted.

"He wasn't as intelligent as Maryanne, and I think the other kids outshone him," said Ginny Droesch Trumpbour, a counselor at the Hillman camps. "He wasn't quick enough to grasp what their father was telling him, which must have been hard given that he was the oldest boy."

What Freddy did have was a sense of humor. He was a wiseguy who specialized in raised eyebrows and double entendres, always ready to poke fun at anyone and everyone, including himself. It was the behavior of a younger child, fitting in where he could; the difficulty was that he was expected to act like a firstborn, to be a leader and a winner, not the class clown. Unlike Maryanne, Freddy did not stay at Kew Forest for high school but instead enrolled at St. Paul's, an Episcopalian boy's prep school on Long Island. Neither a jock nor an academic type, he nonetheless ended up gravitating toward a handful of fledgling intellectuals. They rode the same train to and from school each day and over the years formed a tight group that shared everything—pizzas and Cokes at first, then, as they became older, cigarettes and beer. Often they hung out in the recreation room at Freddy's house, where they played at putting together a band. On nice days they went for rides in Freddy's little red motorboat, *Dixie Cup*.

To his friends, Freddy spoke admiringly of his father as a shrewd, sharp, corner-cutting businessman and boasted that he intended to step into his old man's shoes. But even to them Freddy seemed too much the sweet lightweight, a mawkish but lovable loser, so anxious for attention and approval that often he seemed almost desperate. "He was always trying to play a role, play a game," said one classmate. "He would show his dad he could be a tough little street fighter. But he was a real pussycat, not mean and aggressive, kind of pathetic, really." Among his friends, Freddy's obvious vulnerability elicited protective feelings, but from Fred Sr., who urged his sons to be "killers," these traits seemed to bring a far more harsh response.

"Around us, his dad could be very aggressive, arrogant, and pushy, barely sociable in some ways," said the same friend. "He wanted tough people, that was his bottom line, and he put a lot of pressure on Freddy to achieve these goals." When one of Freddy's crowd mentioned that he was going to study liberal arts at an Ivy League school, Fred Sr. bristled with rage and spoke contemptuously of how little money his own brother made as a full professor at MIT. "I think Freddy's father feared that he would be an aesthete fairy, a little English gentleman," said the friend. "It was almost as though he thought prep school was emasculating his son, that he was having the aggressive instincts schooled out of him and he was being turned into an Ivy League wimp."

When it came time to go to college, Freddy pinned his hopes on Wharton. But unlike Maryanne, who was accepted at her first choice, the prestigious women's college Mt. Holyoke, Freddy was turned down and ended up instead at Lehigh University, a second-tier school in central Pennsylvania. There he enrolled in Air Force ROTC and began to daydream about being a pilot, but when he graduated in 1958 he went to work as his father's general assistant. Finally he was face-to-face with the business he had been slated to take over, and for the next several years he gave it his best.

But his best was not close to good enough for Fred Sr. When Freddy made what his father considered a mistake, such as installing new windows when old ones were still marginally serviceable, his father didn't hesitate to chew him out in public for wasting money; when Fred Jr. did something well, as when he finished off the roof and the final touches on a six-story Brooklyn building called the Falcon, his father never mentioned it. "When I asked him why not," Maryanne recalled, "he said, 'Why? He's supposed to do a good job.' It never occurred to him to actually praise Freddy." Tensions between father and son increased under the stress of the State Investigation

Commission hearings on Trump Village, and they heightened further when Fred Jr. was unable to realize Fred Sr.'s hopes for Steeplechase Park. Freddy oversaw the dismantling of the old pavilion and stoutly defended his father's plans to the press,[37] but he could not go forward when his father's political allies could not deliver the zoning variances needed for more high-rise apartment buildings.

Freddy married a beautiful blonde airline stewardess from the Midwest named Linda Clapp, had two children, and continued trying to fit into the heir apparent role. But the strain was becoming unbearable. The occasional cigarettes of high school had long since turned into chain smoking; the occasional beers, into serious, hard-core drinking. Everyone could see that he would never be able to fill his father's shoes. They could also see that another candidate—a substitute firstborn, as it were—had emerged. "Donald moved ahead as Freddy failed," Maryanne said later. "I don't think there was a connection. Donald was a lot younger, not close enough in age for heavy competition. I don't think Freddy thought Donald was a cold wind at his back, and he wouldn't have cared if he was."

Perhaps. In any event, whether Freddy minded or not, Donald was blowing at his brother's back as hard as he could. "Our family environment, the competitiveness, was a negative for Fred," he told one reporter. "He was the first Trump boy out there, and I subconsciously watched his moves."[38] Donald saw that cowering when his father got mad only made him angrier, that hanging around people who seemed more pointy headed than practical caused his father to fly into a rage, and that showing any vulnerability around his father was a mistake. Smoking and, especially, drinking, both of which Freddy did a lot, were also sure triggers for his father's wrath. The more Donald watched Freddy, the more it looked as if his older brother, sweet and generous and funny guy that he was, would probably be spending his life behind the eight ball. If Donald didn't want to spend his life there, he would have to show his father that he was every bit as tough as he was, that whenever anyone pushed him he would push right back and harder—that he was in spirit, if not in fact, first among the firstborns.

CHAPTER FIFTEEN

MANHATTAN BOUND

ONE MORNING BACK IN JANUARY 1964, when Donald Trump was still a cadet at New York Military Academy, his father had gotten on a plane, flown to Cincinnati for the monthly sheriff's auction, shelled out $5.6 million for a 1,200-unit garden apartment complex called Swifton Village, and flown back home in time for a Madison Democratic Club dinner. "Other men like playing golf, but I like buying apartments," Fred Trump told the man sitting next to him that night.[1]

Swifton, an FHA-backed project that had cost about $10 million to build in the early 1950s, was the largest apartment complex in Cincinnati.[2] It was also one of the most dilapidated and was then more than half-empty. Even though the FHA had cut the unpaid mortgage by one-third, Fred Trump was the sole bidder. It looked like a disaster to everyone else, including his own mother. He told a Cincinnati paper that when he informed her of the purchase, she said, "That's the worst news I've had all day."[3] To Fred Trump, though, it seemed a compelling opportunity. "I don't see how you people can resist a steal like this," he told a local developer standing next to him at the auction.

From Chase Manhattan Bank, where he was a member of an advisory board and reportedly the largest depositor in Queens, Fred Trump obtained a $5.75 million first mortgage, enough to cover not only the purchase price, but also part of the renovation necessary to turn Swifton around. On Tuesdays he flew to Cincinnati to make on-site inspections and take local real estate figures out to lunch. Back in New York, he would phone them and asked how much they paid for a gallon of paint or a yard of carpeting, then check their numbers against what his staff reported to him. At Christmas he put up a huge neon sign wishing Cincinnati a happy holiday from Fred Trump. "This [project] was his baby," Roy Knight, a carpenter at Swifton at the time, later told a reporter.

When Donald was at Fordham, his father occasionally took him on his Tuesday trips to Cincinnati to see how the overhaul was going. While Fred Trump spent what was known at Swifton as "T-Day" charging in and out of buildings and firing questions at employees, his son did yardwork and cleaning with the maintenance crew. As the months went by, he saw how his father's demanding style and insistent focus brought the ailing complex back to life. New paint and appliances, neatly landscaped grounds, and beefed-up security brought up occupancy rates, and Swifton gradually returned to a more even keel—for a while.

In June 1969 Haywood Cash, a black stock clerk at a nearby GE plant, inquired about an apartment at Swifton. After the rental agent told him he did not meet income requirements and there were no vacancies, Cash and his wife contacted a local civil rights organization called HOME, which rented an apartment within the Cash family's income eligibility. When HOME attempted to turn over the apartment to the Cashes, the Swifton general manager called a HOME representative a "nigger lover" and threw her and Haywood Cash off the premises. The Cashes filed a discrimination suit under the Civil Rights Act of 1968, and shortly afterward a lawyer for Swifton, acting on Fred Trump's orders, offered them an apartment. They moved in and dropped the suit. But they asked for damages and eventually settled for the maximum allowable award of $1,000. Outwardly that was the end of the matter, although Donald Trump would continue to insist that his father had done nothing wrong. To the younger man, what had happened was a capitulation and a loss, and he did not take losing well.[4]

In the meantime, however, Fred Trump's makeover had only temporarily arrested the urban problems closing in on Swifton Village. An interstate highway slicing across Cincinnati, plus the waves of unskilled and often unemployable immigrants pouring into the city from Appalachia and points south, had permanently disrupted many formerly stable neighborhoods. Swifton again began to slide down-hill. Tenant turnover accelerated, and this time the absentee landlord from Brooklyn could not stem it. By the fall of 1972 it was time to sell. When a potential buyer, Prudent Real Estate Investment Trust, appeared, Donald Trump called Frank Harkavy, the owner of a nearby apartment complex named Colonial Village, introduced himself as Fred's son, and asked to stop by.

When the young man arrived, Harkavy recalled years later, he brought along three Prudent executives in their sixties. "I'd never met Donald Trump before," Harkavy said, adding that his visitor didn't seem to know much about the neighborhood. "He wasn't im-polite, but he had a lot of presence and assuredness. He wanted me to tell them about the area and sell them on it." Evidently Harkavy did a good job. In December 1972 Prudent announced it had bought Swifton for more than $6.75 million in cash.[5]

At the age of twenty-six Donald Trump had sealed his first multi-million-dollar deal. It was a sweet thing for a young man who had been his father's full-time student ever since graduation from Whar-ton. Every morning he and his father drove from Jamaica Estates to Fred Trump's modest office, located in Beach Haven, one of the large housing developments the older man had built near Coney Island in the early 1950s. Inside a nondescript, three-story brick building on Avenue Z, the headquarters of the Trump family empire still looked like the dentist's office it had once been, with a linoleum floor, shag carpet, and chest-high partitions between cubicles. On the walls were routine announcements, a collage of yellowed newspaper clippings, and the numerous plaques and awards given to Fred Trump for com-munity service. The only unexpected touch was a collection of carved wooden cigar-store Indians, traditional fixtures at barbershops when Friedrich Trump immigrated to New York.

The lessons included everything from where to stand when knocking at the door of a nonpaying and possibly violent tenant to how to handle maintenance contracts, negotiate the purchase of sup-plies, and oversee repairs. After the younger man raised neighborhood hackles with plans to put an off-track betting parlor in a Trump-owned shopping mall and to lease land originally intended for tenant parking to a McDonald's franchise, he got a quick course in using political ties to make things go his way. Similarly, when his father walked into a closing on an apartment complex he was selling and told the buyers, who had already syndicated the deal and could not afford further costly delays, that it was just too embarrassing to get such a low interest rate on promissory notes, he saw how to pull off a last-minute renegotiation.[6] When his father put a plant and a mirror in vacant apartments and got a more favorable response from prospective tenants, he saw how an extra touch can make a difference. Likewise he saw how to pinch pennies when, in order to save on boiler-cleaning bills, his father donned old overalls, climbed inside a boiler for a lesson from an experienced boiler cleaner, and emerged covered with soot but ready to instruct his supers himself. And, always, the son saw the importance of looking professional; like his father, he never appeared in casualwear. Even on weekends he wore a suit or a blazer, with his initials on his shirt and gold cuff links.

The son taught the father a few things, too. Gradually he overcame his father's reluctance to refinance his holdings, then about eighty buildings with an equity value on the order of $200 million, and they raised cash for new investments. But the younger man could not convince his father to operate in Manhattan, where both costs and potential benefits were far higher. Indeed, his father seemed willing to consider getting involved in projects almost anywhere except right across the river. "It wasn't his thing," Donald said in a later interview. "Manhattan just didn't make sense to him. He was familiar with the pricing out in Brooklyn. Why pay thousands of dollars for a square foot of land in Manhattan when out there he paid thirty cents?"[7]

What did make sense to Fred Trump were deals like the one his son heard about from an attorney at a Wall Street law firm's Christmas party in 1973. The lawyer had been working nonstop on negotiations to buy the nation's largest federally funded housing project. Located in Brooklyn and originally undertaken by Fred Trump's one-time competitor, Abraham Kazan, it had changed hands and was now called Starrett City, after the development company that finished it. The problem, the lawyer told Donald Trump, was that financing on

an equity package had come up short. The young man immediately
nipped into an empty office, called his father, who was in Miami, and
got an okay to put in enough money for a minority stake.

That New Year's Eve the developer-in-training got yet another
lesson, this time in patience. To receive the maximum tax benefits,
all the papers for the Starrett City transaction had to be finished by
midnight. This meant that Donald had to spend the evening in a midtown law office. "He obviously had something better to do," recalled
Craig Norville, the attorney handling the procedure. "He was so
antsy to get out of there, he was whining to do it faster, do it faster."
Finally Fred Trump, in one of the few public reprimands he ever delivered to his middle son, turned and quietly told him to calm down
and sit still.[8]

By now, although still operating out of the former dentist's office
on Avenue Z, Donald Trump had a new job description. His father
had kicked himself upstairs to be chairman of the board, and Donald
was now president of the family business. One of his first acts was to
bypass all the pedestrian corporate names used by his father and instead adopt one classy-sounding label, the Trump Organization, as a
sort of umbrella identity.[9]

He had upscaled his own life as well, with a move to Manhattan's
Upper East Side. Settling into a small, dark studio on the seventeenth
floor of a twenty-one-floor building, he blithely referred to his new
living quarters as a penthouse and began carving out a new life as a
debonair bachelor. "Moving into that apartment was probably more
exciting for me than moving, fifteen years later, into the top three
floors of Trump Tower," he wrote later.[10] Every morning he drove a
new, company-owned white Cadillac convertible in a reverse com-
mute to the far end of Brooklyn, but in the evenings he could savor
his new identity as a Manhattanite. A first step was to join Le Club, a
members-only restaurant and nightclub on East 58th Street founded
in 1960 by society columnist Igor Cassini.[11] There the young man became acquainted with various powerful players in real estate and
banking, including the lawyer Roy Cohn.

Short, bald, and heavy lidded, with a permanent tan, a bloodshot,
drop-dead stare, and a pugnacious manner, Roy Marcus Cohn had
been a celebrated bad boy ever since he first burst on the national
scene in the 1950s as Senator Joseph McCarthy's assistant in the re-

lentless hunt for subversives in the U.S. government.[12] A master fixer of all things legal and illegal, he lived a conspicuously lavish life, but because he insisted on cash payment, he paid no taxes and stonewalled his way through IRS audits. Over the years he had faced charges for bribery, conspiracy, and bank fraud, gone to trial three times, and won acquittals three times. Now in his mid-forties, Cohn radiated power in a way that repelled many but drew in Trump, who seemed intrigued to find someone else who would do, literally, anything to win. "I think Donald was attracted by the fact that Roy had actually been indicted," said Eugene Morris, Cohn's first cousin and a prominent longtime New York real estate lawyer.[13]

Morris had met the Trumps in the late 1960s, when Fred Trump retained him to handle his donation of funds for a wing to a Queens hospital. When the attorney asked Donald how he planned to handle his father's mini-empire, the young man looked him in the eye and said he didn't want anything to do with it. "I want to be in mid-Manhattan, where all the top stuff is going on," he told the lawyer. "I'll never be involved with the old man's property except when he needs me."

It seemed to Morris that, perhaps in part because of this independent streak, Fred Trump listened to his middle son in a way he listened to few others. At a later point Morris did a total overhaul of Fred Trump's city tax assessments and obtained what he thought was an impressive rollback. His client peremptorily rejected it as grossly inadequate, and Morris complained to his cousin. Cohn passed on the complaint to Donald, who managed to convince his father to accept the deal he had just turned down. To Morris's amazement, Fred Trump—a man who would still spend an entire afternoon meticulously explaining to a maintenance man how to mix liquid cockroach spray so as to avoid calling an exterminator[14]—promptly signed the paperwork. Afterward he put an arm around the lawyer and said, "Oh, Gene, it's only money, after all."[15]

Once in a while, though, it wasn't just money. On October 15, 1973, the U.S. Justice Department slapped the Trump Organization with a suit charging that blacks seeking apartments in Trump-owned buildings were turned away or quoted inflated rents. The Trumps had faced similar charges in Cincinnati, but the new president of the Trump Organization no longer followed his father's policy of quiet diplomacy. Instead he held a press conference at the New York Hilton and announced that he had hired Cohn to fire back at the government with a $100 million damage suit. Denying any discrimination, Donald said that the government was trying to push major landlords into accepting welfare tenants despite their precarious finances.

Five weeks later the presiding judge dismissed Trump's counter-suit as "wasting time and paper," but Cohn's stalling tactics delayed the federal investigation for another year and a half. Donald Trump testified repeatedly that he had nothing to do with renting apartments, although in an application for a broker's license filed at the same time he said that he was in charge of all rentals. In June 1975 he signed a settlement described by the Department of Justice as "one of the most far-reaching ever negotiated." It required Trump to advertise vacancies in a black newspaper, to give first notice to the Urban League for a certain percentage of vacancies, and to include welfare payments when determining an applicant's income.[16]

This time around, Trump simply declared victory and went on as before. He had seen that such a boast was unlikely to be challenged. He had also seen that being charged with discrimination did not seem to deter anyone in the public or private realm from doing business with him. Indeed, practically speaking, the entire matter appeared to add up to little more than "a spit in the ocean," as Roy Cohn had dismissively characterized it at one point. But perhaps more to the point, Donald Trump now had something far bigger and juicier on his plate.

On January 26, 1968, a chunky, balding man with dark-rimmed glasses and a bulldog set to his jaw stared out from the cover of *Time* magazine.[17] His name was Stuart Thomas Saunders, and he had just pulled off what looked to be the biggest corporate coup of the decade, if not the century: the merger of the Pennsylvania and New York Central Railroads. Labor featherbedding, government red tape, unprofitable passenger service, and competition from trucks, planes, and, especially, each other had pushed these legendary rail giants to the edge of bankruptcy. But now, with Pennsy chairman Saunders at the helm and Central president Alfred Edward Perlman as second in command, the two behemoths would morph into a slimmer, more robust entity called the Penn Central. Headquartered in Philadelphia, the nation's largest rail conglomerate would return America's first major industry to health and profitability. Railroads, which had consolidated the nation as they carried Friedrich Trump and millions of other immigrants across it, would again come into their own.

Headline writers dubbed the Penn Central "the Railroad of the Future," and *Saturday Review* named Saunders "Businessman of the Year." Strategic planners and transportation experts applauded, and business schools, including Wharton, where Donald Trump was finishing his senior year, looked upon Saunders with awe. Preaching the gospel of postmodern railroading—in essence, that the industry would survive only if lines got bigger in size and fewer in number—Saunders had taken over at the Pennsy in 1964 and revived long-stalled plans for consolidation with the New York Central. Four years later the new era began.

It lasted exactly 872 days. Late on the afternoon of Sunday, June 21, 1970, the Penn Central, listing badly since the moment it came into being, went belly up. Although competition between these two lines was gone, the other pressures that had led to the merger remained, and a $300 million bailout loan from a fifty-three-bank consortium had disappeared almost without a trace.

One of the biggest problems was that the merger never went beyond a paper transaction into a truly functional arrangement. Indeed, the two chief executives never had more than chilly relations and long before the end had ceased speaking to each other. Saunders, a Virginia-bred, Harvard-trained lawyer, was used to the Pennsy's massive and WASPy bureaucracy, whereas Perlman, a New York Jew and MIT-schooled engineer who had spent his life making railroads run, worked with a few select advisers and valued quick, decisive action.[18] In turn, their huge joint workforce of ninety-four thousand employees had lacked a common sense of purpose or even a common computer language. As a result, the new line routinely misplaced cars and sometimes whole trains, was almost always late, and lost the large-freight customers on which it had pinned its hopes. Supposedly headed for peak efficiency and profitability, the railroad of the future had instead produced a record-breaking deficit of $4 billion.

The Penn Central bankruptcy would help spawn a profitable new bankruptcy industry, peopled by turnaround specialists, lawyers, assessors, regulators, even publishers of newsletters devoted exclusively to this rapidly expanding field. More than that, though, the Penn Central story would produce important lessons about the modern corporate world, the nature of capitalism, the pace and course of change, and, most important, how to survive and profit from seeming disaster. And, as events in coming years would show, Donald Trump, then only twenty-four years old, would prove to be a particularly apt pupil.

Public admission of insolvency did not solve the Penn Central's problems. Because railroads were considered vital national interests, federal law would not permit them to close up shop even if they were drowning in red ink. Under the Bankruptcy Act of 1898, insolvent lines had no choice but to file for reorganization. Doing so suspended the Penn Central's debts, but it also meant that the railroad had to maintain the passenger and freight operations[19] that had been losing $1 million a day.[20] Ultimately, court-appointed trustees came up with a proposal to transfer the actual rail services to government ownership,[21] pay the Penn Central's debts by selling everything not needed for rail operations, and reorganize the holding company that controlled those few subsidiaries that actually made money.

It was an eminently sensible solution. The remaining problem was getting all the many creditors to sign on—no easy task, given that most were busy maneuvering to push the others further back in the line for the railroad's assets. At times the situation seemed to be deteriorating into what one Penn Central trustee called "trench warfare, right out of World War I";[22] eventually, however, the sheer scale of the overlapping claims convinced banks, institutional investors, stockholders, and federal, state, and local authorities to cooperate and settle for much less than they would have in other circumstances. That is, the Penn Central had "debtor's leverage," meaning that its potential loss was so large, it could cow creditors into accepting crumbs—that is, a smaller than usual percentage of what was owed— for fear that otherwise they would get nothing at all. Knowing about debtor's leverage was something that Donald Trump was, some years ahead, to find particularly helpful.

Once the framework was established, the next task was to come up with the crumbs. The way to do this was to sell off anything not directly involved in running the railroad—which, as everyone knew, meant the vast real estate holdings that both the Pennsylvania Railroad and the New York Central had spent the last century accumulating.[23] To handle the deal, *The New York Times* reported on July 6, 1973, the bankrupt railroad planned to hire a Los Angeles businessman. His name was Victor Palmieri, and he would be marketing properties worth more than $1 billion.

Six months earlier Fred and Donald Trump had told a *New York Times* reporter that the Trump Organization was finally entering the Manhattan market and would be turning a site on the East Side into rental apartments. Although the younger man had been thrilled by the prospect of doing such a deal, it paled in significance as soon as he picked up the paper that July morning. He knew that the list of sites being sold was sure to include the one property he wanted more than anything in the world: the Penn Central rail yards, consisting of two huge parcels of land stretching along the eastern shore of the Hudson River. The total size of the yards was 120 acres, one-seventh the size of Central Park.[24] Remarkably, they were the same sort of undeveloped tracts on which Fred Trump had built so successfully in Brooklyn. The same, that is, in all but one respect: They were in Manhattan, a location that would have ruled them out for Fred Trump but made them a magnet for his son.[25]

As soon as the younger man read the article, he wrote Palmieri a letter, but it would be six months before he received a response. The reason it took so long was that Victor Henry Palmieri, a man known for cutting through complex tasks with singular efficiency, was stumped.[26] Palmieri, then forty-two, had already had his share of high-intensity careers. The son of impoverished Italian immigrants, he had grown up poor in the midst of Southern California affluence, graduated from Stanford Law School, and held a series of jobs, including corporate lawyer, developer of vast Southern California orange groves, and deputy chair of the Kerner Commission, established by President Lyndon B. Johnson in 1968 to investigate urban riots. Along the way he had also been the host of a public TV show and had salvaged one of Penn Central's numerous subsidiaries by paring it down to a string of amusement parks in southwestern states called Six

Flags.[27] Stylish and sophisticated, Palmieri was a Renaissance man, Southern California style. But even he was not prepared for what confronted him when he accepted Penn Central's offer.

Reduced to basics, what most people thought of as a huge railroad with a lot of property turned out to be a huge railroad plus a huge real estate company. Indeed, Penn Central appeared to be one of the largest private, nongovernment landlords in the nation, but its real estate portfolio was so disorganized that no one could be sure exactly what property it owned or exactly where it was. To find out, Palmieri tapped his former assistant on the Kerner Commission, an efficient young Yale-trained lawyer named John Andrew Koskinen. A blond, cherubic-looking information machine, Koskinen hunkered down over old railroad maps and began creating an elaborate system for Penn Central's properties. Because existing records often proved inadequate, obtaining exact coordinates of sites often involved going to them and walking the boundaries. Koskinen was initially told that the Penn Central's holdings amounted to about 450 items, but he ultimately pegged the total at over 8,500 parcels of land, including everything from large sites in midtown Manhattan to thousands of rights-of-way obtained from the federal government during the original construction of the railroads.

Of those properties, nearly one-third were in New York City and were among the most valuable real estate in the world.[28] Ordinarily this enormous asset would be all the rescue package needed by any corporation, no matter how dire its straits. In December 1973, though, New York City was in such poor shape that it seemed all but impossible to cash in these holdings for anything close to their real value. Within the city, the manufacturing sector that had made it a magnet to millions of immigrants, including Friedrich Trump and Abraham Kazan, was shrinking. Major corporations were leaving, construction was at a standstill, public employees were staging bitter strikes over inadequate pay, and communities were protesting declining services. The federal government, staggering under the tab for the Vietnam War, was drastically cutting back on everything, including the federally financed housing programs from which Fred Trump and other developers had made their fortunes. At the same time, New York State, suffering the aftereffects of Nelson Rockefeller's exuberant expansiveness, was also on the ropes. The Mitchell-Lama housing program that had financed both Trump Village and Amalgamated Warbasse Houses had ground to a halt, and the state's Urban Development Corporation, which had used John Mitchell's marvelous moral obligation bonds for hundreds of projects, actually went into default.

Still worse, New York City, long one of the most generous cities in its support for public schools, hospitals, and welfare, was relying increasingly on costly short-term bonds just to finance daily operations. As debts piled up, the underwriting firms issued ever louder alarms over the city's financial condition. To attract buyers, the terms for the city became ever less favorable. Seeing the city spiraling into financial disaster, John Lindsay, the elegant East Sider who had ushered in the era of deficit financing, prudently declined to run for a third term as mayor. By the time his successor, Abraham Beame, moved into Gracie Mansion, the pressures of the fiscal crisis became so severe that he was barely able to exercise his mayoral powers.[29]

In short, it was, to put it mildly, not the best market to sell large real estate parcels in New York City. But the man to whom Palmieri had delegated the initial selection of buyers had a long-term perspective about the future and, as it happened, much in common with Donald Trump. A onetime college professor, Edward Philip Eichler was the son of a successful developer who built what were known as "Eichler homes" near San Francisco at the same time Fred Trump was doing FHA 608 housing in Brooklyn. After college, Ned Eichler, like Donald, had gone to work for his father, expecting to take over the prosperous family business. But in the 1960s his father had ignored his advice and dropped his well-designed single-family houses for high-rise apartment buildings. The two had an enormous row, the younger Eichler left the company, and, shortly afterward, his father went bust.

Hired by Palmieri to help divest Penn Central of its surplus real estate, Eichler had farmed out much of the task but reserved for himself the plum: the New York properties, which were the most valuable as well as the most challenging. Because the West Side rail yards looked like a particularly hard sell, he figured that the best shot was not to think of it as a conventional sale. "When I looked at New York, I saw all these developers who were broke or in trouble and the city falling into the river," he said afterward. "I knew that nobody would buy the yards for cash, that effectively we would be going into a joint venture where we'd be putting up the land and the developer would be putting up the skill."

What he needed, it seemed to Eichler, was a seemingly impossible package: a developer who knew how to do the job and could handle big-city politics but didn't already have other Manhattan projects competing for attention. "I knew we would be riding a horse here," Eichler said. "The only question was which horse—which developer—would be the right one."

One December day he opened a file of correspondence on the yards and found Donald Trump's letter. Ascertaining that no one in his office recognized the name, Eichler then dialed the Trump Organization on Avenue Z in Brooklyn and asked to speak to his correspondent. "Donald just came right through the telephone from the start," Eichler said years later. "He was selling from the beginning of the conversation. He told me about his father, all these buildings they'd built, when was I coming to Brooklyn, he'd show me around, he'd send a car to pick me up, don't worry."

Taken by the sheer energy on the other end of the line, Eichler made the trip in mid-January and took the Donald Trump tour. He was impressed by the real estate he saw, and he was fascinated by the young man spouting off grandiose plans to build an enormous residential development on the site now occupied by the rail yards. "He seemed like an epic character, straight out of Stendhal," Eichler said. "An ambitious boy from the provinces, full of his own ego, wanting to make his way in the city."

But Eichler was unsure that this unknown developer-in-training could take care of the heavy-duty politics, community relations, financing, and rezoning such a massive undertaking would require. When Eichler asked for proof that he could handle these issues, young Trump suggested that he speak to the new mayor, Abe Beame, in office only a few weeks. Playing along with what he assumed was a joke, Eichler said off the top of his head, "Okay, how about tomorrow at one-thirty in the afternoon?" Without an instant's hesitation, Donald Trump said he would send his car so that Eichler wouldn't be late to City Hall. What Eichler didn't know was that the new mayor, a diminutive Brooklyn accountant, had started his political career as a precinct worker in the Madison Democratic Club and counted Fred Trump and Bunny among his closest friends.

The next day Ned Eichler found himself walking into the mayor's office at exactly one-thirty P.M. for a meeting with Abe Beame, Fred and Donald Trump, and John Zuccotti, the newly appointed chair of the City Planning Commission.[30] After a few pleasantries Eichler told the mayor why he was there. To Eichler's astonishment, the tiny chief executive of New York City managed to reach an arm around each of the Trumps, both six-footers, then looked out directly at Eichler and said, "Whatever my friends Fred and Donald want in this town, they get."

The normally voluble Eichler was dumbfounded at what seemed a mayoral blank check. "What else could I ask after that?" he said later. "Beame had answered all the questions in one sentence." Afterward Eichler stood on the plaza in front of City Hall chatting with Fred and Donald Trump. As the older man spoke, Eichler was struck by how comfortable he appeared with his son's aggressive plans and how easily he seemed to cede the spotlight to him.

"Many very successful fathers, self-made men, as I understood Donald's father to be—as my father was—are rather ambivalent about their sons at a very young age becoming big figures and successful," he said later. "But it seemed clear to me that this was a very unusual relationship, that his father seemed totally supportive that this was Donald's project."[31] Seeing Fred Trump's solicitude and encouragement to his son, Eichler mused about how his own father could never have offered such unconditional backing.

What Eichler could not have realized was that for Fred Trump, this was an opportunity to live out his own fantasies and longings, to be the father who could not be there for him, the father who had died in 1918 when Fred was only twelve. In a way, Fred Trump was acting as father both to his son and to himself. This dual identity gave great intensity to their relationship, and it had a powerful effect on a number of observers, including Ned Eichler. Indeed, in the end, what may have sealed Eichler's choice of Donald Trump to develop the rail yards was the close tie he saw between father and son.

Victor Palmieri was less taken than Eichler with the untried neophyte from Brooklyn. For several months the two men argued about whether to back Donald Trump's bid to the Penn Central trustees for the option on the yards. But in the end Palmieri gave his okay to a deal that would allow Donald Trump to pursue financing and rezoning on the yards in exchange for cutting the Penn Central in on future development proceeds. One reason for Palmieri's eventual assent was that there were no other candidates he considered credible; another was that Palmieri's national Democratic credentials were worthless in New York, where what counted were local ties. With the Penn Central trustees on his back and pressure from all sides to act quickly, Palmieri had to find someone who already had the necessary connections in place. He needed what he called "a hard charger"—a risk taker who had both a nose for the market and enough energy to keep pushing for the five to ten years a major development could take. If Donald Trump hadn't appeared, Victor Palmieri would have had to invent him.

The reverse was also true. Although Fred Trump's political connections and real estate portfolio gave Donald Trump crucial legitimacy, they did not provide financing per se. Even if he wanted to put his entire fortune at risk, Fred Trump could not have footed the bill for what his son had in mind. Instead the money would have to come from government programs, then being cut back, or from banks and other such institutions loath to lend even to experienced builders given the city's chancy financial state. Because Donald was still an unknown as a developer, he would come under special scrutiny by lenders. What he needed was someone able to buy into the notion that his intense drive would somehow make up for his lack of cash— someone, that is, like Ned Eichler and, albeit reluctantly, Victor Palmieri. "We were backing him for effort," Palmieri said later. "With us, Donald could operate without money, just energy, and that was key for him at that point."

Over the months that followed, Donald Trump tried again and again to come up with a way to strike a deal on one or another of the railroad's properties. By now Eichler was set up in an old Penn Central building, and every day or two the young developer-to-be would show up and go over all the properties that were potentially for sale. Most of the time, though, he talked about the rail yards, which were bundled together for sale purposes. The smaller parcel and also the one with more rail traffic, known as the 34th Street yards, was 44 acres and extended from 30th to 39th Streets along the Hudson River; the second, known as the 60th Street yards, was about 75 acres (18.5 of them underwater), went from 59th to 72nd Streets, and was partially covered by an elevated section of the West Side Highway.[32] Since the late nineteenth century, both tracts, which sat on top of large portions of landfill, had been used by the New York Central for freight traffic. By the late 1920s urban planners were greedily eyeing the site, which was the last large undeveloped stretch left in Manhattan. But it was not until the 1970s, when almost the only thing still shipped by rail down the West Side was the newsprint used at *The New York Times* printing plant, that the property became available for other uses.[33]

The use Donald Trump had in mind was a gigantic middle-income housing complex, which would require a change of zoning, from industrial to residential, as well as enormous government subsidies. "Donald made all sorts of outrageous demands and had no tolerance when I would say something was impossible," Eichler said later. "But that's true of all successful real estate developers—they don't want to hear the negatives. If they just keep pushing and pushing and don't listen, they'll get there. Lots of times I'd have to yell at him, use profanities—'Just shut up, you son of a bitch!'"

But Trump just kept on talking, trying every which way to get what he wanted. At times his conversation included heavy innuendos—but never concrete offers—that he was willing to pay for favors. "Once we passed a headline about a mayor in New Jersey being arrested for an enormous bribe," Eichler recalled. "Donald looks at the headline and says, 'There is no fucking mayor in America worth that much money—I could buy a U.S. senator for less than that.' He had that way of talking—was he kidding, was he serious, was he sending me a message? It didn't matter, I wouldn't have taken him up on it, but I did wonder." After Eichler sent back a Christmas present of a chauffeur-delivered television set, Trump threw up his arms in exasperation and said, "I don't know how to deal with you, Eichler; anybody else in your position would have $10 million in a cigar box tucked away."

On another occasion the younger man asked Eichler to join him and Roy Cohn for lunch at the fashionable Four Seasons restaurant. Eichler was offended by Trump's many tales of hiring Cohn to keep tenants he considered undesirable out of his properties, but he was also curious to meet the ultimate New York fixer. Their host came late and announced, with such loud enthusiasm that Eichler was sure diners on all sides could hear, that he'd just met with Democratic gubernatorial candidate Hugh Carey, then a member of the House of Representatives from Brooklyn. "He's perfect," Trump declared gleefully. "He'll do anything for money."

Mostly, though, Donald Trump worked harder and was more focused and more competitive than anyone Eichler had ever seen. "I saw it again and again," Eichler said. "He'd be in a meeting, performing and carrying on, and then some guy would ask him a technical question and he'd be on it like a tiger." The only topic of conversation, all day long and during dinner as well, was business. "You didn't talk about any of the ordinary things, like movies or books," Eichler said. "With Donald, there was no small talk."

Eichler often wondered why someone who already had family money would be so driven. Once when they lunched at another elegant Manhattan restaurant, the '21' Club, Trump supplied a clue in an uncharacteristically reflective moment. He told Eichler that he assumed he would not marry and would be dead before he was forty, but in the time he had left he intended to be bigger than Harry Helmsley, then the largest real estate magnate in New York. "I knew that whole world of builders," Eichler said, "and the guys who really cared about making money were very private. Donald was different. For him, the purpose wasn't the money. It was to be famous."

Following his father's example, Trump labored morning, noon, and night. Sometimes he would call Eichler up at one or two in the morning to argue over details. One fall day when they drove out to Winged Foot, the classy Westchester golf club that Trump had joined the year after he graduated from college, Eichler commented about the gorgeous trees alongside the highway. His host interrupted his business spiel long enough to say, "I suppose so, if you like that sort of thing," then plunged back in. Once at the club, it was clear that this was no relaxed, recreational game. Trump was playing not just to win, but to vanquish. For him there was no down time; he was as competitive on the golf course playing for a few dollars as he was making business deals worth millions.

Such behavior didn't make him likable, but Eichler wasn't looking for likable. "I never at any time liked Donald personally, but that never had anything to do with whether he was the right person," Eichler said later. "Other developers wanted to get control of the property, and then whenever all their other problems got worked out this could make a lot of money and be a feather in their caps. I wanted somebody who got up every day thinking this was his main thing in life, what he wanted to make work." And to Ned Eichler, that meant Donald Trump.

Late on the afternoon of Monday, November 11, 1974, Donald Trump, then twenty-eight years old, sat at a table in a nondescript federal courtroom in Philadelphia and watched as a hearing on the disposition of the Penn Central rail yards opened. Seated next to him were his father and the Trump Organization lawyer, Bunny Lindenbaum. Nearby were Ned Eichler, John Koskinen, and nearly a dozen attorneys for various creditors and interested parties. They were there because the Penn Central trustees wanted to grant the Trump Organization an option to buy the rail yards and needed permission from the federal district court handling the reorganization.

Specifically, this and any other deal involving the Penn Central required the approval of Judge John Patrick Fullam, under whose jurisdiction the railroad had come when it filed for reorganization. Naturally enough, Fullam-watching had since become something of a necessity among the dozens of lawyers involved in the case. What they found was a small giant. A former Pennsylvania farm boy, Fullam was a World War II vet and Harvard Law School graduate who ended up on the bench after he lost two races for Congress. "In chambers he was this really little guy who wouldn't stomp a fly," said one Penn Central lawyer. "But he was a terror up there on the bench. He controlled all of the creditors and all of us, kept us all in place."[34] With one of the most valuable sites in the entire Penn Central inventory at issue, the proceeding promised to be long and contentious. To make matters worse, it did not get under way until twilight had already arrived outside the large courtroom windows. Courthouse regulars had anticipated a stressful, drawn-out session, but instead the proceeding unfolded with unaccustomed smoothness. Unbeknownst to them and to the judge, the important deal-making had already occurred before Fullam ever lifted his gavel.

In the weeks leading up to the hearing, most of the people now seated in the courtroom had expected strident opposition to the trustees' request to give Donald Trump the option. They assumed the source would be David Berger, the lawyer for the Penn Central's stockholders, then at the bottom of the creditor heap. A stout man with a penetratingly loud voice and showy offices in a Philadelphia brownstone, he had built a successful practice representing clients in class-action suits. Exploiting their own nuisance value is a key tactic for such lawyers, and being a nuisance was something for which David Berger had a special talent. "His job was to yell and scream," recalled one Penn Central lawyer afterward, "and he was very good at it."[35] Protesting reorganization expenses, complaining about the sale of assets, stringing out decisions, Berger was doing precisely what he was hired to do—making himself so annoying that the other lawyers might cut his low-priority clients into any settlement just to get rid of him.

Eichler had specifically told Donald Trump that Berger could be a problem. Trump said nothing, but a few days before the hearing, Eichler received middle-of-the-night calls from both men informing him that the two had met. They then summoned him to Berger's office. There the lawyer announced that because the developer and he had completely overhauled the terms of the sale, he now favored it. As Berger later explained in court, the price would remain $62 million, but because payment would not occur for some time, it would come with interest, plus a larger portion of any future increase in the yards' value and an option to acquire a larger percent of the equity. The total "improvement," as Berger termed it, could amount to as much as $20.5 million.

There was also an "improvement" for Donald Trump. As before, he would pay no deposit and receive $750,000 in start-up money from the Penn Central, but now he would not have to refund any money if the project went nowhere. And—somehow—he had convinced Berger that a nebulous future promise in return for the cancellation of any refund in the event no development occurred was an excellent deal, all in all, for Berger's clients. "Whatever Donald did, assuming he did anything, it was a very clever accomplishment," Eichler said later. "If someone's in your way, deal with him yourself—kill him, buy him, deal with him however. This wasn't the only problem, but it was a big one. Then all of a sudden it disappeared."

Berger's sudden switch from adamant foe to ardent supporter was, at the least, puzzling. A possible explanation would emerge some years later. In 1979 federal prosecutors investigated allegations that Berger's abrupt turnaround was related to Donald Trump's decision to join several other New York landlords as plaintiffs in a $100 million lawsuit Berger was preparing at the same time. The suit charged major oil companies with fixing the price of heating oil. As was standard in such cases, Berger's fee would be one-third of whatever settlement occurred, and the size of any such settlement would depend on the number of apartments represented by the suit. This number was also the basis for the advance that plaintiffs paid Berger up front. Given that the Trump Organization had more apartments than any other parties to the suit, Trump's participation in the case was clearly to Berger's considerable advantage. The federal probe did not find sufficient evidence of wrongdoing to yield any criminal indictments.[36]

Whatever quid pro quo may have taken place, the deeper explanation for why things ended up going Donald Trump's way had at least as much to do with the two men sitting next to him in the courtroom. Bunny Lindenbaum, who had represented Donald's father for a quarter century, had become a New York legend precisely because he could always figure out how to handle a problem. Fred Trump, too, had nearly always been able to see his way around obstacles. Schooled by these two men in his chosen profession, Donald had already gotten rid of one major party that had showed interest in the yards. Starrett Corporation had withdrawn abruptly from pursuing the site after Donald paid a visit to the company's president and reminded him of the Trump Organization's equity position in Starrett City.

But there was an even sharper parallel. Fred Trump had faced an oddly similar situation forty years earlier, in the spring of 1935, when he, too, had been twenty-eight years old, had been trying to gain control of one of the most valuable parts of a bankrupt empire, and had encountered opposition. Another developer had topped his offer to take over the mortgage-servicing department of the Lehrenkrauss Corporation, and a group of disgruntled creditors had threatened to block the sale of any assets. Fred Trump had quickly neutralized both problems. He joined forces with his rival, gained the creditors' support by including an attractive but meaningless provision in an amended offer, and won the mortgage-servicing contract. Now, in this Philadelphia courtroom, Donald Trump was simply following in the footsteps of his father and his lawyer, doing whatever it took to make things end up where he needed them to be.

With Berger in the Trump camp, the only opposition to the trustees' proposal came from an elderly New York real estate broker and his associate. But because their ostensible client, another New York real estate developer, Richard Ravitch, did not appear at the hearing or send an attorney, Fullam gave this competing bid scant attention, and his decision to postpone a final ruling seemed little more than a formality. Still, Donald Trump left nothing to chance. During one break he went over to the broker's associate and attempted to neutralize him, too. "Bring me deals," young Trump said. "Represent me. I'm interested in expanding, and you seem very knowledgeable about real estate."[37] Afterward the Trumps and Lindenbaum walked out into the night, climbed into the black limousine waiting at the curb, and headed north.

Four months later Judge Fullam awarded the Trump Organization the option to buy the rail yards.[38] Donald Trump could now pursue his own large-scale middle-income apartment complex. He had diverged from his father's model by focusing on Manhattan; now he would make his second departure. He would set out to make a Trump development the biggest such project in the world.

The young developer thought more apartments would net him more money, but it was clear to Ned Eichler that Donald Trump was not interested in money alone. "The biggest project, the one with the most apartments, that's what was exciting to him," Eichler said later. "He thrived on conflict, the bigger the better. He loved it. People like him always do."

CHAPTER SIXTEEN

FROM BRICK BOX
TO GLASS FANTASY

SIX DAYS BEFORE THE PENN CENTRAL hearing in Philadelphia, New York elected a new governor.[1] A Democrat and an Irish Catholic with twelve children, Hugh Leo Carey, a lawyer who worked at his family's fuel oil business, had entered electoral politics in 1960, at the age of forty-one, by winning a seat in the House of Representatives from what had long been a solidly Republican district. In six terms he had nailed down choice committee assignments and consolidated his position on Capitol Hill. By his seventh term, in 1972, he had become so powerful that he had tacit support from the state's Republican governor, Nelson Rockefeller.[2]

Two years later Carey launched his gubernatorial campaign against Rockefeller's handpicked heir apparent. Polls showed that Carey was unknown to nine out of ten Empire State voters, and only a few weeks into the race his wife died from cancer. Carey channeled his grief into his quest for higher office and hired a media consultant. By election night he had lost his spare tire, his graying hair was again brown, and he was jubilantly hosting a crowded victory party at the Commodore Hotel in Manhattan. It was the first time in sixteen years that a Democrat would occupy the governor's mansion in Albany. Moreover, it was a Democrat from Brooklyn, with strong ties to

New York City mayor Abe Beame, former mayor Robert Wagner, and Bunny Lindenbaum. In short, a Trump kind of Democrat.

Earlier that year Donald Trump had hedged his bets by offering support to both Carey and his opponent in the Democratic primary, Howard Samuels, the progressive millionaire who had invented Baggies.[3] "Although I'd never met Donald Trump," recalled Samuels's campaign manager, journalist Ken Auletta, "he kept calling me 'Kenny,' the way people do when they grow up with you on Coney Island. My antenna went up. He was a big developer with big plans, and if he was going to come off as a major contributor, I was worried. What was the money for?" Auletta turned down the developer's offer, but Carey's campaign evidently had no hesitation. Accordingly, the Trumps gave early—they funded the campaign's first phone lines— and often. Carey rolled over Samuels in the primary, and the Trumps and Trump-owned companies would go on to become Carey's second largest source of donations, topped only by the candidate's own brother.[4]

Like any good politician, Hugh Carey knew how to say thank you. In the first round of appointments after the election, the governor-elect named Donald Trump to a blue-ribbon task force on housing, although he had not yet constructed a building.[5] With Hugh Carey in Albany and Abe Beame in City Hall, that would change.

———⁓———

Among the hundreds of supporters gathered to cheer the governor-elect was a tall woman with a round face and an assertive manner. She was expensively dressed and heavily made up, her reddish blond hair well coiffed and heavily sprayed. Her name was Louise Mintz Sunshine, and she would arguably have more influence on Donald Trump than any other woman except his mother. On this victory night she was the executive director of Carey's finance committee, but until the Democratic primary she had been a key fund-raiser for Howard Samuels. Gracious and warm to her wide range of friends and acquaintances, Sunshine could be tough when she deemed it necessary. "She made people pay their dues," recalled one campaign insider. "Fund-raising is full of bullshit artists who want to be at the party but don't want to pay. She wouldn't put up with that."[6] As a result, she was not universally loved, but she was highly valued.

A Brandeis graduate from a prosperous New Jersey real estate family, she had married a successful doctor and had three children. Only a few years earlier, being a parent volunteer at Dalton, a prestigious Manhattan private school, had seemed an adequate outlet for her considerable skills. But when she lost a bid to join the school's board of directors, she had redirected her formidable talents toward politics and developed connections in Manhattan and the Bronx. After seizing the reins in Carey's campaign, she overhauled his precarious finances. Early in 1975 she became treasurer of the Democratic State Committee and a national committeewoman from New York. On the side, she continued to do volunteer work. By now, though, she was not donating her services to education or politics. Instead her cause was helping Donald Trump, whom she had gotten to know as a Carey contributor, to develop the Penn Central properties.

Because Sunshine was still Carey's chief fund-raiser, her work for the Trump Organization had to be on an unpaid basis—a "truly ridiculous" situation, given her political status, as she later commented to *The New York Times*. But like Ned Eichler and Victor Palmieri, she found the Donald Trump mix of high energy and high-level political connections irresistible. The brash go-getter from Queens was "the most incredible person I ever met in my life," she said.[7]

For Donald Trump, Sunshine, a powerful political player who appeared capable of delivering the favorable government treatment he needed, seemed the answer to his prayers. Indeed, Sunshine's access to Carey and other state officials would prove invaluable as the all-but-bankrupt city came more and more under the control of the state. But working with Sunshine proved more than a strategic decision for Trump. It gave him his first opportunity to work with someone whose drive, aggressiveness, and stamina matched his own. Someone who already had the approval of his quasi-mentor, Roy Cohn, a patient of Sunshine's husband. Someone whose advice he could take without offense, because she was an older, married woman. Yet at the same time, someone not that much older, not his father's associate but his own, someone he had found and selected himself. In short, a colleague.

Even with Louise Sunshine's aid, Donald Trump's proposal was far from realization. Although he had managed to obtain an option on the Penn Central rail yards, before he could dig a spadeful of dirt, he would have to convince the city to rezone the site and banks to finance construction. And before he could do either of these formidable tasks, he would need a design for the project.

The logical choice for architect was the firm led by Jordan Gruzen and Peter Samton, who had been fascinated with the yards ever since Leonard Bernstein's *West Side Story* had sparked interest in the area and the new performing arts complex at Lincoln Center had opened the West Side to large-scale development.[8] In 1963 the Amalgamated Lithographers Union hired the two MIT-trained architects to design Litho City, an apartment complex built on an enormous platform over the tracks. That five-thousand-unit project never went beyond the drawing board, but Gruzen and Samton continued to produce designs for the site.[9] As soon as Donald Trump fired off his initial Penn Central yards letter, he summoned Gruzen and Samton to Brooklyn to discuss a small Trump apartment project. It was never built, but the designers evidently passed muster. One year later Trump hired them to produce the first plan for housing on the yards that would not have a railroad running underneath.

What he wanted, he told them, was big. In initial press stories he suggested 20,000 units for the 60th Street yards and 10,000 for the 34th Street yards.[10] Taken together, this two-part, 30,000-apartment complex would be almost twice as large as the gargantuan 15,500-unit Co-op City then being built by United Housing Foundation in the Bronx. Indeed, it would surpass the Trump Organization's entire real estate portfolio, variously estimated at between 15,000 and 20,000 units. Fred Trump's first structure had been a garage for a neighbor; his son's initial venture would be the largest apartment complex in the world. It was a breathtaking display of hubris, but it was also a plan with a built-in conflict. On the one hand, without massive subsidies, the only way to cover the staggering cost of basic infrastructure—waterlines, sewers, streets, and so forth—was to construct far more apartments than the community would accept; on the other hand, without community backing it would be impossible to obtain a zoning change from industrial use to residential.

Trump's vision was almost comically out of synch with what almost everyone else in the city had in mind. City Planning Commission chairman John Zuccotti said flatly that the 34th Street yards should remain dedicated to industry and that the 60th Street yards should be "residential but not monster high-rise."[11] The now-retired Robert Moses, never known for advocating small-scale anything, said in a special report on the West Side that the yards should have no more than a total of 1,300 apartments built solely on the northern yards.[12] Richard Dicker, general counsel for Penn Central's largest creditor and subsequently the head of the reorganized railroad, thought building anything on the yards was impossible and said that Trump's option to do so was like "paying me $1,000 for the option of delivering me to Mars."[13] Even Ned Eichler, for whom more apartments meant a higher sale price and a bigger commission for his employer, the Palmieri Company, said that less density would cause less fuss, get approved faster, and be better for the neighborhood.

Donald Trump didn't even pause. He ignored Gruzen's advice to scale down the project; instead Gruzen and his partners found themselves drawing continuously, turning out sketches, studies, elevations, renderings, and site plans for a client who literally could not wait to see their work. When the architects got to their offices in the morning, they would find him already there, looking over drafting tables and leafing through papers.

"He talked a mile a minute, and he knew everything," recalled Paul Willen, one of the architects working on the rail yards. "Of course he didn't know everything, didn't in fact know very much, but he had that air of confidence."

Although Donald Trump's impatience could be irritating, his overwhelming eagerness was engaging. "He was hot to trot," said Jordan Gruzen. "He was excited and anxious, wanting to see what was going on, how far we'd gotten." Often there would be spontaneous discussions about alternatives and possibilities. "Donald had a quality where on the one hand he was assertive and acted as if he knew what he wanted, but he would also play dumb a lot, ask a lot of questions, what do you think of this or that," Gruzen said. "In a way he was testing you to see if you thought the way he did. After a while I realized he wasn't as uncertain as it seemed, that he was playing a game."

Of all the obstacles facing Donald Trump, two were intractable.

First, because the city and state were almost broke and the federal government was undergoing Nixon-era cutbacks, the once-plentiful housing subsidies that had nourished his father had vanished. Without such assistance, Donald Trump's plan—essentially, to follow in his father's footsteps and build middle-income, subsidized housing— was for all practical purposes impossible. But because a market for nonsubsidized, market-rate housing had not yet emerged, he had no alternative. Second, the 60th Street yards were in the middle of an increasingly prosperous area filled with savvy, well-connected residents unwilling to let a developer decide what would happen to their neighborhood. "We felt this land belonged to us," said Sally Goodgold, member and later co-chair of local Community Board 7. "We would look into it and see what was best. We were not going to have a developer-driven process."[14]

As soon as Goodgold and other community board members heard about Trump's ideas, they obtained a commitment from planning head John Zuccotti that he would not accept any plan the board objected to. They also began a seemingly endless series of meetings with Donald Trump, his architects, his lawyers, and his consultants. The different groups made countless phone calls and wrote an endless stream of letters, questions, recommendations, thank-yous, and you're-welcomes. Gradually the project shrank. From 14,500 units, which the board summarily rejected as a "Co-op City on the Hudson," the project contracted to about 5,000. But this was still too big for the board, and meetings with the developer grew increasingly contentious.[15]

It was Donald Trump's first construction project, and his first dilemma. Needing somehow to produce a project large enough to pay for itself but small enough to be approved by the community, he bobbed and weaved. Again and again he would unveil a new plan and insist that it was ideal for the community and financially feasible, but he declined to provide any specific hows and whys.

"Trump was very young, and he would throw numbers around in ways that seemed to me to make no sense," recalled the community board consultant, an architect named Jonathan Barnett. "The whole thing seemed like a variation on the old joke where a vendor says he's selling potato peelers and he's losing four cents on each one, but he expects to make up the loss in volume."[16] To Barnett, the only strategy that made sense, and what Trump may well have been doing, was to say whatever he had to in order to get the zoning change. Then, with the new zoning in hand, he would be able to obtain financing from a large institutional investor with deep pockets and use the investor's clout to push the city into paying for the infrastructure.

Occasionally Fred Trump attended community meetings. No doubt his son's situation reminded him of his own experience a decade earlier, when he had tried to build apartments at the old Steeplechase site in Brooklyn. He, too, had presented one scheme after another, bobbed and weaved, and ultimately failed to win community backing for a necessary zoning change, in that case from recreational to residential. Now, though, Fred Trump sat in the back row of the auditorium as his son delivered his upbeat spiel and showed slides with leafy trees, beautiful parks, and, in the background, shadowy clusters of buildings.[17] "He let Donald sink or swim on his own," said Jordan Gruzen. "I know they talked at night, but they kept any discussions or arguments away from the public view."

The younger man was not alone when he faced the community board. Louise Sunshine was also in the room, chatting with this person or that one, conveying the message that political approval was in the bag, that the finances were all in order, and that she could handle any other issues that might come up. "It was a very general 'Don't worry about it, we know how to do it' approach—plus 'Don't get in our way or we'll run over you,'" said architect Barnett. "They were both radiating that they had a lot of political power, that we had better negotiate with them, because if we didn't, they could push something through that we'd like even less."

Also present was Donald Trump's publicist.[18] A mild-looking man with thick brown hair, a big square face, and heavy, dark-rimmed glasses, Howard Joseph Rubenstein was then in his early forties. He was the son of a Brooklyn police reporter and had grown up wanting to be a Court Street lawyer. But after two months at Harvard Law School he dropped out, asked his father for tips on eye-catching leads, and launched himself on Court Street not as an attorney but as a publicist. After clients proved scarce, he also enrolled in a local law school. With legal know-how added to his skills, he was soon providing his guidance to a long list of Brooklyn heavyweights that included Fred Trump. By the mid-1970s, when he had moved his business to

Manhattan, the list of people who paid for his services had become so large that he occasionally represented both sides in disputes.[19]

Rounding out the group was yet another son of Brooklyn, Samuel Harvey Lindenbaum.[20] Known as "Sandy," he was a Harvard Law School graduate and—more important in New York City—the son of Bunny Lindenbaum. Like his father, he specialized in real estate and was skillful at navigating political and bureaucratic waters. But Sandy Lindenbaum, a hawklike figure with penetrating blue eyes who was as knife-thin and crisp as his father was plump and jovial, had worked only briefly in his father's Brooklyn office and then joined a top-drawer Manhattan firm. There he had focused on the arcane subspecialty of zoning regulations. It was a shrewd choice, for real estate deals often hung on matters of zoning, and those few lawyers who had mastered New York City's famously complex zoning ordinances were highly prized. "I represent the last of the gunslingers," Lindenbaum once boasted. "Very tough guys."

Despite this all-star team, Donald Trump's plans for the 60th Street yards remained stalled. In the end it was a Manhattan project, and his Brooklyn and Albany ties could not make it happen. But at the 34th Street yards, a far different story was unfolding.[21] It had begun back in the Lindsay administration, when major hotel and business interests wanted to replace the New York Coliseum, located just north of midtown Manhattan at Columbus Circle. When the structure was built, in the 1950s, its multilevel layout was cutting edge, but convention planners now favored placing giant displays on the same floor. By the time of Beame's inauguration, advocates of a new hall were pushing for a huge single-level structure. The leading plan, designed by the prestigious architectural firm Skidmore, Owings & Merrill, spread out horizontally on a spaceport platform that extended out hundreds of feet over the Hudson River at West 44th Street. Despite its Jetsonian design, nearly everyone in the city, including Mayor Beame, had signed on to the 44th Street scheme.[22]

When Ned Eichler and, later, Jordan Gruzen pointed out that the nonresidential neighborhood around the 34th Street yards made more sense for a convention center than housing, Donald Trump insisted that it was out of the question.[23] He wanted to build housing, he said, and the 44th Street project looked like a done deal. Gruzen persevered. Warming up to the prospect of a huge project that would involve tens of thousands of jobs and cost hundreds of millions of dollars to construct, insure, and maintain, Donald Trump told him to work up a sketch and leave it unsigned. Together they showed the drawing to John Zuccotti. When Zuccotti's eyes lit up, so did Donald Trump's. Zuccotti had backed the 44th Street proposal but said it now seemed too expensive to survive the city's financial crisis. "If you have a viable, less costly alternative," Zuccotti told Trump, "here's your chance to prove it—but do so quietly."

This time the group that was stymied at 60th Street moved ahead like a precision drill team. Working at a breakneck pace, the Gruzen firm turned out a design for a two-level structure made of bronze-colored glass.[24] Unlike its 44th Street rival, this building rested squarely on terra firma, was accessible from all four sides, and had space for trucks to load and unload without blocking traffic. A solar collector sat on the roof, as per instructions from Donald Trump, who said he wanted the public relations value.[25] Estimated to cost between $100 million and $140 million, it was vastly cheaper than the $231 million budgeted for 44th Street.

To build support for this new plan, Louise Sunshine worked the phones and pulled together a pro–34th Street coalition of city and state politicians and business leaders. She also kept in touch with local community figures. One colleague later summed up her strategy: "Make them feel important, let them speak out and contribute, listen accordingly, and then do what we want anyhow!"

As Zuccotti had predicted, Mayor Beame eventually shelved the 44th Street center for lack of funds. Three days later Donald Trump began making presentations to select private audiences. "He was young, he was blond, and he had done his homework," said a local Democratic leader who had been a vociferous opponent of the 44th Street center and was invited by Louise Sunshine to one of Trump's first meetings. "He was very polished, but he didn't talk over us."[26] Another Democratic leader and 44th Street foe recalled the meeting as "perhaps the only time the word *humble* was ever applicable to Donald Trump."[27]

On Friday, December 11, just as Donald Trump's campaign was picking up speed, Mayor Beame abruptly endorsed a different alternative: Battery Park City, an enormous and, at the time, faltering state-sponsored development project planned for a landfill area at the

southern tip of Manhattan. One reason for Beame's sudden announcement may have been a concern that promoting a site controlled by the son of his old friend Fred Trump would look like
cronyism. Probably more important, the mayor was under siege from
the governor, who was facing pressure from business and financial
leaders to rescue Battery Park City. And, in fact, there was a certain
logic to putting the convention center there, for construction costs
would be lower than at 44th Street, and parts of the 44th Street design could be recycled. In addition, Battery Park City had development monies that might be available, and a downtown exhibition
center could help jump-start the publicly owned World Trade Center,
opening across the street from Battery Park City and desperate for
tenants.

Undaunted, Donald Trump began drafting press releases with
such headlines as RIP-OFF AT BPC. By the next week the selection of
the convention center had become a major story. "I was driving to
work," recalled Charles Urstadt, then chairman of the Battery Park
City Authority, "and I heard a reporter saying Donald Trump had demanded an investigation of Battery Park City. He said that putting
the convention center there was totally unwarranted. This was news
to me. It was the wildest thing I ever heard."[28]

A few days later, Trump unveiled at a press conference what he
called, with a nod to the popular film of the same name, "The Miracle on 34th Street." Before him were midtown business leaders and
city officials, reporters from every major paper, and TV crews.
Terming the idea of putting the convention center at Battery Park
City "a tragic mistake," Donald Trump claimed that his "Miracle
Center" would be the largest such facility in the country, would be
finished in one-fourth the time scheduled for 44th Street, and would
cost only one-fourth as much. In fact, other facilities were larger,
Trump's cost estimates were low, and his projections of potential revenues were high, but most press coverage omitted these details.[29]

For Howard Rubenstein, the actual press conference was an anti-
climax. He already knew it would be a success. For several hours the
previous day, Donald Trump had gone over possible questions with
Rubenstein and rehearsed his answers. His client, Rubenstein said,
was "a natural." Better yet, that morning *The New York Times* had

run a pro–convention center story, the product of a Rubenstein-arranged briefing, that quoted major New York labor negotiator Theodore Kheel saying that a convention center in Battery Park City would be "like putting a nightclub in a graveyard."[30]

By most accounts Donald Trump's rise to power began when he moved to Manhattan. And indeed, such was the case. But not for the reason usually cited, that he had left Brooklyn behind. His rise came because, over the months to come, he would manage to make his Manhattan projects into Brooklyn projects. The real "Miracle on 34th Street" was not the actual convention center design that was unveiled that day. It was how Donald Trump had managed to combine his father's political connections, his advisers' collective wisdom, and his own budding development acumen to outmaneuver his competitors. The borough he had fled would be among his most important sources of strength.[31]

Although Donald Trump's initiatives on the two West Side rail yards were impressive, they were not what would establish him in the New York real estate pantheon. Instead he would secure his reputation with the redevelopment of another Penn Central property, the Commodore Hotel, which had been the site of Carey's victory party.[32] One of five hotels in Manhattan owned by the railroad, it had opened in 1919 and was named after nineteenth-century tycoon Commodore Vanderbilt. After making a fortune in shipping, Vanderbilt had gone on to railroads, merging several lines into the New York Central and, in the 1870s, beginning construction of Grand Central Depot, which was succeeded in 1913 by Grand Central Terminal.

Located next to this Beaux Art monument, the Commodore had two thousand guest rooms and had offered modest but reliable lodging to several generations of railroad travelers. Now, though, it was falling apart. Hotel management had roped off whole floors as unusable. The occupancy rate had slipped well below 50 percent,[33] a massage parlor had set up shop, and prostitutes occasionally propositioned guests in the lobby. Although it was losing close to $1 million a year, a strong union contract required the hotel to continue paying its workers even if it shut down altogether. After years of nonpayment, the overdue real estate taxes on the building stood at $6.6 million. Given that the building's market value was estimated at no more than $10 million, it was hardly surprising that Ned Eichler viewed the Commodore as a losing proposition. "I felt as though we should pay someone to take it off our hands," he said afterward.

When Donald Trump had first inspected the Commodore, he, too, was repelled by the sleaziness and squalor of both the hotel and the neighborhood. But as he got closer to the building, he noticed prosperous commuters flooding in and out of Grand Central Terminal. "Unless the city literally died," he later wrote, "millions of affluent people were going to keep passing by this location every day. The problem was the hotel, not the neighborhood. If I could transform the Commodore, I was sure it would be a hit."[34]

His plan for how to accomplish such a transformation was relatively simple. He would buy the hotel for $10 million, obtain a tax abatement, and gut-renovate the building into a new hotel. The only problem was that to everyone except Donald Trump, each of these steps, not to mention all of them combined, looked utterly impossible.

He started with the design. Because he had admired a striking skyscraper at 44th and Broadway with a huge diadem projecting from the top, he arranged to meet the architect, Der Scutt, for dinner. When Trump arrived at Maxwell's Plum, a hugely popular singles bar on the East Side, he found a tall, square-faced man with an intense and sometimes abrupt manner. Surrounded by faux Tiffany lamps and baroque mirrors, Trump told Scutt, who was about ten years his senior, what he had in mind. As the younger man unfolded his plan to cover the Commodore's traditional brick-and-masonry facade with glass, the architect covered one of the restaurant's oversize menus with preliminary sketches of a tall, glass-enclosed building rising next to Grand Central Station.

From there they proceeded to Donald Trump's new apartment, a bona fide penthouse a few blocks away on East 65th Street. Perched on the thirty-second floor, it had one bedroom, one and a half bathrooms, and a sweeping view that included the George Washington Bridge to the north and Brooklyn and Long Island to the East. At the moment it also boasted a prodigious amount of large modern furniture, most of it in brown or beige and so new that it still had brown wrapping paper around the chrome legs. "He was very proud," said Scutt. "It was a bit glitzy, and there was way too much of it. Donald said, 'What d'ya think, what d'ya think,' his favorite line throughout his whole life—he usually says it twice, not once. I said there's too much, we could arrange it to make the apartment bigger and more spacious. He loved it, and I pushed the excess out in the hallway."

The two men hit it off immediately, for they spoke the same earthy language, relished confrontation, and admired modern design, mirrored surfaces, and shiny metal. Soon Donald Trump asked Scutt to come up with a few ideas for remodeling the old New York Central office building, which was on Lexington Avenue near Grand Central, and made his own preferences clear. "Nothing old-fashioned or Colonial," he scrawled in the margin of Scutt's drawings. "No cornices, no brick, no round columns."

Trump and Scutt also shared an understanding of marketing and what an audience wanted to hear. "Even at the beginning, Donald had a way of not exactly exaggerating, but issuing public relations statements that were exciting," said Scutt. "If they were slightly exaggerated, okay, that was how he could sell."

Trump would retain Scutt to work on the Commodore project in conjunction with Gruzen and Samton and would also ask him to take a major role in his design for the convention center.[35] But the design was only one part of the complex undertaking the developer faced before he could move forward on the Commodore. He also needed an experienced hotel operator. By late 1974 he had set his sights on Hyatt, the one major national hotel management chain without a New York base.

Hyatt was one of many corporate entities owned by the wealthy Pritzker family of Chicago. It had first come to the Pritzkers' attention in 1957, when Jay Pritzker had stopped at a Los Angeles Airport coffee shop called Fat Eddie's. To his surprise, it was packed with other travelers who were also between flights. Then he noticed that the attached motel, named after its builder, Hyatt von Dehn, had no vacancies. A lightbulb went off. Pritzker scribbled on a napkin an offer to buy the motel and Fat Eddie's, and the Hyatt Hotel chain was born.

Ten years later another lightbulb went off. After every other hotel operator in America had passed on the idea, Hyatt bought its first atrium hotel: a twenty-two-story facility in Atlanta with a vertical atrium that went all the way to the roof and brightly lighted, glass-enclosed elevators. The eye-catching design, by architect John Portman, was perfect for the dawning era of business travel and conventions. The elegant lobby and lavish suites drew journeying corporate executives eager to live it up on their expense accounts, and the huge meeting rooms and splendid banquet facilities attracted convention planners. Soon Hyatt had similar atrium-style facilities in every major city except the one city that counted most, New York.

Trump's first call to Hyatt was hardly promising. The rapid-fire New York–style patter of this unknown figure on the other end of the line made him seem like "a kook," recalled Joseph Amoroso, then executive vice president of Hyatt. When Amoroso met the developer and saw a primitive, pre–Der Scutt sketch, he was even more put off. "Trump showed me this awful-looking drawing in an awful part of town," Amoroso said, "and I wasn't too interested." But then the New Yorker intimated that he had a tax abatement deal with the city, and Amoroso's ears pricked up. He reported back to Jay Pritzker that Trump was "very intelligent, very glib, and very persuasive." He was also very optimistic, for at the time a tax abatement was little more than a gleam in his eye.

The developer's next step was to call up another Le Club member, a sophisticated mortgage banker named Ben Lambert.[36] Like Donald Trump, Benjamin Victor Lambert had grown up rich; his father was a wealthy jeweler. After an upper-class Park Avenue childhood, he had majored in art history at Brown. But instead of becoming a museum curator, he went into real estate finance and changed the basic nature of high-end urban real estate marketing. Until he came on the scene, most real estate sales had been relatively simple exchanges between buyers and sellers; under his influence they became elaborate, complex processes in which real estate became "product," deals were "transactions," and getting the best price involved "strategies for raising the selling price floor." Along the way, prices went up and the business became a field in which everyone, including Ben Lambert, made a whole lot more money.

What mattered to Donald Trump was that Ben Lambert knew Jay Pritzker. Lambert didn't remember the developer from Le Club, but he accepted his invitation for lunch at the '21' Club. "Donald came to my office, and we acted like we'd met before," Lambert said. When they went downstairs and got into the back of Fred Trump's stretch limousine, Lambert discovered that his host had lined up renderings of the Commodore all along the back seat. "He's taking me to lunch by way of his office, which is also his car, which is actually his father's car, and he's really giving me this marketing pitch on the way to this lunch he's supposedly taking me to," Lambert said. When they got to the '21' Club the owner didn't recognize Trump, but he greeted Lambert warmly and showed them to a prime seat.

Despite Trump's gaffes at that first meeting, Lambert was impressed by the younger man. The essence of marketing, he said later, "is creating the environment of doing a deal, of having a situation become more than just your thoughts. Donald is very good at that. That's what he did when he invited me to lunch at '21'." When Trump asked Lambert to help him with Hyatt, Lambert made some introductions, for which he was paid "very nominally." But then Trump asked him to write a letter saying that the renovated Commodore would be the greatest hotel in New York. Lambert balked. "I said, 'I can't write that letter,'" he recalled. "I thought it was a great location, that it had potential, but I couldn't write that letter." Trump exploded, and the two men did not speak again for a year.

By this time, however, the initial groundwork had been laid and more Hyatt officials headed east. Soon the developer and the officials began to hammer out a deal.[37] When they reached a preliminary agreement, *The New York Times* announced it with a full-page article—remarkable given that Donald Trump had never built anything, had obtained neither the tax abatement necessary for the financing nor the financing itself, and did not even have a final design for the hotel.[38] Nonetheless Trump told friends he was disappointed because the article was not on page one.[39] Almost before the ink was dry on the deal, he was exploring using a cheaper facade, saving on escalators, and reusing old Commodore guest rooms and baths as ways to save money on the project. When asked whether this would affect the quality image that he and Hyatt had just endorsed, he replied, "Fuck Hyatt. I have them signed, now I can do what I want."[40]

—⁓—

Hyatt, as Donald Trump knew, had not yet really signed and would not sign until he had the tax abatement. It was time for another trip to City Hall. This time his destination was the office of economic development administrator Al Eisenpreis, a successful department store executive who had accepted the invitation to serve in a Democratic administration out of a sense of civic duty.[41]

Trump was on time, something which was, in Eisenpreis's experience, "not the most usual thing in New York." Better yet, he came in with sketches by Der Scutt, whom Eisenpreis recognized as a respectable professional. "The drawings were dazzling," Eisenpreis said. "Donald spread them all out on the desk and I thought, my God, that could be there." For Eisenpreis it was a good moment at a time when good moments were rare. "Most people coming in were asking me how to pay their light bill," he said. "Suddenly a guy comes in with a city-size project. That hadn't happened in a long time." Moreover this project dealt with a pressing problem—the near bankruptcy of a huge hotel next door to one of the nation's premiere destinations. "All I could imagine was that someone would be sleeping there [in the Commodore] at night, and setting a fire to keep warm, and suddenly we wouldn't have just a dead hotel but a ruined hotel and nobody around to rebuild it."

The meeting grew warm when Eisenpreis told Trump that he thought some of the Commodore purchase price should go to cleaning Grand Central Terminal, the sadly neglected Beaux Arts masterpiece next door, and the developer agreed immediately. Eisenpreis was struck by what he saw as a certain openness and an emphasis on quality, a vision that was not entirely bottom-line-oriented. "In the sixteenth century, someone entering a guild had to present a masterpiece to demonstrate that he was an artisan in his own right," Eisenpreis said. "I had a feeling this project was Donald's masterpiece to show that he wasn't just Fred's boy."

But what may have helped most of all was that the economic development administrator had been trying since his arrival to produce an industrial development policy. As New York competed with other localities for new investments and industries and plants, it seemed to him that the city desperately needed the marketing tool of tax abatement for specific limited periods. "The question is, 'If you had it, what would you do with it?'" he said. "When Donald Trump appeared, we could say, 'Here, we could make *this* happen.' He was the person we'd been looking for, even though we didn't know it."

Eisenpreis's enthusiastic response gave Donald Trump a leg up in talking with Hyatt and looking for financing. But the abatement bill Eisenpreis tried to push through the state legislature made little headway amid the growing alarm in Albany over the city's deteriorating finances. In 1965 the city's short-term, high-interest debt accounted for $526 million, or 10 percent of the city's total debt; by the summer of 1975 it was $5 billion, more than one-third of total debt. New York City could not raise another cent, and even the normally unflappable mayor was distressed. On a visit to Israel, Beame stuck a note in a crevice in the Wailing Wall with a one-word plea: "Help."[42]

Some degree of help was already under way. Under the leadership of real estate magnate Lew Rudin, the city's largest taxpayers agreed to prepay their quarterly real estate taxes. In addition, the state set rescue efforts in motion, and the city had actually fired some civil servants, a huge step in heavily unionized New York City.[43] Nonetheless, the Beame administration had lost all credibility. Panicked business and financial leaders demanded that Governor Carey take effective control of the city.

Some went further, pushing for the removal of the mayor himself, but in the end the man who walked the plank was Beame's top aide, James Cavanagh, a close friend and old Brooklyn hand.[44] To replace him Beame tapped John Zuccotti, who was holding the city planning chairmanship to which he had been appointed by John Lindsay. It was a good move for New York City, for Beame's two harshest critics, the unions and the banks, both favored Zuccotti, a Yale-educated real estate lawyer who had a reputation for calling the shots as he saw them.[45]

Although Zuccotti's ascendancy might be good for New York City, it was not necessarily in the best interests of Donald Trump. Zuccotti, with no Brooklyn ties, had no reason to stick his neck out for an untried developer. It was time to try yet another route. Accordingly, in the fall of 1975 Trump visited the tiny office of Mike Bailkin, an obscure attorney in the mayor's Lower Manhattan Development Corporation. Bailkin, a dark-haired, thickset man in his mid-thirties, was not expecting him. When they had first met a few weeks earlier, Donald had made his usual get-acquainted gesture of inviting Bailkin to lunch at the '21' Club. But Bailkin, a maverick whose colorful past included stints in the army, the circus, the Peace Corps, and even a motorcycle gang, had declined, saying that he couldn't afford it and didn't want Trump to pay. Instead they had sandwiches at a restaurant with Formica-topped tables, and Bailkin turned down the developer's request for help on a side project, a small property at the tip of Manhattan.[46]

It had been the worst sandwich of his life, Trump later told Bailkin. But he said that he was impressed by the lawyer's spunk, so he had come back. It seems likely that he was also impressed with Bailkin's access to John Zuccotti; indeed, Bailkin actually worked closely with the man who now controlled the fate of the Commodore. For his second meeting, the developer unexpectedly appeared in Bailkin's office with a sketch of the renovated Commodore. Before Bailkin could say a word, Trump started rattling off a long list of reasons it was a great idea. A revived Commodore would give a signal that New York was still in business; it would be the first new hotel in almost fifteen years;[47] it would give 42nd Street a shot in the arm; it would revitalize the whole city. The price tag would be $70 million, and he could get a bank loan to cover it—but only with a tax abatement.

The developer then sketched out what Bailkin found a compelling argument. At the anticipated interest rate of 10 percent, the developer said, the debt service on a $70 million loan would be $7 million a year. If, as was the general expectation, the hotel made about $9 million a year and had to pay $2 million in taxes (these would be levied before any other obligations) plus about $2 million in operating expenses, there would be only $5 million to pay the mortgage. This would leave a potential shortfall of $2 million, something that no lender would take on given the possibility that if the city went bankrupt, the trustees who took over city affairs could elect to raise cash by raising real estate taxes.

Thus, Trump concluded, the only way to swing the deal was to abate the taxes until the hotel had the ability to pay them. Indeed, as far as he was concerned, the only question left was how to obtain the abatement, so logical was the scenario he had created.

Bailkin came up with the answer: Have the developer buy the hotel, sell it to the New York State Urban Development Corporation (UDC) for the token sum of $1, then lease it back. The UDC, a Rockefeller-era agency that had issued more than $1 billion in tax-exempt moral obligation bonds for projects across the state, was now facing the reckoning that bond lawyer John Mitchell, the creator of these financial instruments, had said would never come. The market for UDC bonds had dried up, the state legislature and the big banks had scorned its rescue pleas, and in February 1975 the UDC had gone into default.[48]

Yet although the agency itself was now belly up, any property it owned would still be exempt from taxes. And as Mike Bailkin well knew, having once been deputy counsel at UDC,[49] the bureaucrats left minding the empty store were desperate for new projects. Their agency's shell ownership of the Commodore would remove the hotel from tax rolls, allowing it instead to pay rent until its income could cover all real estate levies. Housing programs had used similar tax abatements to pay for residential construction, including Warbasse and Trump Village, but they hadn't been used for commercial deals.

To gain approval, the abatement would have to be available to other developers, but Bailkin thought he could craft such a policy and push it through the inevitable obstacles. And unlike Donald Trump's first proposal to him, Bailkin wanted to do this one. As he had realized immediately, the Commodore would not be just one more deal. It would be the only major development deal in town,[50] and putting it together would put Bailkin in direct contact with key city officials, including the mayor.

Because it seemed to City Hall that the Beame administration was under intense scrutiny, the Commodore abatement received more review than any other deal Bailkin had ever seen. Unusual for the time, the city even retained outside counsel to double-check everything. From all directions, Bailkin received the same message: Take it through cleanly, touch base with everyone, and don't make any mistakes.

As the months went by Bailkin gradually developed a grudging respect for Donald Trump. "Something about the guy intrigued me," he said later. "Once he got his mind made up, he was into it a thousand percent. He was always the salesman, selling all the time, and he never doubted he was right. Even when he'd lost a point, he'd say time would tell that he was really right." Such qualities seemed to Bailkin to make Trump a great businessman; at the same time, though, he saw Trump as a dreadful businessman because of his impatience with details and his assumption that the high-powered experts on his payroll would take care of everything. "In his mind," Bailkin said, "once he had bought the land rights, put up a little money, and gotten a bank to come in, things should have been over and done with."[51]

Bailkin liked the developer personally but was annoyed by his incessant competing, particularly with regard to women. He seemed to date only occasionally, and the women were often models whom he approached because he thought they would make him look good. One reason for Bailkin's exasperation may have been the following story from a knowledgeable source. Reportedly, once when Trump and Bailkin were dining, Trump spotted Jay Pritzker with a striking blonde who nodded at Bailkin. Trump demanded to meet her, and Bailkin managed to arrange a small get-together. Incredibly, Trump arrived late, brought another, younger blonde, and left shortly afterward. The next day he cheerfully explained that although he had originally intended to show Pritzker up by stealing the woman he had assumed was Pritzker's date, he had subsequently learned that she was merely a friend and had lost all interest in her.

As in any major development, each item in the Commodore deal—the design, the tax abatement, the choice of hotel operator—depended on the others. None could be finalized until all were in place. But underlying these three was yet another concern: financing. No matter how gorgeous the design, how generous the tax abatement, or how capable the hotel operator, nothing was going to happen unless Donald Trump lined up some strong backers. To obtain them, Donald Trump would have to hire the most well-established and respectable broker in the city.

His name was Henry Pearce, and he was a real estate industry fixture.[52] Afterward Donald Trump described him as "this white-haired guy with whom [bankers] had been dealing forever." Then in his late sixties, Pearce had first gotten into real estate back before the Depression, when he'd worked as a rental agent to pay for night classes at law school. He had intended to open a law office after graduation, but instead, nearly forty years later, he was running mortgage brokerages in half a dozen cities and directing a staff of more than a hundred employees.

"Donald was young, bright, and a pain in the ass," Pearce said later. But in the mid-1970s even as well established a broker as Pearce was hungry for business, and he immediately got to work on his new client's project. "Forty-second Street was not very attractive then, and the Commodore was a drab hotel," he recalled. "There weren't many institutional lenders for that sort of thing." But he had heard that the Equitable Insurance Corporation, which probably had deeper pockets than any other such lender in New York City, was interested in hotels. So he cold-called Bill Frentz, the point man at Equitable for such projects.

When Donald Trump laid out his game plan, Frentz said that Equitable would be interested, but only if he could deliver all the necessary permits and waivers from the city and state. "This wasn't just a new investment that easily fell into place," Frentz said later. "Lots of folks within Equitable were saying, 'Why should we invest in Manhattan when other insurance companies aren't?'" At that point the odds were running strongly against Trump's proposal making it to the next level of review.[53] But every time Frentz met with Donald, the developer had taken care of two or three more steps. "There was little question he was heading in the right direction, that he could pull it off and put all these pieces together," Frentz said.

Eventually Frentz and Donald Trump brought the proposal to a well-appointed conference room on the thirty-second floor of Equitable headquarters. It was the floor where all the real estate deals were done, and only one out of every twenty proposals that made it to this point went any further. By the time the hour-and-a-half presentation was over, it seemed this could well be the one. "Donald was sort of green then, the newest kid on the block," recalled Ben Holloway, a senior real estate investment manager and second in command of Equitable's vast real estate department. A real estate veteran, Benjamin Duke Holloway had worked at FHA headquarters in Washington a quarter century earlier and had processed Fred Trump's plans for Beach Haven. Although Fred's son was hardly a flower child, his longish hair and flashy clothes seemed jarring to the courtly, patrician Holloway, a member of the North Carolina tobacco family. But when Donald started talking about his elaborate and extensive plans to revamp the Commodore, Holloway forgot all about his appearance. "The fact that he'd really done his homework sold everybody," Holloway said. "His presentation was not as slick as we were used to, but it made a lot of sense. It wasn't as polished as you'd expect, but his enthusiasm overcame all of that."

Alas, not long after the presentation in the conference room, the Chrysler Building, directly across the street from the Commodore and one of New York's signature skyscrapers, went into foreclosure. The consensus in the conference room gave way to second thoughts and backpedaling. "It was kind of herky-jerky, to say the least," said Bill Frentz. "That's just the way those things work. A senior executive wakes up one morning and feels comfortable, and then the next day another company threatens to pull out of the city and that causes concern, so you step back another foot or two." At the end of months of discussion, Equitable was still interested—and still uncommitted.

——— ᨆ ———

All the while, the Commodore itself continued to lose money.[54] A recent refurbishment had little effect in boosting the occupancy rate, and another would cost at least $2 million—one-fifth of the hotel's appraised worth. Taking the building down to the ground and selling the land was not a realistic option, given the high cost of demolition and the vast network of subway and railroad tracks under the building. Even purchase by Donald Trump did not seem a surefire solution, for there was no guarantee that he would obtain financing for the desperately needed renovation.

In December 1975 the Palmieri Company upped the ante in

Trump's favor by announcing that unless the Commodore's cash flow improved immediately, it would close before the expiration of the current union contract the following June 1. This meant that when delegates to the Democratic National Convention arrived, one of the city's largest and most centrally located hotels would have a padlock on the door. In February workers at the Commodore went on a brief strike. Then, as the tax abatement program that was necessary for Trump to get financing took shape down at City Hall, other hoteliers began to complain of unfair treatment and favoritism.

"I was paying over one million a year in taxes and losing my shirt," recalled Mario de Genova, president of the Americana Hotel chain. "I thought the abatement should be extended to us, too." But when Trump met with de Genova and several other major hotel operators over breakfast at an exclusive East Side hotel, there was little common ground in either approach or appearance. To the European-born and -bred de Genova, Trump seemed not only pushy and loud, but overdressed. "The rest of us were Brooks Brothers types," said de Genova. "It was like a dress code, very subdued. We would have dark blues and dark grays, and he would come up with bright colors and flashy ties."

There were other rumblings of discontent. Richard Ravitch, newly appointed chair of the Urban Development Corporation, objected to the whole idea of a tax abatement on a potentially profit-making project. The third-generation scion of a wealthy real estate family, and the innovative developer of two major Manhattan projects, Waterside and Manhattan Plaza, Ravitch had studied law at Yale, sat on the boards of a dozen nonprofit organizations, and toyed briefly with a number of possibilities, including buying the Penn Central rail yards himself. Now he was dipping his toes into the public sector prior to a possible run for political office. When Donald Trump showed up at his office with Louise Sunshine, Ravitch declared that it was completely unethical for the governor's chief fundraiser to lobby a state agency for a commercial project. Sunshine burst into tears and promised she would stay out of the way. Furious, Trump threatened to call Carey and have Ravitch fired. In short order, Ravitch ordered them both to leave.

Ravitch remained troubled and urged two City Council members to make a fuss. They teamed up with a state assemblyman, and the three legislators held a press conference outside the Commodore to ask for better terms. To their surprise, Trump himself bounded up to the podium and declared that no investor would put in ten cents if the legislators' points were included. "We weren't very important in the scheme of things," said one of the protesters, then–City Council member Henry Stern. "He provided some confrontation and drama— he helped make our event." He also helped defuse it. City officials tinkered with the abatement but made no move to drop it. Two weeks later, in early May, time ran out. The board of directors in charge of the Penn Central's hotels voted to close the Commodore in one week. On May 20 the New York City Board of Estimate approved the tax abatement. In September the UDC met for a formal vote on the trans- action whereby it would end up owning the Commodore Hotel and leasing it back to Trump for the next ninety-nine years. Richard Rav- itch still didn't like the deal, but he was under intense pressure from both Albany and City Hall to vote yes. He did. Trump would have forty-one years tax-free, a savings of more than $111 million,[55] and a slowly escalating rent that would never come close to that of the abated sums.

Because the city was acting, in effect, as a joint venture partner with the developer, Mike Bailkin had included a net profit-sharing mechanism in the terms of the abatement. Or so he had thought. Some years later, at Donald Trump's request, he gave a lecture before a real estate industry group and noted that because of this arrange- ment the city was sharing in the project's eventual success. Afterward Trump gleefully piped up, "No, I'm able to write depreciation off as an expense!" It was only then that the aghast Bailkin learned that when the city drew up the abatement, after Bailkin himself had left city government, the developer had managed to insert a depreciation clause.

Because Mike Bailkin believed that keeping the Commodore open had been critical for the city, he had not minded that the agree- ment he had done so much to produce had been a great deal for Don- ald Trump. But the budding young developer, who had learned from his father to never, ever, let up, had made a great deal better.

CHAPTER SEVENTEEN

THE TWENTY-EIGHT-SIDED BUILDING

IN THE FALL OF 1976 DONALD TRUMP was a thirty-year-old licensed real estate broker whose first development project was less than half-done. Despite all the talk, the headlines, the tax abatement, and the UDC agreement, he did not have a valid option on the Commodore Hotel. He had returned the necessary legal papers to Penn Central with only his signature on them and had never produced the required $250,000 deposit. He had to obtain a formal commitment from Hyatt. He needed to line up comprehensive financing. He faced negotiating with nine different governmental bodies, including the relevant local community board, the City Planning Commission, two city bureaus and three departments, the Board of Estimate, and the New York State Urban Development Corporation. Neither he nor any other party had made any binding commitments. Everyone could still walk.

But that December, at a major New York real estate industry event, a benefit dinner dance for a medical research center, he received the annual Honor Award. Real estate leaders, an entrepreneurial breed that tends to shun publicity, did not welcome his flamboyant style and penchant for the limelight. Nor, had they known about it, would they have liked his inquiring whether the award was sufficiently prestigious to bother accepting it.[1] But they respected his ability to pull off a whopping commercial tax abatement and to use the UDC as a vehicle, something none of them had apparently ever thought of trying.

Doing so without putting in any money of his own or having the rest of the deal together, for which Councilman Henry Stern, among others, criticized Donald Trump, impressed the real estate *machers* even more. Keeping up in the air some half a dozen elements, each of which requires all the others to be finished before it can be completed, having the timing to pull separate irons in and out of the fire in the nick of time yet keep everything going until the whole thing is up—they knew that is what real estate development is all about. And they knew that Donald Trump was doing it.

———

In September 1977, Abe Beame, politically tainted by the city's fiscal crisis, suffered a crushing defeat in the Democratic mayoral primary. Two months later, Edward Irving Koch, the five-term Democratic congressman from Manhattan who had beaten him, won election as New York City's 105th mayor.[2] As the year drew to a close, outgoing officials scurried around City Hall wrapping up loose ends before the change of administrations. High on the list of outstanding items was finalizing the tax abatement for the Commodore.

"Everyone in the Beame administration was determined to get it done," said Richard Rosan, then head of the city's Office of Economic Development. "Donald knew he had the momentum, and he and Louise played every angle they could." Once again Donald provided the exuberance and the self-confidence, and Sunshine the access to state officials. "If something didn't happen at the city level," Rosan said, "or I had trouble with the city corporation counsel's office, which always found fifty or sixty things wrong with everything, there would be a call [to the party causing the delay] from the governor's office."[3]

Shortly before Christmas, First Deputy Mayor Stanley Friedman convened the parties. The son of a taxi driver, Stanley Melvin Friedman, who had replaced John Zuccotti as Beame's top deputy, had worked his way through Brooklyn Law School and the Bronx Democratic organization. Along the way he had earned a reputation as someone with singular political street smarts, contacts, and bravado. At the moment, though, the cigar-chomping, goateed Friedman was struggling. As soon as the Beame administration closed down, he was supposed to assume a lucrative position with Roy Cohn's law firm. If he could deliver for Donald Trump, one of Cohn's most highly publicized clients, his prospects at the firm would improve—but if he failed to come through, they could vanish. Worse, leaving any details to be resolved in the new administration could be a disaster, for incoming mayor Ed Koch had campaigned as a reformer, lambasting sweetheart deals and the city's political establishment. He might well scuttle the Commodore abatement as a handout that New York could not afford and should not provide.

In the six weeks since the election, Friedman had been scrambling to make the abatement happen. Like all such complicated arrangements, this one was full of time-consuming details, but there was also one seemingly unresolvable problem: Donald Trump's package still did not have financing. Determined not to let the deal unravel, Friedman went after an unusually open-ended version of what was called "an escrow closing." What this meant, underneath the fine print, was a selective closing—that is, one that bound the city and UDC, but not Donald Trump. The government entities would be committed to the deal, regardless of whether the developer came through or not.

The closing took place at the offices of Dreyer & Traub, where Jerry Schrager, Donald Trump's chief real estate lawyer, was a partner. Unlike Roy Cohn and Stanley Friedman, Gerald Neil Schrager, a graduate of New York University Law School, had a soft voice and a shy manner. But Trump was impressed when, soon after he came to work for his father, he saw Schrager defending the other party in a real estate transaction, and he had retained the lawyer to handle the Commodore deal. From the morning of December 20 until the middle of the next day, lawyers, city and state officials, and representatives of Penn Central roamed around the large conference room and the surrounding hallway, conferring and amending papers. Periodically food from a local delicatessen appeared, and the tables filled with empty soda cans. Jerry Schrager pored over the hundreds of pages of legal documents that would have to be approved and signed. Stanley Friedman buzzed from one group to another, prodding the negotiations.

Louise Sunshine, alternately smiling and scowling, was in and out of the room, scoping out the situation.

Unlike the New Year's Eve closing for Starrett City, where an unwilling and unhappy Donald had been present the entire time, the developer was spending this evening at a Lincoln Center concert. With ten days left to complete the deal, there was not quite the same urgency, and unlike his father, Donald showed he was boss by being absent. But Sunshine insisted he remain on call. At one point she dispatched his chauffeur with instructions to get into the concert hall, find the developer, and drag him to the phone to answer an urgent question. "You belong here," she said. "Get the hell over here now."

After the agreements were finally signed, Councilman Henry Stern recalled, "the deal just sat on the table. It was unusual for the city to be committed for a long while before a developer had his finances [in place]. But of course we didn't know this was the situation at the time." The only reason the deal ever made it through closing, Stern said, was that Stanley Friedman was "the point man for Trump." To Stern, "this did not mean that the deal was bad for the city." It did mean that there would be a deal and that it would be favorable for Trump.

But the developer still had to nail down the financing. It was a daunting task—so daunting, in fact, that for one of the few times in his life, even Donald Trump, the eternal optimist, felt discouraged. To Henry Pearce, the broker who brought Trump to Equitable, that institution delivered "a real karate chop" when it cut the $70 million it had suggested it would put up for permanent—that is, long-term—financing to a more firm $25 million. "It got me crazy," Pearce said. "I was really thrown for a loop." Another bad moment came when an institution Trump was absolutely sure would say yes instead said no. Turning to Pearce, the developer said, "Let's just take this deal and shove it." Pearce, who would not get paid unless he got someone to sign on a bottom line, walked across the street from the Commodore to the Bowery Savings Bank and pointed out to its chairman just how devastating it would be to look at an empty, shuttered building. The chairman agreed and helped Pearce cobble together a consortium of banks to make up the $50 million shortfall.[4]

As was common real estate practice, Trump planned to cover his

$70 million costs with a short-term bank loan, and then, when the construction was done, repay that loan with the permanent one from Equitable and the Bowery group. There was a hitch: So far, he did not have a short-term loan. But there was a solution: Jay Pritzker.[5]

Getting Pritzker on board would require that the hotel bear the name Hyatt—an important asset, given Hyatt's prominence in the field, although Trump complained bitterly about the prospect of "ten-foot-high Hyatt letters across the face of my building" and insisted on naming a restaurant inside the hotel "Trumpets."[6] In addition, Manufacturers Hanover required that Fred Trump and Jay Pritzker co-guarantee the entire construction loan, and in the end each side put up about $2 million.[7] At Donald Trump's prodding, the bank also required Hyatt to sign a noncompete clause, promising that it would not open another hotel within New York City.

At the time, this request apparently seemed relatively innocuous to Hyatt executives, for the chain had noncompete clauses in other cities and evidently assumed that future modifications would be possible if necessary. "Hyatt approached this as, 'Look, this is an upstart young man,'" Schrager recalled. "They were still skeptical about his putting the pieces of the puzzle together." But Pritzker himself never had a chance to argue the point with Trump. Although each partner supposedly had ten days to respond to any suggestion from the other, the developer simply bypassed Pritzker by waiting to bring up the issue until the hotelier was on his way to Nepal and unreachable. Pritzker would keenly regret that he ended up locked out, for New York City was reviving and would soon enter an extraordinary boom period, particularly in the hospitality industry.[8]

The Beame administration simply wanted to save the Commodore; the developer's aim was nothing less than knocking the Waldorf-Astoria off its perch as the city's premier luxury hotel—a goal that conflicted with his plans to do the job on the cheap, and one that would cause the project to go wildly over budget. The first step toward Trump's lavish vision would be to reconfigure the old structure's 2,000 tiny cubicles, which felt more like closets than rooms, into 1,400 larger and more comfortable units. Even for Donald Trump, installing a vertical atrium was impossible at the Commodore because the hotel banquet and meeting rooms were directly over the lobby. Instead the present lobby, basically a large, ugly box, would become an arresting, multileveled space filled with plantings and fountains and connected to a glass-enclosed garden restaurant cantilevered out over 42nd Street.

Behind the scenes, Fred Trump continued to advise his son. "The two of them together in the same room was very strange," recalled Mike Scadron, a New York Military Academy classmate who was briefly involved with the project in the mid-1970s. "They were both talking, supposedly to each other, but I was sure neither heard what the other was saying. They talked right past each other." Yet somehow the collaboration worked. Driving himself in from Avenue Z, the older man kept tabs on the job site and dispensed builder lore, including his practice of adding a bucket of water to every bucket of paint in order to stretch it. "Fred was intense, high energy, the bright blue eyes and the bushy eyebrows like Salvador Dalí," recalled Jeff Walker, then Donald Trump's second in command. "He came through like a rocket ship. He would take the stairs two at a time, and it was all I could do to keep up with him."

Long before the architects had worked out the final design documents, Donald and Fred Trump were busy negotiating a contract with the firm that would do the actual construction, HRH Corporation. Developers commonly used such a contract to pin down costs and tried to leave just enough margin to cover subsequent changes. According to the on-site project architect, Ralph Steinglass, though, the Trump father and son went further and "ruthlessly shaved" the construction budget for the Grand Hyatt in order to comply with the short-term construction loan that had been obtained.[9]

If, as had been the case when Fred Trump beat down costs on his own jobs, Donald had been constructing a type of building father and son were familiar with, they might have been more or less able to keep to the spartan budget.[10] But the Grand Hyatt was a different kind of job. The final design, which bore only faint resemblance to the preliminary versions, was more elaborate than anything either Fred Trump or HRH had ever tackled. Attaching a glass skin to the old brick shell was much harder than anticipated. Reusing existing plumbing systems and partitions made sense on paper, but in reality no one knew exactly what lay behind the walls of the sixty-year-old building. As a result, pipes and fixtures were constantly popping up in unexpected and sometimes disastrous places, requiring expensive changes each time[11]

Even when the situation seemed most dire, though, Trump acted like someone at a combination revival meeting and barn raising. He rolled over Jay Pritzker's objections to the construction budget as unrealistic and stuck to the numbers he needed to get the project up and running. He dashed around town from dawn to midnight, returning calls from his car phone and other people's offices and having anything that needed his signature brought to his restaurant table, often at the '21' Club. He heaped praise on his staffers, huddled on the old hotel's half-demolished top floor in space that was unheated and under a roof that leaked during rainstorms. They were the best, he told them over and over, because only the best worked for Donald Trump; inspired, they redoubled their efforts. Required by his agreement with UDC to turn over a portion of his tax savings for improvements to Grand Central Terminal, he hung a huge TRUMP banner over the station and blithely informed the press that he was donating triple the amount he actually contributed, a boast the papers duly reported. Then when the head of the prestigious, preservation-minded Municipal Arts Society called to chew him out about the offending TRUMP flag, he spoke of his delight that his mirrored hotel would reflect Grand Central's architectural splendor and promptly removed the banner—for a day or two.[12]

Two years earlier, in June 1976, shortly after the New York City Board of Estimate had approved the tax abatement for the Commodore, Donald Trump had his thirtieth birthday. To celebrate the occasion, Louise Sunshine had organized a party at a trendy nightclub.[13] Trump was a Manhattanite now, a man of substance, and it was time that his private life reflected these achievements. Among other things, this meant moving from the bachelor's pad that Der Scutt had visited the night he and the developer met.

"The whole apartment was mirrors, glass, furry furniture, and pictures of buildings," said Mike Scadron. "I always wondered where the person was in all this." When Scadron came over to the apartment, his host didn't offer him anything. "Even a glass of water would have been nice," Scadron said. "I had a feeling no one lived there, that Donald just rented it for an hour."

For his next abode, the developer chose a more spacious apartment on the forty-first floor of Olympic Tower, a new luxury highrise building across from St. Patrick's Cathedral at Fifth Avenue and 51st Street. With two bedrooms, a living room, a dining nook, and a kitchen, it was large enough for two. But the ambition and tenacity that led to one of the biggest real estate deals in recent city history translated into a kind of gauche flashiness that did not endear Trump to women. His dates, which consisted of a ride in a limo, a visible table at a chic restaurant or club, and an expansive monologue about his plans to remake the Manhattan skyline, had the flavor of a sales pitch.

On one double date with Jeffrey Walker, another former NYMA classmate who later came to work for the Trump Organization, the developer pulled out a massive wad of bills to pay the tab. "He didn't have a wallet like a normal person," Walker said later. "He was still - really pretty awful with the clothes, too."[14] Trump seemed drawn to an overdone look, even by flamboyant mid-1970s standards, choosing for his first lengthy interview with *The New York Times* a burgundy suit, a white shirt with his initials stitched in burgundy on the cuffs, and burgundy patent-leather shoes.

One evening during his thirtieth summer, he and another Le Club man about town, a private investment banker named Jerry Goldsmith, stopped off at Maxwell's Plum. Among the usual assortment of bright-eyed singles, several slim, long-legged models from Montreal stood out. The slimmest and most long-legged was a twenty-seven-year-old blonde with hazel eyes named Ivana Zelnicekova Winklmayr. A Czech émigré to Canada, she was in New York to model at a fur show and to publicize the 1976 Olympic Games, to be held that fall in Montreal. "There were lots of pretty girls around," Goldsmith said, "but right away Donald latched on to Ivana."

That night he arranged for a table for Ivana and her friends and picked up their tab. The next day he sent her a dozen roses at the Americana Hotel. A few weeks later he showed up at a fashion show in Montreal where she was working, said hello, and left.[15] Soon she was commuting to New York, riding around town in a silver Cadillac limousine with DJT license plates, dining at Le Club, and driving out to Jamaica Estates to meet Donald's parents. Wherever he went with his "Ivaska," as he called her, he marveled aloud at her appearance. "Isn't she gorgeous?" he would ask everyone within earshot. "Have you ever seen anybody more beautiful?"

At the time, Ivana was living with George Syrovatka, her long-time Czech boyfriend. A champion skier back in Prague, Syrovatka now sold sports equipment in Montreal and was a top contender in European skiing races. Although not on the same level, Ivana, too, was an excellent skier. In the early 1970s the couple had decided to leave Communist Czechoslovakia. On a skiing trip to Austria, Syrovatka defected, which meant that he would not be able to return to his homeland. Ivana chose instead to make a cold war–style marriage of convenience to one of Syrovatka's skiing friends, an Austrian named Alfred Winklmayr. With an Austrian passport, she would be able to return to Czechoslovakia to see her parents.

Divorced from Winklmayr by the time she joined Syrovatka in Canada, Ivana looked for employment in Montreal as a model. She had already done some modeling in Prague; in Canada she changed her dark brown hair to a brassy blond and daubed on heavy makeup for a dramatic older look. She had neither the height nor the cheekbones to be a top fashion model, but because of her athletic training— she had earned a master's degree in physical education from Charles University in Prague—she had a physical self-assurance as she headed down a runway or across a room that made people look and keep looking. In addition, the smile that sometimes looked forced and even harsh in photographs was warm and inviting in person.[16] In Montreal this commanding presence gave her steady work as a showroom model.

Her striking physical self-confidence was more than an attractive feature. It was one of many similarities between these two young - people—so many, in fact, that Ivana would later remark that Trump called her "his twin as a woman." They also shared a sense of the importance of family ties and the experience of having strong fathers. Ivana's father had pushed her extraordinarily hard. Born premature, she spent her first months in a hospital crib but eventually became a daredevil skier who charged downhill and broke both legs repeatedly. Like Donald, she was an indifferent student. Once her alarmed father

yanked her out of school and put her to work on the assembly line in
the Bata shoe factory where he worked as an electrical engineer. She
was back at her books within weeks.

Like the man she would marry, Ivana drove herself, piling on
challenges and working harder than anyone else. In part this was because of her early sports training. "Going down a ski slope at a hundred miles an hour, you have only yourself to count on," she told one
reporter. "Nobody else can do it for you. I learned quickly, and I
haven't forgotten those lessons. Discipline. It takes incredible discipline." But it was also because in Czechoslovakia, although it had
been acceptable to excel at sports, it had been prudent not to display
ambition and instead to remain an anonymous mediocrity; now, like
other refugees from authoritarian regimes, she reveled in the opportunity to stand out. She was intelligent, not brilliant, but she had
something that was perhaps better suited to life in the new world: she
was shrewd. She did not question why things were the way they were;
she sized them up and made them work for her.

Above all, she radiated the raw energy that distinguished Donald
Trump. In her relationship with him, it would be the tie that bound.
"I think what attracts us so much together is not only the love and all
that stuff," Ivana once said. "It's the energy. We are very much alike
in that way. I can't sit still."

On Saturday, April 9, 1977, after a bachelor's party at Maxwell's
Plum, Donald Trump married Ivana Winklmayr at Marble Collegiate
Church in Manhattan. It was the day before Easter, and fragrant white
lilies filled the landmark Dutch Reformed sanctuary. Among those
present at the ceremony and at the reception afterward at the '21'
Club was Roy Cohn. When Donald told him he planned to marry,
Cohn insisted on drawing up a prenuptial contract. An early draft
stipulated that the bride return all gifts in the event of a divorce.
Ivana countered by demanding a "rainy day fund" of $150,000 in cash.
After stormy arguments and lengthy negotiations, the couple finally
found common ground and the ceremony went ahead on schedule.

The Trump family was there in force. Because Ivana could not afford airfare for both parents and was evidently too embarrassed to ask
her husband-to-be for the money, only her father was there. The
groom's brothers, Fred Jr. and Robert, served as best man and usher,

and his sisters, Maryanne and Elizabeth, were bridesmaids. Donald was marrying at thirty, the same age his own father had wed; he had chosen a woman who, like his mother, was not an American citizen; and he told everyone that he, too, wanted five children.* Unlike his father, he took time off and went to Acapulco for a honeymoon—but on his way out of town he put in a conference call to Jordan Gruzen and project architect Ralph Steinglass to tell them exactly what to do in his absence.

The church itself was major Trump territory. Two years earlier Fred and Mary Trump had become members, and they had long felt an affinity for the teachings of head minister Dr. Norman Vincent Peale. Indeed, Peale, who officiated at the ceremony, had provided much of the spiritual underpinnings for the entrepreneurial culture in which the Trumps flourished. Starting out in upstate New York at the same time Fred Trump began building in Brooklyn, Peale put worldliness and godliness together into a practical-minded theology that encouraged self-promotion and valued success. Critics called him crass and commercial and resented what seemed like easily digested sound bites; supporters saw an up-to-date Protestant ethic that promised rewards for hard work in this life as well as in the next. "God's salesman," as he was known, acquired a huge audience through his radio shows, newspaper columns, magazine articles, and books like *You Can Win, Have a Great Day,* and *Enthusiasm Makes the Difference.* His most famous volume, *The Power of Positive Thinking,* which appeared in 1952, was a best-seller for two years and sold an estimated five million copies.[17]

Although the Trump children rarely attended services with their parents at Marble Collegiate, they, too, had joined, and Mary Trump was convinced that they shared her deep faith. After one service, she gave Peale's assistant a ride to the airport in her Rolls-Royce and told him that she had taught her children about faith when they were young. "I tried to get it into their heads that they had to believe," she said. "Whether it shows or not, it's in there because I put it in there."

---

*A man of his word, Donald wasted no time getting started. Nine months after his marriage, on December 31, 1977, his first child, a son, was born and named Donald John Trump Jr.

—m—

Donald seemed to expect a marriage more or less like that of his parents, but what evolved could hardly have been more different. Less than two years after the ceremony at Marble Collegiate, Ivana Trump became involved in the family business.[18] Having provided a son and namesake, she had launched herself into the New York social scene via the usual route of volunteer work for select charities. She had redone both herself, cramming her days with exercise classes, massages, and hairdressing appointments, and her husband, exchanging his flashy outer borough wardrobe for expensive dark suits from exclusive Manhattan stores. She had also revised her résumé, telling *The New York Times* that she had originally gone to Montreal only to visit an aunt and uncle. For the family's new eight-room apartment in an old mansion at 800 Fifth Avenue, she had created a glossy corporate look, with beige velvet sectional sofas and mirrors framed with twinkling lights.[19]

She had even developed a promotional manner that complemented that of her husband. "The Donald is fantastic in the golf and very good in the tennis," she told the *Times*, inadvertently giving her husband his most lasting nickname. But the woman who had been winning athletic competitions since she was six was not satisfied being the stay-at-home wife of a rising developer. She began showing up at the construction site in designer outfits and spike heels, donning a hard hat, and conducting inspection tours.

Like her husband, she was inexperienced and aggressive; unlike him, she was not inclined to listen to others or even to learn their names. To some male observers she made matters worse by an imperious manner; she declared that she had to act extra tough to get the job done. In any event, by being there, clipboard in hand, without any clear authority and yet demanding attention, she was for the supervisors and managers a distraction and often a headache. For her husband, however, Ivana was a crucial part of the operation. Because he was a hands-on manager who liked to know every detail, it was vital to have someone acting as his eyes and ears, constantly pointing, looking over shoulders, asking questions, and taking notes. With Ivana on the case, he could devote himself to the number one task of any entrepreneur—scouting out future deals—and still know exactly what was going on at the current job site.

Ivana was one management tool; another was what students at Wharton would have called "creative conflict." Again and again the developer would hire someone to do a job, then bring in someone else to do the same job, setting them against each other. A Machiavellian tactic, it seemed to him to have many advantages. For one thing, something better often emerged when, as one observer put it, "you put ten people in a bag and hang it over the line."[20] For another, making sure that everyone was being watched by someone else was a time-honored way of watching his own back, for this divide-and-conquer approach kept subordinates running to him to adjudicate their status and left him the only one with clear authority.

There were no exceptions; whether consciously or not, the developer set even Ivana and Fred Trump against one another by soliciting from each whatever on-site intelligence they could provide. Off the job, father and daughter-in-law were dutiful family members who shared meals at the house on Midland Parkway, family events, and visits to what was still Fred Trump's favorite vacation retreat, the Concord.[21] But at the work site they complained constantly about each other's presence. Ivana did not hesitate to take her grievances to her husband, which sometimes led to pitched battles between them. For Donald it became yet another opportunity to reaffirm his authority.

In the later phases of the Commodore reconstruction, Trump supplemented the interiors team, which included the initial interior designer plus a second one he brought in to overlook the first one, by adding Ivana. Her taste, he said, was "tremendous" and "'impeccable." In other words, it was just like his. Although the Grand Hyatt was in the middle of New York City, he was not seeking some quintessential Manhattan ambiance. Rather than pursuing a classically tasteful Upper East Side look or a hip Lower East Side feeling, he sought what *New York Times* architecture critic Paul Goldberger called "an out-of-towner's vision of city life."[22] Neither Trump had an allegiance to old-style, WASPy egg-and-dart molding, to vintage Currier & Ives prints, or to floor-to-ceiling bookshelves filled with leather-bound volumes. They did not subscribe to the notion that old and restrained is good, that less is more, or that quiet elegance is superior to sticking out.

In short, they did not want to fit in. To them, newer was better, more was more, and being noticed was always better than being one of the crowd. They shared the same flashy aesthetic, the same boundless appetite for more marble, more mirrors, more shiny brass, more dramatic lighting. Demanding, insistent, hoarse-voiced from screaming so often and so loudly, Ivana worked eighteen-hour days for months on end to be sure that the new hotel would radiate glitz and glamour in every detail.

But creating an environment of extravagance was not simply a matter of taste; it was also a critical business decision. With the site sitting directly on top of a maze of active subway and railroad tracks, the developer could not demolish the old structure, but instead had to work around it. His solution was to make the Grand Hyatt look different in every possible way from its dowdy predecessor.[23] Thus when the architects suggested saving mementos of the historic hotel, Trump would have none of it. When they proposed using a limestone facade so as to relate to Grand Central Station next door, he said that the way he wanted to relate to Grand Central was to reflect it on the hotel's new glass skin. Because he wanted guests to feel they were up high, he inflated the number of floors. A twenty-six-floor building by conventional measure became a thirty-four-floor structure by the simple expedient of beginning the numbering of the guest room floors with fourteen. Likewise he wanted to have the largest ballroom in the city and did not stop making the claim after a junior designer at the Gruzen firm found that other facilities were larger. "He listened to us about plumbing and code issues," said architect Paul Willen, "but on anything that had to do with marketing or image, he got his way."

It was a way that worked. The Grand Hyatt, Donald Trump's first opportunity to display his own glittering vision, was a grand slam. Construction crews were still in the lobby as guests began arriving for the November 1980 opening, and New York magazine scorned the gold Mylar tablecloths and blond waitresses "lined up like Vegas chorines." But the public drank up all the spectacular, unquiet luxury. The same people who had been unwilling to pay $20 a night at the old brick hotel[24] next to Grand Central eagerly forked over several times that amount now that the same building was sheathed in glass, polished to a high gloss, and touted as new. They took the Grand Hyatt's elevators to what they supposed to be the thirty-fourth floor, and they danced in what they believed to be the biggest ballroom in New York City. And if all that wasn't quite so, they didn't really care. Donald Trump was right: it sounded so much better that way.

The gleaming, almost new structure did not come cheap. During the reconstruction, design alterations and change orders had multiplied, and because they occurred after the signing of the construction contract, they were on the developer's side of the ledger.[25] The final tab was $130 million,[26] almost twice the contract and the construction loan. Going over budget was never good; doubling it would seem guaranteed to create a disaster, plunging the new hotel into a financial hole it could never climb out of.

Instead the Hyatt was a resounding success. In the short term, Fred Trump rescued his son. When the huge bills came due, Donald Trump met his half of the extra cost with help from his father's old bank, Chase, in the form of a $35 million unsecured line of credit and a $30 million second mortgage, plus another loan from one of his father's corporations. But the principal reason for the Hyatt triumph was that the city itself was gradually recovering. From 1970 to 1975, thirty of New York City's largest corporations had left the city; between 1975 and 1978, twelve of them returned.[27] Similarly, hotel occupancy, which was down to 64 percent in 1975, rebounded to 78 percent by 1980. Midtown Manhattan stood at the center of this renaissance, and at the center of midtown was the Grand Hyatt, a shiny and prosperous symbol of urban recovery.

Despite Donald Trump's achievements at the Grand Hyatt, development of the other Penn Central properties, the West Side rail yards, continued to elude him. As it turned out, the 34th Street yards would eventually house the city's new convention center, although Donald Trump's architects would not design it and he would not build it. But not for lack of trying. Early in 1978, while the new Koch administration was still unpacking, the developer was down at City Hall pushing his project. "He sort of burst into the office," recalled

Ron Marino, then deputy to newly elected Manhattan borough president Andrew Stein. "He was this big tall blond guy with this great physical presence, saying he had a great idea, that he would be doing us a favor." Rather than bothering with the time-consuming process of requesting proposals from any other developers, Trump suggested, the city could just turn over the land to him and he'd do the job.[28]

Ultimately the commission to design the convention center went to I. M. Pei, and the joint developers were UDC and another public agency, the Triborough Bridge and Tunnel Authority.[29] However, as stipulated by the agreement Donald Trump had made with Palmieri and Penn Central, he stood to collect a broker's fee. At one point he suggested that he might forgo the money. He would be doing so only to help out the city, he told a reporter, because "from an economic standpoint for me, [waiving the fee] is a foolish thing."[30]

To Peter Solomon, then serving as Mayor Koch's deputy mayor for economic development, the offer seemed worth investigating. Most city officials enjoyed having the public come downtown, and Peter Jacob Solomon, who was a multimillionaire heir to an old department store fortune as well as a Wall Street wunderkind before coming to government, had special boasting rights as the first person in his job to have landed an office within City Hall itself. But he had long since found going to others' offices a more effective way to get what he wanted. When he went uptown to meet with Donald Trump, he found an aspiring multimillionaire as attuned as he was to nuances of psychological one-upmanship. According to Solomon, the developer said that although he was entitled to a fee of about $4 million, he would not collect it if the city put his father's name on the center. For further details, the developer said airily, Solomon could look the matter up in the court records.

"It wasn't, 'Put my name on it,' it was, 'Put my father's name on it,'" Solomon recalled. "Of course, that was his name, too, but he was clever the way he put it." Solomon did look the matter up and found the commission was closer to $600,000. "It was like what Casey Stengel used to say," Solomon recounted. "You know, 'Look it up.' I don't think Donald ever thought we would." When Solomon laid out the facts to the mayor, he dismissed the idea of naming the facility after Fred Trump as ridiculous. "I don't remember any rancor, just humor," Solomon said. "It was great chutzpah, and in those days, in the Koch administration, we were admirers of chutzpah."³¹

Donald Trump continued to express a strong desire to develop the northern section of the yards, at 60th Street, and was scheduled to make a $100,000 payment on the option for the site at the end of 1979. At the appointed hour he walked into the Palmieri offices, pulled out what he said was a check for that amount, and then proceeded to back out of the deal, citing problems with the title.

As he later acknowledged, the project faced tough community board opposition, zoning problems, and financing difficulties, and he was wholly occupied with the Commodore. At the time, though, he insisted that he was not paying for the option because the map of the site showed a 1½-inch strip between the street and the yards that nobody owned. As he well knew, such "gores"—minuscule strips where adjacent plots did not match up exactly—are commonplace technical defects for which title companies routinely provide insurance in the unlikely event that anyone tries to exploit them. "The so-called title problem was not only not insuperable, it was a joke," said one close observer. "He just used it as an excuse because the guy could not admit that he was defeated."³² Even for this most positive of positive thinkers, giving up the option seemed the end of a dream. As fate would have it, though, what seemed the end would turn out to be only an interruption.

———

By the time the ground was broken for the Grand Hyatt, Donald Trump was deeply involved in another project: the structure that would identify him in New York City and, eventually, the rest of the country and the world. In the process he would hone the skills and tactics that would define his way of doing business for the rest of his career. He had learned what he needed from his father, including the need for that extra element that caught people's eye. For his father, it had been the garage under a Flatbush front stoop and the extra closet in a Coney Island apartment; for Donald, it was the marble on marble and the gilt on gilt. From his father he had also learned about making

up for the cost of such visible flourishes by cutting what was invisible—lopping an inch off the width of bathroom doors, say, or reducing
the number of cabinet hinges from three to two.

From now on Donald Trump would be on his own. He would not
be relying on his father's network of aging Brooklyn politicians. Instead he would be operating in an entirely different world, where
wealth, power, and possessions would reach new orders of magnitude
and the klieg lights would be permanently on. He already had bravado
to spare, and with his newly cemented ties in the banking world, he
would have access to financing. He had served his apprenticeship in
the Brooklyn old-boy league; now he was ready to play with the Manhattan big boys.

Up to this point Donald Trump had been learning what he could
do, but now he would be learning what he could get away with. This
knowledge was intoxicating, and it was also dangerous. It would take
him to dazzling heights and help set the stage for a calamitous fall. It
would make him one of the most famous people in the world, able to
sell not only real estate per se, but also magazines, pizzas, cars,
books, sunglasses, and even the notion that losing money is fun. For
better or worse, it would leave an indelible impact on the nation and
help to shape an era.

Initially, the idea for the next project was a simple one: Construct
a big building, name it after himself, and make a lot of money. The
model was Olympic Tower, the fifty-two-story modern luxury building that was then his home. It had replaced the failing flagship store
of Best & Company, the old-line clothier where Mary Trump had
once shopped for her chubby toddler Donald. Across Fifth Avenue
was Rockefeller Center, and next door were the luxury jeweler
Cartier, Inc., and the Olympic Building, which housed ticket offices
for Olympic Airways. In the early 1970s the airline's owner, Greek
billionaire Aristotle Onassis, struck a deal with Meshulam Riklis, a
celebrated manipulator of corporate assets who controlled Best's department store, and replaced its ninety-one-year-old building with a
huge box covered in bronze-tinted glass.[33] The first of what would be
known as "mixed use" projects in Manhattan, it had retail stores on
the first two floors, offices on the next nineteen floors, and, on the top
thirty-one stories, 230 of the city's first condo units.[34]

What most New Yorkers noticed about Olympic Tower was a

large indoor public space that contained an arcade, a café, and a three-story waterfall. What other developers noticed was that Onassis made more money out of the site than anyone had thought possible, essentially by having skilled real estate lawyers, including Jerry Schrager and Sandy Lindenbaum, look for creative ways to use loopholes in city zoning regulations.

One of the largest loopholes had to do with "air rights," or the right to build the largest possible building under existing zoning regulations. Just as the scarcity of water makes the right to its use a negotiable commodity in the American West, the lack of land in Manhattan makes air rights there into a valuable asset. Owners of buildings that are not "built out"—in other words, already the maximum square footage allowable—can sell off unused development or "air rights," which developers of adjacent sites can then use to make their own projects larger than would otherwise be allowed. Quietly buying up adjacent sites and air rights, including those over Cartier, Onassis put together the first large-scale development in this exclusive section of Fifth Avenue. Then, by including public space, he earned further zoning bonuses. In the end he increased his building's size and income-producing floor area by more than one-third, giving Olympic Tower the highest density in the city at the time.*

Because it was a superluxury building, the extra space meant record profits. Making the deal even juicier, Onassis also obtained a ten-year real estate tax abatement under a new state law. Known by its section number, 421a, and designed to spur residential development in commercial areas, the abatement was available for sites that were underutilized or functionally obsolescent. By the letter of the

---

*The size of any building in New York City depends on its floor area ratio, or FAR, which is the ratio of the total floor area to the size of the building lot and is a function of the specific zoning assigned to the lot. At that time, the FAR in most high-density commercial areas in Manhattan was 15. Because Olympic Tower (OT) had public space at the ground level, more than the minimally required retail space, and residential units, the FAR increased to 21.6, the highest permissible ratio of floor area to lot size. As a result, OT was able to maximize its density, or total square footage relative to the size of its building lot. Although the Empire State Building (ESB), 102 stories, is far taller than the 52-story OT, its density is not as large because (1) the ESB spreads out over a far larger building lot; and (2) unlike OT, which is essentially a big rectangular solid sitting on its end, ESB is stepped back, in wedding cake style.

law, Best & Co. qualified, for the twelve-story building was not nearly as large as its zoning permitted, and the retailer had long since lost out to other, more modern outlets.

The spirit of the law was another question. "Each of these measures was done to try to solve a single problem without looking at the rest of the picture," said former New York City Corporation Counsel lawyer Rochelle Corson. "When they were used together, you got a monster, which wasn't contemplated and was grossly undertaxed." But it was a monster with important implications for future New York real estate development. "It was the first time 421a was used on such a huge project," Corson said. "All the real estate people, all the law firms, everybody watched Olympic Tower as the test for how far they could push the envelope on this."[35]

Not one to tamper with success, Donald Trump initially followed the example set by Olympic Tower almost to the letter. The spot he selected for his project currently housed the ailing flagship of another celebrated department store chain, Bonwit Teller; it was next to an exclusive jeweler, Tiffany; and it would be worth a lot more empty. His project would also have the same retail/office/residential mix, the same lawyers, the same bankers, and the same zoning bonuses. Even the address, five blocks north of Olympic Tower on Fifth Avenue, was almost the same.

But there the similarities ended. The most immediate problem was that Bonwit's had almost three decades left on its lease.[36] Trump had written a letter to the store's owner, a Nashville shoe and apparel conglomerate named Genesco, but like the letter he had once written to Victor Palmieri, it seemed to go nowhere. In the spring of 1978 the developer read in *Business Week* that Genesco had a new chief executive named John Hanigan who was eager to unload any assets not contributing to the company's bottom line. After obtaining an appointment with Hanigan, Trump phoned Der Scutt and told him to be in front of Bonwit Teller in twenty minutes. "When his limo pulled up," Scutt recalled later, "he leaned out and said, 'Isn't this the greatest site in the world?'"

Uncharacteristically for Donald Trump, the project was hush-hush at first. He gave it the code name "Project T"—supposedly for Tiffany, not Trump—and warned Scutt not to mention it on the car phone. On the way to Nashville to meet with Hanigan, he asked Phil

Wolf, on-site owner's representative on the Grand Hyatt, to meet him at the airport but did not say where they were going. "It wasn't until we got on the plane that he showed me the letter he'd prepared," said Wolf, a dignified and reputable contractor then in his late forties. "He was renting my gray hair for the day."

He was also renting Wolf's social graces. Upon arrival, Genesco brass whisked developer and contractor off to lunch at a private club, and Wolf exchanged pleasantries and shoe industry shop talk as Trump fidgeted in his chair. "Afterward, Donald said that if I hadn't been there, he would have jumped out the window," Wolf said. "He absolutely cannot do small talk—he wanted to steer the conversation his way all the time." Once at Genesco offices, though, the developer got a head start on the deal he wanted.

In November Genesco gave Donald Trump a six-month option to purchase the Bonwit leasehold for $25 million, even though he had put no money down. The signing took place at Genesco's Manhattan offices, located across the street from Bonwit's in the Crown Building. When the developer and Jerry Schrager walked outside afterward, a light snow was falling. "We looked across Fifth Avenue at Tiffany's, and there was a line of limousines around the block," recalled Schrager. "We couldn't believe what we had just done. Without paying out a cent, we controlled the most fabulous location in all of New York City."

To build condominiums, however, the developer had to own not only the property but also the tenant rights currently held by Bonwit's. In theory, current property owner Equitable Life Assurance Society should have been eager to sell because it was earning only about 4 percent a year on its original investment. This had been a reasonable amount back when Bonwit's leased the site, but not by the late 1970s, when interest rates were 8 to 10 percent and still climbing. Yet Equitable managers had refused offers from other entrepreneurs because they believed that when the lease eventually expired, they would be able to negotiate a new one so profitable it would make the long wait worthwhile.

Undaunted, Trump went to talk to Equitable, which had financed Olympic Tower. Just as the developer had told city officials that he considered taking over the 34th Street Convention Center to be doing New York a favor, he now told real estate executive George Peacock that he wanted to help out Equitable, one of the nation's largest institutional investors, by taking this low-yield site off its hands. When he finished speaking, Peacock burst into laughter. "If you just looked at the income, and not what we'd get when the lease was up, it was pretty miserable pay," Peacock said later. "But Equitable was paying me not to miss these things. At that first meeting, I just dismissed Donald's suggestion."

Unlike other developers George Peacock had brushed off, Donald Trump came back. When he said that he had obtained an option on the leasehold, Peacock's interest was piqued. With the New York real estate market at last picking up, Equitable had begun to think of owning the building itself instead of leasing out the land and letting others collect rent. Soon the owner of the property and the holder of an option on the leasehold were drawing up plans for a joint venture.[37] From the start, the developer insisted that the project should bear his name. "Having his name on the building was one of the things Donald wanted very badly," Peacock told a reporter. "We were able to use that to our advantage in our negotiations with him."[38]

With the Grand Hyatt under way, financing the construction of what would later be called Trump Tower was not a problem.[39] Trump simply went to the place where he had first looked for hotel financing: the office of Conrad Stephenson, regional vice president in charge of commercial real estate loans at Chase Manhattan Bank. Known as Steve, he was a hearty, athletic man in his early fifties, with red hair showing just a hint of gray. A sailor in World War II, he had gone through Fordham on the GI Bill, opted out of law school after sitting in a tiny cubicle writing briefs, and ended up in banking. During a stint at a Long Island bank, he worked with Abe Traub, the legendary lawyer who represented nearly every major developer in New York, and became what was known as a "relationship banker," developing a remarkable rapport with blue-chip clients. In 1976 Chase, the bank where he had started out, rehired him to boost real estate lending.

Stephenson had seen his big chance when Fred Trump, the bank's real estate customer of longest standing, brought in his son to inquire about short-term financing for the Grand Hyatt. "As with a lot of my customers," Stephenson recalled, "I was at an age in between father and son, which made me accessible to both." Eager to get moving, Stephenson quickly came to terms with the Trumps, then went off on a European vacation. In his absence a colleague stepped in, the arrangement collapsed, and Stephenson returned to an empty plate. "Putting it mildly, I was very upset," he said. "We had already agreed on everything, but another loan officer went for that extra ounce." When Donald returned to talk about a $130 million construction package for his second project, Stephenson made sure he handled the negotiations himself.[40]

When Trump had first talked to Der Scutt about the site, what the developer had in mind was a mixed-use structure that would essentially be a variation on Olympic Tower: a big vertical box sitting on top of a big horizontal box. Too boring, Scutt said. He began to sketch out alternatives, including an ugly, chunky box that showed the biggest possible structure that could be put up under existing, or "as of right," zoning. The developer flaunted the sketch at a meeting with Tiffany's patrician chairman, Walter Hoving, a famously haughty octogenarian who banned from his store diamond rings for men, silver plate, and any knots in the white ribbon used to tie Tiffany's robin's-egg-blue gift boxes.[41] Aghast at Scutt's eyesore, Hoving eagerly agreed to sell his company's air rights, which the developer claimed would give him the space necessary to construct a more graceful next-door neighbor.

Then Sandy Lindenbaum realized that the building could go still higher if the design included "public parks" in the form of tiny, nearly inaccessible fifth-floor balconies. Combining purchased air rights, Lindenbaum's parklettes, and the same zoning bonuses for public space used at Olympic Tower, Scutt produced a building that was neither chunky nor boxy. Instead it was a soaring twenty-eight-sided structure with an arresting sawtooth profile. It would provide apartment dwellers with drop-dead views in two directions, one of which was Central Park; it also ignored all manner of city guidelines about how buildings were supposed to fit into neighborhoods and arrange themselves on their sites.

Trump seemed unfazed, even though he would have to undergo a cumbersome review process and obtain multiple zoning variances at the same time that two other huge projects were under construction next door and the head of urban design at the City Planning Commission had ordered a crackdown on large buildings. The developer simply instructed Scutt to produce another hideous as-of-right version, this one a seventy-seven-story monolith cantilevered over Tiffany's. Brandishing it in front of the commissioners, Trump promised to lease space in his preferred design to Bonwit's, a prime retail tenant the city was eager to retain. Crying uncle, they okayed the obviously superior building with twenty-eight sides and passed that proposal on for quick ratification at the Board of Estimate.

Razing of the old building began in December 1979.[42] Although Trump did not have a demolition permit, he hired John Kaszycki to handle the operation. A hard-bitten, white-haired Polish immigrant and former window washer, Kaszycki had never done such a job. But because he could pay undocumented Polish laborers less than half the union rate and make money selling whatever scrap metal he salvaged, he accepted a rock-bottom fee. Before Christmas his crews began sneaking into the building and pulling apart upper floors even though the electricity was on and they had to cut into live wires. Over the next six months nearly two hundred illegal laborers worked with three or four dozen members of Housewreckers Local 95. Readily distinguished by their lack of hard hats, the Polish Brigades, as they came to be called, put in twelve- to eighteen-hour shifts seven days a week and slept crowded together in slum housing, cheap motels, or, in some cases, on the floors of buildings they were tearing down. Despite dreadful working conditions and erratic pay, the Poles did exactly what the developer wanted—which proved calamitous.*

---

*Kaszycki grossly underestimated the cost of this and other contracts. At least once he paid the Polish Brigades in vodka, and eventually he stopping paying them at all. In March 1980 they held a work stoppage, and Kaszycki gave them checks that bounced. Remarkably, given their vulnerability to deportation, half a dozen of the men went to John Szabo, a Queens storefront lawyer. His first case, it would turn into a pitched battle over who was to blame for this exploitation and subject Donald Trump to his third FBI probe (the first was for racial discrimination in Trump-owned housing in Brooklyn and Queens, and the second explored how Donald Trump had obtained the option on the West Side rail yards).

In 1983 the developer, Equitable, and Kaszycki were sued for unpaid union pension benefits, due on all workers regardless of immigration status. When the case went to trial, Szabo testified that he had been threatened with a $100 million lawsuit by a Trump Organization spokesman named "John Barron." Although the identity of the caller was never established, Donald Trump and his construction supervisor admitted using the name on other occasions. Indeed, using a pseudonym was an old Trump fam-

On Bonwit Teller's facade were two notable art deco features: an ornamental grille, fifteen by twenty-five feet and made of solid nickel, that consisted of intricate geometric designs and stretched across the top of the front doors; and, mounted above the eighth floor, a pair of fifteen-foot-tall bas-relief panels, carved in limestone, that portrayed highly stylized, partially draped female nudes. In mid-March of 1980 *The New York Times* ran an article at the front of the Sunday real estate section describing in detail Donald Trump's plans to donate the artworks to the Metropolitan Museum of Art, for which he would receive a tax deduction. Although removing the grillwork in one piece would be a simple matter, taking down the sculptures, which one independent appraiser suggested might be worth about $200,000, would be more complex and would cost perhaps $2,500.

Three months later *The New York Times* ran a second story on the Bonwit Teller artwork. This one, on the front page, said the sculptures had been jackhammered into smithereens and the grille had disappeared and perhaps been sold as scrap. Although museum officials expressed dismay at the loss of promised artwork, one John Barron, who identified himself in phone interviews with the press as a Trump Organization vice president, claimed the reliefs were worth only $9,000 and were "without artistic merit." Removing them, he said, would cost the developer $32,000 plus another $500,000 for project delays. Later Donald Trump said that $32,000 was "nothing" because

ily practice, according to Maryanne Trump Barry, who remembered her father's using "Mr. Green" to obtain information over the phone. "It was like 'John Barron' is for Donald," she said, "a name for an imaginary spokesman who is really Donald. My husband [a lawyer named John Barry] says when he's joking that he's going to call and say John Barron's been given a subpoena, and then we'll see how quickly John Barron falls ill and dies."

Sixteen years later, in March 1999, the case was settled out of court. The Trump Organization and Equitable would pay an undisclosed sum, presumably approximately the $4 million that had already been levied against them plus interest, to the pension and welfare fund of Housewreckers Local 95. The Polish Brigades had long since scattered, the lead plaintiff was dead, and few among the public remembered that the gleaming tower at Fifth Avenue and 56th Street had such an unseemly chapter in its early history.

he contributed that much monthly to artists (although he provided no names), that he'd had the reliefs destroyed to protect pedestrians from falling debris, and that there had been no damage to his project because the whole episode was attracting buyers rather than repelling them.

Unable to admit that removing the badly weathered sculptures was harder and more expensive than he had first thought and that had he consulted with the officials to whom he had promised the work, they might have agreed that he could not keep his promise at a reasonable cost, Trump tried to blame everyone and everything else. There had been no reneging on a promise to the Metropolitan Museum of Art because, he claimed, the museum had actually declined the art, and there had been no destruction of valuable art because the art was not valuable.*

He did not see this as lying. There was no more reason, in his mind, for saving souvenirs of Bonwit's, an outmoded department store, than there had been for saving mementos of the Commodore, an outmoded hotel. Both were old, useless, and broke; his projects would be new, glamorous, and, he was convinced, enormously profitable. "He couldn't stand anything from before," Der Scutt said later. "He wants his own clean image, from A to Z, from inside to outside."

But there were other reasons for his peremptory behavior. He did not want attention drawn to the workers who had torn down the artwork and was eager to end press scrutiny of the episode. In addition, a handful of well-connected East Siders had already formed an organization specifically opposed to the developer's project, which they saw as an ugly successor to a beautiful old structure.[43] "Bomb the shit out of that building!" the developer told his staff, urging them to get word out that it was structurally unsound, that windows were falling out, and that previous renovations had already drastically altered the building's original design.[44]

The most urgent reason was that the delays needed for careful re-

*Oddly, given this public claim as to the art's worthlessness, Trump apparently rescued a piece of the sculpture from under the jackhammer. According to architect Alan Lapidus, during a visit to Trump's office at the time, he saw a four-foot-tall chunk of the bas relief showing part of a stylized human form. "Donald seemed genuinely bewildered by the fuss," Lapidus said later. "When I asked him what the carving was doing there, he leaned toward me and said, 'Shut up.'"

moval of the artwork could end up costing him the 421a tax abatement he was counting on. With the city's financial crisis receding, the abatement, once deemed necessary to encourage housing, now seemed a giveaway to fancy apartment buildings for which the need for taxpayer subsidies was a matter of debate. A decade earlier, Olympic Tower's 421a application had gone through smoothly, but now civic leaders and city officials were pushing hard to eliminate one of the loopholes the developer was relying on. To avoid being caught short, he desperately needed to file his application as soon as possible, but he could not do so until the old building was torn down and construction on the new one had actually begun—a situation that made even a modest delay intolerable. What was at issue for the developer was not $32,000, or even $500,000, but at least $25 million in taxes he hadn't planned on paying.

By 1981 Trump was finally able to submit his abatement application. Soon afterward word leaked out that it was receiving special scrutiny. In the past he would instantly have started yanking strings in Albany and Gracie Mansion. But there was no state involvement in this project, and the current mayor was not a self-effacing accountant and old political crony of Fred Trump's. Indeed, Ed Koch enjoyed confrontation at least as much as Donald Trump did. He had welcomed the developer and his wife to his victory party and had snipped ceremonial ribbons at the Grand Hyatt, but his relationship with the Trump Organization was not a happy one.[45]

One reason was a bitter conflict over a long-stalled pedestrian passageway under the Grand Hyatt, meant to relieve subway congestion. After making a verbal promise to a Koch deputy that he would provide a free easement, the developer procrastinated until he extracted a large condemnation award. To Donald Trump, as to many others in real estate, a deal was not a deal until he signed on the dotted line, and the long delay was no more than his prerogative. To the Koch administration, though, an oral promise to a deputy mayor was a done deal, and the developer's refusal to go forward was infuriating.

The developer made a fence-mending contribution to the mayor's upcoming reelection campaign. But he also turned to another city official, Andrew Stein, the pro-development borough president of Manhattan.[46] Their mutual friend Roy Cohn introduced Trump and Stein, both attractive, highly ambitious sons of highly successful, wealthy, and encouraging fathers, in the early 1970s. Over dinner at Trader Vic's, a trendy Polynesian-themed restaurant, the pro–rent control politician, then a state assembly member, and the anti–rent control developer had spent the evening arguing about whether rent regulation should be abolished. Hardly surprising, neither budged. Nonetheless, the two young men hit it off and remained on good terms.[47]

At the moment, Stein, too, was having trouble. Specifically, he was wrestling with a dire threat from Manhattan's biggest real estate owner, Harry Helmsley. Unless the city handed over a playground of little apparent value, Helmsley said, he planned to build on two small, much loved private parks in the middle of Tudor City, an apartment complex he owned on the East Side near United Nations headquarters. City officials, wary of setting a possibly dangerous precedent by giving in to such blackmail, were reluctantly gearing up to approve the trade-off. Then, on the eve of the final Board of Estimate vote, Donald Trump supplied Stein with the ammunition needed to kill the swap. Trump asserted—correctly, as it turned out—that Helmsley's parks were on nearly unbuildable sites, which meant that his threat to put apartments on them was a bluff. Further, Trump said that because the playground fronted the East River, that site was worth far more than its appraised value, which meant that in a trade Helmsley would come out far ahead. To back up his assertion, Trump publicly offered, at a meeting in Stein's office, to buy the playground for more than Helmsley's assessment.

"This is good," the developer said, pulling out his own checkbook. "You can call the bank to find out."[48]

To Jesse Masyr, the young Stein deputy charged with resolving the dilemma, Trump's sudden appearance was a godsend. Masyr had opposed the swap and was now desperate for a decent argument to back up his stance. "I was looking for any port in a storm, and in walked a big port, someone who could speak with credibility," Masyr recalled later. "I don't think we would have gotten anywhere without Donald's help."

Stein, too, was grateful for Trump's intervention. "It was a real delicate situation, and Donald was helpful," he said later. "I don't know if there was a connection to Trump Tower, but I'm sure he was trying to be as helpful to me as he could. It made sense." Using the developer's argument, the borough president's office was able to round up enough votes to postpone consideration of the proposal, and it never came to a vote.

Helmsley never built on the park land, as Donald Trump had foreseen. As he may also have foreseen, his friendship with Andrew Stein grew warmer. The day after the Board of Estimate delayed voting on the park swap, the borough president hosted a breakfast meeting at his Park Avenue apartment for Trump, Louise Sunshine, and Tony Gliedman, the city commissioner charged with deciding on the 421a issue. Less than two weeks after this morning repast, Trump made an early contribution to Stein's reelection campaign. Three days later Stein provided a notarized letter stating that he had encouraged Trump to make his building residential based on the understanding that it would receive 421a tax benefits.

According to later affidavits from the developer and Louise Sunshine, Tony Gliedman seemed to agree with them that, legally speaking, the new building qualified for tax benefits. But the mayor, who thought luxury apartment houses did not deserve tax breaks, remained unpersuaded and told Gliedman so in a meeting on March 20. Late that same afternoon the commissioner telephoned Trump to tell him that the 421a application had been rejected. To Gliedman's surprise, the developer called back an hour and a half later and denounced the decision as "dishonest." Then he added, "I want you to know that I am a very rich and powerful person in this town, and there is a reason I got that way. I will never forget what you did."

Three days after the application was rejected, Trump and his partner, Equitable, sued both the city and Tony Gliedman. Because he wanted to be sure there were no glitches, Donald sent his brother Robert to serve the papers. The Trump-Equitable attorneys made a letter-of-the-law argument that Trump Tower, which replaced a department store that was sixty-five stories shorter than the maximum allowable height and drowning in red ink, couldn't have been more qualified for a 421a tax break. In response, the city's attorneys countered with a spirit-of-the-law position that granting such a benefit to one of the most expensive buildings in New York was flagrantly contrary to the intent of the law.

The case dragged on for three years, twice going up to the state's highest court. At one point Roy Cohn[49] asked for a meeting with the city's lawyer, a dignified, highly respected septuagenarian named Edith Spivack, to discuss a settlement. It was one of the few times that Donald Trump ever acknowledged considering such a step, and it was certainly the only time anyone ever showed up in Spivack's office dressed like Cohn, who wore a white T-shirt, a purple suit, and loafers with no socks. But no deal was struck.[50] Finally, in July 1984, the court of appeals ruled in Trump's favor. Koch denounced the decision as utterly outrageous and unfair; Trump called it "a very positive thing for the city." Later, in what Koch could not fail to perceive as a pointed rebuke, the developer hired Tony Gliedman for his own staff.[51]

—◆—

To a family that had already known success, Donald Trump brought more. His first deal had been a remarkable triumph, and his second, Trump Tower, seemed likely to do even better. But as his star continued its meteoric rise, that of his older brother, Fred Jr., continued to fall. Fred Sr. "didn't like wimps," his nephew, John Walter, said later. "He thought competition made you sharper." But it made Freddy miserable; before Donald came to Avenue Z, Freddy was in Florida. He failed there as an airline pilot and fishing-boat captain, his marriage collapsed, and he returned north to live in his parents' home on Midland Parkway and to work on one of his father's maintenance crews. He was unable to stop drinking, and reportedly his father found closets stuffed with empty liquor bottles. Neighbors spoke of seeing someone so thin and frail, he seemed a wraith.

In September 1981, Fred Trump Jr., a man who had long been living in the shadows, died at the age of forty-two. The cause was a massive heart attack, brought on by alcoholism so acute that it verged on the suicidal. Donald appeared shaken by his older brother's death and would speak over the years of a deep sense of loss as well as a certain guilt for having benefited from seeing his brother's mistakes. He would also speak, in a manner reminiscent of his reaction to the dedication of the Verrazano Bridge a quarter century earlier, of his renewed determination never to let people treat him as they had his brother. "Freddy just wasn't a killer," he told one reporter. To another he said, "I saw people really taking advantage of Fred, and the lesson I learned was always to keep up my guard 100 percent."[52]

As the tax abatement litigation dragged on, Donald Trump plunged into the construction of what he liked to call "the world's tallest concrete structure." In point of fact, Trump Tower (700 feet) was shorter than Chicago's Water Tower Place (850 feet) and the MLC Center in Sydney, Australia (751 feet).[53] But the sawtooth edifice was the tallest such building in New York City, where using concrete rather than steel beams to support a skyscraper was unusual.[54]

On paper, the choice of concrete made sense. Because concrete, which is made of sand, cement, and gravel, is poured on site and thus can be reconfigured up till the last minute, it offers maximum flexibility. This made it a highly desirable building material at Trump Tower, which was being designed while under construction. In New York, though, the choice seemed dubious for the simple reason that the local concrete industry was notoriously corrupt. Because city concrete firms could ship their ingredients by barge instead of truck or train, their overhead was low compared with that of other northeast cities. But somehow New York concrete cost 70 percent more than it did in, say, Boston. According to reports in *The New York Times* and a later state investigation, a principal cause of the excess cost was the union whose members operated the cement mixers: Teamsters Local 282, led by John Cody.[55]

A broad, burly man of sixty with a receding hairline and thick-lensed glasses, Cody said he knew Trump "quite well," called Roy Cohn "a pretty good friend," and had an arrest record stretching back four decades. By the time Trump Tower was finished, Cody was under indictment for labor racketeering; two years later he would return to jail yet again. While at the helm of 282, he had only to nod his head to slow down deliveries of a material that would be ruined if it was not at a building site within an hour of being mixed. Hardly surprising, the mere mention of his name brought developers to heel.

"A lot of the time it cost money under the table," recalled one Equitable executive closely involved with the Trump Tower construction process. "Donald made a deal with those concrete guys in New York. None of us could figure out why or how he did it, but somehow he conned them into building with reinforced concrete instead of steel." Sometimes the executive wondered if the project was on the right side of the law, but he could do little other than trust that whatever the developer was doing was okay. "You'd hope that he was a magician or walked on water," the executive said, "but the reason [he succeeded] was that he made arrangements."

Among those arrangements, in the view of many people involved in the construction, was a comely blonde from Austria named Verina Hixon. Although she had no visible income or assets, she managed, with Trump's help, to get mortgage financing for three duplex apartments at Trump Tower worth about $10 million. Not satisfied with this accomplishment, she also ordered a staggering list of alterations and additions, including the installation of the building's one swimming pool, which the developer seemed oddly willing to provide. Although she was often seen in Cody's company, she emphatically denied being his mistress. She was not—repeat, not—the reason that the concrete deliveries to Trump Tower flowed smoothly.

Despite Hixon's lack of help, Cody, who was planning a citywide strike in the summer of 1982, obligingly speeded up the Trump Organization's shipments to avoid potential problems. In July, after Local 282 had shut down construction sites across the city, Donald Trump invited seven hundred guests to join him at Trump Tower for a topping-off celebration. Before the champagne brunch, a small number of dignitaries rode a hoist up to the roof for a press conference. Standing next to an American flag and a few dozen of the ten thousand balloons scheduled for release over Fifth Avenue, the developer, Mayor Koch, Manhattan borough president Andrew Stein, Governor Carey, and Fred Trump, among others, hailed each other, the building, and the future.

<hr />

The initial architectural commission at Olympic Tower went to the firm of Morris Lapidus, creator of the flamboyant Fontainebleau and Eden Roc hotels in Miami as well as the more pedestrian Trump Village. Done in conjunction with his son Alan, fresh out of Columbia University School of Architecture, the Lapidus design featured a dark L-shaped base that wrapped around Best's; above it was a glassed-in tower that extended out beyond the walls of the base and looked a bit like a harmonica—or, possibly, a radiator—balanced on end. What it did not look like was anything else in Manhattan.

On the morning of Thursday, October 15, 1970, *The New York Times* editorialized that the new building was a mishmash of "tinsel" and "a glassy death." Among the readers was Aristotle Onassis's new wife, the former Jacqueline Kennedy, an ardent preservationist. Onassis canned Lapidus the next day and hired the highly respectable firm Skidmore, Owings & Merrill. Noted for its many modernist structures, most of them variations on big glass boxes, the company obligingly provided yet another one. When it opened, *The New York Times* noted its "ice-cold dignity."[56]

For better or worse, Donald Trump, the builder of the successor to Olympic Tower, was not married to the high priestess of good taste. He was married to Ivana, whose appetite for the spectacular was, if anything, even greater than his. She never objected to anything as too showy. As at the Grand Hyatt, neither she nor her husband had any interest in rescuing Fifth Avenue from the march of time. Instead they wanted to use that march to their advantage. Even more than the Grand Hyatt, the new building would embody the developer's awareness of the newly emerging market segment that real estate brokers called "high net worth individuals"—that is, very rich people.

Thus when condos at the only competing new luxury building, the Museum of Modern Art Tower, went on the market at lower prices, Donald was positively delighted to find that he was selling the most expensive units in New York City.[57] Trump Tower would be, just as he had intended, a high-water mark in conspicuous consumption. It was for people who took pride in paying the most, who wanted to live in a building so aggressively different from its neighbors that it probably would have looked more at home in Houston than in the midst of limestone-lined Fifth Avenue. Above all, it was for people who never seemed tired of hearing what he never tired of saying, that they were getting "the very best, not second best, the very best."[58]

In order to make it the best, the developer dragged Equitable executives across town to look at bathroom fixtures and filled his conference room with tile samples. He spent hours talking doorknobs. Ivana put weeks into the design of the doormen's uniforms and towering black bearskin hats, custom-made in London. When a scale model of Trump Tower, intended as a marketing tool, showed that it would be shorter than the nearby GM Building, and Louise Sunshine pointed out that it would be illegal to make the Trump Tower model taller for sales puposes, Trump told the model maker to reduce the GM building. Following his Grand Hyatt precedent, he called the top story of his new fifity-nine-story structure the sixty-eighth, a tactic which fetched higher prices but caused confusion when potential buyers saw the true numbers on the side of the unfinished building.[59]

Der Scutt had suggested the use of a sensuous rosy marble called *breccia perniche* to help create the buy-buy-buy and spend-spend-spend atmosphere of ultimate consumption that Trump craved. But to make sure that the lobby would have only the choicest slabs, in late July 1981 Ivana went to the actual quarry in northern Italy and, despite being seven months pregnant, climbed up and down the walls on rope ladders. When much of the stone still proved too blotchy to use, her husband discarded half of it; later he boasted that he had gone through an entire mountaintop and used up the world's supply of this particular material. Similarly, when he decided on the eve of the opening that the $75,000 worth of ficus trees just planted in the atrium hid the marble, he ordered them chopped down with a chain saw and hauled away.

Such efforts paid off big-time. Ice-cold dignity was nowhere to be found; instead Donald Trump had created a dazzling, glamorous beehive that *New York Times* critic Paul Goldberger found, perhaps to his surprise, "warm, luxurious, and even exhilarating." Unlike Olympic Tower, which had an unobtrusive entrance on East 51st Street, the new building's front door, framed with what was surely the shiniest brass in America, opened directly onto Fifth Avenue. Also unlike its predecessor, this skyscraper bore the name of its developer out front in three-foot-tall brass letters so out of scale with the rest of the building that, Der Scutt joked, visitors to New York could see them before their plane landed.[60] In the public space, which seemed cavernous thanks to well-placed mirrors, the warm peach marble covered every surface and an eighty-foot waterfall gushed like a mini-Niagara. Dozens of glittering jewel-box boutiques filled the retail atrium, and a tuxedo-clad pianist at a twelve-foot Steinway sere-naded shoppers streaming up and down on brass-railed escalators.

Before the building opened, the prices for its condos, already the highest in the city, went up again and again and again. Buyers, lured by a presentation that included a special show of views from the building and a recording of Frank Sinatra crooning "New York, New York," put down an unprecedented 25 percent of the purchase price, even though moving in was more than a year away. For months, gossip columns carried items on the residents-to-be, who included Johnny Carson, Steven Spielberg, and Liberace. Then the developer inflated the already impressive celebrity quotient by leaking, then refusing to comment on, a rumor that Prince Charles and his new wife, Diana, were considering buying there. As was expected, the apartment revenues paid the construction costs; what was unexpected was that doing so took the sale of only about 60 percent of the units instead of the usual 75 or 80 percent, although the project was neither on time nor on budget.

Retail rents, too, were the highest in the city, even though most atrium visitors were only window shoppers and many of the ultra-luxury stores did poorly. "Donald was able to sell those merchandisers the idea that if you're not in Trump Tower, you're not in New York," said a knowledgeable Equitable executive. "One retailer told me he just takes three-quarters of his rent out of his advertising budget and tells himself that he's buying a billboard on Fifth Avenue."

Crowning the top of what would become the biggest tourist draw in New York City was Donald Trump's own personal Fontainebleau. Inspired by the palatial digs of Arab billionaire Adnan Khashoggi in Olympic Tower, Trump carved out a sprawling triplex that would eventually total fifty-three rooms plus rooftop garden. At eighty feet in length, his living room was the largest in Manhattan and—literally—the splashiest, featuring its own waterfall and fountain. Overhead was a frescoed ceiling that the developer compared to the Sistine Chapel; along the walls were massive columns, newly carved because the developer found antique architectural elements too used-looking. Elsewhere were crystal chandeliers and a two-story dining room with carved ivory frieze. Everywhere there was marble and onyx, a translucent, multihued quartz that the developer liked to note was even more expensive than marble. Everywhere there were phenomenal views, surrounded by solid brass window frames and protected by remote-controlled, bullet-proof shades. Everywhere there was gilt, on chairs and moldings, column capitals and bathroom faucets.[61]

From bottom to top, from the retail stores to the extraordinary penthouse château, Trump Tower was one humongous, sawtooth advertisement for Donald Trump. What was a triumph for the developer, though, was a problem for his partner. "We were in this to make money, not to serve as a marquee for the Trump Organization," said Doug Healey, who had recently taken over Equitable's investment operation in New York City. With the building done, the condos gone, and everything else leased out, Equitable was ready to sell its interest and move on. "We'd been to the altar, had a nice marriage, and made a lot of money," Healey said. Now it was time for a divorce.[62]

When Donald resisted the idea of putting Trump Tower on the market, Healey and Peacock had the delicate task of persuading him to buy Equitable out. Bad cop Healey fussed about the cost of the pianist and the constant cleaning and polishing of the lobby; nice cop Peacock nodded sympathetically as Donald Trump complained about the new guy who was nickel-and-diming him to death. Three years after the opening, lawyers for the Trump Organization and Equitable found themselves at yet another seemingly endless closing, their own. Equitable walked away with a 378 percent return on their original investment; Donald Trump walked away with his own permanent logo.

The Grand Hyatt had been Donald's first significant move away from his father's approach and accomplishments; now, with Trump Tower, the separation was complete. Fred Trump still called and grilled staffers about projects; "God help you if you didn't know the answer," one Trump Organization executive recalled years later.[63] On weekends his grandson Donny, then an energetic preschooler, would visit the construction site with his own father and pick up used nails, just as Donald had done with Fred years before in Brooklyn and Queens.[64] But now it was Donald who was calling every shot.

Indeed, much as Fred Trump respected his son's success, there was little in this project that made sense to the older man. To someone who had made his reputation and his fortune putting up square buildings, to whom extra corners meant extra leaks, the very idea of a sawtooth building was incomprehensible. Equally mystifying was his son's refusal to rent the empty Bonwit Teller building over the Christmas season to Strawberry's, a down-market women's clothing store temporarily displaced by the Grand Hyatt construction. To Fred Trump this was a chance to use vacant space and turn a profit. To his son, however, renting the location to a working-class store would erode its appeal to a luxury market his father had never dreamed of pursuing.

Later, when Fred Trump visited the building site and saw an expensive glass curtain wall going up, he tried to rein in what he considered a waste of money. "Why don't you forget about the damn glass?" he told his son. "Give them four or five stories of it, and then use common brick for the rest. Nobody is going to look up anyway."[65] The idea of leaving lights on at the site all night to draw attention was similarly problematic to someone who still routinely checked that even the lowest-watt bulbs were turned off in his own buildings in Brooklyn and Queens. Still an outer-borough man at heart, he would find little use for the sixty-third-floor apartment provided for him and his wife in Trump Tower.

———

Although Trump Tower was the most famous building in Manhattan to bear the developer's name, it was not the only one. While Trump Tower was under construction, he had also built a second luxury building, an elegant East Side co-op called Trump Plaza, which also received a 421a tax abatement.[66] And much as the idea of a tax giveaway to either building galled Ed Koch and other city officials, there was justification of sorts. The developer himself argued that he was putting people to work, attracting tourists to New York, and, on a more facetious note, saving the outer boroughs by pushing Manhattan prices so high that even the relatively well-to-do would have to move to Queens, the Bronx, and Brooklyn.[67] But perhaps the most important reason was that fully three-quarters of the sales at Trump Tower were to wealthy nonresidents and out-of-town corporations, both of which would help to galvanize the city's revival. "With manufacturing leaving," George Sternlieb, director of the Center for Urban Policy Research at Rutgers University, told *The New York Times*, "and with Federal and state aid diminishing, our cities desperately need the rich." And the rich—people who would bring with them the high incomes, high spending, and high taxes that New York City required to survive—were precisely what Donald Trump was delivering.[68]

At least so the arguments went. Meanwhile, though, the city was rebounding, and the ground around Trump was shifting. His brash, steamroller style, welcome and even refreshing when the city was on the ropes, began to appear in a different light, particularly after he became involved in a bitter battle to raze 100 Central Park South, a spacious limestone apartment house that had been thrown in when he'd purchased the adjacent Barbizon Plaza Hotel. He planned to replace both structures with a new luxury hotel and shopping arcade. The only problem was the more than one hundred tenants who lived in the apartment building. They had no interest in leaving this prestigious address, and when the relocation firm hired by Trump introduced little unpleasantnesses like taking away lampshades from hallway lights and seats from the lobby, they hired a lawyer and called the press. Frustrated and furious at what he saw as tenant intransigence, Trump complained that arcane city rent regulations were allowing affluent residents, about a quarter of the total, to pay bargain rents; what he didn't mention was that building demographics included an equal number of people who were far from affluent.[69]

In a pro-tenant town like New York City, it was inevitably a delicate and problematic situation. But whatever sympathy Trump might have tapped disappeared after he offered to turn over vacant units to the homeless, a group that included schizophrenics and drug addicts. The tenants saw this as a blatant attempt to scare them; Trump insisted that the invitation had been simple altruism and, digging himself in deeper, noted that the tactics he had used so far were nothing compared with what he could have done. After five years of threats, suits, and countersuits, Trump folded. Scrapping his plans, he left 100 Central Park South a rental building and surrounded it with a Y-shaped luxury condominium tower named Trump Parc. But just as with the 60th Street yards and the Bonwit Teller sculptures, he refused to acknowledge anything that smacked of defeat. Instead he claimed that the tenants had done him a favor. Because he had been forced to hang on to the building, he said, he would now benefit from market changes that made it far more advantageous to renovate than demolish.[70]

Perhaps. But the honeymoon he had enjoyed in the New York press was over. He was no longer the boy wonder, the hyperactive hero. He was still the New York real estate wizard, the man who had helped rescue 42nd Street and created the shiniest, showiest new building on Fifth Avenue. But he was also a breaker of promises and an art vandal, an anti-tenant landlord and an exploiter of immigrant labor. Back in the mid-1970s, his first *New York Times* profile compared him to Robert Redford and intimated that his worst defect was talking too fast. Now the same paper said that he would be a shoe-in for "a stupendous new unpopularity prize." *New York* portrayed him as a tasteless vulgarian, the *Daily News* portrayed him as a sorehead, and the *Village Voice* accused him of being a conniver, a racist, and a liar.

In short, he was a major player, part of the city's power elite. No longer his father's protégé, he had earned his own place at the table, and he would draw all the attention, praise, and fire to which it entitled him.

CHAPTER EIGHTEEN

GAMBLING ON ATLANTIC CITY

ONALD TRUMP WORKED ALMOST AS HARD on his public image
as on real estate development. His father had sent out periodic
press releases about his buildings and, once in a while, his opinion on
public affairs; Donald issued a steady stream of news about his every
move. He returned every call from the press, and when the calls
weren't coming in, he made them himself. No longer the awkward
young man who had embarrassed himself at the '21' Club with investment banker Ben Lambert in the mid-1970s, he had permanent
claim to one of the most visible spots in the restaurant, which allowed him to see and be seen by everyone coming and going. As he
ate, he would jump up to greet those passing by and then sit down
again to answer the phones being brought to the table, sometimes
two at a time, for urgent calls.[1]

In classic American huckster fashion, on every occasion he pronounced his projects and himself as the best, the brightest, the greatest. Trump Tower didn't have a good address; it had "the Tiffany
location." The Grand Hyatt wasn't a successful hotel; it was "incredible, gorgeous, gleaming." His deals, he told *The New York Times*,
"would have taken an older man a lifetime to do, if he could ever get
them done." To *New York* magazine he confided, "No one has done
more than I in the last seven years."[2]

Such efforts bore fruit. In the fall of 1983 *Town & Country* featured a full-length article on Donald and Ivana Trump. A national showcase for the rich and well connected, the magazine presented the couple as healthy, wealthy, and blond. That same year *People* gave the developer its American Image Award for business. The next spring he appeared on the front of *The New York Times Sunday Magazine* as the subject of a story entitled "The Expanding Empire of Donald Trump."[3] Framed by the Trump Tower atrium's rosy marble and shiny brass, he leaned against an elegant glass-enclosed escalator and smiled like the Cheshire cat.

A month later he gazed out with the same self-satisfied look from the cover of *Gentleman's Quarterly*, then the hottest men's magazine in the country. Inside, *GQ* ragged him for his glitzy aesthetic and, especially, his habit of constant verbal inflation (or, when it suited him, deflation). But the profile, spread over ten pages, called him "a remarkably deft dealmaker" and featured half a dozen photographs of his newest purchase, an eleven-bedroom, seven-fireplace, fourteen-bath (nine full and five half) family hideaway on six acres of the tony Connecticut shore.[4]

Real estate and fame had not usually gone together in New York. When developers like Fred Trump courted press attention, it was for their projects, not themselves. They saw little good coming out of having personal information in the paper and often did business under faceless corporate pseudonyms. If they became public figures, they hired Howard Rubenstein to keep their profiles low and calm any troubled waters. "They were an anonymous group," said Jerry Schrager. "You didn't know who built your building or even who owned it. But all of a sudden, you lived at Trump Tower, Trump Plaza. It was unique."

Even more unusual, Schrager noted, a public that ordinarily hated landlords and developers couldn't seem to get enough of Donald Trump. "I was constantly astonished at how people received him and his projects," Schrager said. "I would sit there, sometimes across the table from some pretty sophisticated, intelligent folks, and the majority bought into it. The general public bought into it. The man on the street, the cabdrivers, everybody wanted to touch him and shake his hand."[5] But despite the laudatory press about his successes, Donald Trump did not become a national celebrity until he had his first large-scale failure.[6]

Seven months after the opening of Trump Tower, he paid $9 million—he liked to round down the figure to $6 million to make the deal seem more favorable—for the New Jersey Generals, a second-tier professional football team. The one-year-old Generals belonged to the fledgling United States Football League (USFL), a loosely organized group of clubs, many of them owned by land developers and shopping center czars. Playing in the spring off-season to avoid direct competition with the immensely popular and profitable National Football League (NFL), the USFL was following a prudent strategy of low player salaries and a slow start-up.

Too slow, in Trump's opinion. He wanted to challenge the NFL immediately. Within weeks of his purchase he launched a campaign to move the USFL to the prime fall season and dangled big bucks to lure gridiron stars into signing with the Generals. Taking the USFL big-time fit neatly with his own game plan: building and managing a huge new city- and state-backed stadium in New York City, naming it after himself, and making the Generals the home team. Doing so would raise his own profile and put him in line for the real money in professional sports, the hefty profits from leases on private boxes and lucrative fall television contracts.

The developer's thinking was not as far-fetched as it might seem. Years earlier the NFL had faced a rival, the American Football League (AFL), which played in the fall season. To the immense profit of the AFL's owners, the two leagues had merged. If the developer could force a second merger, he could end up owning a first-tier team for a fraction of the current asking price of $70 million. On the other hand, if there was no merger and the USFL was unable to break into the fall network television market, the upstart league could take the NFL to court for monopolistic practices and rake in a huge settlement. Either way, it seemed to Donald Trump, he was bound to come out ahead.

Seizing the initiative, he had Roy Cohn file a USFL antitrust suit against the NFL in October 1984, asking for $1.32 billion in damages. Cohn, ill with AIDS, would be dead by the final verdict, but remained combative. At a press conference, he claimed, without offering any details, that a "secret" NFL committee had plotted the USFL's demise. But the USFL was nowhere near ready to handle either its newest team owner or the NFL. Instead of steamrolling ahead, the stripling league collapsed almost immediately, $150 million in the red. Although the Generals' owner claimed to have sold 30,000 tickets for a debut fall season, none were seen and no games were played.

The USFL made its final tackle a year and a half later in Manhattan federal district court. Just as the developer had foreseen, the jury held that the NFL was a monopoly. But the five women and one man were less convinced that the monopoly had exerted a deleterious economic impact on the USFL and later awarded it the token sum of $1. Donald Trump had reportedly sunk about $22 million into what turned into his first flop. Characteristically, he refused to acknowledge the defeat, instead calling the outcome "a moral victory."[7] The jury acted as it did, he later wrote in his autobiography, *The Art of the Deal*, not because his case was too weak, but because it was too strong. He had been such a compelling witness, he claimed, and his lawyer so powerful a litigator, that the jurors had simply taken pity on the NFL.

Although the developer's "explanation" of the jury finding was cheerfully wide of the facts, he had indeed scored what was, for him, something like a moral victory. From the moment he first publicly mentioned the idea of buying the Generals, the publicity he received for being associated with a professional sports team far exceeded what he had received for all previous accomplishments. His name, already seen in the news, business, and gossip columns, now became a regular feature in the sports pages, the most read part of every paper in America. Aggressive, arrogant, often amusing, and always ready with a plainspoken zinger of a sound bite, he made great copy.[8]

From now on the name would be an integral part of every project in which he was involved.[9] So would a certain style of deal-making. As Brian Strum, a Prudential vice president involved in one Trump deal, recalled, during negotiations Donald would give his version of the facts while patting his interlocutor on the shoulder and saying, "You know," or "You know what I mean." Although his facts often differed from what those present knew to be the case, they did not want to interrupt him. "You're flattered that he's acknowledging that you know something," Strum explained. "But if he says you know, and you don't say you don't know, you've sort of agreed. The next time you meet, he'll say, 'But we talked about that!' You must be obtrusive to hold your own, and this isn't a style most people take to naturally. Most people are too polite."

As a result, Strum said, Trump tended to get his way. "Donald is the top of his organization, wearing a thousand-dollar tailored suit and talking to you eye to eye, nose to nose, and you're middle or upper-middle management in a lending institution or with the government, and here's this guy treating you as an equal and telling you that you know all this good stuff he's telling you. You've got a lot of things working against saying no, you're wrong."

—⁓—

Being the owner of a professional football team brought Donald Trump the media attention he had sought. But he had to go elsewhere for the money. Despite his rapid rise in New York City real estate and his increasing national fame, he did not have the financial wherewithal his lap-of-luxury style suggested and was essentially marketing himself with bluster. The uncomfortable truth was that he was still heavily dependent on his father's resources and fortune. Although his father never actually seemed to say no, he was a questioning presence, in there kicking the tires on the deal even if he didn't understand it. And that fact chafed his son, who loved his father but did not want him always reading over his shoulder. To become truly independent he needed his own source of cash flow.

He had an idea of where to look. Ever since he had learned that the 150-hotel Hilton chain made more than one-third of its net profits from its two casino hotels in Las Vegas, he had been toying with the idea of owning such a money machine himself.[10] Now, just 125 miles from Trump Tower, a tidal wave of cash was washing over Atlantic City, the second place in the nation to permit games of chance for money.[11]

Gambling was not new to Atlantic City, founded as a health resort on a small barrier island off the coast of New Jersey in the 1850s.[12] But in the past, games of chance had not been legal. Instead, gambling, along with prostitution and bootlegging, had been backroom entertainment in a town whose public face consisted of modest family boardinghouses, elegant hotels, and a four-mile-long boardwalk. By 1900 Atlantic City's wide white beach and various amusements attracted a quarter of a million visitors on hot holiday weekends, and the town's kitschy creations, which included picture postcards, the Miss America Pageant, and saltwater taffy, became part of mainstream American culture. So did Monopoly, the most popular board game in the nation's history, which copied Atlantic City's street names.[13]

After World War II the spread of air-conditioning and the increasing availability of cheap airfares to more exotic destinations cut into the Atlantic City tourist trade. The Chamber of Commerce tried to hold on to what was left; one campaign involved trying to get local media to refer to cloudy days as "partly sunny." But when the resort played host to the 1964 Democratic National Convention, press coverage revealed the city's decay.[14] With nearly one out of four adults unemployed, the year-round population dropped precipitously.[15] In the mid-1970s local legislators, desperate to salvage the old resort, determined that the way to bring the tourists back was to make gambling a legal, taxpaying industry. To do so required a statewide referendum. The first effort failed to pass, but it did get the attention of Resorts, Inc., which had launched its first casino hotel in the Bahamas and wanted to set up shop on the mainland. Noting that Atlantic City was only a few hours' drive from perhaps one-third of the nation's population, in 1976 Resorts bankrolled a second attempt. In November the referendum passed.

Stoutly declaring their determination to keep organized crime out of Atlantic City, state legislators then drew up enabling legislation. Among other provisions, the Casino Control Act established the Casino Control Commission, which would monitor and regulate casino operations, and the Division of Gaming Enforcement (DGE), a permanent investigative body in charge of policing the casinos. In June 1977, when Governor Brendan Byrne signed the act, he shook his fist and warned the Mob, "Keep your filthy hands out of Atlantic City and keep the hell out of our state!"

Unfortunately none of these efforts even remotely prepared the city or the state for what having casino hotels would actually be like. "It was like the scene in *2001: A Space Odyssey* where the cavemen are standing around looking at the monolith and not knowing what to do with it," Jim Whelan, then a city councilman and later mayor of

Atlantic City, told one reporter. "That's what casinos were like in Atlantic City—nobody here was prepared for the economic forces that
were unleashed."[16]

Indeed, before most people in Atlantic City knew what had hit
them, those economic forces had taken over the town. Because little
land was available for casino development, speculators immediately
bought up whatever they could lay their hands on, enriching a fortunate few and driving prices and tax assessments far beyond the reach
of most local residents and small-business owners.[17] For the first time
in years there were thousands of new jobs available for cashiers,
croupiers, dealers, and security guards. But newcomers grabbed most
of them, and Atlantic City residents left, unable to pay the rapidly escalating rents. Impatient to get the casinos up and running and worried about competition from other states, officials did not spell out
how casino taxes would be funneled into city renewal, an oversight
that delayed meaningful civic improvement for many years. Instead
the newly appointed Casino Control Commission waived one shiny
new regulation after another. After a hasty makeover of an old Boardwalk hotel, Resorts slapped on neon lights and opened for business on
Memorial Day weekend of 1978.[18]

Long before Governor Byrne cut the ribbon, the lines for Resorts
stretched down the Boardwalk and out of sight. Inside, the thirty-
thousand-square-foot casino area was packed, and customers could
not move in the aisles. Competition for slot machines was so fierce
that gamblers reportedly peed in their pants rather than surrender a
seat at a one-armed bandit. All day long and into the night, thousands
of people waited to get inside and lose money. Overwhelmed by the
volume of business, Resorts was unable for days to count the bills and
coins it was hauling in or even to fit all the money into a safe.[19] In the
first three months of operation its total win was $62.5 million, nearly
three times the $22 million it took in all year at its Bahamas facility.
At the end of the first year gross revenues of $224.6 million made it
the most profitable casino in the world.[20]

Even the most optimistic casino advocates had not grasped the
depth of the public's appetite for gambling. Although many people objected to gambling as unproductive, immoral, and possibly addictive,
others saw casinos as something very different: a place where they
could safely take risks. Filled with mirrors and gilt and glitter, with

crowds and lights and noise, casinos were a special, extraordinary realm where there were no visible clocks or windows, where time stood still and customers could set ordinary caution aside. Whether they were putting in quarters at a slot machine or a few dollars for a hand of blackjack, they could feel the physical thrill of an adrenaline spike, then do it again, and again, and again, from ten o'clock in the morning until four o'clock the next morning. For a small number of people that experience was habit-forming and dangerous; for most it was a relatively inexpensive, exciting, and totally legal way to feel a fantastic buzz.

In 1976, shortly before New Jersey citizens voted to legalize gambling at Atlantic City, Donald Trump had driven down and taken a look. But he had not been impressed by the shabby old beach town. Rather than pursuing opportunities there, he decided to wait and see if gambling became legal in New York and to reconfigure the Grand Hyatt floor plan so that it would be possible to carve out a large casino space.

Two years later, after seeing the phenomenal success of Resorts, he flew down to Atlantic City by seaplane for another look. He quickly decided that the Tiffany location was the 2½-acre Boardwalk site where the major expressway into town crossed the main street. Meeting with a local broker named Paul Longo, he offered several million dollars for one of the leases on the property. But speculators had already driven prices higher, and his bid went nowhere.

For the next two years other investors went through all manner of intricate maneuvers over the same site. Howard Weingrow, a former hotel chain owner and national treasurer of the Democratic Party, was one of the most dogged. He struck a deal for one parcel with Robert Maheu, chief of staff for the legendary Howard Hughes; tracked down the dozen or so heirs to an adjacent motel and cocktail lounge and convinced them to put aside their squabbles long enough to sell their property to him; negotiated with the owners of half a dozen individual houses; and promised the owner of yet another lot that he would send a car to take her to church every Sunday for five years. But despite relentless effort, control of the site continued to elude Weingrow's grasp.[21]

In February 1980 Donald Trump called Paul Longo again and said he was ready to make a deal. There were several reasons. With the Grand Hyatt finished and Trump Tower under way, he could turn his attention to something else. In addition, the federal probe of how he had obtained the option on the West Side rail yards had ended with no indictments and no publicity, which meant that he could pass muster with the state's investigative agency, the Division of Gaming Enforcement. Moreover, it looked as though New Jersey's hunger for casino revenues would moderate its regulatory bite, for the Casino Control Commission had awarded Resorts a permanent license over vehement DGE objections. "Doing so was politically expedient," said the prosecutor who had presented the state's case against granting a license. "If Resorts hadn't gotten a license, the industry might have dried up."[22]

But probably the most important reason was ABSCAM, an explosive, casino-related federal sting operation in New Jersey that had implicated that state's senior U.S. senator and a host of local politicians. In its wake, casino gambling seemed too tainted an endeavor to gain legal status in New York. If the developer wanted gambling dollars, he would have to go to Atlantic City.

On a gray Saturday in February Donald and Ivana went down to Atlantic City.[23] After a Frank Sinatra concert and dinner, he left Ivana and a friend playing the slots and strolled up the deserted Boardwalk with Longo. A middle-aged, friendly sort who had grown up in Atlantic City and at one time had managed most of the stores along the Boardwalk, Longo pointed out the various casino hotels then under construction. Although it was bitterly cold, they stopped and looked at the same site the developer had tried to lease two years earlier. It consisted of three separate properties, held by thirty separate owners, facts that did not seem to discourage Donald Trump in the least. "This is the best location in Atlantic City," he said. "I want to be right here."

On Monday morning Longo got to work. The next month Trump cut a deal with Howard Weingrow and then hammered out leases with holders of other major parcels. Over the months that followed, Longo filled in the missing pieces, one little postage-stamp-size lot after another. "We were paying the highest price per square foot in the city at the time," Longo recalled later. "But these people weren't selling real estate, they were selling part of their lives."

Plain-talking and direct, Donald Trump told Longo exactly what he wanted, and the broker felt relaxed and comfortable working with him. But Longo was struck by his apparent need to maintain a formal, businesslike image at all times. In early July the developer arranged with Longo to spend a day scoping out recent developments along the Boardwalk. It was blisteringly hot, but the developer wore his uniform of dark suit, dark shoes, and red tie. Longo, who was wearing cutoff jeans and sneakers, told Trump he was surprised that he wasn't dressed more informally. "I came down here for business," Trump replied, "and in New York this is the way we dress for business."

Longo was also struck by how Trump seemed to get even the most unpromising-looking situation to go his way. "I don't think Donald negotiated many deals where he ended up elsewhere than where he wanted," Longo said. "You need a willing buyer and a willing seller, and Donald can tell how willing you are. He will say things like 'Why don't we just remain friends and forget the deal. Just promise to remain friends.'" He seemed particularly adept at making whatever deal was on the table seem like the other party's last chance. "The image is very important, being able to project that he's willing to walk away," Longo said. "He is able to make you believe this is the best deal you're going to get from him—if you don't like it, talk to the next buyer—and he makes you wonder if there is going to be another buyer."

Preparing to make his move on Atlantic City, Donald Trump had added to his small staff two key players. One was attorney Harvey Ira Freeman, a brainy veteran of Olympic Tower whom Trump nicknamed "Harvard" after seeing how quickly he whipped through the *New York Times* crossword puzzle. Known for his dry humor and poker face, Freeman was a teddy bear–like figure in his early forties with short, curly salt-and-pepper hair and crinkly eyes. For more than a decade Freeman would serve Trump as a negotiator, strategist, and investment adviser. His most important role, though, was saying "no." Sometimes by himself, sometimes in concert with the developer's other chief naysayer, lawyer Jerry Schrager, Freeman made it his job to spell out the negative side of potential deals. "Harvey was always negative, gloom and doom," said architect Alan Lapidus, who had worked with Freeman on Olympic Tower and would do so on Trump's first Atlantic City casino. "He would unearth every pitfall in any deal."[24]

The other addition was Donald Trump's younger brother. Like Donald, Robert was tall, blue-eyed, and heavy-browed, but he had an altogether different personality. As one former Trump employee put it, on an intensity scale of 1 to 10, Donald would be 15 and Robert 5.[25] Low-key, soft-spoken, and unassuming, the baby of the family drove a ten-year-old Oldsmobile Cutlass and still lived in the one-bedroom apartment on East 65th Street that his older brother had left behind. After graduating from Boston University, Robert had worked as an investment banker, showing no particular interest in joining the family business. But now that Donald was branching out into a different city, he needed someone he could trust—that is, someone named Trump—to represent him there.

As it turned out, Robert would do far more than that. As Fred Trump's son he was comfortable on a construction site, and as a former banker he could handle number crunching and detail monitoring. Perhaps even more important, he could talk tough when he had to but did not have the same need to win all the time, every time, that fueled his brother. "Robert was the good Trump," said Alan Lapidus. "When there were endless meetings and Donald would come on and do the hard negotiating and be the tough guy, then you'd need the good guy to come in and make everybody feel like his best buddy."[26]

In mid-July there was a marathon closing. In part because the property was still being assembled, the session stretched out nearly twenty-four hours and involved more than one hundred participants, including Fred Trump. Privately he was not enthusiastic about this venture into new and unfamiliar territory; publicly he was at his son's side whenever he was needed. Because Donald did not yet have his own funds, he would be drawing on the same Chase line of credit he had obtained because of his father's long-term relationship with the bank and which he had used for the Hyatt. Accordingly, Fred Trump signed documents as vice president of the new entities created for each transaction. A few weeks later he signed off on what may have been the only part of the whole deal that he actually welcomed. It was the contract for Alan Lapidus, who had known both Trumps when he was an apprentice under his father at Trump Village, and contained the same provisions that had appeared in Morris Lapidus's contract.

At the moment, the definition of high-profile casino design in Atlantic City was what Skidmore, Owings & Merrill did for the new Bally's Park Place casino, a large glass box reminiscent of the firm's earlier work at Olympic Tower. Rejecting that elegant but austere vision, Donald Trump had instead selected an architect whose sense of design was, if anything, anti-Skidmore. In 1970 Lapidus's flashy and obtrusive plan for Olympic Tower had turned Jackie Onassis off. But in Atlantic City, his taste for arresting and unusual shapes that jutted up above the horizon was exactly what Donald Trump wanted.[27]

In mid-1980, two years after casino gambling became legal in Atlantic City, four casinos had opened and five more were under way. But government officials were still in the process of adjusting to the arrival of shiny, Las Vegas–style casinos in a small beach town where everyone was on a first-name basis, no one locked their doors, and the common thread among the power elite was having been lifeguards as teenagers. Feeling overwhelmed by all the changes that had taken place, regulators had defensively hung on to their right to make rules, imposing a sixty-six-page preliminary application for a casino license and unduly rigid rules, including a requirement that casinos locate their gambling operations out of sight of hotel entrances.

Within the industry, it was axiomatic that casinos had to be on the ground floor. On Trump's narrow site, though, the hotel's front desk and concierge booth would take a large bite out of the available floor space. To gain more room for the casino and, not so incidentally, to please regulators, Lapidus made the heretical suggestion of putting the casino one flight up. Donald agreed but decided that, given that a casino's profitability is linked to the size of its gaming floor, even the second floor was not large enough. With Lapidus he proceeded to lay out an alternate plan. An obscure city regulation required passageways between neighboring hotels so that even in bad weather visitors could go from one hotel to the next. Other hoteliers had built narrow, utilitarian tubes across adjacent streets, but Trump suggested expanding the passageway into a huge plaza that hung over the street. By doing so, he would make his second floor larger by some twenty-thousand square feet and create a sixty-thousand-square-foot casino—the largest in Atlantic City and one of the largest in the world.

At ground level, the extra floor space would have cost Trump a fortune, but he unilaterally declared the street overhang an enhanced public amenity, paid a token $100, and had a building with every guest room angled for an ocean view.[28] Like the Grand Hyatt and Trump Tower, the structure was not quite as tall as he liked to say it was—it was only the second tallest in Atlantic City[29]—but there was no doubt that it would have the town's oddest silhouette. Looking like two giant Edsel radiator grilles set end to end, it would be the one casino hotel no one could possibly miss seeing.

Long before, Trump had learned from his father the value of going along with the powers that be. He had done it in New York; now he would do it in Atlantic City. "Donald's attitude was, I'll do anything," Lapidus said. "You want me to stand on my head, fine. You want me to get undressed, I'll get undressed. Whatever you want, I'll do it." Clearly it would not do to send lowly minions to the endless regulatory hearings that stretched ahead. Instead Donald would make sure that either he or Robert was present to answer every question. He would not rely on his usual lawyers but would hire local attorneys. He would make nice to the various political factions in town. Rather than hide behind some corporate moniker, he would do everything in his own name, he would meet with officials in person, and he would be friendly, polite, and, above all, respectful. To handle relations on the state level, he had Louise Sunshine, whose brother was a tennis partner with Governor Byrne, arrange lunch at the Grand Hyatt for the governor and the two of them. Afterward Sunshine accompanied Byrne on a shopping trip along Fifth Avenue and helped him pick out a birthday present for his wife.

At the same time, Donald would keep up the hard sell. When state regulators or casino officials came to New York to introduce themselves, the visit would start with a Trump Tower promotional film strip that heaped praise on the developer and extolled his visionary powers. Later, when he applied for a casino license, he kept up a drumbeat of telephone calls to those in charge. "Instead of asking how much longer it would take or who we were talking to, he'd say was there anything he could do to help, could he make someone available," said Bob Sturges, a former prosecutor then serving as deputy director of the Division of Gaming Enforcement. "The real message was always, 'Don't forget about me, keep pushing this thing along.'" Asked to list character references, a request obviously referring to close business colleagues, the developer listed Norman Vincent Peale. "It seemed typical Trump, hit-you-between-the-eyes-with-a-sledgehammer style," said a close observer of the licensing process. "You know, you want character references, I'll give you a character reference."

And, in the end, Trump would get what he wanted. Once again a city was in distress, and the tall, blond entrepreneur would play the white knight, experienced enough to build a casino, but new enough to the gaming industry to have few, if any, problematic entanglements.[30] With the first wave of casino applications over, anxious regulatory officials eagerly catered to this rich New York developer who promised to bring "some pizzazz" to the Jersey shore. Thus they interpreted his lack of casino experience as an asset—it meant he was untainted by the Mob. When he failed to record in his application that he had been charged with racial discrimination in Trump-owned buildings in Brooklyn, the regulators noted the lapse in a footnote but excused it because he mentioned the incident during an interview. And they evidently ignored the fact that he had been investigated in connection with more than one federal probe. "We were a little shell-shocked at getting so many applicants with licensing problems," Sturges said. "With Donald, it was a pleasure to be looking for skeletons in the closet and for once not finding any."

———

Donald Trump was still a real estate developer. Unlike everyone else who had opened a casino resort in Atlantic City, he would not open for business, hire staff, or begin construction until he had permits and money in place. It would not be easy, for the stigma attached to gambling meant that the banks and institutional investors he had won over in New York were still wary of casinos. Further, he had no experience actually running either a casino or a hotel. There was also the ever-present worry that even the most profitable resort hotel in town could be closed overnight if the operator lost a license because of some infraction. Eventually, Crocker National Bank, a San Francisco–based institution that had already dipped its toes in the gambling industry in Las Vegas, came through as the developer's lead bank, but it would not cover the entire construction loan. As a result, the man who was arguably the hottest name in New York real estate had to go around the country begging financing institutions to put in even relatively small participations of $3 million to $5 million.

Discouraged after months of knocking on doors and having to borrow money from his father to keep going, Donald Trump began looking for ways out.[31] At one point he went to see Bob Guccione, the editor and publisher of Penthouse and the owner of the adjacent casino site, at his lavish East Side town house. Walking past the magazine magnate's beefy security guards and half a dozen Rhodesian Ridgeback hounds, Trump made his way to a walnut-paneled study lined with Impressionist and Post-Impressionist paintings. There the king of glitz proposed that the king of soft-core porn take over his Boardwalk property. But because Guccione's own Atlantic City financing had dried up mid-construction, his Penthouse casino was now a rusting pile of girders, and he passed.

The developer also made a pilgrimage to Los Angeles to visit Drexel Burnham Lambert bond trader Mike Milken, who was already heavily involved with another casino operator, Steve Wynn. The owner of casinos in Atlantic City and Las Vegas, both named the Golden Nugget, Stephen Alan Wynn had a background not unlike Trump's. He had grown up in Utica, New York, attended a military academy, and was a fiercely competitive athlete. After graduating from Wharton, he worked in the same field as his father, a manager of bingo parlors, and had achieved remarkable success at a young age, in his case with his Las Vegas Golden Nugget.

Wynn had been drawn to Atlantic City early on, showing up for Resorts' Memorial Day opening and within days scooping up an old motel property along the Boardwalk. In part because Wynn put up his Las Vegas holdings as collateral, Milken floated a $160 million bond issue to finance his East Coast expansion. The junk bond guru was willing to consider a similar deal with Trump, but Donald balked at the terms. More a developer than a casino man, he would not use his own resources—reportedly Milken asked him to put in $30 million— or provide a guarantee that the project would be completed.[32]

Then, in June 1982, just weeks before Trump might well have had to pull the plug on his Atlantic City dreams, in walked the man who would make it all work out for him.[33] Being Donald Trump's savior was hardly the role that Mike Rose, the Harvard-trained lawyer who was chief operating officer of Holiday Inns, had in mind. Six feet seven inches tall and immaculately groomed, Rose was an imposing figure. He had already established the most profitable casino in Atlantic City, located at a marina across town from the Boardwalk and operated by Holiday's newly acquired gambling subsidiary, Harrah's.[34] This time, Rose wanted to try his luck on the Boardwalk itself. But because he would have to start from scratch, and Donald Trump already had a license, an excellent Boardwalk site, and a hole in the ground, it made sense to Rose to come calling.

"The rule of any major entertainment area is that the first right turn is always the best," explained Richard Goeglein, president and chief executive officer of Harrah's at the time. "We would be the first right turn, and customers could swing around, park, and walk in. We would have a key mousetrap."[35]

Through Paul Longo, Donald Trump had already tried to get Harrah's attention, but to no avail. Now, though, Rose was like Santa Claus, bringing a sack of goodies right to the developer's front door. Through Harrah's he would put up $50 million, out of which the developer would be reimbursed for what he had spent so far. He would also pay the developer a fee as construction manager with a bonus for staying on budget and on time, operate the facility at no cost, cover all losses for five years, and split any profits. Not batting an eye, Donald Trump, who until that moment had been faced with deep-sixing the whole project, said that he wasn't sure he wanted a partner and would have to think the offer over. Meanwhile his staff was dumbfounded, and at least one wondered whether Rose was simply setting Trump up.

He wasn't. To Rose, putting Harrah's casino expertise together with Donald Trump's construction savvy seemed a promising combination. As soon became apparent, though, nothing could have been further from the truth. Rather than being a source of strength, the contrast between Mike Rose, corporate man, dedicated to making money for shareholders, and Donald Trump, entrepreneur, equally dedicated to making money for himself, was a gap too wide to be bridged. The perhaps inevitable result was a near catastrophe.

Rose had made his mark by bringing modern management techniques to Holiday Inns, a large Memphis-based motel chain.[36] Established in the 1950s, when Americans began crisscrossing the country on interstate highways, Holiday had once been an industry leader. A model midcentury American corporation, it had plucked its name from a Bing Crosby film, opened company meetings with a prayer, and constructed chapels next to its motels. Twenty years later the chain had become a disorganized collection of haphazardly assembled properties. Rose swept in, streamlined operations, dumped money-losers, and looked for investments that fit with Holiday's core business of food and shelter.

To Rose this meant casinos—a choice that would end up helping to redefine the entire gambling industry. It was hardly a whim. His father was a slot machine manager in Las Vegas, and he had spent a college summer working at a casino hotel. More recently he had watched as legitimate investors and professional managers transformed the once sordid casino business. First Hilton, one of the top names in the hospitality industry, bought two casino hotels in Las Vegas. Then Harrah's, the classiest casino operator in Nevada, received approval from the Securities and Exchange Commission to go public. Although Wall Street firms remained wary, the first issue of stock sold out immediately, and soon Harrah's had the industry's first institutional investor, a major insurance firm.[37]

Like Donald Trump, Mike Rose saw the legalization of gambling in New Jersey as a golden opportunity. As soon as Resorts opened, he, too, began scouring Atlantic City for a site. Unlike the developer, though, Rose went through a methodical decision-making process before making a move. He commissioned a study to find out what current guests thought about Holiday entering the casino business and found that 94 percent didn't care. Then he prepared the case to go ahead, used it to outflank the antigambling Southern Baptists on Holiday's board of directors, and bought Harrah's. Once in Atlantic City, he continued in the same deliberate fashion, approaching each decision by forming committees, ordering studies, writing reports and memos, then slowly steamrollering ahead.

But what worked at Holiday was anathema to the Trump Organization. "There were no layers of authority," said Jeff Walker, who worked for the developer for more than a decade and never wrote a single memo. "There was just Donald. You went to him for every major decision." In part, Walker said, this was because the developer thought lengthy reports were a waste of time and had learned from his father to retain a remarkable amount of detailed information in his head. But this "no memo" style was also a strategic decision. "We didn't want a paper trail for a lot of things we were doing because we thought paper can come back to haunt you sometimes," Walker said. "If you don't put it in writing, you don't have to produce it or explain it. It was really different from the corporate world, where you have a memo to back everything up."

The developer routinely asked everyone else what they thought, but there was only one vote that counted. Asked what sorts of marketing surveys and other homework he had done before deciding to go into Atlantic City, Trump simply pointed to his nose. "There," he said. "That's all the study I need. The market is here, believe me."

Another problem for the partnership was that Holiday and Donald Trump had a different market in mind. Harrah's had done well at the marina with middle-class, middle-aged slot players and wanted to stick with the same middle-of-the-road customer base; the developer wanted a more sophisticated crowd and an emphasis on high-end table play. Once again the difference between being a public corporation and one that was privately owned was key. Because Holiday wanted stable, predictable income and a consistent earnings picture, it preferred slot machines, whereas Donald Trump was willing to take on high rollers with winning streaks because he was after the more glamorous image of table games and assumed that the house would come out ahead over time.

From the start, Holiday and Donald Trump seemed less like partners than competitors who happened to be temporarily and unhappily yoked together.[38] "The relationship was sour long before the property opened," recalled Darrell Leury, one of the Harrah's executives assigned to the jointly owned facility. "Donald would say something like 'Let's use Cadillac limos, a friend of mine does a great job, So-and-so from the U.N. uses his limos, so let's strike a deal with him.' His decision-making style was, Let's do it." But when Leury would mention the idea to the other executives from Harrah's, they would insist on a complete cost-benefit breakdown that compared using the firm belonging to the developer's friend with buying their own vehicles and hiring their own drivers. "Donald would want to know two days later whether the deal was done," Leury said. "When I said I needed a more complex analysis, he'd blow up. There were two different approaches, and they were at loggerheads all the time on everything."

Donald Trump was partly to blame for the distrust. When Rose first brought his board of directors to Atlantic City to examine the property, the developer faked construction on the site, instructing bulldozers to drive back and forth so as to impress the suits with his progress. In addition, during the actual construction the developer refused to make much needed changes, such as adding more elevators, because the costs would eat into his fee.

But Harrah's executives compounded the problem by, among other things, insisting that they were the experts and acting so disdainful toward the Trump employees that one complained he felt treated like a construction type with a dirty undershirt. Perhaps to Harrah's staff, their casino background was reason enough to make the name noticeably larger than Trump's on the new facility's first official logo. But when the developer, who had expected equal billing, saw it, he was furious—and, ego aside, he had reason. When what was to be called Harrah's Boardwalk Hotel-Casino at Trump Plaza opened, he owned the New Jersey Generals and his name was a major asset. One casino analyst suggested that it might be better known than Harrah's and would be a magnet.[39] Apparently aggreeing, Harrah's emphasized the developer's name in advertising and later agreed to shorten the casino hotel's name to Trump Plaza.

Thoroughly alienated from each other almost from the start, each side sought to undermine the other. Donald Trump did not come through with the parking garage stipulated in the partnership agreement, hobbling the casino but also making it less valuable, and less costly, if he bought Holiday out. In turn, at internal budget meetings at Holiday headquarters Harrah's did not aim for high performance goals, which were the basis for personnel bonuses as well as stock prices. Instead Harrah's set its performance goals low so that it would be sure to meet them and Donald Trump could not exercise his contractual right to buy Holiday out. "In twenty years of gaming, nobody else ever said to me that budgets were too aggressive," said Steve Rosen, one of the Harrah's executives working at Trump Plaza. "I knew at that point it couldn't go on with a joint ownership."

Early in 1985 the relationship between the two partners collapsed. The precipitating reason was the Casino Control Commission's unprecedented—and totally unexpected—refusal to grant a license to the Hilton Hotel Corporation, which had been courted by three New Jersey governors. A leader in the hospitality industry, Hilton had succumbed to their blandishments and had just completed a spanking new $320 million casino on the marina next to Harrah's. Just three months before the scheduled opening, the commission rejected Hilton's application for a casino license. The stated reason for the denial was the unsavory record of a former Hilton attorney, Sidney Korshak, who was a legendary fixer in the entertainment industry; the unstated reason was the refusal of Hilton Hotels and William Barron Hilton, son of the chain's founder, the late Conrad Hilton, to be obsequious to commission members. Without any discussion with Holiday, Donald Trump immediately began negotiating with Hilton to buy the new casino.

The deal had gotten its start when Ben Lambert, then a Hilton board member, told Trump there were licensing difficulties with the just-completed facility.[40] "Many advised Donald not to buy," Lambert said. "But I wanted it to happen because I was looking at [being] $320 million in the hole." As Lambert knew, there were big hurdles, including the fact that the thirty-fifth and final revision of Conrad Hilton's last will and testament placed severe constraints on his heir's financial transactions. In addition, Barron Hilton was the guiding spirit and part owner of a National Football League team called the San Diego Chargers, and Donald Trump had recently slapped the NFL with a whopping antitrust lawsuit. Playing peacemaker and matchmaker, Lambert held a dinner party at his elegant Manhattan town house and introduced the developer to Hilton and the rest of the board. During the course of the evening, Trump and Hilton, a cigar-chomping athlete whose passion was hang gliding, had a private conversation in the garden. But Hilton, still enraged at being denied permission to enter the Atlantic City market, was in no mood to start figuring out an exit strategy.

Soon after the chat in the garden, Golden Nugget owner Steve Wynn made an unsolicited takeover bid for the whole Hilton chain. To fight him off, Hilton would need cash. Suddenly Donald Trump was less unwelcome. But because the opening of the new facility was imminent, everything was on a take-it-or-leave-it basis, with no time

for the master negotiator to employ his bargaining skills or even to in-
spect what he would be buying. Instead Donald Trump would have to
hand over $320 million, trusting his guess that what Hilton considered
the finest structure it had ever built would be good enough for him.

First, though, the developer would have to obtain the $320 mil-
lion. Ordinarily, the last place he would have looked for help was a
big New York bank, because such institutions still had deep reservations about the gambling industry. As it happened, however, Barron
Hilton had a seat on the board of Manufacturers Hanover, the bank
that had given Donald Trump his first construction loan for the
Grand Hyatt. In the past, Manny Hanny president John Torrell had
stoutly insisted that he would not loan money for Atlantic City and
that he required collateral he could see out his window—that is, New
York real estate. But after the developer sent him a sheaf of casino reports, circling the profits with a fat green felt-tip pen, Torrell began to
see certain virtues in faraway New Jersey. After making sure that
seller and buyer were willing to overlook the NFL-USFL fracas, Torrell held his nose and pushed through what would be New York banking's first casino deal, arranging the details so as to avoid public
notice. "I lent him three hundred on the phone," Torrell said later.
"But there were two conditions, that he and Barron were in love and
that he and Ivana would sign the note personally."

There was also a third condition, that the developer look for long-
term financing immediately. Until then only Drexel Burnham had
been willing to underwrite projects in Atlantic City. But after years of
watching Drexel pull in huge fees on its casino deals, Bear, Stearns
and Company, another prominent Wall Street investment firm, was
ready to jump in. When Donald Trump asked Drexel to take on the
entire debt for his second project, and for a second time Drexel refused, Bear, Stearns saw its chance and floated its first issue for a gambling enterprise. The Bear, Stearns deal was also Atlantic City's first
privately placed bond issue, and the first for an individual rather than
a publicly traded company. The result was a $353 million mortgage
bond issue that gave Donald Trump 100 percent financing and a $5
million fee. He would have to meet a higher interest rate than with
the bank, but he would be out from under the personal guarantees, for
these were nonrecourse bonds. In case of default, the holders would
have no claim on any other assets.[41]

Harrah's executives were furious to find their supposed partner in direct competition with their flagship casino. In May, just one year after the opening of what was now Trump Plaza, the sniping became open warfare. On the opening day of the developer's new casino, Trump's Castle, Harrah's filed suit against his use of his own name. The developer retaliated with what might be called his personal trump card: the media. In the tightly regulated, corporate environment of Atlantic City, his breezy, flamboyant style had made him a favorite of the local press. When reporters called, he had one story after another about Harrah's supposed incompetence and mistakes.[42]

Doing so was business as usual for Trump, but for Mike Rose this created a nightmare situation. The chief executive officer of a publicly held company and answerable to stockholders, Rose found himself going toe to toe with an antagonist answerable only to himself and for whom there was no such thing as bad publicity. At the same time, Trump's team launched a direct offensive through long, bristling letters; reportedly Robert was particularly skillful at composing them. Soon nasty missives filled with purple prose were shooting back and forth.[43]

Ultimately Mike Rose was a guy who colored within the lines and followed the rules. Donald Trump was not. He liked fighting in public, he liked dragging his partner through the mud, and, most of all, he liked winning. "Donald doesn't play by the rules," said Harrah's executive Steve Rosen, who saw the developer as a sort of upscale New York street fighter. "He'll say those are the rules, but then right away he'll ignore them because winning is everything." Rose sued for peace, and Donald Trump bought out Harrah's interest in Trump Plaza the next March, using the same financial methods he had put together to buy what would be Trump's Castle from Hilton.

Two years after opening one casino hotel, of which he owned only half, Donald Trump had sole possession of two. In fact, he was the only owner of two casino hotels in Atlantic City. He controlled 120,000 square feet of casino floor space, slightly more than two football fields and double that at Resorts, the second largest of the city's eleven casinos. Together, his two properties were grossing about $30 million per month, or 19 percent of the market, the highest market share of any casino company in town. By just about any index, he was the most powerful person there. It was time to start doing things his way.[44]

On March 14, three days after becoming sole owner of Trump Plaza, he held a press conference to announce that he would begin construction on the very object over which he and Holiday had parted ways, the long-postponed garage. In addition, he told the assembled reporters that he might change the name of Trump Plaza once again, to Trump's Palace. Although he noted that Caesars, which had a second casino in Las Vegas named Caesars Palace, had gone to court to oppose others' use of the word *palace*, he expressed confidence this would not be a problem. "You have the palace and you have the castle, hence you have the kingdom," he explained, sounding like nothing so much as a little boy playing with his favorite toys.[45] Then he denounced a project that he had been obliged to take on when buying Trump's Castle. In order to prepare for future development, the state had required Hilton, and now Donald Trump, to participate in an ambitious and expensive effort to widen and upgrade marina area roads, a plan that the developer refused to follow and dismissed as "a disgrace," "a disaster," and "ridiculous."

Three months later, at license renewal hearings for Trump's Castle, Donald took on the road-widening issue directly. After he testified that there was no need for the road to be widened and that Hilton attorneys had not informed him fully of the obligation, a charge that they heatedly denied, acting Casino Control Commission chair Valerie Armstrong voted against renewal. Calling Trump's behavior "inexcusable," she spoke of a "dark cloud over this license that must be dispelled." But the other commissioners voted in favor. "I think they knew full well that this man hadn't told the truth," said deputy public advocate David Sciarra, who opposed renewal. "But they really wanted his money in Atlantic City. There was a tremendous amount of pressure to keep him in there."[46]

Donald Trump had won the battle and the war. From now on he would handle his affairs in Atlantic City as he saw fit. For all practical purposes he could write his own ticket. He could, for example, obtain approval for a $30 million, eight-floor addition to the Castle with one hundred luxury suites and what he described as a "high French, Louis XV" ballroom, even though he had refused to pay his share of the cost of relieving traffic problems caused by the Castle. He could also quit the Atlantic City Casino Association, an industry trade group. The ostensible reason was that the association was unable to obtain legislative approval for twenty-four-hour gambling, but even if it had been successful, he might well have walked out. He did not need the association to get what he wanted, any more than he had needed the Real Estate Board of New York. More than that, he did not want to belong to any such group. He did not want to recognize the other members as his equals, and he did not want to have anyone else—an individual, a corporation, or a trade group—make decisions for him. He would take care of himself, by himself.[47]

As important, he had learned that his status as a privately held corporation could be advantageous in struggles with corporate America.[48] Three months after he became sole owner of Trump Plaza, he purchased stock in Harrah's parent corporation, Holiday, and started making takeover noises. Holiday's solidly profitable balance sheets and undervalued stock had made it takeover bait; now, to make itself less desirable, it swallowed what was known as a poison pill by floating a $2.6 billion junk bond issue, thereby managing to turn what had been a positive balance sheet an offputting red. Meanwhile, takeover rumors pushed up the price of its stock, and Trump sold his holdings for a profit that he touted as $35 million but reported to the Casino Control Commission as a smaller but still impressive $12.6 million. Better yet, Holiday was too strapped to spend much on the Castle's most direct competition, Harrah's Marina.

Although Trump insisted that he had been making a serious move, he did not act that way. Genuine takeover strategies usually involve keeping everything quiet as long as possible, but Donald advertised his every move, for he had figured out that his gaming license could also serve as a hunting license. Unlike ordinary corporate raiders, he was actually empowered to run a casino property. Accordingly, when he talked casino takeover, the market listened, the stock appreciated, and he could almost automatically count on a quick profit.

Having succeeded once, Donald went on to try again, this time buying stock in Bally's. Like Holiday, Bally's loaded up on debt—in this case, purchasing another Atlantic City casino, the Golden Nugget, from Steve Wynn for an eye-popping $440 million. By so doing, Bally's became the second holder of two casinos in town. As such, it was the one outfit Trump could not take over because state regulations prohibited ownership of more than three casinos, and he already had two. But Donald was scarcely the loser, for Bally repurchased his stock for an inflated price plus a hefty fee. The total profit, Trump boasted to the press, was $21 million, although it appears in Casino Control Commission records as $15 million. Like Holiday, Bally was now too debt-laden to compete effectively in Atlantic City.[49]

Presumably to avert unwelcome shareholder suits, Holiday and Bally's avoided calling the developer's actions "greenmail," the industry term for buying large blocks of stock with the intention of selling them back to the issuing company at a premium. But what he had done, especially with Bally's, was, at the least, extremely close to greenmail. His actions could have met with a strong response from the Casino Control Commission, charged with monitoring possible predatory behavior among casino operators. Indeed, they rang alarm bells in the Federal Trade Commission, which filed a two-count complaint against him for stock manipulation, and he eventually paid $750,000 to settle the case. But aside from a little modest throat clearing, the Casino Control Commission remained silent.[50]

Even if its members had spoken up, however, they could have done little to prevent the deeper problem that emerged in the wake of the Holiday's and Bally's affairs. With its rabid competition and relentless need for capital, the casino industry was electrified to see how easily it could float huge offerings of junk bonds. From the mid- to late 1980s, junk bond issues in Atlantic City increased steadily, but not in order to grow the industry through expansion and new construction; instead four of every five dollars of that new debt went to pay existing debt and cover parent corporations' other financial obligations. In less than a decade, New Jersey attorney general Anthony Parillo told one reporter, Atlantic City's casinos had gone from "a cash-rich and soundly capitalized industry" to "a debtor business hooked on junk." In the short term Donald Trump had enriched himself by $27.6 million; in the long term he had helped open a financial

Pandora's box. In the years to come, he would be among those most deeply affected by the consequences.[51]

---―⚬⚬⚬―

Like his father, Donald Trump did not view his success as a reason to relax. If anything, he worked harder. "Donald is a driven guy," said Jeffrey Walker, the former NYMA classmate who began working for the developer during the construction of the Grand Hyatt. "I've never seen him shut down or stop selling. No matter where you were, he was working, selling, moving things along." Whatever he had done, he wanted to do something more the next time. The exaggerations for which he was known and often ridiculed in the outside world were meant to impress, but they were also a way of challenging himself, of setting up a remote and imaginary benchmark in the sky and then pushing himself to achieve it.

Trump viewed almost any time as potential work time, and he had a strong aversion to wasting it. In practical terms this meant that he had an extremely short attention span. "He gets bored really easily," said Vivian Serota, an acquaintance who first met the Trumps back in the Le Club days. "He cannot sit and make small talk—it makes him fidget. If you talk to him and he isn't interested in what you have to say, his mind is somewhere else. He isn't there, even though he's standing there in front of you. It's a waste of time to him because he could be thinking about money."

Like his father, he spent the day on business, then took a pile of papers home to read over. "Dad was happiest when he was talking real estate, and so is Donald," said his sister, Maryanne Trump Barry. "He never really relaxes—he's always working. We're all like that. You can be sitting watching TV and the mind is going a hundred miles an hour. That's the way Donald is, and the way Dad was." For both men, life was about making deals. "On a day in which I've got good ones in the works," Donald later wrote, "and the phone calls and faxes are going back and forth and the tension is palpable—well, at those times I feel the way other people do when they're on vacation."[52]

It was also the way he wanted everyone around him to be. Like his father, he expected anyone who worked for him to be on duty all the time. "I woke up every morning at five or six, when he'd call with his first idea or his first complaint," recalled Blanche Sprague, a Trump executive whose roles included construction supervisor, apartment broker, and hatchet woman.[53] "Donald would say, 'I just drove by the site and something needs to be taken care of.' He slept only about two hours a night. If you got there at five, he'd been there at four, and he'd catch you." Even an empty soda can in front of a building site brought a predawn call. "He'd be so disappointed, 'Oh, how could you not have taken care of that,'" Sprague said. "Until I met him, I thought I was the most hyper, intense, almost unbelievable perfectionist, but then I realized I was very low down on the ladder."

The organizational model on the twenty-sixth floor of Trump Tower was a cross between a single-parent family and a wheel. At the center was the father/hub, Donald Trump, always demanding from everyone the same all-out, no-excuses effort he put in; next to him was executive secretary Norma Foerderer, a former foreign service staffer in Tunisia who answered a classified ad in the late 1970s and had been working for Trump ever since. A matronly but glamorous figure in designer business suits and spike heels, Foerderer imposed order on the twenty-sixth floor, acted as a filter for the stream of invitations and requests that poured in, and tried to nudge Donald back on track whenever he had, in her estimation, gone too far astray.

Radiating out from the center of the wheel were spokes connecting Donald to each top staffer. Although these key executives, fewer than a dozen in all, had considerable leeway, the developer did not surrender any actual power. He signed checks, read documents, interrogated everyone about assignments, and did not hesitate to call the people they were calling, just as his father had always done.

There was no formal business plan, no development strategy. Instead Donald would come up with ideas, do the preliminary calculations in his head, then tell someone to get moving on it. Usually there was a conversation about the idea with Harvey Freeman; sometimes the developer heeded what Freeman had to say, and sometimes he ignored it. "It didn't make any difference that you had never done something before," Walker said. "He thought you could figure it out.

That's what made him exciting to work for—we didn't fool with bureaucratic red tape. You got an assignment, you went off and did it, didn't let anything get in your way. Move it, knock it down. He wouldn't tolerate it, neither should you."

Most of the time Trump sat behind an imposing burled rosewood desk in his big corner office and talked on the telephone as people walked in and out of the room. Whether they came in answer to his summons on the intercom or on their own, they knew to say what they had to say in a hurry. "They'd stop by my desk and I'd say green light, red light, or amber, depending on his mood," said executive secretary Rhona Graff, who sat outside the developer's door and maintained his schedule. "But even if it was green, they knew they would have only a minute." When things weren't going as Trump thought they should, or fast enough, or both, he might erupt like a volcano, screaming, yelling profanities, hurling accusations of laziness and incompetence; those who lasted were those who learned fast never, ever to argue back. Or he might dispatch someone, most often Blanche Sprague, to irritate staffers and stir them up. "He used me to annoy other people," she said. "He loved to have people mix it up. He really believed that having people fighting and in conflict for approval made them work harder."

He was in control of almost every situation from the start. One way was to turn on the charm. "When he wanted to be attractive, it was like he just pushed a button in his body and became a matinee idol," Blanche Sprague said. "People walked in with a very specific idea of what they wanted and walked out doing just what he wanted and feeling lucky as could be. He can just charitz the shit out of you." Another was to hire those who dared go toe to toe with him, for he admired those who competed well and wanted to surround himself with people whose mettle he had already tested. A third was to include a high proportion of women within the inner circle on the twenty-sixth floor of Trump Tower. It was an enlightened move; it was also smart, for they worked hard to prove themselves in what was still a man's world.

"There was nothing sexual in those relationships, but it was more than employer-employee," said Alan Lapidus. "They all needed Daddy's approval." By being aggressive, competent, and tough, they earned it. But Trump would be a rare man if the calculus of placing so

many women in top slots did not include the notion, however un-
conscious, that it might be easier asserting authority over them than
over men.

If so, Donald Trump encountered at least two exceptions to this
assumption of female pliability. One was Louise Sunshine.[54] In the
early 1980s he had rewarded her years of service with a 5 percent
share of the profits in the Trump Plaza cooperative apartment building in Manhattan. In late 1985 she quit abruptly. According to Donald and Blanche Sprague, Sunshine left because she and Sprague
loathed each other. Sunshine said that she left because Donald had
saddled her with a $1 million tax bill on her share in Trump Plaza and
then told her to sell out to him in order to pay it. "I think it was a
power struggle," Sunshine later told *Vanity Fair*. "I think this was his
way of telling me 'I'm still the boss around here.'" She sued, and the
legal skirmishing went so badly for Trump that he eventually settled
the case for $2.7 million, enough to cover the taxes and give Sunshine
a tidy profit. "Donald never should have used his money as a power
tool over me," she said later. Yet she still called him "the greatest,
most brilliant teacher a person could have," and eventually teamed
up with him again to develop and market several luxury projects.

The other exception was Ivana Zelnicekova Winklmayr Trump.[55]
She had not intended to be an exception; indeed, she had spent years
attempting to mold herself into the perfect consort. An early adapta-
tion was speaking Trump-style, dotting her heavily accented, un-
grammatical sentences with expletives. "The first time we met, she
was saying things like 'It's so incredible fucking party,' and 'Look at
it, it is fucking wonderful,'" said Chicago writer Sugar Rautbord, who
subsequently became a close friend. "She was so beautiful and glossy,
and she spoke in such a soft, silky voice, and then out came these
words that she had obviously borrowed from her husband's business
vocabulary. It was clear that this was not just a husband with an arm-
piece wife—they were very coupled."

Like her husband, Ivana seemed to run on multiple tracks, always
mentally checking off an endless list of tasks—the suitcases unpacked, the holiday cards sent, the brass polished and inspected, the
phone calls made, and, especially, everything kept cleaner than clean.
Obsessed about cleanliness and worried about germs, Donald avoided
shaking hands whenever possible, and when it was not possible, he

washed his hands afterward. Perhaps in part because of his father's meticulousness and his own years in a spit-shined military school, he also demanded that his environment be constantly cleaned and shined. Accordingly, Ivana was fastidious, insisting that carpets be vacuumed immediately before she or her husband stepped on them, that sheets be changed daily, that guests remove their shoes so as not to scuff marble floors.

Her sense of discipline extended to family life as well. When she had a third child, Eric, in January 1984, she kept a full schedule until the last minute, arranging an induced labor late on Friday so as not to interfere with Donald's business day. According to a close friend, society reporter Nikki Haskell, Ivana lunched at Le Cirque, was in the delivery room promptly at six, and by nine was walking around in a black peignoir being toasted with Dom Pérignon champagne.[56] For Donny, six years older than Eric, and Ivanka, three years older, Ivana provided complete schedules; their lives, supervised for the most part by nannies, were full of lessons and sports and the elaborate, expensive birthday parties children of the very rich tend to have in Manhattan. At every school function a parent or, more often, a nanny was present. On Halloween the costumed children paraded around the twenty-sixth floor as the staff oohed and aahed. Before Christmas a nanny would take them over to FAO Schwarz and note which toys they liked, and Ivana would arrange for those that received high marks to be purchased, wrapped, delivered, and placed in readiness under the tree.

Always she did her homework. Wherever she was, she managed to know the names of the maître d's, the captains, the wine waiters, and the photographers, and she also knew the names of their wives and which ones had just had children. Before parties she would learn the names of the guests and a thumbnail sketch so that she could make introductions and small talk. Whatever the occasion, she would play the appropriate role, and if necessary, she would repeat it, as many times as needed. One summer she held a number of ladies' lunches and hired musician Christopher Mason to entertain guests at each one with the same specially composed parody. "Ivana was great," Mason said later. "Every time I'd sing, she'd open her eyes wide and look totally surprised and say, 'Vot! I pay heem money and den he insults me!'" During dinner parties at Trump Tower, Donald would vanish as soon as he'd made whatever contacts he considered useful, while she would play gracious hostess all evening, cementing business connections and extending social networks.

But her efforts were in vain. At one time, the competitiveness that Donald and Ivana both had in such abundance had seemed proof positive that they were made for each other. Both reached automatically for challenges; both seemed to operate only in high gear. They seemed true partners, in work as well as at home. But they were not; they were mirrors. They both wanted to be winners. For a while that was a bond, but eventually it became an obstacle—two people can't both be first.

No matter whom he was with, Donald Trump had to compete, and he had to come out ahead. The primal rival was Fred Trump, against whom he would compete his entire life. As a kid he broke all the rules his father laid down; later he went into the same field and then far outstripped his father's accomplishments. "I'm lucky Manhattan wasn't his thing," he said later. "If he had come to Manhattan, he would have been very successful, but to do my own thing I would then have had to go somewhere else."[57] Hardly unusual, this competitive dynamic turned up elsewhere; in every sphere of his life, the son seemed to reenact this ongoing Oedipal contest. In childhood he chose as his best friend the most competitive kid he could find; as an adolescent he focused on sports, the arena where competition was the most raw; as an adult he invariably opted for the most challenging individuals and situations possible.

Even when the contest was wildly uneven, he still had to win. One such occasion occurred when he played catch with his sister Maryanne's son, David, in the backyard on Midland Parkway. "David was good, and Donald was superb," Maryanne recalled. "Donald kept throwing it faster and faster, harder and harder, until I hear this crack and the ball hit David's head. Donald had to beat the seven-year-old." A close source said that on another occasion Donald played golf with Robert's father-in-law, who was just recovering from hip replacement surgery. When the older man, then in his mid-seventies, hit the ball into a sand trap, Donald walked in and buried it.

"He likes to deal with people who are tough," Maryanne said. "But he also likes hearing about how he's the greatest—not just the greatest, but the best of the greatest." Perhaps if Ivana had been willing to spend her life telling him that, the marriage would have flourished. But the strength that her husband had welcomed when he was starting out at the Grand Hyatt did not disappear. Instead it had grown, making her even more self-confident, more competent. Once held back by her unfamiliarity with American ways and poor language skills, she had become a rival, at least in his mind. Now he had to take control.

"Donald plays head games with people," Blanche Sprague said. "He looks at you and knows within five minutes where your buttons are. I've been with him with the most important people in the world, with a future president, and he pushes everybody's buttons, either to annoy them or make them feel good." Ivana's button was her competitiveness, and her husband pushed it for all it was worth, constantly setting the hurdles higher so that she had to be harder and more combative. Often he set Ivana and the other women on his staff against one another in a more intense version of the creative conflict he had employed in the past. "He'd say, 'Ivana, I want you to go from there to there, from east to west, don't let anything stop you,'" Jeff Walker recalled. "Then he'd say to one of these other women, 'Go from west to east and don't stop,' and he'd sit back and watch the fallout. It could be called creative conflict, but it doesn't work with your wife, whom you have to get into bed with at night."

After a while even this grew old. Sexual passion between the two had apparently waned early on and, on his part, given way to indifference and periodic hostility. He made disparaging remarks about her in public, as well as suggestive and sometimes lewd comments about other women. He suggested an open marriage, but she scornfully rejected the idea. Another man might have pursued a divorce, but this would cause his family and, especially, his parents great pain.

Now, though, he had an offer she couldn't refuse. He would make her the chief executive officer of Trump's Castle. That she had no experience at anything other than modeling and interior design did not seem to bother the developer. Presumably he considered it more important to have a member of his own family in charge of this vital asset. Even more to the point, he wanted her to be out of New York City. He had already established the fact that he could do what he wanted in his business life. Now it was time to do what he wanted in his personal life as well.

CHAPTER NINETEEN

THE TALLEST BUILDING
IN THE WORLD

ALTHOUGH DONALD TRUMP HAD BEEN RICH ALL HIS LIFE, his
assets were not liquid—he could gain access to his own wealth
only by selling holdings. His illiquidity, to use the jargon, was a frustrating limitation. No matter how famous he became, his inability to
raise substantial amounts of cash himself meant that he had to approach bankers, hat in hand, to put together a project. And because
his buildings, though profitable, did not rapidly generate huge sums
of cash, bankers were cautious in lending to him.

His acquisition of the two casinos in Atlantic City changed
everything—perhaps even more than he had imagined. With an annual cash flow in the neighborhood of $60 million and only $30 million in interest payments to cover, one knowledgeable source said
afterward, the casino business seemed to the developer like it was the
greatest thing since sliced bread. If the Trump Organization had been
a conventional public corporation, shareholders might have pressured
him to use the excess cash to retire his growing load of debt. But because the Trump Organization was private, Donald did not have to
worry about whether his balance sheet would look attractive to outside monitors. Instead he could plunge all the remaining money into
new ventures, trusting that they would generate enough money to
pay off his debts when they came due.

The only immediate problem, as far as Donald Trump was concerned, was keeping his success quiet. If the public had any idea how profitable the gambling industry was, the source explained, everyone would want in on it. Then the developer would face more casino competition, pressure for higher taxes, unionization, and even, perhaps, more interest from the Mob. As a result, the source said, Trump was always torn between blaring out how sensationally he was doing or poor-mouthing it and complaining about how bad the licensing process was or how many poor people there were in Atlantic City.

With the casino money washing in at the same time that New York was in the midst of a real estate boom that would greatly increase property values, especially in Manhattan, Donald Trump had become extremely wealthy—the fiftieth richest person in America, according to *Forbes*, which in 1986 estimated his fortune at $700 million.[1] Whether *Forbes*'s evaluation was accurate was impossible for anyone to prove, including the developer himself. In part this was because traditional accounting rules do not fit well with the real estate business. Assets are valued, as a rule, at their cost or their market value, whichever is lowest. Thus if the value of a building increases, as Trump's did, the rise does not show up on a balance sheet, although a decrease in value is reflected. Further, because real estate's book value is also reduced by depreciation of improvements, it is worth less on the books each year even if the market value goes up. On the other hand, because the developer's assets were privately held, he did not have to make his balance sheets public. The only figures he released were his own estimates of the market value of his holdings— estimates that tended to be high.

There was no doubt, though, that Donald Trump was now rich in his own right. He had money, and he had access to more money. Although his life had been thoroughly luxurious, every action and every purchase had been highly strategic—part of a plan to make himself appear richer and more important. Now, though, he was in a position to buy himself a trophy. Although he did not know it, the object he would choose would provide a distant link to the enormous assets that had bankrolled Monte Cristo, where Donald's grandfather had his first mining adventure.

—⁓—

Trump chose a spectacular mansion in Palm Beach, Florida, called Mar-a-Lago. Built at the height of the 1920s boom, the house owed its existence to a puzzling problem that confronted the very richest Americans at the turn of the century: They didn't know what to do with their money. The wealthiest of them all, John D. Rockefeller Sr., actually agonized over what to do with the enormous wealth he accumulated at the helm of Standard Oil. A devout Baptist, he lived relatively moderately and donated vast sums to philanthropy.[2]

Few others among the newly rich followed his example. Even Henry Morrison Flagler, Rockefeller's second in command, had little urge to give away his earnings. Nor did he spend it underwriting friends' get-rich-quick schemes, as Rockefeller had done with Monte Cristo. Instead Flagler moved to Florida and created a new opportunity for conspicuous consumption: Palm Beach. In 1893, when he first came to this barrier island off the east coast of Florida, Palm Beach had one hotel, a small population of year-round residents, and some twenty thousand exotic coconut palms, grown from coconuts washed ashore after the wreck of a cargo ship. After constructing a rail link to the North, Flagler built two enormous ultra-exclusive resorts, at which he enforced a strict social code that required formal dress on the beach. Across the inland waterway, known as Lake Worth, that separated the island from the mainland, he developed a separate town, West Palm Beach, to house the workers needed to staff this new watering hole for the rich. Soon Palm Beach became WASP society's most fashionable winter gathering place.[3]

In 1927 a beautiful blonde cereal heiress named Marjorie Merriweather Post created an $8 million Spanish-Moorish-Romanesque fantasy atop a coral reef, naming it Mar-a-Lago because it stretched from the eastern, ocean side of Palm Beach to Lake Worth on the west.[4] A monstrous 118-room structure built of Italian stone and fifteenth-century Spanish tiles, the mansion had 58 bedrooms, 33 bathrooms, a 29-foot-long solid marble dining table, 12 fireplaces, and a pair of cloisters.[5]

From this grandiose citadel, chockablock with antique furniture, crystal chandeliers, frescoes, porcelains, silver, tapestries, and murals, Mar-a-Lago's owner ruled over Palm Beach society, filling the house with rich and often famous guests for the entire winter season. By the time she died, in September 1973, the era of such unstinting excess was over, and the estate had become an enormous white elephant. She left it to the federal government as a retreat for presidents and foreign dignitaries, but the annual maintenance was more than the bequest provided. Worse, the Secret Service deemed the estate, which lay directly under the flight path from Palm Beach International Airport, too great a security risk for official use. In 1980 the federal government returned Mar-a-Lago to the Marjorie Merriweather Post Foundation, which put it on the market for $20 million.

Unfortunately the mansion was too expensive for the old money in Palm Beach, and Palm Beach itself was too old for most new money. For three years, there were no takers. Then, in 1983, Donald Trump saw the estate for the first time. He immediately made a bid and in December 1985 paid $8 million—what it had cost Post to build the house in 1927—for what he termed "a jewel in my crown," plus $2 million for a strip of adjacent private beach. "I thought I was buying a museum," Donald confessed to a local paper. "I never thought it was going to be a particularly comfortable place, but I thought it was so incredible as a statement that it would be wonderful to own."[6]

So it seemed. The most select spot in the East Coast's most select resort town, Mar-a-Lago was an obvious next step for the man who already dominated the East Coast's most profitable resort town, Atlantic City. Donald Trump now had bragging rights for the Tiffany resort's Tiffany property, an estate that he bragged was even more opulent than the Breakers, the Vanderbilt mansion in Rhode Island, or William Randolph Hearst's San Simeon in California. For many, taking possession of this legendary showpiece would have been the achievement of a lifetime. Being able to buy what Establishment types could no longer afford should have been a moment to savor. So should the lavish twelve-page cover story on Ivana Trump, Mar-a-Lago's new mistress, which appeared in *Town & Country.*[7] Perhaps best of all, because the $10 million Chase mortgage contained an unusual proviso, inserted by the developer's favorite banker, Conrad Stephenson, which allowed it to go unrecorded, the developer was able to give the impression that he had forked over the entire purchase price in cash, even though he had paid only $2,811 out of his own pocket.

Somehow the feeling of triumph did not last. Donald Trump had obtained a certain entrée to the world of Palm Beach, but he did not seem comfortable there. It was stultifying to play lord of the manor in a place so genteel that merchants could not display sale signs in store windows and quality tended to mean old and a little worn—a Persian carpet that had been in the family for decades, say. And it was positively galling to have to be polite to people who scorned his skyscrapers as too glitzy, who were still grousing about the Bonwit Teller sculptures, and whose welcome was decidedly cool. The developer wanted to fly down on his own plane on weekends and bring along his own big names, people like opera diva Beverly Sills and Yankees owner George Steinbrenner and actor Don Johnson, not settle in for the season and cultivate the doyennes of local society. He wanted to wear his usual dark business suit, not the Palm Beach uniform of crested navy blazer and white linen pants. He wanted to tell people his opinion, not stand in little clusters at cocktail parties and chat about gardening and polo.

In this most Jay Gatsby–like of settings, comparisons between the developer and the eponymous hero of *The Great Gatsby* seemed inevitable. Both Donald Trump and F. Scott Fitzgerald's character surrounded themselves with great excess yet seemed emotionally detached from it; both shared a certain faith that somehow they would get what they wanted and everything would work out. But the developer was the anti-Gatsby. He had no desire to pass for old money himself and considered most of those who benefited from it to be phonies; likewise he was not at all reticent about how he made his money but took every opportunity to boast about just how clever he had been. Nor was there a Daisy at whose feet he wished to lay himself and his material possessions; he did not for a minute consider Ivana to be made of finer stuff than himself, and he had been notably ungenerous in the series of nuptial agreements they had negotiated over the years. "I would never buy Ivana any decent jewels or pictures," he told friends. "Why give her negotiable assets?"

So Donald Trump did Palm Beach his way. He installed a large oil painting of himself in a reception area and filled the sterling silver picture frames sitting on side tables with magazine covers featuring him. Near the front entrance he framed a copy of the *Town & Country* cover that showed Ivana on the Mar-a-Lago patio. He lowered the berm Post had installed on the ocean side of the mansion; she had wanted the view from that side of the house to be of water rather than

Route A1A, which ran between the estate and the ocean; he wanted drivers to get a clear view of his newest trophy.[8] Rather than using invitations as a way to ensconce himself in Palm Beach society, he employed them as paybacks for business and political favors and as markers for use in the future.

Ever the savvy entrepreneur, he also sued to have his real estate taxes lowered, claiming in classic Fred Trump fashion that his concern was not the $81,525 under dispute, but the principle at stake. Then he applied for a zoning variance so as to subdivide his property and build mini-mansions. Annoyed by the constant jet traffic overhead, he and neighbor George Petty, a Canadian-born paper pulp magnate, backed two antinoise local political candidates, launched an antinoise organization, and sued the county over the issue. Trump proposed, in all seriousness, that the newly expanded Palm Beach International Airport pick up stakes and move ten miles south. But this was not New York City, and his efforts to flex his political muscle went nowhere. The courts upheld his real estate taxes; he never obtained the rezoning he sought; the candidates lost; the lawsuit fizzled; and the airport stayed put.[9] Heeding, perhaps, the developer's complaints about noise, the airport strictly enforced flight curfews, which meant that Donald could not fly in or out on his own plane at night.

Restless, he looked for new projects—and he found them, or thought he found them, everywhere.[10] He bought a huge, foreclosed, not quite finished, and almost empty condominium complex across Lake Worth in West Palm Beach. Changing the name to Trump Plaza of the Palm Beaches, he announced that Chrysler Corporation president Lee Iacocca was in on the deal, talked grandly of a wall-to-wall makeover, raised prices, and began a national advertising campaign. In Aspen, Colorado, he made a $17.5 million bid on a foreclosed six-acre hotel property that had sold a year earlier for three times that sum, but he was outbid. In Los Angeles he made an offer on the ramshackle Beverly Hills Hotel, a favorite Hollywood hangout for decades, but he bailed out when he learned that the wooden structure would be impossible to fireproof. And back in New York he offered to build a $250 million domed sports stadium and began buying shares in Alexander's, a department store chain that, like Bonwit Teller, was now more valuable for its sites than for its retail business.[11] Facing competition for control of Alexander's, he installed himself, Ivana, and Robert Trump on the retail company's board of directors, all the while talking about opening his own chain of upscale stores, named Trumps, on half a dozen Alexander's locations.

Although Trump went into each deal to make money, he told Jerry Schrager that it didn't matter whether he actually did so. "If I get my name in the paper, if people pay attention, that's what matters," he said. "To me, that means it's a success."[12] By that measure, each of these moves was a triumph. Each produced a flurry of media coverage, fanned by the developer's well-placed calls to reporters who then quoted "a source close to the Trump Organization" and, occasionally, Trump Organization "spokesman" John Barron.

There was an additional reason that these deals were not of earth-shaking importance to the developer. Another deal was already in that exalted position: his long deferred dream of developing the old 60th Street Penn Central rail yards.[13] Five years earlier, facing fierce community opposition and lacking financing, he had dropped his option to buy the property. An Argentine developer named Francisco Macri had gained control of the site and, despite continued community opposition, shouldered a project called Lincoln West through the city's torturous approvals process.

But it was a pyrrhic victory, for the approval came only after Macri agreed to a staggering collection of amenities, including $30 million to repair a nearby subway station. Because these amenities drove the project costs to stratospheric levels, Conrad Stephenson, the Chase banker attached to the project, began to express doubts about Macri's ability to handle the situation. Eventually Stephenson began pushing to bring in a developer from New York, who would presumably cut tougher—and more financially sound—deals for going ahead.[14] In the spring of 1984, after lengthy on-and-off negotiations involving Macri, Stephenson, and Donald Trump, the banker abruptly called for repayment of Macri's $75 million debt.

To Macri—and to many community activists—it seemed clear that Stephenson was trying to deliver the site to his favorite client, who was now ready to pick up where he left off in 1979.[15] Stephenson had a different explanation. Famous for his rapport with clients, he was used to acting as a consultant and to intervening when he saw someone making a misstep. But Macri walked in with a big entourage, Stephenson said, and insisted on doing things his way. When the banker objected, Macri threatened to walk out. "We had run to the end of our court," Stephenson said later. "We'd just had enough." Frantic, Macri tried to put the deal back together, but to no avail. "I do not want anything to do with you!" Stephenson screamed when one of Macri's emissaries tried to lure him back to the negotiating table. "I want out! I want my money!"

In January 1985 Donald Trump bought the 74.6-acre site, of which 18.5 acres were underwater, for $117 million, a sum he immediately rounded down to a better-sounding $95 million. It was, perhaps, a forgivable display of vanity, given the remarkable achievement involved. Forced by circumstances to relinquish the yards, he had used his resources to build his fortune and fame through other projects; now, in a near miracle, he had control of the property once again, and this time he appeared to have sufficient wherewithal to proceed. Unable to get to first base with banks a decade earlier, now he could simply take over Macri's loan.

Unfortunately he still faced the problem of the huge amenity package, but he evidently believed he had the solution in hand: his newest lawyer, Allen Schwartz, who had never handled a development deal but happened to be Mayor Koch's former law partner, former corporation counsel, and closest friend. For insurance, Donald Trump, Fred Trump, and the Trump Management Corporation donated a total of $33,250 to the mayor's reelection campaign.[16] As soon as Koch won his third term, Schwartz convened a meeting at the mayor's office and managed to have the amenities put on long-term hold. In effect, Donald Trump had won the game once again. The amenities remained in limbo for years and eventually underwent big reductions under a different set of city officials.

Meanwhile the developer began laying the groundwork for a new large-scale design.[17] The structures he had in mind would be unlike those he had planned back in the 1970s, which were essentially a greatly expanded version of those built by his father decades earlier. For starters, the new buildings would not be brick. Also, because underwriting from public sector housing programs was no longer available, there would be no rent ceilings and thus no low-income tenants. Towering skyscrapers sheathed in luxury materials, these buildings would be products of the private sector, with rich tenants paying market-rate rents. But the developer was still the son of his father in one crucial respect: He would somehow find a way to get the government to pick up a major portion of the tab.

He had not hidden his intentions. One former colleague recalled Trump's frequent mention of how terrible it was that New York didn't have the world's tallest building—an observation that the colleague translated as a lament over the fact that Trump did not have it. A year earlier the developer had announced his ambition to erect such a building in lower Manhattan; when a *Chicago Tribune* critic called the idea "one of the silliest things anyone could inflict on New York," the developer filed a $500 million defamation suit, which was soon thrown out of court.[18] When he closed on the yards, he hired Chicago-based architect Helmut Jahn, who was already working on the tallest buildings in Houston, Philadelphia, and Frankfurt, Germany.[19] Indeed, the Messe Tower in Frankfurt would be the tallest in all of Europe. Told to create a project that would be two and a half times as large as Macri's, the German-born Jahn, once dubbed Baron von High-Tech because of his futuristic glass-and-stone towers, accepted the challenge with relish.[20]

On Sunday, November 17, 1985, Donald Trump used an interview with Mike Wallace on *60 Minutes* to announce his plan for what the developer described as "the greatest piece of land in the world." At a packed Grand Hyatt press conference the next day, he unveiled a model of what he called "Television City," a massive development of 18.5 million square feet. Sandwiched between the elevated highway on the eastern edge of the site and the surrounding West Side community, the huge complex included the world's largest television studios, the world's biggest shopping center, and, of course, the world's tallest building.

"Do you guys love it?" he crowed exuberantly to then–City Planning Commission chairman Herb Sturz and other officials.[21]

The statistics were mind-boggling. The thirteen-block-long project would have a huge fifteen-story technical center, seven skyscrapers far taller than Trump Tower and most other buildings in the city, and 7,900 apartments. In the center of the complex would be a tapering, triangular, 150-story monolith that looked like a rocket ship and was nearly one-third of a mile high. At 1,670 feet (with a spire and antenna, 1,910 feet), it would restore to New York the world's tallest building title lost to Chicago's Sears Tower (1,454 feet) in 1974. The whole humongous project, which the developer estimated would provide at least 40,000 jobs, sat on a vast platform adjacent to the elevated highway that ran lengthwise across the entire site. Beneath the platform, there was another huge six-story structure that contained the TV studios, the shopping mall, and enough parking spaces for 8,500 cars.

The largest project in New York City since Rockefeller Center, which was built in the 1930s, Television City would have to make its way through the same complex approvals process that Macri had barely survived. Officially titled the Uniform Land Use Review Procedure and known by the inelegant acronym of ULURP, the process included evaluations from the local community board, the borough president, the City Planning Commission, and, ultimately, a vote by the Board of Estimate. Not wasting a minute, the developer got things rolling that same evening at a two-hour local community board meeting.[22] Appearing before an overflow audience, he enthusiastically pitched the project as "a spectacular city within a city," pledged to "work closely with the community," and responded to comments and questions.

"It looks like the quintessential phallic symbol," said one woman. Another queried the developer as to how he planned to bring more people into the already overcrowded area. "What are you going to do, Mr. Trump?" she asked. "Helicopter them in?" A third declared, "You better prepare yourself for a hell of a fight." The developer smiled at each speaker. "Of all the neighborhoods in New York, this is the one I get, right?" he joked. Then he tried charm: "You folks are not known as pussycats, I can tell you." He walked out grinning and waving his hands in the air like a fighter who's just scored a knockout punch. "I don't expect any trouble from the community," he said later. "I expect they'll be very supportive."

During the months that followed, Trump insisted that he would not make a profit on the world's tallest building and was planning it only because New York needed such a monument. "I'd make a lot more money if I built short, efficient, less dramatic buildings on the

West Side," he told one reporter. "But I'd just rather do this." The local residents, he said, would have the benefit of better television reception, a huge new upscale shopping center, and more affluent neighbors. In addition, Television City would bestow architectural distinction, sorely lacking in adjacent Mitchell-Lama-era brick buildings. Given that the developer's father had made the family fortune by constructing just such buildings for moderate-income families in Brooklyn, the claim was surprising. But this was the son, not the father, and in his view the fact that his project did not fit into the local architectural context of Manhattan's Upper West Side was an asset.

"The surrounding area is garbage," he said. "Does that mean everything's got to look like this?"

The press was even less welcoming than the neighborhood.[23] *Time* described the "screwball" project as "chess pieces that have slid off the board." Influential *New York Times* architecture critic Paul Goldberger applauded the creation of the large, horizontal spaces needed for TV and film studios but said that the main rationale for the ugly 150-story building would be to distract the eye from Television City's other ugly towers, which included a 65-story office building and six 76-story apartment buildings. In response, Trump complained to the *New York Post*'s widely read gossip column, "Page Six," that Goldberger had poor taste in clothes. "Donald was frustrated and flailing about," Goldberger said later. "I went to the Television City press conference in a navy suit, looking more like an investment banker than a journalist. I remember Donald saying, 'Oh, nice suit.' I think he concluded I cared about clothes and so I'd be vulnerable about it—he's good at going for people's weaknesses."

The criticisms continued.[24] When a study revealed that at certain times of year the shadow of the 150-story building would reach 96th Street, thirty blocks to the north, and all the way across the Hudson River to New Jersey, the complaints grew louder. In mid-June City Planning Commission chairman Herb Sturz informed Donald Trump that the city would not look favorably on a project that seemed utterly disconnected from the rest of the West Side. To the developer the subtext seemed obvious: "I thought I'd better get rid of the German and get a Jew," he said later. "It'd go over better with Sturz."[25]

Within a week he fired Jahn and hired the anti-Jahn: architect

Alex Cooper, whose far less flamboyant design for the other major Manhattan development project of the era, Battery Park City, had earned universal praise. Unlike Jahn, an autocrat who jetted from one high-profile commission to another, the soft-spoken, easygoing Cooper had spent much of his career in the public sector. There he had earned a reputation for focusing on "the urban fabric"—that is, the scale and feel of whole neighborhoods—and for a design philosophy of thinking smaller instead of larger. In an earlier meeting with the developer, Cooper had pronounced the buildings in Television City "too damn big" and refused to have anything to do with the project. Now, though, Trump was dangling the prospect of designing the biggest undeveloped site in Manhattan from scratch. "Goddamnit, Cooper, you have to change your image," he said. "It's about time you got associated with something huge! And something not so bloody civic!" The arrow hit its target. Shrugging off the horrified reactions of colleagues, Cooper set about trying to make a project big enough for Trump and small enough for everyone else.

Having made end runs around the amenities and design problems, Trump tried to do the same with ULURP and the government subsidies he wanted to underwrite Television City.²⁶ Back in the mid-1970s the threat of a boarded-up Commodore had produced zoning variances and city approval for a sale and leaseback arrangement with the state's Urban Development Corporation that gave the developer an enormous tax abatement. This time Trump hoped to achieve the same results with a different catalyst: the potential loss of NBC. Rated number one in the nation, the network dubbed "the peacock" because of its symbol had long since outgrown its space at Rockefeller Center. Old-fashioned studios with outdated wiring and inadequate mechanical systems made routine operations difficult, and major shows like *Saturday Night Live* had to build sets in Queens and then break them up for transport back to Manhattan. Although NBC's lease would not expire for another dozen years, the network was already hunting for a new home. Several locations across the Hudson River offered the kind of space needed for television production, but the only alternate New York City site on NBC's short list was on Alex Cooper's drawing board.

If Television City could keep NBC and its four thousand jobs in

New York, Trump reasoned, the city would have no choice but to facilitate zoning approvals and a tax abatement. Declaring that NBC's future was tied to that of Television City, he launched a high-pressure campaign to get the city to agree to his terms. "Donald only knows one technique for getting things done," said architect Paul Willen, who worked on the Grand Hyatt and rail yards projects. "That's to push and push and push—and scream and yell. If he wants something, he calls up and demands it, right away—he doesn't hold off." At one point he called Deputy Mayor Alair Townsend and gave her a two-hour deadline to decide. In another phone call he pushed Mayor Koch to make up his mind that day and added, "I can taste the deal in my mouth."

But it was not the mid-1970s, and obtaining City Hall endorsement for a Trump project, especially one as large and controversial as Television City, would require considerable dexterity. Although Donald Trump continued the family tradition of large financial contributions to political campaigns, he no longer had the same network of connections his father had nurtured so carefully. On the city level, Donald Trump and Ed Koch disliked and distrusted each other, and on the state level, then-governor Mario Cuomo did not always cast a favorable eye on the developer's interests. Soon after Cuomo took office, Trump had attended a small dinner party the governor held for major contributors and complained about a 10 percent tax Cuomo had levied on gains from real estate deals of $1 million or more. "Donald, it's one of my favorite taxes," Cuomo had replied. "I call it 'the Trump tax.'"[27]

For months Trump searched for ways to build his case. Then, in the spring of 1986, he found the perfect opening. For six years he and the rest of New York had watched the city's hapless efforts to renovate Wollman Memorial Rink. A large facility in Central Park's southeast corner, it was a gift from Kate Wollman, an eighty-year-old banking heiress who lived in the Waldorf-Astoria Tower and had never been on a pair of skates. A much loved institution, the rink had opened in 1950 and offered ice-skating in winter and roller-skating in the summer. After thirty years of hard use, the rink closed in 1980 for a two-and-a-half-year, $4.9 million overhaul. Six years later the tab was up to $12 million and Wollman was still closed. Worse, the latest prediction was that it would take at least two more years and another

$2 million to finish. To the Koch administration it was a source of frustration and embarrassment; to Donald Trump it was a golden opportunity.

On May 28 he sent a "Dear Ed" letter to the mayor. "I and all other New Yorkers are tired of watching the catastrophe of Wollman Rink," he wrote. "The incompetence displayed in this simple construction project must be considered one of the greatest embarrassments of your administration." The job should take four months, he declared. He offered to do it at cost and to manage the rink and its adjacent restaurant thereafter. In a response dated the same day, the mayor said that he would be "delighted" to accept the developer's offer to fix up the rink, although it would not be renamed and the developer could not operate it. Koch closed by saying, "With bated breath, I await your response." Presumably to his surprise, when he released both letters publicly, instead of hooting at Trump's chutzpah, New Yorkers embraced the idea. City dailies ran editorials in favor; ten days later his makeover was a go and would begin at the end of the summer.

Now Trump had to live up to his own challenge. After wangling an interest-free construction loan from Chase, he pushed contractor HRH to avoid construction delays and used his newest hire, former city commissioner Tony Gleidman, to get through bureaucratic hurdles. Each morning he scrutinized the rink from the high-powered telescope mounted in his sixty-fifth-floor Trump Tower apartment, which was really on the fifty-ninth floor, and throughout the day he monitored progress from the huge windows in his twenty-sixth-floor office. Periodically he hiked over to the rink for unannounced inspections, after which he often called on-site press conferences. At the first, in a gesture reminiscent of the huge TRUMP banner he had flung over Grand Central nearly a decade earlier, he posted next to the rink a large sign that made the bold but inaccurate claim "Owner: Trump Ice Inc." Among the numerous press conferences that followed, highlights included the laying-of-the-pipes press conference one day, followed by the pouring-of-the-cement one the next day.

Although the rink would lack his signature mirrors and gilt, it did have one luxury touch: instead of using pedestrian pine for railings, Trump employed burnished teak. "See this railing?" he pointed out to reporters. "Same railing Onassis had on his boat." The redone rink opened in mid-November, two months ahead of his announced schedule and $750,000 below his announced budget. Like the original benefactor, he was a nonskater; the reason, he said, was that so many people would love to see him fall down. As grateful New Yorkers glided by, he stood in the crisp, sunny weather in his usual dark topcoat, a businessman even on an ice rink.

He had stuck to his word. So did the city. Because Trump did not pay for the restoration, the city did not budge on the renaming—an idea, the developer insisted, that had never crossed his mind. Instead the city awarded him the contract to operate the rink and provided "appropriate donor recognition," a young Japanese Saphora evergreen planted next to the rink. "We thought he had everything else," said Koch's parks commissioner, Henry Stern. "But he wanted a sequoia, something huge. He was outraged. It's like when you first see an infant and it's small and wrinkled. He didn't want his name on anything like that—he thought of it as the 'Trump stump.'"[28]

The renovation was indeed an impressive accomplishment. But it was not, perhaps, quite the superhuman feat it appeared. Trump had given himself a six-month deadline for what he initially called a four-month job, and as a private contractor, he did not face the burdensome regulations imposed on public construction to eliminate corruption.[29] There was also another factor: What the developer did was far easier than what the city had attempted to do.

In the initial design of Central Park by Frederick Law Olmsted, the spot where the rink now stood had been a delicately balanced panorama with a fanciful gray stone structure known as the Dairy up on a hill and a graceful lawn sloping down to a lake and an adjacent pond. A century later Robert Moses had plopped Wollman Rink and several large, squat buildings square in the middle of Olmsted's vista. By 1980, when the city had begun thinking about repairing the rink, then–parks commissioner Gordon Davis had decided to restore what he could of Olmsted's original contemplative ambiance by making the rink a reflecting pond in the summer. Alas, no engineer could come up with a workable design for both functions. Worse, the Parks Department, in an attempt to be ecologically sound, chose to refurbish the rink with a supposedly energy-efficient new refrigeration method based on Freon instead of the usual brine solution.

"We really screwed this up," Davis said later. "It was our version of making the movie *Apocalypse Now.*"[30] When Donald Trump came in, he jettisoned the reflecting pool, poured a new slab over the old rink, and went back to brine. His plan was uglier, more expensive to maintain, and less environmentally conscious—but it worked.[31]

The restoration was a moment of great triumph for Donald. Indeed, although he exploited it for publicity to a degree remarkable even for him, being the can-do hero of Wollman Rink gave him the kind of popular support that could help make Television City happen. Under fire because of political scandals swirling around his administration and the recent loss of the corporate headquarters of Mobil Oil and JCPenney, Mayor Koch seemed favorably disposed to pushing through the deal. For its part, NBC appeared unenthusiastic about crossing the river and sent technical experts to help design Television City's studio space. The press, primed by the developer's frequent calls, put out story after story emphasizing the import of the situation for Television City, NBC, and New York City itself. Meanwhile Trump kept all his options open and played the various parties to the deal against each other. "We thought we had an opportunity for a quick hit," said Jerry Schrager. "It would have been a grand slam home run for Donald."

This time, though, the techniques that had worked so well for Donald Trump in the past would prove his undoing. He could not keep badgering each party and use any differences to his own ends, for instead of dealing through him, NBC, Rockefeller Center, and the city spoke directly with each other and used him to their advantage. NBC found its hand greatly strengthened by all the press attention. "Donald was really an advocate for us," said Henry Kanegsberg, the NBC vice president charged with finding a new location. "He was in the forefront, saying that New York cannot afford to lose NBC. He was doing it for his own benefit, but it helped us." Rockefeller Center also gained. Alerted to the potential loss of its largest tenant, it elbowed its way back into the negotiations and made the case for NBC to stay and remodel. "The city told us they liked dealing with us because they didn't like hearing everything they said in the paper the next day," one Rockefeller Center official said afterward.

New York City came out ahead as well. Already put off by Trump's incessant gloating over the Wollman reconstruction, Koch found his coercive tactics and constant leaks to the press annoying. Then the mayor learned that the developer, claiming that new accounting methods provided more accurate numbers, had slashed his payments to the city from Grand Hyatt profits. Worried about how to safeguard profit sharing at Television City and uneasy about implicitly endorsing zoning approvals for the project, Koch finally rejected Trump's proposal at the end of May 1987. That is, instead of handing the developer the largest tax concessions in city history, he offered a far smaller incentive package that could be used anywhere. Furious, Donald Trump blasted the mayor as "a moron" and "a disgrace" and denounced the city as "a cesspool of corruption and incompetence." Calling for Koch's resignation, he talked impeachment and demanded an investigation of Koch's involvement in his appointees' misdeeds.[32]

"I think I must be doing something right if Donald Trump is squealing like a stuck pig," Koch shot back, and referred to the developer as "piggy, piggy, piggy."[33]

Eventually NBC decided to stay at Rockefeller Center. Publicly the developer shed no tears; instead, in characteristic fashion, he insisted that he had pulled the final plug on the deal because the network "would add nothing to my project [and] I hated the concept of a studio building without windows or life."[34] But he did not concede to Koch; instead he stepped up his attack. His anti-Koch comments and the mayor's responses became regular press features, along with the developer's many protests that he would never, ever think of running for mayor himself. In the months to come he made an insult-laced offer to finish the stalled renovation of the Central Park Zoo, noisily volunteered to fix a major bridge that had been closed, talked about spending $2 million on anti-Koch television advertisements, and, after a young woman was brutally raped and nearly killed in Central Park, ran full-page ads in city dailies spurning Koch's call for understanding and instead demanding the return of the death penalty and more police.[35]

The loss of NBC at Television City had been a stinging defeat, but Donald Trump quickly bounced back. Three weeks after the mayoral no, the developer put himself back on the sports pages by promoting the first of many lucrative Atlantic City boxing matches.[36] The fight between Michael Spinks and Gerry Cooney, staged on a Monday night in the city's Convention Hall, attracted a bumper crop of high rollers. Afterward they strolled across the aerial walkway to Trump Plaza and wagered six times the average take for that night of the week. The precedent-setting event spurred boxing promoter Don King to coin a new word. He declared the developer to be "telesynergistic," which meant "progress ingeniously planned by geometric progression, the capability to translate dreams into living reality in minimal time at megaprofits."

Continuing his telesynergistic rebound, Trump flew to Moscow on his own jet and talked with officials there about building a capitalist-style luxury hotel. He offered the use of the West Side site for the 1988 Olympic Games, scheduled to be held in strife-torn Korea. Repeating his pattern with Holiday and Bally, he purchased shares in Pan Am and Steve Wynn's Golden Nugget casino in Las Vegas (followed later by Federated Department Stores and Gillette), talked takeover, sold off his holdings, made money, and then exaggerated his profits.[37] As usual, he talked—and talked—to reporters about each of these activities. Each conversation seemed to produce a story, another conversation in reaction to the story, a second story, then a third. "He really has diarrhea of the mouth," said one colleague.[38] "He loves the press. Whenever anyone calls him, he's talking, he's on stage. He can be in his own room, but he sees the lights go on and he's rolling."

Two months after the biggest defeat of Donald Trump's career, *Business Week* carried his picture on the cover with a caption that read "Donald Trump has conquered New York real estate."[39] *Newsweek* soon followed; its tag line was "Trump: A Billion-Dollar Empire and an Ego to Match."[40] The day after the stock market crash on Black Monday, October 19, 1987, Trump boasted loudly that he had seen it coming, had sold his entire portfolio, and had made $200 million. In fact, he had hung onto certain shares, including those in Alexander's, and had taken a paper loss of more than $22 million.[41] Soon afterward the developer cheerfully smirked on the cover of *People* under the headline "Too Darn Rich."[42]

In the fall of 1987 he extended the Trump brand in the form of his own book, *The Art of the Deal*, written "with" Tony Schwartz, then a *New York* magazine staffer. Schwartz was not an obvious candidate; two years earlier his article about efforts to oust tenants at 100 Central Park West had helped turn public sentiment against the developer. But once again Donald hired someone he considered a worthy opponent. Audacious and egotistical, the first-person account is a highly selective retelling of the developer's most successful deals, larded with the same faux frank asides and energetic exaggerations that had served him so well at the negotiating table. Donald Trump, one assumes, did not care that his grandfather was not, in fact, Swedish; that his father, not he, had bought and renovated Swifton Village in Cincinnati; that he had not, in fact, given his elementary school music teacher a black eye;[43] or that he had paid top dollar, not below market, for his land in Atlantic City. Instead he was concerned with being engaging and entertaining. And indeed, the combination of mind-boggling brashness and relentless optimism that bowled over so many in person has the same effect on the printed page.

At ten P.M. on Saturday, December 12, klieg lights played over the front of Trump Tower, and a red carpet covered the sidewalk from the curb to the shiny brass entrance. Inside the pink atrium, waiters in white jackets stood at attention, ready to pour champagne. Violinists wearing red sashes played a medley of waltzes and serenades, and disco music blared from the lower level. Christmas lights, red balloons, and red poinsettias were everywhere, and buffet tables were heaped with elegantly arranged platters of food.

As declared at the top of the invitation, it was "The Party of the Year," held to celebrate the publication of *The Art of the Deal*.[44] At the head of the receiving line stood the tuxedo-clad author, flanked by Ivana and Si Newhouse, close friend to the late Roy Cohn and owner of Random House, which published the book. The celebrities filed by: Michael Douglas, Jackie Mason, Cheryl Tiegs, Barbara Walters, Phyllis George, Liz Smith, Joan Rivers, Norman Mailer, Don King. Alongside them came the politicians: Senator Al D'Amato, former governor Hugh Carey, Manhattan borough president Andrew Stein, New York City controller Harrison Goldin, New Jersey governor Tom Kean. Plus the bankers, investors, lawyers, architects, contractors, and, it seemed as the night wore on and the guests kept piling in, everyone else in the greater New York area who had managed to cadge an invitation. The event, planned by Studio 54 co-founders Steven Rubell and Ian Schrager, supposedly cost $160,000. When it was over, an estimated two thousand people had celebrated the print debut of one of the most showy, self-involved, and seductive voices of the era.

Also one of the most marketing-oriented. In the months before publication, the developer plugged his upcoming tome at the annual convention of the American Booksellers Association and flew his helicopter up to Connecticut to push the book to regional executives at Waldenbooks, the country's largest bookstore chain. Then he took Barnes & Noble chief Leonard Riggio to lunch at La Cote Basque and trotted out the same hard-sell tactics he'd used fifteen years earlier during his lunch with investment banker Ben Lambert. "[Donald] gets in touch, tugs you by the collar, and pats you on the back," Riggio told *The Wall Street Journal.* Once again the personal touch paid off, for both chains had special Trump displays.

In addition, the developer and Dan Klores, one of Howard Rubenstein's top publicists, came up with the idea of launching Donald Trump as a possible presidential candidate. The developer's first foreign policy foray had been a deadpan public offer a few years earlier to serve as an arms negotiator with the Soviet Union. Now he paid $94,000 to run a full-page open letter in *The New York Times,* the *Boston Globe,* and *The Washington Post* that began, "There's nothing wrong with America's Foreign Defense Policy that a little backbone can't cure."[45] The press speculated energetically about the developer's political aspirations. He insisted that he was not a candidate but gave a speech in New Hampshire during prime presidential season, distributed "I ♥ Donald Trump" bumper stickers, and commissioned a telephone poll.

When the findings proved promising, the developer's staff deluged reporters with the numbers: Donald Trump had a 75 percent recognition factor, would be competitive in Republican primaries, and might take more than 20 percent of the votes in a general presidential election.[46] Speaker of the House Jim Wright promptly asked him to host a major Democratic fund-raiser. Although Trump declined, he reaped another publicity windfall—and a best-seller. Within a month of publication, the book topped the *New York Times* list and ultimately sold 835,000 hardcover copies, capturing the number nineteen position on the list of best-sellers for the entire decade.[47]

Donald Trump had become a superstar, a megacelebrity. His name appeared so often in newspapers that it was impossible to keep count, and he was on the front of so many magazines that the framed covers filled the wall next to his desk. Although *Forbes* continued to place him around midpoint in its list of the one hundred richest Americans, the public tended to consider him much closer to the top—or, possibly, number one. Similarly, many assumed that he was the largest landlord in New York, although this was not the case.[48] But in these matters perception easily, as it were, outtrumped reality. He received payments and media attention for the use of his name on Cadillac cars, Parker pens, eyeglasses, and business cards, as well as the board game with his face on the cover of the box. He was also the subject—and object—of countless rumors, anecdotes, and jokes, showed up in Gary Trudeau's *Doonesbury* and other cartoons, and played cameo roles on television. In 1988 he made a deal with Ted Turner for *Don Trump: the Movie.* "I want a very good-looking guy to play me," he said.[49] Whenever he made a preannounced appearance to autograph his book, lines stretched around the block and across shopping-mall parking lots.[50]

Donald Trump had spent his entire adult life working to this end. In Atlantic City, already drenched in the Trump name, he had erected billboards dedicated to making a word that was a noun and a verb into an adjective, as in "You're looking very Trump today." Nonetheless he managed to look both pleased and surprised every time he saw the crowds waiting for him. "I had worked for developers before, but now I was working for a rock star," said Blanche Sprague. "He would seem very cool and collected, but he would always turn to you and say, 'Do you believe this, do you believe this is happening?'"

Known for being able to sell just about anything to just about anybody, he was selling himself to everybody, and the reason it worked was that he was also selling himself to himself. Thus he would speak of himself in the third person, as in "Trump says this" or "People say that Trump is the only one who can do it." The consummate salesman, he was demonstrating his product, which happened to be himself, and at the same time managing to suggest that he actually identified more with the consumers out there deciding whether or not to buy.

Yes, he was rich and, for the most part, they were not, but that wasn't what mattered. What counted was that both salesman and consumer saw the huge mansions, private jet, stretch limos, glitzy casinos, blond ex-model wife, and gold-plated everything as the embodiment of quality—that is, what any normal human being who struck it rich would like to have. Refusing to subscribe to the old WASP notion that discretion was the better part of wealth, the developer advertised his possessions and invited the public to admire them with him. Whenever estimates of his wealth appeared, he did not, in classic tycoon fashion, round the numbers down; instead he insisted that he was worth more. After years of boasting and bravado, he had become the people's billionaire. Although his means did not approach those amassed by John D. Rockefeller, the developer rivaled the oil magnate as the touchstone of wealth. Instead of aspiring to be "rich as Rockefeller," people wanted to be "rich as Trump."

Wherever he went, whether it was down the street or to a Michael Jackson concert, he was automatically the center of attention, regardless of who else was present. At one charity function in Los Angeles, Jerry Schrager recounted, the VIP room was wall-to-wall Hollywood greats. "All the childhood stars," Schrager said. "You know, Gregory Peck, Sidney Poitier, Charlton Heston, Bob Hope, Carol Channing, Ronald Reagan, George Burns. And who was the center of attention? It was Donald. In this room, where everybody was a celebrity but me and my wife, he was the one person the press engulfed."

He had become the celebrities' celebrity. When people who were household names themselves came to look at apartments in Trump Tower, they would invariably ask if he was in. "I'd say he was in his office," Blanche Sprague said later. "They'd say, 'Why don't you give him a call, I'd love to meet him,' and they'd sound a little anxious."

Inevitably that megawattage affected the responses he received. It was hard to have a different opinion, much less debate, with a man who presented such an impenetrable, invincible image, who spoke from on high and seemed touched with gold. Although he constantly asked others what they thought, if he heard something he didn't like, he reacted strongly and sometimes explosively. "He was fearsome," said a key staff member. "Everyone was afraid of his tirades and his power to get things in the press. To influence him you would need to be a combination of Machiavelli and Mike Tyson, shrewd enough to come up with a clever strategy and strong enough to punch him in the jaw."

This extraordinary strength of mind could function as a sort of shield, allowing Donald to ignore attacks or distractions and forge ahead to his goal. But it also functioned as blinders and earplugs, keeping out information he needed to hear. On minor matters this was unfortunate; on larger ones it would prove catastrophic.

CHAPTER TWENTY

SPINNING OUT OF CONTROL

THE NIGHT OF HIS BOOK PARTY, Donald Trump received the homage of New York City's glitterati and literati, people who showed up in bold-faced type in gossip columns as well as people who disdained the columns. But the only person he seemed to show any genuine interest in seeing was a twenty-four-year-old aspiring actress from Dalton, Georgia.[1] Her name was Marla Ann Maples, and her idol since childhood had been Marilyn Monroe. Blonde, blue-eyed, and stunningly beautiful, she had a soft southern voice and a warm, friendly manner. She also had a spectacular body: five feet eight inches tall, 125 pounds, long legs, and full breasts. When she was only sixteen her looks had brought her an offer to pose nude for *Playboy*. She refused but did accept first place in a swimsuit pageant, modeled in print ads for airlines and ceramic tile adhesive, and had a bit part in a Stephen King horror movie called *Maximum Overdrive*, in which she was crushed to death by a truckload of watermelons.

Now these same looks brought her Trump's complete and, for once, undivided attention. Over lunch and, soon, late-night dinners, she shared with him her earnest belief that everyone, including him, is on this earth for a higher purpose; he courted her with press clips and reviews of his book. Soon he installed her nearby, at the St. Moritz, a hotel on Central Park South that he had bought with the idea of someday turning it into condominiums. When he was in Atlantic City, she stayed at Trump Plaza. He relished showing off her photograph and boasting of her 37-25-37 measurements, and sneaked away from work whenever possible for a midafternoon rendezvous. He paid her expenses, bought her lavish gifts, gave her cash, and flew her and her family in his jet. When she called his office she used a special code name, and his staff had standing orders to attend to her every need.

Trump's life was already impossibly crowded. Every day he barely made his way through the phone calls, the documents, the employees urgently needing his attention, and all the schemes and dreams that were constantly running through his mind. He gave few people more than a moment or two of his time, slept only three or four hours a night, and, reportedly, for an extra boost took diet pills. The prescription, supposedly written by a doctor who had once been investigated by *60 Minutes*, was for an amphetaminelike substance that suppressed a patient's appetite and produced a sense of euphoria and boundless energy—precisely the sort of manic behavior that staffers often saw their boss exhibit.[2]

Now he was embarking on a second, secret life, with all the claims, conflicts, and confusions that inevitably accompany such a situation. When possible, he dodged his wife; when this was not possible, he became furious at her, setting off hurt feelings, recriminations, self-justifications, and more dodging. Flitting from one illicit love nest to another, he struggled to keep straight the half-truths, careful shadings, and often outright lies he had to tell to keep the two lives going. He began making deals for their own sake, or deals that had no purpose other than self-aggrandizement, or, most worrisome of all, deals that simply made no sense on any level. And as the deals piled up, Donald Trump lost track of what he was all about—a fatal error.

To blame the disaster that would eventually unfold on the curvaceous blonde from Dalton would be a mistake and also a misconception. For all his adeptness at deal-making and his astuteness at reading other people's minds, Donald Trump seemed remarkably unaware of what was going on in his own head. The man who had made being a winner the most important thing in his life would not acknowledge even to himself that he was in the throes of the one thing that, sooner or later, overcomes all creation—aging. Reportedly he had nips and tucks to eliminate wrinkles and sagging jowls and, eventually, liposuction to take away the extra pounds his taste for pizza and chocolate cake from Cakemasters had put on. Acutely aware of his thinning hair, he took to arranging what was left in careful combovers and, by one account, hiding the pink skin of his exposed scalp by tattooing it a darker hue. Equally concerned with graying, he followed his father's example and colored his hair, occasionally turning up with an odd orangish shade.[3]

In classic male midlife-crisis fashion, he looked outside his marriage for affirmation that he was still attractive, vital, and potent. Even before Ivana began commuting to New Jersey to run the Castle, he had pursued other women. Because he was a notorious germ phobe, it seemed doubtful that many of these liaisons involved sexual intimacy. Nonetheless, gossip columnists linked his name with those of actresses, models, and other glamorous celebrities, and he fanned such rumors with selective leaks and innuendos. In turn, as happens with many powerful public figures, other women pursued him—a fact he lost no opportunity to brag about.

On one occasion he gave broker Jack Shaffer a ride to a party and boasted that when he got there every woman in the room would come over to him. "You want to throw up when you hear that," Shaffer said later, "but when he walked in, they did all run over. I felt like I was carrying his briefcase." Such attention was thrilling, but it was also wreaking havoc in the developer's head and his life. "Donald hadn't figured out that he was a powerful man and women would jump all over him," said another colleague. "He would walk one block and twenty-two women would hit on him. He got constant solicitation letters. This availability of other women can be unbearable if you don't have things in balance, and the other women were making him crazy."

—◆—

Eight months before Marla Maples entered the developer's life, while he was in the midst of trying to bring off Television City, by far his biggest deal in New York, and unload the unsold condominiums at

Trump Plaza of the Palm Beaches, he made another, unrelated deal in Atlantic City. It would bring him the largest casino in the nation at the time and eventually lead to his downfall. Named the Taj Mahal, this asset became available in April 1986, after James Crosby, international playboy and owner of Atlantic City's first legal casino, died of acute emphysema. Facing a messy squabble over his estate, his heirs opted to sell off his casino properties. In March 1987 Donald Trump arranged to buy a controlling interest in Resorts International, Inc.; the eventual price would be $96.2 million. For this sum he received Resorts' $600 million in junk bond debt and two gambling facilities: the tired and by then money-losing casino that had opened back in 1978, and the half-finished Taj, which would cost an estimated $525 million to complete.

Already the Taj was overbudget and behind schedule. When it was finished, the three-casino rule would require Trump to sell one of his Atlantic City properties or convert one into a nongambling hotel. The Taj was also likely to steal business from the developer's other casinos, and it would tie him even more closely to a town that sometimes seemed worse off than before the 1976 referendum. Since the arrival of the casinos, the town had lost 20 percent of its population, 15 percent of its already inadequate housing stock, and much of its hope that there was any possibility its fortunes could somehow be restored. At this point Atlantic City had thirty-five thousand residents, eighteen thousand slot machines, and the highest crime rate in the state. Half the city received public assistance, the ex-mayor was in jail for misconduct, and other public officials had set new records for personal greediness. Most of the forty thousand casino jobs had gone to outsiders who commuted from elsewhere, and gambling taxes intended to revive the town had little effect so far. Instead the shimmering casinos had become almost entirely white enclaves strung out along the Boardwalk and on the marina, and most of the black-majority city remained a bleak wasteland of squalid storefront businesses, deteriorating homes, and weedy vacant lots.

Those were the negatives connected with buying the Taj. The positives were a casino in the Bahamas, vast amounts of prime Atlantic City real estate, and, especially, the fact that the Taj would have a casino the size of Trump Plaza and Trump Castle combined. The tallest building in the entire state, the Taj would inevitably dominate the market. "Everything is much bigger than it should be," Trump told one reporter. "It's built as a dream."⁴ Evidently this staggering size, plus the fear that if he didn't buy Resorts someone else would, seemed to him reason enough to act. Against the advice of two of his most trusted associates, Harvey Freeman and Jerry Schrager, he went ahead.

Two months later Mayor Koch turned down Trump's proposal to obtain city subsidies for Television City. To salvage his reputation, the developer quickly produced *The Art of the Deal*. But the same month it came out, he made a deal that was as dubious as his purchase of the Taj: he bought the world's third largest yacht.⁵ Built by arms dealer and financier Adnan Khashoggi in the late 1970s and named after his daughter Nabila, it had cost $30 million to build and another $55 million for superluxury appointments. A decade later Khashoggi was broke, the yacht went to pay off a loan from the sultan of Brunei, and it became clear that, as with Mar-a-Lago, an extraordinary creation had become a gigantic white elephant. In the fall of 1987 Donald Trump bought the boat for $30 million, minus a $1 million discount he wangled to remove the name of Khashoggi's daughter from the hull.

It was a typical Donald Trump transaction. Edward S. Gordon, a major New York real estate broker, recalled receiving a call from him during the negotiations for the yacht. Gordon counseled him to go with the sultan's final offer, which the developer did. "Donald calls me four days later and says, 'It was worth the $40 million I paid,'" Gordon said. "I said, 'What are you—you can't do this to me.' But that's the Donald." By then, though, Gordon was used to the developer's numbers games. "Half the time he's so full of shit," Gordon said. "He'll double the numbers on me, and it's a deal I did for him. I'll say, 'What are you doing, I did the fucking deal'—and he'll say, 'Oh, oh, yes.' But he believes it, he's doubled it and believes it. That's his strength and his weakness."⁶

Renamed *Trump Princess*, the yacht had all the usual super-luxury touches: eleven guest suites featuring bird's-eye maple and gold-plated doorknobs, two waterfalls, a sun deck surrounded by bulletproof glass, a discotheque, and sleeping quarters for a staff of fifty-two. In addition, there were more than two hundred phones, used by Khashoggi and guests for arms deals and commodities trades on the

high seas, as well as secret passageways and pushbutton-controlled
ceiling panels, windows, and doors. The one thing the ship lacked was
any sense of comfort, and it was so large that few marinas could accommodate it. Although its new owner spoke of it often, he never
spent a night there and visited infrequently. When he did venture
aboard, he led guests on tours and pointed out the numerous "quality"
items, including the hull's steel plating, the medical equipment in the
three-room hospital, the hand-carved onyx bathroom fixtures, and the
solid gold sink in the master suite. Calling his new prize "a masterpiece," he declared it "beyond a ship or a boat or a yacht. That's what
I love."

What he did not love were boats themselves. "I'm not exactly
into them," he said. "I've been on friends' boats before and couldn't
get off fast enough." Nonetheless, an hour after he took possession of
the yacht, he was making plans to sell it and build a new 420-foot
Princess, and he would later briefly own the Dutch shipyard he commissioned to construct it. Like Mar-a-Lago, the current *Princess*
would be a place for paybacks and piling up credits, and it would also
spawn a line of *Princess* souvenirs.[7] Although the developer delegated
most details about the boat, he took a direct hand in designing the
ship's logo, a voluptuous mermaid who would appear on T-shirts and
towels as well as crew uniforms. "My marching orders were to make
everything else look the same, just brand new," said longtime deputy
Jeff Walker. "But on the mermaid, we tried contemporary, traditional,
big breasts, small breasts, nipples, no nipples, for hours and hours."

The *Princess*, it turned out, was only a warm-up for the next purchase.[8] The new prize was the Plaza Hotel, the elegant Edwardian-era
landmark at the corner of 59th Street and Fifth Avenue. Built to re-
semble a French château, it had a mansard roof faced with green-
tinged copper, and its lavish interior was filled with crystal
chandeliers, European tapestries, and Oriental carpets. Since its opening day in 1907 the Plaza had been a favorite of the rich and the famous,[9] but in recent years its appearance had slipped, as had its
occupancy rate. Nonetheless, the developer was smitten.[10] In March
1988 Donald Trump bought his heart's desire for $407.5 million—the
highest price ever paid for a single hotel—even though he had not
done a careful inspection of the property.

"Trump wasn't Trump in this deal," said one of his lawyers for the transaction, Norman Bernstein. "Normally we'd tear a property like this apart." Donald was himself in one detail: his $425 million loan from a Citibank-led consortium, almost $20 million over the purchase price. "He was like an international superstar who says, 'I want to do a movie, who wants to pay for it,'" said Blanche Sprague. "Jerry Schrager would have this fabulous way of presenting it to the bankers, Donald would walk in and shake a few hands and smile, and then boom, there was the money."

This time, though, the money came with a condition: $125 million required a personal guarantee from Trump. It was a decisive moment. Within the real estate industry, famous for operating on other people's money, risking your own was seen as folly on such a scale as to be almost a sin. A personal guarantee was something Fred Trump would never have considered, and his son had done it only once before, on Trump Plaza in Atlantic City, and then only for ten days.[11] Worse, he was taking this momentous step on a deal where the property's annual cash flow, less than $20 million, would not come close to covering interest payments.

"I haven't purchased a building, I have purchased a masterpiece—the Mona Lisa," he declared in another full-page open letter in *The New York Times*. "For the first time in my life, I have knowingly made a deal that was not economic—for I can never justify the price I paid, no matter how successful the Plaza becomes."[12]

Actually, the justification had already begun via this faux confession, intended to underscore the hotel's cachet. And, in fact, the status and distinction the Plaza Hotel conferred were enormous—so much so that even Donald Trump made no effort to put his name on the outside. Even though the hotel would never earn out, buying it was arguably the right move because it gave prestige and power and was worth more than the cash flow would ever justify. The problem was that the developer did not stop there.

It could not have helped that he was constantly distracted. For one thing, he was still carrying three as yet unprofitable projects: the rail yards, the Taj, and the West Palm Beach condominiums; also, there was the unresolved problem of Ivana.[13] Commuting by helicopter, she spent three days each week at the Castle, where she had honed herself into an executive machine and copied her husband's hands-on style wherever possible. She signed every check, reviewed in minute detail everything the Castle's managers did, and issued an endless stream of orders that, whatever their ostensible purpose, kept the staff on permanent high alert. She had special high-roller parties and, on one memorable occasion, led a conga line through the casino. Despite her lack of casino experience, she managed to surpass Trump Plaza in monthly revenues, enraging the casino veterans who were her counterparts there.

But with every success she had, her husband grew more alienated. He did not want to be reconnected to her; he wanted out. He had dispatched her to run the Castle because he did not want to be around her in New York, but now it was inconvenient to have her in Atlantic City. Because of his involvement with the Taj, he had to be in Atlantic City himself, and he wanted his mistress with him. Accordingly, and abruptly, he yanked his wife back to run the Plaza Hotel. The gesture might have passed as a reward, but he publicly belittled her by saying that he was paying her $1 a year and all the dresses she could buy. Once again there were hurt feelings, recriminations, and self-justifications; inevitably there was even more dodging.

Ivana kept trying. After her husband complained that she looked old and haggard, she had extensive plastic surgery and emerged looking at least a decade younger, but he seemed unmoved. He had refused to have sex with her for more than two years and complained that she was flat chested; after she made her entire body over, he recoiled from the sight of her implanted breasts. Nothing she could do, or say, or not do, or not say, was right.

The reason he had to pay more attention to Atlantic City was that the Resorts deal had hit a snag. To complete what would be his first takeover of a public company, he had needed Resorts' other outstanding shares.[14] But at a share price of 62, that would cost a lot. So Donald Trump had gotten to work. He had demanded a $1 billion management contract and settled for a still-huge $200 million to $300 million. He had declared that the construction of the Taj would cost hundreds of millions more than current estimates. He had spoken of the whole Resorts situation with uncharacteristic glumness. The share price went to 49 and then, after October 19, the stock market's Black Monday, to 33. Somehow word leaked that he was thinking about putting Resorts into bankruptcy. The share price sank to 22. At state hearings on his new management contract, the developer again painted a bleak picture of Resorts' prospects. The share price hit 13.

Disgruntled shareholders threatened to file suit, and by March 1988 the developer had agreed to settle at 22. As he sat in his Trump Tower office and glanced down at the St. Patrick's Day parade marching up Fifth Avenue, he got some bad news: The Resorts share price, which had been sinking for more than eight months, had turned around.

"What's going on?" he yelled.

The answer was talk-show host Merv Griffin. Flush from selling *Wheel of Fortune* and *Jeopardy* to Coca-Cola for $250 million in cash, the white-haired, ever affable entertainer had made a tender offer of 36 for all of Resorts' outstanding shares. In mid-April he flew to New York in his private plane and met with the developer at Trump Tower. Griffin knocked off a few jokes, then nodded in his best ego-stroking host style as Donald machine-gunned his ideas in rapid, impatient bursts. "I have all the cards," he declared repeatedly, then interrupted himself with his trademark, "You know what I mean?"

For the next month negotiators hammered away at deal points while trying to talk their respective principals out of what Griffin lawyer Tom Gallegher labeled "the deal from hell." Undaunted and unruffled, Griffin listened and smiled; the developer, alternately engaging and aggressive, raced ahead, jumping back and forth between general points and seemingly random details. "There was the good twin and the bad twin," Gallegher said. "In many ways [Donald was] a Jekyll and Hyde guy. He could be enormously charming and you'd almost think, gee, this is a nice, decent, warm guy, and then the bad twin would come out."

Finally the developer and the entertainer cut a deal. Donald Trump would buy the unfinished Taj for $273 million, less than half of what had already been spent on it, and he would also receive $63.7 million in "severance" for his management contract.[15] Merv Griffin would get the original Resorts casino hotel, the Bahama resort, and the Atlantic City real estate. Essentially each party got what he wanted, although Griffin also wound up with what he didn't want, Resorts' existing $600 million debt.

For months the press speculated about who came out ahead and by how much. It was hard to make a strong case for Griffin.[16] He had

immediately piled on another $325 million in junk bonds—a land-
mark of sorts, for it was Drexel Burnham Lambert's last Atlantic City
deal before a securities fraud indictment caused the firm's expulsion
from the New Jersey casino industry. In the months to come, he
would take Resorts in and out of bankruptcy twice.

Then again, Trump also miscalculated. He had assumed that he
could obtain another junk bond issue from Bear, Stearns, which had
stopped writing high-risk paper for Resorts only when, as the investment bank's famously aggressive head Ace Greenberg put it, Jim
Crosby "had the audacity to die on me." It had also provided the financing for Donald Trump's first two casino purchases and acted as
his broker during what many considered his greenmail forays. But the
developer wanted to make the property more highly leveraged than
even Bear, Stearns could handle. When he told Greenberg that Merrill
Lynch would peddle $675 million in bonds, almost twice Bear,
Stearns's top offer of $320 million, Greenberg told him to go ahead.
"The world was offering him deals we could not and would not compete with," Greenberg said afterward.

The developer's second misjudgment was what it would take to
get the Taj Mahal up and running. Under Crosby, its construction had
eaten cash and lurched along uncertainly for years. "We didn't even
have a plan," said Crosby's top aide. "You just [pointed and] said,
'Keep building that way.'" After Crosby died, the estate left the site
exposed to rain, wind, and salt air. In effect, Trump was taking on
Wollman Rink all over again, on a vastly larger scale; this time,
though, instead of paring the job down to the bare minimum, he expanded it. Carrara marble replaced less expensive materials, $250,000
crystal chandeliers from Austria bumped more pedestrian light fixtures, and areas that Resorts planned to leave undone became sumptuous hotel suites.[17]

With Marla, Ivana, the Taj, the yacht, the rail yards project, the
still unsold Trump Plaza of the Palm Beaches, and the Plaza Hotel to
deal with, a mere mortal might have paused. Instead Trump jumped
into yet another folly.[18] It was, in effect, a flying building—or, rather,
a fleet of flying buildings: twenty-one Boeing 727s, plus leases on facilities and landing slots at Washington's National Airport, New
York's LaGuardia Airport, and Boston's Logan Airport. These assets,
previously owned by the Eastern Shuttle, would now be the basis for

a new Trump Shuttle—and for extending the Trump franchise even further.

Indeed, airlines are a superb publicity vehicle. "Everybody is fascinated by planes and travel," said Goldman Sachs airline analyst Glen Ingalls. "There were no profits in the airline industry [then], but there was a glamour to it. You didn't know who ran Procter & Gamble, but you knew that Bob Crandall ran American Airlines." The problem was that airlines are also a poor business proposition for someone whose field is not aviation.

Ignoring Harry Freeman and Jerry Schrager's advice to pass on the deal, Trump set up a meeting with Bruce Nobles, the president-designate of the independent shuttle operation Eastern Airlines had been trying to spin off. Nobles, whose father starting working at American Airlines six months before he was born, had gone into the industry after college. He'd worked his way up to the presidency of the other northeast corridor shuttle, Pan Am, when he was hired to head up Eastern's new operation. But financial and labor pressure had put Eastern's plans on hold for so long that the airline was instead selling its shuttle-related assets to the developer for $365 million. At four o'clock on the afternoon of Wednesday, October 5, 1988, Trump, Freeman, and Nobles sat down together at Trump Tower.

"He asked me a lot of questions," said Nobles, "but he was most interested in how much cash flow the shuttle would throw off. I didn't know why at the time." Evidently his answers were satisfactory. "At five o'clock Donald offered me the presidency of the Trump Shuttle," Nobles said. "At six o'clock he said, 'You can't leave until you agree,' and at seven I said, 'All right.'" One week later the two appeared at a Plaza Hotel press conference to announce the developer's newest venture.

In the meantime, what at first looked like a tremendous stroke of good fortune would have an ultimately bad effect. That same month Donald Trump came across someone who outdid him for reckless behavior: Australian beer baron Alan Bond, who paid him $180 million for the St. Moritz.[19] To hear Trump tell the story, he had paid $31 million for the hotel in 1985 with the thought of turning it into condominiums at some point and thus made a profit of almost $150 million; in fact the property had cost $73.7 million, which meant a still hefty profit of $106.3 million. More important, the developer took the deal as proof that he had not lost his business touch and thus could continue with the string of deals that Freeman and Schrager kept vetoing.

Several court suits and one crippling labor strike later, the Trump Shuttle finally took off the following June. The developer launched an ad campaign and a $1 million-per-plane makeover to make the airline "a diamond, an absolute diamond." To Trump's chagrin, weight problems ruled out marble, and the need to push refreshment carts down the aisles deep-sixed the plush carpeting he preferred. Nonetheless he managed an elegant look, with bird's-eye maple veneer on the cabin walls, chrome seat belt latches instead of polished aluminum, and, in the lavatories, gold-plated fixtures and pink faux marble. "Donald was convinced that people would choose the Trump Shuttle because it was Trump and it was beautiful," Nobles said. "But the product was the product. People flew for pragmatic reasons."

Soon the new airline was close to splitting the market with the rival Pan Am Shuttle. A 50 percent share was all that the developer could reasonably expect; unfortunately he was counting on 60 percent to cover the stiff interest payments on the $380 million in loans he had used to buy and refurbish the planes. As with the Plaza Hotel, Citibank had provided the lion's share, $245 million, and Trump had to make a personal guarantee to cover the balance of $135 million. Nobles, who had never seen such high leveraging in airlines, mentioned his concern. "Don't worry," he was told. "We know what we're doing." Some Citibank lending officers also seemed uneasy, particularly those who handled airlines, but they weren't running the show. Instead the real estate side, where the developer was a big customer, had taken charge. They were used to high-risk clients who routinely put the highest possible leverage on their projects. The critical factor was having enough cash flow to cover interest payments, which is why Trump, Freeman, and, later, the banks, had grilled Nobles closely on this very point.

In November 1989, five months after the Trump Shuttle started flying, a recession hit the Northeast, and business travel contracted immediately. The shuttle market, which had been growing for thirty years, shrank. The next month it shrank again, just as fuel costs went up. Ordinarily the different entities within the Trump Organization upstreamed and downstreamed funds, transferring surplus cash back and forth to cover expenses. But with the recession there was no surplus. Because shuttle costs were fixed, Nobles had to ask the Trump Organization for funds to cover interest payments.

The request made Donald Trump most unhappy. "He wanted each operation to be independent, to live or die by itself," Nobles said. "He wanted everybody competing against each other and beating their brains out. He thought that was the best way to increase profits." Nobles had suggested possible economies of scale and synergies, such as combining information and reservations systems, but the man who had relied on creative competition in every aspect of his business was not interested. The closest the developer would come to letting different operations work together was to have the shuttle give passengers casino vouchers. But shuttle passengers were not casino customers, and of the tens of thousands of coupons that were distributed, few were redeemed. Meanwhile the airline's overhead remained untouched.

Belt-tightening and pulling back did not fit into the developer's strategy. He had come into the world an entrepreneur, and so he remained, always pushing to see if he could get more, thinking of what lay beyond not just the next corner but the one after that. Every deal had to be not just good, or even great, but unbelievable. Because of a labor strike before the deal with Eastern closed, the developer could have dropped the whole thing and taken home a $5 million breakup fee, but he refused. At another point the developer had a solid offer of $107 million for the Alexander's shares that had cost him $50 million. He said yes, then called Robert Campeau, the largest retailer in the United States and owner of Bloomingdale's, who was way over his head in debt but offered to pay $120 million. Instead Campeau filed the biggest retail bankruptcy in the nation's history, and Trump, who had let the first offer go, continued to pay interest on a money-losing investment.

By definition, entrepreneurs are deal makers. They look for markets, decide where there is money to be made, and make their move. Donald Trump had an elegant way of describing his relationship to deal-making; deals, he proclaimed, were his "art form." Others were more blunt: One former Trump executive called Trump "a deal junkie." Part classic entrepreneur, part artist, and part addict, Trump was constantly on the lookout for opportunities to expand. Thus, while still hashing out the shuttle purchase in the spring of 1989, he paid $1 million to get in on a third baseball league;[20] bought stock in American Airlines, Universal Pictures, and MCA, and again talked takeover; put more than $1 million into a pilot for *The Trump Card*, a television quiz show to be produced at Trump Castle;[21] and pledged $750,000 to the Tour de Trump, an eight-hundred-mile bicycle race scheduled to end in front of the Trump Plaza in Atlantic City.

Even in the field he presumably knew best—real estate development—he could not seem to say no. Thus, in Manhattan, where the real estate market was visibly tightening, he plunged ahead on Trump Palace, a large East Side condominium project, and rejected potential Japanese partners for the project. Reportedly, chief saleswoman Blanche Sprague initially came up with a sellout figure of $180 million, $40 million short of the $220 million estimated for construction costs. Supposedly Donald kept after her until she came up with a better-sounding $265 million, but she then refused to endorse the figures and wrote a letter to that effect to attorney Jerry Schrager.[22]

By now Donald had Marla, Ivana, the Taj, the yacht, the rail yards project, the Plaza Hotel, the Trump Shuttle, Trump Plaza of the Palm Beaches, and Trump Palace on his mind. Then, in the fall of 1989, three of his top casino executives died in a helicopter crash on their way back to Atlantic City after meeting with him in New York. Such a loss would have been tragic in the best of circumstances; in the Trump Organization, already stretched paper thin on the management side, it was a disaster from which the business would not recover for a long time.

It also seemed to have left the developer even more unhinged. For nearly two years he had been living a double life. Although there were near leaks, and the occasional not very veiled references in gossip columns, Marla's existence remained more or less secret from the outside world. But the arrangement was taking its toll, and the person who was most affected was the one who was ostensibly in charge: Donald himself. From the *Trump Princess* to the Trump Shuttle, each new purchase and every new venture seemed another, more large-scale version of a little boy asking to be caught. With each grandiose episode he seemed to be risking not just his own fortune but fate itself. He seemed almost begging to be found out and to be stopped, to have the whole huge edifice, built of thousands of lies, massive debts, adulterous behavior, and overcommitted resources, come tumbling down.

But it didn't. Instead he went on and on, finally topping every other outlandish deal so far by opening a casino that was unable to pay what it cost him to build it and would inevitably cause severe and possibly fatal damage to his other casinos.

Donald Trump was able to pull off a remarkable series of moves, but there was one thing he was unable to do: tell his wife it was over. "I have to confess, the way I handled the situation was a cop-out," he later wrote. "I never sat down calmly with Ivana to 'talk it out' as I probably should have." Nor was his wife able to face squarely the disintegrating situation in which she was living. Meanwhile Marla Maples was growing tired of being sequestered, of hiding in the back of the limo, of bringing her own escort to public events and standing across the room from her lover, of having a vacation with him mean traveling separately and staying at a different hotel.

During the Christmas holidays in 1989, Donald's jet brought his family out to a luxury Aspen hotel, Little Nell's, then on a separate trip fetched Marla, who bunked with a girlfriend at more modest quarters a few blocks away. On New Year's Eve Ivana confronted her rival out on the ski slopes and told her to leave Donald alone, giving her a slight shove for emphasis. "Are you happy?" Marla asked as the paparazzi immortalized what was arguably the most well-documented marital confrontation in human history. Soon rumors were flying, and a remarkable number of people in New York and Atlantic City were claiming to have known of the illicit relationship for some time.[23]

But Ivana had not, and the revelation was devastating.

Every unhappy marriage is unhappy in its own way. For Ivana Trump the problem was that although from the outside she appeared to have the perfect life, filled with material possessions and near regal splendor, within her own home she was not free to be a winner and a champion. For Donald Trump it was that he had made the mistake of marrying the wrong parent. Instead of choosing a mate like his mother, eager to play quiet backup to a towering success, he had selected someone more like his father, someone who was a born contender, who could not hold back and go second even if she tried. Worse, Ivana did not seem to grasp that the enormous opulence with which he had surrounded himself and his family was a marketing tool, larger than life and thus, as he saw it, not real life. The Trump Tower triplex, Mar-a-Lago, and the *Trump Princess* were stage sets, backdrops, places to be photographed in and used to create impressions and win points; they were not environments that anyone should consider normal.

Although Donald had long arranged his worldly affairs precisely so that he could live and work in this atmosphere of extraordinary and ultimate luxury, his own personality was all agenda, and his sole aim in most interactions was getting himself where he had to go. Frequently he needed people to help him, and in order to get that help he could be, literally, unbelievably charming; when he did not need anything, though, he often had little warmth to spare. He went to charity events because his name would sell tickets and being at the event sold him, but he did not seem to care much about either the charities or the social acceptance attached to them. What mattered to him was being accepted as a serious businessman, and he already knew that he could have lunch with Saul Steinberg or Henry Kravis or any of the other businessmen present whenever he wanted to. He insisted on leaving early, and he made it clear to Ivana and anyone else within hearing distance that he would much prefer being at home watching television, eating SpaghettiOs or a hamburger and French fries from the New York Delicatessen and drinking yet another diet soda.[24]

But Ivana believed in that lavish, glitzy, gilded image he had created. She loved being at Mar-a-Lago, enjoyed taking long cruises on the *Trump Princess*, relished being part of high society in New York. For Ivana the kingdom of Trump was real, a thing of flesh and blood. And in a way, she was right. As any reader of American newspapers and magazines could attest, although it may have begun as a marketing tool, by now there was, indeed, a Trump kingdom. Unfortunately, though, Ivana was not its queen. "Ivana was a very smart woman," said Blanche Sprague. "But we were working in a kingdom where there was really only room for a king. He would walk into a room of - people all in black tie, and suddenly there would be nobody there but Donald."

The developer did not want a queen; he wanted a concubine. He wanted to come home at night and relax. If there was talk about business, it should be talk about his most recent triumph, not questions about how something had been handled or discussions of problems. "Marla was subdued, not forceful like Donald," said Mai Hallingby, then wife of Bear, Stearns banker Paul Hallingby and a member of the same social set as the Trumps. "Donald would be the star of the group, and she would be a listener. She seemed very willing to take a backseat." Evidently she was also willing to continue a volatile relationship filled with spats, breakups, reconciliations, talk of marriage, and then more spats, many of them in full view of the public eye.

A month after the incident in Aspen, *Playboy* published an interview with the developer in which he refused to say whether or not his marriage was monogamous. Two weeks later Ivana made her move. She consulted a divorce lawyer, hired her own publicist, and, taking yet another leaf from her husband's book, called gossip columnist Liz Smith. More than a dozen years earlier, Jay Pritzker, off on a long-planned trip to Nepal, had been unavailable when Donald Trump had pushed through the noncompete clause for the Grand Hyatt; this time it was Donald who was unavailable for comment at a critical moment. When Ivana phoned the columnist, her husband was twenty thousand feet in the air, flying home from a trip he'd taken to Japan, supposedly to see Mike Tyson fight but which was in fact a desperate attempt to unload the Plaza Hotel. His own wife had scooped him. She had gotten a whole news spin cycle ahead, and he would never catch up. In the world's eyes she would be the victim, he would be the cad, and the man whose access to the press was the stuff of legend would be unable to do anything about it.

For months the nation's press roiled with he said/she said tales. Ivana demanded a larger share of the fortune her husband had once insisted was over $3 billion; the developer refused to pay any more than $10 million, the comparatively modest sum named in their most recent nuptial agreement, which had been renegotiated upward three times. Intent on capturing public sympathy and getting in the last

word, husband and wife threw selective tidbits to a voracious press;
meanwhile the mistress donned a red wig, assumed a false name, and
secreted herself in a series of hideouts that included, at one point, a
Peace Corps encampment deep inside Guatemala. Journalists dug
into her life, and the *National Enquirer* paid a reported $11,000 to her
high school and college sweethearts for the mostly banal details of
her earlier romances. Hundreds of reporters and photographers
followed the bread crumbs, producing forgettable prose but unforgettable headlines, including the memorable BEST SEX I EVER HAD, supposedly a remark made by Marla to a friend.

Donald was thrilled, his parents were distressed, and his executives were appalled. "Businesswomen won't fly your shuttle with you
on the front page of the paper every day [talking] about your sex life,"
Bruce Nobles told the developer. He replied, "Yeah, but the guys love
it." Perhaps, but that admiration did not translate into ticket sales.
The airline's market share continued to decline, possibly because passengers worried, like one respondent in a focus group, that someone
distracted in his personal life might not be paying enough attention to
airplane safety. The banks, too, were unhappy about the headlines.
They had been attracted by the image of a brilliant dealmaker, and
they were troubled by the idea of doing business with someone whose
personal life was in such visible disarray.

Marla's public debut as the developer's mistress was scheduled to
occur on the same day as the opening of the Taj, April 5, 1990. For
weeks beforehand, stories about her planned appearance and, especially, the different outfits she might wear filled the tabloid press. On
the big day, though, Donald's family prevailed, and he appeared alone.
The delay was brief; two weeks later Marla was on *Prime Time Live*
and spoke to interviewer Diane Sawyer about her relationship with
Donald Trump. The interview gave the show the best ratings it had
ever received.

In the end the Taj cost more than $1.1 billion, and Trump personally
guaranteed a loan for $75 million. To meet interest payments, he
would need daily revenues of $1.3 million. It was more than any At-

lantic City casino had made on a regular basis, and impossible unless he could figure out how to bring in stunning numbers of slots players and high rollers—that is, both mass and moneyed customers. His solution: a gaudy, glitzy, grandiose seaside palace carefully engineered to have the drawing power of Trump Tower. A surreal contrast to the original Taj Mahal, a serene and elegant Indian mausoleum, the New Jersey Taj would not be beautiful, peaceful, or even comfortable. But it would be, in its own way, a design triumph, a unique and unforgettable building that performed exactly as intended, attracting paying customers by the hundreds of thousands from around the country and the world.

At Trump Tower the owner's name shone over the entrance in out-of-scale block letters made of brass; at the Taj it blazed from the roof in giant block letters fashioned from bright red neon. In New York Trump had built a glass-sheathed tower precisely because it would contrast with its limestone neighbors; here he covered his new casino with candy-striped onion domes and miniature gold-topped minarets and put big stone elephants next to the entrances, creating a building that looked nothing like the big, boxy casinos next to it.

Inside the Taj he used the same floor-numbering magic as at the Grand Hyatt and Trump Tower, turning what was the forty-second and highest floor into the more dramatic-sounding fifty-first floor. In addition, he also offered a spectacle comparable to Trump Tower's waterfall: the noise and lights of 3,010 constantly clanging slot machines. Similarly, in much the way that Der Scutt had used rosy peach to set a tone of rich abundance for the Trump Tower atrium, the developer coated the Taj interior in bubble-gum pink, using it for overhead acoustic tiles, Oriental-style carpeting, hallways, even slot machines, to create a giddy, carnival-like atmosphere.

The record number of slot machines would pull in low-stakes players; to draw the high-stakes crowd, the Taj offered 160 table games, also a record number, plus special high-roller amenities. Overlooking the baccarat pit, a particular favorite for many wealthy customers, a lavish, pink-chandeliered restaurant called Scheherazade eschewed menus, instead keeping records of guests' preferences and serving them with gold-plated tableware. Upstairs were luxury guest suites, Lucullan penthouse accommodations named after Cleopatra, Napoleon, and other historical figures. The most opulent was the

4,500-square-foot Alexander the Great Suite, listed at $10,000 per night and boasting its own steamroom, sauna, weight room, and white baby grand piano. There was one problem: Guests lolling in the marble Jacuzzi would look out on a particularly squalid neighborhood. Architect Francis Xavier Dumont apologized profusely during one tour. "Unfortunately," he said, "we overlook Atlantic City."

The developer called the Taj the Eighth Wonder of the World; it had to be if he was to recoup his investment and, somehow, avoid cannibalizing his other casinos. But to Philadelphia casino analyst Marvin B. Roffman, the Eighth Wonder of the World was compound interest, not a mammoth facility opening in a shrinking market. An investment analyst for nearly thirty years, Roffman, then fifty, was well respected. Before he and Donald Trump had ever met, the developer called and said, "I just want to let you know I read your reports and I think you're right on the money and one of the best guys on the street."

Unlike many in his field, Roffman was a guy who did his homework not once but twice. "I almost have a curse," he said. "It's this terrible thing where before I do or say anything I have to do my research, almost to the point of nuttiness." When the balding, gregarious Roffman, a faithful reader of Consumer Reports, wanted to buy a car, he would test-drive dozens; when he needed a new coat, he went to ten stores and tried on every style; and when he wrote up a casino, he scrutinized the numbers. After Roffman issued a negative report on the Taj in an industry publication, the developer invited him to come and see for himself. "I'll have my brother take you on a personal tour," he said, "and you'll be so excited that at the end, I want you to pick up any phone in the lobby and tell me how thrilled you are."

Roffman made an appointment with Robert Trump for March 20, 1990. The same day a Wall Street Journal article quoted him as saying that although the Taj would do well in summer months, "once the cold winds blow from October to February, it won't make it. The market just isn't there." When Roffman showed up at the Taj, Robert Trump met him at the door and ordered him off the property. "You're no fucking good," Robert yelled, and then accused him of having stabbed Taj bondholders in the back. After Donald Trump threatened to sue and the analyst refused to apologize, the brokerage house where he had worked for sixteen unblemished years fired him. "Marv Roffman is a man of little talent who disagrees with other people," Donald told a reporter.[25]

Two weeks later, on April 5, the Taj had its opening night. The weather was chilly, and despite claims that there would be celebrities by the yard, only a handful of lesser lights showed up. After a brief walk-through earlier in the day, Governor Jim Florio had departed. The highest-ranking public official to mount the small outdoor stage set up for the evening festivities was the current mayor, then under indictment on corruption charges. He drew a solid round of boos. Then a cheerful Merv Griffin congratulated the developer and joked that he had once owned the Taj for twenty-four hours. Finally Donald Trump, wearing a wide, bright red tie, touched a large Aladdin-style magic lamp, and an enormous televised genie appeared, followed by green lasers and pink-and-purple fireworks.

As Roffman had predicted, the crowds were huge—too huge for the Taj's slot operation, which was unable to keep track of its cash and had to shut down. The same thing had happened at the opening of the developer's first casino, and he had the same reaction, which was to launch a vicious attack on everyone in sight. When he turned on his brother, Robert quit and went home to manage the real estate their father had built. Soon the slots were up and running, but the developer kept the heat on his executives, demoting, reassigning, and in some cases firing them summarily.

But rage, redeploy, and retrench as he might, he could not prevent the coming disaster. Contractors who worked on the Taj filed complaints for nonpayment, and tales of cash flow shortages began to circulate. Workmen removed the Trump name from Castle slot machines, a sign that a sale might be impending. In late April an enterprising young *Wall Street Journal* reporter named Neil Barsky came to Trump Tower for an interview. Barsky, who had written the earlier *Journal* piece quoting Roffman, found the developer sitting at his desk with the reporter's clips spread out before him. Trump greeted him by turning on a tape recorder and saying that he had three sworn affidavits from sources stating that Barsky was spreading rumors of a cash flow problem.

"He also said he'd retained [prominent libel lawyer] Martin Garbus and he'd sue my ass if I mentioned a negative cash flow," Barsky recalled later. "Then the interview began." Barsky had a lot of information, but he did not know that the developer was considering selling, refinancing, or securitizing every asset. In particular, the reporter did not know that the shuttle was on the block. But the developer thought he did, and when Barsky bluffed, asking for confirmation of the potential sale, Trump provided it.

"I really just played poker with him," the reporter said. "I won."[26]

It was a major scoop for Barsky, whose subsequent *Journal* story quoted Trump as saying that he wanted to be "king of cash" so that he could scoop up bargains later. To the financial community, the article was a red-light alert, and the market for Trump casino bonds took a nosedive. A year earlier *Forbes* had ranked the developer's wealth at $1.7 billion, making him one of the country's twenty richest people; now the magazine ran a cover story that estimated his net worth at $500 million.[27] When the numbers from the Taj's first month came in, there was more bad news: although the casino had taken in huge revenues, they had been less than break-even. Worse, the Taj had cut into revenues at Trump Castle and Trump Plaza. The Taj and the shuttle started laying off workers, shuttle passengers found themselves paying for coffee and newspapers, and Trump shut down the small development office he had in Las Vegas. The board game named for him showed up on the remainder shelf in toy departments, and Turner Broadcasting tabled the biographical film it had planned.

On Monday, June 4, 1990, Neil Barsky had another scoop. It was entitled "Shaky Empire," and it was the lead story on the *Journal*'s front page. Less than two months after the Taj had opened, Barsky reported, Trump was desperately struggling for his financial life. His attempts to sell or refinance the pieces of his empire had failed, and he was now holding secret meetings with representatives of Citicorp, Bankers Trust, Chase Manhattan, and Manufacturers Hanover in the conference room at Trump Tower. Dozens of bankers and lawyers pored over numbers that included a staggering $2 billion in bank debt. Perhaps even more stunning, the developer had personal liability on guarantees and unsecured loans amounting to $800 million,[28] as well as more than $1 billion in junk bonds on his casinos.

In less than a decade Donald Trump had become the Brazil of

Manhattan. His annual interest payments, said to be around $350 million or almost $1 million a day, exceeded his cash flow. Worse, only two of his assets, his half of the Grand Hyatt and the retail component of Trump Tower, stood a prayer of making a net profit. "He will have to trim the fat," said one banker, and spoke darkly of selling off the yacht and the mansions and requiring the developer to operate in a more conservative fashion.

It was not, of course, the first time that the Trump family had encountered the shadow of bankruptcy. Back in 1934 the fall of the house of Lehrenkrauss had been the catalyst for the rise of Fred Trump. Forty years later the bankruptcy of the Penn Central Railroad had created the conditions for Donald Trump's entrance into Manhattan real estate. Each time enormous sums of money were involved; each time there were long and intricate negotiations over which creditor would get how much and what would happen with the carcass. Now, though, there was no Trump outsider trying to elbow his way to the table; instead a Trump owned the table, the room, and the debt. Just as Lehrenkrauss had been caught short, and then Penn Central, now the party who could not meet his obligations was a Trump. The debt under discussion was Trump debt, and the assets being picked at by others were Trump assets. The family that had made its fortune taking the offensive was, for the first time, on the defensive, and Donald Trump was fighting to save his own financial skin.

He had gotten into this situation by convincing major banks and other financial institutions that his name made any asset worth more and that they could therefore ignore their usual lending guidelines and demands for collateral. In the late 1980s, when the real estate market was so hot that it seemed to be almost smoking, he could have sold or refinanced assets with relative ease and kept his own financial house in order; now, though, the market was contracting, and banks that until recently had been riding high were now having to scramble to keep their own operations going. Government bank examiners reportedly visited Chase Manhattan, and there was talk of mergers between banks that were beginning to choke on bad real estate loans.[29]

The events unfolding now were the many times removed consequences of events long past. Back when Fred Trump was building with the help of government programs, the division of spoils between banks and savings and loans was a relatively simple matter. Both charged the same interest rates, in the low to middle single digits; however, banks took the most profitable area, real estate and commercial lending, whereas what were known as S&Ls, then a backwater within the financial industry, handled home mortgages and passbook savings accounts. Financial wags joked that the S&L industry ran on the 3-6-3 rule: pay 3 percent on savings, charge 6 percent on loans, and close up shop every day at 3 in the afternoon so as to get in a round of golf before dark. During the 1970s interest rates crept up little by little, but by the end of the decade, in part because of the cost of the Vietnam War, rates started going up more rapidly. Banks, free to charge whatever interest rates the market would bear, were able to get more for their loans; S&Ls, saddled by law with fixed interest rates, were not and found themselves squeezed almost out of the running.

But not quite. During the early years of the Reagan era, large-scale deregulation of the financial industry allowed S&Ls to raise rates and invade traditional bank turf. Stripped of their customary prerogatives, banks then had to cast about for new sources of revenue. They needed to make their money work harder and began to increase their loans and, in turn, their percentage-based fees. Rather than waiting for borrowers to come to them, they went out looking. Competition among banks heated up, and leveraging that would have been unthinkable in the past now became doable. Major banks loaned out not just what was required for a project, but more—in the case of Donald Trump, much more. Then they skimmed off their fees and syndicated—that is, sold off—pieces of loans to other institutions even more hungry for loans and willing to accept a smaller profit.

Such fee-driven practices had allowed real estate departments to report impressive earnings and become dominant forces within their respective institutions—and nowhere more so than in the four banks whose top real estate lending officers were now huddled on the twenty-sixth floor of Trump Tower. They had lined up to lend the developer huge sums, taken most of the fees, and then syndicated the loans to scores of domestic and foreign banks so eager to get in on the action that they accepted deals on which they made far less. In fact, the readiness of other banks, particularly in Japan, to buy Trump loans was the very proof that the name did indeed bestow value on a deal, and in turn led Citibank, among other financial institutions, to "adjust their own risk/reward ratio," as one official described the bank's willingness to take on a level of exposure it would otherwise have shunned.

In the process, the New York banks had put their own assets at what afterward seemed unconscionable risk. But they did something more: in their rush to loan to Trump, they had created what might be called a faux moral hazard. In classical economics the term *moral hazard* refers to a situation in which a third party is encouraged to undertake risky behavior and is guaranteed against any loss. In the case of Trump, however, the banks merely encouraged the dangerous activity; they did not insure him against loss. What they did not realize was that, in a sense, he insured himself by making himself such a big part of the deals that the financing institutions would have to keep him going simply to cut their own losses.

Although the big four had taken the lead on most of the developer's bank debt and were initiating efforts to figure out a settlement, nearly ninety financial institutions would be party to the bailout, and about one thousand bankers, lawyers, and accountants would participate in the marathon negotiations. Bankers from New York, Florida, New Jersey, Illinois, and California would have to sign off; so would their colleagues from Japan, Ireland, Brazil, Italy, South Korea, and France. It was a daunting challenge, for the sums at stake, the amounts of collateral behind loans, and individual lending practices all varied widely. But without each party's approval, Donald Trump stood to lose everything.

As the weeks went by, Trump missed a $43 million interest payment on Trump Castle bonds and a $30 million loan payment to Manufacturers Hanover. The Ohio-based maker of the Taj's onion domes and elephants threatened to remove them unless he received payment. Also citing unpaid bills, Honeywell pulled its computer engineers off the job, leaving the casino's air-conditioning system limping.[30] Bank negotiations, now being held at the separate offices of the lead institutions, went round the clock, and exasperated loan officers tried to coax, then coerce, recalcitrant minority lenders to go along with the plan gradually taking shape. That plan arose from the fact that despite certain similarities between the present set of circumstances and those facing Lehrenkrauss and the Penn Central, there was one overwhelming difference. In those cases the debtor was done for, and the only real issue was how to handle the bankruptcy. This time, though, the debtor was far from finished.

Elsewhere Trump had exhibited a certain strain. He had hovered anxiously when a Japanese high roller who had already won at one of his casinos showed up again; he had been so abusive to employees that, according to one casino regulator, "People are hiding under their desks"; and he was gobbling up the candy and popcorn of his youth at an alarming rate. At the bank workout sessions, though, he was positive thinking personified, upbeat and clear-eyed. When he strode into the room, he radiated that indefinable but palpable glow that sets the famous apart from the crowd. Heads swiveled and eyes opened wide to take in his passage across the room, the nod here and the hello there. The only reason anyone was there was that this man was over his head by an amount that would keep any of a handful of small countries humming for a year, yet everyone in the room still seemed to be a fan.

They had loaned him more than they should have because he was a star; now, when he was on the ropes, he was still a star. It was true outside the meeting room, where reporters and television crews were on perpetual stakeout; when one banker called home to tell his wife that the day's meeting was extended and he wouldn't be home to dinner, she said she'd heard it on the news and then told him what had happened in the supposedly closed-door session that had just finished.[31] And it was also true inside the room, where the developer, coming face-to-face with dozens of people to whom he owed hundreds of millions of dollars, seemed, of all things, to be enjoying himself.

Bizarrely, this may have been the best thing that could have happened to Trump. With a gun at his head, he finally started paying attention. The skillful Donald of old crawled out from under all the wreckage he had made of his life and his business and, once again, found the critical leverage points. His debts were so big that everyone in the room was afraid to see him fall; in addition, they didn't want to admit they had been suckers. He had debtor's leverage, and he played it to the hilt.

When he said the usual pleasantries, the good-to-see-yous and the glad-to-be-heres, he meant them; when he sat down with the bankers and lawyers, he was a model of decorum. He did not slink in late or slouch in his chair or seem distracted; instead, displaying the same courteousness and straightforward manner he had shown at every regulatory hearing in New Jersey, he was respectful, attentive, and visibly professional. He had always been the most important asset, the factor that gave the properties their value by imbuing them with "quality"; now, to their great relief, these financial institutions could see for themselves that he gave every appearance of still being at the top of his game. "He didn't go around ranting and raving and picking the wrong fights with the wrong people," said the head of one Japanese bank's real estate department. "He acted as a businessman."[32]

No one had wished to resuscitate Julius Lehrenkrauss or the Penn Central's Stuart Saunders, but everyone in these negotiations wanted Donald Trump to keep going. In a period in which the real estate market was turning soft, they had little desire to take over major properties and even less desire to become involved in casinos, which being in a regulated industry would require bank personnel to go through the onerous licensing process. Perhaps most of all, though, they did not want to admit that they had been seduced by parties on the *Princess* and lavish receptions at the Plaza Hotel and that the special "quality" that had attracted them was not the same thing as solid, bricks-and-mortar collateral.

Instead they hung on to their belief that eventually the real estate market would recover, and with it the value of things named after the developer. During the negotiations, banks occasionally used the threat of a bankruptcy filing against one another, and the developer himself raised the specter to win a point. But even the most balky parties had no real interest in seeing the problem put in bankruptcy court, which would cost them a fortune in legal fees, expose them to further embarrassment, and severely limit their control over the outcome. Worse, because such a process would take years, it would almost certainly devalue the Trump name and the market price of his properties.

More than a month after they first sat down, the banks finally came to an agreement. Donald Trump would receive an immediate loan of $20 million and a five-year, $65 million bailout. They would lower interest rates, and they would suspend interest on nearly half of his bank debt, although he would have to keep paying the interest on his mortgages and his junk bonds. In addition, he would have to appoint a chief financial officer (CFO), and he would have to live on a budget. Although CFOs were a standard feature in most corporations of any size, and his monthly allowance of $450,000 hardly qualified as draconian, these measures represented a fundamental change for the developer. It was the first time in his adult life that anyone had imposed even the appearance of limitations on how he handled his business and his life.

More important, although Donald Trump remained more than $3 billion in debt, had lost certain freedom, and had suffered significant damage to his superman reputation, he did not have to surrender ownership of any assets. If the market turned around, he could end up paying less for them than if he were not in a financial crisis and still benefit from any increase in value. As he saw the situation, he had emerged "greatly enhanced" by the agreement. "There was a media stampede," he said dismissively. Ignoring the fact that he had survived precisely because of his remarkable ability to make whatever he did the center of public attention, he focused on another, more upbeat message: "When you come through adversity, I think people respect that."

CHAPTER TWENTY-ONE

PULLING BACK FROM THE BRINK

On Wednesday, August 15, 1990, the Casino Control Commission posted its statistics for July, traditionally the best month of the year. The numbers showed an ominous slowdown. The problem was twofold: on the one hand, total July revenues had dropped from a year earlier; on the other, with the opening of the Taj, Atlantic City had actually increased its casino floor space by 14 percent. As a result, nine out of Atlantic City's twelve casinos had posted losses. Trump Plaza revenues were down 24 percent, those at Trump Castle were off by 30 percent, and the Taj, then in its third month of existence, had failed to break even.

The same day, over Donald Trump's vigorous protests, the appellate division of state superior court had permitted the release of documents relating to the $65 million bailout extended by the banks as well as personal financial information. Among the most damaging revelations: the embarrassing specifics of exactly how much each bank had lent him, plus a survey of his assets, prepared by his own accountants, showing a negative net worth of nearly $300 million.

Two days later Trump stood in the lobby of commission headquarters in Lawrenceville, New Jersey, a suburb of Trenton, the state capital.[1] The commission was in the second day of hearings on the banks' rescue effort, after which it would vote on whether to consider him financially stable. Because a negative vote would mean the automatic loss of his casino license, the hearings were a matter of some urgency to the developer. Indeed, the man who had learned positive thinking at his father's knee and had taken it to unimagined heights seemed uncharacteristically subdued. The entire previous day he had sat on a metal folding chair and whispered to his advisers as a stream of witnesses described his financial woes. Ordinarily an immaculate dresser, this morning Donald had on the same suit, dark with white pinstripes, that he had worn the day before, and both he and it were showing signs of wear.

Still, as he spoke to reporters and television crews, he did his best to rally. The reason for his economic difficulties, he announced, had little to do with anything he'd done. Instead the causes included the invasion of Kuwait by "that madman" Saddam Hussein and the major recession—practically a depression—that was gripping the entire country. "It's a great time to buy," he said. "Of course, anyone just starting out couldn't get what I already have."

Warming to the topic, he insisted that his situation was not all that bad. "Overall, we're in really good shape," he declared firmly. The shuttle was "doing really well," and even though the Taj did "cannibalize" his other casinos, it was a surmountable problem. "If one of these properties goes into a Chapter 11 [bankruptcy filing]," he said, "it doesn't lead to Trump. Individual events don't affect Trump, the overall Trump."

As half a dozen flashes went off, he walked into a large, beige meeting room and sat near the front of the chamber. Arranged around him were his advisers, lawyers, and bodyguards. Out in the lobby, journalists waited to see who else would attend the hearings. "Donald's lost weight!" one reporter said in a tone of mock alarm. "He looks really whipped." In a joking reference to the reclusive billionaire Howard Hughes, a second said, "I heard Donald's let his fingernails grow." In fact, as they both knew, the developer did not look gaunt, and his nails were neatly trimmed. But they were not talking about how he actually looked; instead they were enjoying spinning the man who had spun them so often, the man for whom everything might, at long last, be all over.

It was a far cry from the situation three years earlier, when *The Art of the Deal* seemed to seal Donald Trump's reputation as the master business strategist of the era. Soon afterward he had contracted to write a second installment, this time "with" a senior *Newsweek* writer named Charles Leerhsen. Two months earlier, in June, booksellers had flocked to hear the developer at their annual conference in Las Vegas. Now that the new book was in bookstores, however, the title, *Surviving at the Top*, seemed a fantasy to most observers.

At the moment, the real question seemed to be who, exactly, would pull the plug and when. So far some ninety banks had demurred and instead brought out every kind of Band-Aid, glue, tape, and sealing wax they could find. Whether the Casino Control Commission would do the same remained to be seen. The official watchdog of New Jersey's casino industry, it had been created to oversee the legal and financial status of licensed casinos. Although the territory under its scrutiny consisted of a narrow strip of the Atlantic City Boardwalk and a small section of the marina, the commission maintained only a small office in the field and had its main base of operations in a two-story office building some eighty miles to the northwest, in Lawrenceville, an arrangement that forced the commissioners and their staffs to spend much of their time in transit.

More problematic than the physical remove, however, was the inherent conflict of interest in having this body sit in judgment over someone upon whom the economic well-being of Atlantic City depended. If the commission decided that the bailout was not a step toward financial recovery, it would have to find Donald Trump financially unstable and appoint a conservator to run his casinos. Because the developer controlled 30 percent of Atlantic City's casino business, such a step could create economic panic in the town; worse, it could shut off the flow of investment capital necessary for Atlantic City's casinos to remain competitive in an increasingly crowded field. But to overlook Trump's current financial crisis also seemed unpalatable, for it would mean flying in the face of mounting evidence, including a scathing 115-page report from the New Jersey Division of Gaming Enforcement, that confirmed the dire financial picture given by Trump's accountants.

All of which meant that the Casino Control Commission found itself caught in an apparently unavoidable and awkward dilemma. Its very reason for being was to safeguard the legal and financial integrity of casinos, yet to take action in this instance could set off enormous turmoil and possibly destroy the $3 billion industry it was supposed to protect. No one explicitly mentioned this problem during the hearings; there was no need to do so.

In the Lawrenceville hearing room, the mood was skeptical. Indeed, only two people there seemed entirely confident that Donald Trump would surmount his current financial crisis. One was the developer himself, and the other was a man whom he had grudgingly hired the day before the hearings began. As part of their rescue package, the banks had insisted that he take on a chief financial officer. To the banks it was a routine step in straightening out tangled financial affairs; to Trump it meant breaking the habits of a lifetime. For the first time he would not be able simply to embrace his version of reality. Instead someone else would be looking at his deals from the inside, would know what was real and what was embellishment, would see where the facts left off and what Donald called "truthful hyperbole" began.

Still insisting that he would be "the top guy," he had finally bitten the bullet and offered the CFO post to Steve Bollenbach, a financial wizard with a reputation for being able to take care of even the trickiest situations.[2] Equally important for Donald Trump, whose constant hype had eroded his believability, the financial community regarded Bollenbach as forthright and honest, the straightest of shooters. A gentle, soft-spoken man with gray hair, a neatly trimmed beard, and dimples, he had orchestrated the Holiday response four years earlier, when Trump had made takeover noises. "My first day of work at Holiday was when Donald announced that he had bought 5 percent of the company and was planning to clean out its stupid management," Bollenbach said. "I thought, Some welcome!" Forced into defensively restructuring the company by taking on a massive amount of debt, Bollenbach had come to detest the name *Trump*.

Nonetheless, when the developer offered him the job of reorganizing his financial affairs for a salary estimated to be at least half a million dollars, Bollenbach jumped at it. As he later explained, he saw this as an opportunity to make his mark in the ever-growing industry of high-profile "financial workouts"—business-world jargon for figuring out how to make do when a company owes more than it can pay. "This is just like the Super Bowl," he told *The Wall Street Journal*.

His first challenge was to persuade the five members of the

Casino Control Commission to overlook their deep misgivings and allow the bank bailout to proceed. He brought to the task an easy, genial manner. More important, he also brought the credibility he had earned during lengthy commission hearings on the Holiday restructuring.

Yes, he told the commissioners, he was familiar with Donald Trump's situation: he had spoken with Bankers Trust and Citibank.

Yes, he understood big numbers: he had handled the $2.8 billion recapitalization for Holiday.

Yes, he knew from visionaries and huge losses: he had been with Daniel Ludwig when the legendary industrialist had tried—and failed—to carve out a billion-dollar timber empire in the Amazon River basin.

Although Bollenbach had just started working for Donald Trump and didn't know the detailed financials, he assured the commission of the Trump Organization's viability. "With good hard work, the business can be turned around," he said firmly. "I don't think of that as dire straits, but maybe some people do." Again and again he struck his central theme: Donald Trump's major assets—the casinos, the shuttle, the Plaza Hotel, half of the Grand Hyatt, the commercial part of Trump Tower—were sound and simply required consolidation, reorganization, and refinancing.

Evidently this soothing messenger and his calming words were what the regulators had been waiting for. Perhaps even more than the banks, they dreaded shutting down the developer. Intent on keeping casinos free of the Mob, these officials had left the door open to Wall Street, and they now faced debt loads large enough to sink Atlantic City. The previous month the casino industry in New Jersey had its second lowest quarterly profits, mainly because of debt. Caught in an impossible bind, the Division of Gaming Enforcement gave what it termed a "reluctant" endorsement of the bailout but slapped on additional conditions. Sounding equally doleful, the Casino Control Commission met at its Atlantic City office four days after the hearing and voted in favor. "There are no good answers for Mr. Trump or New Jersey," said acting commission chair Valerie Armstrong.

Apparently Donald Trump thought otherwise. This time, dressed in a fresh dark suit, he smiled and called the vote "a great success." Afterward he stood outside and chatted with *Wall Street Journal* reporter Neil Barsky. "It's all going to work out," Trump said grandly.

As he spoke he eyed a buxom young blonde woman in cutoff jeans who was strolling along the Boardwalk. She walked over to a souvenir stand, then walked back. Finally he called out, "Hello!" Apparently assuming that she recognized him, Donald did not introduce himself but did introduce Barsky. "He's an important reporter," the developer said.

She seemed unimpressed, but the developer pressed on. "Hey, you look great—have you been working out?" Next to the curb, his driver and his limousine waited. For once, the man who had been in a rush for two decades seemed to have all the time in the world.

In reality, though, Donald Trump had no time. For the moment, he had taken care of the banks and the Casino Control Commission; now he would have to contend with casino bondholders, who were growing increasingly impatient. The day before the commission okayed the bank bailout, institutional investors holding about half the junk bonds sold to finance the Taj had retained Rothschild, Inc., as their adviser. As everyone in the financial community knew, this meant Wilbur Ross, who had served as adviser for Resorts investors when Merv Griffin took Atlantic City's first casino into bankruptcy the previous fall. A Harvard-trained analyst, Ross, then in his mid-fifties, had made a career out of representing the actual owners of public companies—that is, holders of stocks and bonds. Protecting their interests often meant reviving the companies; he sometimes referred to his work as running "a corporate emergency room [where] when a company gets in trouble, we either fix it and reorganize it, or let it die."

Acting as corporate doctor, he put debtors on the examining table, checked their vital signs to see if there was hope, then figured out how to get them the working capital they needed to keep going and repay their owners' investment. In the case of Donald Trump, the first step in coming up with a treatment plan was a field trip to Atlantic City. Accordingly, Ross paid a visit, flying down with the developer in his helicopter. After they landed on a helipad next to the Boardwalk and Ross saw the crowds surge forward to greet Trump, the adviser quickly came to the same conclusion as that reached by the banks: It made no sense to try to take the Trump name off the Taj.

The trick would be getting angry bondholders to agree with this diagnosis—not an easy task. As was usual in such cases, bondholders and company began far apart. What was not usual was Trump's involvement in the negotiations, which focused an enormous spotlight on every move. The media, with its appetite for conflict, played up even the slightest difference of opinion. In turn, because people dislike changing positions they have taken publicly, it was hard to get those involved to be flexible once they had enunciated a stand. "It complicated my life," Ross said of the media barrage. "But it also helped in a strange way—what better proof [of Trump's drawing power] than the fact that he was all over the papers every day!"

Similarly, Trump's own advisers found both problems and advantages in representing someone so accustomed to overstatement.[3] "He was used to being impressive and exaggerating and blowing everything up," said Ken Moelis, an investment banker at Donaldson, Lufkin & Jenrette who had worked on the Holiday reorganization and had been recruited by Bollenbach to help dig out their former opponent. "Steve had a hard time convincing Donald that this time it was advantageous not to exaggerate," Moelis said. "We kept saying, 'Look, this isn't about getting new money. It's about restructuring loans, about not having to give it all back.'" But much as Trump's habit of inflating numbers sometimes caused problems, at other times his characteristic bombast let his bankers seem reasonable by comparison. Likewise Trump's negotiating style, which included grandiloquence, convenient slips of memory, and liberal doses of flattery, could be embarrassing to his advisers, but it also allowed them to keep renegotiating until the end.

A further complication was the appearance of TWA chairman Carl Icahn, a predatory entrepreneur who made a habit of buying up the stock of distressed companies. Over recent months Icahn had scooped up a reported 22 percent of outstanding Taj junk bonds, said to be worth $100 million, which made him the biggest single bondholder and a major player in the negotiations. Because Icahn insisted on meeting on his own turf, the man who was used to having the world come to the twenty-sixth floor of Trump Tower had to get into a limousine and drive forty miles to the low-rise office building in

suburban Westchester County that served as TWA corporate offices.
"Driving up there, Donald was crazed," Moelis said. "He had to go
see Icahn to try to get his own company back, and he doesn't like to
be in that position."

Then, too, there was Donald's personal style. A man of enormous
self-confidence, he was both extraordinarily astute and oddly adolescent. As his world teetered close to collapse, he reacted with a combination of petulance, denial, and furious intensity. Sometimes he
would focus with such laserlike attention that he seemed about to
burn a hole right through his interlocutor; at other times he simply
ignored all advice and insisted that any strategy be designed around
his own opinions. He would sit at his big rosewood desk hour after
hour; then, with no warning, he would disappear upstairs to the
three-bedroom Trump Tower apartment where he now lived. Lying
on his big bed, he would snack on junk food and watch television
with Marla, leaving those in the office to fend off calls and muddle
through the day's inevitable crises. On still other occasions, sometimes in the middle of the night, he might be seized with energy. Regardless of the hour, he would then call his financial advisers and
launch into a lengthy monologue.

In the early days of his relationship with Marla, he had wanted relief from Ivana and her alternating moods of fierce competition and
desperate subservience. Now, though, Marla seemed his only refuge
from a world spinning out of control. In the middle of conversations
he would pull out her picture and rhapsodize about her physical en-
dowments. Sometimes he would interrupt meetings in his conference
room and put on a videotape of her for everyone to watch. "There
she'd be in a bathing suit, jiggling around," said one participant, "and
he'd be making all these comments about 'nice tits, no brains.' "

Part of the problem was that he had lost his reality check. For
years he had raced ahead at top speed, exploring potential options and
arranging possible deals, knowing that he could afford to do so because the members of his inner circle would act as brakes. Now,
though, most of that inner circle had either left or was in the process
of leaving. In part this was a simple budgetary move, for Trump no
longer had the money to pay them and was scrambling even to cover
Bollenbach's paycheck. But there was another reason: The developer -
could not stand being around eyewitnesses, people who had seen him

create his current crisis and who had every right to say "I told you so." He could not acknowledge his refusal to heed their warnings or accept responsibility for the problems that had resulted from his actions.

For years he had needed these men and women for their skill and judgment; now he needed them as scapegoats. Blanche Sprague, Tony Gliedman, Howard Rubenstein, Harvey Freeman, Jerry Schrager, Jeff Walker, other top employees and casino executives—one by one he had fired them, pushed them out, refused to pay their bills. "He has burned an immense number of bridges in the last six to eight months," one former adviser said at the time. "It's come to be Donald against the world." True to form, however, he refused to acknowledge that the staff departures were linked to his financial problems and at one point threatened the *New York Post* with a $250 million lawsuit for suggesting such a possibility.[4]

Unlike the bank bailout, the settlement he eventually reached with the Taj bondholders and, later, Castle and Plaza bondholders involved filing for bankruptcy. But in the years since Lehrenkrauss and Penn Central had done the same, bankruptcy lawyers and judges had refined this step almost beyond recognition. The developer would be using a "prepackaged" bankruptcy, a legal maneuver that had recently evolved to take care of the technical requirement that all bondholders agree to any settlement. When Lehrenkrauss and Penn Central had declared bankruptcy, they had surrendered everything to the courts; when Donald Trump did so, it would be to maintain his control. He would not have to turn over the asset in question to a bankruptcy judge, and the entire procedure would take only a few months.

Bondholders did have a victory of sorts. As was inevitable in such cases, they had to accept an extension of the maturity date on their bonds and a reduction in their interest rate from 14 to 12 percent, which was still more than the casino might be able to pay. In exchange, however, they now owned half the casino. But in almost - every other respect it seemed that Trump came out ahead. He would chair the board of the legal entity that owned the Taj, he would retain actual ownership of half the casino, and he would be able to recoup up to 80 percent ownership if he met certain performance goals. In addition, he would receive an annual management fee of at least

$500,000, which, as the *Journal*'s Barsky tartly observed, was probably more than he was making from any of his other assets.[5]

It was an early use of such a prepackage, a device that would soon become commonplace. But this was only one of the many ways that losing money had changed over the course of the twentieth century. At its opening, bankruptcy had been a black hole from which few of those touched by it were able to emerge. Indeed, when Lehrenkrauss and Penn Central went under, the creditors were so fearful of seeing vast assets swallowed up the way the Jarndyce fortune disappeared in the Charles Dickens chronicle *Bleak House* that they cooperated on allocating the spoils. Now, though, Donald Trump himself was such a large part of the assets that in order to keep up their value, his creditors had to keep him going.

—⁓—

Donald Trump had won this one. He had gotten his creditors on his side, and they would not let him go under. What for others might have been an even harder struggle—keeping himself going—did not seem to be a problem. Whenever he talked to the press, he said the same thing: He had not lost a night's sleep; things would work out; two years from now he would be worth more than ever. "He never saw this as a game winding up," Steve Bollenbach said later. "From his point of view, he was simply sorting out the credit overloaned to him. The fact that the debt was much larger than the assets were worth was just another business problem, and he was taking a rational approach. He was correct, but that's not the way most people think about it."

Even when he had to auction off an asset, Trump broadcast an upbeat mood. Not long after he acquired Mar-a-Lago, he had ignored Jerry Schrager's protests and paid $41 million for a nearby condominium complex whose bankrupt builder owed Marine Midland $94 million. After announcing a major overhaul, Donald had began advertising what was now called Trump Plaza of the Palm Beaches in upscale national publications.[6] It was the sort of thing Fred Trump would have done: spot a distressed property that locals had ignored; sweep in, buy it for a fraction of what it had cost to build, and, with much fanfare, lay on the spit and polish; then promote it like crazy until the rent rolls filled up. But the older Trump had gone for sturdy, modestly priced apartments that required little more than fresh paint and enthusiasm, not poorly constructed condominiums starting at $300,000 and still needing significant work. For that kind of money people wanted more than a view of Palm Beach; they wanted to be in a prime residential location themselves. Even after Donald Trump bragged of Lee Iacocca's involvement with the project—in fact, the Chrysler president's investment was limited to buying three apartments for a total of $1.1 million and reselling them almost immediately for a grand profit of $41,000, or less than one-half of 1 percent—the units didn't move.

Nonetheless Donald Trump continued to be optimistic. Whenever he sold an apartment at Trump Plaza of the Palm Beaches, he told one reporter, "I'm angry, because I know in four years they're going to be selling, you know, my opinion, for four or five times as much." But after four years more than half of the units remained unsold. During the first eleven months of 1990 there was one sale. When the developer missed an October interest payment, Marine Midland, which had given him a $60 million mortgage on the property, demanded that he do something.

"Something" turned out to be a public auction. Because it was impossible to move the condominium across Lake Worth to Palm Beach, the location Trump needed to get the prices he wanted, he did the next best thing. He held the sale in the main ballroom of the Breakers, the grandiose hotel built a century earlier by Palm Beach founder Henry Flagler. Once again, elegant advertisements appeared in upscale national publications. Shortly before noon on Sunday, December 16, potential bidders drove up the hotel's long drive, past an immaculately manicured lawn, and parked in a lot filled with Mercedes, Rolls-Royces, and a dozen stretch limousines, including Donald Trump's own. Once inside the main building, a palatial cream-colored structure, the bidders made their way through long hallways hung with crystal chandeliers to the vast, salmon-walled Venetian Ballroom. Local high school cheerleaders performed a rousing if incongruous cheer. Then a fast-talking auctioneer, whose patter was being broadcast in simulcast auctions in Boston and Chicago, got going on the thirty-five lots being offered that day.[7]

In novels and films, someone whose property is on the block is instantly recognizable: alone, unkempt, perhaps taking swigs out of a bottle, and almost certainly holding his head in his hands. And, in fact, behind the scenes there were tales of the developer screaming and ranting at the president of the auction house, its sales representatives, and even Louise Sunshine, who had rejoined her former boss for the event. "Sometimes he'd call and be really nice," said Susan Stevens, on-site manager of the event. "The next morning he'd be swearing at us, like someone so out of control he didn't know *what* tack to take."[8]

But in the Venetian Ballroom, Donald Trump, clean-shaven and immaculately dressed, stood at the back of the room, smiling and chomping on Tic-Tacs. He had arrived with a beautiful young woman, tall, slim, and blond. Conspicuously inconspicuous, she now sat next to Louise Sunshine and said, "I'm sorry," whenever anyone asked her name. By the next morning the press had learned that she was Rowanne Brewer, that she was a model, and that she was the developer's companion du jour during one of his many well-publicized splits from Marla Maples. Graciously Donald Trump accepted dozens of business cards, tossing them after their donors walked away. When reporters wandered over, he launched into his familiar stream-of-consciousness press agentry.

"These are great prices, you know," he said. "You know, this is the wave of the future, it's better than taking two years and schlepping to all the buyers. What you have to remember, though, you have to remember I sold 50 percent of the units in the weakest market in the history of Florida—it's not like these are empty buildings. I'm having a party at the end of the year—not what you think, not to toast the future—to curse the bad year out. It's been a disaster for everyone, look at the airlines, for chrissakes."

He paused to accept another business card, then resumed. "You know what I think?" he asked. Without pausing he answered, "I think there's something very sophisticated and intelligent about auctions."

When the auction ended, all thirty-five units had sold, at an average of 40 percent below the original asking price—about what they would have gone for before the addition of the Trump name and elevation to the superluxury price bracket. The developer inspected his appearance before a mirror, then strode into a small reception room and struck a commanding pose in front of a huge carved fireplace.

"This has turned out to be a really great event," he declared to dozens of reporters and a handful of television crews. "We've far exceeded our expectations." Pithily he summed up: "Trump Plaza is the building of the future."[9]

One thousand five hundred miles to the north, a second auction took place the same day. It was a quiet affair. No newspaper reporters were in attendance, and no limousines sat outside. The day was cold and gray. Almost the only spot of color came from the bright scarlet tie worn by Fred Trump, the sponsor of the event.

It took place in a windowless basement room at the JFK Airport Hilton Hotel, a white bunker in the wastes outside John F. Kennedy Airport, and featured one-, two-, and three-bedroom apartments in Brooklyn and Queens. During the late 1980s the real estate frenzy in Manhattan had spread to the outer boroughs, and Fred Trump had converted a number of the properties he had built or acquired over the years into condominiums. Anticipating quick sales, he had instead run full tilt into a real estate slump, and the man who had always refused to tolerate vacancies now had a disturbing number of unsold units. Wanting to cut his losses, he had decided to try offering forty of them up for auction. Unlike the flimsily built condos being sold that day in Florida, these did not have heated towel racks, crystal bathroom fixtures, or ocean views. Instead, as the diagrams taped around the room attested, they were standard layouts in unspectacular buildings in the outer boroughs. That is, they were solid, meat-and-potatoes homes for ordinary people, the kind of housing associated with Fred Trump for his entire career and the financial base on which his son had built his own extraordinary career.

The auctioneer held an armload of brochures describing reserve prices and auction rules. In the back of the room two assistants crouched over the coffeemaker, trying vainly to cajole it into life. Before the sale began, Fred Trump shook hands and answered questions from potential buyers. An erect figure, he wore a dark blue pin-striped suit that was a trifle loose on his eighty-five-year-old body. His hair was thick, though the reddish highlights had an odd, chemical sheen.

When people said they were interested in buying apartments, he reacted with the easy warmth of a good salesman. If he heard the whispers—"You know who that is? That's Fred Trump, Donald's father!"—he gave no sign.

An acquaintance asked him if his son was holding another auction.

"Yes," he said, consulting a heavy watch. "We're holding one in Florida right about now. At the end, we're going to see who sold more, Donny or me." He smiled. "Donny'll be sure to tell the reporters he won."

Eventually the small crowd took seats, the auctioneer cleared his throat, and the sale began, starting in Brooklyn. The first four units went unsold—they did not attract a single bid. As the auctioneer made his way through Lincoln Shore, Sea Isle, Ocean Terrace, and the other Brooklyn buildings, bids came for one unit here, another there, a total of perhaps half a dozen. When he got to Queens, Fred Trump's home borough, the auctioneer went halfway down the list and got nothing. Then he switched to asking if anyone was interested in any unit in a particular building. Finally he asked if there was any interest in the entire borough. When there was no response, he thanked everyone for coming and left the front of the room. The event lasted sixteen minutes.

Fred Trump had sat stone-faced during the proceeding. When it was over he stood and spoke in a low voice to the people seated next to him. The wave of the future had rolled past, leaving him and his properties nearly untouched.

The wave did not rescue his son, either. By April 1991 Trump Plaza of the Palm Beaches still had seventy unsold units, and Donald Trump still had an $18 million Marine Midland loan on the property that he had personally guaranteed and could not repay. Bank and developer struck a deal: In exchange for title to the units, $1 million cash, and the developer's presence at a second auction, the bank would write off the personal guarantee and split with him any eventual profits.[10]

It was Donald Trump's first foreclosure. But instead of appearing devastated, he sounded ebullient. "Talk to Donald and he's *happy* about this," said Rick Edmonds, a publicist assigned by Howard Rubenstein to handle the event. "He's reveling in how much money he'll make."[11] In fact, his optimism turned out to be unmerited; although all the units that were offered sold, the auction revenues did not cover the outstanding debt. "These are the first people in America to take a piece of Donald Trump's empire for as low as sixty cents on the dollar," Edmonds said afterward.

Donald had a more upbeat spin. "It's called 'deleveraging,'" he said. "Everybody's doing it."[12]

—⁓⁓⁓—

Little by little, inch by inch, Donald Trump was extracting more favorable loan terms, renegotiating bond obligations, and shedding his most unprofitable holdings. Indeed, the man who had appeared to be at the mercy of his bankers seemed instead to be getting the better of them.

What he had actually gotten the better of, though, was the bankruptcy system itself. In 1978 Congress had overhauled the old bankruptcy laws, intending to make them less punitive to debtors. But instead of merely giving bankruptees a little help recovering from financial reversals, Congress ended up favoring debtors over creditors to such a degree that debtors could now use the prospect of bankruptcy as a weapon in their negotiations. Helped by this change, Donald Trump, who had leveraged his name and his fame to obtain huge loans and build a mountain of debt, was now able to leverage the bankruptcy system and slide out from under that mountain relatively unscathed.

Steve Bollenbach's basic strategy was to divide the assets between those to which the Trump name added value, principally the casinos, and those to which it did not, such as the yacht, the helicopters, and the block of smaller units in Trump Tower that the developer still owned. "We considered the second group of assets hostages," the CFO said, "and every now and then we'd release one of them to [creditors to] get a concession. The whole idea was to end up with the casinos and whatever else we could keep." Ultimately, as far as Bollenbach was concerned, the most important asset was the casinos, because of their cash flow. To Donald Trump, however, there was another asset of considerable significance: the West Side rail yards, which he still hoped to develop. As his CFO maneuvered to protect his holdings, Donald Trump would reserve his own energy for what he saw as his ultimate chance to get out from under his current debacle.

In the meantime, pulling off what amounted to a cross between hostage negotiations and a chess game took skill, patience, and, often, brinkmanship—what Bollenbach called "keeping an eye on whose interest was at stake at any given moment." When an insurance premium on the yacht had to be paid, he called the bank that had loaned the most money for its purchase, said that it would be a shame if the boat sank without coverage, and forwarded the bill; on the day it was due, the bank angrily coughed up the money. When the banks were dragging their feet on providing better terms, Bollenbach drew up bankruptcy papers and sent Robert Trump to file them at federal court in New Jersey. Robert waited for hours, legal documents in hand, until at the end of the day the banks cried uncle.[13]

The most extraordinary display of ingenuity occurred on December 17, 1990, the day after the first Palm Beach auction, when Trump had to make an $18.4 million interest payment on Castle bonds. Casino analysts were certain that he was several million dollars short and, because his assets were already pledged to creditors, would be unable to get a loan. Somehow, though, he came through with a check. "We don't need an outside infusion," he said smugly to reporter Barsky.

Five weeks later Barsky had another scoop: The reason Donald Trump had not needed "an outside infusion" was that he had received an inside infusion. The day the payment was due, Fred Trump had given his lawyer more than $3 million to buy chips at Trump Castle and told him to leave without playing or cashing them in. In this unorthodox fashion father conveyed funds to son without actually risking any loss, for state law mandated that chip holders be first in line for repayment in the event of default. Financially the maneuver was foolproof. Legally, however, it was a problem, for lending money to a casino requires a license from the Casino Control Commission.[14]

Knowing that such a tactic was, as one Trump colleague put it, "borderline," one of the developer's lawyers called the Casino Control Commission beforehand and got a verbal okay. Eventually this turned into a not-okay, for the ploy was an unauthorized and therefore illegal loan. But somehow the prior, informal notice, combined with the fact that the source of the funds had been the developer's own elderly father, stayed the regulators' hands. Eventually they doled out a fine of $65,000, but they also certified Fred Trump as a casino lending source. As a result, the Castle did not have to return the money that he had advanced right away but could instead repay it over time.[15]

"Sometimes [a confrontation with a creditor] was just a stare-down," Bollenbach said. "I'd say, 'You're right, we should give it back, but guess what, we're not going to.'" Certain stare-downs had an even more blatant "I dare you" quality. Even though Trump had the money, he refused to make mortgage payments on Mar-a-Lago until the bank that had made the loan extended it.[16] On another occasion, Charlie Reiss, a Trump housing consultant, recalled later, the bank that held the mortgage on the yacht wanted to repossess it. "Donald reached into his pocket and handed over the keys," Reiss said. "Then he said, 'Okay, here, it's yours. What are you going to do about it? Are you happy?' They slid the keys back."

Trump's monthly allowance was a particularly sore point for creditors. "It made them wild when Donald wrote a $10 million check for Ivana," Bollenbach said. "'That's our money,' they were screaming. I told them that's the price of keeping Donald from pushing the bankruptcy button." Indeed, as far as the CFO was concerned, the idea that the developer would ever really stick to a budget was a fantasy. "He wasn't in a Long Island bungalow, and he still had a 727," Bollenbach said. "He never changed how he lived at all, but [the provision for an allowance] let them feel he was trying." This apparently was enough, despite the fact that Trump began violating the budgetary guidelines almost immediately and the strategy played out just as Bollenbach had planned. Over time Trump ceded his small apartments, yacht, helicopters, shuttle, Alexander's stake, and half of the Grand Hyatt; he retained the casinos, the rail yards, his residences, and a partial interest in the Plaza Hotel.

In turn, Bollenbach had to accept that the developer had an ego as big as the Ritz. "It's part of who Donald is," he said, "like his height and the color of his hair." During one drive to Atlantic City, he recalled, Trump started telling him the same version of his life story that he had already recounted many times. Bollenbach interrupted. "I said, 'Donald, today we're going to do something novel—I'm going to tell you the story of my life.' I began by telling him I was born in Los Angeles, and right away he interrupted to ask if he'd ever told me about the first time he went to Los Angeles. I gave up and went to sleep."

———

Of the unresolved issues facing the developer, the most perplexing was the West Side rail yards. There had been no shortage of opportunities to share the burden of this most problematic of projects and, more than once, to sell it outright. In 1986 a Japanese construction firm named Kumagai Gumi had offered to buy a 25 percent interest in Television City for $97 million, a deal that would have paid off most of the land cost at a stroke. At the last minute Trump raised the price to $160 million. "The Kuma people just stared at him," said real estate broker Jack Shaffer, who represented the Japanese firm, and whose own office was across the street from Trump Tower. "Then they walked. By the time I got back to my office, Donald had called and asked me to bring them back, but the damage was done." Deeply insulted by what they considered dishonorable behavior, Kumagai Gumi terminated the deal and refused to reconsider. Two years later Donald Trump came even closer to selling the site to another New York developer for $550 million. But he kept upping the ante with certain financial controls and demands that streets be named after himself, and that deal, too, fell apart.[17]

In February 1988, nine months after Mayor Koch nixed Donald Trump's grand plan to make NBC the centerpiece of Television City but more than two years before the opening of the Taj and his subsequent near-bankruptcy, the developer launched a new rail yards initiative. Instead of television studios, the project would now focus on what he called "the largest and most technologically advanced" housing complex for the elderly ever built in New York City. In turn, rather than marketing this development as a center for cutting-edge TV production, he would promote it as a major contribution to the life of the city and the region, on a par with Rockefeller Center.

"Because I'm so happy with the way the job has developed and the tremendous response I've gotten," he declared, he was changing the name from Television City to Trump City. The project was still enormous, the buildings still towered over the surrounding neighborhood, and community opposition remained high. Nonetheless Trump insisted that much of the city was behind him and the complex would benefit the area. In any event, he added, because he could outwait any adversaries, he would eventually get the zoning he required. "Whether it's now or later doesn't matter," he said. "All my life, people have been trying to stop me. Frankly, I look forward to the challenge."[18]

Before any real estate development begins its official passage through the various stages of ULURP, the city's complex zoning approval process, the developer and city agencies usually resolve a number of issues through quiet negotiation. This time, though, there was little pre-ULURP bargaining. In particular, Donald Trump refused even to consider reducing the size of Trump City. Instead he retained Sandy Lindenbaum, the most well-connected zoning lawyer in the entire city, and announced that he would use "underwater zoning"—development rights derived from the underwater portion of the site—to increase the size of what he built on dry land.

On the city's side, too, there was little movement. Although Mayor Koch said flatly that he saw no reason for a project any larger than that planned by the site's previous owner, Francisco Macri, other officials remained silent.[19] In part this was because zoning permits almost always involve last-minute haggling and all parties tend to save their big guns until then. But according to former City Planning Department staffer Tom Glendenning, officials were also concerned that it might be counterproductive to try whittling down the size of the project. Accordingly, he said, planning agency officials decided to follow a convoluted strategy that called for them to surrender to what Glendenning called the developer's "most irrational demands." The idea, he said, was that by letting this absurdly dense project get as far as possible through the approvals process before being killed off, it would then be too late for the developer to do anything else. "We wanted to get Trump going [to] the point where it wouldn't be worth his while to start over," Glendenning said. "That was our strategy to lower the density."[20]

Accordingly, official communication about Trump City became a variation on "The Emperor's New Clothes," in which participants

avoided addressing directly what was on everyone's mind. "The messages about Trump City from downtown were very mixed," said a
former top Trump staffer involved in plans for the West Side site.
"No one in the City Planning Department would say anything
straight. Instead, more subtle signals would come back. City Planning would talk about planning principles, [and] the issue of heights
was never really taken on." Trump's staff kept mum as well. Indeed,
the former top staffer was never sure whether the world's tallest
building was only a chip to be thrown away during negotiations or
something Donald Trump wanted so much that he could not admit
any difficulties. In either case, the top staffer thought, such a structure was not worth the trouble it caused.

"It swallowed almost $1 million for studies, and it was so dumb,"
the top staffer said. "Can you imagine living at the top of such a
place? The windows would shake, it would take several elevators to
get there, your pizza would be cold by the time it arrived, and the dog
would pee in the elevator before you ever got to the ground floor."
Nonetheless Trump's team slogged on through studies and reviews
and meetings, drafting and redrafting the plans and environmental
studies required before ULURP could begin. "Everyone was really
just waiting for ULURP and then getting trashed by the City Planning
Commission," the top staffer said. "Finally, light would have to
dawn."

In part this reticence was because his staff dreaded Donald
Trump's rages. But it was also due to their eagerness to share what
still seemed, at this pre-Taj point, his seemingly endless success.
"Within the office, there was an incredible bullishness," said the top
staffer. "We were always making money, the world would never go
out of business, there was always a place for growth and development—that sort of thing. It was hard to say there was anything to
worry about, because everything he did seemed a success, and people
were throwing money at him."

Although Donald Trump claimed to have community support for his
rail yards project, any such backing was close to invisible. The strong

opposition to his plans, though, was impossible to miss. The community groups who had labored against Macri had now targeted the Trump projects, and once again they were handing out leaflets and newsletters, raising money at street fairs, and issuing loud protests every chance they got. To Donald they seemed a troublesome presence, though not dangerous. But in January 1986, two months after he first presented what was then Television City at a community board meeting, yet another group had formed. It would cause him considerably more difficulties and, in the end, would change the project in ways he had never imagined.

The new group was born when four affluent, civic-minded West Side couples had dinner together in the Central Park West apartment of Roberta Gratz, a former urban affairs reporter for the *New York Post*.[21] One guest was Arlene Simon, a dedicated preservationist who had pushed through landmark status for several buildings and forced her across-the-street neighbor, ABC, to lower its profile on the West Side. Sitting at Gratz's dining room table, Simon described the proposal she had seen Donald Trump unveil at the recent community board meeting. The other guests included Simon's husband, Bruce, a combative labor lawyer for the Teamsters; Victor Kovner, a libel attorney and former law partner of Ed Koch; and his wife, Sarah, a founder of the First Women's Bank and an activist in local Democratic Party circles. Veterans of the civil rights, antiwar, and women's movements, they had helped block smaller construction projects in the neighborhood and a massive highway along the Hudson River. When they heard of this appalling project that would loom over their own neighborhood, it seemed natural to take on Donald Trump.

To Gratz the only choice was to go for total defeat. "There is nothing right about this project that you can fix with a change in scale," she said to her guests. "Everything is wrong." Before the evening was over, they had a name: Westpride. Instead of working through existing neighborhood organizations, volunteer efforts that funded themselves by passing the hat at meetings, they decided to launch an ambitious effort. Starting the next day, they would ask fifty families to donate $1,000 each to stopping what was then Television City. They also proposed to line up against the project the biggest names they could muster.

Within weeks they had enlisted television journalist Bill Moyers, former mayor John Lindsay, photographer Arnold Newman, and best-selling writers Judith Rossner, David Halberstam, and Robert Caro. They had a $125-per-person cocktail party on the roof of the nearby Gulf + Western Building, with a high-profile guest list that included novelist E. L. Doctorow, folk singer Peter Yarrow, feminist Betty Friedan, actor Joel Grey, and dancer Gwen Verdon. Three years and dozens of celebrity-studded benefits later, Westpride had nearly six thousand members, a $200,000 budget, and paid lawyers, environmental experts, and public relations counsel.

Trying to distinguish itself from other anti-Trump efforts, Westpride insisted that it was actually in favor of developing the site with a project more in scale with the surrounding community. "We didn't want to just scream that development is bad and we don't want it," said architect Steve Robinson, Westpride co-chair. "We're in favor of development that makes sense." The real problem, he explained, was that the city itself seemed to have no way—or will—to initiate city planning and to play an active, creative role in shaping the physical environment in which its citizens lived. As result, he said, real estate projects inevitably ended up being designed strictly to maximize profits and/or enhance a developer's stature, and the city played no role other than reacting to whatever the developer set forth.

For help in figuring out alternatives, Westpride hired an environmental engineer named Dan Gutman. A community activist who had graduated from MIT in the mid-1960s, he had become intrigued by the notion of dropping the ugly elevated highway at the edge of the rail yards to ground level and moving it inland, thus eliminating a huge eyesore and freeing up a large chunk of the site to be a waterside park. The idea was not original; indeed, it had already been considered by, among others, Robert Moses and Donald Trump, both of whom had dismissed it as prohibitively expensive. Now, though, the corroded, badly rusting roadway was about to undergo an $85 million rehabilitation. To Gutman the planned repair seemed the perfect opportunity to tear down the highway and rebuild it away from the river's edge. He asked architect Paul Willen to figure out what such a change might look like.

Willen was not a random choice. He had grown up on the West Side and had worked on earlier designs for the site for both Donald

Trump and Francisco Macri. More recently Willen had chaired a pres-tigious American Institute of Architects task force that had studied Trump City and, in an unusual move, had recommended the rejection of the entire project. But the design Willen produced this time was completely different from Trump City and all of its predecessors. By lowering and moving the highway, he was able to create a large river-side park. The housing density used for the plan was 7 million square feet, the same as that approved for Macri and about half the 14.5 mil-lion in the latest version of Trump City. However, instead of a set of monoliths, Willen created a variety of structures in the art deco style characteristic of the neighborhood. Running through the site were streets that connected to the rest of the West Side.

"To our surprise and delight, it worked," Willen said. "Everything fit."

Others agreed. On Sunday, July 1, 1990, a sketch of the new plan appeared in *The New York Times*. It accompanied an article by critic Paul Goldberger, who described it as an "eminently civilized design." For years Goldberger had been ridiculing the developer's plans for the site. But he now wrote that under the Gutman-Willen proposal, "everything on Donald Trump's 72 waterfront acres falls into place logically, even elegantly." The next day Norman Levin, a South African who served as project director at the rail yards site for both Macri and Donald Trump, showed the sketch and the article to Tony Gleidman, then working on obtaining rezoning for Trump City. "This is a winner," Levin said to Gleidman. "We have a problem."

Levin was right. The plan appeared just as Donald Trump and his bankers were in the midst of negotiating the $65 million bailout he needed to hang on to the rail yards and the three casinos. Already rev-elations about Trump's economic woes had spurred Manhattan polit-ical and civic leaders to begin thinking about whether and how they might wrest the West Side site away from him. Now they had a con-crete and attractive alternative to promote. Manhattan borough pres-ident Ruth Messinger and other elected officials called for the city to buy the site and take the lead in producing a new and better design. Optimistically, civic groups declared that the proposal to move the highway would cost less than the $85 million already budgeted to fix it and began lobbying city, state, and federal transportation authori-

ties. David Dinkins, who had defeated Ed Koch to become the city's
first African-American mayor, seemed favorably disposed to moving
the roadway, and Deputy Mayor Barbara Fife, a preservationist who
had been active in urban planning debates, also appeared supportive.

Publicly Donald Trump continued to plow ahead and to discount
the opposition. "You have to understand," he told *Manhattan, inc.*
magazine, "they have zero to do with this process. Zero." But the
process had changed. No longer could problems be fixed by a donation, a promise, or a quiet threat. Instead civic and community groups
tied up developers in court, no matter what the politicians wanted.
The old-line Municipal Art Society (MAS), a ninety-three-year-old
group whose members were more accustomed to lifting sherry glasses
than picket signs, had recently taken on one of the biggest and most
visible projects in the city, a soaring structure on the Coliseum site at
Columbus Circle. MAS board member Jacqueline Kennedy Onassis
and eight hundred other protesters had marched into Central Park
and on cue unfolded black umbrellas to symbolize the huge shadow
the towering skyscraper would cast. A court suit stalled the project
and eventually forced its developer to provide a scaled-down version.[22]

Now an alliance that included Westpride and the MAS and came
to be known as the civic alternative wanted to promote the scheme
Norman Levin had seen in the *The New York Times*. Uncertain how
to proceed, they approached Richard Kahan, who had worked on the
Commodore project and later headed both the Urban Development
Corporation and the authority that built Battery Park City. An amateur wrestler who moved and spoke in a quick, sometimes brusque
manner, Kahan had no interest in participating in a mission that
seemed to him quixotic at best. "These people were from the West
Side," he recalled thinking. "I had heard they were very difficult."

Then he took a look at the sketch that had been in the *Times*. He
liked what he saw: a natural extension of the West Side that would be
cheaper to construct than Trump City and would therefore allow a
developer to accept a lower density and still make money. What he
didn't like was that the group seemed more set on getting rid of Donald Trump than having a great project. "Here were a bunch of people
who despised Donald, who wanted to get him out of the project, see
him go bankrupt, have the bank take the property, and never deal with
him again," Kahan said. "I asked, 'What would happen if Donald Trump

walked into this room and said, "I'll build your scheme?"' It was a very uncomfortable question. Nobody wanted to touch it, but finally Bruce Simon looked at me and said, 'I guess we'd have to do it.'"

Kahan signed on, and under his guidance members of the civic alternative began fleshing out their plan. But even with his help, they made little progress at diverting the highway renovation. The day before Thanksgiving 1990, Barbara Fife delivered the bad news: The Dinkins administration had decided that the highway was in such bad shape that the reconstruction had to proceed without delay. "We were devastated," said Kent Barwick, MAS president. "It looked like an opportunity that had been lost forever." That was not the only bad news. The coalition also learned that Trump City, which in its current version was 14.5 million square feet, would almost certainly obtain city approval for a still-too-large 11 million square feet.

Feeling desperate, the civic alternative groups filed suit to stop the highway renovation. They also began considering the still repugnant idea of asking their nemesis, Donald Trump, to build their plan. Six months earlier they had found such a notion unthinkable; now, though, it might be thinkable for both Westpride and Trump, then in the midst of negotiations with irate Taj bondholders. "He was running out of things to say to the banks," Barwick said. "He was looking down the barrel at potential foreclosure [and] there were sharks in the water. Plus he was also looking at organizations that had already caused him trouble at Television City." Talking to Donald directly would be a high-risk venture that could be a humiliating failure. But it also had the possibility of changing the climate of discussion. Ultimately the groups decided to proceed, but to hide what they were doing from the press.[23]

MAS chair Stephen Swid, a former co-owner of the '21' Club who was friendly with the developer, volunteered to make the first contact. "I went to him, laid out the alternate plan, and said, 'How about it?'" Swid recalled later. "Donald had only one question: 'Who says the West Side will approve it?'" Swid explained that the sponsors of the plan were the same groups who had been fighting the developer's proposals, then again asked if he would do it. Trump did not pause to consider. "I'm not going to change my plan publicly," he said. "But the answer is yes if you can get the West Siders to sponsor it."

Although he did not discuss it with Swid, Trump urgently needed such an opening. Since August, Bollenbach had been maneuvering to retain as many of the developer's assets as possible, but of necessity this had been a holding action. Working with groups who had so far done little but castigate the developer would be, as one civic leader later put it, the municipal equivalent of Richard Nixon's trip to China—a breakthrough that had the potential to move this long-stalled project out of the twin quagmires of zoning difficulties and community opposition.[24] While Bollenbach took care of the past, the developer would be able to go ahead into the future and create something new.

Stunned at Trump's affirmative response, the groups held a flurry of "oh my god, what now" meetings. On a chilly early morning two weeks before Christmas, about thirty civic and community representatives assembled around a large inlaid table in the wood-paneled conference room of Cravath Swaine, the law firm of one Westpride board member. They were waiting for Donald Trump, who arrived promptly at seven A.M. Because the community members had deliberately scattered themselves around the room, the developer's eight or nine aides, including Tony Gleidman and Norman Levin, had to scatter themselves as well. But it was not hard to distinguish the Trump employees from the activists, many of whom worked in the nonprofit sector. "Some of the men had tweed jackets with leather patches actually covering up holes," Swid said, "not Brooks Brothers jackets with preattached patches."

Swid introduced Trump, and then he turned the floor over to him. The man who was about to auction off his West Palm Beach apartment complex and get an unauthorized loan from his father to keep the Trump Castle casino from foreclosure began by announcing, "I want to say that no matter what you read, I'm still worth $1 billion." Swid shrank down in his chair as the leather-patches crowd bristled and rustled papers aggressively. "My god," he recalled later, "if there was one audience who didn't want to hear this, who would have given him more sympathy if he said he was broke and struggling to get back on his feet, it was this one."

But Trump went on, talking for half an hour straight. He, too, hated the highway, he said. He had tried to deal with it, he claimed, by hiding it in plain sight. The only reason he had built a huge platform was to act as camouflage; then, because he had space to fill, he had come up with the idea of TV studios and a shopping mall. "He sort of bowled everyone over with his tirade," Dan Gutman recalled later. "He kept repeating himself and making jokes about his financial problems, and he also kept saying that he could get approval of Trump City."

Then Trump picked up a yellow legal pad and a pencil. "Your idea would be better," he said. "It's an exciting design." On the pad he drew a crude oval and bisected it with an arc. "Okay," he said. "Here's the property. On one side I'll build my development, and on the other side you can build a park."

To Paul Willen, a veteran of so many plans for the site, it was a particularly dramatic moment. "Donald switched a hundred and eighty degrees," Willen said later. "This was everything he had opposed. He liked big, repetitive buildings, and never showed any appreciation whatsoever for the history of the city. This project was historic and organic—it was attached to New York City."

By the end of the meeting it seemed as if something could happen. It seemed even more that way during the discussions that followed. To give themselves maximum flexibility to work out an arrangement, the organizers continued to keep everything under wraps, including their meeting with construction leaders, who had been furious at the prospect of losing the highway reconstruction job. "We said, 'Listen, we think the highway should be rebuilt, just not here, and we also want to build a whole development and a park,'" Barwick said. "They saw the point immediately." There were also visits to city and state officials to say that the groups would drop the lawsuit on the highway if they could get support for moving it.

Then early in 1991, just after Barsky's revelation that Donald Trump had been forced to turn to his father for the money to make an interest payment on Trump Castle, the developer told Swid that he - could not move forward after all. The reason, he said, was that he was personally on the line to Chase for the purchase price of the rail yards, plus about $20 million a year in interest, a total of about $220 million. Swid asked an important political contact to make the case to Chase that the best way for the bank to get the money was to allow the project to go forward, and Chase later let Trump off the guarantee. "It's rare that you get so many disparate parts whose interests are not allied to get together to get something done," Swid said. "But Donald was very smart, because he didn't tell me everything at once. Until the not-for-profits and MAS agreed, he didn't tell me about needing to get the guarantee lifted."

Keeping Chase reassured would be an important task for Trump's new allies.[25] At the developer's behest, Richard Kahan would lunch with bank officials, and the coalition's housing expert, Charlie Reiss, a former city housing official who would later go to work for Donald Trump, would make presentations to them. Nearly fifteen years earlier, when Richard Kahan was a deputy at the Urban Development Corporation, he had seen Donald Trump leverage government support to obtain financing from institutions that were otherwise unwilling to finance the Grand Hyatt. Now that Kahan was serving as adviser to the anti–Trump City groups, it seemed to him that Trump was leveraging community and civic support to get the zoning approval he needed, as well as continued financial support. Rather than go straight for government approvals and risk later lawsuits from the community, he would get the community to fight on his behalf for the official okay. "Donald was the first to understand that the rules had changed," Kahan said, "and that there could be a different way of doing business."

Three months after that morning meeting in Cravath Swaine's conference room, the developer and representatives of a wide number of civic and community groups stood next to Mayor Dinkins and told a packed City Hall press conference that there would be no Trump City.[26] Instead Donald Trump would build the activists' plan. It was a remarkable about-face; *Times* critic Goldberger would later compare its impact to "the news that the Soviet Union had given up on Communism."[27] The lion had lain down with the lambs, and handshakes, smiles, and hugs filled the dais. In an expansive moment, Donald even allowed Westpride's executive director to pin on his lapel a button that had a red circle with "Trump City" written inside and a red cancellation bar drawn across it. After a few moments he removed it.

According to the deal struck by Donald Trump and Richard Kahan, the redesigned project would be a little more than half the size of Trump City and cost about half as much, although it would still be the largest private development project of the decade, and with 5,700 units, far larger than anything Fred or Donald Trump had ever done.[28] There would be no world's tallest building or giant shopping mall or public parking garage, and the developer would donate land to move the elevated highway inland and build a riverside park of 21.5 acres. In return, the civic alternative alliance would support what would now be called Riverside South, and the project would go forward regardless of whether the highway was relocated.

For more than a year the media had provided nonstop coverage of Donald Trump's ongoing financial crisis. *Fortune* kicked him out of the billionaire's club; *Forbes* said he had a negative net worth. Every tabloid and talk show in the nation mocked his personal life, relishing each public incident with Marla Maples, and the mainstream press seemed to be licking its chops at the prospect of his collapse. Now, though, the man who had once been the hero of Wollman Rink reemerged as the hero of the West Side rail yards. "This is the biggest turnout I've ever seen here," Donald said happily, and waved an arm at the rest of the dais. "All you folks have persuaded me to do really what was right."

He had not lost his taste for superlatives; he noted that Riverside South would be "one of the greatest developments anywhere" on "the greatest piece of property anywhere in the world." And the compromise was not—repeat, not—a blow to his ego. Rather, Trump City had been a project for the 1980s. "This is a project for the '90s," he told *Newsday*. "The '90s are less obtrusive."

Seated halfway back in the room, Fred Trump watched his son. The older man had just returned from a trip to Miami, where, as usual, he stayed at the Fontainebleau. When asked about his own career, he declined to comment. "I like to keep low and not have a lot of attention," he said. "Other people can have it, I don't need it." He paused, then added, "As Shakespeare said, Work is what you do while you're waiting to die."

A moment later he took out a photograph of Donald Trump wearing a tuxedo. "I showed this to people in Florida," he said. "They all seemed to know who he is."[29] He sounded genuinely amazed at something that would not have surprised anyone else in the room. But Fred Trump had a different relationship with the man in the tuxedo. When he looked at him he saw a boy in a baseball uniform tagging another player out at first base, a cadet marching at the head of his company, a squash player winning a game, a young man at the topping off of the Grand Hyatt and Trump Tower, the same man later announcing that he'd bought the Trump Shuttle and Plaza Hotel and opening the Taj by rubbing a big lamp as the casino loomed behind him. It did not matter that the man in the tuxedo was a celebrity. What mattered was that he was a champion.

———

All opposition to the project did not disappear. After a brief sigh of relief that the world's tallest building was history, the original anti-Macri coalition came out swinging. Riverside South was still too large, its members insisted, and the park, cut off behind a wall of tall buildings, was too far away and too small to be a remotely adequate trade-off. "People formed Westpride because they said we weren't strong enough to fight Donald Trump," said coalition leader Madeleine Polayes. "Then they went to bed with him."

One by one, local elected officials also refused to support Riverside South. "I remember another council member saying, 'Gee, I wish I had this in my district,' recalled city council member Ronnie Eldridge, who represented the West Side. "I said, 'That's the point, it *should* be in another district.'" Jerrold Nadler, who represented the West Side in Congress, flatly opposed development on the site and pushed instead to rebuild rail freight facilities there in order to retain manufacturing jobs in the city and create new blue-collar employment.

In an effort to expand the range of planning options, Manhattan borough president Ruth Messinger sponsored a four-day workshop in late June 1991 at which urban planners and designers from around the country discussed the site and alternative possibilities. Trump himself turned up during one Saturday afternoon session. Dressed as usual in a dark suit and a striped tie, he stood out against the jeans and T-shirts of the other attendees.

As he walked through the lobby, he stopped here and there for brief exchanges with participants. Upon learning that one consultant was from Buffalo, he asked how the project would go over there, and the consultant replied, "It's as big as Buffalo!" Another planner complained to Trump about the current proposal's density, and Trump dared him to come up with a way to make money on a smaller project. Then local community board member Ethel Scheffer, a longtime critic of plans for the site, launched into an impassioned plea for a greater sense of social responsibility on everyone's part. The developer listened for a few minutes, then tipped back his head and said in mock earnestness, "Ethel, there's one thing you've got to do, you've got to get more *serious* about all this! Get more *into* it!"

As the little group of listeners that had gathered around him chuckled, the developer proceeded to lay out his own prescription for urban ills. "You know," he said, "you know, what New York really needs—besides this project—is to reduce its debt. And let me tell you—this is something I know—it's easy! You just don't pay!"

His listeners grinned at the reference to the developer's most recent failure to pony up what he owed, in this case a total of $41 million in interest and principal payments due June 15 to Trump Castle bondholders. "There's all these stages people go through," Trump went on. "You know, first there's incredulity, then there's rage, frustration, then grudging acceptance."

The grins became guffaws. "It works every time. You just have to be strong enough *not* to pay. Look how often I've done it in Atlantic City, four, five times, and each time people said he'll lose the Taj, he'll lose the Plaza, he'll lose the Castle, and I haven't at all. For the Castle—off the record, I've just got interest payments for the Castle reduced from 14 to 8 percent. This was the punishment I got for saying I'm not paying!"[30]

Just before Halloween 1992, nearly two years after the developer and the civic alliance first met—a long time for many things, but the blink of an eye in the real estate world—Riverside South faced the final vote by the City Planning Commission. Although Westpride still found the buildings too large, other groups belonging to the alliance thought there was too much parking, and Donald Trump wanted the towers higher so there would be more high-priced river views, together they had hammered out a package they could live with. In negotiations with Manhattan borough president Ruth Messinger and the City Planning Commission, Trump had then accepted a slightly lower density, agreed to pay $12 million to fix up nearby subway stations and $7 million for a rail freight facility in the Bronx, and promised to earmark at least 12 percent of the apartments for moderate- and low-income families.

Alighting from his double-parked limousine, Donald Trump

swept into the commission's public hearing room, trailed by a camera crew for *Prime Time Live*, the usual gaggle of reporters, and three Chase bankers. Although there was little expectation that he would not prevail, the developer, his television makeup giving him an orange glow, worked the room until the last moment. Pointing to a *Newsday* reporter, he effusively praised that paper's favorable editorial. He hugged former foes, squeezed elbows, and put his arm around shoulders. Standing next to the bankers, he said loudly, "They've been great, really great, great guys."

Even his most implacable adversaries appeared to blink, if not melt, in the face of this charm offensive; spotting Madeline Polayes, whom he had faced the previous evening in a televised debate, he yelled out, "You looked good, really good, better than me!" Caught off guard, she cracked a smile and shot back, "I'll send you my hairdresser!"

After receiving unanimous approval from the commissioners, the proposal moved on to the city council for more tweaking. At one key subcommittee meeting in late November, construction workers, bused in from all over the city, demonstrated outside City Hall, chanting in favor of the project. Inside, lawyers, experts, community activists, and civic leaders congregated in the lobby, waiting for the meeting to start. City officials dashed back and forth between various offices, and at one point Mayor David Dinkins came out, waved, shook half a dozen hands, and then went back into his quarters.

Among those waiting in the lobby was a participant connected with Chase, whose large and currently nonperforming loan on the property would take a big step toward repayment once zoning approval was granted and the property became marketable. En route to the meeting, this participant, who had worked closely on the Riverside South negotiations, speculated that Trump's mother had told him as a child that he was the greatest and he had always believed it. "He just sees from here to there, and he's willing to put up with whatever he has to put up with to get there," the participant said. "He will ignore anything negative, and he doesn't care about the details. He always thinks positive. If you spend any time with him, you see that he's always pumping himself up, always. He really believes he's the smartest, the best-looking, the best lay."

In the participant's view, such behavior did not necessarily make for happiness, much less niceness. "He can be mean and nasty, and he has horrible attitudes about women," the participant said. "But he - really believes in himself. He has this gut thing, where he goes ahead on his own gut, and it's why he's a successful entrepreneur." It was also why, although Trump had not made a single interest payment on the West Side site, Chase had not yet pulled the plug, why the participant was there, and why the civil alternative coalition had supported the man they once despised and still did not really like.

As the hearing finally began, more than an hour late, Richard Kahan sat up in the balcony and peered down at the scene below, his head whipping back and forth as he tracked the movement of key figures. Nearby, Donald Trump chatted with reporters. Down on the chamber floor, the discussion of the project's merits and demerits proceeded in a desultory fashion. As members from Brooklyn and Queens listened, a handful of representatives from Manhattan asked whether the project would overwhelm a new but problem-plagued sewage plant, what would happen to the space formerly intended for a television studio, whether anything would ever be built given the depressed real estate market, whether it made sense to consider the project in isolation given all the large developments headed for the West Side, and whether, in fact, the whole deal was a setup for the sole purpose of bailing the developer out.

This last was a particularly relevant question. Although Donald Trump had reduced his $900 million in personal debt to approximately $150 million, the Trump Organization still owed over $2 billion.[31] But there were few answers on the council floor or up in the balcony. Smooth-browed and smiling, Trump himself seemed a creature without a care in the world. Roving around the balcony, he munched Tic-Tacs and kept up a running commentary.

"This is going great," he said. "If I want to do anything with the studio space, I have to go back through ULURP, the whole approvals thing—that's fine. What I'm thinking about now is a big sewage plant there that will handle sewage not just for Riverside South, but for the whole West Side. You know, there's lots of money to be made in sewage. The studio was just there because I couldn't think of anything else to do with the space, but in this climate, whew, that's a tough business."

He paused for a handful of Tic-Tacs. "I've already got an Italian contractor in Queens lined up, ready to build the sewage plant. Ten years ago, I said sewage was going to be a big problem. Of course, I mean building a good plant, not something for $1 billion like what the city built, where the tanks are all screwed up."

More Tic-Tacs. "I didn't need to be bailed out, you know. Last year maybe, but not now. Nobody's saying that anymore, are they? This is going to be the greatest job since Rockefeller Center."[32]

At one point a large group of fourth- and fifth-graders on a field trip came in to see where the city's laws are made. Spotting Trump, the students, all of them African-American, squealed and pointed. He walked over and shook a few hands.

"Would you like a photograph?" he asked.

"Yes!" they said enthusiastically, and he posed with them.

"Do you like my project?" he asked as the teacher snapped a shot.

"Yes!" they said even more enthusiastically.

So, apparently, did the subcommittee, for it gave the project its blessing. Three weeks later, on Wednesday, December 17, 1992, the same groups again gathered at City Hall as Riverside South faced its last hurdle in the approvals process. At last Donald Trump was at the final moment of decision on the site that had first brought him to Manhattan nearly two decades earlier.

It was a historic occasion, for Riverside South was the first large project to go through the city's new approvals process. In 1990 a court ruling had eliminated the old Board of Estimate as undemocratic, giving the City Council the final say on land use. There would be no more old-style horse trading, for borough presidents no longer had the veto power Brooklyn borough president John Cashmore had exercised when Fred Trump fought for the site on which he later built Trump Village. Instead there would be multiple small-scale deals, in which individual council members haggled directly with developers. In theory this was a more democratic process; in fact it meant that decision making was more widely diffused and developers had become relatively more powerful.

But although the project was expected to pass, Donald Trump was still using old-style heavy artillery: registered lobbyists, many of them former city officials, who made a career out of buttonholing and chatting up city officials and, especially, city council members. In 1992 Trump shelled out almost half a million dollars to lobbyists working for Riverside South—the highest amount paid to lobbyists that year by anyone in the city.[33] As the council session began, Trump's arm-twisters were still at work, smiling and greeting members as they filed in to take their seats.

Of equal historic note, it was also the first time anybody could remember that a developer and his opponents had jointly asked for approval. Hardly surprising, getting to this point had not been easy. Among other problems, everyone involved had trouble selling the idea of working with the enemy to their home base. Westpride and MAS had lost some members, and even Trump found himself on the defensive. "He got tremendous flak from everyone working for him," Kahan said. "His lawyers, everyone thought it was dangerous to share so much control. 'How can you give up this power?' Sandy Lindenbaum was dead set against it."

Within the alliance there was shouting, cursing, well-timed temper tantrums and threats to resign, and, occasionally, near-fistfights.[34] There had been moments of incomprehension, as when Donald Trump insisted on defending Mike Tyson, then on trial for rape, to the incredulous women in the alliance, and again when he said, as proof of his dedication to the project, that he had made a very beautiful young woman wait more than an hour late one Saturday night while he answered questions from a member of the City Planning Commission. There had also been second thoughts when, out of nowhere, Trump would suddenly say that he wanted the buildings to be eighty stories high after all or that the banks were really supporting him and things were looking up, so why should the buildings be so small.[35]

And, always, there had been suspicions. The developer wondered whether, even if he compromised, those opposed to the project would litigate, and the civic groups did not know whether, once Trump had the rezoning, he would forget about the relocated highway and park. "Sincere is an irrelevant concept with Donald," Claude Shostal, president of the Regional Plan Association, one of the constituent groups, said later. "He insisted he wanted to do the right thing, but I think he wanted to be admired for seeming to do the right thing."

Once again Donald Trump sat in the balcony above the council chamber and watched legislators decide the fate of his project. After noting that this was one of the many days he had planned to marry

Marla Maples, he said that he planned to start building "as soon as we have an uptick in the real estate market," that this would be "my most successful project ever," and that there was "lots of interest in financing it."

Down below, a series of members addressed the council. A large clock kept track of the time, and a bell rang when the three minutes allotted to each speaker expired. Most who spoke favored the project; the most passionate opposition came from Ronnie Eldridge, the member from the West Side, who said that Riverside South was too large and was being pushed through too quickly. She predicted that it would now be sold off piece by piece "to bail out Donald Trump" and charged that by approving it, the council "permitted the taxpayers of New York to be played for small-town suckers."

"That's all just bullshit!" Trump said loudly to no one in particular. "That woman is a fat pig who doesn't know what she's talking about. It's a pack of lies!"

He switched to a happier topic, an upbeat report published the previous day on a proposed refinancing of the Trump Plaza casino.[36] "D'ja see the article in the *Times*? A $375 million bond issue—the article said $300 million, but they didn't know the real number—it's 375. I'll be out of personal bankruptcy by the end of the year. I'll have my casinos back by 1995. I didn't lose a thing, I've got it all. What did I lose? I don't have the shuttle and I don't have the boat, but what else?"

The truth was that he had also lost his stake in Alexander's, his half of the Grand Hyatt, part ownership of his casinos, most of the Plaza Hotel, and most of the residential units he owned in Trump Tower. But he gave another answer, one he evidently found more satisfactory.

"I've got *everything* else!" he crowed. "Everything!"

As expected, the vote was a landslide in his favor, 42 to 8. Afterward Trump stood on the floor of the council chamber for press interviews. "This could look like just a political payoff, like you just gave political campaign contributions and people paid you back with your votes," said a local television news reporter.

Knitting his brows in concentration, the developer looked straight into the camera and spoke with a sincerity worthy of the young Jimmy Stewart. "Well, that would be a fair conclusion, I guess," said the man

whose father had been notably generous to politicians and had benefited greatly from their favor, and who in turn had himself been among
the highest donors to political campaigns and the frequent beneficiary
of official largesse. "But it wouldn't be true. They supported this because it's a great project and it's good for New York and they know it."

The debts of Riverside South could have finished Donald Trump; instead he used the project to pull himself back from the brink. In July
1994, a year and a half after obtaining the zoning approvals he had
sought for two decades, he sold control of the site and its development to a Hong Kong consortium. Publicly the price was $88 million
plus his $250 million debt on the property.[37] He would build and sell
what was now an eighteen-building development, for which he would
earn a handsome salary, and he would also receive a share of the profits that could be as high as 50 percent depending upon performance.

Leading the new owners was a father-son team. Their publicly
traded company, New World Development, owned real estate, power
companies, telecommunications firms, and hotels, including the Ramada and Stouffer hotel chains in the United States. New World's reported holdings were far larger than Donald Trump's had ever been,
but the company's disciplined, low-key, parsimonious style was more
akin to that of Fred Trump than of his flamboyant, impulsive son. "In
Hong Kong, China, we've done bigger projects than this," said Henry
Cheng, the son, sounding for a moment oddly like the man from
whom he was buying the site. "Much bigger."

In March 1997, after beating back lawsuits from those community
groups that had rejected the Riverside South compromise, New World
broke ground. By 2000, two apartment buildings were finished, a third
was under way, a fourth was scheduled, and the project had obtained a
421a city real estate tax abatement.[38] To the dismay of many on the
West Side, the finished structures looked much bigger in the concrete,
as it were, than in the guidelines that were drawn up under the civic alternative alliance. One reason was that many preliminary sketches depicted the project from above, which diminishes building heights;
another was that the most widely distributed drawing, that published

in *The New York Times*, had the Macri density of 7.3 million, not the ultimate compromise of 7.9 million, and almost the entire extra space went into additional height. "Everyone says the buildings are much larger than they are supposed to be, but we went back to the plans and showed that they were within the guidelines," said architect Philip Johnson, whom the developer hired to do the detailed design for the first four structures and, not so incidentally, lend his name to the project. "They just didn't imagine how high forty stories is."

Nearly ninety, the elfin, owlish Johnson, who had been kicked out of his own firm, had entered the 1990s in a bind something like that of the developer: world famous but cash poor. Now the Riverside South commission helped to relaunch him, for which he was grateful. Unfortunately, however, having the same architect for all four buildings, then stripping the structures of their initial art deco details—a pineapple top here, a stylized triangular pediment there—meant that the ensemble lacked the variety that was an important hallmark of buildings on the West Side. The buildings were not the enormous, arrogant monoliths once proposed by Helmut Jahn, but Johnson's boxy structures, far larger than their neighbors, seemed rather bland, almost institutional.[39]

More disturbing to Donald Trump's allies, the highway was still in place, covering a wide swath of the park. The civic and community groups that had backed Riverside South were deeply chagrined. "I will consider it a total failure if the highway doesn't get taken down and the park built as intended," Kahan said. "None of us would have spent five minutes on it otherwise. The civic groups would have gone to the barricades, and I wouldn't have gotten involved."

Probably the most insurmountable obstacle to moving the highway was Representative Jerrold Nadler. He and Trump, who loathed each other and frequently traded barbed remarks, disagreed about everything, including the cost of moving the highway. Trump's experts pegged it at about $120 million, whereas Nadler, noting that it cost $85 million just to rehabilitate the roadway in the early 1990s, insisted that relocating it would be more like $350 million.

Unlike Richard Kahan, who described the cooperation of civic groups and developer as a new urban planning model, Nadler saw the participation of outside groups in West Side affairs as colonialism. "Who the hell gave them the right to do the negotiating?" he said, pointing out that Westpride was the only local group involved and that its members and contributors were given no opportunity to vote on the matter. "Someone in a closed room just decided that it was a good deal." It wasn't, in Nadler's view. As he saw it, moving the highway was a waste of taxpayer money that should go for more pressing needs; worse, doing so would create a walled-off facility that amounted to little more than a glorified backyard for Riverside South.

Perhaps predictably, the man who could never admit defeat did not do so when the road did not come down. Instead he professed his pleasure when Nadler engineered the defeat of federal funding for moving the highway in July 1998. "The job is a much simpler one for me if we leave the highway in place," Trump said. "Jerry Nadler is my best friend, economically. He's played right into my hands." Given that he was making a profit from the development with the highway in place, the developer bragged, he would just as soon it stayed right where it was so people could drive past and see what he'd achieved. "When the highway remains, everyone sees the great job I've built," he said. "If it goes underground, no one will see what I've done."[40]

Twenty years earlier Donald Trump had taken on one of the most undoable projects in New York City; now, one by one, actual buildings were rising on the site. Whether the project would ultimately elevate him to master-builder status remained unclear. So did the question of which side ultimately got the better deal, the developer who pulled out of the fire a project far smaller than he had wanted but still immense, or the civics, who had traded a horrendous project for one that was still too large in the expectation of obtaining a park that so far remained stubbornly unattainable. What was clear was that although the project was no longer Trump's, and its new owners talked of selling some or all of it, in the public mind the project would remain linked to him. When he teamed up with the civics he had dropped the "Trump City" name, and the legal documents providing zoning approvals called the project "Riverside South"; nonetheless, in July 1998 he unilaterally announced plans to market the new buildings under yet another title, "Trump Place." The civics continued to refer to the project as Riverside South, but the large bronze letters over the entrances said "Trump Place," as did coverage in the city's journal of record, *The New York Times*.

By imposing his name on the project he no longer owned, Donald

Trump had completed the process of reinventing himself as a human logo. He would be his own marketing gimmick, charging premium prices for condos and rentals in buildings bearing his name. But meanwhile roles would have shifted; he was no longer a developer in the old sense, someone who came up with the money and constructed the building. He had become a different sort of developer. He was the person the public associated with the project, the one the world thought of when they thought of that site and that address. What he possessed was not the project, but the idea of the project. At one time he had made himself into a virtual billionaire, someone whose appearance of limitless resources had taken him remarkably far; now he was a virtual developer, and this status, too, would have remarkable rewards.

CHAPTER TWENTY-TWO

TRUMP™

FREDERICK CHRIST TRUMP DIED AT THE AGE OF NINETY-THREE on June 25, 1999. He had lived almost twice as long as his own father and left an estate estimated at $250 million to $300 million. For many years he had not constructed or bought any buildings. Stricken with Alzheimer's disease, he had his good days, his not-so-good days, and, increasingly, his bad days. But he still lived with his wife, Mary, in the big house on Midland Parkway, he still had a navy blue Cadillac with the license plate FCT, and almost every day he still went to Avenue Z, greeted his secretary of the last fifty-nine years, and sat at his desk.

The obituary in *The New York Times* occupied half a page, and the funeral took place four days later at Marble Collegiate Church. Norman Vincent Peale had died, and Fred and Mary Trump had long since been too frail to attend Sunday services. But Fred had remained a firm believer in the power of positive thinking, and Marble Collegiate remained his church to the end.

More than 650 people attended the service, filling every pew. They included politicians, a sprinkling of celebrities, other developers and builders, Trump Organization employees, journalists, and the curious. Joan Rivers, former senator Alphonse D'Amato, and Ivana Trump, accompanied by her widowed mother, were there. Louise Sunshine and attorney Sandy Lindenbaum sat near the back. Across the way was Donald Trump's current girlfriend, a twenty-six-year-old model named Melania Knauss, whose plunging neckline would be prominently featured in the tabloids the next day. Business colleagues and social acquaintances nodded and waved to each other, stopping occasionally to shake a hand or exchange remarks.

Sunlight filtered in through the large stained-glass windows, and huge sprays of miniature white roses flanked the sanctuary and covered the casket. The massive organ and two violins played a selection of sacred music, and the Marble Sanctuary Choir joined in for elaborate arrangements of "A Mighty Fortress Is Our God" and other standard Protestant hymns. Just before the service began, the Trump family, including Fred Trump's children and their spouses, his grandchildren and great-grandchildren, his nieces and nephews, filed in. Mary Trump, eighty-seven, was in a wheelchair.

The Reverend Arthur Caliandro, Peale's successor, thanked Fred Trump for his contributions to the church, and Mayor Rudolph Giuliani offered a brief tribute to the man who had built homes for thousands of New Yorkers. Then Elizabeth Trump Grau, a banker, recited what she described as one of her father's favorite poems, entitled "Don't Quit." One grandson, a surgeon, made a virtue of Fred Trump's fabled penuriousness with a childhood anecdote about his grandfather's frequent offer to give him a one-dollar bill. Each time, though, his grandfather would describe how hard he'd worked for it, and the boy felt obliged to decline. Finally he decided to accept it, and his grandfather never offered him another, thus providing what the grandson now called "an important lesson." Fred Trump III, a real estate broker whose father, Fred Trump Jr., had died in 1981, said that although people thought of his father and grandfather as very different, what they had in common was a sense of connection to ordinary people.

Robert Trump, manager of the Trump Organization's extensive real estate holdings outside Manhattan, called his father his hero and recalled hearing his whistle when he came home at night, taking two steps at a time because "when you do that, the staircase is only half as high." Maryanne Trump Barry, a federal judge in New Jersey, read a letter she had written to her wealthy father during college asking his permission to wait on tables. Fred Trump's response had been on the back of the same paper. "Hiya, Babe," he began, and thanked her for doing her part to share the load of supporting their large family.

None of these heirs mentioned their own accomplishments.

When it was Donald's turn to speak, he said it was the toughest day of his life. It was ironic, he said, that he had learned of his father's death just moments after he'd finished reading a front-page story in *The New York Times* acknowledging the success of his biggest development, Trump Place. On this project, as on the Grand Hyatt, Trump Tower, Trump Plaza, the Trump Taj Mahal, Trump Castle, and everything else he had ever done, his father had been totally supportive. When he had been on the financial ropes in the early 1990s, when the press and the public and even his own colleagues said he was finished, his father had insisted he'd come back. Whatever the deal, whatever the project, Fred Trump had always known that Donald would be able to pull it off.

In short, that warm spring day at Marble Collegiate Church did not belong to Fred Trump after all. It belonged to Donald. At his own father's funeral, he did not stop patting himself on the back and promoting himself. The first-person singular pronouns, the I and me and my, eclipsed the he and his. Where others spoke of their memories of Fred Trump, he spoke of Fred Trump's endorsement. Donald Trump had never been defeated in the past, and he was not defeated now. There was to be no sorrow; there was only success. It was the power of positive thinking squared.

Donald Trump's unrelenting, unapologetic focus on his own accomplishments had alienated many people; others, drawn to winners, found this self-absorption appealing. Early on it had made him his father's favorite child. Although it had been Fred Trump's lot in life to be a plow horse, to go up and down the rows and get the job done, he had yearned to be a racehorse. To his obvious delight, his middle son was born a racer, and Fred Trump had rooted for him in every contest he ever ran.

That insistence on always putting himself first propelled Donald Trump to fame so extraordinary that fame itself became his greatest asset. He was always competing, always selling himself, always concentrating on how to make whatever he was doing seem bigger and better than what anyone else had ever done. No matter what happened, including the death of the person who meant more to him than anyone else in the world, from whom he had learned everything he needed to know, to whom he had turned when he needed counsel or comfort or bailing out, he would never relinquish being the center of attention. He would never give up, he would never let go. When he lost, he would say he won. When he won, he would say he won more, or bigger, or faster. For him the race would never, ever be over. He would never stop.

Indeed, he must not stop. His business was to sell himself, a job that required burnishing his own image day in and day out, week in and week out, at work and at play—the latter two categories being, in his case as well as that of his father and, in all likelihood, his grandfather, indistinguishable. The funeral oration had been an astonishing display of self-absorption; more than that, though, it was a remarkable illustration of the journey taken by this family and, by extension, this nation over the past century. Despite obvious differences in lifestyle and affect, Friedrich, Fred, and Donald were similar types. All three were energetic people who would do almost anything to make a buck; all three possessed a certain ruthlessness; all three had a free and easy way about the truth; and all three had a range of solid, practical skills. How these traits played out in different eras is, in its own way, a vest-pocket history of America.

During Friedrich's first two decades in the New World, he made a living by providing services that were as concrete as could be imagined. They ranged from haircuts to food to sex, and customers returned not because he was the vendor but because they were satisfied with his work. The value he added was not his name but his skill at barbering, cooking, and keeping order in the side and back rooms of his establishments. The name over the door meant so little to him that he did not bother to change it when he purchased already existing businesses, and those he started himself—the Monte Cristo and, later, the Arctic—were named after their location. At the end of his life he moved into another field, real estate, but that, too, involved physical goods and services in the form of buying plots of land and building houses.

Friedrich's son Fred followed in his father's footsteps but created further value in his own way. By establishing a network of political contacts, he managed to obtain government housing subsidies, then released a stream of press releases designed to give his solid but conventional developments a special shimmer. A man of his era, he named these projects after their location, but on the last one he placed his own name, giving that shimmer a specific identity that his son Donald would develop in ways Fred never dreamed of.

Unlikely as it might have seemed from the outside, Donald shared much with his father and grandfather. He, too, knew how to read a blueprint, frame a building, and lay bricks; he knew how to retar a roof and how to lay a plumb line. But Friedrich's grandson would not employ this practical knowledge to build anything with his own hands; instead he would use it to connect with the contractors and laborers who actually put up his buildings, the maintenance men he encountered in the lobby of Trump Tower, the retired blue-collar workers he greeted warmly as they played his slot machines in Atlantic City. Although these skills would be helpful in hiring and firing those who did this work and, especially, in negotiating contracts, the special value he would add to his projects would be his own name. Seemingly the simplest of acts, it was, in fact, quite arduous, for keeping that name going, constantly protecting and buffing it, required vigilance and intensity and energy of the highest order.

It was an activity that his grandfather could not have understood. Indeed, to Friedrich his grandson might well have seemed like a hired gun, doing what he did best for the benefit of someone else. But this was not the beginning of the twentieth century, it was the end; just as Friedrich had shrewdly adapted to his era by leaving Germany and coming to America, his grandson had skillfully adjusted to the modern world, a place where intangibles matter enormously, where a name or a trademark can mean everything, can in fact be everything, where *Time* magazine's prestigious Man of the Year award can go to the head of a company that has never made a nickel but is worth billions on paper.[1] Indeed, in such a world, to devote one's highest energies to polishing and shining the name *Trump* might well be the most practical and sensible thing a man could do.

Donald Trump had begun burnishing his name as soon as he got to Manhattan and had always considered it the highest of priorities. He invariably covered his own achievements with a thick coating of superlatives, but sometimes he also attached a string of -ests, as in "greatest," "tallest," or "biggest," to other people and their attainments. Doing so served the dual purpose of flattering them while suggesting that the presence of people of such accomplishment was still further proof of his own outstandingness.

But after pulling himself back from the edge of financial disaster in the early 1990s, he went about the task of polishing his name with a special urgency. Because of his still enormous burden of debt and the fact that his assets were heavily collateralized, he could not obtain mortgages on his own behalf. For the foreseeable future he would not be able to put significant equity into deals even if he wanted to; his name was all he had.

Accordingly, doing a deal meant finding a partner with deep pockets. It did not take him long to locate one. In the summer of 1993 he once again made a pilgrimage to the provinces. Pulling up at a nondescript suburban office building in Stamford, Connecticut, Donald Trump paid a call on Dale Frey, chairman of General Electric Investment Corporation.[2] Sitting in Frey's large corner office, the developer made a case that sounded remarkably similar to the one he had once made at City Hall regarding the site for a new convention center and then at Equitable involving the land under Bonwit Teller. He'd heard that Frey had a problem and he was there to take it off his hands.

The problem had to do with a well-known, although not well-loved, New York City landmark, a forty-four-story skyscraper at the southwest corner of Central Park. Built in 1969 as corporate headquarters for the multibillion-dollar conglomerate Gulf + Western, the silver-and-black-striped slab now belonged to the General Electric Pension Trust, one of Frey's many responsibilities. Because the building's floors were small, it was ill suited for modern office usage, yet it seemed a bad bet for conversion to apartments, mainly because on blustery days it swayed so much in the wind that people on upper floors could not have a bowl of soup without getting drenched. The obvious move was to tear down the building and start over, but a replacement would face newer and more restrictive zoning and the loss of a dozen floors. Trump had driven up to Stamford because he had figured out a solution: strip the old structure to the steel frame so as to retain the current zoning, then construct a new and stable building that, for zoning reasons, would be two-thirds condominiums and one-third hotel. "He tried to blow us away with his knowledge of what we should do," Frey said later.

A gruff-sounding fireplug who had spent nearly forty years working in corporate finance at General Electric, Frey managed $70 billion in assets, of which real estate was a relatively small part. Although he was not about to hire anyone after one brief chat, he was impressed and made inquiries. To his surprise, real estate brokers told him that despite the developer's financial problems, the Trump name was still magic in the target market of wealthy foreign buyers and would bring an extra $150 per square foot in condo sales. Among bankers, too, the developer's name was good, for although he could not borrow money directly, he remained an astute deal maker. In the rapidly expanding economy of the mid-1990s, the fact that three years earlier many in the banking community had spent the summer digging out from under wildly overleveraged loans to Donald Trump seemed to have little bearing. What mattered was the simple fact that the financial industry makes money off people who do deals, not people who don't. Like any other business, banks would always need new product, which in their case meant new loans, and Trump still remained a man with the potential to deliver it.

On Wednesday, March 23, 1994, a front-page article in *The New York Times* announced the planned renovation of the Gulf + Western Building.³ The more important story was that Donald Trump, the man who had been considered a goner only a short while before, was back. He would be part of one of the most prominent projects in the just reviving construction industry, and General Electric Investment Corporation, one of the nation's largest corporate investment divisions, was trusting him with its pension fund resources. Unlike any project in which the developer had ever been involved, he would not be an owner. He would not control the project, and his share would be limited to the building's restaurant, retail, and roof space, plus a fee for his role on the development team. But it was a golden opportunity to relaunch himself, for he would not have to put one cent into the deal, and soon another large, highly visible New York building would bear the Trump name.⁴

The burnishing continued. A few months later Donald Trump obtained a highly attenuated ownership stake in one of the most famous buildings in the world, the Empire State Building. Until the expiration of the current lease, which had another eighty years to go and paid a minuscule rent, he would reap only bragging rights, but such rights were precisely what he was after.

Still further visibility came with the purchase of an office building at 40 Wall Street, just yards from the now demolished building at 60 Wall Street where his grandfather had once had a barbershop.[5] In this one case the developer did not have a partner, but he did not need one, for the building, shabby and half-empty, cost him a total of $10 million to buy and refurbish. One more restrained neoclassical limestone facade on a street lined with them would not seem the sort of exposure the developer craved. But he had found an inexpensive, simple way to be conspicuous yet compatible with the area's landmarked status: he covered the facade's hitherto all-but-invisible rosettes and papyrus fronds with shiny gold paint and affixed the new name, The Trump Building, over the door in bright gold letters.

Suddenly the same building that had been indistinguishable from its neighbors popped out; no one on Wall Street could miss what amounted to a neon sign announcing that Donald Trump was back in the running. The building reopened nearly fully rented, and Deutsche Bank provided a staggering $125 million mortgage. In the summer of 1990 the same bank had sat in the Trump Tower conference room and contemplated the near wreckage of the developer's empire; now it had made the Trump Building one of the most heavily leveraged buildings of the developer's entire career.

More visible still, in 1998 the developer announced plans for what he proudly described as "the world's tallest residential building." By adroitly buying up air rights around a large site on First Avenue between East 47th and 48th Streets, he managed to control enough square footage to begin Trump World Tower.[6] Whether the building would be ninety stories tall, as described in glossy advertisements, or seventy stories, the number given in official documents on file with the city, it would dwarf its neighbors, including the U.N. headquarters. Because no rezoning was needed, protests led by area resident Walter Cronkite and U.N. secretary general Kofi Annan could not stop the building, but did spark a proposed rewrite of zoning rules to prevent such projects in the future. Again, Trump's partner—in this case, Daewoo, a huge Korean conglomerate with interests in construction—put up major funding, some $58.5 million. Trump provided his name and $6.5 million, managed the project, and would receive a performance-based profit share.

Further contributing to the luster of the name were smaller projects, including three Trump country clubs and golf courses outside Manhattan in Westchester County and appearances in commercials for Pizza Hut. The first ad, shown in 1995, featured the developer and Ivana making double-entendre remarks about sharing a pizza, a tongue-in-cheek reference to their bitter divorce. Four years later Pizza Hut tapped him to introduce their newest pie, the Big New Yorker Pizza, to the two hundred million viewers of the Super Bowl. "We only had thirty seconds, so we needed someone very famous, [with] an over-the-top quality," said Charlie Miesmer, the BBDO executive who pushed for putting Trump in the spots. "We knew if we chose him, it would generate a lot of attention, and it did."[7]

But the name would receive what was literally its most radiant glossing just two blocks from Trump Tower. In the spring of 1998 Donald Trump made a deal to buy the General Motors Building. Like the Gulf + Western Building, this fifty-story white marble behemoth was an unloved landmark, designed by Edward Durell Stone and Emery Roth and built in 1968. But because the General Motors Building occupied a square block at one of the city's premier locations, the corner of 59th Street and Fifth Avenue, it commanded a premier price: $800 million, the highest sum on record for a Manhattan building. Trump would put in $20 million and revamp the structure; Conseco, an Indiana-based insurance and financial services company, which managed $100 billion in assets and had been the top-performing stock in the Fortune 500 for the previous ten years, would pick up the rest of the tab.[8]

Because of lease restrictions, the structure's official name would continue to be the General Motors Building, but there would be a new twist: it would be the General Motors Building at Trump International Plaza. Or, at any rate, that would be the official name. From the outside, the first half of the name, which appeared in small letters inside a small porch on the Fifth Avenue side, was invisible. By contrast, the second part of the clumsy new moniker, Trump, was impossible to miss. Because there were no contractual arrangements regarding the presence of the developer's name on the building, he promptly mounted it across the front in shiny gold-colored letters four feet high.[9]

In Atlantic City, too, Donald Trump continued to protect and promote his name, which loomed over the city in huge red neon letters. In 1995, taking advantage of a long-delayed surge in casino revenues, he began to take his operations public. Starting with Trump Plaza, going on to the Taj, and then finally to Trump Castle, since renamed Trump Marina, he put his holdings into a public company, Trump Hotels and Casino Resorts (THCR), and made enough in a series of public offerings to pay down his own Atlantic City debts. There was a certain amount of controversy over the price he paid himself for Trump Castle, the least profitable of his operations, but he weathered it, in part by his well-timed mention of the fact that the Hard Rock Cafe was considering coming there. It didn't, but bondholders, buoyed by the prospect, backed up the developer.

Like the bankers, they, too, were always in search of new deals and new fees. Thus, after the yelling and screaming of 1990 had subsided, they were ready to sign up again. And, in fact, although it was a bumpy ride, in the end most Trump casino bondholders had been able to get out more or less whole. True, repayment was delayed, and those who sold—mainly small investors who could not afford to hold on—lost money; however, by definition, bonds that yield high rates carry high risks. Investors who had bought such bonds knew there was a reason they were referred to as "junk," namely that they were volatile and that only a few years down the road it would almost inevitably be necessary to do another deal to get the developer out of the one they were doing then.

With the Castle deal done and his remaining share of the Grand Hyatt sold to his estranged partner, Donald Trump was in the clear—such an unaccustomed situation, one of his lawyers told *The New Yorker*, that the developer could not sleep at night.[10] But the purported insomnia was worth it. In October 1996, after six years of exclusion from lists of the wealthiest people in the land—the equivalent of magnate Siberia—he landed back on the annual *Forbes* ranking of the country's 400 richest individuals. According to the magazine, which ranked him as the 368th wealthiest American, his net worth was $450 million; as usual, his own calculations, based on his own accountants' estimates of confidential and hence unverifiable figures, provided a higher number, in this case $2.25 billion.[11] Whatever the total, the virtual developer had restored lost luster to his name, and it shone even more brightly over what was now a virtual empire.

Specifically, much of his net worth derived from his Trump Hotels and Casino Resorts holdings, which amounted to about 40 percent of the company's stock—a significant asset, given that it was the largest casino company in Atlantic City and dominated the gambling industry there. Unfortunately, however, Trump Hotels and Casino Resorts owned not only the developer's former casinos but also his former debt load. When THCR went public, its shares rose to 34, but then sank to about 3 and sat there. Worse yet, because the company owed too much money to borrow more, it could not expand. The only way growth could occur was if the company could do as Donald himself had done, find a partner for whom using the Trump name would be worth picking up the tab. In the meantime, the Trump-filled skyline of Atlantic City continued to be one of the developer's most important tools for the never-ending task of keeping his name going.

Donald Trump had made his name into a remarkably successful marketing device. Among the many reasons, one of the most important was that it actually represented something to which he was deeply and passionately attached, his own family. Even in the midst of marital collapse, he was a fond, if sometimes distracted, father, allowing his children free run in his office, talking to them on the telephone regardless of whether he was in meetings, taking them with him on trips whenever possible.

The oldest, Donald Jr., twenty-one, compact and dark haired, was by nature what the family called a Boston Trump, referring to the wing of the family headed by Fred Trump's now deceased brother John, a physics professor at MIT. Quiet and reserved, Donny studied business at Wharton and seemed likely to play a key role in the Trump Organization, although it would probably be out of the limelight. The more outgoing Ivanka, nineteen, who was the second oldest child, handled the public eye with ease; in imitation of both parents, she had posed expertly in front of cameras from early childhood and now had a budding career as a model, although she also showed periodic interest in the family business. It was the younger son, Eric, fifteen, who had his father's looks and impish personality, doing exactly what he had been told not to and then charming adults into forgiveness, but it was unclear whether he would use this legacy to pursue a role in business, entertainment, or both.

Almost ten years after Eric's birth, Donald Trump had become a father for a fourth time. In October 1993, after ten hours of labor, with new age music playing and scented herbs and oils wafting through the air, Marla Maples gave birth to Tiffany Ariana Trump. Her arrival gave new attention to the question of when, or if, her father would marry the woman who was invariably referred to as his Georgia peach.

Donald Trump had been grateful to Marla for sticking by him. Year after year she had been at his side for marketing pitches and casino receptions, for all the openings and parties and get-togethers and meals that were necessary to polish the Trump name and keep it out there in the world. "If you had a real tough nut to crack, an invitation to have dinner with Donald and Marla went a long way," recalled a top Trump casino official. "There you were, sitting down to dinner with them in a public place, lots of people saw you, and you would be a celebrity, too. Marla's just as nice as she can be, can make you feel real comfortable real quick, not standoffish. It worked well. Before that dinner, it was Mr. Trump and Mr. Banker; afterward, it's Joe and Donald and Marla."[12]

But Marla was more than a helpmate; she was also his lover. "She did something to him sexually that he just couldn't resist," said one close observer. "Deep down, this guy is really just a horny teenager." Six years into the relationship, Donald still could not keep his hands off Marla's curvaceous body; during one business trip in August 1993, when she was eight months pregnant, he was constantly fondling her in the presence of other members of the party. Still, although there had been several announcements of engagements and even wedding dates, the two had never gotten close to the altar. Year after year, periods of intimacy continued to alternate with bickering, accusations, slammed doors, and separations.

Now, though, Donald Trump had a pressing reason to reconsider his position: Before he made a public offering on his casinos, he needed to polish up his name to the brightest possible sheen. He made no bones about the fact that his second trip to the altar was a marketing decision. Even after he and Marla appeared on the front page of *The New York Times* getting a marriage license, he was still asking family and friends about whether tying the knot would help or hurt his business prospects and whether it might be better for his public image if he reconciled with Ivana.

Instead, on December 17, 1993, he sent Ivana a dozen red roses. The next day, in a lavish ceremony at the Plaza Hotel, before 1,300 guests and with his frail father as best man, he said, "I do." *Entertainment Tonight* had exclusive video rights to the rehearsal; the groom sold the wedding photos to magazines and newspapers and said that he would donate the proceeds to charity. Prominently featured in news reports was the staggering amount of food and drink and the nine-tier wedding cake. Seven tiers and more than five hundred pounds of food were left over and reappeared in the city's soup kitchens over the next several days.

The wedding ring may have helped with the initial public offering for the casinos, but it did not make the man who had always put himself first stop doing so. At one time Marla's lack of high-level involvement in business affairs had been a relief of sorts for Donald, burdened by his collapsing empire. Now, though, when Marla pushed him to balance his time between his work and his new family—that is, to give something of himself back—he had little interest. Still a workaholic, he was totally caught up in his business and, especially, his comeback, from the moment he woke until he went to sleep at night.

In April 1996 news accounts appeared about a Palm Beach cop's report that he had encountered a "rumpled and sandy" Marla on the

beach in the wee hours with her bodyguard.[13] She explained the com-
promising circumstances by claiming that she had simply been taking "a bathroom break," and her husband made no public comment.
A year later, when the developer announced that he and Marla were
separating, he did not mention the incident. Instead the man who
could never acknowledge defeat, or failure, or even regret, said that
ending his marriage was a business decision. According to their
prenuptial agreement, the amount Marla would receive in case of a
divorce would soon grow significantly larger. He was, he insisted,
simply cutting his losses.

In dollars and cents, the loss to Donald Trump amounted to about
$1 million plus child support; in personal terms, it seemed to add up
to something far less. His parents, his siblings, and, now, his children
had always been his main support system, what mattered most to
him. They had always been there, and they always would be. Although there would be periodic strains, their relationship to him was
constant. They provided a kind of connectedness that he could tolerate, a relationship that was direct, warm, and accepting, but not inti-
mate or probing. For all the running after supermodels, after women
of extraordinary beauty and physical perfection, he was basically a
no-touch person, someone who did not, except with his children, en-
gender physical closeness. His insistence on wearing business clothes
was only partly for the professional image; it was also the wardrobe of
choice because of the distance it provided. Similarly, the security
guards who had accompanied him for years were a way of keeping the
world at a remove that was psychological as well as physical.

Trump had an enormous number of acquaintances who enjoyed
coming to his office for a visit and, maybe, a little business. Sharp and
witty, a clever mimic and an engaging storyteller, he could be fun to
be around. "He'll be sitting with you and say, 'Let's call Don King,'"
said broker Jack Shaffer, who dropped in occasionally at Trump
Tower. "Before you know it, Don King is on the speakerphone. I never
met Don King, but there I was talking to him." He could also be abra-
sive or thoughtless, but somehow he would make up for it. "He calls
and excuses himself for his jerkiness if he's been majorly bad," Shaffer said, noting that sometimes Donald let Abe Wallach, his chief of
staff, smooth things over or take the blame. "He'll say, 'I didn't do

that, Abe did.' The whole thing is childish and immature, but most of the time it's fun and sometimes you even make money."[14]

To be a lasting presence in Donald Trump's life, one had to be able to take the long view. "You know with him you'll get the bum's rush at some point, then he'll be all over you," said another person who had known Trump since the developer first arrived in Manhattan. "All you have to do is keep your eye on the heart-rate graph printout, or on the applause meter, because that's where his eye is. He'll be charming, you'll be the greatest, then he'll say something neutral, then something negative. It will be a whole package. This is understood with someone like this, that everything is marketing."

As a result, Trump seemed to have few truly close friends. One reason was that he was too busy working; another may have been that traditional men's culture does not often encourage such relationships or the sharing of personal thoughts. "He talks about whatever is going on in the world," said yet another acquaintance. "Not personal things. He doesn't need that one-to-one. I don't think he approaches his personal feelings because he doesn't need that emotional outlet. He gets along best with people who are very direct—straightforward, unemotional people because it's uncomplicated and you can get straight to the point. He can be kind and funny, but he's not embracing."

But perhaps the most important reason was that in any relationship he always had to be in charge, to a degree that precluded the give-and-take that intimacy requires. Thus a favorite way to be with friends was at the U.S. Open tennis tournament, held in Forest Hills, Queens, in late summer. Each year Donald would hold court in a large private box, eating hot dogs and French fries and watching the world's best tennis players compete only a few yards away. In the box with him would be a handful of celebrities, assorted useful business contacts, and his children.

As at that lunchtime table back at the '21' Club, he was right where he wanted to be, right in the middle of everything. In the course of the afternoon or evening, everyone who was anyone would stop by and say hello. Because the event was televised, millions of others would see this, would nod to him in their heads, would think to themselves, Donald Trump is there, this must be important.

Ultimately, though, he found an even better way to socialize, at

Mar-a-Lago.[15] The mansion's builder, Marjorie Merriweather Post, had ruled Palm Beach by inviting the wealthy and well known of her day and providing lavish entertainment. A hostess in the old sense, she had picked up the tab for everything. Now he, too, would invite the most well-connected and well-known people he could think of. He would meet, greet, talk, give a squeeze on the arm and, sometimes, a peck on the check. But he would be a different sort of host from his predecessor, for he would be charging his guests admission. He would be, as it were, a virtual host.

Unable to get the grounds of Mar-a-Lago rezoned for a luxury subdevelopment, Donald Trump had instead turned the old estate into a private club for tycoons and magnates who flew down to Palm Beach for winter weekends on their own jets. A more glamorous version of the Concord, the Catskills resort where Fred Trump and his colleagues had once congregated, Mar-a-Lago served a similar purpose: a place where the nation's most-high-net-worth individuals, tired out from the week's wheeling and dealing, could get together and socialize with their own kind. To join they paid an initiation fee, officially listed as $100,000 but waived in the case of extremely high-profile types whose names on the membership list were worth far more to Trump. The privileges of membership included use of a spa, a three-hole mini–golf course, tennis courts, a strip of ocean beach, a pool, dining facilities, and, mainly, the opportunity to be part of a social set every bit as exclusive as that which Donald Trump had found so offensive when he first arrived.

Presiding over it all was Donald Trump, entrepreneur and master of ceremonies, virtual developer and virtual host. At night, sometimes with his beautiful teenage daughter, Ivanka, on his arm, he would move through the room like a turn-of-the-century grandee, charming and attentive to everyone he encountered. Even among this group, heads turned to follow his progress, and somehow there seemed to be a spotlight on him, even though in fact there was none. By his presence and, even more, by his name, he was proof that the men and women there were in the most important place they could possibly be, in the company of the most important people they could possibly be with.

All evening long he would be the center of attention in a room full of people who had spent much of their lives being the center of attention. Then, when he wanted to go home, he would wave good night and mount the stairs to his private living quarters. Alone upstairs in his palatial suite, he would check closing market prices, watch a talk show or a video, nibble on snack food, and talk on the phone, while below him the party would go on, the guests would keep laughing and eating and drinking and dancing, and he would keep making money, all night long.

NOTES

INTRODUCTION

1. In 1984, Donald Trump sued Julius and Edmond Trump over their use of "The Trump Group" to designate their real estate company. Ultimately they were enjoined from using their own family name as a trademark. See chapter 19.

2. *Newsweek*, 2/20/89; Reuters, 2/7/89.

CHAPTER 1: THE NEW WORLD

1. The complex housed fireworks, wrestling matches, tightrope walkers, Indian war dances, a park with swans and deer, and, most famously, Jenny Lind, the Swedish Nightingale, who sold out the six-hundred-seat auditorium in 1850. Sources for this section include Ann Novotny, *Strangers at the Door*, pp. 40ff.

2. During the Civil War, the Union Army had set up a recruiting stand and attracted so many immigrants with a $600 enlistment bounty that they constituted a hefty portion of the Grand Army of the Republic.

3. LaVern Rippley, *The German-Americans*, Twague Publishers, 1976, p. 96.

4. Ernst Merk, *Heimatbuch des Edelweindorfes Kallstadt*. Property transfers dropped to almost nothing. According to the *Uffagabebuch*, in which such actions were recorded, real estate sales plummeted from an average of three to five per year to only three in the twenty-four-year stretch from 1632 to 1655.

5. Golo Mann, *The History of Germany Since 1789*.

6. Merk, *Heimatbuch*.

7. Worried that the colonies might become German in language and culture, Benjamin Franklin supposedly muttered darkly about sending "the Palatines" back where they came from, and in London Edmund Burke made the same suggestion. Sources in this section include Roland Paul, *300 Years Palatines in America*, 1983, pp. 46ff., and interviews with Christian Freund, 5/91.

8. Wilhelm Heinrich Riehl, *Die Pfalzer*, 1857, p. 220.

9. P. G. J. Pulzer, "From Bismarck to the Present," in *Germany: A Companion to German Studies*, Malcolm Pasley, ed., p. 260.

10. Charlotte Erickson, *Emigration from Europe*, 1976, pp. 39ff.

11. Bob Larson, *It's All Your Pfalz*, 1982, p. 90.

12. Otto Roller, *Die Schoene Pfalz*, p. 33.

13. Her dowry included property worth 6,000 marks, a considerable sum when a laborer's weekly wage was perhaps 5 marks, but it was mortgaged to the hilt.

14. Wolfgang Glaser, p. 120.

15. *America & the Germans*, ed. by Frank Tommler and McVeigh, vol. 1, 1985, p. 76.

16. The railroad hired 124 agents, who distributed 623,590 copies of publications and placed ads in sixty-eight German-language papers. Sources include Roland Paul, *300 Years*, pp. 90–95.

17. Merk, *Heimatbuch.*

18. Sources include Edward R. Hewitt, *Those Were the Days*, 1943, pp. 158–159.

19. Sources for this section include Leslie Allen, *Liberty: The Statue and the American Dream*, 1985, p. 66.

20. Roland Paul, *300 Years*, p. 93.

21. *Valentine's Manual of Old New York: 1927*, ed. Henry Collins Brown.

22. *Eider* passenger list.

23. Leslie Allen, *Liberty*, p. 80.

24. Stan Fischler, *Uptown Downtown: A Trip Through Time on New York's Subways*, 1976, p. 18.

25. Sources for this section include Stephan Longstreet, *City on Two Rivers: Profile of New York: Yesterday and Today*, 1975; Lloyd Morris, *Incredible New York: High Life and Low Life of the Last Hundred Years*, 1951; and Edwin G. Burrows and Mike Wallace, *Gotham: A History of New York City to 1898*, 1998.

26. Sources for this section include Hewitt, *Days*, pp. 57 and 113; Longstreet, *City*, pp. 52ff., and Morris, *Incredible*, p. 112.

27. Anthony Jackson, *A Place Called Home: A History of Low-Cost Housing in Manhattan*, p. 78.

28. *Valentine's Manual of Old New York: 1926*, pp. 41, 204, 206.

29. Sources for this section include John Robertson Henry, *50 Years on the Lower East Side*, pp. 6–11; Valentine, *1926*, p. 19; Morris, *Incredible*, pp. 88 and 124–54, and Longstreet, *City*, p. 29.

30. James McCabe, *Lights and Shadows of New York Life*, quoted in Longstreet, *City*, p. 66.

31. McCabe, quoted in Longstreet, p. 77.

32. The 1811 New York City commissioners' map set the groundwork for the modern metropolis, laying out streets and carving the vast emptiness into blocks and lots, even though few expected all the neatly ruled rectangles on the zoning maps ever to be inhabited. "To some," the commissioners conceded, "it may be a subject of merriment that the Commissioners have provided for a greater population than is collected at any spot on this side of China." Sources include William Thompson Bonner, *New York, the World's Metropolis*, R. L. Polk & Co., 1924, p. 355.

33. Valentine, *1926*, p. 21.

34. Sources for this section include Ann L. Buttenweiser, *Manhattan Water-Bound*, 1987, p. 42.

35. Except where specifically noted otherwise, most of what follows comes from conversations with Benjamin Miller, director of public policy for the Office of Resource Recovery at the New York City Sanitation Department. He was extremely generous with his time and expertise, and I am most grateful.

36. Valentine, *1927*, pp. 3–11.

37. Jackson, *Place*, p. 77.

38. *New York Panorama: WPA Guide*, pp. 100, 138–139.

CHAPTER 2: SEATTLE DAYS AND NIGHTS

1. Yesler Way was also known as Skid Road, for this was where early settlers rolled logs down the hill from Henry Yesler's sawmill to the water. Sources for this section include William C. Speidel, *Sons of the Profits*, pp. 1ff., 291.

2. Sources for this section include Murray Morgan, *Skid Road*, 1971; Gordon Newell & Don Sherwood, *Totem Tales of Old Seattle*, 1974; Roger Sale, *Seattle: Past to Present*, 1976; Carlos A. Schwantes, *The Pacific Northwest: An Interpretive History*, 1989; and William C. Speidel, *Sons of the Profits*, 1967.

3. According to Morgan, *Skid*, p. 18, the Indians on the Sound were all part of the Salish family.

4. When it became clear that the pounding storms at the first location would make it impossible to found a metropolis, the name was altered to "New York-Alki," meaning "New York bye-and-bye," and then eventually to just "Alki." Meanwhile most of the settlers moved across the bay to the spot, empty but for a deserted Indian longhouse, that would become Seattle. Relations between settlers and Salish remained uneasy, despite the choice of the name of a local Indian chief, Sealth, for the new town. Sealth himself was reportedly horrified by the gesture because Salish myth holds that the dead are disturbed whenever their name is uttered. Nor did the name reflect any significant change in attitude on the part of the settlers. Seattle's white majority retained its initial prejudices and in 1865 banned Indians from residing within city limits. Sources include *New York Times*, 4/21/92, p. 1, and Newell & Sherwood, *Totem*, p. 11.

5. John F. Storer, *The Life & Decline of the American Railroad*, p. 64.

6. Supposedly said by Commodore Vanderbilt, the railroad magnate who greatly expanded the New York Central Railroad and made it one of the era's most powerful lines. Chamberlain, *Enterprising*, p. 134.

7. Sources for this section include William A. McKenzie, *Dining Car Line to the Pacific*, 1990. The lengthy and elaborate menu featured duck, trout, venison, and salmon; the wine list consisted of vintages from Bordeaux, the Rhine, Moselle, and Champagne. "There was nothing to indicate the great distance from markets and cities, save the occasional necessity of resorting to condensed milk for the coffee," editor Eugene V. Smalley wrote in his magazine, *The Northwest*, as quoted in McKenzie, p. 60. The ongoing celebration, which lasted for days, included a twenty-mile-long parade in St. Paul, a Crow Indian tribal council, and festive arches, bunting, and processions in every major stop all the way to the West Coast.

8. David Chalmers, *Neither Socialism nor Monopoly*, 1976, p. 4. Estimates on railroads and land vary. Chalmers reports that eighty railroads received 180 million acres; Schwantes, pp. 142–143, reports that from 1864 to 1871, congressional land grants totaled 131,350,534 acres to sixty-one railroads.

9. Storer, *American Railroad*, p. 83.

10. Sources include John Chamberlain, *The Enterprising Americans*, 1974, pp. 171ff.

11. William A. McKenzie, *Dining Car*, p. 63.

12. Northern Pacific R.R. timetable, Spring–Summer 1891, kindly provided by Larry Shrenk.

13. Storer, *American Railroad*, p. 75.

14. Northern Pacific R.R. timetable, Spring–Summer 1891.

15. Interview with Gary Tarbox, February 1992.

16. Julian Ralph, "Washington—The Evergreen State," *Harper's New Monthly Magazine*, September 1892, pp. 595–596.

17. Sources for this section and the one following include Speidel, *Sons of the Profits*, pp. 237ff., and interview with Jeff Oechsner, 8/90.

18. Sources include Alexander Norbert MacDonald, "Seattle's Economic Development, 1880–1910," Ph.D. dissertation, 1959, pp. 293ff., and Morgan, *Skid Road*, p. 78. For this section, I am particularly grateful for interviews with Tim O'Brien on 2/28/92 and 3/30/00.

19. Schwantes, *Pacific*, p. 184. A census included 21 banks, 105 restaurants, 64 barbershops, 33 publications including 4 daily newspapers, 3 dancing academies, 13 public baths, and 36 dentists, whose services included full sets of rubber teeth for only $3.

20. Sources include *Seattle Press-Times* election coverage, October and November 1892.

CHAPTER 3: TALES OF MONTE CRISTO

1. Sources for this section include David A. Cameron, "The Everett and Monte Cristo Railway: A Lifeline to the Mines of Eastern Snohomish County," *Journal of Everett & Snohomish County History*, Winter 1988–89; Norman H. Clark, *Milltown*, 1970; Philip R. Woodhouse, *Monte Cristo*, 1979; Murray Morgan, *Mill on the Boot*, 1982; and *Everett Times*, 9/20/1893. I am indebted to David Cameron for his assistance with this material and numerous interviews in 1991–93 and 2000, and to Douglas McNair for a tour of Monte Cristo in 1990.

2. *Everett Times*, 7/4/1889.

3. Woodhouse, *Monte Cristo*, pp. 13–15.

4. *Everett Times*, 7/4/1889; and Woodhouse, p. 27.

5. Clark, *Milltown*, pp. 25ff.

6. Interview with David Cameron, 5/91.

7. Sources for this section include Ron Chernow, *Titan: The Life of John D. Rockefeller Sr.*, passim; and Allan Nevins, *John D. Rockefeller: The Heroic Age of American Enterprise*, vol. 1, pp. 191, 266, 268.

8. *Everett Times*, 2/15/1893.

9. *Everett Times*, 10/12/1892.

10. Quoted in Woodhouse, *Monte Cristo*, pp. 44, 79. The Comstock Lode was the richest known U.S. silver deposit, discovered in western Nevada in 1857.

11. Morgan, *Mill on the Boot*, p. 114.

12. Clark, *Milltown*, p. 15.

13. Sources for this section include Woodhouse, pp. 45ff., and Cameron, pp. 4ff.

14. Sources for this section include letter from David Cameron, 7/10/91; and *Everett News*, 6/16/1894.

15. Clark, p. 25.

16. Woodhouse, p. 54.

17. Interviews with Gary Tarbox, 1/25/92, and Lorenz Shrenk, 3/1/92.

18. Interview with Gary Tarbox, 2/92.

19. Speidel, p. 272.

20. Woodhouse, p. 37.

21. *Everett News*, 9/17/1892.

22. *Everett News*, 7/11/1894.

23. *Seattle Press-Times*, 4/21/1893.

24. Further, if he proved that the claim was a moneymaker, he could file for a patent, or ownership of all rights. This process entailed performing a mineral survey, installing $500 in improvements, and completing numerous complex applications. At Monte Cristo this lengthy rigmarole discouraged many claim holders, most of whom were small operators whose sole intent was to sell off their holdings to larger outfits for cash or a percentage of profits. But for Frederick Trump, filing such a claim was a preemptive move that would block other such attempts. Further, if the claim did somehow go through, he could then patent it and have the property at a relatively small cost.

25. Seattle directory, 1893.

26. Charitably, one can imagine that Frederick Trump hoped that Rudebeck had not renewed his claim, making the land available. Sources include interview with David Dilgard, 7/90.

27. Sources for this section include Jeffrey Karl Ochsner and Dennis Alan Anderson, "Adler and Sullivan's Seattle Opera House Project," *Journal of the Society of Architectural Historians*, vol. XLVIII, no. 3, September 1989, p. 229; and Milton Friedman and Anna Jacobson Schwartz, *Monetary History of the United States*, 1963.

28. *Seattle Times*, 5/4/1893.

29. *Seattle Press-Times*, 5/5/1893.

30. *Seattle Press-Times*, 5/12/1893.

31. Woodhouse, *Monte Cristo*, p. 89.

32. Ibid., p. 90.

33. Ibid.

34. *Everett Times*, 9/20/1893.

35. *Everett Herald*, 8/3/1893.

36. *Everett Herald*, 12/7/1893.

37. *Everett News*, 9/23/1893.

38. *Everett News*, 9/23/1893.

39. Woodhouse, p. 80.

40. *Everett News*, 8/19/1893.

41. *Everett News*, 9/30/1893.

42. Cameron, "Railway," pp. 4ff; Woodhouse, *Monte Cristo*, pp. 52ff.

43. Woodhouse, *Monte Cristo*, p. 90.

44. *Everett News*, 1/6/1894.

45. David Cameron, letter 7/10/1991.

46. *Everett News*, 6/16/1894.

47. *Everett News*, 6/23/1894.

48. *Everett Herald*, 12/18/1893; Morgan, *Mill on the Boot*, p. 124.

49. Clark, *Milltown*, p. 32.

50. Woodhouse, *Monte Cristo*, p. 101; Morgan, *Mill on the Boot*, p. 126.

51. Clark, *Milltown*, p. 31.

52. Sources include Woodhouse, p. 44, and interview with David Cameron, 4/9/00. The real problem was the lack of knowledge at the time about the nature of Cascade deposits. The debate about how valuable the deposits at Monte Cristo were was not finally resolved until a 1902 report by geologist Josiah Sparr concluded that mining there could not be a paying proposition with existing technology.

53. *Everett News*, 8/25/1894.

54. *Everett News*, 11/24/1894.

55. Woodhouse, *Monte Cristo*, p. 103.

56. Ibid., pp. 114–115.

57. *Everett News*, 7/7/1894.

58. *Everett News*, 7/11/1894.

59. Deed recorded 12/1/1894, Snohomish County, Washington.

60. *Everett News*, 2/9/1895, 2/23/1895; *Everett Times*, 2/13/1895, 2/27/1895, 3/13/1895, 10/16/1895.

61. *Snohomish Democrat* 12/21/1895; *Everett News*, 12/7/1895; *Everett Times*, 10/16/1895.

62. *Everett Herald*, 1/01/1896.

63. Roger Sale, *Seattle*, pp. 14ff.
64. From the start, America had a long and tangled history with money. When
Henry Hudson sailed up the river that was to bear his name, the Indians standing along the shore used clamshells and periwinkles woven into strings and mats
for buying and selling. Crude as this system looked to the Europeans, it was
admirably simple and stable compared with the unholy hodgepodge of coins,
made by everyone from emperors to common tinkers, that circulated on the
continent. Even after other European countries got their monetary systems in
some kind of order, and Great Britain introduced paper money, Germany was
still awash in coins of all shapes, sizes, and materials, issued by every princeling
in the realm.

   Hardly surprising, buying and selling in the New World was also a cumbersome affair. Many transactions used beaver, tobacco, wheat, beef, or pork as legal
tender, but a more convenient and large-scale medium of exchange was needed.
Colonies and then states printed their own money, but because it lacked backing
and depreciated rapidly, Americans used foreign currencies when possible. Until
as late as 1825, there were 174 varieties of foreign silver coins in Manhattan
alone, and in gold there was the Spanish pistole, Venetian sequin, Portuguese
Johannes, German carolin, and a dozen others. Plus, of course, bills of credit for
armies raised for various wars, small notes and bills of private parties, loan office
certificates, notes of trading companies and, later, banks, and currency issued by
the various states.

   Gradually the American monetary system stabilized, only to be destabilized
all over again during the Civil War. To cover the cost of the war, which totaled
about $4 billion, the federal government issued $449 million in unsupported
greenbacks, sold bonds, and imposed an income tax. Disappointing revenues and
complaints meant an early end to the tax, but rounding up the greenbacks took a
decade and a half. In the meantime, local and national economies used "shin-
plasters," fractional paper currency issued by banks, railroads, corporations, even
individuals, in denominations of 3, 5, 10, 15, 25, and 50 cents.

   Until nearly the end of the century, the struggle to control and define the
nation's monetary system continued. Roughly speaking, this conflict pitted
eastern bondholders against western plowholders—that is, bankers, industrial-
ists, and institutional interests, based mostly in the East, against farmers, settlers, and the newer cities to the West. Put simply, the former, who were
epitomized by the banker J. P. Morgan, wanted their money to be worth as much
as possible and so opposed efforts to put any more currency in circulation; this
was the "hard" or "tight" money position. They favored high interest rates—that
is, they wanted their money to make a lot of money—and a return to the gold
standard, which would mean that the federal government stood ready to back up
all currency with gold reserves. Most often Republicans, these "goldbugs"
wanted to protect their position as "haves."

   By contrast, the other side was basically the "have-nots" of the day, although
its ranks included such famous "haves" as Philadelphia banker Jay Cooke, who
proclaimed the need for both gold and silver "to oil the machinery of exchange"
and facilitate development. The have-nots wanted more money in circulation so
that they could have some; this was the "soft" money point of view. Their two
main goals were low interest rates, so that they could borrow to finance their

own growth and development, and bimetallism, which would expand the money supply by pegging currency to silver as well as gold.

Voters who favored this view tended to support the Democratic Party. Along the way, however, those who were fed up with establishment politics altogether left to form the Populist movement and the Greenback Party. Both groups advocated inflating the currency as a way of allowing workers to share more fully in the fruits of their labor, rather than letting those profits go to make a small number of millionaires even more wealthy.

In response to these fiercely competing pressures, U.S. monetary policy zigged and zagged, accommodating one side and then the other. In 1878 the United States adopted a limited bimetallic standard; a year later the nation was back on the gold standard. A decade afterward, in 1890, the Sherman Silver Purchase Act once again authorized the federal government to buy a certain amount of silver to be made into coins. Then, in November 1893, Congress repealed the Sherman Act's purchase clause. The government pegged silver to gold coins at forty to one, which drastically limited the amount of silver in circulation; by contrast, the "free silver" opposition was pressing for a silver to gold ratio of sixteen to one.

The stage was set for a showdown. It arrived in 1896, when William Jennings Bryan's candidacy split the nation as well as the Democratic Party into hard and soft money camps. Bryan's remarkable ability to speak to the feelings of depression and discontent sweeping the nation had already won him a seat in Congress from normally Republican Nebraska. His eloquent speeches to the House opposing repeal of the Sherman Act made him the leader of the free silver movement and champion of bimetallism. In 1896 he went as a delegate to the National Democratic Convention in Chicago, wrote the party platform, and delivered his most celebrated oration. It culminated with an unforgettable manifesto: "You shall not press down upon the brow of labor this crown of thorns; you shall not crucify mankind upon this cross of gold." The speech was electrifying and gave the Democratic Party's presidential nomination to Bryan on the spot.

65. Friedman and Schwartz, *History*, pp. 112ff.

66. *Everett News*, 8/2/1896.

67. General Election Abstract of Votes 1896 of Snohomish County.

CHAPTER 4: MINING THE MINERS

1. Sources for this section include Pierre Berton, *The Klondike Fever: The Life and Death of the Last Great Gold Rush*, 1958, pp. 99ff.; William C. Speidel, *Sons of the Profits*; David and Judie Clarridge, *A Ton of Gold*, 1972.

2. MacDonald, dissertation, p. 134.

3. Clarridge, *Ton of Gold*, pp. 5–6.

4. Berton, *Klondike Fever*, pp. 110ff.

5. Victoria Hartwell Livingston, "Erastus Brainerd: The Bankruptcy of Brilliance," master's thesis, University of Washington, 1967, pp. 27ff.

6. MacDonald, dissertation, pp. 138ff.

7. Livingston, master's thesis, pp. 28–29. Sources include Morgan, *Skid*, pp. 158–159, and Speidel, *Sons*, pp. 318–319.

8. Speidel, *Sons*, pp. 319ff.

9. Morgan, *One Man's Gold Rush*, p. 38.

10. Clarridge, *Ton of Gold*, p. 8.

11. Interview with Tim O'Brien, 2/28/92.

12. Chattel mortgage filed in Kings County, Washington, 9/29/1897.

13. The same facility subsequently became Manca's Cafe, which can be seen in photographs in Paul Dorpat, *Seattle Now & Then*, vol. III, 1989, pp. 106–107.

14. Morgan, *Skid Road*, pp. 124ff. The restaurant sat on land owned by Amos Brown, who had been lured from New Hampshire by a small gold rush on the Fraser River in 1858. Ten years later he had been a beneficiary of a somewhat embarrassing adventure in Seattle history, when an enterprising Seattle resident named Asa Mercer raised money by public subscription to import marriageable maidens from back east. But New York papers did not discern civic virtue in Mercer's plan; instead they saw it as tantamount to white slavery. Seattle got a black eye, Mercer lost his shirt, and the Illahee went on to prosper. One of the few dozen maidens who reached Seattle wed Amos Brown, who later on became a major property owner, city father, and trustee of the Seattle Opera House Company. He lived around the corner from Trump's restaurant in a Victorian mansion considered the finest house in town. Sources include Paul Dorpat, *Seattle*, pp. 84–85.

15. R. C. Coutts, *Yukon: Places & Names*, 1980, p. 133.

16. Coutts, *Yukon*, p. 79.

17. Woodhouse, *Monte Cristo*, p. 164ff.; Schwantes, *Pacific Northwest*, p. 179.

18. Cameron, "Everett and Monte Cristo Railway," p. 15; Clark, *Milltown*, p. 33.

19. In the years that followed, Monte Cristo was the site of sporadic mining efforts. Although the railroad finally closed down permanently in 1933, the town still attracts adventure-seeking tourists. Sources for this section include Woodhouse, *Monte Cristo*, pp. 153ff.

20. Clark, *Milltown*, p. 33.

CHAPTER 5: KLONDIKE FEVER

1. Juliette C. Reinicker, *Klondike Letters*, printed in *Alaska Journal*, 1984, p. 18.

2. E. Hazard Wells, *Magnificence & Misery*, p. 32.

3. Such strictness was understandable; in 1898–99, 48 percent of total government expenditures in the Yukon Territory went to the care of indigent prospectors. Ken S. Coates and William R. Morrison, *Land of the Midnight Sun: A History of the Yukon*, 1988, p. 10.

4. Hazel T. Proctor, *Tenderfoot to Sourdough*, 1975, passim.

5. Archie Satterfield, *Chilkoot Pass*, 1978, p. 2. Satterfield notes that the Chilkoot Pass was called the "meanest 32 miles in history."

6. Sources include Coates and Morrison, *Land of the Midnight Sun*, p. 91; Wells, *Magnificence*, p. 214.

7. S. H. Graves, *On the "White Pass" Payroll*, 1908, pp. 36–37.

8. Roy Minter, *The White Pass: Gateway to the Klondike*, 1987, p. 139.

9. Reinicker, *Klondike*, p. 31.

10. *Victoria Colonist*, 5/28/1898. At the same time Fred Trump was setting up shop, a group of English investors, under the leadership of financier William Brooks Close, embarked on the considerably larger project of constructing a railroad through the White Pass. It would run from Skagway through the mountains, alongside Bennett Lake and then more or less due north to the point where the Yukon became navigable, a total distance of 110.7 miles. Unlike the Rockefeller-backed builders at Monte Cristo, who in a disastrous attempt to economize bypassed their own engineers' recommendations and laid down a track that could not survive the harsh winters of the region, those who constructed the White Pass & Yukon route produced an engineering marvel. Rising from sea level at the coast to 2,880 feet at the summit of the White Pass, it looped back and forth across the narrow canyons and barely clung to steep cliffsides. A 250-foot tunnel had to be blasted out of solid granite, and the 215-foot-high trestle bridge over Dead Horse Gulch was among the world's highest for some time.

  Like many engineering marvels, the WP&YR took far longer than originally projected, and local wags joked that its initials meant "Wait Patiently and You'll Ride." A major problem was finding enough men to build the line. The job required two thousand workers, but as soon as laborers accumulated any pay, they headed off for the gold fields that were the only reason they had come so far north. But finally, in mid-1899, the section from Skagway to the town of Bennett was completed. The next year, the line made it to its terminus in White Horse. Sources include Minter, *White Pass*.

11. John Alexander Sinclair papers, 1898–1902, misc. 5/29/1898, pp. 70–71.

12. Mary Louise Black, *My 90 Years*, 1976, pp. 35ff.

13. Robert G. McCandless, *Yukon Wildlife: A Social History*, 1985, p. 48; Martha Louise Black, *My 90 Years*; *Yukon Sun*, 4/17/1900, reprinted in *Atlin Claim*, 5/5/1900.

14. Sinclair diary, 1/4/1900.

15. *Yukon Sun*, 4/17/1900, reprinted in *Atlin Claim*, 5/5/1900.

16. *Victoria Colonist*, 6/7/1898, p. 5.

17. Berton, *Klondike Fever*, revised edition, p. xvi.

18. *Dyea Press & Trail*, special illustrated edition, August 1898.

19. Berton, *Klondike Fever*, revised edition, p. xiv; Coates and Morrison, *Land of the Midnight Sun*, p. 104.

20. The spelling of the town's name is sometimes White Horse, other times Whitehorse. I have chosen White Horse in accordance with contemporary local newspapers. Current Canadian usage is Whitehorse.

21. Even in the Yukon, the final "golden" spike in railway construction was made of material more base and also more sturdy.

22. Minter, *White Pass*, p. 347. Hardly surprising, Mrs. Wood's own first name is not included in any contemporary accounts. Her husband's background, however, is extensively covered. He was a grandson of Zachary Taylor, twelfth president of the U.S., and a nephew of Jefferson Davis, president of the Confederacy. After the South lost the war, Wood's father, like many Confederate military men, emigrated to Canada and became part of the military establishment there.

23. Paul M. Koroscil, "The Historical Development of Whitehorse," *The American Review of Canadian Studies*, vol. XVIII, no. 3, pp. 271–292.

24. Interview with Linda Johnson, 8/90.

25. Minter, *White Pass*, pp. 35off.

26. *Dawson-Daily News*, vol. 2, no. 1, 1/31/1900

27. Minter, *White Pass*, pp. 35off.

28. *Bennett Sun*, 7/7/1900.

29. If anything, Dawson's gold dust was circulating too much. According to the *Dawson Daily News* of August 25, 1900, gold dust, which was used in commerce at a par value of $16 per ounce, often underwent so much "doctoring with black sand, white iron, brass filings, and even fine bird shot" that it was not worth even $13 an ounce.

30. Sources include the Honorable Stratford Tollemache, *Reminiscences of the Yukon*, 1912.

31. Graves, *Payroll*, p. 141.

32. *Dawson Daily News*, 7/6/1900.

33. According to Coates and Morrison, *Land of the Midnight Sun*, p. 114, production of Klondike gold in 1900 was $22 million, versus $2.5 million in 1897 and $10 million in 1898.

34. Other events were also overshadowing the Klondike. The Spanish-American War had broken out, and the attention of the notably fickle American public turned to the front. Despite the enormous revenues pouring out of the far North, the Yukon dropped out of the spotlight. It was old news. "Go to the Klondike!", formerly a cheerful salutation, had changed to mean something more like "Drop dead!" Berton, *Klondike Fever*, p. 411.

35. Richard Mathews, *The Yukon*, 1968, pp. 142–143.

36. Whitehorse Heritage Buildings pamphlet, Yukon Historical and Museum Association, 1983, p. 60; Jane Gaffin, correspondence with author, 7/7/91.

37. Interview with Linda Johnson, 8/90.

38. *Bennett Sun*, 7/7/1900.

39. *White Horse Star*, 2/2/01, p. 2.

40. *White Horse Star*, first anniversary edition, 5/1/01.

41. Jane Gaffin, correspondence with author, 7/31/91.

42. *White Horse Star*, 2/13/01, 2/20/01, 2/27/01, 3/06/01, 3/20/01.

43. David R. Morrison, *The Politics of Yukon Territory, 1898–1909*, pp. 4ff.

44. By 1900 the cheaper transport available on the railroad balanced off the gradual
emptying out of placer deposits. Within two years the very nature of gold mining
had changed; with placer mining played out, what was needed was capital, not
workers. Gold mining was no longer a situation involving hundreds of individual
digs worked by one or two people. To get the remaining gold out of the ground
required expensive hydraulic and dredging equipment, which meant large-scale
commercial operations. The day of the cheechako was over, and thus the days of
restaurants like the Arctic were also. The population of White Horse and Dawson fell precipitously. Dawson never revived, but White Horse came back to life
during World War II, when the United States routed the Alaska Highway through
the town and reestablished it as a regional center.

45. *White Horse Star,* 3/5/02, 3/15/02, 3/22/01.

CHAPTER 6: HERE TO STAY

1. Interviews with Christian Freund, May 1991. Nicknames were common among
villagers. One Trump relative was Hinkel ("Chicken") Hartung, because he
raised fowl for a living; another was "Crazy" Hartung because instead of working in the field he preferred to read and play music. Because the Trumps were the
only family in the area with that surname, they did not need a nickname.

2. Gary Hermalyn, "The Bronx at the Turn of the Century," *The Bronx County
Historical Society Journal,* Fall 1989, p. 96.

3. Sources include Jill Jonnes, *We're Still Here: The Rise, Fall, and Resurrection of
the South Bronx,* 1986, p. 11; Edward Wolf, "Adam Hoffmann: Master Brewer,"
n.d., courtesy of John McNamara, Bronx County Historical Society.

4. Sources include Jonnes, *Still Here,* pp. 22, 25ff.; Evelyn Gonzales, *Building a
Borough,* 1986, p. 21; Bert Sack, "Growing Pains of the Bronx," n.d., and Leo
Weigers, "Growing Up in Morrisania," n.d., courtesy of John McNamara.

5. Bert Sack, "Life in the Bronx: 1900," in Lloyd Ultan and Gary Hermalyn, eds.,
The Bronx in the Innocent Years: 1890–1925, 1985.

6. Census and voting records and New York City directories.

7. According to Professor Michael Edelstein, Department of Economics at John Jay
College, 80,000 German marks in 1904 would be worth $355,000 in 1999 dollars.

8. Sabine Baring Gould and Arthur Gillman, *Germany: The Kaiser and His Times,*
1901, p. 421.

9. Sources include Otto Hinze, "Military Organization and State Organization," in
The Historical Essays, Otto Gibert, ed., n.d.; Gould and Gillman, *Germany,* pp.
139ff.; P. G. J. Pulzer, "From Bismarck to the Present," in *Germany: A Companion to German Studies,* Malcolm Pasley, ed., 1982, pp. 286–295; Golo Mann,
History of Germany Since 1789, pp. 262ff.

10. German federal archives, Speyer, Friedrich Trump papers and correspondence,
document y, September 21, 1904.

11. German federal archives, documents 15/16, December 24, 1904.

12. German federal archives, documents 65–67.

13. German federal archives, documents 15/16.

14. Sabine Gould and Arthur Gillman, *Germany*, passim.

15. German federal archives, document 42.

16. German federal archives, documents 31–34.

17. German federal archives, document 36.

18. William Carr, *A History of Germany 1815–1945*, 1969, pp. 224–226.

19. Whether Wilhelm and Bernard von Bulow, his chancellor from 1900 to 1909, really wanted such arrangements is an intriguing question, for clear opportunities to arrive at some sort of entente, including a bid at the turn of the century from the other superpower of Europe, Britain, were allowed to fizzle out. The power behind this policy was von Bulow, a smart and supremely egotistical diplomat who assumed there was nothing he could not arrange. "Bernard Bulow is clean-shaven and flabby, with a shifty look," Geheimrat Holstein, minister of foreign affairs and an archrival, confided to his diary. "[He] usually has a smile on his face . . . [and] no ideas in store. . . . If Bulow wants to set one man against another, he says with a charming smile to the one that the other does not like him. The method is simple and almost infallible." Sources include Louis Snyder, "William II's visit to Tangier, March 31, 1905," *Documents of German History*, 1958, pp. 288–289; Carr, *History*, pp. 224–226, and Golo Mann, *History*, pp. 264ff.

20. German federal archives, document 40.

21. German federal archives, documents 24/25.

22. German federal archives, documents 65–67.

CHAPTER 7: BORN TO WORK

1. Sources include *Brooklyn Times Union*, 1/5/34, and motion by Isador Neuwirth to set aside the election of Charles H. McDermot [sic], Frederick S. Martyn, and Charles H. Kriger as trustees. January 19, 1934, Lehrenkrauss, file B.

2. *Brooklyn Eagle*, 1/16/34.

3. *Brooklyn Eagle*, 1/25/34.

4. Interviews with Nat Sobel, 3/11/94, and Gene Morris, 3/9/94; *Brooklyn Eagle*, 1/4/34.

5. *Brooklyn Eagle*, 12/16/33.

6. U.S. Supreme Court, Brooklyn, Lehrenkrauss bankruptcy documents, Lehrenkrauss Summary, box 324, folder 61. In 1932 the business had even launched a new venture, the Lehrenkrauss Corporation, and sold $1.6 million in preferred stock to willing buyers, most of them German-Americans. *Brooklyn Eagle*, 12/14/33, p. 1.

7. *Brooklyn Eagle*, 12/2/33.

8. *Brooklyn Eagle*, 12/22/33 and 12/24/33.

9. Interviews with Nat Sobel, 3/11/94, and Conrad Duberstein, 3/28/94.

10. Lehrenkrauss, First Meeting, 1/15/34, pp. 5, 29; *Brooklyn Eagle*, 12/20/41.

11. *Brooklyn Eagle*, 12/23/33.

12. Lehrenkrauss, First Meeting, pp. 9–10.

13. Ibid., p. 11.

14. *New York Times*, 6/20/69.

15. Lehrenkrauss, First Meeting, pp. 12–13.

16. Ibid., p. 15; *Brooklyn Eagle*, 1/16/34.

17. Lehrenkrauss, First Meeting, p. 20.

18. Ibid. pp. 28–29.

19. Robert A. Olmstead, "A History of Transportation in the Bronx," *Bronx County Historical Society Journal*, pp. 8off.

20. Interview with John McNamara, 2/91.

21. Walter Propper, "Growing Up in the Bronx," Ultan and Hermalyn, *Bronx*, p. 2.

22. Interview with John Trump Jr., 1/91, and New York City directories.

23. Vincent Seyfried, *Queens: A Pictorial History*, 1982, preface.

24. Clifton Hood, *722 Miles: The Building of the Subways and How They Transformed New York*, 1993, p. 168.

25. Horse racing, illegal in the rest of the state, brought enormous crowds to the huge oval track at Union Course from the 1820s until the Civil War. In 1845 a southern horse, Peytona, trounced a northern steed, Fashion. Currier and Ives depicted the victory in a print that hung in thousands of southern homes and, according to some historians, fed the hostilities that led to the Civil War. *New York Sun*, 1/31/33; *New York Daily News*, 5/1/83,10/6/84; *Richmond Leader-Observer*, 11/22/79.

26. One reason real estate had become a red-hot commodity among New York financiers and entrepreneurs was the Flatiron Building, standing in all its tricorner glory at 23rd Street and Fifth Avenue, one block from the Medallion Hotel. Finished in 1902, it had already inspired plans for nearly one hundred more skyscrapers in Manhattan as well as heavy condemnation. Armchair architects argued that the three-sided edifice would either fall down or create terrifying gusts that would blow down pedestrians and blow up women's skirts. An additional argument, presumably facetious, was that it would produce vicious neck strain among passersby who couldn't help looking up at it. Sources include Eugene Rachlis and John E. Marqusee, *The Landlords*, 1963, pp. 198ff.

27. *Richmond Leader-Observer*, 4/11–17/85.

28. Interview with Dorothy Austen Haas, 3/90.

29. Interview with John Murphy, 2/90.

30. Interview with Hedwig Brautigam Cloos, 2/90.

31. The last few old Dutch farmhouses, decrepit and boarded up, were disappearing, along with the meadows full of daisies. As land values rose so did taxes, and landowners could no longer afford to leave lots empty or even to raise crops. A small farm at the edge of Brooklyn still provided fresh milk and butter to western Queens, but these last rural remnants were being replaced by businesses like Hillside Bank, which was less than a year old when Trump made his first deposit there. With the introduction of trolley service across the Queensboro Bridge in

September 1909, Queens was open to the world. Sources include Jeffrey A. Kroessler, "Building Queens: The Urbanization of New York's Largest Borough," Ph.D. dissertation, City University of New York, 1991, p. 347; interviews with Sibyl Hogan and John Murphy, 2/90, and Hillside Bank incorporation papers.

32. William Kroos, "A Peek at Richmond Hill through the Keyhole of Time," privately published paper, 1983, p. 29; Kroessler, "Building Queens," pp. 348ff.

33. Kroessler, "Building Queens," pp. 352ff.

34. Interview with Jessie Voeller Conrad, 10/24/91.

35. Erik Kirschbaum, "The Eradication of German Culture in the United States: 1917–1918," *American-German Studies*, vol. 2, p. 13. Stuttgart: Hans-Dieter Heinz, 1986.

36. Triangle Hofbrau commemorative booklet.

37. Interview with John Trump, 1/91.

38. For example, in the mid-teens, rapid transit—and the five-cent fare zone—finally reached deep into Queens and changed life along Jamaica Avenue. Seyfried, *Queens*, p. 48.

39. With the building of a second span between Manhattan and Queens, the Hell Gate Bridge, Queens seemed headed toward a future of unstoppable growth and prosperity. The bridge, which finally opened in 1917, was the longest steel span in the world, and its engineer, Gustav Lindenthal, boasted that he could span the Atlantic. Somewhat more realistically, there was talk of making Jamaica Bay into a deepwater port larger than the ports of Liverpool, Hamburg, and Rotterdam. Although technically possible, such a step would have wreaked ecological disaster and left canals in Queens filled with sewage; fortunately it never went beyond the talking stages. Kroessler, "Building Queens," pp. 341ff.

40. Kirschbaum, "Eradication of German Culture," pp. 54ff and Alfred W. Crosby, *America's Forgotten Pandemic: The Influenza of 1918*, Cambridge University Press, New York, 1989, p. 46.

41. Interview with Arthur Bender, 5/91.

42. Crosby, *America's Forgotten Pandemic*, pp. 17ff.

43. Ibid., pp. 7ff.

44. Interview with Fred Trump, 3/1/91.

45. Crosby, p. 171. In Woodhaven there were funeral wreaths on every block and black armbands on many pedestrians. Funeral directors were constantly corraling neighborhood kids to march in the sad processions that seemed to stream to the cemetery almost nonstop. Interview with Felix Cuervo, 3/90.

46. When Fred Trump's sister Elizabeth entered Richmond Hill in 1917, the school was a beehive of patriotic activity. Eager to sacrifice beef, flour, and oil for the soldiers on the front, students boasted that their school was "meatless, wheatless, and heatless." They saved peach pits for use as gas mask filters, collected shirt and coat buttons for Red Cross reuse, and moved graduation to midafternoon to conserve coal and electricity. Boys trained in their own battalion, the first in a Queens school. Girls made clothing for war orphans, knitted sweaters and socks for the troops, and promised to substitute rye flour, cornmeal, and

molasses for supplies diverted to the war effort. Richmond High School Annual for 1901 and June 1905, *Richmond Hill High School Dome*, seventy-fifth anniversary issue, pp. 3ff.

47. *Dome*, anniversary issue, pp. 3ff.

48. *As You Like It* meant "no homework," one newspaper article explained, and *Much Ado About Nothing* referred to "reciting when unprepared." As for pedagogy per se, New York City's schools in the first quarter of the twentieth century did not do a notably better job than at the close. Before World War I, most students never made it to high school, and in 1923, the year Fred Trump graduated from high school, the president of the Carnegie Commission lamented that in many schools "the teaching has become enormously diluted." Six years later the *Elementary School Journal* worried about the large number of children "practically unable to read" after attending public schools. *New York Times*, 2/24/90.

49. Although cars had made an appearance, there were still horse-drawn carts and stables. Victorian-era formality still obtained, which meant that men did not appear in public without a coat, tie, and stiff collar, nor women without hat and gloves. With a vast pool of unskilled but eager labor right at hand, menial tasks remained manual. Even households of modest means had servants, elevators had operators, and a uniformed attendant raised and lowered the gates at each Long Island Railroad grade crossing.

50. Initiated in 1829 in Brooklyn as a festival for Protestant Sunday schools, Anniversary Day gradually became a day of local recognition and celebration in Brooklyn and Queens and remains a school holiday in those two boroughs. *New York Times*, 2/5/95.

51. Interviews with Mildred Spillman Berndt, 2/11/90, and Ethel Shoge Kern, 2/90.

52. According to Professor Michael Edelstein, Frederick Trump's estate, valued at $31,359 after estate taxes, would be worth $344,745 in 1999 dollars. Professor Edelstein's figures are derived from "A Bicentennial Contribution to the History of the Cost of Living in America," by Paul A. David and Peter M. Solar, published in *Research in Economic History*, vol. 2, 1977, pp. 1–80, and current bulletins of the Bureau of Labor Statistics, U.S. Department of Labor.

53. For much of the following account I am indebted to Robert Trump, whom I interviewed on 2/3/94 and 2/16/95, and John Walter, whom I interviewed on 7/26/91 and 2/16/95.

54. Sources for this section include *New York Daily News*, 6/26/99; press release from David O. Albert Associates, 9/11/50; Harry Hurt, *Lost Tycoon*, p. 68; interviews with Robert Trump, 2/3/94, Fred Trump, 3/1/91, and Matilda Schaaf Timmerman, 2/90.

55. *New York Journal-American*, 8/6/53, and *New York Times*, 1/28/73.

56. Interview with William Kroos, 3/16/90.

57. Albert press release, 9/11/50.

58. *Journal-American*, 8/6/53.

59. Interview with Fred Trump, 3/1/91.

60. *New York Times*, 1/28/73; *Brooklyn Eagle*, 5/14/50; *New York Journal-American*, 8/6/53.

61. Interview with Ceil Raufer, 2/90.

62. *New York Times*, 1/5/64.

63. *New York Herald Tribune*, 3/13/31 and 5/8/31.

64. Interview with George Aslaender, 3/14/90.

65. Interview with Robert Trump and John Walter, 2/16/95.

CHAPTER 8: SAVVY IN A BROOKLYN COURTROOM

1. *New York Times*, 1/22/34.

2. Sources for this section include Kathryn B. Yatrakis, "Ballots and Bosses in Brooklyn," paper for American Political Science Association Annual Meeting, 8/3–9/4/88, pp. 16ff.; Jerome Krase, *The Italians and Irish in America*, 1985, pp. 191ff.; Jerome Krase and Charles LaCerra, *Ethnicity and Machine Politics*, 1991, pp. 29ff.; *New York Times* 1/22/34; and interviews with state supreme court judge Nat Sobel, 3/11/94; Anthony Jordan Jr., 12/27/89; Alfred Levingson, 6/14/89. McCooey's nickname may refer to the character Little Buttercup in *H.M.S. Pinafore*, the operetta by Sir William Gilbert and Sir Arthur Sullivan, first produced in London in 1878 and an enormous success in the United States. Little Buttercup, a street vendor of notions and snacks, is a "gay and frivolous" matron who is rosy, round, and a superb dissembler—all characteristics of the Brooklyn political boss. My thanks to Katherine Blair Salant for drawing this reference to my attention.

3. McCooey's most famous predecessor was George Washington Plunkitt, a canny Tammany boss half a century earlier who coined the memorable phrase "honest graft." Sketching out his notion of the ideal politician, Plunkitt scorned dishonest behavior as foolish when "there is so much honest graft lyin' about." To Plunkitt, in return for helping others, a politician had a right to use whatever information came his way to enrich himself. "I seen my opportunities and I took 'em," Plunkitt declared, a forthright and, as it turned out, immortalizing statement.

McCooey, too, took such opportunities as came his way. In addition to whatever "contributions" he might pick up by way of recompense for his labors—$50 was considered an appropriate donation in return for a favor—he gleaned useful information and acted on it. When, for example, the IRT dug a line along Eastern Parkway, McCooey reportedly made money from the excavation contracts and the sale of the excavated dirt. Much of this landfill ended up in East Flatbush on the very land on which Fred Trump would build his first major project. Among those whom McCooey's methods benefitted were family members. His sister was associate superintendent of schools, his brother had a law firm that received over 90 percent of the borough's lucrative construction bonds, his son was a federal judge, and the law firm of his son and son-in-law received forty-nine appointments as guardian or referee, more than all other firms in the borough combined. The biggest job, borough president, went to McCooey's brother-in-law, James J. Byrne. When Byrne died in office in 1930, McCooey promptly replaced him with another old Madison Club buddy. *Brooklyn Eagle*, 1/22/34; *New York Times*, 10/19/29.

4. Henceforth, federal patronage for New York State would go through U.S. Postmaster General James J. Farley, and that for the city would be controlled by Bronx Democratic boss Edward J. Flynn. Krase and LaCerra, *Ethnicity*, p. 52.

5. Warren Moscow, *Last of the Big-Time Bosses*, 1971, p. 50.

6. *Brooklyn Eagle*, 12/7/33.

7. Krase and LaCerra, *Ethnicity*, pp. 84–86.

8. Sources include *New York Times*, 1/22/34, and Krase and LaCerra, *Ethnicity*, pp. 50, 77.

9. *New York Times*, 12/1/33 and 12/7/33.

10. *Brooklyn Eagle*, 12/13/33.

11. *Brooklyn Eagle*, 12/16/33.

12. *Brooklyn Eagle*, 12/26/33, 12/27/33.

13. Lehrenkrauss, Adjourned First Meeting, p. 42.

14. Sources include Wayne Barrett, notes from an interview with Brooklyn politician Joe Sharkey, and interviews with Nat Sobel, 3/1/94 and 11/94; *New York Times*, 6/16/49; Krase and La Cerra, *Ethnicity*, p. 86.

15. *Brooklyn Eagle*, 1/24/24, 1/29/34, and 3/1–3/9/34.

16. Lehrenkrauss, Adjourned First Meeting, March 12, 1934, p. 94.

17. Letter, Fred C. Trump to Trustees in Bankruptcy of Julius Lehrenkrauss, et al., March 9, 1934.

18. Letter, William A. Demm to Trustees in Bankruptcy of Julius Lehrenkrauss, et al., March 9, 1934.

19. March 12 meeting, p. 100.

20. Adjourned First Meeting, pp. 103–105; *Brooklyn Eagle*, 3/13/34; *New York Times*, 3/13/34.

21. Wayne Barrett, notes from interview with John Hyman, n.d.

22. Letter, Fred C. Trump to Trustees in Bankruptcy of J. Lehrenkrauss & Sons, March 13, 1934.

23. *Brooklyn Eagle*, 3/16/34.

24. Lehrenkrauss Meeting, March 26, 1934, p. 186.

25. Lehrenkrauss Meeting, March 26, 1934, p. 179.

26. Lehrenkrauss Meeting, March 26, 1934, p. 189.

27. Lehrenkrauss Meeting, March 26, 1934, p. 181.

CHAPTER 9: WASHINGTON TO THE RESCUE

1. *Brooklyn Eagle*, 3/27/34.

2. Milton Friedman and Anna Jacobson Schwartz, *A Monetary History of the United States, 1867–1960*, 1963, p. 301. Sources for this section include Marriner Eccles, *Beckoning Frontiers*, 1951.

3. Eccles, *Beckoning Frontiers*, p. 144; National Emergency Council release, 3/14/34, cited in Hilbert Fefferman and Mary Fruscello's Memorandum to Gary Kopff, vice president for policy development, FNMA, 3/9/83.

4. John Davies, *Housing Reform During the Truman Administration*, p. 16; National Emergency Council release 3/14/34, cited in Fefferman and Fruscello, p. 2. A year before the 1929 stock market crash, building contracts dipped precipitously and did not rebound. Ben B. Seligman, *The Potentates*, 1971, p. 312.

5. The Hoover administration tried to rescue banks and financial institutions by establishing the Reconstruction Finance Corporation (RFC), which provided handsome bailouts to a fortunate few; for example, three weeks after Charles Davies resigned as RFC president, his Chicago bank, which held a total of $95 million in deposits, received a remarkably generous $90 million loan. But most financial institutions struck out. In May 1932 the House of Lehrenkrauss applied for a $1 million loan based on bogus mortgage certificates; fortunately for both the RFC and Fred Trump's future interests, Lehrenkrauss got a thumb's-down. Sources include Seligman, *The Potentates*, p. 317.
   Although the RFC later served a major role, at this point it had too little money and too many restrictions (for example, loans for industry, for states or cities, for public relief works, or for public relief were prohibited). Worse, the RFC policy of making loans public made banks reluctant to borrow for fear of seeming shaky, while the RFC practice of using the best assets as collateral left banks that did obtain loans without any working capital to get ahead. Seligman, *Potentates*, pp. 316–317; Friedman and Schwartz, *History*, pp. 320–325.
   In July 1932 Congress tried to prop up the collapsing mortgage market with the Federal Home Loan Banking System. But it was too little too late, and the market continued its downward slide. Eccles, *Beckoning Frontiers*, p. 145.

6. Friedman and Schwartz, *History*, p. 316.

7. Ibid., pp. 328–330. In June 1933, in yet another attempt to revive construction, President Roosevelt signed legislation creating the Home Owners Loan Corporation. It helped bail out those who had defaulted on their mortgages, but lacking financing for new construction, it failed to generate an economic turnaround. Eccles, *Beckoning Frontiers*, p. 144.

8. Eccles, *Beckoning Frontiers*, pp. 58–62.

9. Ibid., pp. 91–115, 132–133.

10. Ibid., p. 133.

11. Ibid., pp. 145ff.

12. Interview with Chester Rapkin, 9/22/94.

13. Interview with Allan Thornton, 12/20/94.

14. Richard O. Davies, *Housing Reform During the Truman Administration*, 1968, p. 5.

15. The federal government, which had a $200 million subsidy for the purpose, promised to repay up to 20 percent of total losses to any one institution. However, the default rate was so low that the program cost the government only a fraction of what had been anticipated.

16. Roosevelt's short-lived real estate rescue effort, the Home Owners Loan Corporation, had used a similar approach but did not evaluate the borrower's ability to pay and did not apply to new construction. M. Carter McFarland, *Federal Government and Urban Problems: HUD: Successes, Failures, and the Fate of Our Cities*, p. 117; Allan Thornton, interview.

17. Robert M. Fisher, interview, 12/13/94.

18. Miles Colean, *A Backward Glance: The Growth of Government Housing Policy in the United States 1934–1975*, interviews done for the Oral History Research Office of Columbia University and published by the Research and Educational Trust Fund of the Mortgage Bankers Association of America, 1975, p. 17.

19. A more incongruous setting could hardly be imagined. On pediments outside the new facility, carrier pigeons, ancient Indians, the sun god Helios, and seahorses surrounded huge nudes representing human and divine history. Eagles, symbolizing airmail, swooped overhead. Inside, each floor had cut-glass chandeliers and art deco murals depicting the history of communication in the New World since early colonial days. On the third floor, Postmaster General James Farley, who took over federal patronage from John McCooey and the Madison Club after Roosevelt's election, held court. His inner office was a tennis-court-size mahogany-paneled chamber with walk-in fireplaces at each end and carved ceiling medallions. The capital's most opulent cabinet room, it was also the largest until Interior Secretary Ickes reportedly measured it and made his own office two feet longer. Allan Thornton, interview, 12/20/94.

20. Interview with Helena Casey Kadow, 1/10/95.

21. Interview with Margaret Babcock, 12/23/94.

22. Ernest M. Fisher, "Memories of an Octogenarian, 1893–1975," unpublished memoir, 1970.

23. Colean, *A Backward Glance*, p. 36.

24. Interview with Claire Blumberg, 12/21/94.

25. Interview with Buzz Bazan, 9/94.

26. Colean, *A Backward Glance*, p. 34.

27. McFarland, *Federal Government and Urban Problems*, p. 119.

28. Sources include Colean, *A Backward Glance*, pp. 54–56, and interview with Morton Schusheim, 10/23/93.

29. Brownstein was at the FHA because the Depression forced him to delay college and law school. After starting out as a truck driver's assistant, he worked his way up to filing reports on FHA efforts to enroll lenders and nearly thirty years later was appointed FHA commissioner by President Kennedy. Sources include

Washington Post, 9/23/99; *New York Times,* 9/23/99; and an interview with Philip Brownstein, 10/18/93.

30. McDonald guarded the FHA's integrity with passionate zeal. When one senator promoted legislation McDonald thought damaging to the FHA, he hunted the legislator down in a Capitol Hill corridor, grabbed him by the lapel, and said, "If you pass this amendment, you can kiss my ass in Macy's window and that will be the end of the FHA." Once on an airplane trip McDonald sat next to department store heir Nathan Straus, Public Housing Authority head and a rival in the housing arena. When Straus asked him how things were at the FHA, McDonald growled, "Does Macy's tell Gimbel's?" When Roosevelt set up a committee to coordinate housing policy, McDonald sent Colean to meetings of what he called "the Three Hours of Lost Motion Club" with strict orders to knock out anything that might get in the FHA's way. Colean, *A Backward Glance,* pp. 38–43.

31. Interview with Jim Lamb, 10/10/94.

32. Colean, *A Backward Glance,* p. 38.

33. McFarland, *Federal Government and Urban Problems,* p. 115.

34. McFarland, *Federal Government and Urban Problems,* p. 119; interview with Alan Thornton, 12/29/94.

CHAPTER 10: HOME BUILDING'S HENRY FORD

1. The stories that pushed Fred Trump off the first thirty-five pages of the paper included a report from Spain that German and Italian planes had joined Franco's assault on Madrid. At home, Hollywood studio heads, dreading the reaction of the Legion of Decency, tried frantically to quash public testimony in actress Mary Astor's racy divorce case. *Gone With the Wind* continued its reign as the best-selling book in American publishing history, and nearly a million cars used New York City's Triborough Bridge in the first month it was open. *New York Times,* 8/12/36.

2. She arrived on the SS *Transylvania* on May 11, 1930. Sources for this section include Certificate of Arrival, INS; and interview with Robert Trump, 2/3/94.

3. Hearing as to proof of value of mortgages, in the Matter of Julius Lehrenkrauss, et al.

4. When John McCooey finally stepped aside as Brooklyn's Democratic boss in early 1934, Bay Ridge chief Tom Wogan, one of three party heavyweights who shared the county leader position for an interim period, made sure that Tommy Grace had a lock on the upcoming appointment as FHA director. Sources include *New York Times,* January 9, 1958, and Wayne Barrett, notes for interview with Joe Starkey, n.d.

5. Others who got started at the Madison Club included Murray Feiden and Nat Sobel, struggling lawyers and later state supreme court judges. Long afterward Feiden said that he resented having to be involved with the clubhouse system. "I hated politics and politicians," he said. "But you didn't have any choice about getting involved if you wanted to get anywhere." Sobel, who first went to a club

when he needed someone to fix a ticket for the then illegal offense of appearing shirtless on the beach at Coney Island, seemed to find the experience more positive. "I liked the way these people operated," he said years later. "They had one line here for this problem, another line there for that problem." Sources include interviews with Murray Feiden, 11/93, and Nat Sobel, 7/90.

6. Interview with John William Hyman, 10/23/93.

7. Wayne Barrett, notes from interview with David Hyman, n.d.

8. Sources include McFarland, *Federal Government and Urban Problems*, pp. 118–119.

9. Many of the Italians lived nearby in an area of old wooden houses and unpaved lanes popularly known as Pigtown because residents raised animals for food. Sid Frigand, press secretary to Mayor Abe Beame, recalled playing baseball there as a kid and tripping over a goat in the outfield. Sources include the *New York Herald Tribune*, 5/19/40; interviews with Anthony Jordan, 12/90, and Sid Frigand, 5/13/96.

10. *Brooklyn Eagle*, passim, 1936–37.

11. Irene Fischl, "A Taj Mahal in Brooklyn," *New York Newsday*, 8/28/90.

12. Three years after moving in, the Kelleys had finally scraped together the money to buy a car, the first on the entire block. Marian's husband, Frank, had to read the manual to learn how to operate it. Sources include *Brooklyn Eagle*, 2/18/39, and interview with Marian Kelley, 8/91.

13. Marie Brenner, "Trumping the Town," *New York*, 11/17/80.

14. Nostalgic evocation of her Trump home would form the centerpiece of Schwartz's 1989 novel, *Leaving Brooklyn*.

15. Sources include Irene Fischl, "A Taj Mahal," *New York Newsday*, 8/28/90, and interviews with Phyllis Becker, 3/90; Marian Kelley, 8/91; Howard Mendes, 3/90; Frieda Mendes, 3/90; Lynne Sharon Schwartz, 3/90; Sam Silber, 3/90; and Beverly Ziegler, 3/90.

16. Although it is hard to quantify, many who were once again employed seemed still shell-shocked from the Depression and unwilling to spend as they had in the past. Another component was the start-up of the Social Security system. Paycheck deductions removed $2 billion in wages and salaries from circulation, and because the program was new, not a penny was paid out in benefits. In addition, a major reason for the upturn in consumer spending had been the 1936 soldier's bonus, which pumped $1.7 billion into the economy that year. A one-shot payment, it did not recur in 1937. Americans' disposable income, which had spiked up for a year, now plummeted back to earth, dragging the barely revived economy with it. Sources include Friedman and Schwartz, *Monetary History of the United States*.

17. Sources include Eccles, *Beckoning Frontiers*, pp. 287ff; Colean, *A Backward Glance*, pp. 39–47.

18. *New York Times*, 3/6/38; *Brooklyn Eagle*, 3/6/38.

19. *Brooklyn Eagle*, 7/10/38.

20. *Brooklyn Eagle*, 2/25/39.

21. *New York Evening Post*, 2/7/38.

22. *Brooklyn Eagle*, 10/12/41.

23. *New York Herald Tribune*, 12/15/40.

24. *Brooklyn Eagle*, 4/27/41.

25. Interview with Conrad Duberstein, 2/14/95; *Brooklyn Eagle*, 4/9/39; *New York Herald Tribune*, 10/1/39; *New York Times*, 5/14/39, 1/2/00.

26. *Brooklyn Eagle*, 11/10/40.

27. *Brooklyn Eagle*, 9/14/41.

28. *Brooklyn Eagle*, 12/10/39.

29. *Brooklyn Eagle*, 6/27/37 and 12/04/43.

30. *New York Herald Tribune*, 4/27/41.

31. *New York Herald Tribune*, 4/20/41; *Brooklyn Eagle*, 10/28/41.

32. *Congressional Quarterly Almanac*, 1954, p. 227.

33. *New York Herald Tribune*, 4/12/42; Thomas C . Parramore, *Norfolk: The First Four Centuries*, University Press of Virginia, 1994, pp. 331ff.

34. Interview with Carol Melton, 1/12/95.

35. Thomas J. Wertenbaker, *Norfolk: Historic Southern Port*, Duke University Press, 1962, p. 348.

36. *New York Herald Tribune*, 4/12/42.

37. Interview with David Hyman, 10/12/93.

38. On one of the car trips, Fred Trump brought along some Brooklyn political pals, including Abe Beame. As they sped south to Norfolk, Trump explained how he used FHA mortgage insurance to avoid putting a penny of his own into his projects. Deeply involved in the conversation, he never noticed the speedometer needle creeping upward or the police car in hot pursuit. When a sheriff pulled the car over for speeding, it turned out that neither Trump nor any of his well-connected passengers had thought to bring along identification. Interview with Nat Sobel, 7/90.

39. On March 10, 1942, Mary Anne Macleod Trump became a U.S. citizen. A patriotic move, it was also prudent for the wife of a man doing wartime construction for the Department of Defense.

40. Interview with David Hyman, 10/12/93.

41. Interviews with John Walter, 7/26/91 and 2/16/95.

42. One of the earliest occasions was in December 1941, when he served on the dinner committee for the annual fund drive of the New York and Brooklyn Federations of Jewish Charities. *New York Times*, 12/14/41.

43. After the war, the two brothers visited Kallstadt and found the village heavily damaged and the Trump and Christ families battered. Elizabeth Christ Trump's older brother, Philip, who was in his late sixties, had been drafted, captured by the British, and forced to walk home across Europe. Another relative, who was crippled, was raped by an SS officer and had a child afterward. That traumatic visit would further distance Fred Trump from the birthplace of his parents. In the late 1940s, as Fred Trump became involved in building apartments in Brook-

lyn, his brother John started High Voltage Associates with Vandergraf and Dennis Robinson. Sources include Dr. C. M. Cooke, *Tech Talk*, MIT publication, February 1985; and interviews with Christian Freund, 5/91, and John Walter, 7/26/91.

44. Interviews with James Rosati Jr., 11/17/93, and Joseph Rosati, 1/17/93.

45. Interview with W. Taylor Johnson Jr., 10/22/93.

46. Interview with David Hyman, 10/12/93.

47. *Norfolk Ledger-Dispatch*, 3/9/46.

48. Interview with Bill Levitt, 11/93.

49. Six months after Fred Trump came to Norfolk, he and Rosati bought land in Chester, Pennsylvania, and obtained priority approvals and FHA mortgage insurance. They immediately began construction of 50 eight-family buildings intended for defense workers at shipyards and war production plants nearby. Sources include *New York Herald Tribune*, 6/7/42; *New York Times*, 6/21/42; and interview with W. Taylor Johnson Jr., 10/22/93.

50. *New York Times*, 4/18/43.

51. *New York Herald Tribune*, 2/28/43; *Brooklyn Eagle*, 2/28/43, 3/27/43, 5/2/43; *New York Times*, 4/18/43.

52. *Brooklyn Eagle*, 3/27/43.

53. Wertenbaker, *Norfolk*, p. 357.

54. *New York Herald Tribune*, 4/12/42.

55. *Brooklyn Eagle*, 2/28/43.

CHAPTER 11: PUTTING A ROOF OVER GI JOE'S HEAD

1. Richard O. Davies, *Housing Reform During the Truman Administration*, pp. 42–53.

2. According to the U.S. Census Bureau, 2.2 million GIs who took off their uniforms in early 1946 wanted another type of housing right away, and another 4 million wanted to change within a year. With only 94,000 houses for sale and 166,000 units for rent in the entire country, most of these 6 million returning vets were out of luck. Sources include *Washington Post*, 8/16/54.

3. Davies, *Housing Reform*, p. 41; Irving Welfeld, *HUD Scandals: Howling Headlines and Silent Fiascoes*, 1992, p. 16.

4. Frederick M. Kaiser, "Past Program Breakdowns in HUD-FHA: Section 608 Multifamily Rental Mortgage Insurance Program of the 1940s," Congressional Research Service, Library of Congress, p. 4; interview, H. Fefferman, 5/19/00.

5. *Brooklyn Eagle*, 1/20/46.

6. Davies, *Housing Reform*, pp. 46, 52.

7. Colean, *A Backward Glance*, p. 80. Support for Wyatt eroded further after a letter he received from ad executive Chester Bowles was leaked to the press and published in the *Congressional Record*. A patrician New Englander who headed the Office of Price Administration during the war, Bowles had been the top enforcer of wartime price controls. His letter suggested ways to implement

peacetime price controls and consolidate government influence over the construction industry. There was no evidence Wyatt planned to follow this unsolicited advice, but big business denounced it as a blueprint for socialism, and the construction industry, already smarting about government intrusion in its affairs, stepped up its assault on Wyatt's program. *Current Biography*, pp. 63–65; Colean, *A Backward Glance*, pp. 74, 80.

8. *New York Times*, 4/14/46.

9. Unwilling to work with Wyatt, the plant's owners instead leased to the Tucker Automobile Company—an unfortunate choice, for the production record of the short-lived Tucker company would prove to be even more dismal than Wyatt's. Davies, *Housing Reform*, pp. 52–53.

10. *Brooklyn Eagle*, 4/21/46.

11. *Brooklyn Eagle*, 10/13/46.

12. *Brooklyn Eagle*, 4/14/46.

13. *Brooklyn Eagle*, 1/20/46.

14. *New York Times*, 4/21/46.

15. *Brooklyn Eagle*, 7/17/46, 7/21/46.

16. *Current Biography*, 1946, pp. 669; Davies, *Housing Reform*, p. 54.

17. Colean, *A Backward Glance*, p. 80.

18. *New York Times*, 11/10/46.

19. *Brooklyn Eagle*, 10/13/46; *New York Herald Tribune*, 9/10/46.

20. Davies, *Housing Reform*, pp. 11–28.

21. *New York Herald Tribune*, 1/20/46; *New York Herald Tribune*, 11/10/46.

22. While the administration and Congress debated how to get the housing industry moving, Joseph Raymond McCarthy, who had just beaten Robert LaFollette to become the junior senator from Wisconsin, took another tack. If the nation that had won the war could not put a roof over its veterans' heads, McCarthy reasoned, something must be wrong. Assisted by his staff attorney, a young and still unknown Robert Francis Kennedy, McCarthy launched an investigation of the housing industry and called his first public hearings. There he hauled building materials manufacturers onto the carpet and accused them of price gouging but was unable to charge them with any actual crime. He attracted little press attention and, after a brief inquiry, left the veterans to their fate. Sources include Colean, *A Backward Glance*, pp. 78–79; and interview with Philip Brownstein, 10/28/93.

23. Davies, *Housing Reform*, pp. 60–62.

24. Sources for this section include Irving Welfeld, *HUD Scandals*, p. 7; *Current Biography*, 1949, p. 201.

25. "Details Supporting the Findings of Fact in the Special Investigation of the Federal Housing Administration: April 12, 1954–August 31, 1954," p. 36. Cited in Welfeld, *HUD Scandals*, p. 7.

26. Sources include Franklin D. Richards, assistant FHA Commissioner, memo to field office directors, 1/8/47.

27. Raymond M. Foley, memo to field office directors, 1/1/47.

28. *Brooklyn Eagle*, 6/22/47.

29. Raymond M. Foley, letter to directors and chief underwriters of all field offices, 1/1/47.

30. *Brooklyn Eagle*, 6/22/47.

31. *New York Herald Tribune*, 7/18/48.

32. Trump and most other builders of multifamily housing made their buildings six stories because of a wrinkle in the New York City Building Code. Structures up to six stories in height were considered "fireproof" if builders followed certain procedures, including wrapped window lintels and enclosed elevator shafts. Although these measures did not make the buildings fireproof, they did allow builders to use highly inflammable wood floor construction, which was far less expensive than steel. Sources include interview with John William Hyman, 10/9/93.

33. *Brooklyn Eagle*, 3/5/48.

34. Interview with George Grace, 1/94.

35. *Brooklyn Eagle*, 8/1/47.

36. *New York Times*, 6/22/47; *New York Herald Tribune*, 6/22/47; *Brooklyn Eagle*, 6/22/47; *Housing Progress*, fall 1947; *Brooklyn Eagle*, 8/1/47.

37. *Brooklyn Eagle*, 8/1/47.

38. Interviews with Ben Holloway, 1/94 and 11/9/98.

39. *New York Times*, 8/30/47.

40. *Brooklyn Eagle*, 2/8/48.

41. *Brooklyn Eagle*, 6/1/49.

42. *Brooklyn Eagle*, 12/21/47.

43. *New York Times*, 8/15/48.

44. *Brooklyn Eagle*, 9/11/49.

45. Wayne Barrett, *Trump: The Deals and the Downfall*, 1992, pp. 42ff., 45; interviews with Murray Felton, 1/94, and Judge Louis L. Friedman, 12/93.

46. Interview with Alex Naclerio, 3/92.

47. Interviews with Ben Holloway, 1/94 and 11/9/98.

48. *Brooklyn Eagle*, 5/14/50.

49. Interview with John Hyman, 10/9/93.

50. Sources for this section include Barrett, *Trump*, pp. 52–53. Just how powerful was suggested years later by another Brooklyn real estate operator, Salvatore Grieco. "When Freddy Trump built Beach Haven there was quite an upset between its residents and those of a nearby area [called Gravesend]," he said. "Between the little Jewish boys and girls and the little Italian American boys. A little Jewish girl was accusing some one of our boys in Gravesend of molesting her, and I called up Freddy Trump and told him that people here resented that and I'd like to see if we could make amends. And we did. He gave us the privilege of creating a recreational hall where boys and girls can get together. We

created more or less of an understanding between the children in Beach Haven and those in Gravesend. We put out press releases about the cooperation we got from Freddy Trump, and the family [of the girl] moved out the next day. So there was no lawsuit or any police interest. We created a very good social atmosphere ourselves." Interview with Salvatore Grieco, 12/31/93.

51. Fred C. Trump, testimony before the Senate Banking and Currency Committee, 1/12/54, p. 419.

52. Barrett, *Trump*, pp. 52–53; interview with John Hyman, 10/9/93.

53. According to a story in the *Brooklyn Eagle*, 5/14/50, in 85 percent of Trump's rentals, wives cast the deciding vote.

54. *New York Herald Tribune*, 1/15/50.

55. *Brooklyn Eagle*, 5/14/50.

56. *New York Times*, 7/1/51; *New York World-Telegram*, 7/12/51; *Brooklyn Eagle*, 7/22/51.

57. *New York Times*, 9/11/49; *New York Herald Tribune*, 1/15/50.

58. *Brooklyn Eagle*, 1/2/50.

59. *Brooklyn Eagle*, 5/25/50.

60. *Brooklyn Eagle*, 5/13/50.

61. *New York Herald Tribune*, 5/5/50.

62. *New York Times*, 9/9/51.

63. *New York Times*, 4/29/51.

64. *Brooklyn Eagle*, 12/3/50.

65. *Brooklyn Eagle*, 5/25/50.

66. *Brooklyn Eagle*, 10/8/52.

67. *New York Times*, 10/25/50.

68. *Brooklyn Eagle*, 11/5/50.

69. *Brooklyn Eagle*, 10/15/50.

70. Barrett, *Trump*, p. 48.

71. Interview with Nat Sobel, 2/91.

72. *Brooklyn Eagle*, 5/24/52, 11/30/52. Afterward Fred Trump was honored for his work for the Federation of Jewish Philanthropies.

73. *Brooklyn Eagle*, 1/7/53.

CHAPTER 12: THE PERILS OF SUCCESS

1. *New York Times*, 6/12/54.

2. *Brooklyn Eagle*, 6/12/54; Senate Committee on Banking and Currency hearing, 1/12/54, p. 409.

3. Section 608 was originally drafted by this same Senate Committee on Banking and Currency that was now denouncing it. Welfeld, *HUD Scandals*, p. 16.

4. *Washington Post*, 7/13/54.

5. The broker was W. Taylor Johnson. The scandals also left other witnesses emotionally stricken. Gustave Berne, a New York developer who testified just before Fred Trump, was devastated by the occasion. "When he saw himself being accused in those huge headlines, he just never forgot," his son, Bob Berne, recalled years later. Interviews with Bob Berne, 3/96, and W. Taylor Johnson Jr., 10/22/93.

6. Attorney Gerald L. Marcus, as reported in *The New York Times*, 7/13/54.

7. Miles Colean, *A Backward Glance*, pp. 101ff, and interviews with William McKenna, 6/91, and Guy T. O. Hollyday Jr., 9/29/95.

8. *Washington Post*, 10/24/54; interview with William McKenna, 6/3/91.

9. *HUD Scandals*, Welfeld, pp. 5–6; *Congressional Quarterly Almanac*, 1954, pp. 227–228.

10. Interview with Hilbert Fefferman, 9/94, and unpublished interview with Guy T. O. Hollyday, conducted by Guy Hollyday Jr., 1984.

11. Miles Colean said that back in 1940 he heard rumors of questionable FHA activity and passed them on to Abner Ferguson, Stewart McDonald's successor as FHA administrator. Colean, *A Backward Glance*, p. 109.

12. *Architectural Forum*, the first national publication to blow the whistle on questionable 608 practices, was most concerned with mediocre design and the wasted opportunity to create innovative multifamily housing. But it also questioned loopholes that let builders make enormous profits with almost no risk or investment of their own funds and the gimmickry that allowed builders to pay architects only a portion of the allowable fee but write off the whole amount as an expense. *Architectural Forum*, January 1950.

13. FHA programs also included Title I home improvement loans. Each year the FHA underwrote more than one million such loans, which by 1954 totaled some seventeen million loans for almost $8 billion. Although these loans averaged only about $400, there were so many and the default rate so low that they provided hefty profits for bankers and builders. Welfeld, *HUD Scandals*, p. 18.

14. *Architectural Forum*, January 1950, p. 97.

15. Interview with Hilbert Fefferman, 11/15/93.

16. Interviews with Hilbert Fefferman, 2/95 and 11/93.

17. *Current Biography*, 1955, pp. 90–92; *New York Times*, 10/21/66.

18. Interview with William McKenna, 10/27/93.

19. A descendant of U.S. president John Quincy Adams, Sherman Adams had been the manager of a lumber mill and owned little more than a modest Colonial-style home back in the Granite State. Stern faced and ramrod straight, he combed his gray hair the same way every day, weighed exactly what he had in college, and was the most powerful unelected official in American history. He had gained Ike's favor as an early backer in the 1952 primaries and now controlled all access to the chief executive. Famous for cold-blooded efficiency, he ended telephone calls by the clock and went to bed with dinner guests still present—behavior which contributed to keen public interest when, in 1958, the press revealed that Adams accepted gifts, including a vicuna coat, from a Boston manufacturer seeking special government favors, and he was forced to resign.

20. Interview with William McKenna, 6/3/91.

21. *Washington Post*, 10/24/54.

22. Interview with William McKenna, 6/3/91.

23. Builders routinely bypassed the $5 million ceiling, originally intended to prevent huge projects from dominating the program. Fred Trump received three mortgages on Shore Haven and six on Beach Haven, although the supposedly autonomous parts of each were separated only by thin strips of lawn. In one notorious case, Ian Woodner, a Washington, D.C., builder, divided a 1,139-unit apartment building by erecting two parallel walls, one inch apart, across the middle. Although doors linked the two "halves," which meant that entrance to either project automatically gave access to the other, Woodner was able to obtain two mortgages. Sources include *Architectural Forum*, January 1950, and interview with Alfred Levingson, 6/14/89.

24. William McKenna, Details Supporting the Findings of Fact in the Special Investigation of the Federal Housing Administration, 4/12/54–8/31/54.

25. Interview with Maurice Paprin, 11/93.

26. McKenna Report, 8/31/54, p. 22.

27. Welfeld, *HUD Scandals*, p. 12.

28. In the postwar period, Grace & Grace handled sixty-four large-scale FHA housing projects, involving nearly $85 million in FHA mortgage insurance and providing between two-thirds and nine-tenths of the firm's income. McKenna estimated 90 percent; Grace said 65 percent. William F. McKenna, testimony before Senate Banking and Currency Committee, pp. 1,127ff.

29. Hearings, Senate Banking and Currency Committee, August 8/24/54.

30. An Irishman with twinkling blue eyes and a booming voice, George had naturally ruddy cheeks that got even ruddier every day at lunch. "You made sure you saw George before noon if you wanted to get anything done," said Alex Naclerio, Tom Grace's successor at the New York FHA office. As George described it, he and his brother were basically facilitators. "My forte was getting applications through the FHA," he said. "I knew exactly what to do. When a guy made out a form, I could say that number isn't right, or change this." Tommy handled the administrative end of things. "The underwriters were the ones who put all the figures together and actually ran the FHA office," George said. "Tommy was just a fountain pen, signing papers that underwriters told him added up." Interview with George Grace, 1/94.

31. *New York Herald Tribune*, 2/6/54; George Grace, testimony before the Senate Banking and Currency Committee, August 24, 1954; Barrett, *Trump*, pp. 56–57.

32. Interview with George Grace, 1/94.

33. Sources include interviews with Donald Greenberg, 12/93, and Murray Feiden, 12/93.

34. About half a dozen lawyers left Dreyer & Traub at this time and set up their own firms, one of which was the firm that became Lindenbaum & Young. Interviews with Murray Felton, 1/94; Murray Feiden, 11/93; Philip Birnbaum, 12/93; and Sidney Young, 6/11/96.

35. Interview with Alex Naclerio, 3/92.

36. Further corroboration came from Alex Naclerio in an interview in 1/94. "When a guy makes maybe $10,000 a year and lays down one $200 bet after another all afternoon, what are you supposed to think?" he said. "Powell had tremendous power. His salary was only $10,000, but he was making decisions every day that involved millions of dollars. That's a bad setup for anybody to be in, and lots of federal workers were in it. What do you think happens when political appointees leave private jobs for government jobs where they make half as much or less? There's a lot of opportunity for enrichment in the government, a lot."

37. Philip Birnbaum, interview, 12/93.

38. *Washington Post*, 7/15/54, 7/20/54, 9/15/54, 10/6/54, 2/26/55; Final Report on FHA Investigation, 8/31/54, submitted by William F. McKenna, p. 5 and passim; interviews with Hilbert Fefferman 9/94; W. Taylor Johnson Jr., 10/22/93.

39. Correspondence, Clyde Powell and Fred C. Trump, 3/30/51.

40. McKenna Preliminary Report, p. 22.

41. William McKenna, Report to the Senate Committee on Banking and Currency, 6/29/54.

42. *New York Times*, 6/29/54.

43. A member of an old and distinguished New York family, Judd was tall and lanky with black curly hair, bushy dark eyebrows, and olive skin. Famous at Harvard for making *Law Review* and being the only summa in his class despite never taking notes and devoting every Sunday to Baptist church activities, he was a protégé of law professor and later U.S. Supreme Court justice Felix Frankfurter. After clerking for Judge Learned Hand, he became a successful lawyer in New York and an active Republican. *Brooklyn Eagle*, 5/5/46; *New York World Telegram & Sun*, 10/5/64; *New York Times*, 7/8/76; *New York Law Journal*, 7/12/76; interview with Nat Sobel, 2/14/95.

44. *Current Biography*, 1947, pp. 90–92; interview with William Simon, 12/90.

45. Hearings, p. 409.

46. Hearings, pp. 408–409, 417.

47. Friedman and Schwartz, *Monetary History of the United States*, pp. 597ff.; interview with Hilbert Fefferman, 9/94.

48. *Washington Post*, 8/19/54.

49. Interview with Bob Berne, 3/96.

CHAPTER 13: CLASHING VISIONS

1. Sources for biographical details on Abraham Kazan include interviews with Ben Kazan, 7/24/89; Sandra Kazan Pomerantz, 3/9/98; Alene Marx, 3/5/98; Leon Kazan, 4/89; Donald Martin, 3/31/89; Harold Ostroff, 4/7/89 and 6/96; Irving Alter, 3/12/96; Julius Goldberg, 4/18/89; Ralph Lippman, 4/89; Sol Shaviro, 2/1/96; Harvey Segelbaum, 5/15/89; Herman Jessor, 9/89; Roger Starr, 2/89, 3/10/89, 3/21/89; Roger Schafer, 4/4/89. Other sources include Eugene Rachlis and John E. Marqusee, *The Landlords*, 1963; Abraham Kazan, "Co-operative

Housing," and "Amalgamated Warbasse Houses . . . A Private Builder Opposes a Development," both unpublished manuscripts; Sol Shaviro, Ph.D. dissertation, "Cooperation: A Theoretical Model and a Practical Example," Fordham University, 1969.

2. That Kazan found a job in the clothing industry was hardly an accident. A growing need for ready-made clothes and plenty of skilled immigrants living within walking distance of large industrial buildings had made the Lower East Side the nation's garment center by the turn of the century.

3. What came to be known as Amalgamated Houses, the first project under the new Limited Dividend Law, received financial backing from the Metropolitan Life Insurance Company and the *Jewish Daily Forward*, a labor-oriented paper published in Yiddish.

4. Like the owners of the homes Fred Trump built later, the tenant-cooperators in Kazan's mid-20s apartments took great pleasure in the detailing of their new homes. All apartments had kitchen windows, cross-ventilation, tiled bathrooms, and a dining area; most had three exposures and rooms coming off a large central foyer and hall rather than strung out railroad-car-style as in many tenements. The complex also had an auditorium, a dance hall, a cafeteria, a library, a nursery, a commissary room, a kindergarten, and five laundries. Outside, the central courtyard had an elaborate ornamental garden and sculptured fountain, and playgrounds and dozens of trees dotted the grounds.

5. Rachlis and Marqusee, *The Landlords*, p. 157.

6. The tightly knit group of tenant-cooperators started classes in music, photography, and art, shared child care, arranged for summer day camp, and organized theater parties. They also entertained each other with musical performances, plays, and public meetings. Forums and a wide variety of lectures were frequent. On one occasion, economist Scott Nearing, then a resident, and Socialist Party leader Norman Thomas led a formal debate entitled "Socialism and Communism, Which?" Even regular cooperative meetings routinely erupted into fierce confrontations along political and ideological lines. Sources include Rachlis and Marqusee, *The Landlords*, pp. 155ff.

7. Kazan obtained tax abatement for Amalgamated Houses in the Bronx, his first construction project, under the 1926 Limited Dividend Law. This law provided for a twenty-year tax abatement on residential buildings (but not the land under them) provided rents did not exceed a fixed ceiling and landlords limited their dividends to 6 percent (considered a reasonable percentage at the time). Starting with Hillman House, built on the Lower East Side in 1947, Kazan received tax abatement under the Redevelopment Companies Law. This 1942 New York State statute, pushed through the legislature by Robert Moses for a pet project called Stuyvesant Town, allowed for the use of eminent domain, or the power of condemnation, to obtain sites. It also provided tax concessions for twenty-five years, allowing builders to pay at the rate assessed before they had added improvements to the site.

8. *Encyclopedia of New York*, edited by Kenneth T. Jackson, p. 774.

9. Letter from Robert Moses to City Planning Commission, 5/25/45.

10. Interview with Herman Jessor, 9/89.

11. As quoted in Robert Caro, *The Power Broker*, 1975, p.12.

12. Title I, part of the 1949 National Housing Act, allowed the federal government to pay two-thirds of the cost of the big-ticket items in slum clearance, namely the relocation of site tenants and the demolition of existing buildings. The other one-third would be divided between the state and the city, with the latter acting as the interface between the federal government and the eventual site developer. As city construction commissioner, Robert Moses both designated sites and selected the developers for them—a position of unparalleled power and influence that allowed him to dominate New York City politics and made him an enormously valuable ally.

13. *New York Times*, 7/5/58.

14. Rachlis and Marqusee, *The Landlords*, p. 161.

15. Interview with Homer Godwin, 4/2/98.

16. Interview with Sally Wiseman, 6/26/98.

17. *New York Post*, 9/21/54; *New York Herald Tribune*, 7/30/55 and 12/9/55; *Encyclopedia of New York*, ed. by Kenneth Jackson, pp. 272–274; *New York Times*, 12/9/55.

18. Fred Trump bid $3,336,000 for Grymes Hill Gardens in May 1955. The garden apartment complex consisted of thirteen buildings containing 416 apartments. In September 1956 he purchased the complex. *New York Herald Tribune*, 5/10/55; *New York Times*, 9/25/56.

19. Pro-Trump and pro-Kazan allies kept up a flurry of letters and press releases. In Trump's corner, the City Taxpayers League (CTL), which identified itself as a Brooklyn-based civic organization, blasted the United Housing Foundation (UHF) proposal as "a brazen steal." In a press release dated July 21, 1958, CTL spokesman Sidney Young, who was Fred Trump's lawyer and whose office served as CTL headquarters, called Warbasse Houses "a well-camouflaged gimmick to plunder the city's depleted treasury." Meanwhile the Citizen's Housing and Planning Council, a prestigious Manhattan civic group, accused Trump of exploiting the UHF's careful planning without adding any improvements. In a letter to Mayor Wagner, quoted in *The New York Times* on April 13, 1959, Roger Starr, council president and a prominent figure in civic-minded circles, charged that Trump's proposal "proves merely that high taxes can be paid if higher rentals are charged." *New York Post*, 2/6/59.

20. The expansionist vision of longtime Amalgamated Clothing Workers (ACW) president Sidney Hillman was crucial for the first cooperative housing projects built by Kazan. After Hillman's death in 1946, the ACW left the housing business, and Kazan formed a new entity, United Housing Foundation. He also found important new allies, including David Dubinsky, president of the International Ladies Garment Workers Union (ILGWU). This tie eventually led to the construction of Penn South, built with the sponsorship of the ILGWU just south of Penn Station in Manhattan. But that union, too, was not interested in the Coney Island project, which meant that for the first time Kazan was without any effective allies in the allocation of a site. Interview with Philip Blumberg, 6/3/96.

21. Both Trump and Kazan originally relied on tax abatements through the Redevelopment Companies Law, a Robert Moses–backed program passed in 1942 to facilitate the construction of an 8,750-unit complex called Stuyvesant Town by Metropolitan Life Insurance Company.

22. Abraham Kazan, "Amalgamated Warbasse Houses . . . A Private Developer Opposes a Development," unpublished manuscript, p. 7.

23. Ibid., pp. 6-7.

24. When Fred Trump's plans to build on the Luna Park site had collapsed, Cashmore went to bat for him. "You've got to take care of my friend Fred Trump," he told a top official in Mayor Robert Wagner's administration in 1955. "I want you to talk to Fred about his site in Luna Park." Barrett, *Trump*, p. 58.

25. Sources for the material that follows include Barrett, *Trump*; and interviews with Sidney Young, 12/20/93, 12/24,93, 6/11/96; Murray Feiden, 11/93; and Sidney Frigand, 6/96.

26. Interview with Murray Feiden, 11/93.

27. During the war, when Fred Trump drove a car full of well-connected Brooklyn cronies to Norfolk and got a speeding ticket, Lindenbaum was one of the party (chapter 10, note 38). "Even at that time, Bunny knew how to get things done," his brother-in-law and fellow Madison Club regular Murray Feiden said later. "He could make anyone like him. He just had something, he was able to be the best friend of just about anybody." After the war Feiden obtained a judgeship and turned over his modest law practice to Bunny, who then invited Young to join him. Expecting a cushy setup, Young was greatly disappointed. "Bunny sold us a bill of goods," Young said many years later. "The firm had no business, nothing. We had to pay for everything down to pencils and paper." Interview with Sid Young, 12/20/93.

28. After Abe Traub overextended himself financially, disappeared, and then called the office from a Philadelphia hotel room and threatened suicide, Young was one of the lawyers who walked out of Dreyer & Traub and had to start over.

29. Bobby Brownstein, then a member of the New York State Assembly, recalled meeting a dapper Fred Trump at the Lindenbaum & Young office on Court Street. "I had on an off-the-rack suit from Klein's that went three for a hundred bucks," recalled Brownstein, a street-smart type who had grown up over a Brooklyn candy store, "and here was this tall, imposing guy with impeccable tailoring." Afterward Brownstein said, "Whenever Fred Trump needed something in my district, he wouldn't call me himself. Instead he would call someone who knew me better. But I could write to him for contributions, and he would respond." Interview with Bobby Brownstein, 12/12/93.

30. These included the Metropolitan Fair Rent Committee and the Brooklyn Real Estate Board, both industry organizations, as well as the Mayor's Committee for Better Housing, the New York City Housing Authority (NYCHA) and the New York City Planning Commission. *New York Times*, 2/13/51, 11/20/51, 1/29/56, and 7/8/60.

31. Noting that he had represented Fred Trump on matters other than Luna Park, Lindenbaum recused himself from this vote, taken at the first NYCHA meeting he attended. Whether Lindenbaum remained entirely hands off with regard to a

large and problematic piece of property belonging to his major client is unknown. Then again, perhaps Lindenbaum's clout was not necessary, given that Brooklyn borough president John Cashmore had already asked NYCHA head Warren Moscow to help Trump in this matter.

32. Philip Blumberg, at the time a young partner in the firm representing UHF, recalled discussing Kazan's plan for Warbasse with his father, the executive vice president of Amalgamated Clothing Workers. "Kazan is operating in a fairyland," the senior Blumberg said. "He's not going to get that land." When young Blumberg remonstrated and pointed out that one of the most powerful men in New York City, Robert Moses, was on the Warbasse board, his father replied, "That's all very well, but Abraham Lindenbaum has a louder voice in Brooklyn than Abraham Kazan. And there's some real estate fellow there who's provided Abraham Lindenbaum with enough money to see that he gets the land." Philip Blumberg, interview, 6/3/96.

33. Abraham Kazan, Columbia University Oral Biography, 1968, pp. 476ff., and "Amalgamated Warbasse Houses," pp. 10ff.

34. *New York Post*, 12/9/58, 2/5/59; *New York Times*, 6/25/59; *New York World-Telegram*, 3/24/61.

35. Lawrence Ettore Gerosa owed his own fortune to having figured out early on that trucks could haul a lot more waste than horses could and then wangling the necessary permits to send extra large loads across city streets and bridges. In 1954 city controller Gerosa demanded that an abandoned hospital site next to Riis Park in Queens should be sold and returned to the tax rolls. Wearing his city parks commissioner hat, Robert Moses insisted that the property belonged to the parks department and should be added to Riis Park. Ultimately both parties compromised on using the site for a home for the aged. *New York World Telegram*, 1957; *New York Times*, 6/25/72.

36. Exactly what role Robert Moses played in the matter remains an intriguing question. In the past Moses had backed Kazan because he delivered the Title I projects Moses wanted, but he had no reason to support the non–Title I Warbasse. In addition, Moses and Trump both used lawyer Richard Charles and worked well together on the Title I Brooklyn Civic Center; also, Moses had an unerring instinct for ending up on the winning side. On July 24, 1959, more than three months before the conflict over the Coney Island site was resolved, Moses, wearing his city construction coordinator hat, submitted a report to the Board of Estimate. In it he opined that both Trump's and Kazan's plans were "well conceived," that it was to the city's advantage to have as many developers working on "substandard" land as possible, that UHF was also working on another project at the former Jamaica Race Track but Fred Trump was not pursuing any other redevelopment plans, and that therefore Moses recommended giving the Coney site to Trump. Robert Moses letter to Board of Estimate, July 24, 1959.

According to Bunny Lindenbaum, as reported in Barrett, *Trump*, pp. 61–62, Moses supervised the final division of the site, now expanded to about seventy acres, nearly forty of which went to Fred Trump. One possible scenario is that Moses backed Trump and made his own seat on the City Planning Commission available for Bunny Lindenbaum as part of a quid pro quo through which Moses would be appointed president of the World's Fair. As chronicled by Robert Caro in *The Power Broker*, pp. 1060ff., Moses desperately wanted the fair post by way of a golden parachute after decades of public service.

Evidently as part of the process of hammering out a compromise, Amalgamated Clothing Workers became a Warbasse sponsor and the project's name changed to Amalgamated Warbasse Houses. Kazan complained in his unpublished memoir and in an interview conducted by Columbia University's Oral History Project that the ACW provided no funds and did nothing to help him hold on to the original site; he did not address the fact that he needed the official presence of organized labor to preserve even part of the site. Kazan, "Amalgamated Warbasse Houses," pp. 11–15; Oral History, pp. 477–478, 481.

37. Three weeks after his inauguration, Rockefeller appointed a commission, headed by General Otto L. Nelson Jr., to study housing needs throughout the state. In response to Nelson, Mayor Wagner fired off a preliminary report that found a housing gap in New York City of 430,000 units, expected to grow to 730,000 over the next seventeen years. Closing the gap, the report estimated, meant a 50 percent increase in the rate of construction and would cost $12,173,000,000. Other governors would have stopped there, but to Rockefeller it was apparently just one more invigorating challenge. A year later he launched his own super-agency, HFA, to solve the problem. *New York Post*, 2/5/59.

38. Legally speaking, the HFA, which was an independent agency, was considered a municipality—that is, a subdivision of the state and thus not subject to federal taxes. Interview with Irving Alter, 3/12/96.

39. Harriman had promoted housing subsidies for middle-income families—those not poor enough for public housing, but not well-off enough for market-rate homes—and lent his support to the Limited Profit Housing Companies Law, passed in 1956. Referred to by the names of its co-sponsors, Senator MacNeil Mitchell, a Manhattan Republican, and Assemblyman Alfred A. Lama, a Brooklyn Democrat, the bill authorized loans for up to 95 percent of construction costs for co-ops and rentals. The term of the loan could be as long as fifty years, and the interest rate was to be approximately that paid by the state on its own obligations. Builders, who were limited to a profit of 6 percent, were eligible for a 50 percent tax abatement for up to thirty years; in turn, tenants, whom Harriman referred to as "the forgotten families," had to observe income restrictions that on average meant they could make no more than $4,000 to $5,500 a year.

In the fall of 1956, as the UHF was breaking ground on the first Mitchell-Lama housing development, Park Reservoir, located in the Bronx, real estate interests joined forces to oppose any further expansion of the program. Industry groups and real estate boards around the metropolitan New York area campaigned vigorously against an upcoming proposal that authorized a bond issue for more Mitchell-Lama projects. One advertisement showed a cigar smoker clad in a luxurious smoking jacket, lounging in an easy chair, and patting his stomach in contentment. The caption read, "Stop Supporting this $7,500 a Year Man." Although this was the maximum income allowed for Mitchell-Lama applicants and applied only to large families, the ad evidently struck a chord, for the public voted down the proposal at the polls. *New York Times*, 10/28/56, 10/30/56, 11/7/56.

Interestingly, those against the proposal said they opposed it because the tax abatements available to builders under the Mitchell-Lama Act imposed an unfair burden on other home owners. (Fred Trump made the same charge against UHF's original Warbasse proposal the next year, but then, apparently upon reflection, decided that tax abatements were not such a bad thing after all and applied for one himself.) Those who supported the proposal pointed to what they considered the desperate need of people living in substandard housing. But apparently neither side was concerned that Mitchell, a prominent real estate lawyer, and Lama, an architect, kept up their practices throughout their time in the state legislature, which would be considered a blatant conflict of interest today. While Mitchell was head of the Joint Legislative Committee on Housing and Multiple Dwellings, its New York City office was within Mitchell's own law firm. The name of the firm and that of the committee were both on the front door, and Mitchell's law partner was executive director of the committee—only fitting, perhaps, given that during this period the firm received $427,633 in fees to process developers' applications for construction loans under the Mitchell-Lama Act, including $128,000 for work on Trump Village. Similarly, Al Lama, co-sponsor of the law, bagged at least four contracts for Mitchell-Lama projects for his architectural firm.

During the State Investigation Commission's hearings on the Mitchell-Lama Act, held in 1966, Mitchell was asked whether he considered his firm's participation in the program while he was committee chair a conflict of interest. He replied that in his view it was not a conflict but "a public service" and that the committee worked in his firm's office because this would save travel time for Mitchell and space in the state office building in New York City (which would have been free) was not available. Sources include New York State Investigation Commission Hearings, 1/27/66, p. 511ff.; *New York Post*, 2/8/66; *New York Times*, 1/29/66; *New York Herald Tribune*, 6/28/63, 8/7/63.

40. *New York Times*, 11/10/88; *Current Biography*, 1969, pp. 291–293; Annual Report of the New York State Housing Finance Agency for Fiscal Year November 1, 1960 to October 31, 1961; interviews with Al Walsh, 5/24/96, and Rich Marrin, 10/20/97. Following up on the previous footnote, we may note that John Mitchell, creator of the moral obligation bond, earned impressive fees from HFA bond work. A week after the 1968 presidential election, Rockefeller summarily fired HFA head James Gaynor after learning of the lucrative HFA business that had gone to Mitchell, then campaign manager for Rocky's nemesis, Richard Nixon.

41. Interview with Harold Liebman, 4/30/90.

42. Press release, New York State Housing Finance Agency, 12/7/62.

43. Annual Report, New York State Housing Finance Agency, 1962, p. 7.

44. The concrete slabs that served both as floors and as ceilings were reinforced with steel rods and with welded steel wire mesh. Sources include *New York Times*, 5/1/63, and interview with Harold Liebman, 4/30/90.

45. Sources for this section include interviews with Roger Starr, 2/89, 3/10/89, 3/21/89, and 4/4/89.

46. The following is based on *New York Times*, 6/10/51; *Brooklyn Eagle*, 6/8/52; and interviews with Alan Lapidus, 4/18/90, 4/23/90, 5/7/90, and Morris Lapidus, 1/94.

47. Supposedly at least one prominent architect was not entirely negative about Lapidus. Philip Johnson reportedly told interviewer Mike Wallace that Lapidus's work was "not all bad" and that he was dazzled by his use of twenty-seven colors in one building.

48. Both projects had tiled bathrooms, balconies, picture windows, and ocean views (although residents of Warbasse had a more distant look at the water). Warbasse buildings were divided into three sections, each of which had two skip-stop elevators; Trump Village buildings had four elevators that stopped at every floor and were available to the entire building. Interview with Marvin Pomerantz, 6/5/98; *New York Herald Tribune*, 9/22/63; *Brooklyn Bulletin*, 5/6/64, 7/2/64.

49. Soon afterward Fred Trump received Board of Estimate approval to change the status of Trump Village so that he could obtain a low-interest HFA mortgage. *New York Times*, 9/28/61, 10/4/61, 10/5/61; *New York Post*, 9/28/61, 9/29/61, 10/1/61, 10/3/61, 10/6/61; *New York World-Telegram*, 9/30/61; *New York Herald Tribune*, 9/30/61, 10/4/61, 10/5/61.

50. George Tilyou, an inventor of carnival rides, founded Steeplechase in 1897. In 1907 the park burned down, and the next day Tilyou started charging passersby ten cents to look at the smoking ruins. He rebuilt on the same spot and three years later, in 1910, opened the Pavilion of Fun, a glass dome covering all the rides.

51. For generations of New Yorkers, Steeplechase, Dreamland, and Luna Park, the three major amusement parks on Coney Island, were about the most wonderful places in the world. Eleanor Guggenheimer, a member of the City Planning Commission in the mid-1960s, remembered going to Steeplechase as the high point of the summer when she was a teenager. "It was an escape to a lovely, romantic world," she recalled later. "The racetrack ride was just a little scary, so you could count on a moment or two of clutching the opposite sex, which in those days was intimacy. My husband and I cemented that we'd go together forever at Coney Island." Interview, 6/11/98.

52. *New York Times*, 7/4/72, and interview with Dick Bernstein, 5/20/96.

53. *New York Herald Tribune*, 12/4/65.

54. Interviews with Leo Silverman, 11/28/97 and 6/12/98, and Judge Joseph Fisch, 6/7/96.

55. Apparently unfazed by the SIC or any other law enforcement mechanisms, major underworld figures held their largest known meeting at the upstate hamlet of Apalachin in 1957. Dewey's successor, Governor Averell Harriman, promptly expanded the SIC and strengthened its mandate to investigate (but not prosecute) "any matter concerning the public peace, public safety, and public justice." Ninth Annual Report of the Temporary Commission of Investigation of the State of New York to the Governor and the Legislature of the State of New York, February 1967, pp. 15–20.

56. Ibid., p. 113. According to Fisch's investigation, cited in the SIC's Ninth Annual Report, Trump sometimes used this expensive equipment for his other, private work and did a better job and provided higher-quality equipment for the rental sections, which he would keep, than on the co-ops, which he would sell. He also

collected all taxes and interest estimated for two years of construction, although the project was half done at mortgage closing and he finished early.

57. Fred Trump, testimony before the State Investigation Commission, pp. 343–344 and passim.

58. For the five 24-story buildings containing 2,484 apartments at Warbasse Houses, UHF received $350,000 for the builder's fee and overhead. Kazan, SIC testimony, p. 248.

59. SIC, Ninth Annual Report, pp. 109, 116.

60. Fred Trump was legally required to repay any overestimation on funds needed for land purchase, and he did so.

61. This was hardly as unlikely a possibility as it may seem, given how skillful Fred Trump was at saving large sums out of what were presumably reasonable project budgets. But according to Leo Silverman, of the thirty projects he audited, nineteen, or almost two out of three, lost money, and the builders were unable to collect fees or expenses. SIC investigation, testimony of Leo Silverman, p. 279.

62. Although the SIC was not able to prosecute anyone, the investigation cast a shadow on participating developers and on the New York State Housing Finance Agency. "Nobody was fired, and nobody was prosecuted," said agency director Paul Belica afterward. "But there was damage by insinuation and second-guessing." He claimed that many developers subsequently steered clear of the program because they faced the prospect of an investigation if they managed to do what all private developers aimed to do—namely, come in under budget. Interview with Paul Belica, 6/96.

63. After Warbasse, Kazan went on to build Rochdale Village, a six-thousand-unit complex in Queens, and then Co-op City, at fifteen thousand units the largest cooperative project in history.

64. Interview with Sidney Young, 12/24/93.

65. Interview with Lou Powsner, 6/98; interview with Michael Onorato, 6/98; interview with John Manbeck, 6/98; *New York Herald Tribune*, 2/26/66; *Newsday*, 7/22/66; *New York World Journal Tribune*, 9/15/66, 3/8/67; *New York Times*, 9/22/66, 10/5/66, 10/20/66, 1/6/68, 3/10/68, 5/23/68, 12/20/74, 4/3/77, 6/16/77; *New York Post*, 1/5/67, 2/6/68.

66. "Steeplechase Park: Sale and Closure, 1965–1966; Diary and Papers of James J. Onorato," Michael P. Onorato, ed., 1998, pp. 57–58.

67. In 1905 George Tilyou designed and copyrighted the somewhat grotesque face, with its extra teeth and leering expression. According to historian John Manbeck, it was the inspiration for the Joker character in the Batman comic series.

68. Office of the Comptroller, City of New York, March 17, 1980.

CHAPTER 14: BORN TO COMPETE

1. Flag Day was first celebrated on the centennial of the U.S. flag's existence, June 14, 1877. In 1949 President Truman signed legislation making it a day of national observance; however, it had been celebrated in New York for some years prior to this official recognition.

A key element in what became known as the baby boom was the Census Bureau's ability to register it. Until the early twentieth century, high levels of infant mortality and the lack of age-related benefits such as Social Security meant that keeping track of births was not a high government priority. In 1915, however, growing public health concerns led to the creation of a nationwide birth registration system, and by 1933 paper copies of every new birth certificate in America were flowing to a single large room in the Census Bureau. There clerks keypunched the information onto stiff file cards that were tabulated on the world's only unit counters. Bureau technicians had invented these unwieldy contraptions, which could not add, subtract, multiply, or divide. But they could count, which meant that the nation could know for the first time precisely how many children were born each year.

Until the end of World War II the numbers were unremarkable, with increases during seven years and decreases during five. But then, in 1946, there was an abrupt shift. At midyear the number of births suddenly spiked up by 40,000, more than double any previous monthly increase that year. Over the next twelve months 553,000 babies were born in the United States, nearly twice the largest number in any year since the birth registration system began; what was later dubbed "the baby boom" was under way. Sources include interviews with Jay Olshansky, 7/1/98; Carol De Vita, 7/7/98; Manning Feinleib, 7/7/98; Martin O'Connell, 7/7/98; Sam Shapiro, 7/7/98; Eric Kingson, 7/7/98; I. O. Moriyama, 7/8/98; Howard West, 7/9/98; and Frank Sulloway, 7/15/98. Other sources include Leon F. Bouvier and Carol J. De Vita, "The Baby Boom—Entering Midlife," *Population Bulletin*, November 1991; Carol J. De Vita, "The United States at Mid-Decade," *Population Bulletin*, March 1996; "IIVRS Chronicle," November 1991; and *Vital Statistics of the United States, 1950*, vol. I, pp. 1–19.

2. That is, if pre-1946 birth levels had continued. The UNIVAC, on which statisticians tracked much of the boom and now on display at the Smithsonian Institution in Washington, D.C., requires a floor space of 25 by 50 feet, or 1,250 square feet.

3. According to Frank Sulloway, author of *Born to Rebel: Birth Order, Family Dynamics, and Creative Lives*, 1996, everyone has the innate capacity to develop all of these characteristics. But the reason that firstborns tend to be more assertive and successful and later-borns to be more adaptive and creative is that firstborns start out the focus of parental attention, whereas later-borns have to compete for it. Unlike their older siblings, who by definition are first in line for parental time, energy, and resources and therefore tend to feel self-confident and entitled, later-borns must develop flexibility and attractiveness to have access to that same parental notice.

4. Interview with Robert Zajonc, 2/3/00.

5. Audrey Leibovich, Magali Rheault, and Dan Wilchins, "An Amazing Half Century of Progress," *Kiplinger's Magazine*, January 1997.

6. Elsewhere Americans were figuring out how to adjust to peacetime. Members of Congress were arguing about whether to draft eighteen-year-olds, the United States was offering to turn over all its atomic warfare information to an internationally supervised commission while at the same time reserving the right to continue atomic bomb tests at Bikini Atoll in the Pacific, and maritime workers,

no longer forced to observe wartime prohibitions against strikes, were preparing to walk out at midnight.

7. Sources for this and the following sections include interviews with Robert Trump, 2/3/94; Maryanne Trump Barry, 2/9/98; Louis Droesch, 7/23/98; Nancy Boyd Tickel, 7/17/98; Heather Hayes MacIntosh, 8/10/98; Jan van Heinigen, 6/5/98; Harold Liebman, 4/30/90.

8. Interview with Florence Stelz Spelhouse, 2/90.

9. Interview with Bob McKinley, 10/7/97. As McKinley related the story, Fred Trump usually pledged about $200 to the church. One year, when the lawyer who usually made pledge calls was sick, McKinley substituted for him and visited the Trump home himself. "We sat down and I said, 'Mr. Trump, why don't you write me a check for ten thousand dollars?' He stopped and looked up at me and said, 'You've got a lot of nerve, and I admire you for it so much, I'm going to write a check for that amount.'" But after writing the check, Fred Trump then lapsed back into his usual shyness. "When you talked to him, you'd almost think he didn't know what to say to you," McKinley recalled.

10. Interview with Linda Strauss Kearns, 8/3/98.

11. Thomas J. Lovely, *The History of the Jamaica Estates, 1929–1969*, 1969; interviews with Bernice Able MacIntosh, 2/90; Dorothea Kuritzkes, 2/90; Heather MacIntosh Hayes, 7/25/98.

12. "We wanted to introduce children to experiences without putting labels on everything the way they do now," Greene said. "The idea was to expose children to as many things as possible and then let their own imagination and creativity take over." Interview with Shirley Greene, 3/24/98.

13. So Donald Trump later reported in his autobiography, *The Art of the Deal*, written with Tony Schwartz, pp. 49–50.

14. Interview with Ann Rudovsky Kornfeld, 12/1/93. The oldest Presbyterian church in North America, First Presbyterian was one of the largest in Queens, and its congregation consisted mainly of teachers, bank tellers, salespeople, and other midlevel office workers. "There were a few lawyers, and some securities dealers, but the Trumps were the only ones in their income bracket," recalled former minister Reverend Carl Smith. "They were way off the graph." Sources for this section include interviews with Bob McKinley, 10/7/97; Carl Smith, 10/8/97; Chris Ferro, 10/10/97; and Olive Messenger, 10/10/97.

15. Sources for this section include interviews with Fina Farhi Geiger, 6/5/98; Peter Brant, 5/11/98; Linda Dufault, 1/27/98; Philip Rogers, 3/24/98; Charles Walker, 2/6/98; Ann Rudovsky Kornfeld, 12/01/93; Michael Corbisiero, 11/1/97; Dave Rudovsky, 12/5/93; Joe Sukaskas, 3/24/98.

16. Both men would be high school sports stars and, in later years, keenly competitive athletes. Donald is a low-handicap golfer; Peter, a newsprint magnate and publisher, is a top-ranked polo player and owner of his own polo club. Touted by *Polo*, a magazine devoted to the sport, as "polo's most competitive amateur," he is renowned for a bare-knuckles style that has included brazenly hitting opponents with his mallet and cutting off their horses. Eric O'Keefe, "The Peter Principle in Polo," *Polo*, March/April 1998.

17. Sources include *New York Times*, 1/20/99; interview with Marty Goldensohn, 8/17/98.

18. Sources for this section include Nancy Boyd Tickel, 7/17/98; Ginny Droesch Trumpbour, 7/14/98; Richard Hillman, 7/9/98; Phyllis Grady, 7/15/98; Stanley Hillman, 8/91; Raymond Hillman, 8/91; Kathy Young, 8/91; Heather Hillman Adams, 7/30/98; Betty Miles, 7/31/98; Brian Goldin, 7/23/98; Fred Briller, 7/23/98; Larry Strauss, 7/23/98; Mary Roche Cossman, 7/14/98.

19. Brochures described Hilltop as "a summer camp for Christian boys," and religious observances consisted solely of Protestant and Catholic services on Sundays. According to Raymond Hillman, one of the owners' sons, Hilltop and Hill Manor, like many Gentile camps of that era, discouraged Jewish children from applying and assumed that any who wanted to attend summer camp could do so at one of the many Jewish camps located in Pennsylvania's Pocono Mountains.

20. Conversation with Mary Trump, 5/17/98. Apparently, even at that time, such close supervision was remarkable.

21. Sources for this section include interviews with Paul Bekman, 4/15/98; Bernie Blum, 1/14/98; John Brugman, 1/13/98; Colonel Anthony Castellano, 4/16/98; Francis Diotte, 4/21/98; Major Theodore R. Dobias, 3/24/98; Warren Goodwin, 3/18/98; Stan Holuba, 2/2/98; Mike Kabealo, 2/3/98; Ted Levine, 1/14/98; David Smith, 8/23/98; Robert V. Ward, 3/18/98; George White, 8/11/98; Mike Scadron, 8/29/98. I am also indebted to Lieutenant Colonel Dan Keenan.

22. Horseplay was a regular feature of life at NYMA, and occasionally groups ambushed one another with, for example, a trash can full of water poised to tip over when a cadet answered a knock at his door. A favorite bit of cadet mischief was to sneak over to the Ramble, a nearby stream that had a series of cascading waterfalls and pools. Officially off-limits, it was a magnet for boys in the spring and fall, a place to fish, hunt snakes, stash beer, and, occasionally, meet town girls, known among the cadets as "Ramble rats." The standard punishment for misdemeanors, like talking during study hours or being late to mess, was pushups and marching back and forth outside barracks. "Donald did his share of walking," coach Dobias said. "The real punishment was that it was so boring." Donald's military career ended with NYMA graduation; despite his athletic prowess, in 1968 he received a medical deferment from the military draft.

23. According to dormmate Frances Diotte, Donald once refused to go downstairs to meet his parents because they had, as usual, driven up in their chauffeured limousine. "A lot of people there were wealthy, but they came up in private cars, not limousines," Diotte said. The next time, he recalled, Donald's parents came up in an ordinary Cadillac convertible, with Fred Trump at the wheel, and Diotte was invited to join them for dinner. The drive to the restaurant was "kind of harrowing," Diotte recalled. "Donald had never been in a car with his father driving, and after that he allowed his parents to come up with the chauffeur after all." Interview with Frances Diotte, 4/21/98.

24. Interview with Mike Scadron, 8/29/98.

25. Donald Trump, *The Art of the Deal*, p. 50; conversation with Mary Trump, 5/17/98.

26. Sources for this section include interview with Donald Trump, 12/17/97. The standard joke at Gregory Estates, he recalled, was that Seat Pleasant got its name "because that's where they had the largest toilet seat manufacturer."

27. Interview with John Meyers, 2/12/99.

28. Interviews with Marcy Feigenbaum, 12/24/93, and Morris Lapidus, 10/28/98.

29. Sources for this section include interviews with Steve Lesko, 3/26/98; Bob Hawthorne, 7/23/98; Don Robinson, 3/3/98; Artie Storrs, 5/28/98; Rich Marrin, 11/20/97; Peter Shapiro, 3/9/98.

30. Sources for this section include interviews with Donald Trump, 12/17/97 and 1/12/98.

31. *New York Times,* 8/26/80 and 4/16/00. Ammann, whose name is often mispelled Ammerman, also designed the Triborough and Bayonne Bridges and consulted on the Lincoln Tunnel and the Golden Gate Bridge, among others.

32. Interview with Steve Lesko, 3/26/98.

33. Sources for this section include interviews with John A. Cantrill, 2/3/98; Joe Cohen, 4/21/98; Herbert Denenberg, 2/3/98; Peter Gelb, 1/29/98; Marty Golden-sohn, 8/24/98.

34. Trump, *The Art of the Deal,* p. 53.

35. Sources for this section include interviews with Jim Nolan, 3/29/98; Karl Walther, 3/29/98; Homer Godwin, 4/2/98; Maryanne Trump Barry, 2/9/98; Jan von Heinigen, 6/15/98; Louis Droesch, 7/23/98; Ginny Droesch Trumpbour, 7/14/98; and David Smith, 8/28/98; Harry Hurt, *Lost Tycoon,* 1993, p. 13.

36. "My father was a very formal guy, very proper, with fixed ideas about how things should be," recalled Maryanne Trump Barry. One fixed idea was that business—especially the building business—was the province of men. Although Maryanne worked in Fred Trump's office in the summers (and became a lawyer and, eventually, a federal judge in New Jersey), she never saw herself as a candidate for taking over for her father. "I never tried to get involved in any important way," she said. "But even if I'd been the greatest thing, Dad was an old-fashioned guy, and he thought women were mothers or teachers. If they worked, they worked in a bank. For me to be in line as his right hand wouldn't have occurred to him, or to me, either." Interview, 2/9/98.

37. *New York Herald Tribune,* 12/2/65.

38. Glenn Plaskin, "Playboy Interview: Donald Trump," *Playboy,* March 1990.

CHAPTER 15: MANHATTAN BOUND

1. The name Swifton alluded to the fact that the land where the apartment complex now stood had been a generous wedding gift from one Briggs Swift to his daughter Eunice back about 1880. Ian Woodner, a developer in Washington, D.C., completed Swifton Village in 1953 and one year later stood accused, along with Fred Trump, of windfall profits on FHA projects. A few weeks after Fred Trump testified before the Capehart committee on Capitol Hill, Woodner did the same and admitted that he had skirted FHA mortgage ceilings on a project in Washington by putting an inch of caulking compound between the two halves of

a large building and then obtaining a separate mortgage for each side. Sources for this chapter include *Cincinnati Enquirer*, 6/28/90; *Cincinnati Post*, 5/28/51, 8/5/54; *Cincinatti Post & Times Star*, 4/15/64; *New York Times*, 6/7/64; *New York Herald Tribune*, 4/2/64; several conversations with Donald Trump, particularly in 12/97 and 1/98; Murray Feiden, 12/93; Jerry Robinson, 10/26/97; Franklyn Harkavy, 10/10/97.

2. The 1,200-unit complex had 57 two-story, garden-style buildings spread out over 41 acres.

3. *Cincinnati Post & Times Star*, 4/15/64.

4. HOME had received other complaints of discrimination at Swifton, but these were settled by compliance and did not go to court. Sources for this section include HOME records and interviews with Jerry Robinson, 10/26/97; Franklyn Harkavy, 10/10/97; Heywood Cash, 8/21/97; Lee Hereth, 8/21/97.

5. *Cincinnati Enquirer*, 12/23/72.

6. The property being sold was Gregory Apartments in Maryland, where Donald Trump had worked one summer. Sources for this section include interviews with Gerald Schrager, 5/17/99, and Brad Zackson, 2/9/95.

7. Interview with Donald Trump, 12/17/97.

8. Interviews with Leonard Boxer, 11/97, and Craig Norville, 1/6/99.

9. A Fred Trump favorite at this time seemed to be Trump Village Construction Corporation. In Cincinnati alone, the Trump interests were variously known as the Swifton Land Corporation, Swifton Realty Corporation, and Fred Trump's New Swifton Village Apartments.

10. Sources include Donald Trump, *The Art of the Deal*, p. 65.

11. Its first board had included Cassini's fashion designer brother Oleg, Italian industrialist Giovanni Agnelli, and actor Rex Harrison, and it still offered a heady mix of exclusivity and glamour to a wide range of socially ambitious New Yorkers.

12. In "Fifth Avenue Coach Lines," a chapter of an unpublished autobiography, Cohn's legal colleague Milton Gould wrote of meeting him in the 1940s when his father, Albert Cohn, an appellate court judge, brought Roy, then a college student, to lunch with a group of highly respected jurists. Gould was too intimidated by the company to speak, but Cohn had no such inhibitions. "Within minutes this brash stripling was lecturing these hoary veterans at the table on the state of the nation or some other weighty issue," Gould wrote. "It was a portent of the future. For the next few decades, Roy Cohn would be talking down to his elders and betters, judges and lawyers, with the same arrogant self-confidence, the same aplomb, without reservation or shame." Gould, "Fifth Avenue," p. 1.

13. Nicholas von Hoffman, *Citizen Cohn*, 1988, passim; interview with Eugene Morris, 12/22/93.

14. Interview with Alan Weiselberg, 2/3/98.

15. A few years later Fred Trump retained Morris's firm to handle its city real estate tax assessments. While Morris was preparing the case, Fred Trump seemed to gravitate toward Morris's associate, David Benjamin, a retired judge who had

specialized in such cases. When the reassessment claim Morris was preparing
went to trial, the presiding judge, Benjamin's former boss, held a settlement
conference with Morris, Benjamin, Trump, and a city representative. As Morris
recollected the story, "Benjamin said to the judge, 'Look, Sam, I want this much
on this case. We'll give you all the evidence you need, but this is what we want.'
Fred Trump never forgot it and always referred to it afterward. He almost had an
orgasm over it. We got a big reduction, and he loved us." Interview with Eugene
Morris, 12/7/93.

16. Sources include *New York Times*, 10/16/73, 12/13/73, 1/26/74, 6/11/75; *New
York Daily News*, 12/16/73; Barrett, *Trump*, pp. 85–88.

17. *Time*, January 26, 1968. Sources for this section include *Time*, January 26, 1968,
and June 22, 1970; *Saturday Review*, January 11, 1969; *Fortune*, August 1970;
New York Times, 2/9/87; *Corporate Reorganization Reporter*, passim; Eric Posner, "The Political Economy of the Bankruptcy Reform Act of 1978," *Michigan
Law Review*, October 1997; Joseph R. Daughen and Peter Binzen, *The Wreck of
the Penn Central*, 1971; Robert Sobel, *The Fallen Colossus*, 1977; interviews
with Eric Posner, 10/7/98; Fred Rovet, 9/17/98; James Blair, 8/28/98; Cary Dickieson, 9/22/98 and 9/30/98; Newell Blair, 12/26/90; Robert Blanchette, 10/5/98;
Paul Duke, 9/30/98.

18. The difference in working styles, so pervasive as to be nearly paralyzing from the
moment the merger took place, is reflected in this later comment from longtime
New York Central attorney Fred Rovet: "At New York Central, we were guys
who went into the office and took off our jackets and got to work. But when we
went down to this austere Philadelphia office with these big boardrooms, we
almost had to genuflect to see their vice presidents." Interview with Fred Rovet,
9/17/98.

19. Presumably because many colonists fled harsh debt laws in Europe and many
founding fathers had their own cash flow headaches here, the Constitution
specifically enables Congress to write bankruptcy laws. This power to override
the states was little used until a major depression in 1897 threw the entire economy for a loop. Congress responded with the Bankruptcy Act of 1898, which
basically gave debtors the option of reorganizing and continuing in business
rather than selling out to pay bills. In the case of railroads, though, lawmakers
nixed the idea of folding and marketing assets to satisfy creditors. Section 77,
which assumed the railroads' inherent importance and profitability, required
them to reorganize and chug on. During the reorganization period, their debtors
would have to hold off; afterward they could collect according to a set of priorities that favored those who extended goods or services during reorganization and
put the original owners—that is, the shareholders—last.

By the 1960s authorities still assumed that with enough help a troubled
railroad could, as it were, get back on track, even though numerous rescue attempts had failed to stabilize the New Haven Railroad, which went bust in 1961.
The Interstate Commerce Commission resolved this vexing problem by requiring the Penn Central to buy the New Haven as a condition of the merger that
created the new line. Years of litigation followed over what price Penn Central
should pay for this unwanted purchase. Finally, after a second appearance before
the Supreme Court, the New Haven's own figure was upheld; unhappily for the

winning side, however, the decision was rendered moot eleven days later, when the Penn Central went broke. The practical result was that the New Haven's creditors would now spend years more trying to collect what they were owed.

20. Estimates of the daily losses vary widely. The *New York Times* pegged it at $600,000 a day (7/6/73), whereas it is put at more than $1 million every twenty-four hours in *The Wreck of the Penn Central*, p. 255.

21. A major problem for U.S. railways was that many services, especially passenger service, were inherently unprofitable. Government regulators pegged ticket prices too low to cover the real costs, but if the lines charged the true cost, passengers would bolt for cheaper and/or faster transport, such as buses or, in some cases, planes. Still more uneconomical, old regulations required railroads to continue little-utilized routes. Most other industrialized nations maintained reasonable passenger ticket prices and comprehensive services only because they were nationalized. Eventually the Penn Central adopted a modified version of the same solution, with one government-owned corporation, Amtrak, taking over interstate passenger service, and another, Conrail, taking over commuter and freight service.

22. Interview with Robert Blanchette, 10/5/98.

23. Sources include *Forbes*, April 17, 1978; *New York Times*, 7/6/73; and interviews with John Koskinen, 8/28/98, and Morris Raker, 10/7/98.

24. Central Park comprises 840 acres.

25. Sources include interviews with Morris Lapidus, 10/18/98; Alan Lapidus, 11/6/98; Larry Schafran, 9/2/98; Milton Braverman, 10/10/97; Donald Trump, 12/12/97. By the end of the nineteenth century, the New York Central, like all U.S. railroads, owned immense amounts of property, including rail yards, terminal areas, and, in Manhattan, a wide ditch down the middle of the island used to accommodate coal- and wood-fired steam locomotives. After electric locomotives replaced those powered by steam, the New York Central Railroad covered over this ditch, created modern Park Avenue, and built luxury apartment houses down each side. At the same time, the railroad also built a new Grand Central Terminal at 42nd Street as well as hotels and other facilities for travelers.

For decades the income from these properties only partly offset the enormous maintenance costs for Grand Central. After World War II, however, Park Avenue became home to new office buildings built on ninety-nine-year ground leases with escalation clauses, and the income flowing to New York Central began to rise steadily. With the 1964 World's Fair, hotel occupancy and income also rose significantly. Gradually the real estate operations that had always been considered subordinate to the main business of running a railroad began to play a major role. One of the first developers to recognize this historic shift was William Zeckendorf, but he went bankrupt before he could realize his plans for Penn Central properties. Donald Trump, who also saw this change, got much farther before encountering economic reversals and has had a far more successful recovery.

26. Sources for this section include interviews with Edward Eichler, 9/20/98 and 11/28/98; John Koskinen, 8/28/98; Peter Martosella, 9/2/98; Victor Palmieri, 9/8/98; Larry Schafran, 11/90; and an interview with Edward Eichler conducted by *Inside Story* on April 19, 1989.

27. Great Southwest was a land development company gone amok that was purchased by a rail conglomerate that also went amok. By 1970 Great Southwest owned, among other things, a wax museum, mobile home communities, and cattle ranches. Palmieri's successful restructuring of this subsidiary was key to his later appointment to handle Penn Central's nonrail assets. Sources include *Fortune*, 2/13/78.

28. *New York Times*, 10/29/76.

29. It didn't help the new mayor that *The New York Times*, which would have preferred a Lindsay-style WASP as mayor, viewed Beame as little more than a party hack from the outer boroughs. When Beame asked why the *Times* was so hostile to him from the start, his press secretary, Sid Frigand, recalled, "I explained to him that if he worked for the *Times*, he would be known as A. D. Beame because anyone named Abraham couldn't use it as a first name. Just look at [*Times* veterans] A. H. Raskin and A. M. Rosenthal." Interview with Sid Frigand, 9/1/98.

30. Zuccotti, a liberal Democrat and highly successful real estate lawyer, had his first political experience serving on the Kerner Commission with Victor Palmieri and John Koskinen.

31. Interview conducted by *Inside Story*, 3/19/89.

32. Construction on the highway, a viaduct stretching from 59th to 72nd Streets and spanning what was then the New York Central rail yards, began in 1929 and was finished in 1932. Named for Manhattan borough president Julius Miller, the Miller highway is reportedly the first urban elevated highway in the country. *New York Times*, 2/17/91.

33. After World War II annual traffic at the two yards reached more than two hundred thousand carloads, but by 1973 it had declined to fewer than twenty-five thousand carloads. Converting the yards to other uses was difficult, however, because the railroad planned to continue running trains through the property. In theory it seemed possible to sell the yards' air rights—that is, the right to build up to a certain size depending on the relevant zoning—with the expectation that any development would be on a platform. (For further discussion of air rights, see the section on Olympic Tower and Trump Tower in chapter 17.) The problem was that no one knew how much of the air rights would be used by railroad operations below the platform because they didn't know how high the platform had to be. Unable to proceed without some number, Fred Rovet, an attorney who was assistant vice president of the Penn Central's own real estate department, went to the railroad's engineers and asked what clearance would be needed for a man hunched over the top of a freight car. After some hemming and hawing, the engineers came up with a guesstimate of twenty-two feet above the ground, which promptly became the industrywide standard. "When you're in bankruptcy," Rovet said afterward, "you're not surrounded with eight thousand consultants to help you figure these things out. You have to say to the last guy who hasn't already left to work for a profit-making operation, 'Let's take a guess—what can they do, kill us?'" *New York Times*, 7/30/74; interview with Fred Rovet, 9/17/98.

34. *New York Times*, 11/29/80. Interview with Fred Rovet, 9/17/98.

35. Interview with Cary Dickieson, 9/22/98.

36. Sources for this section include Wayne Barrett "Like Father, Like Son," *Village Voice*, 2/15/79, "Donald Trump Cuts the Cards," *Village Voice*, 1/22/79, and *Trump: The Deals and the Downfall*, chapter 4. Apparently Donald Trump had a deep appreciation for David Berger's legal skills, for five years later, in 1984, he hired the Philadelphia attorney to represent him on yet another matter; see chapter 19, note 25.

37. Interview with Herbert Chason, 5/22/89. During the hearing the young developer could barely sit still. "Donald was right next to me," recalled attorney Arthur Arsham, who represented *The New York Times*, which owned a small site on the edge of the rail yards. "He didn't hesitate to make his position known. He poked me with his elbow every time someone said something on the witness stand that he didn't like." At the end of the hearing, Arsham said, it was clear that the agitated young man couldn't bear to stand by any longer. Jumping to his feet, he walked up to the judge and asked for permission to speak. When the judge nodded, Donald Trump made what Arsham remembered as a brief but effective argument. "He knew what he was talking about," Arsham recalled. "He touched all the right notes on the piano."

38. Ravitch did not pursue his interest in the site with vigor. As he later recalled, he was preoccupied with his pending appointment by newly elected New York governor Hugh Carey as head of the New York State Urban Development Corporation, as well as the death in a plane crash of his cousin and partner in the family-owned construction business HRH. Ravitch's own West Side project, Manhattan Plaza, was also in serious trouble—a factor, Ned Eichler said later, that inclined him to favor granting the option on the yards to the unencumbered Donald Trump. Interviews with Richard Ravitch, 9/28/98, and Ned Eichler, 9/20/98 and 11/27/98.

CHAPTER 16: FROM BRICK BOX TO GLASS FANTASY

1. Sources for the following section include *The New York Times*, 11/6/74, 11/3/82, 10/30/98.

2. Appointed to the powerful House Ways and Means Committee in 1970, Carey had forged strong ties with its chair, Representative Wilbur Mills of Arkansas. In the 1972 election Mills suggested to Governor Rockefeller that it would be in New York's best interests if Carey stayed in office. In response Rockefeller told Carey's Republican opponent to decline Conservative Party support, thereby contributing to Carey's victory amid the statewide rejection of the Democratic presidential candidate, George McGovern. *New York Times*, 11/6/74.

3. Interview with Ken Auletta, 11/14/89.

4. Wayne Barrett, *Village Voice*, 1/22/79.

5. Such postelectoral committees, which Donald Trump's fellow task force member Richard Ravitch summed up as "all b.s.," are usually little more than public opportunities to say thanks and/or to line up contacts for the future. This particular group apparently never met; afterward several members had no recollection of its existence. Interview with Richard Ravitch, 12/11/98.

6. Interview with Matthew Lifflander, finance chair of the Democratic State Committee 1973–74, conducted on 10/20/97.

7. *New York Times*, 3/10/85.

8. On August 2, 1962, Gruzen and Samton were among the small but noble group of architects who picketed against the demolition of the old neoclassical Pennsylvania Railroad Station. Although the protesters wore suits and ties—newspapers wrote of "the best-dressed picket line ever"—and their signs were beautifully lettered, they failed to save the elegant McKim, Mead & White rail depot. Soon afterward it was razed to make way for a presumably more functional office building and the Madison Square Garden entertainment arena. Sources for this section include Wayne Barrett, *Trump*, chapter 4; Elliot Wilensky and Norval White, *AIA Guide to York City*; and interviews with Jordan Gruzen, 11/22/98, Peter Samton, 1/4/99, Paul Willen, 9/13/91 and 9/22/91, Scott Keller, 4/24/90 and 1/2/99, and Stuart Sheftel, 3/7/89.

9. A few years later a state education agency hired Gruzen & Partners to expand the Litho City plan to nearly double its size, with nine thousand apartments and two huge new public high schools. Because of the astronomical cost of air rights and platforming, this proposal also went nowhere.

10. *New York Times*, 6/30/74 and 3/11/75.

11. *Westsider*, 3/20/75.

12. Robert Moses, "West Side Fiasco: A Practical Proposal for the Restoration of the West Side Highway and Parkway to Public Use," 11/25/74.

13. *Forbes*, April 17, 1978; interview with Richard Dicker, 3/22/89.

14. Interview with Sally Goodgold, 6/5/89.

15. At one community presentation, a Gruzen representative complained to a community board co-chair, shouting, chanting, and "general chaos pervaded the meeting," and "it was effectively impossible to have any rational discussion." Letter from Amanda Burden, community liaison for Gruzen & Partners, to Doris Freedman, Community Board 7 co-chair, July 11, 1978.

16. Interview with Jonathan Barnett, 11/5/98.

17. *Westsider*, 5/6/76.

18. Sources for this section include *New York Times*, 10/3/84; *New York Daily News*, 3/5/89; *Manhattan, inc.*, September 1988 and September 1989; interviews with Howard Rubenstein, 9/16/98, and Breina Taubman, 3/8/89.

19. A classic workaholic, Rubenstein began his fifteen-hour workdays by rising before dawn, jogging while dictating memos into a tape recorder, then packing in scores of phone calls and half a dozen meetings. But when talking to clients, he spoke in the low, reassuring tones of a psychotherapist. His advice, to tell the truth and be direct, was simple, but it calmed out-of-control egos and restored self-control to business magnates and political big shots who could never openly admit to having gone off the rails. Even after moving to Manhattan, Rubenstein retained and polished his ties to Brooklyn, helping Abe Beame become mayor and Hugh Carey become governor. "Howard had become someone people called because he could make a call," said former Rubenstein employee Breina Taubman. Interview with Breina Taubman, 3/8/89.

20. Sources include *New York Times*, 11/23/92 and 10/6/99, and "The New Fixers," by Peter Wilkinson, *Manhattan, inc.*, January 1988.

21. Sources for this section include "How to Get Things Done in New York: A Case History," by Nicholas Pileggi, *New York*, November 1973; "The Bottom Line," *New York*, November 13, 1975; *New York Times*, 10/8/75, 10/17/75, 12/12/75, 12/13/75, 12/18/75; *Chelsea-Clinton News*, 11/13/75, 12/18/75, 12/25/75; *New York Post*, 12/18/75; *New York Daily News*, 12/19/75. Also, interviews with Howard Rubenstein, 9/16/98; Mary D'Elia, 2/2/99; Charles Urstadt, 5/14/96; John McGarrahan, 9/23/98; Der Scutt, 9/24/98; Breina Taubman, 3/8/89; Joe Walsh, 2/4/99; Jordan Gruzen, 11/28/98; Dan Gutman, 2/2/99. I am grateful to Der Scutt for allowing me to read and quote from his private, unpublished diary covering the years from 1974 on.

22. Area residents bitterly opposed the proposal and enlisted Representative Bella Abzug, the feisty New York congresswoman known for combative stances and large hats, to hold up necessary congressional approvals. They also suggested using the 34th Street yards, but to no avail. Now, though, these opponents had received guarantees of neighborhood preservation and had relaxed their opposition.

23. Ned Eichler also remembered mentioning to Donald Trump that the 34th Street yard would be a great site for the convention center. As Eichler recalls the conversation, Trump asked if he was kidding, then said, "You start talking about the convention center on the 34th Street yards and you'll be dead in a month because so many people have put together this whole package around 44th Street." Interview with Ned Eichler, 9/20/98.

24. The lead designer, Der Scutt, was not a member of the firm, but rather a consulting architect on this project. *Interiors*, February 1976.

25. Der Scutt diary, 10/4/75.

26. Mary D'Elia, 2/2/99.

27. Joe Walsh, 2/4/99.

28. Urstadt apparently had no idea that his accuser was promoting his own site. To Urstadt, Donald Trump was still the young kid who came along with his father when Urstadt was deputy commissioner of the state Mitchell-Lama housing program and Fred Trump was pressing for payment of the $520,000 bill submitted by Bunny Lindenbaum in the mid-1960s for relocation of tenants living on the site used for Trump Village. Because of numerous objections by government officials to paying the fee, the largest ever submitted for such work, the bill remained unpaid until the 1970s (see chapter 13). As deputy commissioner of the state Mitchell-Lama program, Urstadt declined to pay because it appeared to him that Lindenbaum's relocation work had been done not for the co-op sections of Trump Village, which Urstadt oversaw, but for the rental section. Thus, in Urstadt's opinion any fees should be paid out of the rental revenue—in other words, Fred Trump's pocket—instead of state funds.

29. Donald Trump's 34th Street proposal called for a 540,000-square-foot convention center. The McCormick Place Convention Center in Chicago, built in 1960, had been expanded in 1971 to 644,000 square feet.

30. Then again, with Howard Rubenstein pushing the site, there wasn't all that much doubt where the convention center would end up. He had steered the 44th Street plan right up to the finish line, and the only reason it stopped short of completion was the city's fiscal crisis. When 44th Street went belly-up, Rubenstein cut his losses and joined forces with Donald Trump to put the complex at 34th Street. Sandy Lindenbaum, who had also worked on 44th Street, did the same. To those left at 44th Street, such switches were a dire portent. "When Howard left, it was a sign that the center of gravity in this thing had shifted," said John McGarrahan, attorney for the 44th Street project. "The convention center had become a Brooklyn project, that's what happened. Howard's moving over told us the decision had been made."

31. Among the other key players in the Brooklyn network, two of the most important were City Council president Tom Cuite and state assembly Speaker Stanley Steingut, both long-term friends and colleagues of Howard Rubenstein's and Fred Trump's.

32. Sources for this section include newspaper articles of the period; Tom Shachtman, *Skyscraper Dreams*, 1991; Der Scutt diary; letter from John Koskinen to Wayne Barrett, 2/6/79; interview with John Koskinen, 8/28/98; memo from Mike Bailkin to John Zuccotti, 1/9/76. In April 1975 the projected loss for the year for the Commodore was $840,000, but by December the predicted shortfall had grown to $1.2 million.

33. *New York Post*, 12/12/75.

34. Donald Trump, *The Art of the Deal*, p. 82.

35. Although Donald Trump had a reputation for being cheap, Scutt was unprepared for how hard a bargain the developer would drive on the Commodore. As Scutt recalled, Donald Trump sat down across from Scutt and Gruzen and told them he would give them the job for about 10 percent less than they had expected and dismiss the firm he had already spoken with. Then he moved the phone to the corner of the desk and asked for the other firm's phone number, a gesture Scutt found "incredible and enticing." With much discussion, Trump increased the fee slightly, but said he would not pay unless they cut the total construction costs, and he also added on more expenses. When they agreed he slapped on one last item, making the final fee only slightly higher than the offer with which he began. Interview with Der Scutt, 9/24/98.

36. Sources for this section include Karen Cook, "Street Smart," *Manhattan, inc.*, December 1986, pp. 43–54 and interviews with Ben Lambert, 8/5/98 and 8/7/98.

37. According to Henry Benach, head of the Starrett Corporation, whose subsidiary HRH was the contractor on the reconstruction of the Commodore, several possible arrangements came up in early discussions and involved both Donald and Fred Trump. Early on, Hyatt Hotel Corporation declined to invest in the deal and instead agreed to take a management role. Henry Benach considered becoming a partner in the deal and asked Donald Trump to see the management contract Jay Pritzker had provided. Benach then called Jay Pritzker, told him it was a "very tough document," and said that he was considering entering the deal because he knew Fred Trump and the Trump Organization. Pritzker said that he didn't

know Donald Trump, but if Benach said he and his father were okay, Pritzker would become a third partner. Pritzker and Benach met with Donald and his father and began negotiating. Soon afterward it became clear that Benach, as owner of a public company, wanted to build and then sell, whereas the Trumps and Pritzker, owners of private companies, wanted to build and hold on, using the tax depreciation as a write-off for other properties. Accordingly, Benach backed off and, after Starrett purchased HRH from Richard Ravitch in 1977, served as the builder, while the Trump Organization and Jay Pritzker proceeded to have a two-way partnership. Interviews with Henry Benach, 4/20/98, 5/29/98, 7/7/98, 1/24/99.

38. *New York Times,* 5/4/75.

39. Der Scutt diary, 5/4/75.

40. Der Scutt diary, 5/24/76.

41. "Beame used to introduce me as the man who took a $100,000 cut to work for the city," Eisenpreis said later. "I didn't have the heart to tell him it was more." As soon as he arrived at City Hall, he made his priorities clear by declining the usual perk of new furniture. "I said let's get two cheap chairs from other offices," he recalled afterward. "We weren't there to make some Louis XVI quarters." Accordingly, Eisenpreis worked in a large, mostly empty room with a desk, a few flags, and hand-me-down seats for visitors. "It wasn't a hotel lobby for people to relax and enjoy themselves," he said. Interview with Alfred Eisenpreis, 10/1/98.

42. Sources for this section include Shachtman, *Skyscraper Dreams,* chapter 14, and *New York Times,* 7/19/96.

43. Rudin, head of an old Manhattan real estate family, persuaded large taxpayers, including Consolidated Edison, New York Telephone, and Rockefeller Center, to join his company and other real estate firms (which did not include the Trump Organization) in this civic gesture. Meanwhile the state established a new entity called the Municipal Assistance Corporation (MAC), a consortium of banking and financial interests led by investment banker Felix Rohatyn and empowered to sell bonds for the city. But despite the credentials of MAC's directors, its bonds didn't move on the market.

44. James Alfred Cavanagh, then sixty-one, had been a civil servant for thirty-seven years and was Abe Beame's closest friend at City Hall. One of Beame's first appointments after his election, Cavanagh was a rumpled, plain-talking, old-style Brooklynite, which endeared him to the mayor but not to the financial forces who had gained ascendancy in the midst of New York City's financial crisis.

45. At his first press conference as deputy mayor–designate, Zuccotti wore a tie covered with tiny gold Don Quixotes, which was widely interpreted as a sign of his determination to follow his own path.

46. Sources for this section include *New York Times,* 1/6/74, 1/17/75, 7/2/85; *Barron's,* August 20, 1979; Barrett, *Trump;* and interviews with Mike Bailkin, 2/22/89 and 3/7/89, and John Zuccotti, 9/30/98.

47. The last had been the New York Hilton, built in 1963.

48. Specifically, the UDC issued $1.3 billion in bonds and in 1975, unable to meet $135 million in short-term obligations, went into default. *Barron's*, August 29, 1979.

49. Perhaps Bailkin's tenure at this state agency, to which Louise Sunshine would presumably have access, was yet another reason Donald Trump came back to see him.

50. John Portman, innovative architect of the Hyatt Regency in Atlanta, was promoting another large hotel for 42nd Street, but the project was stalled and would never be built.

51. Sources for this section include an interview with David I. Stadtmauer, 4/11/89.

52. Sources for this section include interviews with Henry Pearce, 2/3/94; Bill Frentz, 4/6/98; Claude Morton, 3/7/98; Ben Holloway, 11/1/98; Frank Bryant, 3/2/98.

53. Interview with George Puskar, 11/17/97.

54. Sources for this section include letter from John Koskinen to Wayne Barrett, 2/6/79, and interviews with Henry Stern, 11/17/98, Richard Ravitch, 9/30/98, Mark Alan Siegel, 10/9/98, Mike Bailkin, 2/22/89, and Mario de Genova, 9/18/98. Ravitch eventually decided that the UDC was merely acting as a conduit and that a state agency had no standing to veto what was, at heart, a city project.

55. *Dun & Bradstreet Reports*, November/December 1978, p. 10.

CHAPTER 17: THE TWENTY-EIGHT-SIDED BUILDING

1. Every year in December, the real estate and construction industries held a dinner dance to benefit the National Jewish Medical and Research Center in Denver, Colorado. Previous recipients included Sam Lefrak, who had carved out a development path in Queens parallel to that of Fred Trump in Brooklyn; World Trade Center architect Minoru Yamasaki; HRH partner Saul Horowitz; and Manhattan real estate heavyweights Sylvan Lawrence, John Larsen, James Gorman, and Bernard Rosen. Interview with Lenny Boxer, 11/28/97.

2. The first was Thomas Willett, elected in 1665.

3. Sources for this section include Barrett, *Trump*, and interviews with Richard Rosan, 2/1/99; Richard Kahan, 9/29/98; Gerald Schrager, 5/17/99; Henry Stern, 11/17/98 and 11/18/98; Hadley Gold, 10/5/98.

4. Ultimately, Equitable Life plus the Bowery, Manhattan, Greenwich, Lincoln, Dry Dock, and Central Savings Banks came up with the permanent financing. Sources include Trump, *The Art of the Deal*, chapter 6; "Private Enterprise Breathes New Life into Old Cities," *Dun & Bradstreet Reports*, November/December 1978.

5. Sources for this section include Barrett, *Trump*, chapter 5; and interviews with Ralph Steinglass, 1/4/99, Joe Kordsmeier, 1/22/99, Bill DiGiacomo, 10/16/98, Harriet Economou, 1/12/99, and Lowell Goldman, 1/14/99.

6. Hyatt called its atrium-style luxury hotels "Hyatt Regency" to distinguish them from the other lodgings in its chain, known as "Hyatt Hotels." However, in New York City the name *Regency* was already being used by the Tisch hotel chain, whose head, Robert Preston Tisch, a backer of the 44th Street convention center and opponent of the 34th Street site, had complained that the tax abatement given the Commodore was unavailable to other hotels. The Tisches did not care to share the name *Regency*, and Trump also objected to the name because it made it seem that the former Commodore was merely part of a chain. Thus the Commodore became the Grand Hyatt, reflecting its proximity to Grand Central Station, which was next door. Sources for this section include Der Scutt diary, 5/24/77.

7. Michael Stone, "Clash of the Titans: Business Tycoons Donald Trump and Jay Prizker," *Chicago* magazine, October 1994.

8. Sources for this section include Marie Brenner, "After the Gold Rush," *Vanity Fair*, September 1990; interviews with Gerald Schrager, 5/17/99; Sugar Rautbord, 2/27/99 and 3/6/99.

9. Concerned about underbudgeting, Steinglass tried to bump up the contract to what he considered a more realistic level. "I've got a Christian project manager architect with a Jewish name," Donald Trump joked. Top HRH executive Irv Fisher shot back, "And we've got a Christian owner with a Jewish head!" Der Scutt diary, 11/23/77.

10. On Shore Haven and Beach Haven, which were modeled after the garden apartments Fred Trump had built in Norfolk during World War II, it was to the developer's advantage to make actual costs as low as possible. After covering those charges, he could "mortgage out"—that is, use the balance of his construction loan to pay off the mortgage—then issue dividends out of rental income to the sponsor of the projects (in other words, himself). He ran into trouble at Trump Village because he was putting up an unfamiliar building type, high-rise apartment towers, and had to call in HRH for help. Fortunately for the developer, he had figured in such an ample profit margin that despite having to pay another builder, he still collected a handsome profit.

11. According to Phil Wolf, the on-site owner's representative on the Grand Hyatt, construction crews found that in certain areas of the Commodore cinder fill had been used to make up for differences in floor thickness. At the time the hotel was built, cinders, produced by the locomotives next door at Grand Central, were plentiful. Because they are not as heavy as concrete or sand, they made good filler; unfortunately, however, they are corrosive and thus had to be removed. Another surprise was the corrosion in steel beams adjacent to ice-making machinery. The cause was the salt used in the production of the vast quantities of ice needed for iceboxes and to cool large common areas, where fans blew over large blocks of ice to produce a rudimentary form of air-conditioning.

12. Sources include Barrett, *Trump*, p. 161; interview with Margo Wellington, 4/12/99.

13. Sources include interview with Rich Rosan, 2/1/99.

14. Interview with Jeffrey Walker, 3/17/98.

15. Sources for this section include "The Two Faces of Ivana—Model and Sports-woman," *Montreal Gazette*, 12/31/75; Marie Brenner, "Trumping the Town," *New York*, November 17, 1980; Jonathan Van Meter, "Ivana! Ivana! Ivana!" *Spy*, May 1989; Glenn Plaskin, "Queen Ivana Approximately," *New York Daily News Magazine*, 12/17/89; Norma King, *Ivana Trump: A Very Unauthorized Biography*, 1990; Wayne Barrett, *Trump*; interview with Jerry Goldsmith, 3/20/99; Ivana Trump, speech, Church of the Holy Apostle, 11/19/99.

16. Like many people, Ivana tended to look better in person than she did on film. In photographs her wide smile showed too much tooth and, even worse, too much gum. A further problem was that at a little over five feet seven, Ivana fell about two inches short of the minimum requirement for top-of-the-line modeling work but was tall enough for runways.

17. Carol V. R. George, *God's Salesman*, 1993; interview with Arthur Caliandro, 10/27/97.

18. Sources for this section include Marie Brenner, "After the Gold Rush," *Vanity Fair*, September 1990; *New York Times*, 8/30/79; and the notes of the *Times's* reporter, Patricia Lyndon.

19. One of the few personal touches was a small bedside photo of Donald in the nude, with his back to the camera. "It was like a secret piece of intimacy in the room," said reporter Lyndon, "and it stood out from the rest of the impersonal decor."

20. Interview with Andre d'Usseau, the Hyatt vice president in charge of technical assistance, 10/21/98. Thus, for example, Donald Trump retained Der Scutt as well as Jordan Gruzen as architects on the Grand Hyatt and the convention center and fanned the competitive flames between them with selective praise, credit, and payment.

21. Interview with Alan Lapidus, 5/7/90.

22. Quoted in "Trump: The Development of a Manhattan Developer," by Howard Blum, *New York Times*, 8/26/80.

23. This meant, among other things, an aggressive effort to get rid of on-site retailers he considered not classy enough for the image he wanted to create. In one instance, Trump insisted on the right to review the display windows of a sporting goods store he considered tacky; in another, he decided that in order to be prepared for the possible legalization of casino gambling in New York, he would install escalators in the space occupied by Strawberry's, a moderate-price women's clothing store. Negotiations between the developer and many site tenants were long and often bitter and in some cases led to court suits. Eventually, Strawberry's and some, but not all, of the site tenants returned. Sources for this section include "Trumping the Town," by Marie Brenner, *New York*, November 17, 1980; interviews with Paul Willen, 11/27/98, Richard Rice, 1/4/99, Peter Samton, 1/4/99, Rich Rosan, 2/1/99, and Arthur Emil, 2/25/99.

24. *Dun & Bradstreet Reports*, November/December 1978.

25. For HRH, which figured the construction would cost about twice as much as the $35 million the Trumps had insisted on, this was not unexpected. But for many of those on the job who were used to building on time and on budget, the experience of being constantly behind the eight ball was dismaying. "I was nervous,"

said Joe Kordsmeier, a Hyatt vice president assigned to the construction site. "I knew we were going way over budget, and it was nerve-racking and scary. It was the first time any of our projects had gone over budget, and if it hadn't been for the tax abatement, it would have been a disaster." Another Hyatt executive, John Nichols, recalled the problems caused by the project overshooting both its budget and its deadline. "There was tremendous pressure to get it completed," he said, "but the trades didn't want to finish the job because it was a nice warm place to work in the winter and there was still a recession in New York. Our people became frustrated, so we just decided on an opening date and did it." The solution was a "soft opening," which meant going ahead and renting rooms while imposing strict work rules, such as no beer or food on the job, so as to encourage workers to finish the job and move on.

26. This figure includes land costs of $10 million. Sources include Barrett, *Trump*, p. 160.

27. *Dun & Bradstreet Reports*, November/December 1978.

28. "He wasn't the only one promoting himself," Marino said, "but he did it with more flair. Most of the developers were these nice older Jewish guys—we called Donald 'the Golden Goy.'" Interview with Ron Marino, 3/5/99.

29. The new mayor announced in April 1978 that the new convention center would be built at the 34th Street site. Within a week Donald Trump told Der Scutt that he was no longer in the running for developer but wanted a percentage of any architectural fees collected by Scutt's firm on the project. Scutt objected indignantly, and the issue became moot when the design commission went to I . M. Pei. Perhaps one of the reasons the young developer withdrew so precipitously was that the U. S. Department of Justice was again breathing down his neck with claims that the Trump Organization was still discriminating against blacks in its Brooklyn apartments. Sources include *New York Times*, 4/29/78; Der Scutt diary; Jerome Tuccille, *Trump*, 1987, p. 131.

30. *New York Daily News*, 11/22/78.

31. Sources include interview with Peter Solomon, 3/29/99.

32. Five years later Peter Martosella, the Palmieri executive in charge of closing the 60th Street yards deal, sent Donald Trump a note congratulating him on a recent acquisition and saying that the developer had succeeded at everything he tried to do except the 60th Street yards. "Within a second of his receiving the letter," Martosella said years later, "he was on the phone with me explaining why he couldn't go ahead." Sources include interviews with Larry Shafran, 9/27/98; Peter Martosella, 9/2/98; Fred Rovet, 9/17/98; and John Koskinen, 8/28/98.

33. Artistotle Onassis's partner on Olympic Tower was Arlen Realty and Development Corporation, headed by Arthur Cohen, owner of E. J. Korvette's, among other enterprises. Riklis later leased office space on two floors in Trump Tower for a monthly rent of $100,000. In 1991, after five years as a tenant, he and his wife, singer Pia Zadora, skipped out, stiffing the Trump Organization for many months of rent. Vowing revenge, Donald Trump eventually won a judgment against him for $750,000. Sources include *New York Times*, 10/3/70, 10/7/70, 10/15/70, 2/10/71, 9/1/71, 6/24/73, 10/5/91, 1/10/92; interviews with Alan Lapidus, 5/13/99, and Jerry Shrager, 5/17/99.

34. *New York Times,* 9/6/74.

35. Interview with Rochelle Corson, 2/25/99.

36. Sources for this section include *Business Week,* January 29, 1979, and April 5, 1978, and Der Scutt diary, 1/22/79 and 1/23/79. One day after the appearance of this article, planted by an Equitable executive on the Genesco board of directors and the first to describe a possible Genesco sale to Donald Trump, the Equitable board approved Project T.

37. Because it was obvious that the deal hinged on the developer's participation, Equitable took out a $20 million life insurance policy on him, payable to the partnership.

38. *New York Times,* 8/26/80; *Los Angeles Times,* 4/7/85.

39. Sources for this section include Barrett, *Trump;* Hurt, *Lost Tycoon,* 1993; and interviews with Bill Frentz, 4/6/98, Ben Holloway, 11/9/98, Conrad Stephenson, 5/28/98, George Puskar, 11/17/97, George Peacock, 5/16/98, John Minikes, 12/9/98, Claude Morton, 3/7/98, Tim Welch, 6/30/98, Doug Healey, 4/21/98, and Wally Antoniewicz, 5/11/98.

40. The experience would do more than curtail Stephenson's travel schedule. His disappointment over the loss of the Grand Hyatt loan would lead him to develop new ways to lend money and earn him the nickname "Mr. Real Estate." Up until this time, a bank either handled an entire loan or, if it lacked adequate financial resources or was getting close to its loan limit, passed altogether. "We were opening the door for competitors to take a customer over and we wouldn't get him back for maybe three years, because that was the typical length of a construction loan," Stephenson said afterward. "I thought that was crazy, so I developed a group of banks that shared loans, with the customer continuing to be the prime customer of the lead banks." Making large loans to Donald Trump and other developers, keeping a portion of the interest, and then selling off the rest to smaller banks who wanted to be in New York and part of the lending scene made Chase the leader of the real estate pack, handling up to three-fourths of the loans in that era. But the pattern Stephenson did so much to establish also set off a spiral of lending on ever-shakier grounds. "The other banks had redlined Manhattan because of what happened in the mid-seventies," Stephenson said, referring to the city's fiscal crisis. "But then they said, 'Hell, look at all this money Chase is making, we're going to do it, too.' That's when the whole thing fell apart, because it got very competitive and people made loans that weren't sound."

41. Sources for this section include *New York Times,* 11/28/89; interview with Thomas Hoving, 9/9/98; Der Scutt diary, 12/13/78.

42. Sources for the following sections include *New York Times,* 3/16/80, 6/6/80, 6/7/80, 6/9/80, 6/15/80, 7/13/90, 4/27/91; *Newsday,* 1/15/84, 8/29/88, 7/8/90, 7/13/90, 4/27/91; *New York Daily News,* 8/10/80, 4/15/90, 7/20/90, 3/8/99; U.P.I., 7/12/90; *New York Post,* 6/10/80; Sy Rubin and Jonathan Mandell, *Trump Tower,* 1984; interviews with Tom Macari, 4/14/99, Alan Lapidus, 2/01/00 and 5/10/00, Ashton Hawkins, 7/11/99, and Wendy Sloan, 3/17/89.

43. In September 1979, the New York Committee for a Balanced Building Boom, whose members included an investment banker, stockbroker, and real estate developer, opposed rezoning for Trump. Sources include *New York Times*, 9/6/79; interviews with William Hubbard, 3/4/99, and Hal Negbaur, 3/2/99.

44. Der Scutt diary, 3/30/79, 4/2/79.

45. Sources for this section include press accounts at the time and interviews with Hadley Gold, 10/5/98; Jesse Masyr, 3/12/99, 6/7/99; Edith Spivack, 3/23/99; Rochelle Corson, 2/25/99, 5/12/99.

46. Sources for this section include interviews with Jesse Masyr, 3/12/99, and Andrew Stein, 6/8/99.

47. Andrew Stein was head of a state assembly commission that was critical of a new program to phase out rent control in New York City, whereas Donald Trump vigorously supported the phase-out. Although the developer actually lived in a rent-regulated apartment himself at that time, his family real estate business would realize enormous benefits from the end of rent control. Sources include interview with Andrew Stein, 6/8/99.

48. As quoted by Mitchell Moss in *Palace Coup: The Inside Story of Harry and Leona Helmsley*, p. 158. In helping out Stein, Donald Trump was also evening out a score with Harry Helmsley's wife, Leona. Hostility between the two dated back at least four years, to one of Leona's annual birthday parties for her husband. Donald Trump, then busy pushing the 34th Street site for the new convention center, and Robert Preston Tisch, a major backer of the 46th Street site, had earned her ire when they spent the party lobbying for their respective plans. Sources for this section include "Will New York Get a New Hotel?" by Dan Dorfman, *New York*, 4/26/76; *Trump: Surviving at the Top*, by Donald J. Trump with Charles Leerhsen, 1990; Moss, *Palace Coup*, pp. 145–159.

49. According to the unpublished memoir of Milton Gould, who represented Equitable in the 421a abatement case, Equitable's general counsel told him that Donald Trump insisted that Cohn handle the appeal because "Mr. Cohn had assured him that he had the judges of that court in his pocket." Gould further said that Equitable's council would authorize hiring Cohn only if the lead lawyer was someone respectable—for example, Gould—because Equitable did not want to be involved in any "rinky-dink." Gould, "Fifth Avenue," p. 10.

50. Interview with Gary Schuller, 3/2/99.

51. A no-holds-barred fighter himself, Donald Trump admired and, in some cases, hired those who opposed him with particular vigor. An early example occurred in 1975 when he accompanied his father to Norfolk in an effort to quell a rent strike at a Trump-owned property. Tempers were running high, and at a poolside meeting one tenant threatened to throw Fred Trump into the water. At a negotiating session between the two sides, Donald told his own lawyer to sit down and shut up. Putting his arm around the tenant's representative, a local lawyer named O. L. Gilbert who went by the nickname "Buzz," Donald said, "Buzz and I are going to settle this." Gilbert turned to him and said, "It's Mr. Gilbert, not Buzz, and I'll speak to your lawyer, not you." After the strike was settled, Donald Trump called Gilbert and put him on retainer for a year. A dozen years later

the developer tapped Tony Schwartz, who had done a critical and widely circulated article about him for *New York* ("A Different Kind of Donald Trump Story," February 11, 1985), to co-author his autobiography, *Art of the Deal* (see chapter 19). Recent top aides have included Charlie Riese, former aide to Tony Gleidman and consultant to groups opposed to Trump's plans for the 60th Street yards, and Abe Wallach, vehement critic of Trump during his financial crisis in the early 1990s. Sources include interview with O. L. Gilbert, 10/23/93.

52. Sources include *New York Times Magazine*, 1/2/00; "The Playboy Interview," Glenn Plaskin, *Playboy*, March 1990; Hurt, *Lost Tycoon*, p. 126.

53. Roger E. Nelson, Letters, *New York Times*, 7/25/82. Sources for this section include Wayne Barrett, *Trump*, pp. 193–201; Hurt, *Lost Tycoon*, pp. 131–132; *New York Times*, 4/25/82, 4/26/82, 7/11/82; and interviews with Claude Morton, 3/7/98, Wally Antoniewicz, 5/11/98, Frank Alleva and Frank Cardile, 3/13/98, and Der Scutt, 9/24/98.

54. One of the few to do so was Olympic Tower. The lower floors, which contained offices and retail space, were steel frame, but the upper or residential section used reinforced concrete. Sources include *New York 1960*, by Robert A. M. Stern et al.

55. The high price of concrete in New York was also due to bid-rigging. Sources for this section include *New York Times*, 4/25–26/82; Barrett, *Trump*, pp. 193ff.

56. Sources include Stern et al., *New York 1960*, and *New York Times*, 7/21/75.

57. Unlike Olympic Tower, where the developers used the zoning bonuses for a retail arcade but did little to develop it or invite the public inside, Donald Trump actively pursued retailers. Charging up to $300 per square foot, he attracted European merchants for the most part, including Hermès (French scarves), Lowey's of Madrid (leather), and Fred Jouillier (French jeweler). One reason was that Europeans had the money, another was that vertical malls had a poor track record. And, in fact, many of the Trump Tower boutiques were money losers and served essentially as expensive advertisements for those stores' other locations. *New York Post*, 10/10/89; *New York Times*, 8/15/89.

58. Sources include William Geist, "The Expanding Empire of Donald Trump," *New York Times Magazine*, 4/8/84; Michael Sorkin, *Village Voice*, 6/11/79; *New York Times*, 4/4/83, 11/2/83, 5/6/84; interview with Der Scutt, 9/28/98; Der Scutt diary, passim.

59. His rationale for essentially skipping floors, he told Equitable officials, was that if the entire building were residential, the lower ceiling heights would result in more floors. To implement this creative approach, he simply used one set of elevators, accessible from Fifth Avenue, for the office floors, and another set, accessible from 56th Street and starting with a much higher number, for the residential floors. Sources include Hurt, *Lost Tycoon*, p. 136; interview with John Minikes, 12/9/98, and John d'Alessio, 10/89.

60. Early in the planning stages, the developer told the architect he intended to use the name *Trump Tower* but would not do so publicly until Equitable agreed. He told Scutt to place the name on the renderings to look "natural" and to begin

using the name "unobtrusively," as in "Trump Tower will be an exciting building," but to avoid suggesting a decision had actually been made. Once the decision had been announced, Scutt incorporated the name over the entrance in discreet eighteen-inch-high letters. Trump said nothing but quietly bypassed the architect and doubled the letter size to thirty-six inches.

By the opening in February 1983, the developer seemed to have half forgotten he had a partner and planned to run a newspaper ad on behalf of Trump Tower in which he thanked a number of subcontractors and Equitable for making the new building possible. When Tim Welch, Equitable's representative on the project, reminded him that Equitable was a co-owner and thus a co-extender of thanks, Trump "was in a snit for about a day, but then he agreed." Sources include Der Scutt's diary, 3/1/79, and interview with Tim Welch, 6/30/98.

61. John d'Alessio, a designer for the apartment, called it "Louis XIV on LSD." Sources: Leslie Marshall, "Breakfast Above Tiffany's," *In Style*, December 1995; Marie Brenner, "After the Gold Rush"; interview with John d'Alessio, 10/89.

62. This was principally a decision to go for immediate gain instead of long-term income. But Equitable, noting the number of retailers falling short of their staggering overhead, was also worried about the long-term future for the retail component. Sources for this section include interview with Doug Healey, 4/21/98.

63. Interview with Blanche Sprague, 4/13/99.

64. Interview with Ed Murphy, 6/14/99.

65. Donald Trump, *The Art of the Deal*, p. 54.

66. Trump Plaza was a $125 million project, financed by a construction loan from Manufacturers Hanover. The lawyers retained by the developer for Trump Plaza used the Trump Tower conflict to their advantage, arguing that the city could show its good faith—that it wasn't discriminating against him on Trump Tower—by granting him a tax abatement for Trump Plaza. Sources for this section include Tony Schwartz, "The Show Must Go Up," *New York*, 1981; and interview with Scott Mollen, 4/5/99.

67. Sources include Tony Schwartz, "A Different Kind of Donald Trump Story," *New York*, 2/11/85.

68. Sources include William Geist, "The Expanding Empire of Donald Trump," *New York Times Magazine*, 4/8/84.

69. Of the tenants in the building's sixty occupied apartments, approximately one-quarter earned $75,000 a year (in 1985 dollars), one-quarter lived on fixed incomes of less than $15,000 a year, and the rest fell in between. Tony Schwartz, "A Different Kind," p. 36.

70. In 1998 the building finally became a condominium. By the terms of the final negotiation, tenants were able either to buy their apartments at a 33 percent discount or keep renting and remain exempt from certain rent increases for the next eight years. The tenants claimed a victory, in that forty-three of the building's eighty apartments would still be occupied by rent-regulated tenants, of whom many would pay less in rent than the owner forked over in monthly condominium carrying charges. But as far as Donald Trump was concerned, the

victory was his. Even with a discount, the apartment prices were quite high, and he predicted that he would eventually make $50 million from a building that was essentially thrown in when he bought the hotel next door. *New York Times*, 3/26/98.

CHAPTER 18: GAMBLING ON ATLANTIC CITY

1. Donald Trump was proud of having snagged what he obviously considered the Tiffany location of restaurant tables. Richard Dicker, head of the reorganized Penn Central Transportation Company, recalled having lunch with Donald Trump at the '21' Club in the mid-1980s. When Dicker saw that they were seated right between two rooms, he told the developer he should get to know the maître d' better so that he could get a more secluded table and have private conversations. "No, no," Donald Trump replied. "I'm just where I want to be, where I can see everybody in the place." On another occasion Donald Trump took Robert Sturges, a former casino regulator in New Jersey, to lunch at '21.' When the developer asked him if he noticed where they were seated, Sturges said yes, at a small table. "No, Bob," the developer said. "What's important is we're between the columns. Don't ever let them sit you anywhere but between the columns, because if you're not between the columns, you're nobody." Interviews with Richard Dicker, 3/22/89, and Robert Sturges, 12/22/98.

2. Sources include Marylin Bender, "The Empire and Ego of Donald Trump," *New York Times*, 8/7/83, and Marie Brenner, "Trumping the Town," *New York*, November 17, 1980.

3. William Geist, "The Expanding Empire of Donald Trump," *New York Times Magazine*, 4/4/84.

4. Graydon Carter, "Donald Trump Gets What He Wants," *Gentleman's Quarterly*, May 1984.

5. Interview with Jerry Schrager, 6/10/99.

6. Sources include Robert H. Boyle, "The USFL's Trump Card," *Sports Illustrated*, 2/13/84; Jim Byrne, *The $1 League*, 1986; Barrett, *Trump*; *New York Times*, 10/19/84; *New York Post*, 10/18/84, 10/19/84.

7. *New York Times*, 7/30/86.

8. Although the developer had been asserting the value of the Trump brand for years, he could not get his name on the Grand Hyatt and had to bow to Equitable's conditions to have it on Trump Tower. But in the wake of his newfound USFL notoriety, Prudential Securities, one of the largest investment companies in New York, asked the developer to construct and market a residential project on Madison Avenue and to name it after himself. "We went to Trump because his name had magic in it," recalled Brian Strum, Prudential vice president at the time. Such magic, in fact, that Prudential was willing to hand over 49 percent of the project without requiring the developer to put up a cent. Soon afterward architect Philip Johnson sketched out Trump Castle, a residential apartment building with arched windows, gold-leaf turrets, spires, crenellated towers, and a miniature moat. Ultimately Prudential sold the site to another party and gave Donald Trump a commission rather than a building with his name across the

front. But although this particular deal remained unconsummated, it confirmed that Trump had indeed become a valuable label. Sources for this section include *Los Angeles Times*, 4/7/85, *New York Times*, 4/8/84, and interview with Brian Strum, 11/17/97.

9. By 1984 Donald Trump deemed his name valuable enough to go to court to protect it. That year he filed suit against two South African brothers, Julius and Eddie Trump, Orthodox Jews who had opened offices in New York under the name the Trump Group and were involved in various investments and real estate transactions around the country. See chapter 19, note 47.

10. In 1975 the two Hilton casino hotels in Las Vegas provided 35 percent of total Hilton Hotel Corporation revenue ($124,440,000 out of a total of $351,121,000) and 43 percent of the total HHC cash flow, then called "income contributions" ($16,683,000 out of a total of $39,153,000). Source: Hilton Hotel Corporation.

11. According to Whittier Law School professor Nelson Rose, the United States is now in what he calls the third wave of legal gambling. Lotteries helped fund early American settlements and were a regular part of colonial and postcolonial life until scandals and Jacksonian moralism led to antilottery legislation. After the Civil War the South turned to lotteries to rebuild its shattered economy, and gambling was a way of life on the frontier. Once again, however, scandals and a wave of moral fervor led to a second prohibition against betting, and by 1910 the United States was once again free of this supposed vice. The third wave began in response to the Depression. In 1931 Nevada reauthorized casino gambling, and in the 1930s and 1940s other states approved pari-mutuel betting. The pace picked up in 1963, when New Hampshire opened the first legal state lottery, and by 1997 only Utah and Hawaii had no form of legal gambling. Perhaps the biggest change of all, Rose notes, is that state governments, influenced by the enormous tax revenues gambling provides, have actively backed it through advertising and extensive promotion. Sources include Nelson Rose, "Gambling and the Law: Recent Developments, 1998," unpublished paper, and interview with Nelson Rose, 6/4/99.

12. Sources for this section include Gigi Mahon, *The Company That Bought the Boardwalk*, 1980; Timothy L. O'Brien, *Bad Bet: The Inside Story of the Glamour, Glitz, and Danger of America's Gambling Industry*, 1998; David Johnston, *Temples of Chance: How America Inc. Bought Out Murder Inc. to Win Control of the Casino Business*, 1992; Ovid Demaris, *The Boardwalk Jungle*, 1986; and Gwenda Blair, *Almost Golden: Jessica Savitch and the Selling of Television News*, 1989.

13. The game used names of bodies of water for avenues and omitted certain of the resort city's streets, such as Adriatic, Drexel, and Congress, because blacks lived on them.

14. One formerly posh hotel started giving guests paper towels, and the owners of another once classy resort eventually dynamited it because they could no longer afford the upkeep. The Traymore, the first poured-concrete building in the country, was blasted into nonexistence in 1972 because its owner, the Loew's Corporation (itself owned by Larry and Bob Tisch), could not afford to keep it up. An expanded version of a nineteenth-century boardinghouse, the six-hundred-room hotel, with its four gilded, concrete domes towering over the beach, looked like a classic sandcastle and had been the centerpiece of the Atlantic City skyline since

its completion in 1916. It became nationally famous after President Herbert Hoover stayed there. Sources include *Atlantic City Press*, 5/9/82, and Vicki Gold Levi and Lee Eisenberg, *Atlantic City: 125 Years of Ocean Madness*, 1979.

15. Between 1960 and 1970 the year-round population of Atlantic City went from 59,544 to 47,823, a decline of 20 percent. By 1977 the unemployment rate hit 23 percent. Sources include *New York Times*, 6/24/96; George Sternlieb and James W. Hughes, *The Atlantic City Gamble*, 1983, p. 30; and interviews with Pete Murphy, 5/24/99, Steve Perskie, 11/16/98, and Fran Freedman, 12/9/98.

16. Quoted in O'Brien, *Bad Bet*, 72.

17. Approximately the northern half of Absecon Island, Atlantic City comprises 6.7 square miles, two-thirds of which consists of federally protected wetlands. By way of comparison, Atlantic City is more than five times as large as Central Park (840 acres, or 1.3 square miles) and less than one-third the size of the island of Manhattan (22.6 square miles). With the legalization of casino gambling, job opportunities and, in turn, the population, increased. But the amount of housing, especially at low rents, plummeted as speculators rushed to tear down marginal properties. Citywide, vacant land, which was only 4 percent of the city's real property in 1977, jumped to 17.6 percent in 1980. Nonetheless, the area zoned specifically for casinos remained small, and property within those borders became phenomenally valuable. Sources include the *Philadelphia Inquirer*, 6/16/85, and Sternlieb and Hughes, *Atlantic City*, pp. 100–101.

18. A standing joke at the time, according to one Atlantic City insider, was that the old Chalfonte-Haddon Hall used to be a shithouse, and now it was a shithouse with carpeting. Because retrofitting an old hotel was the cheapest and fastest way to get up and running, other casinos followed Resorts' lead, buying up shabby old facilities and planning to expand them with additions. But then a Resorts-friendly amendment to the Casino Control Act upped the minimum number of rooms from 400 to 500, leaving Resorts, which had carved 566 rooms out of an original 1,000, the only facility large enough to qualify. Instead of renovating existing structures, newer casinos tore them down and erected new buildings. More rapidly than anyone had ever anticipated, Atlantic City's old landmarked buildings vanished; in their stead appeared impersonal, modern skyscrapers, unconnected architecturally, historically, or culturally to the city in which they were located.

Atlantic City's nearness to major population centers had made it attractive to the casino industry, but the same geography would produce a market strikingly different from that in Las Vegas. On the one hand, being within easy driving distance meant that more people would come to Atlantic City than to Vegas; on the other, such customers, most of whom came by bus, were less affluent than Vegas customers, who had to fly to get there. Because Atlantic City lacked a commercial airport or direct rail connections to anyplace but Philadelphia, jet-setters sometimes skipped going there altogether. Similarly, most Atlantic City gamblers came just for the day, heading straight for the casinos and spending little or nothing in the rest of the town. Unable to tap into these new sources of revenue, the noncasino areas of town remained shabby, and visitors had little incentive to be anything more than day trippers.

Had they wanted to stay more than a few hours, they might have had trouble doing so. Unlike Las Vegas, which had 42,620 rooms in 1978 and 120,205 by the end of 1999, Atlantic City still had fewer than 12,000 rooms twenty years after Resorts opened. Again this was, in large part, a result of geography. Las Vegas casinos could expand into the desert and build as many hotel rooms as they wanted, whereas Atlantic City was a small island on which the supply of available land was extremely limited. As the result of these and other factors, two decades after Resorts opened, the two largest gambling markets in the nation had diverged sharply. Atlantic City was number one in casino revenues, whereas Las Vegas, which took in more from noncasino sources than the actual casinos themselves, came in number one overall.

19. Bill Cosby, who opened a show at Resorts within a few weeks of the casino's opening, joked that people used to come to Atlantic City for the beach, but now they were lined up around the block to get away from it.

20. Nelson Rose, "Gambling and the Law: Recent Legal Developments, 1998," p. 17.

21. Interview with Howard Weingrow, 11/18/98.

22. Interview with G. Michael Brown, 12/17/98.

23. The Trumps took along a real estate broker named Richard Levy, who had done business in New York and Atlantic City and was a close friend of Robert Trump's. According to Levy, Donald Trump drove his own limousine, Ivana sat next to him in the front, and Levy was in the back. When they arrived in Atlantic City, a man stuck his hand into the rear window and said to Levy that he had always wanted to met him. Surprised, Levy asked why. "I wanted to meet the guy Donald Trump chauffeured," the man replied. Introducing himself as Mickey Rudin, Frank Sinatra's attorney, he ushered the party into Resorts, where they sat at a table with Faye Dunaway and watched Sinatra perform. Sources for this section include interviews with Paul Longo, 11/23/98, and Richard Levy, 11/17/98.

24. Interview with Alan Lapidus, 4/18/90.

25. Interview with Jeff Walker, 10/98.

26. The Trump presence in New Jersey would be enhanced a few years later. In 1983 Donald Trump managed to have his sister, Maryanne Trump Barry, then an assistant U.S. attorney in Newark, appointed to the federal bench. Married to John Barry, an ex-prosecutor who represented major corporate clients as well as the developer, the oldest Trump child had been a lawyer only nine years and could not leapfrog over senior colleagues by herself. "There's no question Donald helped me get on the bench," she said. "I was good, but not that good."

For this coup, which needed support from the governor, nomination by the president, and approval by the U.S. Senate, Donald Trump needed help. He got it from Roy Cohn and Cohn's old pal Roger Stone. A Republican political analyst and Washington insider, Stone had a long client list that included, among others, Richard Nixon, Ronald Reagan, and Brendan Byrne's successor, Tom Kean, and in 1987 and 1999 he would manage Trump's own brief presidential forays. Trump, an early Reagan supporter, had met Stone when he was running Reagan's 1980 New York campaign out of Cohn's town house. In 1981 Stone produced a squeaky 1,797-vote margin in New Jersey for Kean, a liberal Republican million-aire with a gap-toothed smile, a nice-guy persona, and razor-sharp political instincts. Ultimately Donald Trump, Cohn, Stone, and Kean all played a part in the effort to put the developer's sister in judicial robes. When the appointment finally came through, the developer reportedly declared, "Roy can do the impossible," and the new judge called Cohn personally to say thank you. In subsequent years a sister on the bench and a brother-in-law arguing cases around the state would add still more clout to the Trump name in New Jersey. Sources include *New York Times*, 10/9/86; *Bergen Record*, 10/27/91; Barrett, *Trump*, pp. 248–249; and interview with Maryanne Trump Barry, 2/9/98.

27. Like Donald Trump, Alan Lapidus spent his childhood in a home built by his father and began learning about his future profession before he could walk. Outside, the house was an eye-catching red, white, and blue; inside, it had Morris Lapidus's signature touches, including curving interior walls, low planters, then-novel Plexiglas fixtures, and, in the dining room, a custom-made, zebra-striped linoleum floor that stayed immaculate because everyone was under strict orders to walk only on the black stripes.

28. Building such a large passageway was an engineering challenge. Because the building was within one hundred feet of the beach, supporting the street overhang on columns meant sinking piles into the sand, a method that would require a lengthy federal review. The other standard approach, attaching it to an adjacent building, would require the owner's permission. Instead Lapidus cantilevered the passage from Trump's structure, so that it would literally hang out over Mississippi Avenue without touching any other surface. Interview with Alan Lapidus, 4/18/90.

29. A nearby condominium, the Ocean Club, was a few feet higher.

30. Regulators might have had problems with certain entanglements, such as having Roy Cohn as his lawyer. But the developer apparently did not mention his ties to Cohn, and officials later said that Cohn, who was not working directly on the developer's Atlantic City deals, seemed basically a figure out of the nation's political past and thus irrelevant—despite having been charged with bribery, conspiracy, and bank fraud. Nick Ribis, the local lawyer who would be Donald Trump's major representative in Atlantic City, had worked for a firm linked to Cohn, but that, too, seemed to be of little interest. Sources for this section include interviews with Ben Borowski, 12/2/98, and Robert Sturges, 12/22/98.

31. Sources for this section include *Los Angeles Times*, 4/7/85.

32. When Wynn was about eleven years old, his father took him on his first visit to Las Vegas. When his father died at age forty-six, he left a legacy of gambling debts. Wynn, who was not a gambler, took several years to pay them off and then in 1967 moved to Las Vegas. After establishing himself there with the Golden Nugget, he got in on the ground floor of the next gambling opportunity, Atlantic City. Only a few days after Resorts opened, he paid $8.5 million for a Boardwalk site and then put all he could raise, some $2 million, behind the Drexel junk bond offering. Sources include O'Brien, *Bad Bet*, pp. 47ff.; John L. Smith, *Running Scared: The Life and Treacherous Times of Las Vegas Casino King Steve Wynn*, 1995, pp. 35ff.; and Connie Bruck, *The Predators' Ball: The Junk Bond Raiders and the Man Who Stalked Them*, 1985, pp. 58ff.; *New York Times*, 7/6/97.

33. For this section I am particularly indebted to David Johnston's *Temples of Chance*. Sources also include interviews with George Rinaldi, 5/28/99; Jeffrey Walker, 10/20/98; Bob Sturges, 12/22/98; Richard Goeglein, 12/18/98; and Daryl Leury, 1/6/99.

34. In February 1980 Holiday bought Harrah's and used that name for its first Atlantic City casino, already under construction at a marina across town from the Boardwalk. The location was risky, for Harrah's Marina Hotel and Casino was the only operation so far away from the historic tourist magnet, the beach. But the bet paid off, for the Queen of Resorts was no longer about the beach. Instead it was about gambling in the most appealing possible surroundings. Indeed, middle-class, middle-aged patrons who drove their own cars preferred to keep some distance from the legendary but seedy Boardwalk. They also favored Harrah's relatively low-key, restrained decor, which featured the usual mirrors and marble but was less flashy than the competition. Most of all they liked the fact that Harrah's, unlike every other casino hotel in town, had its own garage. Within a year after its November 1980 opening, Harrah's was well on its way to becoming the most profitable casino in town. By 1983 Harrah's four casinos, including three in Nevada and Harrah's Marina in Atlantic City, provided 40 percent of Holiday Inn's net profit of $124.4 million. Sources include *Nation's Restaurant News*, 8/27/84.

35. Interview with Richard Goeglein, 12/18/98.

36. Sources for this section include Johnston, *Temples of Chance*; O'Brien, *Bad Bet*.

37. Sources include Johnston, *Temples of Chance*; and interview with Richard Goeglein, 12/18/98.

38. Attorney Craig Norville, who had handled a New Year's Eve closing for an impatient Donald Trump a decade earlier and now represented Harrah's, called the partnership "a clash of hubrises."

39. Daniel Lee, casino analyst for Drexel. Although Lee did not work for Donald Trump in a paid capacity, he advised him on several key moves against other casino corporations and then earned large fees for Drexel advising those targets on how to counter Trump's offensives. Sources include Barrett, *Trump*, passim.

40. Sources for this section include Trump, *The Art of the Deal*, chapter 9; Johnston, *Temples of Chance*, chapter 10; interviews with Frank Bryant, 3/2/98 and 9/10/99; Ben Lambert, 8/5/98; and John Torrell, 6/10/98; *San Diego Union-Tribune*, 12/12/93.

41. A year later, when the developer bought his partner's half of Trump Plaza for $223 million, he used essentially the same tools, an initial Manufacturers Hanover bridge loan followed by a $250 million bond issue from Bear, Stearns. Again the developer had complete financing, plus, in this case, a $20.7 million payment made directly to him. Sources include John Connolly, "All of the People, All of the Time," *Spy*, April 1991.

42. Regardless of whether the blame belongs to Harrah's for poor management or to the Trump Organization for not making the changes that would have made the facility run more smoothly, there were significant problems at the opening and afterward. Perhaps the biggest was the crowds, far larger than had been expected, putting a strain on the already inadequate elevator system. To add to the chaos,

the fire alarms rang constantly, each time necessitating evacuation of the entire facility, and significant malfunctions in the accounting systems required closing slot machines and, in turn, losing potential revenue. To have such problems at the opening of a complex, major facility is not unusual, as the Trump Organization learned later at the opening of the Taj, but at the time Trump executives assumed the cause was Harrah's sheer incompetence.

43. In one four-page, single-spaced letter from Donald Trump to Philip G. Satre, president and chief executive officer of Harrah's, the developer claimed, among other things, that Harrah's operated in a "purposefully negative way," was in "a disgraceful situation for which you should be ashamed," that employees at the joint facility were "unhappy working for Harrah's [and] who can blame them," and that matters were now in a "deplorable" state.

44. A U.S. football field, including the end zones, is 360 feet long and 160 feet wide, a total of 57,600 square feet; Resorts had a 59,857-square-foot casino. Sources for this section include *New York Times*, 3/16/86; *Atlantic City Press*, 3/15/86, 3/18/86; and *Variety*, 3/26/86.

45. Caesars World, Inc., defended its right to the word *palace* by emphasizing the motif of Greco-Roman splendor in its three casinos, including Caesars Atlantic City Hotel Casino. Caesars' obviously tireless lawyers found evidence of this motif in the faux roman-style lettering used in Caesars' signage; the reproductions of sculptures with what might be loosely termed "antique" themes (thus Michelangelo's *David*, a sixteenth-century rendering of a biblical subject, is included); a Chinese restaurant, inaccurately linked to the Roman Empire through reference to Marco Polo; and advertisements showing comedian Buddy Hackett as Caesar in a palace. Perhaps the most startling citation is the use of pig Latin in radio ads for Caesars. U.S. Court of Appeals judge Dickinson R. Debevoise dismissed these arguments but seemed impressed by polls that showed that the public associated the word *palace* with Caesars' operations. On May 14, 1987, he held that although Donald Trump didn't intend to steal any of Caesars' goodwill because he had plenty through the use of the name *Trump* alone, he would not allow the developer to use the word *palace* because it would inevitably infringe on Caesars' turf and cause confusion. Sources include 1987 U.S.App.LEXIS 6988; 1 U.S.P.Q.2D (BNA) 1806. I am indebted to Leon Friedman for pointing out this material to me.

46. The original idea had been to tap New Jersey casino reinvestment taxes—a 2 percent levy on each casino's gross win—to pay for the reconstruction project. Now, though, the developer offered one reason after another why he should not have to pick up the tab, including his claim that there was no traffic problem and the project was overkill ("a howitzer to kill a fly," as Robert Trump put it). He also testified that Hilton attorneys had glossed over the commitment and failed to hand over key papers on time. Hilton lawyers denied this and noted a bill, still unpaid, sent to Donald Trump for copies of 4,993 pages of relevant documents. Interview with David Sciarra, 8/16/99.

47. There were a few disappointments, including the fact that Caesars prevailed in its court suit to protect the word *palace*. In addition, the reinvestment authority would not let Trump write off the $30 million cost of his gleaming new parking

garage as a civic improvement, even though he had a horse and carriage specially painted along one wall. But Trump could console himself with the increase in revenues the garage brought, just as Harrah's had predicted.

48. Sources for this section include John Connolly, "All of the People, All of the Time," *Spy*, April 1991, and Harry Hurt, *Lost Tycoon*, pp. 179–181.

49. In addition, the deal neatly removed Steve Wynn, the only figure who offered real competition to Donald Trump as Mr. Atlantic City. Long before the developer's arrival there, Wynn had promoted himself along with his casino. He played the winsome foil to tough-guy Frank Sinatra in television ads, mixed with the crowds on the casino floor, and successfully targeted the same upscale, high-roller market Donald Trump wanted for Trump Plaza. Now Wynn, who had complained loudly about the Casino Control Commission's constant micromanagement, happily took himself and the $250 million he made on the Golden Nugget sale back to Las Vegas, leaving the field wide open for the New Yorker.

50. Sources include Application of Trump Plaza Associates and Trump's Castle Associates for casino license renewal, 4/4/88.

51. Sources include Lenny Glynn, "Blowout on the Boardwalk," *Institutional Investor*, December 1989.

52. Donald J. Trump, with Charles Leerhsen, *Surviving at the Top*, 1990, p. 6.

53. In the early 1980s an old family friend, prominent hotelier Robert Tisch, arranged a job for Sprague with Trump. Although the two men had tangled about the convention center site, Tisch told her that Donald Trump was the only game in town, the only high-profile developer, and the only one doing anything interesting. Interview with Blanche Sprague, 4/13/99.

54. Sources for this section include Marie Brenner, "After the Gold Rush," *Vanity Fair*, September 1990.

55. Sources for this section include interviews with Ana Zanova Steindler, 3/18/99; Mai Hallingby, 3/17/99; Nikki Haskell, 2/28/98; Vivian Serota, 12/15/98; Sugar Rautbord, 1/14/99, 2/14/00; Fran Freedman, 2/9/98; Hurt, *Lost Tycoon*, passim.

56. Interview with Nikki Haskell, 2/28/98.

57. Interview with Donald Trump, 12/12/97.

CHAPTER 19: THE TALLEST BUILDING IN THE WORLD

1. UPI, 1/7/87.

2. For some years Rockefeller gave money away on an ad hoc basis and attempted to diversify through friends' business propositions, including Monte Cristo, the ill-fated mining venture in the Pacific Northwest where Friedrich Trump sought his fortune. Eventually the oil tycoon resolved the issue of how to spend what he had made by pouring vast sums into large-scale philanthropy, bankrolling the University of Chicago and the largest nonprofit organization in history, the

Rockefeller Foundation. His other two major philanthropic projects were Spelman Seminary, a black institution now known as Spelman College, in Atlanta, and the Rockefeller Institute for the Study of Medicine, a large research facility in Manhattan.

3. A lean, handsome man with intense blue eyes, thick black hair tinged with gray, and a headstrong manner, Flagler was the bold innovator behind the system of illegal rebates from northeastern railroads that established the mighty Standard Oil monopoly. He used the same force of will to develop the east coast of Florida and to build resorts at St. Augustine, Daytona, Miami, and Palm Beach. In 1901, at the age of seventy-one, he made his final lavish gesture. On the occasion of his third marriage, he presented his thirty-three-year-old bride with an enormous neoclassical mansion called Whitehall. Immediately dubbed "the Taj Mahal of North America," it cost $2.5 million to build and another $1.5 million to furnish. The huge white mansion, roofed with red Spanish tiles and surrounding an enormous open courtyard, contained fifty-five rooms stuffed with art and antiques and set a standard of ultimate personal luxury that would last for a quarter century. The architects, John M. Carriere and Thomas Hastings, had built Flagler's first grand hotel in St. Augustine and would later design the New York Public Library, the Henry Clay Frick mansion, the U.S. House and Senate Office Buildings, and the Memorial Amphitheater in Arlington Cemetery. Sources for this section include "Whitehall: The Henry Morrison Flagler Museum," a brochure published by the museum in 1988; Ron Chernow, *Titan: The Life of John D. Rockefeller, Sr.*; Edward N. Akin, *Flagler: Rockefeller Partner & Florida Baton*; and James R. Knott, *The Mansion Builders*.

4. Marjorie Merriweather Post, born in 1887, was already rich when she married her second husband, Edward F. Hutton, founder of the first wire brokerage service in history, in 1920. Together they went on an extraordinary shopping spree, buying Jell-O, Baker's chocolate, Hellmann's mayonnaise, Log Cabin syrup, Maxwell House coffee, and Birds Eye, maker of the world's first frozen foods. Post's original legacy, the Postum Company, became the food conglomerate General Foods, and she became even richer. Her only child was born during this marriage; her other husbands included Edward Bennett Close, whose descendant is the film star and actor Glenn Close; Joseph Davies, ambassador to the Soviet Union; and Herbert May, a prominent industrialist.

5. Noted Palm Beach architect Marion Sims Wyeth designed Mar-a-Lago. Joseph Urban, who had helped stage Florenz Ziegfeld's Follies and went on to be art director of the Boston Opera and a set designer for Covent Garden and the Paris Opera, did the interior detailing, and his theatricality and extravagance are everywhere apparent. Occupying a seventeen-acre site, the estate is a source of staggering statistics. They include boatloads of Dorian stone imported from Genoa and used on the exterior (3); total room count (118); bedrooms (58), bathrooms (33), and servants' rooms (27); Spanish tiles dating back to the fifteenth century (36,000); fireplaces (12); flower pots on outside terraces (700); the solid marble dining table's full length (29 feet), weight (2 tons), and number of place settings (50); separate staff residences (5); greenhouses (4); bomb shelters (3); and cloisters (2).

The quarters designed for Marjorie Merriweather Post's daughter, Nedenia (an actress known in her adult life as Dina Merrill), include a silver-plated, elaborately carved canopy bed, silver-squirrel doorknobs, and hand-loomed carpets with fairy-tale themes. The living room's thirty-foot-tall ceiling is covered in gold leaf in imitation of the "Thousand Wing Ceiling" of the Accademia of Venice, and the loggia features a copy of the Benozzo Gozzoli frescoes from the Medici Palace in Florence. Every room in the house contains wood carvings and stone sculptures and the dance pavilion doubles as a movie theater. The dining room is a copy of the dining salon at the Chigi Palace in Rome, and the massive marble table is inlaid with more marble and semiprecious stones arranged in a complex floral pattern. Outside, the pavement of the patio contains thousands of glacially polished stones shipped from Mrs. Post's Long Island hunting preserve. In addition, the estate includes a seventy-five-foot tower, a small "pitch and putt" golf course, citrus groves, cutting gardens, guest houses, a superintendent's residence, a steward's residence, a watchman's cottage, chauffeur's quarters, staff residences, and a tunnel underneath the main road that gives access to a private beach. The only thing missing when Donald Trump bought Mar-a-Lago in late 1985 was a swimming pool, which he added soon afterward.

6. Sources for this section include *Palm Beach Life*, July 1986; and Marie Brenner, "After the Gold Rush."

7. *Town & Country*, March 1986.

8. *Playboy*, May 1997.

9. It had been public knowledge for years that Mar-a-Lago was squarely in the airport's flight path. What is curious is that deal-making legend Donald Trump apparently did not know this, chose to ignore it, or thought that he would somehow be able to change it.

10. As with Bonwit Teller, the jewel of the sixty-eight-year-old, sixteen-store Alexander's chain was the flagship, located at the corner of 59th Street and Lexington, directly across from Bloomingdale's. For years brokers and developers had been vying to pull off the ultimate Alexander's deal. "It was one of those classic undoable deals everybody took a shot at," recalled investment banker Peter Solomon, who after finishing a stint as deputy mayor under Koch had made his own unsuccessful effort. "It always looked like somebody should be able to do it, like it should happen." Rising to the challenge, Donald Trump paid more than $40 million to the bookish Texas investor and oil heir Robert Bass for about 20 percent of the outstanding stock. But the other major shareholder, a tough-talking New Jersey strip-mall czar named Steven Roth, was just as determined to pull off the ultimate deal as the developer—and just as competitive. A friend reportedly once said that Roth, a compact figure with a blunt manner, was only half kidding when he told his golf teacher he would give him a small shopping mall if he could lower Roth's handicap. Sources for this section include *New York Post*, 12/9/86; *Aspen Times*, 2/6/86; and interview with Peter Solomon, 11/24/99.

11. Interview with Peter Solomon, 11/24/99.

12. Interview with Gerald Schrager, 5/7/99.

13. Sources for this section include Barrett, *Trump*; Hurt, *Lost Tycoon*; Carlos Macri, "Lincoln West or Who Trumped Whom," from an unpublished autobiography written with Judith Murphy; and interviews with Conrad Stephenson, 5/28/98, 6/12/98.

14. They included a twenty-six-acre park, low-income housing, a new smokestack for an adjacent power plant, and funds for redoing nearby subway stops and a new rail freight depot in the Bronx.

15. Community activists discerned the heavy hand of Donald Trump in the complicated scenario that followed. After he surrendered his $400,000 option, the Palmieri Company, hired to sell off Penn Central properties at the highest possible prices, made no effort to solicit interest among other developers. Instead Palmieri official Larry Schafran sold the option for the same price to Abraham Hirschfeld, a parking-garage czar, Lindenbaum client, and Fred Trump associate known for bizarre antics in his many runs for public office. Hirschfeld then sold 65 percent of his interest to Francisco Macri, who managed to obtain the necessary rezoning for the site—at which point Donald Trump resurfaced. The financially pressed Macri eventually sold the property to Trump. Hirschfeld retained a 20 percent interest, but sold it to Trump some years later.

    According to one anti-Trump line of thought, Hirschfeld, with the cooperation of the Palmieri Company, was a stalking horse for a Chase-backed attempt to retain the yards for Donald Trump, and Macri, perhaps unwittingly, became part of that effort. Schafran said that the sole reason Hirschfeld got the option was that Palmieri was facing a tight deadline and Hirschfeld was ready to deal. Hirschfeld insisted that although he was a longtime friend of Fred Trump's, he had pursued the yards on his own. Macri later wrote that he, too, had launched the project on his own, that community suspicion had contributed to his difficulties, and that the constant collusion between Stephenson and Donald Trump had made his situation impossible. Conrad Stephenson said that he simply acted appropriately in the face of mounting uncertainty that Macri could handle the project. Whatever the merits of these various claims and counterclaims, it is at the very least a measure of Donald Trump's stature that everyone involved seemed to consider him the critical figure. Sources include Barrett, *Trump*; Macri, "Lincoln West"; and interviews with Larry Schafran, 9/2/98, Abraham Hirschfeld, 12/90, and Conrad Stephenson, 5/28/98, 6/12/98.

16. *New York Daily News*, 11/24/85; *New York Times*, 12/23/86; *Newsday*, 5/15/86.

17. Sources for this section include Jonathan Greenberg, "Clash of the Titans," *Manhattan, inc.*, January 1986.

18. Donald Trump announced his intention to build the world's tallest buildings on lower Manhattan sites in 1983 and 1984. *Chicago Tribune* architecture critic Paul Gatt panned the second proposal, and the developer sued him for defamation and asked $500 million in damages. David Berger, the developer's last-minute ally back in 1974 when he was maneuvering to land the rail yard option, served as his attorney. The claim was that Gapp's critique subjected the developer "to ridicule, contempt, embarrassment and financial harm" and "had a devastating effect" on the project. In September 1985 U.S. District Court judge

Edward Weinfeld, citing the Latin proverb *De gustibus non est disputandum* ("There is no disputing about taste"), dismissed the developer's complaint. I am grateful to Leon Friedman for bringing this material to my attention.

19. Sources for this section include Joshua Hammer, "He Wants to Take You Higher," *Manhattan, inc.*, January 1986.

20. Donald Trump's first assignment for Jahn was to create a version of the world's tallest building for a competition to develop the old New York Coliseum site on Columbus Circle. The city and the Metropolitan Transit Authority, joint owners of the site, had requested bids on the site in February 1985. Donald Trump and Peter Kalikow—like Donald Trump, a successful New York developer, member of an old real estate family, and client of Jerry Schrager—teamed up and presented two entries, Jahn's design for a 121-story building and another, by architect Eli Attia, for a 137-story building. The winner was Mort Zuckerman, in large part because he had a commitment from Salomon Brothers to be a primary tenant. Later, Donald Trump would tell one interviewer that he was the "biggest winner" of the process and had entered it only to ensure that something good would be built near his rail yard site.

21. Sources for this section include Frank Rose, "Celebrity Zoning," *Manhattan, inc.*, November 1989.

22. Sources for this section include *New York Daily News*, 11/19/85, 11/21/85 (Bob Herbert column); *New York Post*, 11/19/85; *New York Times*, 11/19/85.

23. Sources include *Time*, December 2, 1985; *New York Times*, 11/19/85, 12/22/85; *New York Post*, 12/31/85; interview with Paul Goldberger, 2/26/99.

24. Sources for this section include *New York Post*, 6/25/86; Karen Cook, "Trumping Trump," *Manhattan, inc.*, November 1986; Frank Rose "Celebrity Zoning."

25. Interview with Dan Gutman, 4/91.

26. Sources for this section include interviews with Henry Kanegsberg, 7/30/99, and Bill Maloney, 8/20/99.

27. Interview with Mathew Lifflander, 10/20/97.

28. Sources for this section include *Time*, November 10, 1986; *New York Times*, 11/15/86; and interviews with Henry Stern, 11/24/98 and 12/1/99, Kent Barwick, 8/24/99 and 11/24/99, Bronson Binger, 11/30/99, and Gordon Davis, 11/26/99.

29. In a meeting of USFL owners in 1984, Donald Trump said, "When I build something for somebody, I always add $50 million or $60 million onto the price. My guys come in, they say it's going to cost $75 million. I say it's going to cost $125 million, and I build it for $100 million. Basically I did a lousy job. But they think I did a great job." During the Wollman reconstruction, he said that the job was simple so he would not need to add contingency money; if he actually refrained, it was apparently an unusual and possibly unique move. *New York Times*, 7/1/86.

30. He was referring to the famously disaster-plagued Francis Ford Coppola film, which was finally completed in 1979. Scheduled to take six weeks, it ended up requiring sixteen months, and the budget, originally projected at $12 million to $14 million, more than doubled to $30 million, a colossal sum at the time.

31. Instead of becoming a reflecting pond in warm months, Wollman returned to being a roller rink. Three summers later it became a miniature golf course adorned with models of Manhattan landmarks—including, of course, everything that bore the name *Trump.*

32. Soon after Ed Koch was reelected for a third term in November 1985, his administration became engulfed in a series of corruption scandals that swirled around, among others, former deputy mayor Stanley Friedman and Queens borough president Donald Manes. Although Koch himself was not tied to the scandal, his leadership came under heavy fire.

33. This was a rewarding victory for Mike Bailkin, the former Beame administration lawyer who had authored the Grand Hyatt tax abatement. Although he was proud of his Grand Hyatt work and remained friendly with Donald Trump, the lawyer had been annoyed that after he left city government the developer had slipped in a more favorable profit-sharing arrangement. In late 1986 Rockefeller Center retained Bailkin for what both center and lawyer considered a long-shot effort to hold on to the network. "Trump had a lock on NBC," Bailkin later told the *New York Post.* "He could have pulled that one off." But having worked with the developer, Bailkin told the center that Donald Trump was likely to overreach himself. "I told my client we should wait this one out," he said later. "A problem might arise, and we might get some reconsideration." When Trump and Koch began feuding publicly over the matter, the lawyer knew he was right. As the Television City deal fell apart, he sprang into action and retained the network for Rockefeller Center. Sources include *New York Post,* 5/5/96; Barrett, *Trump;* interview with Mike Bailkin, 4/12/00.

34. *New York Daily News,* 11/8/87.

35. In December 1987 Donald Trump offered to complete the renovation of the Central Park Zoo, saying that otherwise his children would outgrow the zoo before they could see it. Declining the offer, parks commissioner Henry Stern said that the developer's help was unnecessary because the long-delayed project was nearly finished. The next April, inspectors found hazardous conditions at the Williamsburg Bridge, which links lower Manhattan to Brooklyn, and the eighty-five-year-old suspension bridge was abruptly closed. Alfred Delli Bovi, head of the Federal Urban Mass Transit Administration and a former Republican state legislator from Queens, asked Donald Trump for help. Seizing the opportunity, the developer invited the news media to accompany him on a visit to the bridge and then offered to carry out—but not pay for—the job himself. Again the city declined the offer and handled the repair itself. A year later, after a gang of young men raped and critically injured a jogger in Central Park, the developer ran full-page ads in all four New York dailies denouncing the crime, disagreeing with Koch's stance, and saying that he wanted not to understand criminals but to hate, frighten, and punish them. *New York Times,* 5/1/89.

36. Since time immemorial, boxing and gambling have gone together, presumably because both involve risk-taking behavior. For most of this century Las Vegas had a hammerlock on both pursuits. Casinos put up the purses for bouts, originally to entice high rollers who would then gamble, but later because the fights

themselves generated profits. On June 15, 1987, Donald Trump backed a Michael Spinks–Gerry Cooney bout at Atlantic City Convention Hall and recouped his $3.5 million investment from the gate receipts. On fight night he reaped a $7.2 million spike in gaming revenues at Trump Plaza, which he had linked to Convention Hall by an overpass in order to maximize the casino's floor space. Over the entire four-day fight weekend, the total increase in Trump Plaza revenues was about $10 million The following October the developer staged his second lucrative match, between Mike Tyson and Tyrell Biggs, then a third four months later between Tyson and Larry Holmes. He subsequently went on to promote a number of other matches and to become a major player in the boxing industry. Sources for this section include *New York Times*, 1/18/88, and *Wall Street Journal*, 10/8/87.

37. His account of the profits he made on the Golden Nugget was $2 million, but the actual amount was $100,000; on Gillette, he claimed to have netted $2 million, but the real number was $1.1 million; on Federated, he asserted that he made $22 million, as opposed to his actual profit of $14.7 million.

38. Interview with Edward S. Gordon, 2/5/98.

39. *Business Week*, July 20, 1987.

40. *Newsweek*, September 28, 1987.

41. *New York Post*, 10/20/87; *Newsday*, 10/27/87.

42. *People*, December 7, 1987.

43. Interview with Charles Walker, 2/6/98.

44. Sources for this section include *Wall Street Journal*, 9/5/90, 11/30/87, Der Scutt diary, 12/12/87.

45. In an open letter published September 2, 1987, and addressed "To the American People," Donald Trump charged that "Japan and other nations have been taking advantage of the United States" and called on the nation to stop "protect[ing] ships we don't own, carrying oil we don't need, destined for allies who won't help." Sources include *New York Times*, 9/2/87; and Hurt, *Lost Tycoon*, p. 190.

46. "Report to Donald Trump on Public Opinion in America," Penn + Schoen Associates, Inc., October 1988; interviews with Doug Schoen, 8/20/99, 11/5/99.

47. All of which made Donald Trump's name even more valuable than before—and more worth protecting. Periodically he threatened suits against those who made unauthorized use of it, most notably two South African brothers, Julius and Edmond Trump. They were involved in large real estate transactions and investments around the country for years and in the early 1980s opened offices a few blocks from Trump Tower under the name the Trump Group. In 1984 Donald Trump brought suit against them and lost. Four years later the U.S. Trademark Trial and Appeal Board ruled that although the South African Trumps could use what was, after all, their own name in the ordinary course of business, Donald Trump had the exclusive right to its use as a trademark. *New York Times*, 2/7/88. Sources for this section include *New York Times*, 1/16/90; and interview with Charles Walker, 2/6/98.

48. In 1988 the city's largest private landlord was Samuel LeFrak, who housed one out of every sixteen New Yorkers; builders for four generations, the LeFrak family constructed more than two hundred thousand apartments. UPI, 7/24/88. Reliable numbers for the Trump Organization are hard to obtain. The usual figure is twenty-five thousand, which is almost certainly inflated; an educated guess is in the neighborhood of fifteen thousand.

49. *New York Post,* 7/1/88.

50. Sources for this section include interviews with Blanche Sprague, 4/13/99, and Gerald Schrager, 5/7/99.

CHAPTER 20: SPINNING OUT OF CONTROL

1. Sources for this section include Marie Brenner, "After the Gold Rush"; Donald Trump, *Surviving at the Top;* Hurt, *Lost Tycoon;* and interviews with Jack Shaffer, 7/30/99, and Edward S. Gordon, 2/5/98.

2. Sources include John Connolly, "Just Say 'Please,'" *Spy,* February 1992; and Hurt, *Lost Tycoon,* pp. 136–137.

3. Hurt, *Lost Tycoon,* pp. 52ff.

4. Mary Billard, "The Art of the Steal," *Manhattan, inc.,* April 1988.

5. The *Nabila* came in behind King Fahd's *Abdul Aziz* (482 feet) and Queen Elizabeth's *Britannia* (412 feet). Sources for this section include John Taylor, "Trump's Newest Toy," *New York,* July 11, 1988; *Newsday,* 5/16/90; *Newsweek,* July 18, 1988; and interview with Jeff Walker, 3/17/98.

6. Interview with Edward S. Gordon, 2/5/98.

7. It would also provide still more bragging rights. Soon after the developer acquired the yacht, he met with Tom Messer, director of the Guggenheim Museum, to discuss underwriting an exhibit of the museum's paintings in Czechoslovakia. When Messer, an erudite art historian, began to describe the works in the show, the developer interrupted and said, "I'd like to show you something." Then he pulled out a package of photographs of the *Trump Princess* and began passing them around, pointing out the lines of the boat, the distance between bow and stern, and other particularly fine details. Interview with Stephen Swid, 9/99.

8. Sources for this section include William H. Meyers, "Stalking the Plaza," *New York Times Magazine,* 9/25/88; John Connolly, "All the People All the Time," *Spy,* April 1991; interviews with Alan Lapidus, 11/6/98; Blanche Sprague, 4/13/99.

9. The Vanderbilts had a permanent apartment, Frank Lloyd Wright lived there while designing the Guggenheim Museum, the duke and duchess of Windsor made it their New York base, and Elizabeth Taylor and Richard Burton used it to hold court.

10. His purchase of stock in United Airlines' parent corporation in March 1987 was an early effort to get the hotel, then owned by a UAL Inc. subsidiary, the Westin chain, but instead he sold the stock for an estimated profit of $50 million.

11. See Chapter 18 for Donald Trump's purchase of the Hilton casino in 1985.

12. *New York Times*, 9/14/88.

13. Sources include Michael Schnayerson, "Power Blonde," *Vanity Fair*, January 1988; Hurt, *Lost Tycoon*, passim; Barrett, *Trump*, passim.

14. Sources for this section include Mary Billard, "The Art of the Steal," *Manhattan, inc.*, April 1988; Maggie Mahar, "The Merv and Donald Show," *Barron's*, 5/23/88; Mary Billard, "Revenge of the Merv," *Manhattan, inc.*, June 1988; Evan Simonoff, "Deal of Misfortune," *Investment Dealers' Digest*, July 3, 1989; Lenny Glynn, "Blowout on the Boardwalk," *Institutional Investor*, December 1989; Connolly, "All the People, All the Time," *Spy*, April 1991; *Time*, September 25, 1989; *Atlantic City Press*, 12/8/86; Johnston, *Temples of Chance*, chapter 21; Barrett, *Trump*, chapter 13; and interviews with Ace Greenberg, 8/18/99, Jonathan Arneson, 1/6/99, Tom Gallegher, 5/4/99, Kevin de Sanctis, 6/23/99, Marvin Roffman, 4/16/99, Ken Platt, 3/30/99, Mitchell Etess, 1/11/99, and Jack O'Donnell, 7/29/88.

15. Donald Trump would also receive an adjacent retail and entertainment complex known as the Steel Pier and the estate's helicopters, on which he had already painted his name.

16. Griffin would have to make $133 million in debt service payments in 1989, his first year out. Because he could expect a cash flow of only about $55 million, he would face a shortfall of $148 per minute, or $214,000 each day. To stay afloat he would need a major miracle; instead he encountered an epic disaster. In a replay of the faked construction activity once used to impress Harrah's executives, Donald Trump had persuaded Griffin of Resorts' potential through a carefully orchestrated tour of a small area that had been repainted and fixed up for the occasion. In fact, the facility was so dilapidated that it required immediate and costly first aid to remain even moderately competitive. Worse, because the market for both the Bahamas casino and the Atlantic City real estate was poor, these assets could not bail Griffin out. In August 1989, just months after the deal with Donald Trump finally closed, Griffin suspended interest payments. Soon afterward he asked bondholders for a pared-down rate—a "haircut," in Wall Street parlance—and he would proceed to take Resorts in and out of bankruptcy twice.

17. To fend off a possible Steve Wynn purchase, the developer put out another $115 million to buy two more properties for use as noncasino hotels: the never finished Penthouse casino (plus an associated parking lot) and the Atlantis, a bankrupt casino once owned by Playboy and now renamed the Trump Regency. He also continued a $90 million remodeling of the Castle. Reportedly, the Penthouse purchases were in part a response to implications that the magazine planned an exposé of the developer's extramarital life. Sources include Barrett, *Trump*, pp. 446–447; and Hurt, *Lost Tycoon*, p. 246.

18. Sources for this section include interviews with Glen Ingalls, 11/17/99; Michael Conway, 1/17/99; and Bruce Nobles, 11/19/99.

19. Hotel experts were surprised at the price Bond paid, although he had already made jaws drop with a winning $53.9 million bid for Vincent van Gogh's *Irises*

at a Sotheby's auction. Bond made jaws drop again when word leaked out that a secret Sotheby's loan had figured in the astronomical bid, which had an inflationary effect on art prices in general. Because Bond was unable to pay for the masterpiece, it remained at Sotheby's, which eventually repossessed it.

20. Interview with David Lefever, 11/22/99.

21. Interviews with David Saltzman, 10/19/99, and Scott Carlin, 11/18/99.

22. Hurt, *Lost Tycoon*, p. 245.

23. Sources include Hurt, *Lost Tycoon*, chapter 8.

24. Among its other distinguishing characteristics, the New York real estate community is known for its generosity to charity. Fred Trump regularly donated space, services, and, often, funds to a number of causes, and his youngest son, Robert, and his wife, Blaine, have long been heavily involved in organizing efforts to assist the sick and the homeless. By contrast, Donald has avoided major charity commitments and instead tended toward occasional and usually highly publicized gestures, such as providing a plane ride to a hospital for a sick child, donating book and product royalties to charity, helping pay off a farm mortgage for a Georgia widow whose husband killed himself to fend off bank foreclosure, and contributing to a Big Apple Circus tent provided it bore his name.

25. For Roffman, who could not find another job, the episode seemed a disaster. As it turned out, however, he collected a $750,000 arbitrator's award from his former employer. After suing Donald Trump and receiving a handsome out-of-court settlement, he opened his own money-management company and wrote a popular investment guide. Like Bunny Lindenbaum before him, Roffman discovered that an unimaginable crisis can turn into even more unimaginable success.

26. *Wall Street Journal*, 4/27/90; and interview with Neil Barsky, 5/1/90.

27. *Forbes*, May 14, 1990.

28. He had $320 million in personally guaranteed loans from Citicorp, including $135 million for the Trump Shuttle, $125 million for the Plaza Hotel, and $60 million as part of a $220 million construction loan for the Trump Palace condominiums in New York. He also had an unsecured loan of $104 million from Bankers Trust and $47 million from Boston Safe Deposit & Trust Co. for Mar-a-Lago, the *Trump Princess*, and "personal use." *Wall Street Journal*, 6/4/90, 6/18/90, 8/16/90.

29. Sources include *New York Post*, 9/14/90, and interview with Harry Blair, 2/9/00.

30. *Philadelphia Inquirer*, 7/1/90.

31. Interview with Sandy Moorehouse, 3/9/99.

32. Interview with Jerry Jagendorf, then head of real estate for the Bank of Tokyo, 3/17/99.

CHAPTER 21: PULLING BACK FROM THE BRINK

1. Sources for this section include newspaper clippings of the period and Casino Control Commission hearings, August 16–17 and 21, 1990, Lawrenceville and Atlantic City, N.J.

2. Sources include *Wall Street Journal*, 8/13/90 and 8/15/90, and interview with Steve Bollenbach, 8/12/99.

3. Sources for this section include Marie Brenner, "After the Gold Rush"; *Forbes* October 1990; and interviews with Steve Bollenbach, 8/12/99; Wilbur Ross, 8/23/99; Ken Moelis, 8/27/99, 9/19/99, 12/1/99.

4. *Bergen Record*, 8/5/91; *New York Post*, 8/8/91.

5. *Wall Street Journal*, 11/19/90.

6. The Plaza's twin towers, gleaming white and, at thirty-two stories, the tallest buildings in the area, looked like a slice of Manhattan transplanted to south Florida. Not long after the complex was finished, its builder had defaulted on $94 million in obligations, reportedly the largest foreclosure in Palm Beach County history. Poor construction, lack of maintenance, and the fact that only 6 out of 221 units had sold had discouraged other potential buyers. Undaunted, Donald Trump eagerly snapped up the complex for $41 million, financing the deal with a $60 million mortgage from Marine Midland Bank. Sources for this section include *The Wall Street Journal*, 11/7/76, and interview with Charles Kimball, 12/18/90.

7. Unfortunately for Donald Trump, there was no simulcast auction in New York City, which presumably would have been an important market. The reason had to do with a series of complications related to his newest Manhattan project, the 283-unit Trump Palace. Usually buildings of this size were sponsored by a partnership or a corporation with a number of partners; in this case, however, there was only one sponsor, Donald Trump. This fact was disclosed in Trump Palace's 1½-inch-thick offering plan, and, until recently, had apparently been of little concern to buyers, almost all of whom were Asians buying the condominiums as investments. Now, though, the developer was facing severe financial problems; in addition, he was the defendant in more than one hundred court actions, including suits by Taj contractors, Resorts bondholders, Merv Griffin, Ivana Trump, and Blanche Sprague, that sought awards totaling hundreds of millions of dollars. Purchasers were concerned that Donald Trump would not be able to meet his obligations on Trump Palace, that the building, which was less than one-third sold, would go into default, and that the value of their units would plummet. Accordingly, even though the developer was current with all Trump Palace obligations, purchasers complained to state attorney general Robert Abrams, whose office oversaw all condominium sales within the state, and asked to be released from their contracts.

   It was against this background that the Palm Beach auction took place. As a matter of course, the attorney general's office required disclosure of the developer's liabilities before approving a simulcast auction of condominium units. Given recent events, such a disclosure would be, at best, a complicated and lengthy undertaking; ultimately the auction house handling the sale said it could not comply with the requirement, and thus no New York simulcast auction occurred. Sources include interview with Frederick K. Mehlman, assistant attorney general, Real Estate Financing Bureau, Office of the New York State Attorney General, 4/17/91.

8. Interview with Susan Stevens, 4/3/91.

9. The second auction occurred at the PGA National Resort, which was not in Palm Beach itself but rather in the nearby resort town of Palm Beach Gardens. By holding the first auction at the Breakers, Donald Trump had tried to blur over the fact that Trump Plaza was not actually in Palm Beach; this time the auctioneers took a more positive approach and positioned the complex as a way for people to have access to Palm Beach and its fabled lifestyle without paying Palm Beach prices. Sources include interview with Donald Trump and Trump press conference, 12/14/90.

10. Interview with Edward J. Meylor, vice president, Real Estate Industries Division, Marine Midland Bank, 5/91.

11. Interview with Rick Edmunds, 4/91.

12. Sources include *Newsday*, 4/29/91; *Palm Beach Daily News*, 4/29/91.

13. Meanwhile Trump also had to dodge all his other financial obligations. One of the more pressing was the $11 million he had agreed to pay for a heavyweight title fight between Evander Holyfield and George Foreman, scheduled for the Atlantic City Convention Center in April 1991. Usually such big-name bouts drew business to Trump Plaza, which was next door, but because of the dampening effect of the Gulf War on the casino business, it seemed possible that Trump might actually lose money on the deal. Accordingly, he called a meeting of the various fight promoters involved and announced with a straight face that he was going to invoke "the war clause." Asked what he was talking about, he said that every contract stipulates that if the United States is at war, the signatories have a right to cancel the fight.

"Everyone said, 'Who are we at war with?'" recalled Trump Plaza executive Kevin DeSanctis. "When Donald said, 'We're at war in the Persian Gulf,' those guys just freaked, called him every name in the book. We walked back into Donald's office, and he said, 'They want to do it, they want the fight.' Sure enough, they called us back and let us off the hook. Anybody else would have had an $11 million problem, but he made it go away. They made a ton of money anyway, and we didn't get killed." Sources include *New York Times*, 2/7/91, and interview with Kevin DeSanctis, 6/23/99.

14. *Wall Street Journal*, 1/21/91. Later that year Donald Trump struck back at Barsky, who had received the prestigious Gerald Loeb Award for Distinguished Business and Financial Journalism for his reporting on the developer's financial meltdown. In April the developer offered the reporter a $1,000 ticket to an Evander Holyfield–George Foreman fight in Atlantic City. Barsky asked to buy another ticket, and the developer offered him two more for free. Having received permission from his editor to accept the first one, Barsky assumed there would be no problem taking the others for his father and brother. Evidently it was the opening Donald Trump had been waiting for. The next month the developer complained that Barsky had squeezed him for the tickets. Barsky had not, but he was in an awkward position. The *Journal*, too, was in an awkward position, for

its editor-in-chief, Norman Perlstein, had accepted a ticket and a helicopter flight for the same fight. Ultimately the *Journal* defended Barsky but, apparently by his request, reassigned him to another beat. Eventually he left the profession altogether and became a financial analyst. Sources for this section include Hurt, *Lost Tycoon*, chapter 12.

15. UPI, 6/26/91.

16. *Washington Post*, 11/29/92; interview with Charlie Reiss, 3/12/98.

17. Sources for this section include *Wall Street Journal*, 12/24/86 and 12/12/88; *New York Daily News*, 11/8/88; and interviews with Jack Shaffer, 7/30/99, and William Stern, 1/15/99.

18. Sources includes *New York Times*, 2/13/88, and *Wall Street Journal*, 3/23/88.

19. The hush was also a reflection of a widespread unwillingness to take on someone who did not hesitate to take on adversaries in print. He had launched dozens of lawsuits over alleged offenses to his well-being, zapped the mayor whenever possible, and taken potshots at any number of other opponents in his books. One of the more visible examples of the lengths to which Donald Trump would go to get even was a pet food billionaire and New Jersey real estate developer named Leonard Stern. He was the owner of two publications, the *Village Voice* and *7 Days*, which had published scathing attacks on Donald Trump, and was also financing an anti-Trump television documentary called *Trump: What's the Deal?* In February 1989 Donald Trump apparently told a *New York Daily News* reporter that Stern's second wife, a filmmaker whom the publisher had recently married and who was at least twenty years his junior, had phoned Donald Trump for a date. The ensuing news coverage humiliated and infuriated Stern—but perhaps also contributed to his eventual decision to end his support for the film. Sources include *New York Daily News*, 2/26/89 and 2/28/89; *New York Post*, 2/28/89; *Newsday*, 3/1/89.

20. Sources for this section include *New York Daily News*, 12/2/88; interview with Tom Glendenning, 7/89.

21. Sources for this section include Frank Rose, "Celebrity Zoning"; *Wall Street Journal*, 3/23/88; interviews with Charlie Reiss, 3/12/98; Marla Simpson, 8/8/99; Madeleine Polayes, 4/12/00; Jerrold Nadler, 4/4/00; Ronnie Eldridge, 4/8/00; Roberta Brandes Gratz, 8/23/99; Anne Sperry, 12/6/99; Stephen Swid, 9/7/99 and 4/10/00; Linda Davidoff, 8/30/99; Richard Kahan, 9/29/88 and 9/8/99; Kent Barwick, 8/24/99; Dick Anderson, 8/4/99; Claude Shostal, 7/29/99; Philip Howard, 8/3/99 and 8/17/99; Mary Frances Shaughnessy, 8/4/99; Catherine Cary, 11/27/99; Ruth Messinger, 8/11/99; Richard Bass, 1/2/00; Steve Robinson, 7/7/91; Dan Gutman and Ethel Scheffer, numerous interviews beginning in 1990.

22. The protest occurred on October 18, 1987. Speakers at a rally beforehand included Bill Moyers and David Dinkins, then Manhattan borough president. *New York Times*, 10/19/87.

23. Estimates of just how far in the red Donald Trump was continued to grow. By March of 1992 *Business Week* pegged it at a negative $1.4 billion (*Business Week*, March 23, 1992).

24. Interview with MAS board president Philip Howard, 8/17/99.

25. Although the developer was the one in fiscal hot water, he seemed to have less difficulty with the situation than the bankers who were questioning him. "If Donald didn't have an answer," Charlie Reiss said later, "it didn't matter. He just put more words on the table, made a joke, said something diversionary. He understood that no one really understood anything." In fact, it seemed to Reiss that he and the developer knew far more about the bankers' business than they did. "They really weren't very prepared for those meetings," Reiss said. He recalled being surprised "at how little they knew about their own quarter-of-a-billion-dollar loan. It became sort of a joke for me, and I think for Donald, too." Reiss, who was a consultant for the civic group at the time, later came to work for Donald Trump. Interviews with Charlie Reiss, 3/12/98, and Richard Kahan, 9/8/99.

26. Just five days earlier such an event had seemed out of the question. When West Side elected officials and community groups had a breakfast meeting with Dinkins to discuss the issue, the most low-key mayor in city history, dressed in his usual blue satin baseball warm-up jacket, blew up. To him the paramount issue was not the future potential for a smaller project and a park, but the immediate potential for the elevated highway to give way and cause a tragedy from which the city and its mayor might never recover. But the next day Kahan and Trump reached an agreement. When told that there would be a press conference at the governor's office to announce a historic agreement within his own city, David Dinkins had no choice but to climb aboard and host it himself.

27. Sources for this section include *New York Times*, 3/6/91, 3/17/91, and 8/11/91; and *Newsday*, 3/5/91 and 3/6/91.

28. The final version of Riverside South would be 7.9 million square feet, down from Television City's 14.5 million square feet, the estimated cost would be $2.4 billion, and the commitment to subway renovation would be $12 million, down from Macri's promise of $30 million. In exchange, the city had extended the usual three-year deadline for commencement of construction to seven and a half years, a change that could make a big difference if the real estate market's recovery was slow.

29. Interview with Fred Trump, 3/15/91.

30. In fact, the most recent restructuring plan for the Castle, which subsequently underwent numerous revisions, called for a reduction of interest rates from 13.75 percent to 9.5 percent and required the casino to file for Chapter 11 reorganization in U.S. Bankruptcy Court. UPI, 6/26/91. In their final report, the planners deemed the Riverside South proposal a good one but suggested that it be cut 16 percent to fit into the "spatial character" of the West Side. Sources include *Newsday*, 7/1/91.

31. Because property valuation is a highly subjective enterprise, estimates of just how much the developer owed at any particular moment vary widely. These numbers, cited in *The Washington Post*, 11/29/92, appear to be consensus figures adopted by most of the press.

32. Interview with Donald Trump, 10/26/92.

33. $447,145, according to *Newsday*, 8/22/93.

34. The constituent members of Riverside South, Inc., the not-for-profit corporation formed to guide the development process, were the Trump Organization, Westpride, the Municipal Art Society, the Parks Council, the Riverside Park Fund, the Natural Resources Defense Council, and the Regional Plan Association.

35. Interview with Paul Willen, 12/92.

36. *New York Times*, 12/16/92.

37. Evidently attracted to the Trump name, wealthy Asians had purchased many luxury condominiums in the developer's earlier buildings. But apparently it was the low price and the opportunity to diversify their portfolio that attracted the father-and-son team who headed New World to the rail yards, not the name of its owner. Henry Cheng and his father, Cheng Yu-tong, whose first job was as an apprentice jewelry maker, ran a publicly traded company that owned real estate, telecommunications, power projects, and hotels, including the Hong Kong Grand Hyatt and the Ramada and Stouffer hotel chains in the United States. Sources include *New York Times*, 7/15/94; and interview with Sin-ming Shaw, 7/19/94.

38. Because the project was on underutilized land, it received the same 421a city tax abatement that Trump received for Trump Tower and Trump Plaza. However, at least in part due to Jerry Nadler's vigorous opposition, Riverside South failed to obtain HUD mortgage insurance—the current version of the same FHA mortgage insurance that Fred Trump had used decades earlier in Brooklyn. *New York Times*, 7/24/98; and interview with Jerry Nadler, 4/4/00.

39. Johnson himself was not thrilled with the finished product. "Donald says these buildings are great architecture, but I don't agree," he said. "There were too many rules and too many previous architects—too many cooks in the broth, including the investors, [and] the West Siders also had a lot to say." Interview with Philip Johnson, 3/99.

40. Sources include *New York Times*, 7/31/98 and 6/25/99.

CHAPTER 22: TRUMP™

1. *Time*'s Man of the Year for 1999 was Jeff Bezos, founder of Amazon.com, which during that year lost an estimated $350 million. Chapter sources include Jerry Useem, "What Does Donald Trump Really Want," *Fortune*, April 3, 2000.

2. Sources for this section include interviews with Peter Ricker, 2/19/99; Dave Wiederecht, 5/11/99; Mike Simmons, 2/16/99; John Meyers, 2/12/99; Sandy Moorehouse, 3/9/99; Scott Coopchick, 4/30/99; Dale Frey, 3/8/99; Charlie Reiss, 3/12/98; Abe Wallach, 1/98; and Donald Trump, 12/12/97.

3. Soon after Donald Trump met with Frey, the chairman called him and said it was time to start working on the building. "Then I said we would be pleased to accept a bid from him and incidentally there were seven other people asking," Frey said. "That really set him back—he thought he should just win." Although the developer was offended by being asked to compete for the job, he still wanted the deal. Accordingly, he, too, did some homework. What he found was that the Galbreath Company, a mainline development concern that had an inside track because it had already been consulting with Frey's office on the project, was

interested in doing the job itself but lacked actual experience producing luxury condominiums in New York City. Recognizing the potential fit between them, Galbreath and Trump then teamed up and submitted what turned out to be the winning proposal.

4. In this and subsequent projects, Trump proved adept at a peculiar New York art known as "remeasuring"—increasing the square footage in rentable areas by charging tenants for what in other cities would be considered common space and also measuring space from the outside walls of a building. Then, to justify far higher prices for Trump International Hotel and Tower than anyone else had thought possible, the building's old low-cachet One Columbus Circle address became higher-cachet One Central Park West, subsequently touted in ad copy as "the most important address in the world," and Philip Johnson became the architect. After Johnson updated the exterior with bronze columns and a curtain wall of champagne-colored glass, the developer slashed the expected price of the curtain wall by waiting until three days before Christmas to let the contract. "He called the contractor and said, 'I know it's your year's end, you want to wind things up, I'll book it at this price,'" recounted Abe Wallach, Trump's chief of staff. "The guy was so desperate to land the job, he took it. Where did Donald learn this? From his dad—he instilled these ideas in Donald."

5. A seventy-two-story office building, 40 Wall Street had a distinctive pyramid top and a brief reign as the world's tallest structure before being eclipsed in 1929 by the Chrysler Building and, soon afterward, the Empire State Building. Now what would be known as the Trump Building was, as the developer liked to point out, "the tallest building in downtown Manhattan after the World Trade Center."

6. To obtain air rights over an adjacent Roman Catholic church, the developer promised that Trump World Tower would ban discussion of condoms or birth control pills in public areas.

7. Sources include *Los Angeles Times*, 2/14/99; interview with Charles Miesmer, 7/8/99.

8. After the debt was paid off, the partners would share any subsequent profits fifty-fifty. To outsiders, the financial arrangement looked decidedly lopsided, but to Steve Hilbert, founder and president of Conseco, it seemed eminently fair. Not because he didn't know about the importance of branding—he had recently forked over $40 million just to put his company's name on a new field house in Indianapolis. But here, he said, it made more sense to ride on someone else's coattails. "This isn't part of our branding," he explained. "It's about making money." Using the Trump name would allow the partners to bring in premium rents; better yet, the developer's innovative plan to sell office space on a condominium basis could have the entire building paid off in record time. Interview with Steve Hilbert, 11/18/99.

9. The Trump name also appeared on the corners of the building in shiny letters about two feet high. A few of the tenants, a high-profile list that included Estée Lauder and the toy store FAO Schwarz, complained, but to no apparent avail. Then CBS, which had leased the old General Motors auto showroom for a broadcast studio for the network's early morning show, weighed in. CBS chairman Mel Kamarzin gave the developer a call and said that a corner *Trump* would be

visible in any external camera shots. Kamarzin said that this would be a problem for CBS, and he asked the developer to take care of it.

Although Steve Hilbert sprang to the developer's defense and told Trump the letters should be bigger, the developer, who had recently bragged that the four-foot letters were made of titanium and "really expensive," backed down. "Mel is a great friend of mine, and he said it was directly in the line of their vision, and I really thought to myself, I have the right to do it," the developer told the *New York Observer*. "But every time they panned back around the building, that's all you could see, which I thought was terrific for me, but I understand the difficulty it is for CBS." He told Hilbert that even though they were in the right, he would take the name down on the corners and replace the titanium letters plastered across the building's facade with ones of the same size and design but made of antiqued—that is, dulled—bronze. Showing unprecedented diplomacy, he later told the *New York Times* that the shinier version was "too glitzy" and that "I don't love it." Sources include *New York Times*, 10/18/99.

10. Mark Singer, "Trump Solo," *New Yorker*, May 19, 1997.

11. By 1997, *Forbes* pegged Trump at 105th richest American, with $1.4 billion (Trump's figure: $3.7 billion); in 1998, *Forbes* put him at 110th richest, with $1.5 billion (Trump's figure: $5 billion); and in 1999, although *Forbes* upped its estimate of his assets to $1.6 billion, his rank had slipped to 145th richest (Trump's figure: $4.5 billion). Sources: *Forbes*.

12. Interview with Kevin DeSanctis, former president of Trump Plaza, 6/23/99.

13. *New York Post*, 4/27/96 and 4/28/96.

14. Interview with Jack Shaffer, 7/30/99.

15. Sources include interviews with Sugar Rautbord, 1/14/99, 2/27/99, and 2/14/00. I am particularly grateful to Ms. Rautbord for her keen observations of high society in New York and Palm Beach.

BIBLIOGRAPHY

BOOKS

Akin, Edward N. *Flagler: Rockefeller Partner and Florida Baron*. Gainesville: University Press of Florida, 1992.

Allen, Leslie. *Liberty: The Statue and the American Dream*. New York: Statue of Liberty–Ellis Island Foundation, 1985

Auletta, Ken. *The Streets Were Paved with Gold*. New York: Random House, 1975.

Baida, Peter. *Poor Richard's Legacy: American Business Values from Benjamin Franklin to Michael Milken*. New York: Quill/William Morrow, 1990.

Balfour, Michael. *The Kaiser and His Times*. Boston: Houghton Mifflin, 1964.

Baring-Gould, Sabine, and Arthur Gillman. *Germany: The Kaiser and His Times*. London: S. Low, Marston, Searle and Rivington, 1901.

Barkin, Kenneth D. *The Controversy over German Industrialization, 1890–1902*. Chicago: University of Chicago Press, 1970.

Barlett, Donald L., and James B. Steele. *Empire: The Life, Legend and Madness of Howard Hughes*. New York: W.W. Norton and Company, 1979.

Barrett, Wayne. *Trump: The Deals and the Downfall*. New York: HarperCollins, 1992.

Bayor, Ronald H. *Neighbors in Conflict: the Irish, Germans, Jews and Italians of New York City*. Baltimore: Johns Hopkins University Press, 1978.

Benecke, Gerhard, ed. *Germany in the Thirty Years War*. New York: St. Martin's Press, 1979.

Berton, Pierre. *The Klondike Fever: The Life and Death of the Last Great Gold Rush*. New York: Knopf, 1959.

Bonner, William Thompson. *New York, the World's Metropolis*. New York: R.L. Polk & Co., 1924.

Brown, Henry Collins, ed. *Valentine's Manual of Old New York: 1926*.

———. *Valentine's Manual of Old New York: 1927*.

Bruck, Connie. *The Predators' Ball: The Junk Bond Raiders and the Man Who Stalked Them*. New York: American Lawyer/Simon & Schuster, 1988.

Burrows, Edwin G., and Mike Wallace. *Gotham*. New York: Oxford University Press, 1999.

Buttenwieser, Ann L. *Manhattan Water-Bound*. New York: New York University Press, 1987.

Byrne, Jim. *The $1 League: The Rise and Fall of the USFL*. New York: Prentice Hall Press, 1986.

Caro, Robert. *The Power Broker*. New York: Vintage Books, 1975.

Carr, William. *A History of Germany, 1815–1945*. New York: St. Martin's Press, 1969.

Chalmers, David. *Neither Socialism nor Monopoly*. Philadelphia: Lippincott, 1976.

Chamberlain, John. *The Enterprising Americans: A Business History of the United States*. New York: Harper & Row, 1974.

Chernow, Ron. *Titan: The Life of John D. Rockefeller, Sr.* New York: Random House, 1998.

Clark, Norman H. *Milltown*. Seattle: University of Washington Press, 1970.

Clasen, Claus-Peter. *The Palatinate in European History, 1559–1660*. Oxford: Basil Blackwell, 1963.

Coates, Kenneth S., and William R. Morrison. *Land of the Midnight Sun: A History of the Yukon.* Edmonton: Hurtig Publishers, 1988.

Colean, Miles. *A Backward Glance: The Growth of Government Housing Policy in the United States, 1934–1975.* Washington: The Research and Educational Trust Fund of the Mortgage Bankers Association of America, 1975.

Connery, Robert H., and Gerald Benjamin. *Rockefeller of New York.* Ithaca: Cornell University Press, 1979.

Coutts, R. C. *Yukon: Places and Names.* Sidney, B.C.: Gray's Pub. Ltd., 1980.

Crosby, Alfred W. *America's Forgotten Pandemic: The Influenza of 1918.* New York: Cambridge University Press, 1989.

Daughen, Joseph R., and Peter Binzen. *The Wreck of the Penn Central.* Boston: Little, Brown, 1971.

David, Paul A., and Peter M. Solar. "A Bicentennial Contribution to the History of the Cost of Living in America." In *Research in Economic History,* edited by Robert E. Gallman. Greenwich, Conn.: JAI Press, 1977.

Davies, John. *Housing Reform During the Truman Administration.* Columbia: University of Missouri Press, 1966.

De Schweinitz, Karl. *Industrialization and Democracy.* New York: Collier-Macmillan, 1964.

Demaris, Ovid. *The Boardwalk Jungle.* New York: Bantam Books, 1986.

Doerries, Reinhard R. "Empire and Republic: German-American Relations Before 1917." In *America and the Germans,* edited by Frank Tommler and Joseph McVeigh. Philadelphia: University of Pennsylvania Press, 1985.

Dorpat, Paul. *Seattle Now & Then,* Volumes 2 and 3. Seattle: Tartu Publications, 1984.

Eccles, Marriner. *Beckoning Frontiers.* New York, Knopf, 1951.

Eldot, Paula. *Governor Alfred E. Smith: The Politician as Reformer.* New York: Garland Publishing, 1983.

Elkins, T. H. *Germany: An Introductory Geography.* New York: Praeger, 1968.

Eller, Karl. *The Palatinate: Heartland on the Rhine.* Muenchen: Bruckmann, 1971.

Erickson, Charlotte. *Emigration from Europe, 1815–1914.* London: Adam and Charles Black, 1976.

Fischer, Fritz. *From Kaiserreich to Third Reich.* London; Boston: Allan and Unwin, 1986.

Fischler, Stan. *Uptown Downtown: A Trip Through Time on New York's Subways.* New York: Hawthorn Books, 1976.

Freund, Christian. *Kallstadt in alten Ansichten.* Kallstadt, 1985.

Friedman, Milton, and Anna Jacobson Schwartz. *Monetary History of the United States.* Princeton: Princeton University Press, 1963.

Gancarz, Jack Andrzej. *Palm Beach: Florida's Riviera.* Lake Worth, Fla.: Downtown Photo Service Press, 1989.

George, Carol V. R. *God's Salesman.* New York: Oxford University Press, 1993.

Gibert, Otto, ed. *The Historical Essays,* n.d.

Gilbert, Felix, and Stephen R. Graubard, eds. *Historical Studies Today.* New York: W.W. Norton, 1972.

Gonzalez, Evelyn. *Building a Borough.* Bronx, N.Y.: Bronx Museum of the Arts, 1986.

Gould, Sabine Baring, and Arthur Gillman. *Germany: The Kaiser and His Times,* 1901.

Graves, S. H. *On the White Pass Payroll.* Chicago: The Lakeside Press, 1908.

Grossman, Harold J. *Grossman's Guide to Wines, Beers and Spirits.* Revised by Harriet Lembeck. New York: Charles Scribner's Sons, 1983.

Henry, John Robertson. *Fifty Years on the Lower East Side of New York.* 1966.

Hewitt, Edward R. *Those Were the Days.* New York: Duell, Sloan and Pearce, 1943.

Himmelspach, Rainer. *Die Schoene Pfalz.* Neustadt/Weinstrasse: W. Graeber GMBH, n.d.

Hood, Clifton. *722 Miles: The Building of the Subways and How They Transformed New York.* New York: Simon & Schuster, 1993.

Hornickel, Ernest. *The Great Wines of Europe.* New York: Putnam, 1965.

Hurt, Harry. *Lost Tycoon.* New York: W.W. Norton, 1993.

Ingersoll, Ernest. *Gold Fields of the Klondike.* Langley, B.C.: Mr. Paperback, 1981.

Institute for Policy Studies. *America's Housing Crisis.* Edited by Chester Hartman. Boston: Routledge & Kegan Paul, 1983.

Jackson, Anthony. *A Place Called Home.* Cambridge, Mass.: MIT Press, 1976.

Jacobs, Jane. *The Death and Life of Great American Cities.* New York: Vintage Books, 1961.

Johann, Ernst. *German Cultural History from 1860 to the Present Day.* Munich: Nymphenburger Verlagsbuchhandlung, 1983.

Johnson, David. *Temples of Chance: How America Inc. Bought Out Murder Inc. to Win Control of the Casino Business.* New York: Doubleday, 1992.

Johnson, Hugh. *The Atlas of German Wines and Traveller's Guide to the Vineyards.* New York: Simon & Schuster, 1986.

Johnston, Alva. *The Legendary Mizners.* New York: Farrar, Straus & Giroux, 1953.

Jonnes, Jill. *We're Still Here: The Rise, Fall, and Resurrection of the South Bronx.* Boston: Atlantic Monthly Press, 1986.

King, Norma. *Ivana Trump: A Very Unauthorized Biography.* New York: Carroll and Graf, 1990.

Kirschbaum, Erik. "The Eradication of German Culture in the United States: 1917–1918." In *American-German Studies, Vol. 2.* Stuttgart: Hans-Dieter Heinz, 1986.

Knott, James R. *The Mansion Builders, Palm Beach Revisited III.* Palm Beach: The Best of the Brown Wrappers, 1990.

Koch, Edward I. *Mayor.* New York: Simon & Schuster, 1984.

———. *Politics.* New York: Simon & Schuster, 1985.

Kramer, Michael, and Sam Roberts. *"I Never Wanted To Be Vice-President of Anything!"* New York: Basic Books, 1976.

Krase, Jerome. "The Missed Step: Italian Americans and Brooklyn Politics." In *The Italians and Irish in America,* edited by Francis X. Femminella. Staten Island: American Italian Historical Association, 1985.

Krase, Jerome, and Charles LaCerra. *Ethnicity and Machine Politics.* Lanham: University Press of America, 1991.

Larson, Bob. *It's All Your Pfalz.* Stuttgart: Schwaben International Verlag, 1982.

Levi, Vicki Gold. *Atlantic City: 125 Years of Ocean Madness.* New York: C. N. Potter, 1979.

Littlefield, Henry W. *History of Europe 1500–1848: Digest of Political, Military, Economic, Social and Cultural Events.* New York: Barnes and Noble, Inc., 1939.

Longstreet, Stephen. *City on Two Rivers: Profiles of New York—Yesterday and Today.* New York: Hawthorn Books, 1975.

Lovely, Thomas J. *The History of the Jamaica Estates, 1929–1969.* Jamaica, N.Y.: Jamaica Estates Association, 1969.

Mahon, Gigi. *The Company That Bought the Boardwalk.* New York: Random House, 1980.

Mann, Golo. *The History of Germany Since 1789.* New York: Praeger, 1968.

Mathews, Richard. *The Yukon.* New York: Holt, Rinehart and Winston, 1968.

McCandless, Robert G. *Yukon Wildlife: A Social History.* Edmonton: University of Alberta Press, 1985.

McCullough, Edo. *Good Old Coney Island.* New York: Charles Scribner's Sons, 1957.

McFarland, M. Carter. *Federal Government and Urban Problems: HUD: Successes, Failures, and the Fate of Our Cities.* Boulder, Colo.: Westview Press, 1978.

McKenzie, William A. *Dining Car Line to the Pacific.* St. Paul: Minnesota Historical Society Press, 1990.

Merk, Ernst. *Heimatbuch des Edelweindorfes Kallstadt.* Verlag: gemeinde Kallstadt, 1952.

Milward, Alan S., and S. B. Saul. *The Development of the Economies of Continental Europe, 1850–1914.* Cambridge, Mass.: Harvard University Press, 1977.

Minter, Roy. *The White Pass: Gateway to the Klondike.* University of Alaska Press, 1987.

Mollenkopf, John Hull. *Power, Culture, and Place.* New York: Russell Sage Foundation, 1988.

Morgan, Murray. *Skid Road.* New York: Ballantine, 1971.

———. *Mill on the Boot.* Seattle: University of Washington Press, 1982.

———. *One Man's Gold Rush.* Seattle: University of Washington Press, 1967.

Morris, Lloyd. *Incredible New York High Life and Low Life of the Last Hundred Years.* New York: Syracuse University Press, 1951.

Morrison, David R. *The Politics of Yukon Territory, 1898–1909.* University of Toronto Press, 1968.

Moscow, Warren. *Last of the Big-Time Bosses.* New York: Stein and Day, 1971.

———. *Politics in the Empire State.* New York: Alfred A. Knopf, 1948.

Moss, Mitchell. *Palace Coup: The Inside Story of Harry and Leona Helmsley.* New York: Doubleday, 1989.

Neuwirth, Art. *The German Wines.* Publ. by Mr. A. C. Neuwirth, 1977.

Nevins, Allan. *John D. Rockefeller: The Heroic Age of American Enterprise.* New York: Charles Scribner's Sons, 1940.

Newell, Gordon, and Don Sherwood. *Totem Tales of Old Seattle.* New York: Ballantine, 1971.

Newfield, Jack, and Wayne Barrett. *City for Sale: Ed Koch and the Betrayal of New York.* New York: Harper & Row, 1988.

Newfield, Jack, and Paul DuBrul. *The Permanent Government: Who Really Runs New York?* New York: The Pilgrim Press, 1981.

Nichols, John Alden. *Germany after Bismarck.* Cambridge, Mass.: Harvard University Press, 1958.

Norman, Elof. *The Coffee Chased Us Up: Monte Cristo Memories.* Seattle: The Mountaineers, 1977.

Novotny, Ann. *Strangers at the Door.* Riverside, Conn.: Chatham Press, 1971.

O'Brien, Timothy L. *Bad Bet: The Inside Story of the Glamour, Glitz, and Danger of America's Gambling Industry.* New York: Times Business, 1998.

O'Donnell, John R., with James Rutherford. *Trumped! The Inside Story of the Real Donald Trump—His Cunning Rise and Spectacular Fall.* New York: Simon & Schuster, 1991.

Onorato, Michael P. *Another Time, Another World: Coney Island Memories.* Fullerton: California State University Oral History Program, 1988.

———. *Steeplechase Park: Sale and Closure, 1965–1966; Diary and Papers of James J. Onorato.* Bellingham, Wash.: Pacific Rim Books, 1998.

Parramore, Thomas C. *Norfolk: The First Four Centuries.* Charlottesville: University Press of Virginia, 1994.

Pasley, Malcolm, ed. *German: A Companion to German Studies.* New York: Methuen, 1972.

Paul, Roland. *300 Years Palatines in America.* Landau/Pfalz: Pfaelzische Verlagsanstalt, 1983.

Persico, Joseph E. *Rockefeller: A Biography of Nelson A. Rockefeller.* New York: Simon & Schuster, 1982.

Pink, Louis H. *The New Day in Housing.* New York: Arno Press, 1974.

Polisensky, J. V. *Thirty Years War.* University of California Press, 1971.

Proctor, Hazel T. *Tenderfoot to Sourdough.* New Holland, Pa.: E.C. Procter, 1975.

Rachlis, Eugene, and John E. Marqusee. *The Landlords.* New York: Random House, 1963.

Raff, Diether. *A History of Germany.* New York: Berg: St. Martin's Press, 1988.

Ranum, Orest, and Patricia Ranum. *The Century of Louis XIV.* New York: Walker, 1972.

Reinicker, Juliette C., ed. *Klondike Letters: The Correspondence of a Gold Seeker in 1898.* Anchorage: Alaska Northwest Publishing Company, 1984.

Riehl, Wilhelm Heinrich. *Die Pfalzer.* 1857.

Rippley, La Vern. *The German-Americans.* Boston: Twayne Publishers, 1976.

Rubin, Sy, and Jonathan Mandell. *Trump Tower.* Secaucus, N.J.: Lyle Stuart, Inc., 1984.

Sale, Roger. *Seattle: Past to Present.* Seattle: University of Washington Press, 1976.

Sanders, Ronald. *The Lower East Side. A Guide to Its Jewish Past in 99 New Photographs.* New York: Dover Publications, Inc., 1979.

Satterfield, Archie. *Chilkoot Pass, the Most Famous Trail in the North.* Anchorage: Alaska Northwest Pub. Co., 1978.

Schlegel, Marvin W. *Conscripted City: Norfolk in World War II.* Norfolk: The Virginian-Pilot and The Ledger-Star, 1991.

Schwantes, Carlos A. *The Pacific Northwest: An Interpretive History.* Lincoln: University of Nebraska Press, 1989.

Schwartz, Joel. *The New York Approach: Robert Moses, Urban Liberals, and Redevelopment of the Inner City.* Columbus: Ohio University Press, 1993.

Seligman, Ben B. *The Potentates.* New York: Dial Press, 1971.

Seyfried, Vincent. *Queens: A Pictorial History.* Norfolk, Va.: Donning Co., 1982.

Shachtman, Tom. *Skyscraper Dreams.* Boston: Little, Brown, 1991.

Smith, John L. *Running Scared: The Life and Treacherous Times of Las Vegas Casino King Steve Wynn.* New York: Barricade Books, 1995.

Snyder, Louis, ed. *Documents of German History.* New Brunswick, N.J.: Rutgers University Press, 1958.

Sobel, Robert. *The Fallen Colossus.* New York: Weybright and Talley, 1977.

Speidel, William C. *Sons of the Profits*. Seattle: Nettle Creek Pub. Co., 1967.

Stern, Robert A. M., et al. *New York 1960*. New York: Monacelli Press, 1995.

Sternlieb, George, and James W. Hughes. *The Atlantic City Gamble*. Cambridge, Mass.: Harvard University Press, 1983.

Stover, John F. *The Life and Decline of the American Railroad*. New York: Oxford University Press, 1970.

Sulloway, Frank. *Born to Rebel: Birth Order, Family Dynamics and Creative Lives*. New York: Pantheon Books, 1996.

Sutcliffe, Serena. *The Art of the Winemaker: A Guide to the World's Greatest Vineyards*. Philadelphia: Courage Books, 1981.

Tollemache, Hon. Stratford. *Reminiscences of the Yukon*. London: E. Arnold, 1912.

Tommler, Frank, and Joseph McVeigh, eds. *America and the Germans*. Philadelphia: University of Pennsylvania Press, 1985.

Treasure, Geoffrey. *The Making of Modern Europe, 1648–1780*. New York: Methuen, 1985.

Trump, Donald, and Kate Bohner. *The Art of the Comeback*. New York: Times Books, 1997.

Trump, Donald, and Charles Leerhsen. *Trump: Surviving at the Top*. New York: Random House, 1990.

Trump, Donald, and Tony Schwartz. *The Art of the Deal*. New York: Random House, 1987.

Trump, Donald, and Dave Shiflett. *The America We Deserve*. Los Angeles: Renaissance Books, 2000.

Ultan, Lloyd, and Gary Hermalyn. *The Bronx in the Innocent Years: 1890–1925*. New York: Harper & Row, 1064.

Vexler, Robert I., ed. *Germany: 1415–1972; a Chronology and Fact Book*. Dobbs Ferry, N.Y.: Oceana Publications, 1973.

Villard, Henry. *Memoirs of Henry Villard*. Westminster: Archibald Constable & Co., Ltd., 1904.

von Hoffman, Nicholas. *Citizen Cohn*. New York: Doubleday, 1988.

Welfeld, Irving. *HUD Scandals: Howling Headlines and Silent Fiascoes*. New Brunswick, N.J.: Transaction Publishers, 1992.

Wells, E. Hazard. *Magnificence and Misery*. Garden City, New York: Doubleday, 1984.

Wertenbaker, Thomas J. *Norfolk: Historic Southern Port*. Durham, N.C.: Duke University Press, 1962.

Wilensky, Elliot, and Norval White. *AIA Guide to New York City*. San Diego: Harcourt Brace Jovanovich, 1988.

Wirsing, Dale R. *Builders, Brewers and Burghers: Germans of Washington State*. Olympia: The Washington State American Revolution Bicentennial Commission, 1977.

Woodhouse, Philip R. *Monte Cristo*. Seattle: Mountaineers, 1979.

Zeckendorf, William, and Edward McCreary. *The Autobiography of William Zeckendorf*. New York: Holt, Rinehart and Winston, 1970.

ARTICLES

Architectural Forum. Coverage of FHA, January to December, 1949.

Barrett, Wayne. "Donald Trump Cuts the Cards." *Village Voice,* January 22, 1979.

———. "Like Father, Like Son." *Village Voice,* January 15, 1979.

Basque, Garnet. "Bennett City." *Canadian West,* May 1989.

Bender, Marylin. "The Empire and Ego of Donald Trump." *The New York Times,* August 7, 1983.

Billard, Mary. "The Art of the Steal." *Manhattan, inc.,* April 1988.

———. "Revenge of the Merv." *Manhattan, inc.,* June 1988.

Bouvier, Leon F., and Carol J. De Vita. "The Baby Boom—Entering Midlife." *Population Bulletin,* November 1991.

Bowden, Mark. "The Trumpster Stages the Comeback of a Lifetime." *Playboy,* May 1997.

Boyle, Robert H. "The USFL's Trump Card." *Sports Illustrated,* February 13, 1984.

Brenner, Marie. "After the Gold Rush." *Vanity Fair,* September 1990.

———. "Trumping the Town." *New York,* November 17, 1980.

Burlingame, Virginia S. "John J. Healy's Alaskan Adventure." *The Alaska Journal,* Autumn 1978.

Byron, Christopher. "Other People's Money." *New York,* September 17, 1990.

Cameron, David A. "The Everett and Monte Cristo Railway: A Lifeline to the Mines of Eastern Snohomish County." *Journal of Everett & Snohomish County History,* Winter 1988–89.

Carter, Graydon. "Donald Trump Gets What He Wants." *Gentleman's Quarterly,* May 1984.

Connolly, John. "All of the People, All of the Time." *Spy,* April 1991.

Cook, Karen. "Street Smart." *Manhattan, inc.,* December 1986.

———. "Trumping Trump." *Manhattan, inc.,* November 1986.

Cox, Hank. "Greed Is Good." *Regardie's,* July 1989.

De Vita, Carol. "The United States at Mid-Decade." *Population Bulletin,* March 1996.

Dorfman, Dan. "The Bottom Line." *New York,* November 13, 1975.

———. "Will New York Get a New Hotel?" *New York,* April 26, 1976.

Edwards, Owen. "All the King's Women." *Savvy Woman,* November 1989.

Friedrich, Otto. "Flashy Symbol of an Acquisitive Age." *Time,* January 16, 1989.

Gardiner, Nancy Tuck. "Mistress of Mar-A-Lago." *Town & Country,* March 1986.

Geist, William. "The Expanding Empire of Donald Trump." *New York Times Magazine,* April 8, 1984.

Gerard, Jeremy. "Trumped Up." *Fame,* Summer 1989.

Goldberger, Paul. "Zone Defense." *The New Yorker,* February 22 & March 1, 1999.

Greenberg, Jonathan. "Clash of the Titans." *Manhattan, inc.,* January 1986.

Glynn, Lenny. "Blowout on the Boardwalk." *Institutional Inventor,* December 1989.

Hammer, Joshua. "He Wants to Take You Higher." *Manhattan, inc.,* January 1986.

Hermalyn, Gary. "The Bronx at the Turn of the Century." *The Bronx County Historical Society Journal,* Fall 1989.

Horowitz, Craig. "Trump's Near-Death Experience." *New York,* August 15, 1994.

Klein, Edward. "Trump Family Values." *Vanity Fair,* March 1994.

Koroscil, Paul M. "The Historical Development of Whitehorse." *The American Review of Canadian Studies,* Vol. XVIII.

Kunen, James S. "Pop Goes the Donald." *People*, July 9, 1990.

Leibovich, Audrey, Magali Rheault, and Dan Wilchins. "An Amazing Half Century of Progress." *Kiplinger's*, January 1997.

Lieblich, Julia. "The Billionaires." *Fortune*, September 12, 1988.

Mahar, Maggie. "The Merv and Donald Show." *Barron's*, May 23, 1988.

Marshall, Leslie, "Breakfast Above Tiffany's," *In Style*, December 1995.

Meyers, William H. "Stalking the Plaza." *The New York Times Magazine*, September 25, 1988.

Mumford, Lewis, "In Defense of the Neighborhood." *Town Planning Review*, Vol. 24, January 1954.

"Now Is the Time to Speak Up for FHA." *House and Home*, May 1954.

Ochsner, Jeffrey Karl, and Dennis Alan Anderson. "Adler and Sullivan's Seattle Opera House Project." *Journal of the Society of Architectural Historians*, September 1989.

O'Keefe, Eric. "The Peter Principle." *Polo*, March/April 1998.

Olmsted, Robert A. "A History of Transportation in The Bronx." *The Bronx County Historical Society Journal*, Fall 1989.

Pileggi, Nicholas. "How to Get Things Done in New York: A Case History." *New York*, November 1973.

Plaskin, Glenn. "Playboy Interview: Donald Trump." *Playboy*, March 1990.

———. "Queen Ivana Approximately." *New York Daily News Magazine*, December 17, 1989.

———. "The People's Billionaire." *New York Daily News Magazine*, February 26, 1989.

Posner, Eric. "The Political Economy of the Bankruptcy Reform Act of 1978." *Michigan Law Review*, October 1997.

Powell, Bill, and Peter McKillop. "Citizen Trump." *Newsweek*, September 28, 1987.

"Private Enterprise Breathes New Life into Old Cities." *Dun & Bradstreet Reports*, November/December 1978.

Propper, Walter. "Growing Up in the Bronx." *The Bronx in the Innocent Years: 1890–1925*. New York: Harper & Row, 1964.

Pulzer, P. G. J. "From Bismarck to the Present." In *Germany: A Companion to German Studies*, edited by Malcolm Pasley. London; New York: Methuen, 1982.

Ralph, Julian. "Washington—The Evergreen State." *Harper's New Monthly Magazine*, September 1982.

Rose, Frank. "Celebrity Zoning." *Manhattan, inc.*, November 1989.

Ryan, Michael. "Building Castles in the Sky." *People*, December 7, 1987.

Sack, Bert. "Growing Pains of the Bronx." *The Bronx County Historical Society Journal*, Fall 1989.

Schayerson, Michael. "Power Blonde." *Vanity Fair*, January 1988.

Schwartz, John. "The Stars of Brick and Mortar." *Newsweek*, September 28, 1987.

Schwartz, Tony. "A Different Kind of Donald Trump Story." *New York*, February 11, 1985.

Sheffer, Ethel. "The Lessons of Lincoln West." *New York Affairs*, Vol. 8, no.3, 1984.

Simonoff, Evan. "Deal of Misfortune." *Investment Dealers' Digest*, July 3, 1989.

Singer, Mark. "Trump Solo." *The New Yorker*, May 19, 1997.

Stern, Richard L., and John Connolly. "Manhattan's Favorite Guessing Game: How Rich Is Donald?" *Forbes*, May 14, 1990.

Stone, Michael. "Clash of the Titans: Business Tycoons Donald Trump and Jay Prizker." *Chicago*, October 1994.

Taylor, John. "Trump's Newest Toy." *New York*, July 11, 1988.
Tell, Lawrence J. "Holding All the Cards." *Barron's*, August 6, 1984.
Useem, Jerry, and Theodore Spencer. "What Does Donald Trump Really Want?" *Fortune*, April 3, 2000.
Van Meter, Jonathan. "Ivana! Ivana! Ivana!" *Spy*, May 1989.
Weigers, Leo. "Growing Up in Morrisania." *Bronx County Historical Society Journal*, Fall 1989.
Weiss, Philip. "The Fred." *The New York Times Magazine*, January 2, 2000.
Wilkinson, Peter. "The New Fixers." *Manhattan, inc.*, January 1988.
William, Edwin Ernest. "The Flight from Laissez-Faire." In *Made in Germany*. London: W. Heinemann, 1896.

DISSERTATIONS

Kroessler, Jeffrey A. "Building Queens: The Urbanization of New York's Largest Borough." Ph.D. dissertation, City University of New York, 1991.
MacDonald, Alexander Norbert. "Seattle's Economic Development, 1880–1910." Ph.D. dissertation, University of Washington, 1959.
Shaviro, Sol. "Cooperation: A Theoretical Model and a Practical Example." Ph.D. dissertation, Fordham University, 1969.

GOVERNMENT DOCUMENTS

Belcher, Inspector, Inspector A. M. Jarvis, Inspector D'A. E. Strickland, and Superintendent C. Constantine. *Annual Reports of the North-West Mounted Police*, Yukon Territory, 1898.
Corruption and Racketeering in the New York City Construction Industry. Interim Report by The New York State Organized Crime Task Force. Ithaca, N.Y.: ILR Press, 1988.
Details Supporting the Findings of Fact in the Special Investigation of the Federal Housing Administration, April 12, 1954–August 31, 1954.
German Federal Archives, Speyer, Friedrich Trump, papers and correspondence.
Housing and Development Administration Study Group. "New York City's Mitchell-Lama Housing Program: The Management of the Middle Income Housing Program." New York: The Housing and Development Administration of New York, January 1973.
Kaiser, Frederick M. "Past Program Breakdowns in HUD-FHA: Section 608 Multifamily Rental Mortgage Insurance Program of the 1940s." Congressional Research Service, Library of Congress.
McKenna, William F. *Final Report on FHA Investigation*, August 31, 1954.
——. *Report to the Senate Committee on Banking and Currency*, June 29, 1954.
——. *Summaries of Federal Housing Section 608 Case Investigations Presented to the Senate Banking and Currency Committee*, n.d.
New York State. "Recommendations of the New York State Commission of Investigation Concerning the Limited-Profit Housing Program," April 1966.

New York State Housing Finance Agency Annual Report for Fiscal Year November 1, 1960, to October 31, 1961.

Ninth Annual Report of the Temporary Commission of Investigation of the State of New York to the Governor and the Legislature of New York. February 1967.

U.S. District Court, Eastern District of New York, Archives relating to *In the Matter of Julius Lehrenkrauss et al.*, 1934.

U.S. Senate, FHA Investigation, Hearings Before the Committee on Banking and Currency, Testimony of Fred Trump, July 12, 1954, pp. 395–420.

———. Testimony of Ian Woodner, August 4, 1954, pp. 1021–1123.

MISCELLANEOUS

American Institute of Architects, New York Chapter. "Report of the Sixtieth Street Yards Task Force." New York: June 1990.

Buckhurst Fish Hutton Katz & Jacquemart Inc. "Review of Riverside South Proposal." New York: July 1992.

Clarridge, David, and Judie Clarridge. *A Ton of Gold: The Seattle Gold Rush, 1897–98.* Seattle, 1972.

Columbia University's Oral History Project, interviews with Abraham E. Kazan, 1968.

Community Board Seven/Manhattan. "Draft Report of Community Board Seven/Manhattan on the Riverside South Proposal for the Uniform Land Use Review Procedure." July 22, 1992.

Cooke, Dr. C. M. *Tech Talk.* M.I.T. publication, February 1985.

Corporate Reorganization Reporter (Penn Central).

De Vita, Carol J. "The United States at Mid-Decade." *Population Bulletin.* Washington, D.C.: Population Reference Bureau, Inc., March 1996.

Encyclopedia of New York City, edited by Kenneth T. Jackson. New Haven: Yale University Press, 1995.

Fisher, Ernest M. "Memories of an Octogenarian, 1893–1975." Unpublished memoir, 1970.

Gould, Milton. "Fifth Avenue Coach Lines, Trump Tower and Roy M. Cohn." Chapter from an unpublished autobiography.

Kazan, Abraham E. "Co-operative Housing." Unpublished manuscript.

———. "Amalgamated Warbasse Houses . . . A Private Builder Opposes a Development." Unpublished manuscript.

Kelsey Story. Kelsey, New York History Committee, Kelsey Community Group, 1980.

Kroos, William. "A Peek at Richmond Hill through the Keyhole of Time." Published by Richmond Hill Savings Bank, 1983.

Livingston, Victoria Hartwell. "Erastus Brainerd: The Bankruptcy of Brilliance." Master's thesis, University of Washington, 1967.

Macri, Carlos. "Lincoln West or Who Trumped Whom." Unpublished autobiography written with Judith Murphy.

Moses, Robert. "West Side Fiasco: A Practical Proposal for the Restoration of the West Side Highway and Parkway to Public Use." November 25, 1974.

New York Panorama: WPA Guide, n.d.

Northern Pacific R.R. timetable, Spring/Summer 1891.

Penn & Schoen Associates, Inc. "Report to Donald Trump on Public Opinion in America." October 1988.

Richmond Hill High School Annual, 1901 and 1905.

Rose, Nelson. "Gambling and the Law: Recent Developments, 1998." Unpublished paper.

Scutt, Der. Unpublished professional diary, 1974–present.

Sinclair, John Alexander. Correspondence, diaries, et al. during his mission to Skagway, Alaska, and Bennett, B.C., 1898–1902. British Columbia Archives.

"The 'Force' in the Yukon." Produced by the Public Relations Branch of the Royal Canadian Mounted Police, 1979.

The Henry Morrison Flagler Museum. "Whitehall: The Henry Morrison Flagler Museum." Brochure published by the museum in 1988.

Vital Statistics of the United States, 1950, Volume 1.

Whitehorse Heritage Buildings Pamphlet. Yukon Historical & Museum Association, 1983.

Yatrakis, Kathryn B. "Ballots and Bosses in Brooklyn." Paper presented at American Political Science Association Annual Meeting.

ACKNOWLEDGMENTS

I first started working on this book in 1988, and started many more times in the twelve years that elapsed before I finished. Without the patience and assistance of family members and friends, I would never have completed it. I am also much indebted to a number of other individuals, beginning with Donald Trump and other members of the Trump family. They have been gracious and helpful, as have Trump Organization staff, especially Norma Foerderer and Rhona Graff. Christian Freund, David Cameron, Roger Starr, Nat Sobel, Eugene Morris, and Hilbert Fefferman were invaluable guides for historical material, and Paul Willen, Daniel Gutman, Ethel Scheffer, Sugar Rautbord, Alan Lapidus, and Ken Moelis helped with more recent periods. I am especially thankful to Der Scutt for allowing me to read and quote from his professional diaries; Cate Breslin for news clips; the Cristliebs for their hospitality; Richmond Hills High School alumni for their recollections; Avis Lang for copyediting savvy; Emilie Storrs for indexing; Natalie Goldstein for photo research; and Wayne Barrett for extraordinary generosity with research materials; and Peter Mezan for help getting where I needed to be to finish.

Editor Alice Mayhew and agent Gloria Loomis have been most understanding and supportive during this lengthy process; Ana Debevoise, Roger Labrie, and Anja Schmidt provided vital support. Cam Mann helped shape the book and did a heroic edit; Caroline Mann, Mark Plummer, Richard H. Levy, and Matt Stolper filled in gaps; David Cameron, Hilbert Fefferman, Philip Blumberg, Alan Kleiman, Irving Alter, and Harvey Schultz reviewed manuscript sections. I am deeply grateful to them all, and to many talented researchers: Jennifer Chen, Marcia Dennis, Kim Dixon, Bill Egbert, Felix Ensslin, Ben Field, Jane Gaffin, Linda Johnson, Gayanne Keshishyan, Suzanne Koudsi, Simon Lerner, Robin Letourneau, Lucy Maher, Tim Noy, and Eric Unmacht.

In addition, I owe deep thanks to many others who spoke with me for the book. The following list is only partial, for many asked that I not use their names. Thanks to Mike Abeloff, Heather Hillman Adams, Mark Advent, Frank Alleva, Irving Alter, Joe Amoroso, Dennis Anderson, Dick Anderson, Engler Anderson, Wally Antoniewicz, Jonathan Arneson, Arthur Arsham, Valerie Asciutto, Ken Auletta, Pat Auletta, Mark Bachmann, Mike Bailkin, Jerry Ballan, Jonathan Barnett, Ben Barowski, Neal Barsky, Kent Barwick, Richard Bass, Foster Beach, Abraham Beame, Laurie Beckelman, Phyllis Becker, Paul Bekman, Paul Belica, John Belmonte, Henry Benach, Arthur Bender, Milton Berger, Ted Bergman, Stanley Berman, Bob Berne, Dick Bernstein, Daniel Biederman, Bronson Binger, Philip Birnbaum, Harry Blair, James Blair, Newell Blair, Bob Blanchette, Ron Bleecker, Bernie Blum, Philip Blumberg, Stanley Blumberg, Charles Boch, Joe Boling, Steve Bollenbach, Patricia Bosworth, Leonard Boxer, Lily Brant, Peter Brant, Jeff Breslow, Fred Briller, Bonnie Brower, Michael Brown, Bobby Brownstein, John Brugman, Frank Bryant, Horace Bullard, Karen Burstein, Clayton Burwell, Javier Bustamente, Brendan Byrne, Conrad Cafritz, Arthur Caliandro, John Cantrill, Frank Cardile, Hugh Carey, Larry Carlet, Scott Carlin, Rafael Carmona, Catherine Cary, Haywood Cash, Anthony Castellano, Joe Center, Herbert S. Chason, Andrew Chertoff, Joe Coccimiglio, Joseph Cohen, Joseph M. Cohen, Matthew Coleus, Michael Conway, Peter Coombs, Scott Coopchick, Michael Corbisiero, Philip Corbisiero, Rochelle Corson, Mary Roche Cossman, Gaylen Crantz, Felix Cuervo, Ngaire Cuneo, Jim Czajka, John d'Alessi, Linda Davidoff, Howard Davidowitz, Gordon Davis, Mary D'Elia, Michelle DeMilly, Herbert Denenberg, Kevin DeSanctis, Mario di Genova, Ken di Pasquale, Stanley Diamond, Richard Dicker, Cary Dickieson, John Digges, Bill Digiacomo, David Dilgard, Frank Diotte, David Dischy, Ted Dobias, Paul Doocey, Paul Dorpat, Louis Droesch, Linda Dufault, Paul Duke, Seymour Durst, Andre D'Usseau, Paul Dworin, Harriet Economou, Julius Edelstein, Michael Edelstein, Rick Edmonds, Owen Edwards, Bill Ehlers, Ned Eichler, Al Eisenpreiss, Stan Ekstut, Arthur Emil, Paul Erlham, Spencer Ervin, Mitchell Etess, Stu Faber, Murray Feiden, Marcy Feigenbaum, Murray Felton, Chris Ferro, Joe Fisch, Al Formicola, Cathleen Fostini, Molly Foti, Tim Frank, Fran Freedman, Bill Frentz, Dale Frey, Fred Fried, Bernard Frieden, Louis Friedman, Steve Friedman, Hugo Friend, Sidney Frigand, Charles Frowenfeld, Bart Frye, Roy Gainsburg, Tom Gallegher, Martin Gallent, Alex Garvin, Bernie Gavser, Fina Farhi

Geiger, Peter Gelb, Jeff Gerson, Victor Gerstein, Marvin Gersten, Mae and Moe Gherman, Jack Gibson, Andy Giffuni, D. L. Gilbert, Frank Giordano, Bob Giraldi, Stephen Girard, Ginny Gleidman, Norman Glickman, Homer Godwin, Richard Goeglein, Hadley Gold, Marty Goldensohn, Julius Goldberg, Paul Goldberger, Charles Goldie, Brian Goldin, Lowell Goldman, Jerry Goldsmith, Pat Goldstein, Sally Goodgold, Warren Goodwin, Edward S. Gordon, Dick Gottfried, Martin Gottlieb, George Grace, Gertrude Grady, Phyllis Grady, Ross Graham, Roberta Brandes Gratz, Ace Greenberg, Donald Greenberg, Shirley Greene, Libby Greenwald, Jordan Gruzen, Eleanor Guggenheimer, Michael Guider, Fred Halla, Mai Hallingby, John Halpern, Franklyn Harkavy, Chester Hartman, Nikki Haskell, Ashton Hawkins, Bob Hawthorne, Don Hayes, Heather Macintosh Hayes, Judge John Hayes, Doug Healey, Dan Heneghan, Lee Hereth, Bob Herman, Philip Hess, Jud Higgins, Steve Hilbert, Raymond Hillman, Richard Hillman, Stanley Hillman, Dieter Hoch, Alan L. Hoffman, Archie Holeman, Ben Holloway, Myron Holtz, Stan Holuba, Tom Hoving, Dave Howard, Philip Howard, Bill Hubbard, Gertrude Rice Hughes, John W. Hyman, Glen Ingalls, Steve Jacobson, Jerry Jagendorf, Herman Jessor, Philip Johnson, Richard Johnson, W. Taylor Johnson Jr., Anthony Jordan, Mike Kabealo, Richard Kagle, Richard Kahan, Henry Kaningsberg, Joe Kanter, Teddy Katsoris, Sandor Katz, Richard Katzive, Ben Kazan, Leon Kazan, Scott Keller, Tom Keller, Charles Kimble, Jeanne King, Eric Kingson, Jeff Kone, Arthur Kopit, Oliver Koppell, Joe Kordsmeier, Ann Rudovsky Kornfeld, John Koskinen, Victor Kovner, Howard Kramer, Richard Krauser, William Kroos, Ted Krukel, Irwin Kuhn, Donald Kummerfeld, Dorotha Kuritzkes, Benjamin Lambert, Alan Lapidus, Morris Lapidus, David Lefever, Samuel LeFrak, Ken Lehrer, Franz Leichter, Henry A. Leist, Florence Lemle, Henry Lemle, Steve Lesko, Daryl Leury, Joel Levin, Ted Levine, Alfred Levingson, Bill Levitt, Dick Levy, Harold Liebman, Matthew L. Lifflander, John V. Lindsay, Ralph Lippmann, Clem Long, Paul Longo, Mike Lunsford, Patricia Lynden, Tom Macari, Bernice Able MacIntosh, Maggie Mahar, Bill Maloney, John Manbeck, Norman Marcus, Peter Marcuse, Ron Marino, Rich Marrin, Donald Martin, Dr. Alexander Martone, Peter Martosella, Arlene Marx, Robert Masello, Christopher Mason, Jesse Masyr, Al Maurer, Ted Maylor, John McAnally, Tex McCrary, Patrick McGahn, John

McGarrahan, Sean McGowan, Bill McKenna, Bob McKinley, Frances McNulty, Carol Melton, Bill Merusi, Olive Messenger, Ruth Messinger, John Meyers, Charlie Miesmer, Betty Miles, Ben Miller, David Miller, Ron Millican, John Minikes, Ken Moelis, Milton Mollen, Scott Mollen, Sandy Moorhouse, Alex Mooring, Tom Morgan, I. M. Moriyama, Eugene Morris, Mark Morris, Claude Morton, Eric Moskowitz, Ed Murphy, Gerard Murphy, Peter Murphy, Michael Musaraca, Mary Musca, Hal Negbaur, Donald Neier, Martha Nelson, Jay Neveloff, Barbara Nevins, Jesse Newman, John Nichols, Jerry Nisman, Bruce Nobles, Jim Nolen, Don Noonan, Enid Nordland, Craig Norville, Jay Noyes, V. L. Nussbaum, Tim O'Brien, Timothy L. O'Brien, Martin O'Connell, Jack O'Donnell, Paul O'Dwyer, Jeffrey Oechsner, Michael Onorato, Allen Ostroff, Harold Ostroff, Sen. Frank Padavan, Thomas Palmer, Victor Palmieri, Maurice Paprin, Roland Paul, Charles Payton, George Peacock, Ruth Peale, Henry Pearce, Charles Perkins, Steven Perskie, John Phillips, Frank Pino, Ken Platt, Sandra Kazan Pomerantz, Eric Posner, Lou Powsner, Bill Price, George Puskar, Alex Quint, Richie Rada, Morris Raker, Raquel Ramati, Julian Rashkind, Arthur Ratner, Ceil Raufer, Sugar Rautbord, Richard Ravitch, Walter Reade, Charlie Reiss, Barbara Res, James Revson, Jack Reynolds, Everett Rhinebeck, Richard Rice, Marty Riche, Bernard Richland, Peter Ricker, George Rinaldi, Don Robinson, Jerry Robinson, Steve Robinson, Marvin Roffman, Philip Rogers, Lewis Roper, Richard Rosan, James Rosati, Irwin Rose, Nelson Rose, Steve Rosen, Bart Rosenberg, Bob Rosenberg, Wilbur Ross, Fred Rovet, William Ruben, Howard Rubenstein, Dave Rudovsky, George Ruebel, David Saltzman, Peter Samton, Phil Satre, Mike Scadron, John Scanlon, Roger Schafer, Jack Shaffer, Larry Schafran, Alison Rhoades Schechter, Stuart Scheftel, Dan Schiffman, Doug Schoen, Gerald Schrager, Henning Schroder, Gary Schuller, Harvey Schultz, David Schuster, Edward Schuster, Conrad Schwartz, Gail Schwartz, Harry Schwartz, Joel Schwartz, Lynn Sharon Schwartz, David Sciarra, Mark Scott, Robert Selsun, Paul Selver, Lloyd Semple, Lou Sepersky, Vivian Serota, Graham Shane, Peter Shapiro, Richard Shapiro, Sam Shapiro, Mary Frances Shaughnessy, Sol Shaviro, Sin-ming Shaw, Ivan Shomer, Paula Shore, Claude Shostal, Lorenz Shrenk, Fred Siegel, Mark Alan Siegel, Steve Siegel, Harvey Sieglbaum, Lisa Sihanouk, Sam Silber, Leo Silverman, Larry Silverstein, William Simon, Mike Simmons, Marla Simpson, Marilyn Singer, Dusty Sklar, Wendy Sloan, Carl Smith, David Smith, Nathan R. Sobel, Donald Soffer, Peter Solomon, Florence Stelz Spelshouse, Jerry Speyer, David Spiker, Edith Spivack, Blanche Sprague, David Stadtmauer, Roger Starr, Martin Steadman, Andrew Stein, Ralph Steinglass, Robert Steingut, Conrad Stephenson, Henry Stern, Jeff Stern, Paul Stern, William Stern, Charles Stocker, Roger Stone, Artie Storrs, Larry Straus, Brian Strum, Robert Sturges, Phil Suarez, Joe Sukaskas, Frank Sulloway, Betty Swetz, Stephen Swid, George Syrovatka, Myles Tannenbaum, Gary Tarbox, Breina Taubman, Larry Tell, Niles Thompson, Nancy Boyd Tickel, Elizabeth Tilyou, Jack Toby, Ernest Todham, Patrick Too, John Torrell, Henry Trefousse, Jane Trichter, Matthew Troy, John Trump Jr., Ginny Droesch Trumpbour, Stan Turetsky, William Bruce Turner, Margaret Uhl, Charles Urstadt, Jonathan Van Meter, Jan Van Heinigen, Carmine Ventiera, Jessie Voeller Conrad, Arnold Vollmer, Nicholas von Hoffman, Charles Walker, Jeffrey Walker, Abe Wallach, Al Walsh, Joe Walsh, John Walter, Karl Walther, Stanley Waranch, Robert V. Ward, Marvin L. Warner, Howard Weingrow, Andy Weiss, Allen Weisselberg, Rick Welch, Tim Welch, Margo Wellington, William Wenk, Celeste Wesson, Howard West, George White, Dave Wiederecht, Mike Wiener, Bob Wildermuth, Murray Weinstein, Louis Winnick, Sally Wiseman, Ivan Wohlworth, Phil Wolf, Philip Woodhouse, Donald Woodward, Sidney Young, Brad Zackson, Robert Zajonc, Aja Zanova-Steindler, Lillian Zeh, Carl Zeitz, Beverly Ziegler, Howard Zipser, John Zuccotti, and Howard Zuckerman.

INDEX

PHOTO CREDITS

ABOUT THE AUTHOR

Gwenda Blair is the author of the bestselling *Almost Golden: Jessica Savitch and the Selling of Television News*. She has written for *The New York Times*, *Esquire*, *The Village Voice*, *Ms.*, and many other magazines and newspapers. She lives in Manhattan with her two sons.